Physical and Chemical Sciences Research Report 1

The goal of the Dahlem Workshop on
The Nature of Seawater:

to seek out from the information base
of present-day chemistry those novel
techniques and concepts that may deepen
our knowledge of the nature of seawater
and of the chemical reactions occurring
within the marine environment.

Physical and Chemical Sciences Research Reports
Editor: S. Bernhard

Dahlem Konferenzen is supported by the
Stifterverband für die Deutsche Wissenschaft,
the science foundation
of German industry, trade, and commerce,
in cooperation with the
Deutsche Forschungsgemeinschaft,
the German organization
for promoting fundamental research.

The Nature of Seawater

Report of the Dahlem Workshop on
The Nature of Seawater
Berlin 1975, March 10 to 15

Editor: Edward D. Goldberg

Rapporteurs: J. M. Edmond
                        D. J. Faulkner
                        I. Hansson
                        D. R. Kester
                        P. S. Liss

Program Advisory   E. Bayer
Committee: M. Bernhard
                        K. Bertine
                        M. Branica
                        E. D. Goldberg
                        A. E. Martell
                        G. H. Morrison
                        G. H. Nancollas
                        J. P. Riley
                        P. W. Schindler
                        J. M. Wood

Dahlem Konferenzen Berlin

1975
All rights reserved
© 1975 by Dr. S. Bernhard, Dahlem Konferenzen, Berlin.

Copy Editors: K. Bolstad, B. Lewerich

Produced for Dahlem Konferenzen by Abakon Verlagsgesellschaft
D - 1 Berlin 45, Söhtstr. 3A

Printed in Germany (FRG)

ISBN 3 - 8200 - 1201 - X

Table of Contents

Physicochemical Conventions

Kinetics

Colloidal State and Surface Phenomena

Introduction

Edward D. Goldberg
Scripps Institution of Oceanography
P.O. Box 1529, La Jolla, CA 92037, USA

Herein are an unusual set of presentations. In the main they
were written by some of the world's most distinguished chemists,
who describe the areas of research that they are pursuing.
These articles in pure chemistry were prepared for a group of
marine chemists who assembled in March 1975 in Berlin, Germany
to consider new approaches which might yield a better understanding of the compositions and reactions of oceanic systems. Now
they are being presented to a wider audience of marine chemists
with the same aim in mind. Why was it necessary to bring together marine chemists with their colleagues from the mainstream
of chemistry itself? The simple answer is that at the present
time a lack of communication exists between these groups. To
better understand how this situation developed it is worthwhile
to review the history of marine chemistry.

Chemical descriptions of the oceans have reflected not only the
scientific concepts and techniques of the times that generated
them, but also the social and economic involvements of man with
the domains of nature. The birth of marine chemistry was a natural byproduct of the scientific revolution that promoted chemistry as an integrated discipline during the latter part of the
eighteenth century. Through experimentation, doctrinaire concepts (often derived from the Greeks) were tested and found want-
ing. Some of the first chemists, asking why the oceans were
salty, included Robert Boyle, Antoine Lavoisier, and Tobin
Bergman, the so-called father of analytical chemistry. Curiosity

about their surroundings motivated these pioneer chemists. For example, the first researches of Lavoisier were concerned with the composition of surface waters of France and stemmed from the chronic shortage of water in Paris.

Chemistry grew from these initial investigations with the discovery of the elements. As each new member of the periodic table was identified, its concentration in natural waters was sought. In 1922 the chemist Marcet suggested, "For the ocean having communication with every part of the earth through the rivers, all of which ultimately pour their waters into it; and soluble substances, even such as are theoretically incompatible with each other, being almost in every instance capable of co-existing in solution, I could see no reason why the ocean should not be a general receptacle for all bodies which can be held in solution." Today, only about a dozen of the stable elements have not as yet been analyzed in seawater. Two elements were initially discovered in the marine environment: iodine and bromine.

This period, in which the chemistry of natural waters was an integral part of chemistry itself, extended up to the beginning of the twentieth century. The climax to this work occurred with the very careful analyses of large numbers of samples from different regions and from different depths by the Scotch chemist Dittmar. His exacting work on 77 samples of seawater collected during the world-encircling cruise of the H.M.S. Challenger established the constancy of the relative ionic composition of seawater with respect to its major components.

The first estrangement between those chemists concerned with the oceans and those in more basic lines of research occurred when the former group became interdisciplinary and joined forces with the biologists, geologists, and physicists. During this phase, which began in the early 1900s, marine scientists found two general fields of inquiry to be stimulating, (a) the interactions of the marine biosphere with ocean waters; and (b) the role of the oceans in the major sedimentary cycle. The possibility

that life processes in the ocean waters might govern in part
their compositions would have appeared strange to the pioneer
marine chemists. Yet the relationship between the extent of photosynthesis and the levels of carbon dioxide and oxygen in surface seawaters, established in 1912, directed marine chemists to
ask what other substances might be involved in plant growth and
consequently have their marine concentrations affected. Geologists were concerned with the role of the oceans in the major
sedimentary cycle. What factors governed the marine concentrations of substances whose ultimate source was rock weathering
processes? Were all of the species in the oceans derived in this
way? The bookkeeping of elements moving about the surface of the
earth was attempted by such distinguished chemists as V.M.
Goldschmidt of Germany, F.W. Clarke of the United States, and
V.I. Vernadsky of Russia. In some cases a return to pure chemistry itself was made to interpret findings in nature.
Goldschmidt developed his set of ionic radii on this basis.
Physical oceanographers were seeking methods to accurately determine the density of seawater so that they could ascertain the
stability of water masses in the oceans. They sought the chemists' aid in the determination of the salinity of seawaters from
which densities could be ascertained.

Three groups were asking the marine chemists to become their
handmaidens: the biologists, the geologists, and the physical
oceanographers. Unfortunately, many were thus diverted from pure
chemical research into these interdisciplinary areas.

The field of marine chemistry has witnessed a dramatic growth
since World War II. Both closer contacts with chemistry and a
further estrangement from it have occurred in the field during
this period. Many of the techniques of chemistry and physics
developed in the 1950s were brought to bear upon problems of me-
teorology, geology, and oceanography. Mass spectrometric analyses of light elements such as carbon, oxygen, hydrogen, and
nitrogen gave new insights into the movements of materials about
the surface of the earth. The parameter of time was introduced
into natural systems through the use of radioactive nuclides,

now readily measurable in extremely low concentrations by sophisticated counting equipment. The students of this generation
were drawn into oceanographic institutions, where they brought
with them the ideas and methodologies of modern chemistry. Marine chemical problems were being undertaken in chemistry and
earth science departments in universities, where the investigators had close contacts with practicing chemists.

The activity was intense. While the knowledge of marine chemistry had been published in thin volumes before World War II, it
now takes five large volumes to cover the wide spectrum of work
/5/. A quarterly journal came into being which was dedicated
solely to marine chemistry /7/. Some recommended readings in
marine chemistry are listed here in closing. However, as this
growth continued, there were fewer and fewer contacts between
the practitioners of marine chemistry and chemists. Oceanographic institutions spawned marine chemistry departments which sent
their own brand of chemists out into the world with masters or
doctorate degrees. The students from these departments often
had very little graduate training in chemistry from chemistry departments. Instead, their formal classes involved marine chemistry, biology, geology, and physics to a large extent. This has
been particularly evident at my own institution, where the youn-
ger faculty place far less importance upon training in pure chemistry than do their more senior colleagues. These students now
largely staff the departments of marine chemistry, and unfortunately they have lost contact with the modern moods of chemistry.
Due to time or economic restrictions, marine chemists were often
forced to choose between going to chemical or oceanographic meet-
ings. More often than not they chose the latter. As one of the
former students from my institution commented to me after the
Dahlem meeting, "In my graduate student days I remember you used
to bewail the fact that modern chemistry was leaving you behind.
From Dahlem I am beginning to see what you mean."

The concept of the Dahlem Workshop was to counteract the trend
of an increasing lack of dialogue between marine chemists and
pure chemists. From the point of view of the former, it may

have seemed a selfish concept since they obviously gained much
from discussions with the leaders in the field of chemistry. On
the other hand, non-marine chemists were exposed to interesting
chemical problems in the "real world" of natural seawater.

At the workshop itself, as recorded in the group reports, the
chemists, deliberating upon the problems of the oceans as presented to them by some of the participants, were able to point
out tools available today that might solve the problems. Their
published presentations and their evaluations of the present in-
adequacies in oceanic studies clearly point out new paths and
dimensions that might evolve in marine chemistry.

The Dahlem Workshop on the Nature of Seawater was convened by
Dahlem Konferenzen in Berlin, Germany on March 10 - 15, 1975.
Scientists from 14 countries participated. The majority of the
participants was about equally divided between the fields of
pure chemistry and marine chemistry. The rest belonged to related fields such as biochemistry, marine ecology, and microbiology.

Background papers concerned with recent developments in chemistry
were prepared by the chemists and distributed several weeks before the workshop. These provided the basis for discussions at
the workshop, which centered about five general areas: chemical
speciation; the formulation of conventions to describe seawater
equilibria; kinetics; the colloidal state and surface phenomena;
and biosynthesis and biodegradation. The prevailing mood among
the chemists was the expectation that several obvious voids in
knowledge about the composition of seawater could be filled by
the application of existing techniques.

For the record, the series of events that led to the workshop
took place as follows: Dr. Michael Bernhard and I discussed
these general problems at a Conference on Modelling of Marine
Systems in Ofir, Portugal in June 1973. Our ideas were forwarded
to Dr. Silke Bernhard of Dahlem Konferenzen, who suggested we
translate them into a workshop. The first meeting of the three

of us took place in Paris in June 1974. A program advisory meeting with 11 scientists from different disciplines was held one month later in Berlin.

Credit for the creation of this book is due the program advisory committee, the moderators, provocateurs, rapporteurs, and all workshop participants.

RECOMMENDED READINGS

Books:

/1/ Goldberg, E.D., ed. 1974. The Sea, vol. 5.
         New York: Wiley-Interscience.

/2/ Hill, M.N., ed. 1962. The sea, vol. 2.
         New York: Wiley-Interscience.

/3/ Horne, R.A. 1969. Marine Chemistry.
         New York: Wiley-Interscience.

/4/ Riley, J.P., and Chester, R. 1971. Introduction to
         Marine Chemistry. London: Academic Press.

/5/ Riley, J.P., and Skirrow, G., eds. 1975. Chemical
         Oceanography, 5 vols. London: Academic Press.

/6/ Stumm, W., and Morgan, J.J. 1970. Aquatic Chemistry.
         New York: Wiley-Interscience.

Periodicals:

/7/ Marine Chemistry. A quarterly journal published since
         1972 by Elsevier-North Holland, Amsterdam and New
         York.

Chemical Speciation in Seawater
Group Report

D. R. Kester, Rapporteur
S. Ahrland   K. Kremling
T. M. Beasley   F. J. Millero
M. Bernhard   H. W. Nürnberg
M. Branica   A. Piro
I. D. Campbell   R. M. Pytkowicz
G. L. Eichhorn   I. Steffan
K. A. Kraus   W. Stumm

SCOPE AND IMPORTANCE OF CHEMICAL SPECIATION IN MARINE SYSTEMS

Chemical speciation in the marine environment consists of distinguishing the chemical forms of an element in solution, colloidal, and particulate phases. This overview paper considers a series of chemical techniques and the information gained therefrom primarily on the solution chemistry of seawater. Chemical species in seawater may be classified according to the following types of reactions:

a. Ion association by some of the major components in seawater;

b. Dissociation of weak acids in seawater;

c. Complexation of minor constituents by inorganic and by organic ligands;

d. Oxidation-reduction reactions of multivalent state elements;

e. Biosynthetic formation of substances which would not occur by spontaneous chemical processes;

f. Distribution of chemicals between solution and solid phases by adsorption-desorption, precipitation-dissolution, and ion exchange processes.

Figure 1 provides a schematic illustration of the relationship between these chemical reactions and geochemical processes. Five variables are summarized also which are important in determining the chemical form of many constituents in the marine environment.

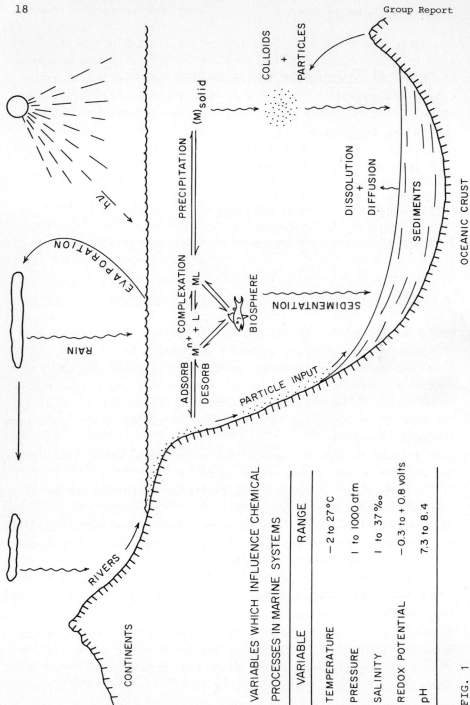

VARIABLES WHICH INFLUENCE CHEMICAL
PROCESSES IN MARINE SYSTEMS

VARIABLE	RANGE
TEMPERATURE	−2 to 27°C
PRESSURE	1 to 1000 atm
SALINITY	1 to 37‰
REDOX POTENTIAL	−0.3 to + 0.8 volts
pH	7.3 to 8.4

FIG. 1

The extent to which the occurrence of identifiable species in seawater is resolved depends upon the objective of the analysis. For example, if the objective is to partition the total carbon dioxide concentration into its principal forms which affect the pH buffering of seawater, it is sufficient to describe the equilibrium in terms of an apparent equilibrium constant K'

$$2HCO_3^- \rightleftharpoons CO_2 + H_2O + CO_3^{2-} \qquad K' = \frac{m_{CO_2} \; m_{CO_3^{2-}}}{m_{HCO_3}^2}$$

where m denotes the analytical molality of each of the three forms of carbon dioxide. On the other hand, if the objective is to relate the effect of magnesium ions on the carbonate system, it is useful to obtain a finer resolution of species which may be represented by:

$$m_{CO_3}^- = [CO_3^{2-}] + [NaCO_3^-] + [MgCO_3^0] + [CaCO_3^0]$$

where the brackets indicate molalities of the enclosed chemical species. These individual species molalities may be obtained from calculations using stoichiometric association constants.

Another factor encountered in defining chemical speciation in marine systems is limitation in separating dissolved and particulate phases. The most common approach to the separation of these phases is by filtration. A filter of a specific pore size does not provide a simple sieving of particulate forms, because particles finer than the pore size may be retained. Particle size distinction is a significant factor in chemical speciation because it is likely that some chemical processes are surface area dependent, and the chemical reactivity of some solid phases is particle size dependent. A possible improvement over filtration for future studies may be obtained by the use of centrifugation separation over a range of accelerations and with density gradient separation.

The importance of speciation considerations is that the chemical behavior of an element in the marine environment depends on its form. For example, the toxicity of copper to some marine

organisms is altered by the formation of copper organic complexes (Steeman Nielsen and Wium-Anderson, 1970; Davey et al.,
1973); the rate at which an element participates in a chemical
process depends on its form (Pytkowicz, 1965, 1973; Stumm and
Lee, 1961); and speciation influences the participation of an
element in geochemical processes such as precipitation-dissolution (Goldberg and Arrhenius, 1958; Garrels et al., 1961) and
adsorption-desorption (James and Healy, 1972; O'Connor and Kester,
1975). An understanding of these processes is essential to determining the impact of man's activity on the marine environment. A
geochemical approach considering various environmental reservoirs
and rates of exchange between them provides information on the
overall fate of pollutants. Chemical speciation and the reactions
by which species are transformed from one to another are required
in order to understand the mechanisms by which pollutants affect
the marine environment. Thus chemical speciation is significant
relative to biochemical and geochemical processes in the marine environment. However, knowledge of the reactions involved in chemical speciation must be pursued for its own sake in addition to its
importance to presently recognized problems. Only by gaining an
understanding of specific chemical processes can we hope to be prepared to handle future problems in the marine environment which
are presently unperceived.

MINOR CONSTITUENT SOLUTION SPECIATION

There are two basic approaches to identifying minor constituent
chemical species. One is to devise techniques which can distinguish different chemical forms present in a sample of seawater;
the other is to develop models which are applicable to the marine
environment based on knowledge of the chemistry of an element.
Examples of the first approach include (1) analytical measurements following various types of physical or chemical separation
such as filtration, centrifugation, dialysis, chromatography, and
solvent extraction; and (2) measurements of the response of a particular form (e.g., "ionic") to various chemical perturbations
such as pH shifts and oxidation of organic material. This approach leads to chemical speciation which is operationally defined
rather than molecularly described. The second approach seeks to

obtain chemical information about the constituent through a
variety of techniques (spectroscopic, thermodynamic, and kinetic)
usually under synthetic conditions in order to chemically understand the analytically and operationally observed quantities.
For example, equilibrium and rate constants for specific reactions
may be defined in ways that are independent of reactant concentrations, and in many cases, in ways that are insensitive to variations in medium composition. Under these conditions it is possible to relate to the ocean chemical information obtained in
relatively simple solutions at reactant concentrations greater
than occur in natural marine systems. The use of these two approaches in an iterative manner provides a means of determining
minor element speciation in seawater. Operationally defined speciation identifies those chemical processes which should receive
the most intensive study under synthetic conditions. The resulting chemical model may then lead to refinements in the design
of analytical methods for natural systems.

The formulation of an equilibrium model is one of the simplest
methods to begin a consideration of minor element speciation. At
the present time this procedure requires selecting stability constants for potential element species which are based on data obtained by a variety of methods under various conditions (Morgan,
1967; Schindler, 1967; Morel et al., 1973; Lerman and Childs,
1973). Table 1 summarizes some of the models which have been developed for metals in seawater. Considerations of metal speciation by two investigations are shown for a number of metals. In
most cases there are major differences in the results of different calculations for a single metal which stem primarily from differences in the selection of species to be considered. Models of
this type are useful for identifying those metal species which
are likely to be important in marine systems and therefore worthy
of further experimental studies. Gardner (1974) concluded from
an analysis of this type that bisulfide and polysulfide complexes
are likely to be more important than simple organic complexes in
reducing marine environments. Some metals tend to form polynuclear complexes ($M_n L_i$ species, $n > 1$). It is unlikely that these
species are important in marine systems in which the metal

TABLE 1 - Inorganic speciation of some trace metals in marine systems at 25°C, 1 atm pressure, 35°/oo salinity, and pH ≈ 8.

Metal	Major Forms	Ref.
Al^{3+}	$Al(OH)_3^{\circ}$	8
Cr^{3+}	$Cr(OH)_2^+$ 85%, CrO_2^- 14%	4
CrO_4^{2-}	CrO_4^{2-} 94%, $HCrO_4^-$ 2%, $KCrO_4^-$ 2%, $Cr_2O_7^{2-}$ 2%	4
Mn^{2+}	Mn^{2+} 58%, $MnCl^+$ 30%, $MnSO_4^{\circ}$ 7%	2
Fe^{2+}	$FeOH^+$ 84%, $FeCl^+$ 7%, Fe^{2+} 7%	6
Fe^{3+}	$Fe(OH)_3^{\circ}$ 95%, $Fe(OH)_2^+$ 5%	6
Fe^{3+}	$Fe(OH)_2^+$ 60%, $Fe(OH)_4^-$ 40%	5
Co^{2+}	Co^{2+} 54%, $CoCl^+$ 31%, $CoCO_3^{\circ}$ 7%, $CoSO_4^{\circ}$ 7%	1
Ni^{2+}	Ni^{2+} 53%, $NiCl^+$ 31%, $NiCO_3^{\circ}$ 9%, $NiSO_4^{\circ}$ 6%	1
Cu^{2+}	$Cu(OH)_2^{\circ}$ 83%, $CuCO_3^{\circ}$ 11%	9
Cu^{2+}	$CuOHCl^{\circ}$ 65%, $CuCO_3^{\circ}$ 22%, $CuCl^+$ 6%, $CuOH^+$ 4%	3
Zn^{2+}	$Zn(OH)_2^{\circ}$ 50%, Zn^{2+} 22%, $ZnCl^+$ 8%, $ZnCO_3^{\circ}$ 6%	9
Zn^{2+}	$ZnCl^+$ 44%, Zn^{2+} 16%, $ZnCl_2^{\circ}$ 15%, $ZnOHCl$ 13%	3
$Mo(VI)$	MoO_4^{2-}	8
Ag^+	$AgCl_4^{3-}$ 54%, $AgCl_3^{2-}$ 24%, $AgCl_2^-$ 17%	1
Cd^{2+}	$CdCl_2^{\circ}$ 50%, $CdCl^+$ 40%, $CdCl_3^-$ 6%	9
Cd^{2+}	$CdCl_2^{\circ}$ 38%, $CdCl^+$ 29%, $CdCl_3^-$ 28%	3
Au^+	$AuCl_2^-$ 91%, $AuClBr^-$ 9%	7
Hg^{2+}	$HgCl_4^{2-}$ 66%, $HgCl_3Br^{2-}$ 12%, $HgCl_3^-$ 12%	3
Pb^{2+}	$PbCO_3^{\circ}$ 76%, $PbCl^+$ 11%, $PbCl_2^{\circ}$ 5%	9
Pb^{2+}	$PbCl_2^{\circ}$ 42%, $PbCl^+$ 19%, $PbOH^+$ 10%, $PbOHCl^{\circ}$ 9%	3

1. Ahrland (1975)
2. Crerar and Barnes (1974)
3. Dyrssen and Wedborg (1974)
4. Elderfield (1970)
5. Kester and Byrne (1972)
6. Kester et al. (1975)
7. Peshchevitskiy et al. (1965)
8. Sillen (1961)
9. Zirino and Yamamoto (1972)

concentration is less than 10^{-7} m, because the abundance of poly-nuclear complexes varies with the nth power of the free metal concentration.

In order to obtain useful precision in an equilibrium model, it is necessary to acquire measurements of the stability constants for species of significance in a seawater medium (e.g., with the ligands OH^-, Cl^-, CO_3^{2-}, HCO_3^-, $B(OH)_4^-$, SO_4^{2-}, and F^- for metal ions as well as mixed ligand species). These measurements must be obtained in a self-consistent manner for each minor element and under conditions of solution composition, temperature, and pressure characteristic of marine systems. An equilibrium model provides a useful reference for comparison with operationally determined species. Discrepancies between these two sets of results may be used to identify marine chemical processes requiring further investigation.

The formation of organic complexes has been one of the most difficult factors to evaluate adequately in equilibrium models. It has therefore been convenient to attribute to organic complexes the differences between equilibrium calculations and analytical observations. Based on the stability constants for metal ions with some types of organic functional groups which may be expected to occur in seawater, one concludes that only a few metals are likely to be significantly affected by organic ligands. Cu(II) forms relatively stable organic complexes, and thermodynamic calculations indicate that these species may be an important form of copper in marine waters (Stumm and Brauner, 1975). This conclusion based on a chemical model for copper is consistent with analytical studies which show that about 50% of the copper in seawater is organically complexed (Williams, 1969; Foster and Morris, 1971; Zirino et al., 1973). Model calculations also indicate that organic complexes may be significant for Fe(II) speciation (Kester et al., 1975), and this result is also supported by chemical observations (Theis and Singer, 1974). There are two reasons why equilibrium organic species are not likely to be significant for many other metal ions. One is that the organic ligands must compete with inorganic ones such as OH^- and Cl^- which either form

very stable species or are present in seawater at much higher concentrations than are the organic ligands. Secondly, the metal
ions must compete with the much more abundant Mg^{2+} and Ca^{2+} ions
for the organic functional groups. Overcoming this factor requires attributing very unusual properties to the selectivity of
seawater organic matter for metal ions relative to alkaline earth
cations. This analysis does not pertain to biochemically synthesized materials such as siderochromes which may form very stable
complexes.

Equilibrium models are most successful in describing rapid chemical processes. For slow reactions it is necessary to consider
kinetic factors in addition to thermodynamic data. Nevertheless,
equilibrium models are important for systems which involve both
rapid and slow reactions. A metal ion may form kinetically slow
species over periods of hours to days or longer, as well as species
with anions such as Cl^- or OH^- which typically achieve equilibrium
in times less than a second. It is impossible to disregard the
fast reactions and expect to explain the metal's chemical behavior solely on the basis of its kinetically slow species, because
a competition exists between all ligands regardless of their
kinetics which must be recognized in order to describe the response of speciation to environmental variables such as salinity
or pH.

It should be useful to distinguish between two types of metal-
organic species. One type is a _labile_ complex which forms by an
equilibrium between the metal ion and the organic ligand. The
second type is an _inert_ complex that is not in equilibrium with
the metal ions in solution, but has been formed biosynthetically
or was formed prior to entering the marine system (e.g., formed
during rock weathering or by continental biochemical processes).
The inert metal-organic complexes owe their existence to kinetic
stability rather than to thermodynamic stability. Such compounds
will not be reflected in equilibrium models. The paper by
Bernhard et al. (this volume) provides evidence for a presumably
inert zinc-organic complex in seawater.

With the presently inadequate knowledge of organic substances in
seawater, it is difficult to experimentally establish that a nonequilibrium form of a metal is an organic rather than inorganic
species. The most obvious approach to distinguish between organic
and inorganic forms is to carry out an organic oxidation process
and observe whether the metal enters an equilibrium form. For
this test to be valid it must be shown that the oxidation procedure (or some portion of it such as acidification) does not affect
inorganic matrices. One possible procedure for the decomposition
of some types of organic material which may be more selective relative to inorganic substances than persulfate oxidation or ultraviolet photochemical oxidation could be to expose the material
to a mixture of enzymes. Even if an analytical procedure is devised which would attack only organic material, it could be hypo-
thesized that the metal is bound within an inorganic matrix
which is protected from equilibrium with the solution phase by
an organic coating.

Many of the ambiguities in marine chemical speciation arise from
lack of knowledge of metal-organic species in seawater. These
species are especially difficult to ascertain because the metals
occur in the concentration range of 10^{-10} to 10^{-7} M in a 0.7 molal
ionic medium, and numerous organic ligands are present at concentrations less than 2×10^{-5} M. Conventional chemical techniques
for the characterization of these organic ligands require concentration and fractionation procedures in order to obtain the metal-
organic substance in a suitable quantity and form. One of the initial features to determine is the type and concentration of functional groups. Structural information would be helpful in evaluating the chelating ability of functional groups, but the major
portion of the dissolved organic matter which has not yet been distinguished as identifiable compounds is probably a heterogeneous
mixture of various components. There are likely to be significant
contrasts in chemical behavior of organic material found in the
biochemically active upper layer of the ocean and the refractory
substances which persist in deep regions of the ocean.

There are a number of types of organic compounds which could account for the observed nonequilibrium characteristics of zinc in marine waters. For example, several well known enzymes form very stable zinc complexes. Specific and sensitive tests are available for zinc enzymes such as carbonic anhydrase and carboxypeptidase (Bergmeyer, 1974). Biological systems also incorporate other metal ions into very stable organic complexes including porphyrins (Schneider, this volume) and siderochromes (Eichhorn, this volume). Chitin and "dead" protein material may be significant complexing substances in marine waters, and it would be useful to assess their concentrations in seawater.

A number of potentially useful spectroscopic techniques are available for speciation studies (Campbell and Dwek, this volume). With the possible exception of some of the major constituents of seawater, it is generally necessary to obtain solute concentrations higher than occur naturally in marine waters in order to apply most spectroscopic methods. This limitation may be overcome either by preconcentration procedures or by the use of synthetic solutions to obtain information which can be related to natural seawater. One attractive system for study, after some concentration and purification, could be iron complexes. Such systems may be investigated by ESR, Mössbauer resonances, Raman, UV and visible spectroscopy. These techniques have proved valuable in the study of iron in biological systems. Consideration must be given to the possibility that concentration and purification procedures prior to chemical characterization may alter the chemical form of the metal. For the identification of small organic compounds, the techniques of gas and liquid chromatography coupled with mass spectrometry are particularly attractive (Blumer et al., 1973).

The sensitivity, precision, and resolution of suitable polarographic and voltammetric methods offer new dimensions with respect to the determination, speciation, and physico-chemical characterization of various species in seawater. The high reliability of electrochemical techniques based on Faraday's law permits reliable measurements at low concentrations which are difficult to achieve by other methods. Reports of artifacts and erroneous results by these electrochemical methods can be eliminated by giving careful attention to the pitfalls common to all trace analyses, e.g., contamination and alteration during sampling, sample storage, and chemical treatment prior to analysis.

It is possible to relate the half-wave potentials on a current-potential curve to free energy of particular species, provided that the electrode reaction is reversible. Even though the electrode mechanism involves mass transfer via diffusion, the condition of reversibility assures equilibrium between the interfacial concentrations of the oxidized (ox) and reduced (red) components. The influence of diffusion rates and the relationship between the observed half-wave potential $E_{1/2}$ and the electrode potential E_o is:

$$E_{1/2} = E_o + \frac{RT}{nF} \ln \frac{D_{red}}{D_{ox}}$$

In practice it is frequently possible to set the two diffusion coefficients D_{red} and D_{ox} to be equal and therefore, $E_{1/2}$ is equivalent to E_o which is relatable to a free energy of reaction. Alternatively, a correction may be applied for the diffusion coefficient term if it is significant.

In considering the range of applications of polarography to seawater, it is suggested that this approach may be applicable to measurements of As(III) and of H_2O_2. Attention should be given to the possibility of artifacts arising in anodic stripping techniques due to the concentration of organic substances on the surface of the electrode producing metal-organic interactions on the electrode which are not characteristic of the solution phase.

The principal characteristics of polarographic and voltammetric techniques and their applicability to seawater have been considered by Bubić and Branica, (1973); Bubić et al., (1973); Zirino et al., (1973); Nürnberg and Kastening, (1974); and Nürnberg and Valenta (this volume).

MAJOR CONSTITUENT SOLUTION SPECIATION

The speciation of major constituents in seawater (those solutes
with concentrations greater than 1 mg/l) has been considered
more extensively than other types of speciation. Table 2 provides a summary of the major ion species in seawater. The range
of percentages listed for most of the species indicates the agreement (or disagreement) of evaluations based on different methods.
Even though speciation is the major concern of this paper, it
should be recognized that the chemical characteristics of some of
the major constituents can be treated by general interaction models which are an alternative to speciation models. It is possible to quantitatively describe the thermodynamic properties of
major cations and anions by general ionic interactions (Whitfield,
1973). These properties have also been described in terms of ion-
pair formation primarily on the basis of potentiometric studies
(Kester and Pytkowicz, 1968, 1969; Pytkowicz and Hawley, 1974;
Byrne and Kester, 1974). One approach to test and improve the
reliability of a major ion speciation model for seawater is to
employ a variety of experimental methods in addition to potentiometry, such as ultraviolet spectroscopy (Elgquist and Wedborg,
1974), solid phase solubility (Pytkowicz and Gates, 1968; Elgquist
and Wedborg, 1975), Raman spectroscopy (Daly et al., 1972), and
ultrasonic relaxation (Fisher, 1967).

Specific ion electrodes have been used extensively as a means
of characterizing chemical species in seawater (Warner, this volume). For many applications of potentiometric techniques, it
is necessary to make some extra-thermodynamic assumptions which
differ depending on whether cells with or without liquid junctions
are used. Some approaches use conventionally assigned single-ion
activity coefficients, whereas others use assumptions about the behavior of mean ionic activity coefficients in multicomponent electrolyte solutions. Additional calibration procedures which should
be considered include variations in temperature and pressure, non-
selectivity of specific ion electrodes in multicomponent solutions,
and maintaining consistency through a series of measurements so

TABLE 2 - Summary of major ion speciation in seawater

Constituent	Species				Reference
Sodium	Na^+: 98%	$NaSO_4^-$: 2%			1, 3, 6, 8
Magnesium	Mg^{2+}: 87-92%	$MgSO_4^\circ$: 8-12%	$MgHCO_3^+$: 0.1-0.5%		1, 3, 6, 8
Calcium	Ca^{2+}: 85-92%	$CaSO_4^\circ$: 8-13%	$CaHCO_3^+$: 0.1-0.5%	$CaCO_3^\circ$: 0.1-0.9%	1, 3, 6, 8
Potassium	K^+: 98-99%	KSO_4^-: 1-2%			1, 3, 5
Strontium	Sr^{2+}: 86%	$SrSO_4^\circ$: 12%	$SrHCO_3^+$: 0.4%		1
Chloride	Cl^-: 100%				1, 5, 6
Sulfate	SO_4^{2-}: 39-46%	$NaSO_4^-$: 26-40%	$MgSO_4^\circ$: 15-22%	$CaSO_4^\circ$: 3-5%	1, 3, 6, 8
Bicarbonate	HCO_3^-: 63-81%	$NaHCO_3^\circ$: 11-20%	$MgHCO_3^+$: 6-14%	$CaHCO_3^+$: 1.5-3%	1, 8
Carbonate	CO_3^{2-}: 8-9%	$NaCO_3^-$: 3-16%	$MgCO_3^\circ$: 44-50%	$CaCO_3^\circ$: 21-38%	1, 8
		$Mg_2CO_3^{2+}$: 7%		$MgCaCO_3^{2+}$: 4%	
Boric acid	$B(OH)_3$: 100%				2
Borate	$B(OH)_4^-$: 56-76%	$NaB(OH)_4^-$: 15%	$MgB(OH)_4^+$: 22-24%	$CaB(OH)_4^+$: 7%	2, 3
Bromide	Br^-: 100%				1
Fluoride	F^-: 48-50%	NaF°: 1%	MgF^+: 47-49%	CaF^{2+}: 2%	4, 7

1. Atkinson et al. (1973)
2. Byrne and Kester (1974)
3. Dyrssen and Wedborg (1974)
4. Elgquist (1970)

5. Garrels and Thompson (1962)
6. Kester and Pytkowicz (1969)
7. Miller and Kester (1975)
8. Pytkowicz and Hawley (1974)

that conventionally defined parameters are obtained within the
reproducibility of the measurements.

The speciation of weak acids such as carbonic, boric, phosphoric
acids and H_2S in seawater has been described (Pytkowicz and
Hawley, 1974; Hansson, 1973; Mehrbach et al., 1973; Lyman, 1956;
Kester and Pytkowicz, 1967; Goldhaber, 1974). Speciation determinations are needed for organic acids, ammonia, and silicates.
The differentiation of S^{2-} and HS^- has not been achieved for seawater systems.

Additional progress is required in the description of ion-water
interactions (Horne, 1965; Duedall, 1973; Millero, 1974). In
terms of speciation, these interactions may be expressed by hydration numbers, but it is generally recognized that the significance of a hydration number depends on the method used to characterize it (Kortüm, 1965). Many ions may possess a fairly well-
defined primary hydration sphere, but in addition to this type
of ion-water interaction, there are longer range effects of ions
on water molecules which require consideration. A question of
importance in marine systems is the extent to which ions compete
with each other for solvation by water molecules and the salinity
dependence of this competition. Ion-water interactions may also
have special significance for chemical processes in the interstitial solutions of sediments (Horne et al., 1968).

In order to advance the understanding of seawater as a chemical
medium, more attention should be given to the interactions between chloride ions and the major cations. Overall consistency
should exist between chemical speciation in seawater and in other
electrolyte media, and the parameters used to treat the thermodynamics of seawater should be consistent with information available for aqueous systems at infinite dilution.

SOLUTION-SOLID PHASE SPECIATION

Formalistically, heterogeneous phase reactions may be examined
in the same way as solution reactions, but experience in marine
systems has shown that reactions between seawater and solid
phases can be very complex (Weyl, 1967). It is important to

recognize that the chemical properties of the solid phase can
be a variable which is influenced by the exchange with seawater.
The free energy of constituents at the surface of a solid may
differ from that of the bulk solid phase due to dissolution-
precipitation reactions. This lack of equilibrium within a solid phase may persist even over geological periods of time. This
effect can be evident from differences in the approach to solubility equilibrium from supersaturated or from undersaturated
conditions for calcite, but aragonite solubility does not show
this behavior. One problem with chemical speciation between
aqueous and some solid phases is that the kinetics of the interchange between phases becomes very slow as equilibrium is ap-
roached (Berner and Morse, 1974; Morse, 1974), so that it is
possible to form meta-stable states. The surface chemistry of
phases such as calcium phosphate is very complex, revealing
chemical heterogeneities which cannot be treated in terms of a
single solubility product. Electron microprobe analysis provides
a useful method for examining the chemical characteristics of
surfaces. For solid phases with hydrated surfaces, it is possible to infer chemical changes by using a large amount of the
solid relative to the solution and examine chemical alterations
of the aqueous phase.

There are two types of solution-solid phase reactions which require investigation for marine problems: solubility reactions
and adsorption-desorption reactions including ion exchange. The
precipitation of a solid phase from an aqueous solution involves two distinct processes. One is nucleation and the other
is particle growth. The supersaturation of surface oceanic waters with respect to calcite and aragonite is due to nucleation
inhibition and to the effects of inorganic and organic substances
which prevent crystal growth on carbonate surfaces (Pytkowicz,
1965, 1971, 1973). Kinetic studies of crystal growth processes
reveal that they may be controlled by either diffusion or a surface chemical process (Liu and Nancollas, 1971; Nancollas and
Reddy, 1971; Nancollas, 1973). Particle size is likely to be significant in determining the chemical reactivity of solid phases (Langmuir,
1971) and the distinction between crystallite particle size and

agglomerated particle size should be considered. Organic material is significant in determining the properties of a solid phase and the chemical exchange between the solid phase and seawater (Chave, 1965). Radioactive tracers provide a useful means of determining the exchange between solid and solution phases (Duursma and Bosch, 1970).

OXIDATION-REDUCTION SPECIATION

Redox reactions are of great significance in determining the chemical properties of constituents in marine systems. There has been considerably less progress in the quantitative description of these types of reactions than for the other speciation processes considered above. This lack of understanding may be attributed to the nonequilibrium of many marine redox systems. The presence of biological processes precludes complete redox equilibrium and in addition, some chemical systems do not achieve equilibrium for kinetic reasons. Departures from equilibrium can imply two types of chemical conditions. One type is the existence of meta-stable species; the N_2-NO_3^- system provides an example in which N_2 is meta-stable. The second condition is the occurrence of unstable species due to a biogeochemical dynamic steady state. There are reports that Fe^{2+} occurs in marine waters even though Fe^{2+} will normally oxidize to Fe^{3+} at the pH of seawater in the presence of oxygen (Lewin and Chen, 1973). The existence of Fe^{2+} may be due to a biological cycling of Fe^{3+} to Fe^{2+} which results in a steady state concentration of Fe^{2+}.

The chemical approach to treating a nonequilibrium system is different for meta-stable and steady state species. Meta-stable species may be treated by thermodynamic methods, provided a distinction is made between chemical activity and equilibrium activity. For example, the thermodynamic activity of N_2 and NO_3^- can be considered even though these two species are not in equilibrium with each other. The characterization of steady state species requires kinetic considerations of the processes which maintain the dynamic balance.

Assessment of the redox potential of marine systems has been
based primarily on thermodynamic and kinetic inferences (Breck,
1974; Parsons, this volume). Significant advances could be
realized by the further development of experimental approaches
to redox processes (Breck, 1972; Liss et al., 1973). Information required includes a reliable determination of the redox potential and its variation in seawater and identification of the
redox couples which establish this potential.

EFFECTS OF TEMPERATURE AND PRESSURE ON SPECIATION

As one considers the chemical speciation of elements in the ocean,
it is necessary to evaluate the effects of temperature over the
range $-2^{\circ}C$ to $30^{\circ}C$ and of pressures from 1 to 1000 atmospheres.
Disteche (1974) provided a recent review of this topic. Techniques have been developed to determine some types of speciation
over the oceanic range of pressure, such as weak acid dissociation (Disteche and Disteche, 1967; Culberson and Pytkowicz, 1968),
ion-pair formation (Kester and Pytkowicz, 1970), and solid phase
solubility (Hawley and Pytkowicz, 1969; North, 1974). These
and other methods can be applied to other types of speciation reactions in future work (Whitfield, this volume). It has been
found that discrepancies exist between the effect of pressure on
speciation based on partial molar volume data and the experimental determination of equilibrium constants as a function of pressure. These discrepancies occur for heterogeneous solution-solid
phase equilibria such as the solubility of calcite in seawater
and pure water, and possibly calcium phosphate phases, but not
for homogeneous solution reactions such as weak acid and ion association equilibria (Millero and Berner, 1972; Millero, 1971).
These observations indicate that the surface of a solid obtains
a different free energy than the bulk solid phase during dissolu-
tion-precipitation reactions near equilibrium. The occurrence
of this discrepancy in pure water suggests that it is due to a
hydrated surface layer rather than to chemical complexities associated with the components in seawater.

RELATIONSHIP BETWEEN SPECIATION AND MARINE PROCESSES

Speciation provides a basis for specifying thermodynamic activity and for identifying nonequilibrium chemical forms in marine systems. It is essential to establish the relationship between speciation and the biochemical and geochemical reactivity of a constituent. It is possible to postulate that the adsorption of a metal onto a solid phase occurs because the metal exists as some particular species such as a hydroxide complex (James and Healy, 1972). It is also possible to develop an adsorption mechanism in which the aqueous metal ion, rather than its complexes, is the active species in the adsorption process (O'Connor and Kester, 1975). This distinction is of great importance in obtaining a predictive model of the influence of variations in solution speciation on adsorption processes. In the case of biological processes, there is evidence that calcium and magnesium ion pairs of phosphate may be preferentially assimilated relative to unassociated phosphate (Chambers and Whiteley, 1966). The toxic effect of metals is also species dependent; free copper is more toxic than organically inert complexed copper, and methyl mercury is more toxic than ionic mercury. The extent to which these examples of chemical form specificity in biological systems are representative from one type of organism to another has not been established.

In relating speciation to natural processes it is useful to identify whether the process responds to the concentration of a species or to the capacity of the system to maintain that concentration. The toxicity of ammonia to fish is directly related to the amount of NH_3 present, rather than to the presence of NH_4^+. Knowledge of the speciation of NH_3 and NH_4^+ thus leads to the realization that ammonia toxicity will be a function of both pH and the sum of ammonia and ammonium ion concentrations, and as pH decreases, the biological system can tolerate greater amounts of total ammonia-ammonium.

For natural processes that respond to the free ionic form of a constituent, it is sufficient to know only the ratio between that form and the total constituent concentration. Uncertainties in the individual complex species concentrations are unimportant for that particular process. However, if one wants to predict or describe the variations in the ratio of free to total forms with environmental variables such as pH, salinity, or competing ligand concentrations, then it is necessary to recognize the specific types of complexed species in the system. For example, changes in the chemical behavior of a constituent due to variations in the concentrations of marine water components will be greatly different for chloro, hydroxy, carbonato, and organic species. There is also fundamental chemical significance in being able to specify as reliably as possible the individual chemical forms of a constituent.

REFERENCES

Ahrland, S. 1975. Metal complexes present in seawater. In Dahlem Workshop on the Nature of Seawater, ed. E.D. Goldberg. Berlin: Dahlem Konferenzen.

Atkinson, G.; Dayhoff, M.O.; and Ebdon, D.W. 1973. Computer modeling of inorganic equilibria in seawater. In Marine Electrochemistry, eds. J.B. Berkowitz, R. Horne, M. Banus, P.L. Howard, M.J. Pryor, G.C. Whitnack, and H.V. Weiss, pp. 124-138. Princeton: The Electrochemical Society.

Bergmeyer, H.U.(ed.) 1974. Methods of Enzymatic Analysis, Vols. 1-4. Weinheim/New York: Verlag Chemie/Academic Press.

Berner, R.A., and Morse, J.W. 1974. Dissolution kinetics of calcium carbonate in sea water. IV. Theory of calcite dissolution. Amer.J.Science 274: 108-134.

Bernhard, M.; Goldberg, E.D.; and Piro, A. 1975. Zinc in seawater - An Overview 1975. In Dahlem Workshop on the Nature of Seawater, ed. E.D. Goldberg. Berlin: Dahlem Konferenzen.

Blumer, M.; Ehrhardt, M.; and Jones, J.H. 1973. The environmental fate of stranded crude oil. Deep-Sea Res. 20: 239-259.

Breck, W.D. 1972. Redox potentials by equilibration. J.Mar.Res. 30(1): 121-139.

Breck, W.D. 1974. Redox levels in the sea. In The Sea: Ideas and Observations on Progress in the Study of the Sea, Vol. 5, ed. E.D. Goldberg, pp. 153-179. New York: Wiley-Interscience.

Bubić, S., and Branica, M. 1973. Voltametric characterization of the ionic state of cadmium in sea water. Thallasia Jugoslavica 9: 47-53.

Bubić, S.; Sipos, L.; and Branica, M. 1973. Comparison of different electroanalytical techniques for the determination of heavy metals in seawater. Thallasia Jugoslavica 9: 55-63.

Byrne, R.H. Jr., and Kester, D.R. 1974. Inorganic speciation of boron in seawater. J.Mar.Res. 32(2): 119-127.

Campbell, I.D., and Dwek, R.A. 1975. Application of physical methods to the determination of structure in solution. In Dahlem Workshop on the Nature of Seawater, ed. E.D. Goldberg. Berlin: Dahlem Konferenzen.

Chambers, E.L., and Whiteley, A.H. 1966. Phosphate transport in fertilized sea urchin eggs. I. Kinetic Aspects. J. Cell. Physiol. 68: 289-308.

Chave, K.E. 1965. Carbonates: Association with organic matter in surface seawater. Science 148 (3678): 1723-1724.

Crerar, D.A., and Barnes, H.L. 1974. Deposition of deep-sea manganese nodules. Geochim. et Cosmochim. Acta 38(2): 279-300.

Culberson, C., and Pytkowicz, R.M. 1968. Effect of pressure on carbonic acid, boric acid, and the pH in seawater. Limnol. Oceanog. 13(3): 403-417.

Daly, F.J.; Brown, C.W.; and Kester, D.R. 1972. Sodium and magnesium sulfate ion-pairing: evidence from Raman spectroscopy. J.Phys.Chem. 76(24): 3664-3668.

Davey, E.W.; Morgan, M.J.; and Erickson, S.J. 1973. A biological measurement of the copper complexation capacity of seawater. Limnol. Oceanog. 18(6): 993-997.

Disteche, A. 1974. The effect of pressure on dissociation constants and its temperature dependency. In The Sea: Ideas and Observations on Progress in the Study of the Sea, Vol. 5, ed. E.D. Goldberg, pp. 81-121. New York: Wiley-Interscience.

Disteche, A., and Disteche, S. 1967. The effect of pressure on the dissociation of carbonic acid from measurements with buffered glass electrode cells. J.Electrochem.Soc. 114: 330-340.

Duedall, I.W.   1973.   Some ideas on the molecular structure of
   seawater based on compressibility measurements.   In   Marine
   Electrochemistry, eds. J.B. Berkowitz, R. Horne, M. Banus,
   P.L. Howard, M.J. Pryor, G.C. Whitnack, and H.V. Weiss,
   pp. 256-268.   Princeton: Electrochemical Society.

Duursma, E.K., and Bosch, C.J.   1970.   Theoretical, experimental
   and field studies concerning diffusion of radioisotopes in
   sediments and suspended particles of the sea.   Part B. Methods
   and experiments.   Netherlands J.Sea Res. $\underline{4}$(4): 395-469.

Dyrssen, D., and Wedborg, M.   1974.   Equilibrium calculations of
   the speciation of elements in seawater.   In The Sea: Ideas
   and Observations on Progress in the Study of the Sea, Vol. 5,
   ed. E.D. Goldberg, pp. 181-195. New York: Wiley-Interscience.

Eichhorn, G.L.   1975.   Organic ligands in natural systems.   In
   Dahlem Workshop on the Nature of Seawater, ed. E.D.
   Goldberg.   Berlin: Dahlem Konferenzen.

Elderfield, H.   1970.   Chromium speciation in sea water.   Earth
   and Planetary Science Letters $\underline{9}$:   10-16.

Elgquist, B. 1970.   Determination of the stability constants of
   MgF^+ and CaF^+ using a fluoride ion selective electrode.
   J.Inorg.Nucl.Chem. $\underline{32}$: 937-944.

Elgquist, B., and Wedborg, M.   1974.   Sulphate complexation in
   seawater.   Mar.Chem. $\underline{2}$(1): 1-15.

Elgquist, B., and Wedborg, M.   1975.   Stability of ion-pairs from
   gypsum solubility.   Manuscript, personal communication.

Fisher, F.H. 1967. Ion pairing of magnesium sulfate in seawater:
   Determined by ultrasonic absorption. Science $\underline{157}$ (3790): 823.

Foster, P., and Morris, A.W.   1971.   The seasonal variation of
   dissolved ionic and organically associated copper in the
   Menai Straits.   Deep-Sea. Res. $\underline{18}$(2): 231-236.

Gardner, L.R.   1974.   Organic versus inorganic trace metal complexes in sulfidic marine waters - some speculative calculations based on available stability constants.   Geochim. et
   Cosmochim.Acta $\underline{38}$(8): 1297-1302.

Garrels, R.M., and Thompson, M.E.   1962.   A chemical model for
   seawater at 25°C and one atmosphere total pressure.
   Amer.J.Science $\underline{260}$(1): 57-66.

Garrels, R.M.; Thompson, M.E.; and Siever, R.   1961.   Control
   of carbonate solubility by carbonate complexes.
   Amer.J.Science $\underline{259}$(1): 24-45.

Goldberg, E.D., and Arrhenius, G.O.S. 1958. Chemistry of Pacific
   pelagic sediments. Geochim. et Cosmochim.Acta $\underline{13}$: 153-212.

Goldhaber, M.B.   1974.   Equilibrium and Dynamic Aspects of the
     Marine   Geochemistry of Sulfur.   University of California,
     Los Angeles: Ph.D. Thesis.

Hansson, I.   1973.   A new set of acidity constants for carbonic
     acid and boric acid in sea water.   Deep-Sea Res. $\underline{20}$: 461-478.

Hawley, J., and Pytkowicz, R.M.   1969.   Solubility of calcium
     carbonate in seawater at high pressures and $2^{o}C$.
     Geochim. et Cosmochim.Acta $\underline{33}$: 1557-1561.

Horne, R.A.   1965.   The physical chemistry and structure of sea-
     water.   Water Resources Res. $\underline{1}$(2): 263-276.

Horne, R.A.; Day, A.F.; Young, R.P.; and Yu, N.T.   1968.   Inter-
     facial water structure: the electrical conductivity under
     hydrostatic pressure of particulate solids permeated with
     aqueous electrolyte solution.   Electrochim.Acta $\underline{13}$: 397-406.

James, R.O., and Healy, T.W.   1972.   Adsorption of hydrolyzable
     metal ions at the oxide-water interface.   Parts I, II,
     and III.   J.Colloid and Interface Science $\underline{40}$(1): 42-81.

Kester, D.R., and Byrne, R.H.Jr.   1972.   Chemical forms of iron
     in seawater. $\underline{In}$ Ferromanganese Deposits on the Ocean
     Floor, ed. D.R.Horne, pp. 107-116. New York: Columbia
     University, Lamont-Doherty Geological Observatory.

Kester, D.R.; Byrne, R.H. Jr.; and Liang, Y.-J.   1975.   Redox
     reactions and solution complexes of iron in marine systems.
     $\underline{In}$ Marine Chemistry in the Coastal Environment, Symposium
     Series. Washington, D.C.: Amer.Chem.Soc. In press.

Kester, D.R., and Pytkowicz, R.M.   1967.   Determination of the
     apparent dissociation constants of phosphoric acid in sea-
     water.   Limnol.Oceanog. $\underline{12}$(2): 243-252.

Kester, D.R., and Pytkowicz, R.M.   1968.   Magnesium sulfate as-
     sociation at $25^{o}C$ in synthetic seawater.   Limnol.Oceanog.
     $\underline{13}$(4): 670-674.

Kester, D.R., and Pytkowicz, R.M.   1969.   Sodium, magnesium, and
     calcium sulfate ion-pairs in seawater at $25^{o}C$.   Limnol.
     Oceanog. $\underline{14}$(5): 686-692.

Kester, D.R., and Pytkowicz, R.M.   1970.   Effect of temperature
     and pressure on sulfate ion association in sea water.
     Geochim. et Cosmochim.Acta $\underline{34}$(10): 1039-1051.

Kortüm, G.   1965.   Treatise on Electrochemistry, 2nd edition,
     revised. Amsterdam: Elsevier.

Langmuir, D.   1971.   Particle size effect on the reaction
     goethite = hematite + water.   Amer.J.Science $\underline{271}$: 147-156.

Lerman, A., and Childs, C.W. 1973. Metal-organic complexes in natural waters: control of distribution by thermodynamic, kinetic, and physical factors. In Trace Metals and Metal-Organic Interactions in Natural Waters, ed. P.C. Singer, pp. 201-235. Ann Arbor: Ann Arbor Science Publishers.

Lewin, J., and Chen, C.-H. 1973. Changes in the concentration of soluble and particulate iron in seawater enclosed in containers. Limnol.Oceanog. 18(4): 590-596.

Liss, P.S.; Herring, J.R.; and Goldberg, E.D. 1973. The iodide/iodate system in seawater as a possible measure of redox potential. Nature,Physical Science 242(120): 108-109.

Liu, S.-T., and Nancollas, G.H. 1971. The kinetics of dissolution of calcium sulfate dihydrate. J.Inorg.Nucl.Chem. 33: 2311-2316.

Lyman, J. 1956. Buffer Mechanism of Seawater. University of California, Los Angeles: Ph.D. Thesis.

Mehrbach, C.; Culberson, C.H.; Hawley, J.E.; and Pytkowicz, R.M. 1973. Measurement of the apparent dissociation constants of carbonic acid in seawater at atmospheric pressure. Limnol.Oceanog. 18(6): 897-907.

Miller, G.R., and Kester, D.R. 1975. Sodium fluoride ion-pairs in seawater. Mar.Chem.: In press.

Millero, F.J. 1971. Effect of pressure on sulfate ion association in sea water. Geochim. et Cosmochim.Acta 35(11), 1089-1098.

Millero, F.J. 1974. The physical chemistry of seawater. Ann.Rev.Earth and Planetary Sciences 2: 101-150.

Millero, F.J., and Berner, R.A. 1972. Effect of pressure on carbonate equilibria in sea water. Geochim. et Cosmochim. Acta 36(1): 92-98.

Morel, F.; McDuff, R.E.; and Morgan, J.J. 1973. Interactions and chemostasis in aquatic chemical systems: role of pH, pE, solubility, and complexation. In Trace Metals and Metal-Organic Interactions in Natural Waters, ed. P.C. Singer, pp. 157-200. Ann Arbor: Ann Arbor Science Publishers.

Morgan, J.J. 1967. Applications and limitations of chemical thermodynamics in natural water systems. In Equilibrium Concepts in Natural Water Systems. Advances in Chemistry Series No. 67, ed. R.F. Gould, pp. 1-29. Washington, D.C.: American Chemical Society.

Morse, J.W. 1974. Dissolution kinetics of calcium carbonate in sea water. V. Effects of natural inhibitors and the position of the chemical lysocline. Amer.J.Science 274: 638-647.

Nancollas, G.H.   1973.   The crystal growth of sparingly soluble
    salts.   Croat.Chem.Acta $\underline{45}$:   225-231.

Nancollas, G.H., and Reddy, M.M.   1971.   The crystallization of
    calcium carbonate.   II. Calcite growth mechanism.
    J.Colloid and Interface Science $\underline{37}$(4): 824-830.

North, N.A.   1974.   Pressure dependence of $SrSO_4$ solubility.
    Geochim. et Cosmochim.Acta $\underline{38}$(7): 1075-1081.

Nürnberg, H.W., and Kastening, B.   1974.   Polarographic and
    voltammetric techniques. $\underline{In}$ Methodicum Chimicum, Vol. 1,
    Part A, ed. F. Korte, pp. 584-607. New York: Academic Press.

Nürnberg, H.W., and Valenta, P.   1975.   Polarography and voltam-
    metry in marine chemistry. $\underline{In}$ Dahlem Workshop on the
    Nature of Seawater, ed. E.D. Goldberg. Berlin: Dahlem
    Konferenzen.

O'Connor, T.P., and Kester, D.R.   1975.   Adsorption of copper
    and cobalt from fresh and marine systems. Geochim. et
    Cosmochim.Acta: In press.

Parsons, R.   1975.   The role of oxygen in redox processes in
    aqueous solutions. $\underline{In}$ Dahlem Workshop on the Nature of
    Seawater, ed. E.D. Goldberg. Berlin: Dahlem Konferenzen.

Peshchevitskiy, B.I.; Anoshin, G.N.; and Yereburg, A.M.   1965.
    Chemical forms of gold in sea water. Doklady Acad.Sciences
    USSR, Earth Science Sec. $\underline{162}$(1-6): 205-207.

Pytkowicz, R.M.   1965.   Rates of inorganic calcium carbonate
    nucleation.   J.Geol. $\underline{73}$(1):   196-199.

Pytkowicz, R.M.   1971.   Sand-seawater interactions in Bermuda
    beaches. Geochim. et Cosmochim.Acta $\underline{35}$: 509-515.

Pytkowicz, R.M.   1973.   Calcium carbonate retention in super-
    saturated seawater. Amer.J.Science $\underline{273}$: 515-522.

Pytkowicz, R.M., and Gates, R.   1968.   Magnesium sulfate inter-
    actions in seawater from solubility measurements.
    Science $\underline{161}$: 690-691.

Pytkowicz, R.M., and Hawley, J.E.   1974.   Bicarbonate and carbon-
    ate ion-pairs and a model of seawater at 25°C. Limnol.
    Oceanog. $\underline{19}$(2): 223-234.

Pytkowicz, R.M., and Kester, D.R.   1969.   Harned's rule behavior
    of $NaCl-Na_2SO_4$ solutions explained by an ion association
    model.   Amer.J.Science $\underline{267}$: 217-229.

Schindler, P.W.   1967.   Heterogeneous equilibria involving oxides,
    hydroxides, carbonates, and hydroxide carbonates. $\underline{In}$
    Equilibrium Concepts in Natural Water Systems, Advances in
    Chemistry Series no. 67, ed. R.F. Gould, pp. 196-221.
    Washington, D.C.: American Chemical Society.

Schneider, W. 1975. Kinetics and mechanism of metalloporphyrin
     formation. In Dahlem Workshop on the Nature of Seawater,
     ed. E.D. Goldberg. Berlin: Dahlem Konferenzen.

Sillen, L.G. 1961. The physical chemistry of seawater. In
     Oceanography, Publ. No. 67 of the American Association for
     the Advancement of Science, ed. M. Sears, pp. 549-581.
     Washington, D.C.

Steeman Nielsen, E., and Wium-Anderson, S. 1970. Copper ions
     as poison in the sea and in freshwater. Mar.Biol. 6: 93-97.

Stumm, W., and Brauner, P.A. 1975. Chemical speciation. In
     Chemical Oceanography, 2nd edition, eds. J.P. Riley and
     G. Skirrow. New York: Academic Press, in press.

Stumm, W., and Lee, G.F. 1961. Oxygenation of ferrous iron.
     Industr.Engin.Chem. 53(2): 143-146.

Theis, T.L., and Singer, P.C. 1974. Complexation of iron(II)
     by organic matter and its effect on iron(II) oxygenation.
     Env.Science and Techn. 8(6): 569-573.

Warner, T.B. 1975. Ion Selective electrodes in thermodynamic
     studies. In Dahlem Workshop on the Nature of Seawater,
     ed. E.D. Goldberg. Berlin: Dahlem Konferenzen.

Weyl, P.K. 1967. The solution behavior of carbonate materials
     in sea water. Studies in Tropical Oceanography, Vol. 5.
     Proceedings of the International Conference on Tropical
     Oceanography, University of Miami, pp. 178-228.

Whitfield, M. 1973. A chemical model for the major electrolyte
     component of seawater based on the Brønsted-Guggenheim
     hypothesis. Mar.Chem. 1(4): 251-266.

Whitfield, M. 1975. The effects of temperature and pressure on
     speciation. In Dahlem Workshop on the Nature of Seawater,
     ed. E.D. Goldberg. Berlin: Dahlem Konferenzen.

Williams, P.M. 1969. The association of copper with dissolved
     organic matter in seawater. Limnol.Oceanog. 14(1): 156-158.

Zirino, A.; Lieberman, S.H.; and Healy, M.L. 1973. Anodic
     stripping voltammetry of trace metals in seawater. In
     Marine Electrochemistry, eds. J.B. Berkowitz, R. Horne,
     M. Banus, P.L. Howard, M.J. Pryor, G.C. Whitnack, and
     H.V. Weiss, pp. 319-332. Princeton: The Electrochemical
     Society.

Zirino, A., and Yamamoto, S. 1972. A pH-dependent model for
     the chemical speciation of copper, zinc, cadmium, and lead
     in seawater. Limnol.Oceanog. 17(5): 661-671.

Zinc in Seawater-an Overview 1975

M. Bernhard, E. D. Goldberg and A. Piro
Laboratorio per lo Studio della Contaminazione
Radioattiva del Mare, CNEN-EURATOM, Fiascherino,
La Spezia-Italy and Scripps Institution of Oceanography,
La Jolla, California-USA.

Abstract: Research on zinc speciation in the seawater and marine organisms is reviewed in order to exemplify the general problems concerning
detection and identification of chemical species in the marine environment.
Various physico-chemical forms of zinc in seawater are experimentally
distinguishable. The transformation of one form into another is slow, i.e.,
in the order of days. Exchange of radioactive zinc with stable zinc, which
is bound to natural complexes, is so slow that even after one year the exchange is not complete. This behaviour explains the observation that the
specific activity of marine organisms which preferentially accumulate certain physico-chemical states can be different from that of their environment.

Introduction

A knowledge of the physico-chemical forms of heavy metals is necessary

in order to understand their roles in biological and geochemical reactions

in the ocean system. These metals exist in sub-micromolar concentrations

in seawater, an electrolyte solution which may be considered to be appro-

ximately 0.5 molar in sodium chloride with millimolar contributions of ma-

gnesium, calcium, potassium, sulfate and bicarbonate ions. The analysis

of the total content of a trace metal and its isolation from seawater has

taxed the abilities of our environmental science community. In addition,

attempts to describe the marine chemistry of zinc have have been complicated by the fact that seawaters collected from various parts of the
world oceans exhibit not only slightly different compositions, but also
a range of temperatures (0-25°C) and pressures (1 to slightly over
1000 atmospheres). The first indications that trace metals in seawaters
existed in different chemical forms came a little more than a decade ago
in some pioneering studies of Professor Donald Hood and his collabora-
tors at Texas A and M University (15). The individual techniques employed to separate manganese and zinc from other metals were never completely effective, indicating that such metals might exist in a variety of chemical forms, some of which were resistant to the separation techniques.
A second major impetus to study the different physico-chemical states of
zinc came from the discovery that marine organisms and especially marine unicellular algae preferentially accumulated particular forms of zinc
(3). This work led to a close collaboration between the Institute Ruder
Boskovic (Zagreb, Yugoslavia) and the Fiascherino Laboratory in applying polarography to the identification of zinc species.

In the intervening years to the present, a number of other studies have
been carried out in laboratories about the world, yet the exact nature
of the chemical forms of these metals still eludes us. This presentation
will describe the various contributions to our present knowledge of trace
metal speciation in seawater using zinc as an example. The fact that zinc
is one of the most thoroughly studied metals may be due to several fac-
tors- its involvment in enzyme systems, its production as the radioactive pollutant Zn-65 from nuclear reactors and from bomb tests, and its
accumulation in such marine minerals as ferromanganese nodules and
phosphorites. It is markedly enriched in many marine organisms (5).

An understanding of its chemical forms in sea water will facilitate an
an understanding of its chemical behaviour in marine biology and ecology.

Zinc Speciation in the Natural Seawater

Until the late 1950s the marine chemist's understanding of zinc in seawater was limited to measurements of its concentrations, which appeared to be in the range of 0.1 to 0.2 micromolar. In 1959 at the Oceanographic Congress in New York, the celebrated inorganic chemist, Lars
Gunner Sillén, posed the problem of the association of inorganic and organic ligands with metal ions and indicated their implications to chemical
processes in the oceans (16).

The first experimental work on zinc speciation was carried out by Rona
et al. (15). They determined zinc by neutron activation analyses in seawater from the Redfish Bay (Mississipi delta) utilizing four pre-analysis
preparative steps: (i) seawater buffered with citrate to a pH between
5.5 and 6.5 was extracted with sodium diethyldithiocarbamate (DEDTC),
(ii) seawater was filtered through a 10 mμ (= nm)membrane filter, (iii)
seawater was dialysed in viscose sausage skins of an average pore size
of 4.8 mμ after filtration through a 10 mμ membrane filter (iv) acidified
seawater was precipitated with iron hydroxide at a pH between 9 and 9.5.
Two samples analysed from the Redfish Bay gave the following results
(in μg-at/l):

Extracted	Ultrafiltered	Non-dialysable	Coprecipitated
0.028 (5.5 %)	0.19 (38.1 %)	0.23 (45.7 %)	0.50
0.028 (5.5 %)	-	-	0.50

If the author's assumption that the coprecipitated zinc constitutes the total zinc is correct,about half of the total zinc present in the seawater
from Redfish Bay is non-dialysable but passes a 10 mμ Millipore filter.
Hence, in a complex form it may possibly be chelated by some organic
ligand. The ultrafiltered fraction, i.e., particles greater than 10 mμ in
diameter, represent about 40 % of the total zinc, and the extractable
zinc at pH 5.5-6.5 about 5 %.

M. Bernhard et al.

Slowey and Hood (19) applied the technique of Rona et al. (15) to open seawater samples from the Gulf of Mexico. A typical depth profile of the amounts of total, extractable, particulate, and non-dialysable zinc is given in Fig. 1. Most of the zinc appeared to be in an extractable form. Significant quantities were found to be non-dialysable, indicating again the presence of complexed zinc. Further evidence of this complexed form came from the observation of an increase in extractability of zinc after oxidation with peroxydisulfuric acid. Zinc was also shown to be associated with particulate phases.

It is interesting to note that the distribution of the extractable fraction and to a lesser extent also that of the non-dialysable fraction paralleled the vertical distribution of coprecipitated zinc. Slowey and Hood found the following concentrations (µg-at/l):

| | Extracted | Ultrafiltered | | Non dialysable | Total (est.) |
		> 450 mµ	10-450 mµ		
Coastal:					
average	0.038 (59.5 %)	0.017 (26.2 %)	0.0	0.014 (21.4 %)	0.064
range	0.003 -0.13	0.005 -0.028		0 -0.034	0.032 -0.153
Open sea:					
average	0.040 (74.3 %)	0.005 (8.6 %)	0.0015 (2.9 %)	0.023 (42.6 %)	0.054
range	0 -0.25	0 -0.015	0 -0.018	0 -0.081	0.003 -0.23

Slowey and Hood found much more extractable zinc, especially in the open oceans, than Rona et al. (1962). The sum of the amounts of the different zinc forms amounted to only 89.3 % of the total content in the analyses of Rona et al., while in Slowey and Hood's analyses the sum of all fractions comes to 107.1 % for coastal water and to 128.1 % for

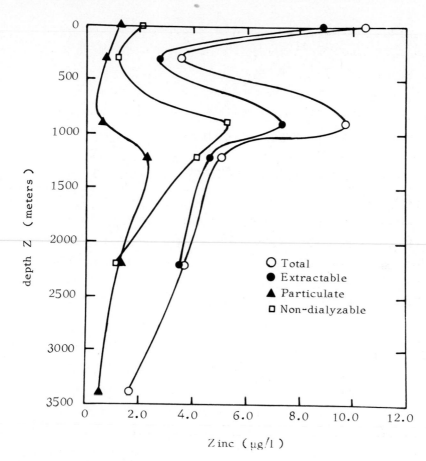

FIG. 1 - Vertical profile for zinc in various chemical forms at station
62 H 13-1 in the Gulf of Mexico. ref. (19).

the open sea. This indicates that in Rona's analyses not all fractions
were determined quantitatively, while in Slowey and Hood's analyses
fractions may have been considered more than once.

The distribution of different zinc species was also investigated by Bernhard et al. (2) in the western Mediterranean sea. Utilizing a polarographic method which allows the determination of ionic and labile zinc at
different pH levels they were able to distinguish three different forms:
(i) ionic zinc and zinc bound to labile complexes ('ionic zinc') deter-

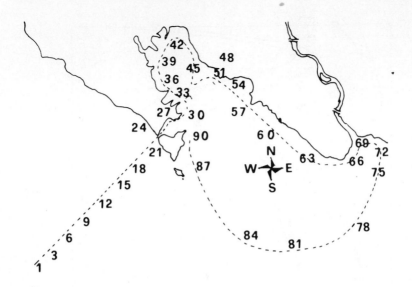

FIG. 2 - Sampling stations in the Gulf of La Spezia (Ligurian Sea).

mined at pH 8.1, (ii) particulate zinc plus 'ionic zinc' determined at
pH 6.5, and (iii) total dissociable zinc determined at pH 1.5, i.e., a
complexed form plus the particulate and the 'ionic zinc'. By computing
the difference one obtains the amounts of particulate and complexed zinc.
The sampling area near the town of La Spezia in northern Italy included
open waters up to 10 kilometers off the coast as well as the outer and inner part of the Gulf of La Spezia. As shown in Fig. 3 the concentrations
of the total and the 'ionic zinc' increase as the coast line is approached.
It is interesting to follow the ratios $\frac{\text{Zn determined at pH 6.5}}{\text{Zn determined at pH 1.5}}$ and the
ratio $\frac{\text{Zn determined at pH 8.1}}{\text{Zn determined at pH 1.5}}$. The first ratio is remarkably
constant in the open waters and in the inner and outer Gulf of La Spezia.
The latter ratio is constant in the open waters but scatters in the inner
and outer Gulf. This suggests that the complexed form of zinc is a constant fraction of the total zinc, while the 'ionic zinc' fraction varies
near sources of contamination such as the numerous shipyards of the
Gulf.

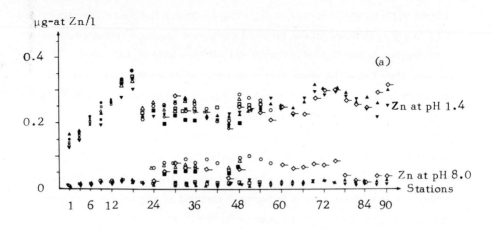

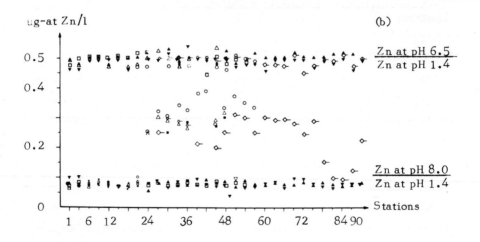

FIG. 3 - Horizontal distribution of (a) total (pH 1.4) and ionic (pH 8.0) zinc. (•: Mean value 1067; o: Feb. 1968; Δ: Mar. 1968; ◊ : Apr. 1968; □ : May 1968; ■: Oct. 1968; ▲ Dec. 1968; ▼ : Feb. 1969) and (b) of the ratios $\frac{\text{Zn at pH 6.5}}{\text{Zn at pH 1.4}}$ and $\frac{\text{Zn at pH 8.0}}{\text{Zn at pH 1.4}}$ in the area of

La Spezia (•: Mean value 1967; o: Feb. 1968; Δ : Mar. 1968; ◊ Apr. 1968; □ : May 1968;■: Oct. 1968; ▲ : Dec. 1968; ▼ : Feb. 1969) ref. (2). The sampling stations are shown in Fig. 2.

In open waters the constancy of the ratios between the three zinc fractions is also reflected in the zinc/pH curves of samples collected at various depths in the Gulf of Taranto and off the coast of La Spezia. Fig. 4,
in fact, shows that the mean values of the zinc determinations carried
out at various pH on the two groups of samples gave two identical Zn/pH
curves, even if the absolute zinc concentrations were different (11). The
mean value of 121 total dissociable zinc determinations in various depths
in station 1 of Fig. 2 resulted in a mean of 0.117 µg-at Zn/l with a range of 0.013-0.193 µg-at Zn/l. The mean concentration of total dissocia-
able zinc at various depths in various stations in the Gulf of Taranto
was 0.155 µg-at Zn/l with a range of 0.090-0.306 µg-at Zn/l.

Preferential Chemical Reactivity of Different Zinc Species with Marine Organisms

The chemical forms of radioactive and stable zinc, if different, may result in a preferential uptake of one isotope over another by marine algae
(4, 20). In the experiments described below, ^{65}Zn was added to natural
and artificial seawater in which the diatom Phaeodactylum tricornutum
was cultured.

For both types of seawater only one batch was prepared for all experiments. Glassware was exposed to the radioactive culture medium prior
to the algae inoculation in order to minimize any preferential adsorption
of zinc upon the walls of the glassware during the investigation. Depending on the chemical forms in which the radioisotope and stable element
were added to the culture medium, the radioisotope was taken up more
rapidly or less rapidly than the stable zinc. In practically all cases,
however, the chemical forms containing the radioisotope were taken up
in larger amounts than the stable zinc. This resulted in a higher specific
activity in the algae than in the surrounding seawater medium (Fig. 5).
The experiments continued for about 20 days. These observations can be
explained if one assumes that (i) the algae accumulated the labelled forms
of zinc preferentially, (ii) the ^{65}Zn did not label all chemical forms of

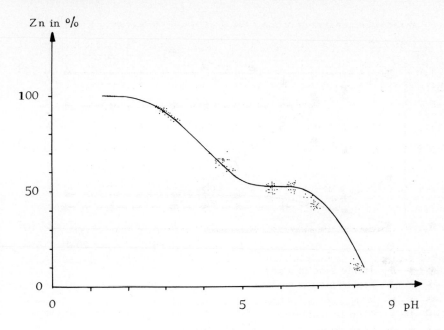

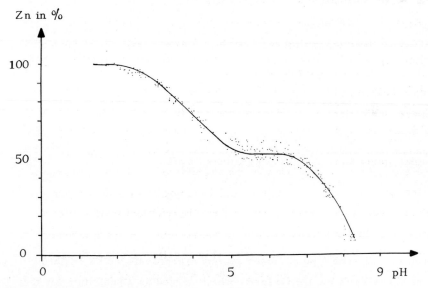

FIG. 4 - Zn^{++} versus pH curves for samples collected near Taranto (upper graph) and near La Spezia (lower graph) during cruises Taranto I and II and Spezia I and II. ref. (12).

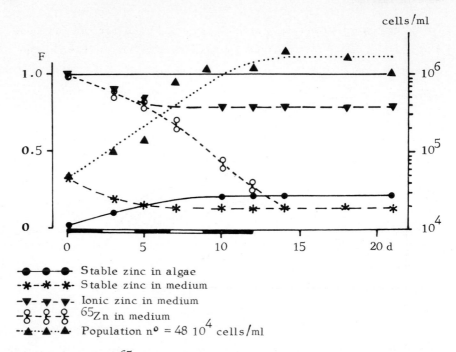

● ● ● Stable zinc in algae
-*-*-*- Stable zinc in medium
-▼-▼-▼- Ionic zinc in medium
-ϕ-ϕ-ϕ ^{65}Zn in medium
··▲··▲··▲ Population n° = 48 10^4 cells/ml

FIG. 5 - Uptake of ^{65}Zn and stable zinc by Phaeodactylum tricornutum in successive days (d) and generations from natural seawater medium plus cysteine (2.36 10^{-6}M/l). Expressed in fractions (F) of total ^{65}Zn and total stable zinc. In the medium at t_0:

$$\frac{\text{ionic stable zinc}}{\text{total stable zinc}} \qquad \frac{0.59 \ \mu\text{g-atom Zn}_I/l}{1.76 \ \mu\text{g-atoms Zn}_T/l}$$

$$\frac{\text{total } ^{65}\text{Zn}}{\text{total stable zinc}} = \frac{3.6 \times 10^{-4} \ \mu\text{g-atom } ^{65}\text{Zn}_T/l}{1.7 \ \mu\text{g-atoms Zn}_T/l} = 2.0 \times 10^{-4}$$

the zinc present in seawater and (iii) the transformation of one form into another is very slow.

Repeating the same type of closed system experiments with a chelating resin (Chelex-100) in the Ca form, which served as a substitute for the algae population, ionic ^{65}Zn was taken up preferentially to the other forms (Fig. 6). The zinc speciation of the stable isotopes in the marine waters also may be influenced by the elimination of the element in a form different from 'ionic zinc' by marine organisms, especially the more abundant ones. Kuenzler (10) noted that, although zooplankton eliminate primarily inorganic zinc, significant amounts of the element discharged passed through cationic exchange resins. Kuenzler suggested that some of the zinc leaving the plankton was inorganically complexed.

In the natural environment, Carey and Cutshell (8) observed that benthic organisms had different specific activities of ^{65}Zn than did the sediments from which they were taken. This may reflect preferential uptake of different species of zinc by the organisms and by the sedimentary phases. Or, there may be a dilution effect by the mixing of ^{65}Zn with different amounts of sedimentary materials.

A further bit of evidence comes from the work of Robertson et al. (14) who noted that the specific activities of ^{65}Zn in several northeast Pacific ocean pelagic organisms were approximately two orders of magnitude higher than those in the surrounding seawater. Robertson et al. were unable to distinguish between the relative importance of dilution and speciation effects.

These field studies are less definitive than the laboratory experiments because they involve open systems, i.e., parts of the marine environment, adjacent to the Washington coast in the northeast United States, which received the pollutant ^{65}Zn. This pollutants, carried down by rivers was produced by neutron activation processes in the coolant waters of nuclear reactors at Richland, Washington. Two phenomena influence the specific activities of zinc (disintegrations of ^{65}Zn per gram of stable zinc isotopes) found in marine organisms and in sedimentary phases. First of all, there is the difference in the speciation of the different zinc isotopes. The speciation of the stable zinc isotopes in seawater is determined by a variety of inorganic and biochemical processes. On the other hand, the forms of radioactive zinc result from the process that gave rise to its formation in the nuclear reactors and its reactions in river waters. By

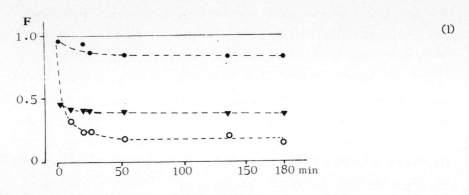

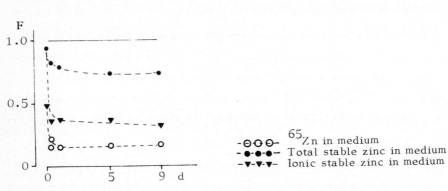

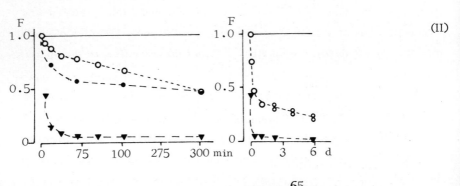

the time the ^{65}Zn reaches the ocean system, its distribution among different chemical forms probably differs markedly from that of its stable
counterparts. Secondly the amount of <u>dilution</u> of the chemical forms of the
radioactive zinc with those of the natural zinc is unknown. The extent of
this dilution clearly depends upon the amount of mixing with stable zinc in
the river waters.

FIG. 6- ^{65}Zn and stable zinc uptake by the chelating resin (Chelex-100)
in time in natural seawater. In (I) ^{65}Zn is added as ionic zinc and in
(II) as ^{65}Zn-EDTA complex. ref. (4).

$$\frac{\text{ionic stable zinc}}{\text{total stable zinc}} - \frac{0.49 \text{ µg-atom } Zn_I/l}{1.0 \text{ µg-atom } Zn_T/l} - 0.5$$

$$\frac{\text{total } ^{65}Zn}{\text{total stable zinc}} - \frac{7.2\ 10^{-4} \text{ µg-atom } ^{65}Zn_T/l}{1.0 \text{ µg-atom } Zn_T/l} - 7 \times 10^{-4}$$

Cysteine: $2.6\ 10^{-6}$ M/l; Ca-Chelex: 0.23 g/l

(II) $\dfrac{\text{ionic stable zinc}}{\text{total stable zinc}} - \dfrac{1.52 \text{ µg-atoms } Zn_I/l}{3.3 \text{ µg-atoms } Zn_T/l} - 0.5$

$$\frac{\text{total } ^{65}Zn}{\text{total stable zinc}} - \frac{1.66 \times 10^{-3} \text{ µg-atom } ^{65}Zn_T/l}{3.3 \text{ µg-atoms } Zn_T/l} = 5.0$$

EDTA: 2.4×10^{-6} M/l; Ca-Chelex 0.31 g/l
Experimental procedure:

5.I $\{[(ZnSO_4 + \text{Cysteine})_{24h} + NSW]_{30\ min} + (^{65}Zn + \text{carrier})\}_{1d} +$

+ Chelex

5.II $\{[(^{65}Zn + Zn_{carrier}) + EDTA]_{30\ min} + ZnSO_4\}_{24h} + NSW_{1d} +$

+ Chelex

Experimental procedure:

$\{[(ZnSO_4 + \text{cysteine})_{1d} + (NSW + Zn_{NSW})]_{30\ min} +$

$+ (^{65}Zn + Zn_{carrier})\}_{4d} + \text{algae. ref. (4)}.$

Carey and Cutshell (8) did not explicitly acknowledge these two phenomena which would influence the interpretation of their results upon the
specific activities of [65]Zn in benthic organisms and in sediments nevertheless, a ready recognition of both phenomena in their results is perhaps apparent. The highest [65]Zn activities were found in benthic fauna
and sediments on the inner continental shelf directly west of the Columbia
river mouth. There is a general decrease in the activities for materials
taken at greater distances or transport times from the coastal areas. This
most probably reflects dilution effects.

Mathematical models of Zinc Speciation

A theoretical approach to describe the speciation of zinc in seawater due
to the interactions of the metal with the natural complexing agents, has
been made by Zirino and Yamamoto (21) and Dyrssen and Wedborg (9).
Both papers are based on the same methodology, i.e., the solution of a
system of several equations describing the formation of metal complexes
between zinc and some selected ligands. The formation or stability constants and the activity coefficients were estimated or directly taken from
literature (17, 18).

Nevertheless as can be seen from Tab. 1, the fractions of the various
species calculated for equilibrium conditions are remarkably different in
the two models.

The differences between the numerical values of the various species in
the two models are mainly due to different values of the formation constants used. Zirino and Yamamoto (21) emphasized the pH dependence of
the chemical speciation by noting that practically all zinc is in the Zn
$(OH)_2^o$ form at pH 9, while at pH 7 nearly half of the zinc is in the ionic
form. They did also not consider in their model the mixed complex Zn
(OH) Cl. Recalculating Zirino and Yamamoto's model with their values
for the formation constants except, for the formation constant of Zn $(OH)_3^o$,

TABLE 1 - Fractions of the chemical species of zinc in seawater at
pH 8.1

	Zirino and Yamamoto	Dyrssen and Wedborg	Piro (personal communication)
Zn^{++}	15.0	16.1	39.0
$ZnCl^{+}$	6.1	44.3	15.8
$ZnCl_2^{o}$	2.6	15.4	6.8
$ZnCl_3^{-}$	1.0	1.7	2.7
$ZnCl_4^{---}$	0.4	2.3	1.1
$ZnSO_4^{o}$	6.1	1.9	15.8
$ZnOH^{+}$	0.2	2.3	0.6
$Zn\,(OH)_2^{o}$	62.8	-	0.1
$Zn\,(OH)_3^{-}$	~ 0	-	~ 0
$Zn\,(OH)_4^{--}$	- 0	-	~ 0
$Zn\,(OH)\,Cl$	-	12.5	3.2
$ZnHCO_3^{+}$	0.7	0.3	1.8
$ZnCO_3$	5.0	3.3	13.0

for which a more recent value was used (6) and including the species
ZnOHCl with the formation constant given by Dyrssen and Wedborg (9),
showed that the species $Zn\,(OH)_2^{o}$ becomes neglectable (Piro, personal
communication). Neither model considered polynuclear and organic complexes such as those with hydrocarbonates and with humic acids.

Electrochemical Experiments

Polarographic methods aided substantially in the study of the zinc speciation, especially the anodic stripping polarography. This technique has
the great advantage that introduction of reagents into the seawater samples is limited (the seawater itself acts as supporting electrolyte) and
the possibility of contamination is reduced. The initial entries were made
by Baric and Branica (1) who used dropping amalgaman electrodes con-

taining zinc. The electrochemical oxidations resulted in the formation of free or complexed metallic ions;

$$Zn\,(Hg) = Zn^{2+} + 2e^- + Hg \quad \text{and}$$
$$Zn\,(Hg) + X^- = ZnX^+ + 2e + Hg, \text{ etc.}$$

The complexing ability of a ligand with zinc could be ascertained through shifts in the half-wave potentials as a function of the concentration of the ligand, holding other variables of the system constant. From laboratory investigations, Baric and Branica suggested that zinc does not form any chloro-complex up to 0.5 M chloride concentration and that the species $ZnOH^+$ predominates at pH values higher than 8.3. On this basis, it is assumed that zinc is present in seawater predominantly in the form of the hydrated ion Zn^{++} with minor contributions of the monohydroxycomplex.

Successively, Branica et al. (7) extended the polarographic investigation of zinc in seawater to the pH range from 8.1 to 1.4 by adding pure hydrochloric acid to the sample. Plotting the percentage of zinc reduced on a mercury electrode as a function of pH, they obtained a typical curve, which was found common to more than 200 samples collected in the Ligurian Sea and in the Gulf of Taranto (see Fig. 4).

The constancy of the curve's shape and the analogy with the Zn^{2+} %/pH curves obtained by addition of complexing agents or ionic zinc to NaCl solutions or to seawater (see Fig. 7) led the authors to propose that at least three groups of zinc species exist in seawater:

1) An ionic form of zinc, usually 10-20 % of the total zinc, directly reducible on the electrode at pH 8.

2) A particulate form of zinc (zinc adsorbed on particles or particulate itself), usually 30-40 % of the total zinc, which is transformed into the ionic form by acid dissolution and corresponds to the difference between the values measured at pH 6.0-6.5 (the plateau zone) and pH 8.1.

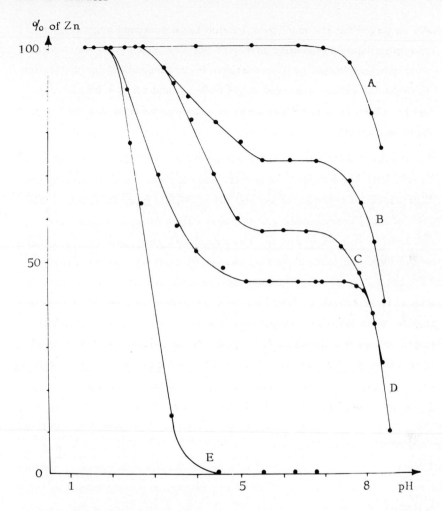

FIG. 7 - Zn^{2+} %/pH curve of a 3.8 % NaCl solution containing 100 μg of Zn^{2+} with and without various complexing agents. A: Zn^{++} alone; B: Zn^{++} + Cysteine (1:2); C: Zn^{++} + Cysteine (1:4.6); D: Zn^{++} + + EDTA (1:0.5); E: Zn^{++} + EDTA (1:10). The values in brackets indicate the molar ratios of ionic zinc to the complexing agent. ref. (6).

3) A complexed form of zinc (zinc bonded to unidentified organic or inorganic ligands), usually 50 %, of the total zinc, from which ionic zinc can be released by dissociation. It corresponds to the difference between the values measured at pH 6.0-6.5 and pH 1.4 (the lowest pH at which zinc can be measured in seawater medium on a mercury drop electrode).

Several experiments were carried out in order to verify this hypothesis of speciation. The existence of particulate zinc was demonstrated by centrifugation of seawater at its natural pH at 20,000 g for 20 minutes. The amount of zinc, corresponding to the particulate form, could be centrifuged down in such experiments. The complexed zinc could be separated from the ionic and particulate zinc phases by dialysis, after conversion of the particulate into the ionic one by changing the pH to pH 6. Dialysis appeared to be complete when the tubes (retention for molecules greater than 1200 mean molecular weight) containing seawater were left in contact with demineralized water for 6 days. An amount of zinc corresponding to complexed fraction remained inside the tubes. It is important to note at this point that the ionic form, as defined here, includes Zn^{++} together with those labile complexes that dissociation in the short time period of the polarographic measurements, i.e., those complexes defined by Taube that undergo ligand replacement within 1 minute at 25°C and 0.1 M reactant concentrations. The zinc complexes in oxygenated seawater were found to be somewhat liable to destruction when exposed to UV irradiation. As can be seen from Fig. 8, total destruction of the complexes was not obtained even after 27 hours of irradiation. The total destruction would have yielded the dashed curve of Fig. 8.

The dialysis and irradiation experiments indicate that the complexed zinc has several components which are high enough in molecular weight and size that they do not dialyse through conventional dialysis membranes. Nevertheless, these components are not necessarily solely organic substances; probably some of the zinc complexes are highly polymerized inorganic species.

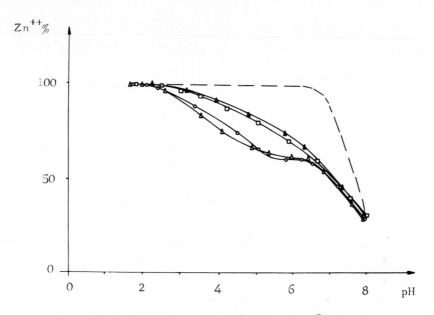

FIG. 8 - Effects of UV irradiation on the typical Zn^{2+} %/pH curve of a seawater sample (o: before irradiation; Δ : 3.5 h after irradiation; ▫ : 19 h after irradiation; ▲ : 27 h after irradiation; the dashed curve represents the curve theoretically expected) ref. (7).

A remarkable difference between the natural zinc complexes in seawater and the artificial one (ZnEDTA, ZnCysteine, etc.) is evident when one compares the Zn/pH curves obtained by changing the pH from 8 to 1.4, back to pH 8, and again to pH 1.4. In natural seawater (Fig. 9) ionic zinc released by dissociation at the acid pH is again bonded by the com-plexing agents when the pH is brought back to pH 8. The extent of com-plexing is the same as that originally, because, after the equilibrium has been reached, the measured ionic zinc is the same as that initially (see the coincidence of the points from pH 6 to pH 8). However, when hydro-chloric acid is again added zinc is released more easily than in the first measurements, indicating that even if the overall complexing capacity has not changed, some differences in the bonding strengths are apparent.

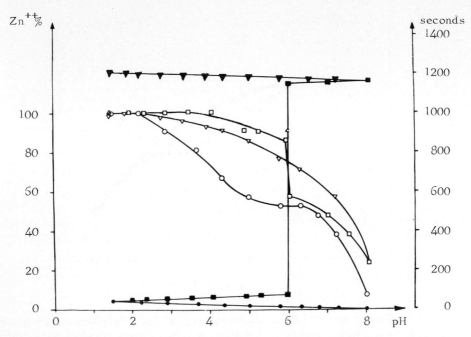

FIG. 9 - Zn^{++} % /pH curves of a seawater sample (o: from pH 8.0 to pH 1.4; □ : from pH 1.4 to pH 8.0, with 16 hours of equilibrium time at pH 6; ▽ : from pH 8.0 to pH 1.4. The time of each measurement is indicated by the corresponding black signs). ref. (7).

Kinetic Considerations

In order to assess the analytical methodology, Rona et al. (15) carried out some experiments with ionic ^{65}Zn which gave some indications on the rates of reaction for the different physico-chemical forms. Seawater, after the addition of ionic $^{65}Zn^{++}$, was stored for 72 hours at pH 8. An extraction with DEDTC at pH 6.1 showed that 100 % of the radioactive zinc could be extracted. This suggests that the ionic radioactive zinc did not exchange rapidly with the stable zinc present in the other non-extractable forms. Similarly, seawater was dialyzed after the addition of ionic ^{65}Zn. All the radioactivity passed the dialysis membrane, indicating again that during the time period between the addition of the $^{65}Zn^{++}$ and

the end of the dialysis (presumably a few days), the radioactive zinc did
not exchange with the stable zinc in the non-dialysable forms.

Similar results were obtained by Marchand (11) using columns of Dowex
50 X-8 resin for the separation of the various zinc forms. In natural seawater, three days after the introduction of the radionuclide, zinc was
found mainly in the soluble cationic form and, to a lesser extent ($\sim$ 10 %),
in particulate phases. By introducing radioactive ^{65}Zn to seawater and by
following the distribution of the ^{65}Zn among the various groups of chemical species through their radioactivity, Piro et al. (13) were able to study the exchange reactions among these groups.

A seawater sample free of both particulate and ionic zinc could be prepared by electrolysis at pH 6. Ionic zinc, liberated from the complexes,
attained an equilibrium with the complexed zinc in about 16 hours. If after the electrolysis, the pH is brought back to pH 8, an equilibrium is
reached among the three forms in about 24 hours. Seawater samples,
electrolysed at pH 8 in order to remove the ionic zinc, did not show any
formation of ionic zinc three hours after the electrolysis had been stopped,
indicating that the complexed and particulate forms are very stable at the
natural pH of seawater and that the rates of transformation are slow with
respect to time.

In a few experiments the exchange of ^{65}Zn against stable zinc was examined at different pHs. Ionic ^{65}Zn, added to seawater at pH 6, entered into
complex formation after 90 days only to an extent of 10 %. As can be seen
from Fig. 10, nearly all the radioactive zinc has been reduced during the
electrolysis, while the natural stable zinc is reduced to only 50 % of its
original value. This remaining part is complexed and thus not reducible
under the experimental conditions employed. If, on the other hand, the
added radioactive zinc had exchanged completely with all the natural zinc
species present, the reduction curves for the radioactive and stable zinc
would coincide. On the other hand, ^{65}Zn complexed with EDTA reached
exchange equilibrium with ionic zinc at pH 6 very rapidly, i.e., within
half an hour in NaCl (36 % S) (Fig. 11).

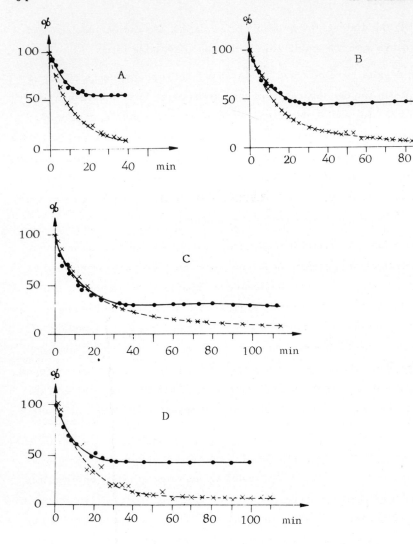

FIG. 10 - Percentage of Zn^{2+} (•) and $^{65}Zn^{2+}$ (x) during electrolysis at pH 6 of a seawater sample at which $^{65}Zn^{2+}$ has been added (A: 2 d after mixing; B: 39 d after mixing; C: 82 d after mixing; D: 90 d after mixing) ref. (13).

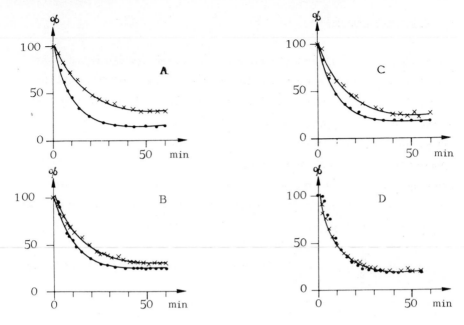

FIG. 11 - Percentage of Zn^{2+} (-•-) and $^{65}Zn^{2+}$ (-x-) during electrolysis at pH 6.0 of zinc solution in 3.8 % NaCl to which ^{65}Zn complexed with EDTA in excess has been added (A: 15 min after mixing; B: 20 min after mixing; C: 25 min after mixing; D: 30 min after mixing) ref. (13).

Radioactive zinc added to seawater at pH 8 did not exchange with the complexed stable zinc even after 1 year, although it was partially transformed to and/or exchanged with the particulate form. The zinc complex involving the natural ligands must have much higher stability constants than the Zn-EDTA complex. Also the exchange reactions between ionic zinc and zinc bound to natural complexes are very slow as compared to those involving the Zn-EDTA complex. This interpretation supplies an explanation for the experiments with phytoplankton which we described earlier. The ionic ^{65}Zn added to the culture medium labelled only the stable ionic and particulate zinc during the 20 days duration of the experiment, but did not exchange with the stable zinc bound to naturally occurring complexes. Thus, the algae which preferentially accumulated ionic zinc had a higher specific activity than the surrounding medium.

Future Investigations

Our present understanding of zinc in marine chemistry can serve as an example of how to investigate the distribution between different physico-chemical forms and the reaction kinetics of trace metals. But more than this, it provides a spring-board for future investigations of zinc species in seawater. What is the nature· of the particulate phase and of the complexed species of zinc? Both categories of zinc can be isolated. The former by centrifugation, the latter by dialysis. What existing techniques can be used to identify more intimately the forms of zinc in these two categories of compounds and their rates of formation?

Acknowledgement: This work has been performed under the Association Contract CNEN-EURATOM.

REFERENCES

(1) Baric, A., and Branica, M. 1967. Polarography of seawater. I. Ionic state of Cadmium and Zin in Seawater. J. Polarog. Soc. 13: 4-8.

(2) Bernhard, M.; Branica, M; and Piro, A. 1975. Zinc in seawater: Distribution of zinc in the Ligurian Sea and Gulf of Taranto, with special consideration of the sampling procedure. (Submitted to Marine Chemistry).

(3) Bernhard, M., and Rampi, L. 1967. First trophic level of the food chain. In Studies on the radioactive contamination of the sea, Annual Report 1965, Euratom Technical Report Eur 3274e, ed. M. Bernhard, pp. 14-17. Bruxelles: Euratom.

(4) Bernhard, M., and Zattera, A. 1969. A comparison between the uptake of radioactive and stable zinc by a marine unicellular alga. In Symposium on Radioecology, Conf. - 670503 (TID-4500), eds. D. J. Nelson and F.C. Evans, pp. 389-398. Springfield, Virg. 22151: Clearing House Fed. Sc. Techn. Information, U.S. Depart. Commerce.

(5) Bernhard, M., and Zattera, A. 1975. Major pollutants in the marine environment. In Proc. Second International Congress on Marine Contamination and Disposal of Wastes into the Sea, Sanremo 17-21 December 1973, Pergamon Press, Oxford pp. 195-300.

(6) Bradford, W.L. 1973. The determination of a stability constant for the aqueous complex $Zn(OH)_2$ using anodic stripping voltametry. Limnol. Oceanog. 18: 757-762.

(7) Branica, M.; Bernhard, M.; and Piro A. 1975. Zinc in seawater: Determination of the physico-chemical states of zinc in seawater. (Submitted to Marine Chemistry).

(8) Carey, A.G. Jr., and Cutshall, N.H. 1973. Zinc-65 specific activities from Oregon and Washington continental shelf sediments and benthic invertebrate fauna. In Radioactive Contamination of the Marine Environment, Proc. of Symposium Seattle 10-14 July 1972, ed. IAEA, pp. 287-304. Vienna: IAEA.

(9) Dyrssen, D., and Wedborg, M. 1974. Equilibrium calculations of the speciation of elements in seawater. In The Sea 5, ed. E.D. Goldberg, pp. 181-195. New York: Wiley-Interscience.

(10) Kuenzler, E.J. 1969. Elimination of iodine, cobalt, iron and zinc by marine zooplankton. In Symposium on Radioecology, Conf. 670503 (TID-4500), eds. D.J. Nelson and F.C. Evans, pp. 462-474. Springfield, Virg. 22151: Clearing House Fed. Sc. Techn. Information, U.S. Depart. Commerce.

(11) Marchand, M. 1974. Considérations sur les formes physico-chimiques du cobalt, manganèse, zinc, chrome et fer dans une eau de mer enrichie ou non de matière organique. J. Cons. Int. Explor. Mer. 35: 130-142.

(12) Piro, A. 1971. Chemical environmental factors in marine contamination. In Studies on the radioactive contamination of the sea, Annual Report 1968-69, Euratom Technical Report Eur. 4508e, ed. M. Bernhard, pp. 11-22. Bruxelles: Euratom.

(13) Piro, A.; Bernhard, M.; Branica, M.; and Verzi, M. 1973. Incomplete exchange reaction between radioactive ionic zinc and stable natural zinc in seawater. In Radioactive Contamination of the Marine Environment, Proc. of Symposium Seattle 10-14 July 1972, ed. IAEA, pp. 29-45. Vienna: IAEA.

(14) Robertson, D.E.; Rancitelli, L.A.; and Perkins, R.W. 1968. Multi-element analysis of seawater, marine organisms, and sediments by neutron activation without chemical separation. In Proc. International Symp. on the Application of Neutron Activation Analysis in Oceanography, pp. 143-212. Bruxelles: Inst. Royal Sci. Naturelles de Belgique.

(15) Rona, E.; Hood, D.W.; Muse, L.; and Buglio, B. 1962. Activation analysis of manganese and zinc in seawater. Limnol. Oceanog. 7: 201-206.

(16) Sillén, L.G. 1961. The physical chemistry of seawater. In Oceanography, ed. M. Sears, pp. 549-582. Washington D.C.: Amer. Assoc. Adv. Sci.

(17) Sillén, L.G., and Martell, A.E. 1964. Stability constants of metal-ion complexes. Special Publ. 17. London: The Chemical Society.

(18) Sillén, L.G., and Martell, A.E. 1971. Stability constants of metal-ion complexes (Supplement) Special Publ. 25. London: The Chemical Society.

(19) Slowey, J.F., and Hood, D.W. 1971. Copper, manganese and zinc concentrations in Gulf of Mexico waters. Geochim. Cosmochim. Acta 35: 121-138.

(20) Zattera, A., and Bernhard, M. 1969. L'importanza dello stato fisico-chimico degli elementi per l'accumulo negli organismi marini. II. Accumulo di zinco stabile e radioattivo in Phaeodactylum tricornutum. Publ. Staz. Zool. Napoli 37 (2 suppl.): 386-399.

(21) Zirino, A., and Yamamoto, S. 1972. A pH-dependent model for the chemical speciation of copper, zinc, cadmium, and lead in seawater. Limnol. Oceanog. 17: 661-671.

Nuclear Magnetic Resonance Techniques for the Determination of the Structure of Molecules

António V. Xavier
Universidade Nova de Lisboa and Laboratório de Química
Estrutural, Complexo Interdisciplinar, Instituto Superior
Técnico, Lisboa -1, Portugal.

Abstract: The scope and limitations of the use of nuclear magnetic resonance spectroscopy for the determination of chemical
and molecular structures are discussed. The methods reviewed
are generally applicable to studies of structures in solution
and are intended to demonstrate the great potential of the
technique in this field. In particular, a procedure is described whereby the quantitative conformation of a flexible
molecule in solution can be found.

INTRODUCTION

Since an understanding of chemical and biochemical processes
requires an extensive knowledge of molecular structures, the
development of physical techniques which can provide structural information is of great importance. The X-ray diffraction method has been the most useful technique for obtaining
the necessary parameters for the determination of the structure of molecules. Besides being time-consuming and laborious,
however, this method has other disadvantages. The resolution
obtained in large molecules (even up to 0.5 A of magnitude) may
not be enough to explain certain processes. Also, the X-ray
method is restricted to the crystalline state. This limitation
can cause serious difficulties, since the structure of the

crystal may not be maintained in solution. Thus, for the study
of structures in solution other methods must be used.

Even though a structure may exist for only a very short time
period, it must be defined. On the one hand, X-ray crystallography cannot hope to achieve this objective, for its time
scale is hours rather than micro-seconds. On the other hand,
the fastest methods of inspection ($<10^{-10}$ sec) are not very
structure specific, for they must use high energy radiation
which may perturb the system during observation (e.g., ultra
violet spectroscopy). The examination of a structure which is
in the micro-second range is possible through the use of low
energy methods such as nuclear magnetic resonance (NMR) and
electron spin resonance (ESR). Due to the comparatively small
value of the energies involved in the resonance condition, a
subtle change in the system can be studied. Since the energy
of molecular magnetic resonance and the time of nuclear relaxation are very much dependent on the environment of the nucleus,
NMR turns out to be a most useful technique for structural
studies.

As it will be shown, the full potential of the technique is
only realized with the use of paramagnetic ions, since they
alter these parameters (chemical shift and relaxation times) in
such a way as to make molecular structure studies possible.

This article will indicate how the NMR techniques can be used
for structural studies. These studies may have two aims -
determination of chemical structure or determination of molecular (three dimensional) structure. The chemical structure
provides a chemical description of the molecule (e.g., functional groups) and the molecular structure provides a three
dimensional picture of the molecule by giving the co-ordinates
in space of its atoms. In essence, a combination of NMR
methods will allow definition of these co-ordinates, but a
great number of precautions are necessary in carrying out the
experimental work and in interpreting it.

THEORY

I shall now analyse those aspects of the NMR theory which have
direct implications for obtaining structural information
[12,15,25,30]. First, the influence of the structure of the
molecule will be summarized in parameters such as chemical
shifts, coupling constants, and relaxation rates. I will also
examine perturbations of the values of the chemical shifts and
relaxation rates by paramagnetic metal ions [10] and show how
these perturbations can be used to obtain geometric information.

Chemical Shift

Due to the applied magnetic field B_o, the electrons around a
particular nucleus will have a circulation which induces a
magnetic field B_{ind} opposed to B_o. Thus, the nucleus will experience a field B_{local} which is modified by the screening of
the electrons. The induced field is proportional to B_o:
$B_{ind} = \sigma B_o$, where σ is a dimensionless constant of proportionality, the shielding constant. Hence, the local field at the
nucleus is given by $B_{local} = B_o (1-\sigma)$. As chemically distinct
nuclei have different values of σ, their resonances will occur
in different parts of the spectrum. The resonance positions
of nuclei thus depend on the chemical structure as well as on
the molecular environments and are known as the "chemical
shifts" [12]. In principle, the measurement of these chemical
shifts allows the identification of each type of proton of the
molecule, thus allowing the identification of H-bonds or of
the different functional groups of the molecule. This identification can be obtained by comparison with the data in published tables. The quantum mechanics treatment is not sufficiently developed so that one can use the values of chemical
shifts for accurate molecular structure determinations.
However, in the case of ^{13}C the effects of substituents have
been found to be largely additive [12,23], which, together with
a larger absorption window, is the reason why ^{13}C NMR has a
greater potential than ^{1}H NMR for the studies of organic

diamagnetic systems. One way of getting detailed geometric
information is to selectively perturb the chemical shifts with
the use of structural probes. The most useful probes are the
anisotropic diamagnetic groups (e.g., aromatic groups, i.e.,
ring current probes) and the paramagnetic metal ions. These
probes can already be part of the molecule (intrinsic probes)
or may have to be introduced in the molecule to make the
structural studies possible (extrinsic probes).

An example of the anisotropic diamagnetic probes are the so-
called ring current probes [15,24,3]. It is not easy to express quantitively the values of the perturbations on the
chemical shifts of the nuclei neighbouring on an aromatic
region. However, for cases where the nuclei are sufficiently
far from these probes, it is possible to calculate the anisotropic contribution to the shielding constant σ_{ani}. This
allows a semiquantitative estimation of the shift experienced
by a nucleus placed in a particular orientation in relation
to the aromatic group [17].   Due to the angular dependence of
σ_{ani} [25] we can then place a cone, whose axis coincides with
the direction of the principal symmetry axis and for which
the cross section is circular with a half-angle of $54^{\circ}44'$.
The surface of this cone separates the shielding and deshield-
ing regions. This means that the shielding can be positive or
negative depending on the geometric relation of the nucleus
and the probe. The example of ring current shifts serves as
a general introduction to problems of mapping, for it stresses
that we need to know the equation giving the perturbation
(i.e., its dependence on direction and distance) and we need
to know the position of the perturbing group. We should
stress, however, that there are several difficulties in making
quantitative estimates for aromatic ring systems other than
benzene [33,35].

The resonance positions of nuclei in paramagnetic complexes
often show large shifts from their corresponding positions in
diamagnetic complexes [10,11]. These shifts result from

nuclear interaction with the unpaired electron and are called isotropic (or average) nuclear resonance shifts. They are of two types:

(1) Contact Shifts - resulting from the delocalization produced, directly or indirectly, by the electron spin density at the resonating nucleus.

(2) Pseudo-contact or Dipolar Shifts - resulting from the combination of the dipolar interactions electron spin-nuclear spin, and the electron orbit-nuclear spin. These shifts ar only observed if the magnetic susceptibility produced by the unpaired electron is anisotropic.

This type of probe can be likened to introducing in the neighbouhood of the resonating nucleus (with a magnetic moment!) a much stronger magnetic moment. (The magnetic moment of the electron is $\sim 10^3$ times greater than that of the nucleus.) The perturbations caused by this probe in the spectral parameters of the nucleus, namely in its chemical shift and its relaxation time, can be used to obtain geometrical information.

These perturbations are not, however, always easy to measure. One of the most common troubles arises from the increase in the relaxation rate of the nucleus under observation. Clearly, for any isotropic shifts to be easily detectable, any effects of the broadening must be less than those of the shift. The most common case is for the electron spin relaxation time τ_s to be very short, as it is for Co(II), Ni(II), low-spin Fe(III) complexes, and most of the lanthanide ions. The bound and unbound species will give two separate peaks or a weighted average peak depending on the exchange rate.

Since only the pseudo-contact shifts have direct relations with the geometrical parameters, I will not deal with the contact shifts [26] in this paper.

Because the dipolar interactions between the unpaired electron spin of some paramagnetic ions (which have anisotropy in the

susceptibility) and a given nucleus fail to average to zero,
a net shift results - the dipolar or pseudo-contact shift.

The magnitude of this shift is given by [22]

$$\frac{\Delta \nu}{\nu_o} = D<\frac{3 \cos^2\theta-1}{r^3}>_{av.} \quad + \quad D'<\frac{\sin^2\theta\cos2\Omega}{r^3}>_{av.} \quad (1)$$

where D and D' are constants for each system at a given temperature, θ is the angle between the principal symmetry axis
($\vec{k}$ axis) of the complexed ion and the distance vector $\vec{r}$, and
Ω is the angle between the equatorial projection of $\vec{r}$ and the
$\vec{i}$ axis. The average is taken over the nuclear motions of
the molecule which are rapid on the NMR time scale. If the
symmetry of the complexed ion can then be taken as axial
(which is the case in reference [2]),then D' = O.

The exact nature (and formulation) of D depends of the particular system studied. It was first derived for certain
special systems by McConnell and Robertson [28] who used an
anisotropic g-factor. Jesson [16] has shown that this
approach could be used for the case of a number of doublets
of different energy. He derived a series of different values
of D valid for various relative values of τ_S, τ_R and of the
Zeeman anisotropy energy. This study, however, neglects the
matrix elements due to the second order Zeeman effects,
arising from interaction between the various energy levels
[4,29]. Recent work invoking this interaction results in
the addition to D of a term in T^{-2} without changing the first
term in T^{-1} derived by McConnell [28].

For the case of the lanthanide [4] at room temperature, there
is no anisotropic g-factor. The splitting of the (2J+1)
levels by the ligand field is so small that all the states
are effectively equally populated. For this case Bleaney [4]
has recently derived the value of D given in equation (2.31)
for the various lanthanide ions.

$$\frac{\Delta\nu}{\nu_o} = \frac{\beta^2}{60(kT)^2} \cdot <\frac{3\cos^2\theta-1}{r^3}> \cdot 2\ A_2^o<r^2>g^2\{J(J+1)(2J-1)(2J+3)$$

$$\cdot <J||\alpha||J>\}\ .$$

(2)

D is proportional to T^{-2} since the term in T^{-1}, being iso-tropic, is zero (the cases of Sm^{3+} and Eu^{3+}, however, are exceptions [4]).

The lanthanide ions probably constitute the most useful ions for obtaining structural information via the pseudo-contact shift mechanism [2]:

(1) Because the 4f electron shell is well screened, the chemi-cal shift that the Ln ions induce is that of the pseudo-contact interaction, at least for nuclei not in the immediate vicinity of the metal ion.

(2) The choice of the metal in the lanthanide series is such that one can pick either those with very short τ_s which give appreciable shifts with negligible line broadening (e.g., Pr^{3+} and Eu^{3+}) or those with larger values of τ_s but very big values of D which give very large shifts but also a certain degree of line broadening (e.g., Dy^{3+}, Ho^{3+}, and Yb^{3+}).

(3) Since it is possible to make isomorphous replacement among them, one can usually measure all the pseudo-contact shifts in relation to proper diamagnetic "blanks" (La^{3+} and Lu^{3+}). In order to obtain the absolute value of the pseudo-contact shift induced, any extra contribution to the observed shift (e.g. due to conformation changes and/or electric inter-action [7]) must be subtracted from the total induced shift. Also, as the value of the susceptibility anisotropy changes sign when going through the lanthanide series, it is possible to use probes that shift the resonance lines either up or downfield suiting the requirements of the system.

Furthermore, this isomorphous substitution allows:
(i) the verification that the shifts obtained are only due to
pseudo-contact interaction [2] and that conditions of axial
symmetry are verified, by comparison of the ratio of the shifts
of various nuclei to a given one, using different lanthanide
ions which induce shifts in opposite directions;

(ii) the checking of the values of r, by binding in the same
site an isotropic broadening probe Gd^{3+} (negligible D and long
τ_s). In particular, one can use a shift and a broadening probe
simultaneously so that a simpler spectrum can be obtained before the broadening experiments are carried out.

(4) Since some of the lanthanide ions give negligible line
broadening,it is very easy to do spin decoupling assignments
on the simplified spectrum obtained after the shifts are induced.

Coupling Constants

Two inequivalent nuclei present in the molecule often interact
giving rise to spin-spin coupling [12]. The dipolar interaction between the nuclei depends on their mutual orientation and
on the nature of the chemical bonds between them. It gives
rise to splitting of the resonance lines. The magnitude of
this splitting is usually small and, in contrast to the
chemical shift, is independent of the applied field. It is
given in frequency units and is known as the "coupling constant." When the value of the coupling constant is much
smaller than the value of the chemical shift between the
coupled nuclei, the spectrum will be a first-order spectrum.
The resonance of a spin - $\frac{1}{2}$ nucleus coupled to n equivalent
spin - $\frac{1}{2}$ nuclei is split into (n+1) lines which have intensity
rates corresponding to the coefficients in the binomial expansion. The value of the coupling constants depends on intimate details of the structure and can be used to obtain
precious information on the chemical structure of the molecules
and, in principle, to obtain geometric information. Again it

should be mentioned that the quantum mechanics treatment is not
sufficiently developed so that accurate conformational information can be obtained. However, in many cases the problem is
not to determine a precise conformation but rather to distinguish between two conformational possibilities or to investigate conformational changes upon variation of physical parameters.

An example of the use of coupling constants to obtain molecular
geometric information is the use of the Karplus equation
[19, 20] for the determination of the dihedral angles ϕ from
the value of vicinal coupling constants

$$J = A + B\cos\phi + C\cos2\phi .$$
(3)

The value of the constants A,B and C will be best determined
from model compounds since these constants cannot be predicted
accurately, particularly in the presence of electronegative
substituents and in cases of departure from tetrahedral angles
at carbon.

Also, great care should be taken in extrapolating geometric
information of this type to more than one dihedral angle,
since any tolerance or error which one usually gets in the
calculation obtained from J becomes, of course, multiplicative.

Relaxation Rates

After perturbation of the Boltzmann populations due to transitions between states induced by radiation, relaxation phenomena
occur which attempt to restore the Boltzmann population difference. The nuclear "relaxation rates" can give valuable information on molecular structure and motion. The approach to
thermal equilibrium has two mechanisms which are measured by
two relaxation times. The spin-lattice relaxation time T_1
measures the time required for the nuclei to achieve an equilibrium population among the allowed energy levels in the

applied magnetic field; it is sometimes referred to as the
longitudinal relaxation time, as it is concerned with the relaxation of the nuclear magnetization along the direction of
the applied field usually called the "z direction." T_1, then,
is a measure of the time required for the nuclei to equilibrate
energy with their surroundings. The spin-spin relaxation time
T_2 measures the time taken for the nuclear magnetization in the
(xy) plane to decay by a loss of phase; it is sometimes referred
to as the transverse relaxation time.

These times depend on the magnitude of the dipolar interactions
[13]. The study of the relaxation times makes it possible to
obtain information on the mobility of the nucleus or group of
nuclei [35]. The contribution from dipole-dipole interactions
may be deduced from the nuclear Overhauser effect, i.e., the
change in the integrated NMR absorption intensity of a nuclear
spin when the NMR absorption of another spin is saturated
[21,32].

The enhancement of the absorption intensity may be used to determine the distance between two protons [3], as the magnitude
of the dipolar interaction depends on the 6th power of the distance between the dipoles.

However, unless we use a paramagnetic centre (e.g., metal ion
[9] or spin label [18,27]) it is very difficult to obtain
enough accurate values for determining the molecular structure
of the whole molecule.

I shall now review the basic equations for nuclear relaxation
of nuclei in systems containing paramagnetic centers.

The spin-lattice and spin-spin relaxation rates for these type
of nuclei are respectively [6]:

$$\frac{1}{T_{1M}} = \frac{2}{15} \frac{\gamma_I^2 \mu_{eff}^2 \beta^2}{r^6} \left(\frac{3\tau_c}{1+\omega_I^2 \tau_c^2} + \frac{7\tau_c}{1+\omega_s^2 \tau_c^2} \right)$$

$$+ \frac{2}{3} s(s+1) \left| \frac{A}{\hbar} \right|^2 \left(\frac{\tau_e}{1+\omega_s^2 \tau_e^2} \right) \tag{4}$$

$$\frac{1}{T_{2M}} = \frac{1}{15} \frac{\gamma_I^2 \mu_{eff}^2 \beta^2}{r^6} \left(4\tau_c + \frac{3\tau_c}{1+\omega_I^2 \tau_c^2} + \frac{13\tau_c}{1+\omega_s^2 \tau_c^2} \right)$$

$$\tag{5}$$

$$+ \frac{1}{3} s(s+1) \left| \frac{A}{\hbar} \right|^2 \left(\tau_c + \frac{\tau_e}{1+\omega_s^2 \tau_e^2} \right).$$

where ω_s and ω_I are the electronic and nuclear Larmor precession frequencies, γ_I is the magnetogyric ratio, β is the Bohr magneton, μ_{eff} is the effective magnetic moment, r is the distance between the nucleus and the paramagnetic ion, $A/\hbar$ is the electron-nuclear hyperfine coupling constant in Hz, τ_c the correlation time for dipolar interaction and τ_e the correlation time for isotropic spin exchange.

τ_c and τ_e are defined as

$$1/\tau_c = 1/\tau_s + 1/\tau_M + 1/\tau_R \tag{6}$$

and

$$1/\tau_e = 1/\tau_s + 1/\tau_M \tag{7}$$

where τ_M is the lifetime of a nucleus in the bound site, τ_R is the rotational correlation time of the bound paramagnetic ion, and τ_s is the electron spin relaxation time.

The temperature variation of these correlation times is usually assumed to be of the form

$$\tau_i = \tau_i^{\circ} \exp (E_i/RT) \qquad i = R,M \tag{8}$$

and

$$\tau_s = \tau_s^{\circ} \exp (- E_s/RT) \tag{9}$$

where E_i and E_s are activation energies.

For τ_s the theory is not fully understood, but equation (9) is often found satisfactory.

If the bulk molecules are in rapid exchange with those attached to the paramagnetic ion (only one average resonance peak is observed for each nuclei), its effect is shared over all the molecules, and the observed spin lattice relaxation rate and $1/T_1$ for any of the nuclei cf the molecule is [9]

$$\frac{1}{T_1} = \frac{P_M q}{T_{1M}} + \frac{1-P_M q}{T_{1(0)}} \tag{10}$$

where P_M is the mole fraction of the bound ligand to the metal ion, q is the number of molecules co-ordinated to the paramagnetic ion (in the case where the molecule is water - the number of water molecules in the first hydration shell of the paramagnetic ion) and $1/T_{1(0)}$ represents the normal diamagnetic contribution to the relaxation rate.

The equations for cases in different conditions of exchange have been discussed in reference [9]. Particularly for slow exchange, if $P_M q \ll 1$ (i.e. for a small fraction bound)

$$\frac{1}{T_1} = \frac{P_M q}{T_{1M}+\tau_M} + \frac{1}{T_{1(0)}} . \tag{11}$$

APPLICATIONS

The previous section demonstrates that by using a combination
of NMR methods one can obtain the parameters necessary for
defining the structure of molecules in solution. Depending
on the system under study and on the degree of structural information needed, several approaches may be chosen. However,
a great number of precautions are necessary in carrying out
the experimental work and in interpreting it.

As I pointed out before, the full potential of the technique
is only realized with the use of paramagnetic ion probes.
Therefore, I shall now describe in more detail how to use these
probes. First, I shall show that relaxation methods can place
a nucleus relative to a relaxing centre on the surface of a
sphere of distance r from the centre. Relaxation studies by
themselves allow no further definition of the co-ordinates
unless a new relaxation time is measured from a second site of
known position with respect to the first. The second relaxation
measurement places the observed nucleus on a second sphere.
The intersection of the two spherical surfaces restricts the
position of the inspected nucleus to a circle in space. Two
more relaxing sites (probes) are required to give, by the intersection of spherical surfaces, a position of a nucleus in
space. Now the equation relating distance from the probes to
the inspected nucleus contains constants relating to the
occupancy of the probe site in solution (the binding constant
and concentration of the probe), as well as certain correlation
times. The methods for determining the binding constants will
be outlined. In principle, the spheres (r) can be absolutely
defined.

It is obviously easier to work with more than one nucleus in
the molecule whose structure is to be found, for the inter-
relationship of the nuclei, assuming a rigid molecular frame,
will restrict the number of probe positions needed. For
example, relaxation data on four nuclei in a rigid frame are

sufficient to locate the position of the probe atom relative to
this frame, since we are again dealing with the intersection of
four spherical surfaces which must interact at a point - the
probe. Clearly, it is a further considerable improvement to
take many more reference points and oversolve the structural
problem. In any event, a computer search may be involved in
order to find the best solution for the structure.

Assistance in locating one nucleus, e.g., a proton, with respect to another, can always be had from the analysis of
coupling constants, or from using the Overhauser effect by
analysing the relaxation of a given proton while irradiating a
neighbour. While the use of coupling constants is on somewhat
uncertain theoretical ground, the through space effect of one
nucleus upon another's relaxation is really just a second
relaxation probe.

For a long time, relaxation procedures were the only methods
used in studying structures. The number of water molecules
associated with bound metals in enzymes were obtained that
way [9]. More recently the relaxation measurements have been
greatly extended, and as I shall show, there is promise of a
very general advance using these methods. Relaxation methods
by themselves, however, will always be suspect, for the NMR
methods only give average distances. To position atoms more
definitely or to know something of their thermal motions, other
procedures have been developed.

The shift of a resonance line by a paramagnetic centre depends
upon the vector between the perturbing cation and the perturbed nucleus. The inspected nucleus now lies on a surface
of a figure not unlike a d_{z^2}-orbital, taking both positive and
negative values of the shift. Again, it requires four probe
positions or the inspection of a minimum of four different
resonance shifts of nuclei in a rigid frame to define a structure. A structure can always be obtained, but it may represent
some average over a sum of many geometries in thermal equilibrium unless it is proved to be a rigid frame. Now, the

added angular dependence and the different distance dependence
of the shift perturbation as compared with the relaxation perturbation means that a good agreement between the two methods
will only be found when a rigid structure is inspected, rather
than an average one. This is of extreme importance. We shall
therefore give an outline of the procedures which must be
followed when a search is being made for a structure.

The constants in the equations relating the observed shift to
the position of the probe are quite complicated. The binding
strength of the probe must be known (when conditions of fast
exchange are observed) and the physical cause of the shift
thoroughly investigated before the equations are applied. Because of the complexity of relaxation and shift equations,
methods in which ratios of measurements on different nuclei
are used are of considerable importance.

I shall now describe the routine of a method to determine the
quantitative three dimensional structure of flexible molecules
in solution [2].

The first step in the routine of this method is to measure the
specific shifts of each of the observed resonance lines induced
by the lanthanide ions bound to a specific site of the molecule.
This study must be done with at least two different lanthanide
ions, which must be carefully chosen so that it can be easily
proved that the contact contribution to the observed shift is
negligible. One way is to choose a pair for which the expected
direction of the pseudo-contact shifts [5] is opposite, and the
expected direction of the contact shifts [8] is the same. An
example of such a pair is Eu(III) and Ho(III). Since the shift
ratios R_i are only independent of the metal ion when
(1) The contact contribution is negligible,
(2) The value of D' is negligible, and
(3) The metal ions bind in the same way,
analysis of the relative values of R_i obtained for different
lanthanide ions shows immediately if the method is applicable.

In principle, as many different lanthanide ions as possible
should be used.

The second step is to plot the observed shifts for a range of
lanthanide ion concentrations so that a titration curve is
obtained and the value of the association constants can be calculated, i.e., the solution chemistry of the system is studied.

The third step is to calculate the ratios R_i of the observed
shifts of each nuclei to that of a given one at each metal ion
concentration.

These ratios are then extrapolated to zero metal ion concentration. In this way, any contribution to the shifts from a much
weaker binding site and/or any variation on the shifts due to
conformational changes caused by increasing ionic strength can
be minimized. If these ratios are sufficiently similar, it
proves that both the value of the contact contributions and
the value of D' can be neglected. Also, the supposition that
binding sites of the lanthanide ions are similar is then sub-
stantiated.

The fourth step involves the relaxation studies. These experiments are carried out with a broadening probe such as Gd(III),
and the selective broadening of the peaks is measured. Again,
the ratios of the perturbations of the relaxations are calculated.

At this stage the data are sufficient to apply the computer
treatment described in reference [2] so that the conformation
of the molecules can be obtained. The solution will be that
one which agrees with the ratios obtained experimentally.

REFERENCES

(1) Amos, A.T.; and Roberts, H.G.F. 1968. In Quantum Theory of Magnetic Resonance Parameters, ed. J.D.Memory, McGraw-Hill Inc., New York.

(2) Barry, C.D., Glasel, J.A., Williams, R.J.P., and Xavier, A.V. 1974. J.Mol. Biol. **84**: 471.

(3) Bell, R.A., and Saumders, J.K. 1970. Can. J. Chem. **48**: 11 14.

(4) Bleaney, B. 1972. J.Mag. Res. **8**: 91

(5) Bleaney, B., Dobson, C.M., Levine, B.A., Martin, R.B., Williams, R.J.P., Xavier, A.V. 1972. Chem. Comm.: 791.

(6) Bloembergen, N., and Morgan, L.O. 1961. J.Chem. Phys. **27**: 842.

(7) Buckingham, A.D. 1960. Can. J.Chem. **38**: 300

(8) Dobson, C.M. Williams, R.J.P., and Xavier, A.V. 1973. J.Chem. Soc. (Dalton): 2662.

(9) Dwek, R.A.; Williams, R.J.P.; and Xavier; A.V. 1974. In Metal Ions in Biological Systems 4, ed. H. Sigel, pp.61-210. Marcel Dekker, Inc. New York.

(10) Eaton, D.R., and Phillips, W.D. 1965. Adv. Mag. Res. **1**: 119.

(11) Eaton, D.R., and Zaw, K. 1971. Coor.Chem. Rev. **7**, 197.

(12) Emsley, J.W.; Feeney, J.; and Sutcliffe. 1965. In High Resolution Nuclear Magnetic Resonance Spectroscopy. Pergamon Press. Inc., New York.

(13) Gutowsky, H.S., and Woessener, D.E. 1956. Phys. Rev. **104**, 843.

(14) Horrocks, Jr., W. de W. 1970. Inorg. Chem. **9**, 690.

(15) Jackman, L.M.; and Sternhell, S. 1969. In NMR Spectroscopy in Organic Chemistry, 2nd Ed. Pergamon Press Ltd., Oxford.

(16) Jesson, J.P. 1967. J. Chem. Phys. **47**, 579.

(17) Johnson, C.E.,and Bovey, F.A. 1958. J.Chem. Phys. **29**, 1012.

(18) Jost, P., and Griffith, O.H. 1972. Methods in Pharmacology, 2, 31.

(19) Karplus, M. 1959. J. Chem. Phys. 30, 11.

(20) Karplus, M. 1963. J.Am.Chem. Soc. 85,287o.

(21) Kuhlman, K.F., and Grant, D.M. 1968. J.Am. Chem.Soc. 90,7355.

(22) LaMar, G.N., Horrocks, Jr., W. de W., and Allen, L.C. 1964. J.Chem. Phys. 41, 2126.

(23) Levy, G.C.; and Nelson, G.L. 1972. In Carbon-13 NMR for Organic Chemists. Wiley-Interscience New-York.

(24) Lipscomb, W.N. 1966. Adv. Mag. Res. 2, 138.

(25) Lynden-Bell, R.M.; and Harris, R.K. 1971. In NMR Spectroscopy. Nelson, London.

(26) McConnel, H.M., and Robertson, R.E. 1958. J. Chem. Phys.28,107.

(27) McConnell, H.M., and McFarland, B.G. 1970. Quart. Rev. Biophys. 3, 91.

(28) McConnel , H.M., and Robertson, R.E. 1958. J.Chem. Phys.29,1361.

(29) McGarbey, B.R. 1970. J. Chem. Phys. 53,86.

(30) McLauchlan, K.A. 1972. In Magnetic Resonance Clarendon.Press,Oxford.

(31) Musher, J.I. 1966. Adv. Mag. Res. 2, 177.

(32) Noggle, J.H.; and Schirmer, R.E. 1971. In the Nuclear Overhauser Effect. Academic Press, New York.

(33) Roberts, H.G.F. 1970. Theoret. Chim. Acta. (Berlin).17, 151.

(34) Wallach, D. 1967. J. Chem. Phys. 47, 5258.

(35) Wu, T.K, and Dailey, B.P. 1964. J. Chem. Phys. 41, 2796.

Polarography and Voltammetry in Marine Chemistry

H. W. Nürnberg and P. Valenta
Institute of Applied Physical Chemistry, Nuclear Research
Centre (KFA), Juelich, Federal Republic of Germany

Abstract: One of the areas in marine chemistry gaining increasing importance is represented by inorganic and organic microconstituents in sea water. Polarography and voltammetry offer unique potentialities with respect to the analysis, speciation, and physicochemical characterization of these substances. The scope and the general aspects of those techniques are described. Besides the presently popular technique of stripping voltammetry, attention is drawn to further possibilities offered by other new advanced methodologies. The great and stimulating potentials of the treated electrochemical methods are emphasized and illustrated by a review of various applications to marine trace chemistry. A carefully selected compilation of references provides an entry to the field.

INTRODUCTION:

The electrochemical methods of polarography and voltammetry have, in their advanced versions, great potential for the study of a number of trace metals contained in sea water. These metals, well accessible to polarography and voltammetry, belong mainly to the transition metals (Table 1 and Fig. 6), among them the toxic metals Cd, Pb, Hg. The usual natural concentration levels of all metallic microconstituents in the sea are very low (typically 20 to 0.01 ppb, i.e., 2×10^{-7} to 1×10^{-10} M or less) and cor-

respond thus to the ultra trace range. Due to pollution, their
concentrations may be locally up to 3 or 4 orders of magnitude
higher but usually remain in the trace range, i.e., below 10^{-4}M
or 10 ppm. Although their concentrations are low, many of
these trace metals are of particular interest since they enter
and affect the life cycles of marine organisms and tend to accumulate at certain stages of the marine food chain. Also, they may
play an important role in marine sedimentation processes /46,93/.

The application of suitable polarographic or voltammetric methods
offers a very versatile, and frequently the only, way to determine not only the total elemental concentration of the respective metal but also to identify its chemical state and to investigate its physicochemical properties, such as the stability of
the formed complexes, the kinetics of their formation and dissociation, and the values of the effective diffusion coefficient.

Furthermore, the amount of some organic substances mainly entering the sea as pollutants and acting, for instance, as ligands
for metals may be determined, and their physicochemical properties may be studied in the matrix sea water, at least at deliberately elevated concentrations. /37, 75, 82, 85, 125-128/.

The aim of this article is to illuminate the manifold possibilities offered by polarography and voltammetry for the determination, speciation, and physicochemical characterization of microconstituents of sea water which are accessible to these electrochemical methods.

In polarography and voltammetry, the substance studied is either
reduced or oxidized at an inert test electrode under transfer
of n electrons per elementary step in the electrode reaction,
which can be generalized as

(I) $Ox + ne^- \rightleftharpoons Red.$

The corresponding current-potential-characteristic (i-E-curve)
is recorded. The electrode potential E is the adjusted, and the
current i is the measured, quantity. For applications in sea water, the test electrode is always a microelectrode (typical area
$< 3 \times 10^{-2} cm^2$, except the mercury film electrode), most frequently
of mercury or at least mercury coated which has the advantage of
a smooth surface and a rather high hydrogen overvoltage. Thus,
in slightly acid and neutral solutions a rather wide cathodic
potential range up to -1.8 volts (SCE) becomes accessible before
the deposition of Na^+ tends to mask the i-E-curve of the substance studied. However, in the anodic direction, the potential
range is rather limited and ends at about -0.1 V (SCE). These
limits refer to the matrix seawater containing Na^+ and Cl^- as
major constituents. Among the test electrodes made from other
materials the carbon paste electrode /68, 69/ promises good application potential for the study of inorganic and organic constituents of sea water (Table 1).
If the test electrode is a dropping mercury electrode (DME) (typical drop time t_1 = 3-5s), which has a significant advantage
in that every few seconds a fresh and thus uncontaminated electrode surface of reproducible qualities is available, the method
belongs to polarography. All techniques with stationary test
electrodes are termed voltammetric.

In general, the polarographic and voltammetric methods are based
on a remarkably complete and well established, detailed theory
of electrode processes. They combine high sensitivity - emerging
from the equivalence of the enormous electric charge of n.96500
Coulomb with 1 mole substance - with good precision and the absence of fundamental standardization problems due to their foundation on Faraday's law. Even at the trace level these properties secure a rather good chance of achieving accurate and reliable results. Furthermore, the pronounced selectivity makes
the simultaneous determination of several metals in the same solution in one run possible, even if these are present in different quantities. Particularly for sea water samples the preli-

TABLE 1

element	mercury electrode	carbon paste electrode	element	mercury electrode	carbon paste electrode
Ag^+	e	a	Mn^{2+}	a	a,b
As^{3+}	a	–	MoO_4^{2-}	d	–
Ba^{2+}	a,e	–	Ni^{2+}	a	a,b
Bi^{3+}	a	a,b	Pb^{2+}	a	a,b
Br^-	d	–	S^{2-}	d	–
Ca^{2+}	e	b	Sb^{3+}	a	b
Cd^{2+}	a	a	Se^{4+}	a	–
Cl^-	d	–	Sn^{2+}	a	a,b,c
Co^{2+}	a	a,b	Sr^{2+}	a,e	–
CrO_4^{2-}	d	b	Tl^+	a	a,b
Cu^{2+}	a	a,b	UO_2^{2+}	a,c	–
Fe^{2+}	a,b,e	a,b	VO_3	d	–
Ga^{3+}	a	a	WO_4^{2-}	d	b
Ge^{2+}	a	b	Zn^{2+}	a	a
Hg^{2+}	e	a,b			
In^{3+}	a	a			
I^-	d	b			

a: reduction to the metal
b: oxidation or reduction followed by a chemical reaction
c: reaction in adsorbed state
d: formation of an insoluble product with the mercury
e: indirect determination

minary preparations are rather simple. However, of paramount importance with respect to speciation is that these electrochemical methods are unique compared to various highly sensitive and popular methods in trace analysis, such as atomic absorption, emission spectroscopy, neutron activation, mass spectroscopy, etc., in that they are specific not only to the element but to the chemical state of the substance studied.

METHODOLOGY

General Aspects

The solution usually contains only the oxidized form Ox or the
reduced form Red of the substance studied in low concentration
(10^{-3} to 10^{-10}M). The other form is produced at the test electrode in situ. If Red is a metal Me^{o}, it diffuses into the test
electrode or into the solution if Red is, for instance, an ion
Me^{z+} of lower oxidation state than Ox or an organic substance.
Consequently, relatively small currents (μA to nA) are flowing,
and the amount of substance consumed for the recording
of the i-E-curve remains very small, usually causing no alteration of the bulk concentration. It is obvious that the
solution would have an intolerably large ohmic resistance if it
did not contain, in addition, an inert supporting electrolyte
such as alkali or earth alkali salts in a much larger concentration (0.1 to 1 M). In this respect sea water (ionic strength
I = 0.7 and pH = 8) is an ideal matrix for polarography and
voltammetry as it already contains, due to its major constituents, the supporting electrolyte. On the other hand, its major cationic and anionic components Na^{+} and Cl^{-} also define a
priori the available potential range of the test electrode between those of the electrode reactions of Na^{+} and Cl^{-}. Furthermore, a Cl^{-} concentration of about 0.53 M, and thus a corresponding ligand concentration for chlorocomplexes of metal ions, is
fixed in sea water.

To avoid contamination it is advisable to use cells made of
pyrex of quartz, and to avoid chemisorption of metal traces, polyethylene or even teflon might be useful /1o1/. Usually solution volumes $\leq$ 3o ml are used. The 3-electrode cell (test electrode, counter electrode, and reference electrode which are separated by diaphragm and connected by a salt bridge) is becoming
more and more common since potentiostatic adjustment /78a/ of a
electrode potential is usual with the modern polarographic instruments. Common reference electrodes are the saturated calomel
(SCE) or the Ag/AgCl electrode. Cells have to be thermostated to
$\pm$ 0.5^{o}C. Sample solutions usually have to be deaerated before

measurement by bubbling pure inert gases (N_2, H_2, Ar) through
the solution for a couple of minutes to avoid interfering responses due to reduction of oxygen and H_2O_2. Care has to be exer-
cised that these inert gases are saturated with sea water vapour
to avoid CO_2 losses and resulting alterations in carbonate concentration and pH of the sample solution.

Table 2 gives a survey on the techniques having significant potential for sea water studies. The limiting or peak currents,
i_{lim} or i_p, are proportional to the concentration of the substance studied, while the half-wave, peak or half-peak potentials,
$E_{1/2}$, E_p, $E_{p/2}$, are correlated to the chemical nature and structure of the determined species (Fig. 1).

For direct determinations of metal traces, sufficient sensitivity of the applied technique combined with reasonable precision
and good resolution is demanded. In this context it has to be
noted that the measured current i, according to

$$i = i_C + i_F \qquad\qquad (1)$$

is always the sum of two components. The faradaic current i_F is
due to the transfer of electric charge through the interface
electrode/solution in the electrode reaction, while the capacity
current i_C is caused by the alteration of the charge of the double layer capacity of the electrode when its potential E is adjusted to new values. Only one component of the measured total
current i is of interest, and this is usually i_F. Therefore, the
respective technique reaches its fundamental sensitivity limit
if i_C and i_F become of equal magnitude. There are three kinds of
instrumental approaches to cope efficiently with this problem. In
ac-techniques with superimposed sinusoidal frequency, selective
recording of i_F and i_C becomes possible due to their different
phase relations /26, 72, 78b/. The discrimination between i_C
and i_F is very efficient based on their different time laws. i_C
decays exponentially with time, while $i_F \sim t^{-b}$ with $b \leq 0.5$, where
b equals 0.5 for diffusion controlled electrode processes. Use
of these relationships is made in the pulse techniques /78b/,

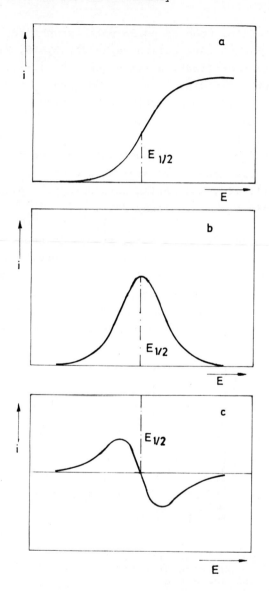

Fig.1

Shapes of the current-voltage curve at the Dropping
Mercury Electrode (DME). (a) normal mode, (b) first
derivative, (c) second derivative.

among them the very important methods of pulse polarography /8, 13, 72, 78b/ (Fig. 2) and square wave polarography /6, 7, 18, 72, 78b/. However, the faradaic rectification techniques /8, 9, 11, 18, 27/ attain the most efficient discrimination between i_F and i_C. As 2nd order techniques they are selectively sensitive to the 2nd derivative of the i-E-characteristic, i.e., to the nonlinearity of the electrode reaction, while the double layer capacity is a rather linear component. Further advanced 2nd order techniques of potential use in marine chemistry are: square wave intermodulation polarography /11, 18/, modulation polarography /14, 17, 18, 116/, and second harmonic ac-polarography /73/.

With the very low concentration level of metal traces in sea water, only the more advanced techniques offer enough sensitivity for direct measurements and determinations. Even the most advanced methods have to be driven frequently to the limits of their sensitivity potential for this purpose, and this always means, of course, some sacrifice in precision. Thus, the main

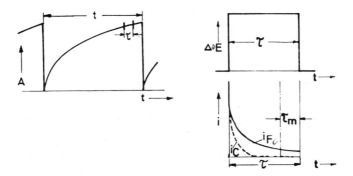

Fig.2

Principle of differential pulse polarography. The dc-electrode potential E of the DME with drop time t is altered by a slow dc ramp voltage (cca 2 mV/s) with a superimposed pulse (τ = 2 to 60 ms, height ΔE = 10 to 40 mV) applied almost at the end of the drop time where the area of the electrode remains practically constant. The charging current i_C is decaying more rapidly than the faradaic current i_F. The mean current i during the measuring interval τ_m recorded as a function of the dc electrode potential E partically consists of the component i_F only.

application areas for direct polarographic and voltammetric studies are the important model experiments at higher concentration
levels in the matrix sea water for solving speciation problems
of assumed species - complexes and organic substances - and for
studying and characterizing some of their significant physico-
chemical properties in true sea water milieu, i.e., with respect
to real conditions concerning ionic strength and composition of
the excess salts.

Furthermore, direct determinations become, of course, very convenient and versatile for samples of toxic metal pollution or
a variety of organic substances, as the concentration level is
then shifted well into the sensitivity range of the available
techniques (Table 2). It should be also noted in this context
that polarography and voltammetry have great potential in the
determination of the metal content in various marine organisms
where several metals, expecially those known as toxic, tend to
accumulate. Of course, the biological material has to be digested
and ashed by reliable methods before the metals contained (after
being brought into solution) may be determined.

Chemical Preconcentration

Despite these numerous and important potentials one of the
most significant tasks remains the determination, speciation,
and physicochemical characterization of metal species at their
natural concentration level in sea water. For sensitivity reasons,
this problem has been solved hitherto often only after preconcentration steps of the substance studied. There are the well known
chemical possibilities of accumulation via extraction, ion exchange or extraction chromatography, etc. Yet this approach has
the fundamental disadvantage that it allows only the elemental
content to be determined while the species present in sea water
remain inaccessible.

By combining chemical methods of preconcentration with subsequent
polarographic determination, a number of reliable data on ele-

mental concentration of metals have been obtained in the past.
The uranium level of the English Channel was determined to
3.37 $\pm$ 0.08 μg/l by solvent extraction from 4 l sea water with
di-(2-ethylhexyl)-phosphoric acid in CCl_4,   following separation
from molybdenum by extraction with ethyl acetate and subsequent
pulse polarography in aqueous $HClO_4$-tartrate buffer. The method
is precise but very time consuming. Cu, Pb, and Cd might be determined simultaneously, and Mo in a separate run /67/.

Ni was determined in the Baltic to 0.36 $\pm$ 0.01 μg/l after extraction with dimethylglyoxime /91/. For this particular metal,
conventional dc-polarography could be applied because the catalytic hydrogen evolution, due to the catalysis of the Ni-dime-
thylglyoxime complex, increased the sensitivity sufficiently.

For sea water from Liverpool Bay /1/, chelating resins of the
iminoacetate type in the calcium form (Chelex-100) with subsequent pulse polarography have been used to preconcentrate and
determine Cu, Cd, and Pb simultaneously in acid milieu; after
addition of ammonia to the same solution, Zn and Ni have been
determined and finally, after further addition of dimethylglyoxime, also Co.
A report from a recent workshop of Pb analysis of seawater /49/
recommends as a standard method preconcentration by extraction
with dithizone in $CHCl_3$, masking of unwanted elements by added
cyanide, and after extraction with HNO_3 determination by pulse
polarography.

If one is only interested in the overall elemental concentration of Cu, Pb, Cd, Zn in sea water, storage and conservation
of sea water samples with their corresponding error sources[+]
might be circumvented by preconcentrating those elements rapidly on Chitosan columns immediately after sampling and storing
only those loaded columns, for instance during a longer trip of

---

+   For error sources due to adsorption of trace metals in sea
    water on various materials of storage containers,(a signifi-
    cant problem in sample treatment) see refs. /55,97,107/.

a research vessel. Later, the metal content may be determined by
polarography after eluation in the laboratory /71/.

Electrochemical Preconcentration

The electrochemical method of preconcentration by applying the
various versions of stripping voltammetry /5,74/ has proved to
be much more efficient and rapid. This rather simple approach,
which is much faster, and in many repects less subject to contamination problems than chemical preconcentration and separation, allows the analysis of trace metals at the natural sea
water concentrations. In this context it must be noted that
practically every polarographic technique listed in Table 2 may
be operated in its stripping voltammetric version as well. This
means that the remarkably high principal potential of stripping voltammetry to be outlined later may be coupled with the a-
bilities of the advanced polarographic techniques, leading to
striking potentials in the ultra trace analysis of metal species
with respect to sensitivity, precision, resolution, and thus, the
capability for simultaneous determination and study, important
aspects also concerning speciation.

Meanwhile, efficient and reliable multimode instruments[+] are on
the market offering to the experimenter selection between a variety of powerful polarographic techniques including their stripping versions. This allows the application of the most suitable
technique to the respective problem in a tailored manner. For
field studies, the rather compact polarographic equipment may
also be installed in laboratories on research vessels in a manner securing reliable results, as longer experiences from Yugo-
slavian[++], American /122,123/, and German /59/ marine research
stations show.

[+] Well-approved multimode instruments are manufactured by Prince-
     ton Applied Research, Corp. (PAR) Mod. 170, USA, /40, 87/, the
     Metrohm E 506, Switzerland, the Tacussel Mod. PRG 3, /113/
     France and the Bruker E 310, Germany. The new multimode po-
     larograph of Barker /15,16,18/ will attract special inter-
     est, due to its unique combination of very advanced techni-
     ques.

[++] M. Branica, private communication

TABLE 2 - Survey of the polarographic and voltammetric methods
applied in trace analysis.

Method	Typical Detection Limit (for Cd^{2+})	Form of the i-E-curve

A. Direct methods
  (DME)

1. Pulse Polarography (PP)	50 ppb	a
2. Differential Pulse Polarography (DPP)	5 ppb	
3. Square Wave Polarography (SWP)	5 ppb	b
4. Phase Sensitive Polarography (ACP)	20 ppb	
5. Radiofrequency Polarography (RFP)	5 ppb (0,1 ppb)[+]	
6. Square Wave Inter-modulation Polarography (SWIP)	100 ppb	c
7. Modulation Polarography (MP)	5 ppb	

(100 kHz current modulated
with 225 Hz square wave
voltage version)

[+] Values in parentheses with tailored data processor in
Barker multimode polarograph /18/.

TABLE 2 continued.

Method	Typical Detection Limit (for Cd^{2+})	Form of the i-E-curve
B. Indirect methods (Stripping Voltammetry)		
1. HMDE with Single Sweep Polarography (SSP)		**d**
a) normal mode	10 ppb	
b) differential mode	2 ppb	
2. HMDE with DPP or SWP	0.1 ppb	as A.2.
3. HMDE with ACP	0.2 ppb	
4. Carbon Paste Electrode with SSP	5 ppb	as B.1.
5. MFE on graphite with SSP	0.2 ppb	
6. MFE on rotating glassy carbon electrode (RGCE) with SSP		**e**
a) normal mode	0.02 ppb	
b) differential mode	< 0.01 ppb	

General Theoretical Aspects

Any attempt to elaborate on the theory and details of the methodology of polarography and voltammetry is beyond the scope of
this review [+]. A few more general theoretical remarks have to be
made here. With the techniques considered here for marine applications, one frequently records the i-E-response in unstirred
solution, and thus diffusion is the only form of mass transfer
to or from the test electrode (Fig. 3a). At the DME, one has a
more slowly expanding diffusion layer than at stationary electrodes due to the growing drop. After each drop life, the ex-

---

[+] See for details /30, 47, 65, 66, 92/ textbooks; /26, 74, 99/
monographs; /5, 68, 69, 72, 76-79, 82, 84/ general reviews.

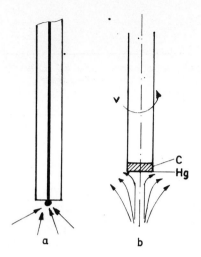

Fig.3
Types of electrodes used in
trace analysis.
a) mercury dropping electrode.
The electrode is used as a
stationary electrode (HMDE) or
as a dropping electrode (DME).
b) rotating glassy carbon
electrode (C) coated with a thin
layer of mercury (Hg). v–speed
of rotation (1000 to 2000 rpm).

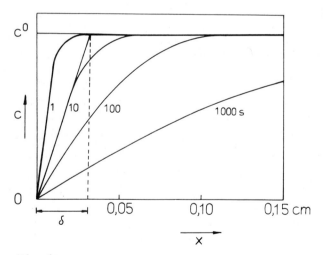

Fig.4a

Dependence of the concentration c of the reducible ion
on the distance x from the electrode (without stirring).
c^0 - the bulk concentration, δ - the diffusion layer.
At the stationary electrode, the diffusion layer expands
with $\sqrt{t}$, and the concentration gradient at the electrode
and the current decays with $\sqrt{t}$. At the dropping electrode
a mean current is recorded which corresponds to an
average value of the diffusion layer expanding to the
same value during each drop life.

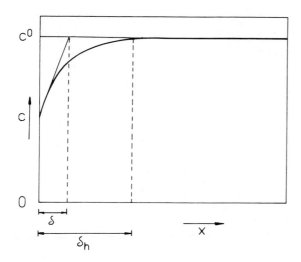

Fig.4b

Dependence of the concentration c of the reducible ion
on the distance x from the rotating electrode. δ-diffusion
layer, δ_h – hydrodynamic layer. At the rotating electrode
a stationary diffusion layer is soon established and the
current does not then depend on time.

pansion of the diffusion layer is terminated, and the interfacial concentration becomes nearly equal to the bulk concentration. Thus, for a given electrode potential E the concentration
gradients towards the electrode, and consequently the diffusion
rate, are reproducibly the same at each drop for the substance
studied. In contrast, at a stationary electrode in unstirred
solution, the diffusion layer expands and the concentration gradient decreases continously over the polarization time at a given E, leading to a current i decreasing with $t^{0.5}$ (Fig. 4a). At
rotating electrodes (Fig. 3b) the diffusion layer thickness
attains a small steady state value after a brief induction period, due to the stationary mass transfer invoked by convection
(Fig. 4b).

Another important aspect influencing the behavior and shape of
the recorded i-E-curves is the kinetics of the overall electrode
process, or more particularly, of its elementary steps contributing to the control of its overall rate. The most straightfor-

ward situation is the common one in which the electrode process
behaves reversibly. Then the current is diffusion controlled
over the whole i-E-curve,and the half-wave potential $E_{1/2}$ or its
analogue peak potential is closely related to the standard redox
potential E_o of the respective electrode process.

The situation for irreversible electrode processes is more involved. Irreversibility might be caused by slow rate of the electron transfer step itself and/or by an insufficiently fast prior
chemical step forming from the substance present in the bulk, the
form undergoing the electrode reaction proper. An example would
be partial ligand dissociation from a complex before electron
transfer. This prior chemical step may be fast or slow. If the
electron transfer itself still behaves reversibly, $E_{1/2}$ is still
correlated to E_o; otherwise it depends on the kinetics of the
electron transfer step. If the kinetics of prior chemical steps
contribute to the control of the overall rate, the corresponding
current i will be smaller than the purely diffusion controlled
current. This makes it possible to determine the kinetics of prior
homogeneous and heterogeneous chemical steps up to very fast rates
according to the time constant of the applied polarographic
technique /76b, 79/.

The adsorption of substances at the electrode surface may also
have a significant influence on the magnitude of the current as
well as on the shape of the i-E-curves /51, 62, 76c, 83/. This
adsorbed material may often inhibit the electrode process,but
sometimes it may also catalyze certain electrode reactions. Both
effects may be used under suitable circumstances.

Furthermore, it should be noted that adsorption of the substance
itself will influence the shape of the responses obtained
with more advanced methods such as differential pulse and square
wave polarography and the 2nd order techniques /12, 14, 17/, because they are particularly sensitive to adsorption of the reactant reduced in the electrode reaction due to their small polarization times. There are also tensioactive substances, usually
organic compounds, which undergo no electrode process but cause

significant changes in the double layer capacity due to their
adsorption. The resulting capacity current i_c may be exploited
for their determination /17, 18, 26, 76c/.

From the recorded i-E-responses, the following entities and parameters relevant to problems in marine chemistry are obtainable.
First, there is the determination of the concentration c of trace
metals, often as more or less identifiable species, and of a number of organic substances if those are present at sufficient
concentration. As $i \sim \sqrt{D} \, c$, the overall diffusion coefficient D
of the studied substance may be determined in addition to the
concentration. The potential range in which the i-E-response
of a metal appears may already give a superficial indication of
the nature of its chemical species. Quantitative information
on stability constants, ligand numbers, and thus the structure
of complexes, are available via the dependence of $E_{1/2}$ of reversible electrode reactions on the concentration of the respective ligand. Sometimes these data may also be obtained via the
alteration of D with the ligand concentration. From the limiting
or peak current, i_{lim} or i_p, the formation and dissociation kinetics of metal complexes and of many weak acids may be determined.

The following part of this article will be devoted to illustrating the previous general discussion on the potential of polarography and voltammetry of microconstituents of sea water by a
review of selected applications. In this context some further
methodological and theoretical aspects of importance will also
be outlined in more detail.

DIRECT DETERMINATIONS

The determination of substances will be treated first. The first
attempts in simultaneous direct determinations of trace metals
(Cu, Pb, Cd, Zn, Ni, Co, Mn, CrO_4^{2-}) and of IO_4^- have been reported for samples of surface and of deep water from the Atlantic, Pacific, and Artic Sea /118, 119/. Single sweep polarogra-

phy in the differential mode with two matched DME was employed.
In this technique, for which the author reports high sensitivity down to 1 ppb, one cell contains the sample and the other
cell the sample plus a standard addition of the metal to be determined. Only the current difference between both cells is
measured, in this manner efficiently eliminating the capacity
current which is equal for both cells. Although the differential
principle is a sound and reliable approach, especially if the
DME is substituted for by stationary electrodes, the results in
these early papers have to be regarded with reservations concerning accuracy. Nevertheless, this work has contributed significantly to demonstrating some of the important possibilities
offered by polarography to oceanography.

Reliable direct determination of the Zn content in sea water
from the North Adriatic by pulse polarography has been reported. This work also made evident the importance of speciation
for more complete solution of the problem, since obviously different Zn-species (ionic, complexes of various stability, and
particulate Zn) are to be expected /24/.

Although direct trace metal determinations by advanced polarographic methods are presently few in number, important future
applications for direct polarographic trace studies in chemical
oceanography can be expected. We have experiences from our routine application of radio frequency polarography and pulse polarography for trace metal analysis in other non-marine matrices. Therefore, we conclude that the advanced techniques of the
2nd order type as improved forms of radio frequency polarography,
square wave polarography, and the new mode of square wave intermodulation polargoraphy will also be applicable for marine chemistry. All these new techniques are incorporated besides a very
efficient version of single-sweep polarography in the new Harwell multi-mode instrument[+] /15,16,18/. The same argument is also

---

+ The further implemented mixed mode RF/SW-polarograph offers
  special resolution and discrimination potentialities with
  respect to resolving overlapping responses /132/.

valid for the new modulation polarograph recently introduced by
Barker as well /14,17,18,116/.

One can see that within the next decade these new, instrumentally
sophisticated techniques in conjunction with tailored modern di-
gital data processing might gain the same importance and wide
application in this and other areas of trace analysis as is
enjoyed today by pulse polarography and the stripping techniques.

Organic Pollutants

An important further application field is the determination of
organic pollutants. They consist of many different organic materials such as detergents, oils, components of petroleum, waste
products from fish factories, natural degradation products of
marine organisms, etc. The pollution levels differ but may reach
intolerable values locally in coastal waters or along highly fre-
quented shipping routes. These organic pollutants are more or
less surface active. Therefore, although they usually are not
electrochemically reactive, conventional dc-polarography offers
an efficient and simple, rapid determination of their total concentration. This approach is based on the suppression of the polarographic maxima occurring in the reduction of oxygen or of Hg^{2+}.
If current flows through a liquid electrode, such as the DME,
motions of the surface and the adhering solution layers may be
easily initiated due to surface tension differences created between neck and basis of the drop. This convection causes additional mass transfer of reducible O_2 or Hg^{2+} to the electrode
and consequently, significant exaltations of the current termed
maxima /105, 106/. They are suppressed by small amounts of surface active substances which, due to their adsorption, tend to
equalize the surface tension over the whole drop surface, thus
slowing down its motion and stopping it finally at a certain degree of coverage. Of course, the determination based on this effect cannot be selective for a certain organic component but responds to the total amount of all surface active organic material
dissolved in seawater. The measurements are calibrated with the
uncharged surfactant Triton-X-100, i.e., $(C_8H_{17}(C_6H_4)(OCH_2)_{7-10}-OH)$,

dissolved in artificial sea water /129/. The measurement of natural samples is very simple and rapid. Using the oxygen maximum
(Fig. 5), the sea water sample only has to be diluted with very
pure distilled water, as the high salinity of sea water itself
tends to suppress the maximum for reasons of high interfacial
conductivity. Then the suppressing of the maximum is measured
and evaluated in mg/l equivalents of the calibrator Triton-X-100.
The sensitivity is high and goes from g/l to 0.1 mg/l Triton-X-
-100 equivalents. This approach may be used in automatic devices
for continuous pollution control /117/. A detailed and extended
study /31, 13o/ of the pollution of the North Adriatic due to
oil detergents and other surface active organic material, including concentration profiles to the depth of the sea, has demonstrated convincingly the monitoring potentialities of this simple
but efficient approach. Even more sensitive has been the recent
use of the Hg^{2+} maximum, which has the additional advantage that
the added Hg^{2+} ions act as a preserving agent of stored sea water
samples against microbiological infections /131/.

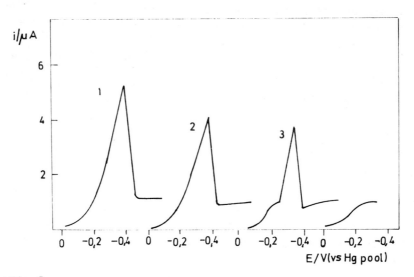

Fig.5

Determination of the total amount of organic substances
in sea water by means of a suppression of polarographic
maxima for oxygen with increasing amounts of Triton-X-100;
(1) -0; (2) -3; (3) -5; (4) -7 mg/l.

Another efficient way to determine surface active substances
undergoing no electrode reaction is offered by the tensammetric
version of the various ac-techniques /26, 76c/. The adsorption
and desorption of substances ocurring at certain potentials E
causes significant alterations of the double layer capacity of
the electrode due to changes in the dielectric, and the resulting changes in charge density lead to corresponding peaks of
the capacity current i_C. The height of this nonfaradaic response
depends on the concentration of the dissolved surface active material. Here again is a potential field of application for the
new Barker techniques incorporated in the multi-mode polarograph
/18/, because these methods are also very sensitive to rather
small amounts of nonreducible surface active organic substances
in their tensammetric version (see also ref. 17). As the faradaic responses of these techniques are very sensitive to inhibition by adsorbed surfactants, a further possibility is to study
the suppression of the response of a pilot metal ion, comparing
the results for surfactant free artificial and for natural con-
taminated sea water. Interesting possibilities for specific determinations of many reducible organic compounds are to be expected via the application of advanced polarographic methods
such as normal and differential pulse polarography /133/, modulation polarography /17, 18/, and the improved versions of square
wave- and RF-polarography incorporated in the Barker multi-mode
instrument/18/.

STRIPPING VOLTAMMETRY

General Aspects

At present, the most widely applied and most popular electrochemical approach to trace metal studies in sea water is certainly stripping voltammetry (SV) in its various versions /5,
53, 54, 74/.

Electrochemical preconcentration is achieved in a simple and
rapid manner by cathodic deposition of the metal studied into a
stationary microelectrode, usually of mercury. Versions of the

hanging mercury drop (HMDE) or mercury film electrodes (MFE)
having an even smaller volume are mainly used. Significant potential applications can be predicted for the carbon paste electrode which expands the number of determinable metals and possibilities for simultaneous determinations (Fig. 6) as has been
demonstrated recently for many cases in other areas of trace
metal analysis /68, 69/. Due to the much smaller volume of the
test electrode compared with the volume of the solution in the
cell (10 to 50 ml), the concentration in the test electrode increases with the HMDE by a factor 10^2 to 10^4, and even more with
the MFE. It is this higher concentration in the test electrode
which determines the height of the response recorded during the
subsequent anodic redissolution of the metal to its ionic state
in the solution. This anodic redissolution has also been termed
anodic stripping, because usually all the metal deposited into
the test electrode is redissolved. In this way the sensitivity
is pushed to the ultra trace range of 10^{-9}M, making even 10^{-10}M
or less, detectable with the MFE. It is obvious that with mercury
electrodes hitherto favored for reasons of reproducibility, the
application is limited to metals being reduced to the metallic
state Me^0 in the deposition step and further capable of forming
amalgams at least for the time of deposition and stripping. In
this respect the reproducible carbon paste electrode offers attractive future extensions of these applications.

Other electrode materials made of graphite, glassy carbon, and
noble metals have also been used. These electrodes might be considered for special cases, particularly if a metal can only be
reduced from a higher to a lower valency state, and the latter
may be fixed on the electrode surface in a compound forming a
sparingly soluble layer which is completely and aptly redissolv-
able in the subsequent anodic reoxydation step /23/. Of course,
one faces severe reproducibility problems with solid electrodes
with respect to the behaviour of the electrode. Special experience and know-how with these solid electrodes seems to be an
almost indispensable prerequisite for obtaining meaningful results.

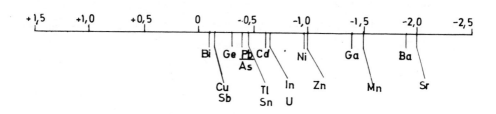

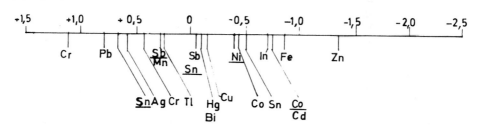

Fig.6

Peak potentials of uncomplexed hydrated metal ions determinable by stripping voltammetry at (a) the HMDE and (b) the
carbon paste electrode.

Further discussion will be focussed on electrodes with a mercury surface.

In anodic stripping voltammetric experiments one generally dis-
tinguishes three stages. In the first stage, the test electrode
is cathode, and the metals present in the solution in some ionic
form or complex are reduced and deposited in the mercury. The
solution is stirred or the electrode rotated to speed up mass
transfer. The deposition potential E_d is usually adjusted 300
or 400 mV more negative than $E_{1/2}$, but for certain speciation
problems every value in the potential range of the i-E-curve of
the deposited metal may be selected. The deposition time t_d de-

pends on the concentration level in the solution and on the volume of the test electrode. Complete exhaustion of the solution
by the cathodic pre-electrolysis is usually avoided. For the HMDE
in conventional stripping voltammetry, typical t_d-values between
5 and more than 30 minutes are adjusted for concentrations between 10^{-7}M and 10^{-9}M. If more sensitive techniques, e.g., pulse-
or square-wave polarogaphy, are coupled, t_d may be lowered significantly. For mercury film electrodes (MFE), usually having a
film thickness l between only 10^{-5} and 10^{-8} cm (larger l-values
are pointless and create the danger that the film sags), smaller
t_d-values are selected, but here also they should exceed 60 sec.
For the theory of MFE, reference is made to the work of DeVries
<u>et al</u> /33-36/.

The next stage is a rest period t_r of 30 to 60 sec. during which
the solution comes to rest and the deposited metal concentration
in the mercury homogenizes. In comparison the rest period may be
only several seconds for the MFE. Subsequently, in the stripping
stage, an anodic potential is applied to the test electrode. The
whole amount of the deposited metals is reoxidized and redissolved (stripping), (with the MFE, at sufficiently low scan rate),
and the corresponding i-E-response is recorded. Frequently, the
solution is unstirred in the stripping stage, but to decrease analysis time, the rotating HMDE fitted to Pt-wire /38/ and the rotating
carbon paste electrode /70/ have been introduced (see also RGCE
among the MF-electrodes). Generally, the stripping process and
its i-E-response depend strongly (in an indirect manner) on the
parameters of the deposition process. Although the first true
stripping voltammetric measurements have been made with square
wave polarography[+] /6/, the linear dc-sweep technique with moderate sweep rates v = dE/dt is most frequently applied at present. One obtains peak shaped i-E-curves (Fig. 7). Their most
important parameters are peak potential E_p and peak current i_p
and their width b at $i_p/2$.

+ For further applications in conjunction with square wave polarography see refs. /7, 20, 109/

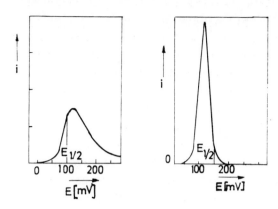

Fig. 7

Current potential curves at stationary electrodes:
(a) HMDE, (b) thin MFE. $E_{1/2}$ - polarographic half wave
potential for the DME. The narrow peak with a limiting
width of about 37 mV at half-height shifted to more positive
potentials against $E_{1/2}$ enhancing a good separation of
metals with closely adjacent half-wave potentials.

The peak current i_p is proportional to the concentration of the
metal deposited in the mercury c_M, which is uniform in the thin
MFE and rather uniform in the HMDE after a prolonged electrolysis (3 min. or more). At the HMDE, the peak current increases
for the usual conventional stripping voltammetry with single-
sweep stripping in unstirred solution with the square root of
the scan rate v following

$$i_p = \text{const } A\, v^{1/2}\, c_M \qquad\qquad (2)$$

whereas at the thin MFE, the peak current increases linearly
with the scan rate v following

$$i_p = \text{const } A\, v\, l\, c_M \qquad\qquad (3)$$

where A = the area of the electrode and l = the film thickness.

The concentration of the metal c_M is proportional to the number
of coulombs involved in the electrodeposition process Q given
by

$$Q = \int_0^{t_d} i_{dep}\, dt = n\, F\, V\, c_M \qquad (4)$$

where i_{dep} = the electrolysis current, t_d = the deposition time,
F = one Faraday, n = number of electrons consumed, and V = the
volume of the MFE or HMDE. As the current during cathodic preconcentration is proportional to the bulk concentration of the
metal ion to be determined, the peak current i_p during anodic
stripping is also proportional to this bulk concentration via Q.
The sensitivity of the MFE is based on a small volume V and a
large area A in comparison to the HMDE. With respect to the
magnitude of v, simultaneous determinations require a compromise between the desire to push up response height and the de-
mands of resolution. Thus, v around 25 mV/sec and less than
200 mV/sec is usually adjusted.
Of course the previously mentioned combination of the stripping
principle with the advanced polarographic techniques will offer
significant improvements with respect to resolution, tolerabil-
ity of components in large excess (discrimination), precision,
and also sensitivity (see example in Fig. 8). Results with good
precision for Cu, Pb, Cd, and Zn in the Oslofjord are reported
/98/ with the application of an advanced phase sensitive sinusoidal ac-technique in the stripping stage. The in-phase component of the ac current is recorded. We have had particularly
satisfying experiences by coupling differential pulse polarography with stripping from the HMDE and MFE in tackling determination and speciation problems of trace metals in sea water
and in environmental research in general.

Striking progress in performance of the i-E-response and in
attainable sensitivity (even $< 10^{-10}$M) with good precision has
been recently demonstrated by using the differential approach
with two matched rotating glassy carbon electrodes with very
thin mercury film /58,102/. Also, a differential arrangement of

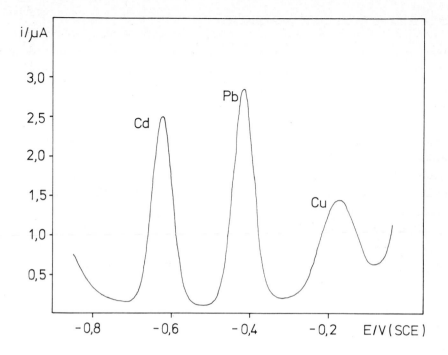

Fig.8

Current-potential curve of acidified sea water with added
Cd^{2+} (2 ppb), Pb^{2+} (3 ppb) and Cu^{2+} (2 ppb) and 0,5 M
HCl as a supporting electrolyte HMDE, 10 min pre-
electrolysis with stirring. Anodic stripping with
differential pulse polarographic mode.

two HMDE suspended on Pt worked satisfactorily, even under the
more stringent conditions aboard a research vessel during a
field study on the level of Cu, Pb, Cd, and Zn in the Pacific.
References/122, 123/ also discuss in detail various aspects of
sample preparation, storage, and pH influences on results.

Stationary Mercury Drop Electrodes

Some further points on test electrode types are to be made. Among
the HMDE, the widely used extrusion electrode of Kemula /52-54/
has the advantage of consisting only of mercury. Disadvantages
are the temperature sensitivity (thermometer effect) and the
danger of deposited metal entering the mercury thread if long
t_d-periods have to be applied causing further progressive contamination of the electrode for subsequent runs at freshly ex-
truded drops. There is also some danger that at negative potentials ($< -1,2$ V), fractures of the thread due to hydrogen evolution, or creeping of solution into the capillary, may occur.
In conjunction with conventional single-sweep voltammetry for
the stripping stage, the Kemula-HMDE has been applied in an extended study on the level of many trace metals in the English
Channel /104/.
The Kemula-HMDE has also been succesfully applied in an extensive field study in the Baltic on Cu, Cd, Pb, and Zn. A cardanic
installation of the cell allowed satisfactory voltammetry on
board the research vessel /59/.

Some workers prefer the HMDE formed by suspending a drop on a
mercury wetted pure Pt- or gilded Pt-wire /5, 115/. This version has proved useful, due to the strong adherence of the suspending Hg-drop, for increasing sensitivity by rotation /38/ and
improving selectivity by solution change between deposition and
stripping stage /112/.

Successful applications of this HMDE type to the trace metal
level in Dead Sea brines have been reported /3, 4/.

In a study of the content of Cu, Pb, Cd, and Zn off the California coast, the potential of stripping voltammetry with this
HMDE type is compared with the results obtained by direct measurement with single-sweep polarography /120/. The surprising
agreement obtained with both techniques casts severe doubt on the
accuracy of the data measurement with the direct approach.

However, for this HMDE type, the risks of solution coming into
contact with Pt seem to be more pertinent than the dangers mentioned for the Kemula-HMDE. This is true at least at the trace
and ultra trace level, i.e. for bulk solution concentration
$< 10^{-7}$M, which is the appropriate application range of all
stripping techniques. Due to the resulting low amalgam concentration ($< 10^{-3}$M), neither the previously mentioned migration of
amalgam into the mercury thread nor all the problems connected
with formation of intermetallic compounds with mercury or among
the deposited trace metals /5, 56, 74/ have significance for
the HMDE except in particular cases (e.g., tendencies toward
intermetallic compound formation of Fe, Co, Ni, Mn with Hg for
$t_d > 2$ min). On the other hand, the MFE more frequently can face
problems connected with intermetallic compound formation if its
application is not restricted to the ultra trace range, i.e.,
$< 5 \cdot 10^{-8}$ to 10^{-9}M.

An attractive variant of the HMDE deserving more attention is
the slowly dropping mercury electrode (SMDE) /61/ with drop
times ($t_1 \approx 68$ sec), since it combines the potential of the HMDE
with the purity of the DME. In sea water, the SMDE has been
used hitherto only for Zn studies /61/, where the MFE cannot be
used because of a smaller hydrogen overvoltage.

Applications of Mercury Film Electrodes

In marine chemistry two types of the MFE have found successful
application. The first is the composite graphite mercury coated
electrode (CGME) /48/64/. Above $5 \cdot 10^{-7}$M the electrode tends to
be overloaded. Microscopic inspection shows that the mercury
forms a layer of small mercury droplets (diameter ≤ 0.01 mm) on
the graphite-wax surface /48/.It is assumed that the mercury
droplets define the active area of this MFE. While the electrode
has been successfully applied /44/ to the determination of Bi and
Sb in surface and depth water from the Atlantic, Gulf Stream of Florida, Caribbean, and Pacific, it behaved unsatisfactorily with respect to time stability in a recent detailed comparative study on
traces of Cd, Pb, Cu, and Zn from the Adriatic /29/.

However, this study /29/ reconfirmed the high quality of performance and reproducibility offered by the rotating glassy carbon
electrode (RGCE) covered by a very thin mercury film formed in
situ /41/. A mercury film with thickness l between $4 \cdot 10^{-7}$ and
10^{-6}cm, i.e.≤ 100 Å, is formed during the deposition stage at
the glassy carbon electrode (rotating with 2000 rpm) by adding
about 10^{-4}M Hg^{2+} to the sample solution. Extensive studies /42,
43/ on the trace metal content (Bi, Cu, Pb, Zn) in Australian
and New Zealand coastal waters and on their accumulation in marine organisms demonstrated convincingly the high potential of
this electrode. Our present studies with Mediterranean water
have also confirmed this, while also revealing that the in situ
coating with mercury leads to a uniformly spread film only for
a thickness >100 Å /103/. Meanwhile, the differential approach
has also been successfully applied to this electrode, pushing the
sensitivity to values below 10^{-10}M /58/. Reliable matching of
both electrodes is achieved by dividing their surface in two
parts by an epoxy barrier, thus enabling both to rotate on the
same axis in equivalent position /102/. Among the electrodes
from other materials, the promising features of the carbon paste
electrode /68, 69, 70/ have already been noted.

SPECIATION

The key role of speciation of trace metals for better understanding
the biological, biophysical, geochemical, oceanographic, ecological, and pollution problems in the sea and marine organisms
is stressed in a recent review /108/. Polarography and voltammetry are very efficient and versatile tools for understanding
speciation /2, 23, 25, 124/.
Complexing of trace metals by natural and pollutional ligands
and its equilibria and kinetics form an important research in
this context. For the details of the involved but complete
theory of the polarographic characterization of metal complexes,
consultation of the general references /32, 50, 57, 114/ is
recommended.

Stability and Properties of Complexes

Significant entities with respect to speciation are the overall
stability constants β_j of metal complexes and their coordination numbers j. Both parameters are attainable from the shift
of the half-wave potential $E_{1/2}$ as function of the logarithm
of the free ligand concentration $\lg c_X$ (Fig. 9). The latter
is usually present in significant excess, so that for c_X the
analytical ligand concentration may be inserted. Since, in principle, activities are involved in the complex equilibria, the
stability constants obtained are conditional data which ignore
activity coefficients and refer to the ionic strength and ionic
composition of the excess electrolyte. If the central metal ion
of the complexes formed is reduced to the metallic state, one
generally has eq. (5) for the half-wave potential shift $\Delta E_{1/2}$
between the aquo complex of the metal and the complex with ligand X at the respective value of c_X :

$$\Delta E_{1/2} = - \frac{RT}{nF} \ln \sqrt{\frac{D_C}{D_M}} \sum_{o}^{m} \beta_j (c_X)^j \tag{5}$$

where R is the gas constant, T the temperature in $^\circ K$, n the number of electrons transferred per elementary reduction step, F
the Faraday, D_C and D_M the diffusion coefficients of the complex and the hydrated uncomplexed metal ion, respectively, and j
the coordination number of which m is the largest value.

From eq. (5) follow the Leden-functions /60/ (Fig. 10):

$$F_o(X) = \sum_o^m \beta_j (c_X)^j = \sqrt{\frac{D_M}{D_C}} \exp - \left(\frac{nF}{RT} \Delta E_{1/2} \right) \tag{6}$$

$$F_j(X) = \frac{F_{(j-1)}(X) - \beta_{(j-1)}}{c_X} \tag{7}$$

with $\beta_o = 1$, and one has

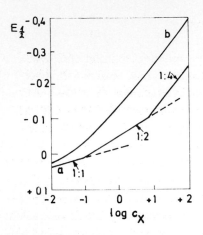

Fig.9

Dependence of half-wave potential on free ligand concentration. a) Simultaneous presence of all possible complexes
due to series of complex equilibria; b) predominant presence
of complex species with indicated ligand number (j - 1 to 4)
in respective range of c_X.

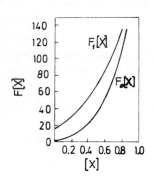 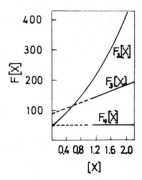

Fig.10

Leden plots for the evaluation of stability constants and
coordination numbers of complex ion. [X] is the free ligand
concentration.

$$\frac{\beta_j}{\beta_{(j-1)}} = K_j \tag{8}$$

With the aid of these equations, the overall stability constants
ß, the coordination numbers j, and the consecutive stability
constants K_j of a series of successively formed complexes may
be evaluated either by a graph method or preferably with the
aid of computer programs /88/. Accurate data have been obtained
for a number of complexes, provided the precision in the measurement of $E_{1/2}$ is $\pm$ 1 mV or better. A fundamental prerequisite
is a reversible electrode reaction; all complex equilibria
should also be sufficiently mobile to behave reversibly as well.
If the latter are sluggish, but the electrode reaction itself
remains reversible, the $\Delta E_{1/2}$-approach still remains applicable,
but now eq. (9) has to be used:

$$\Delta E_{1/2} = -\frac{RT}{nF} \ln \frac{\bar{i}_k}{\bar{i}_d} \sqrt{\frac{D_C}{D_M}} \sum_o^m \beta_j \, (c_X)^j \tag{9},$$

where $\bar{i}_k$ is the limiting current of the wave of the complex obtained for the given kinetic control, due to slow adjustment of
the successive complex equilibria prior to the electrode reaction, and $\bar{i}_d$ the limiting current for pure diffusion control of
this complex reduction.
If the complex equilibria adjust rapidly, but the electrode
reaction is irreversible, no information on the stability constants is available directly from half-wave potential shifts
$\Delta E_{1/2}$.

However, the indicator ion method (Fig. 11) may then be employed
/39,96/. The prerequisite is that the indicator ion N must form
a complex with the same ligand X. This complex is reduced reversibly at more positive potentials whereas the metal complex
studied undergoes an irreversible electrode reaction.

For further methods not related to $E_{1/2}$-shifts but useful for
particular cases, reference is made to monograph /32/.

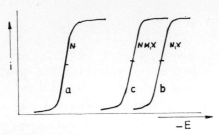

Fig.11

Indicator ion method for the determination of the
stability constant of a complex metal ion undergoing an
irreversible reduction at the DME. (a) hydrated indicator
of N; (b) N in the presence of a known excess of ligand X,
(c) as in (b) but after addition of competing ion M.

In addition to the determination of the concentration c to establish substance quantities, important information on characteristic physicochemical parameters of complexes are obtainable
from the limiting current i_{lim} or analogue currents, as i_p, resulting from methods other than dc-polarography.

It should be added that generally the diffusion coefficient also
indicates complex formation /45/ with excess constituents as D
is correlated to the stability constants of the existing complexes of the metal studied /32/. If one particular complex predominates, one has eq. (10) for the effective mean value $\bar{D}$,
while in the more general case of a series of different complexes
present in the solution simultaneously in noticeable amounts at
a given ligand concentration c_X, the value of $\bar{D}$ is defined by the
general eq. (11).

$$\bar{D} = \frac{D_M + D_{MX_j} \cdot \beta_{MX_j} \cdot (c_X)^j}{1 + \beta_{MX_j} \cdot (c_X)^j} \qquad (10)$$

or

$$\bar{D} = \frac{\sum_0^m D_{MX_j} \cdot \beta_{MX_j} \cdot (c_X)^j}{\sum_0^m \beta_{MX_j} \cdot (c_X)^j} \qquad (11)$$

These relations show also that via D obtained from precise measurements of the dc-limiting currents, i_{lim}, or analogue current values resulting with other techniques, a determination of the stability constants is feasible.

The precision demanded in $E_{1/2}$-shifts or $\bar{D}$-values presently requires experiments to be performed at metal concentrations two or three orders of magnitude higher than their natural trace levels in sea water. However, results rather close to reality are to be expected if all major parameters of the sea water sample, particularly pH and the concentration of the major constituents, are held constant while only the concentration of the metal studied, for instance Cd or Cu, is raised by 3 orders to the 10^{-6}M or 10^{-5}M level. This increase in the central ion concentration will not noticeably affect equilibrium parameters of the complexes, as the complexing macroconstituents of sea water (Cl^-, CO_3^{2-} etc. and organic ligands) still remain present in excess by several orders of magnitude. Here is a wide field of future application for direct measurement with advanced polarographic techniques, which already offer sufficient precision for those studies down to the 10^{-8}M level.

In sea water, the anions Cl^-, OH^-, HCO_3^-, and SO_4^{2-} are the most important inorganic ligands. Although there is a significant excess of Cl^- due to the pH of 8, hydroxide complexing will compete severely with chlorocomplexes of many metals depending on the stability constants of both complex types /100/. Besides these inorganic macroconstituents, a number of strong complexing organic ligands play an important role, even if they are present at only rather low concentration levels.

By employing an advanced version of phase sensitive ac-polarography, the dominating Cu complexes in coastal water from the Bretagne have been identified at their natural level (about 5×10^{-8}M), and their stability constants were determined /86/ via $E_{1/2}$-shifts and pH-dependence. Cu is present mainly as $[CuCl]^+$ and $[Cu(HCO_3)_2(OH)]^-$ in addition to hydrated Cu^{2+}.

The complicated speciation of Zn has been attempted by a number
of groups /124/ for several years; however, the problem remains
unsettled. With lowering of pH, an increased release of voltam-
metrically detectable Zn is observed /122/. A detailed study on
various Zn species detectable as a function of pH adjustment has
been performed in samples from the Mediterranean /89, 90/. The
results were later criticized as artifacts due to adsorption
effects at the wall of glass cells, since the reported findings
could not be reproduced with polyethylene cells /29/.

Model studies employing dc-polarography with prepared Zn and
Cd amalgams in 0.5 M NaCl and in sea water allowed the determination of the stability constants of the dominating complex
species $[ZnOH]^+$ and $[CdCl]^+$ /135/. From these results it was predicted, and recently confirmed /28/ at the low natural concentration level for $[CdCl]^+$ that those complexes are the dominating
complexed forms of both metals in sea water. With respect to
Zn, other authors /21, 124/ claim that $Zn(OH)_2^O$ is the dominating complexed form in sea water. A number of speciation problems on the biologically important metal Zn are still unsettled
and the reader is referred to the review in the paper of Bernhard et al. (this volume).

Meanwhile, the complex formation of the toxic metals Cd and Pb
with inorganic and organic ligands has been extensively studied,
employing stripping techniques at the HMDE and RGCE with application of linear sweep /28, 29/. Recently differential pulse
polarography in the anodic redissolution stage has also been
used /95, 103/.

Of paramount importance with respect to complexing studies at
the natural trace level in sea water is the following finding
/28/. If the anodic peak currents $\bar{i}_p$ (from measurements at the
natural ultra trace level 10^{-8}M to 10^{-9}M) are plotted as function of the deposition potential E_d, a sigmoid curve with a
shape analogous to a conventional dc-polarogram is obtained.
From plots of the $E_{1/2}^+$ values or the tangent potentials E_p^+ at

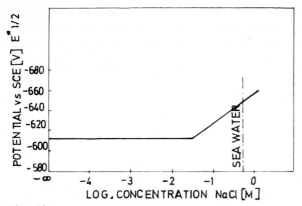

Fig.12

Determination of the stability constant and the coordination
number of the chlorocomplex of cadmium.
$5 \cdot 10^{-9} M$ Cd^{2+}, ionic strength ($NaClO_4$ + NaCl) -
0.7 M, pH - 8,0, HMDE, deposition time - 15 min
After ref.28).

the foot of these dc-polarogram analogues versus the ligand concentration c_X, the stability constants of the respective complexes may be evaluated in the manner previously discussed for
the dependence of true $E_{1/2}$ shifts on the ligand concentration
(Fig.12). In this way the goal is reached of identifying via the
stripping techniques at the natural metal trace level in sea
water, the complexes formed with the respective investigated
ligand and determination of their stability constants. This important new approach has served to elucidate the chlorocomplexes
of Cd in sea water /28/. Quite recently in our laboratory, preliminary data on the carbonatocomplex of Pb and the bicarbonato-
complex of Cd prevailing in sea water and their stability constants have also been obtained /103/.

KINETIC STUDIES

Rate Monitoring of Conventional Slow Reactions by Diffusion
Controlled Responses

The study of Maljković and Branica /63/ on the complex formation
kinetics of Cd-EDTA in sea water and in model solutions containing similar amounts of NaCl and $CaCl_2$ is an example for the

monitoring of the course of a slow homogeneous chemical reaction via a diffusion controlled i-E-response. The cationic excess constituents compete with Cd for EDTA and the Cl^- excess competes with EDTA for Cd. Both effects slow down further the formation kinetics in sea water. After adding the reactant EDTA to a 10^{-6}M Cd-solution at the low concentration level 10^{-5}M to 10^{-6}M and mixing, the time function of the decrease of the response due to the free Cd^{2+} is monitored by square wave polarography (Fig. 13). The formation rate of the nonreducible Cd-EDTA-complex is so slow that during the recording of each polarogram the respective free Cd^{2+} concentration remains virtually unchanged. The latter is a fundamental prerequisite for this approach. Generally, at least the monitored reactant concentration has to remain unchanged over 3 to 4 drop lifetimes of the DME. Conse-

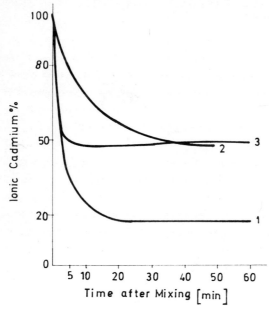

Fig.13

Determination of EDTA complex formation rate.
Decay of the concentration of ionic cadmium after addition of EDTA followed by square-wave polarography.
(1) $2 \cdot 10^{-5}$M Cd + sea water + $2 \cdot 10^{-5}$M EDTA,
(2) $2 \cdot 10^{-6}$M Cd + sea water + $2 \cdot 10^{-6}$M EDTA,
(3) $2 \cdot 10^{-6}$M Cd + 0.59 M NaCl + 10^{-2}M Ca^{2+} + $2 \cdot 10^{-6}$M EDTA,
pH - 7.8. After ref.63).

quently, the half-time of the reaction $t_{1/2}$ should exceed 15 sec, assuming about 3 sec /47, 76b/ as typical drop time. If $t_{1/2}$ approaches this limit, the recording of polarogram may be substituted by the recording of voltammograms at an elevated scan rate. Ample applications in marine chemistry for kinetic studies by this approach can be predicted. As the reactant concentrations (trace metals and organic ligands) are both small in natural sea water, the kinetics of systems which are relatively fast at higher reactant concentrations will remain rather slow and easily accessible in natural sea water.

Fast Reactions - Kinetic Limiting Currents

The recent model study of Raspor and Branica /94/ on the stability and the dissociation kinetics of $[Cd-NTA]^-$ chelates in chloride supporting electrolyte at pH 8 is an example for the method of kinetic polarographic limiting currents /47, 76b/. The ligand nitrilotriacetate (NTA) is considered a substitute for the polyphosphate in detergents to cope with the problem of eutrophication. Due to the chloride excess, the strong ligand NTA has to compete somewhat with the labile ligand Cl^- for the Cd. The technique employed consisted, in direct measurement, of a dc- and a simple version of square wave polarography.

The system is also an example when the electrode reaction is reversible while the dissociation equilibrium of the $[Cd-NTA]^-$ complex is sluggish. In dc-polarography a double wave is obtained (Fig.14). The more positive reversible wave corresponds to the reduction of the free Cd^{2+} (partially diffusing to the electrode as labile $CdCl^+$ complex. The stability constant of the NTA chelate follows from the shift of $E_{1/2}$ of the wave of the free Cd^{2+} with the NTA concentration (NTA in excess), while the limiting current is partially controlled by the kinetics of the prior homogeneous chemical reaction of the $[Cd NTA]^-$ dissociation and thus permits the determination of the rate constant of this step. With 1,6 sec^{-1} it has a value well within the kinetic resolution range of kinetic limiting currents in conventional dc-polarography /79/. In the second, more negative wave $[Cd NTA]^-$ is reduced directly in an irreversible electrode process. The study described has now been systematically extended in our insti-

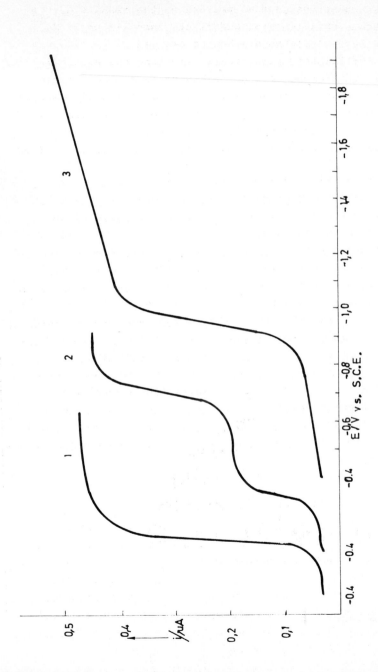

Fig.14

Reduction of ionic cadmium and of cadmium complexed with NTA. $2 \cdot 10^{-4}$M Cd^{2+}, 0.1M NaCl, pH −8.1.

(1) without NTA;
(2) $4 \cdot 10^{-4}$M NTA, first reversible wave with kinetic limiting current due to ionic Cd, second irreversible wave corresponds to Cd-NTA-complex;
(3) $2 \cdot 10^{-3}$M NTA, all Cd complexed (after ref.94).

tute/95/ to sea water and its natural Cd level, employing pulse polarography. While the general pattern of the results of the former study is confirmed, the additional competition of Mg^{2+} and Ca^{2+} for the NTA ligand has been clarified.

The approach of polarographic kinetic limiting currents /47, 76b/ introduced in the foregoing example has to be applied if the prior chemical reaction is so rapid that the monitored reactant alters its concentration during the drop life. The resulting limiting current corresponding to the overall rate is then controlled by the diffusion rate and the rate of the prior chemical step.

For the study of very fast homogeneous chemical reactions via coupled electrode reactions, advanced voltammetric relaxation methods based on μsec-pulse techniques are available today /10, 79/.

Extensive studies on the important proton transfer reactions of dissociation and recombination of carboxylic acids have been performed via the coupling of the electrolyte reaction of hydrogen evolution at the mercury electrode /10, 80, 81, 134/. The medium conditions (aqueous 1 M LiCl for experimental reasons) were not too distant from the ionic strength in sea water. Precision determinations of the conditional equilibrium constants and the conditional values of the related thermodynamic parameters /81, 110, 111/ , and dissociation enthalpy ΔH^O and dissociation entropy ΔS^O for acid dissociation by nonvoltammetric but electrochemical methods (emf-measurements in cells without liquid junction) have now been extended to sea water milieu in our institute.

CONCLUSIONS

The applications of polarography and voltammetry in marine chemistry are still in their very beginning stage. But the trends and developments now predictable show that these electrochemical methods will play a very important, or perhaps even the key role in the determination, speciation, and characterization of traces and microconstituents of sea water and will consequently make major contributions to important aspects of our future knowledge about the sea.

REFERENCES

Full title is cited only for textbooks, reviews, etc. References particularly referring to marine applications are marked +).
The support of Dr. L. Sipos, temporarily attached to our institute,
in compiling those references is gratefully acknowledged.

1)+) Abdullah, M.J.; Royle, L.G. 1972. Anal. Chim.Acta 58:
     283-288.

2)+) Allen, H.E.; Matson, W.R.; and Mancy, K.H. 1970.
     Trace Metal Characterization in Aquatic Environments by
     Anodic Stripping Voltammetry. J.Water Pollut.Contr.Fed.
     42: 573-581.

3)+) Ariel, M.; Eisner, U. 1963. J.Electroanal.Interfac.
     Electrochem. 5: 362-374.

4)+) Ariel, M.; Eisner, U.; and Gottesfeld, S. 1964. J. Electro-
     anal.Interfac.Electrochem. 7: 307-314.

5)   Barendrecht, E. 1967. Stripping Voltammetry. In Electro-
     analytical Chemistry 2, ed.A.J.Bard, pp.53-109. New York:
     M.Dekker.

6)   Barker, G.C.; Jenkins, I.L. 1952. Analyst. 77: 685-696.

7)   Barker, G.C. 1958. Square Wave Polarography and Some Related
     Techniques. Anal. Chim. Acta 18: 118-131.

8)   Barker, G.C.; Gardner, A.W. 1960. Pulse Polarography.
     Z.Anal.Chem. 173: 79-83.

9)   Barker, G.C. 1961. Faradaic Rectification. In Transactions
     of Symposium Electrode Processes, ed. E.Yeager, Ch. 18.
     pp.325-367. New York: J. Wiley.

10) Barker, J.C.; Nürnberg, H.W. 1964. Naturwissenschaften
     51: 191.

11) Barker, G.C. 1966. Non-Linear Relaxation Methods for the
     Study of Very Fast Electrode Processes. In Polarography
     1964, ed.G.J.Hills, Vol.I., pp.25-47, London: MacMillan.

12) Barker, G.C.; Bolzan, J.A. 1966. Z.Anal.Chem. 216: 215-238.

13) Barker,G.C. 1972. Square Wave and Pulse Polarogaphy. In
     Progress in Polarography 2, eds. P.Zuman, I.M.Kolthoff,
     pp.411-427. New York: Interscience.

14) Barker, G.C.; Gardner, A.W. 1972. Chem.Ing.Techn. 44:
     211-216.

15)   Barker, G.C.; Gardner, A.W.; and Williams, M.J. 1973.
        J. Electroanal. Interfac. Electrochem. 42: App. 21-26.

16)   Barker, G.C. 1973. The Multi Mode Polarograph. Harwell
        Information.

17)   Barker, G.C.; Bolzan, J.A.; and Gardner, A.W. 1974.
        J. Electroanal. Interfac. Electrochem. 52: 193-208.

18)   Barker, G.C. 1975. Some Developments in Polarographic
        Instrumentation. Proc. Anglo-Czechoslovakian Conference
        Electrochemistry, London 1973, ed. B. Fleet, in press.

19)+)   Bernhard, M.; Goldberg, E.D.; and Piro, A. 1975. Zinc
        in Seawater - An Overview 1975. In Dahlem Workshop on
        the Nature of Seawater, ed. E.D. Goldberg.
        Berlin: Dahlem Konferenzen.

20)   Bersier, P.; Finger, K.; and v. Sturm, F. 1966. Z. Anal.
        Chem. 216: 189-202.

21)+)   Bradford, W.L. 1973. Limnol. and Oceanogr. 18: 767-762.

22)   Brainina, Kh.Z. 1971. Film Stripping Voltammetry.
        Talanta 18: 513-538.

23)+)   Branica, M.; Petek, M.; Barić, A.; and Jeftic, L. 1968.
        Rapp. Comm. Int. Mer. Medit. 19: 102-106.

24)+)   Branica, M. 1970. In Reference Methods for Marine
        Radioactivity Studies. pp. 243-259. Vienna:IAEA.

25)+)   Branica, M.; Sipos, L.; Bubić, S.; and Kozar, S. 1974.
        Electroanalytical Determination and Characterization of
        some Heavy Metals in Seawater. Proc. 7th Materials
        Research Sympos., Gaithersburg, Ma..

26)   Breyer, B.; Bauer, H.H. 1963. Alternating Current Polaro-
        graphy and Tensammetry. New York: Interscience.

27)   Brocke, W.A.; Nürnberg, H.W. 1967. Methodik und Instru-
        mentation faradayscher Gleichrichtungsverfahren.
        Z. Instrumentenkunde 75: a) I. Grundlagen 291-299;
        b) II. Low Level-Techniken 315-325; C) III. High Level-
        Techniken 355-364.

28)+)   Bubić, S.; Branica, M. 1973. Thalassia Jugoslavica
        9: 47-53.

29)+)   Bubić, S.; Sipos, L.; Branica, M. 1973. Comparison of
        Different Electroanalytical Techniques for the
        Determination of Heavy Metals in Sea Water. Thalassia
        Jugoslavica 9: 55-63.

30)   Charlot, G.; Badoz-Lambling, J.; and Trémillon, B. 1962.
        Electrochemical Reactions. 376 p. Amsterdam: Elsevier.

31)+) Cosović, B.; Žutić, V.; Zvonarić, T.; and Kozorac, Z. 1974.
      Electroanalytical Estimation of Seawater Pollution by
      Aromatic Hydrocarbons. XXIV. Congrès Assemblée plénière
      C.I.E.S.M., Monaco.

32)   Crow, D.R. 1969, Polarography of Metal Complexes. 203 p.
      London: Academic Press.

33)   DeVries, W.T.; van Dalen, E. 1964. Theory of Anodic
      Stripping Voltammetry with a Plane Thin Mercury Film
      Electrode. J. Electroanal. Interfac. Electrochem. 8: 366-377.

34)   DeVries, W.T. 1965. Exact Treatment of Anodic Stripping
      Voltammetry with a Plane Mercury Film Electrode.
      J. Electroanal. Interfac. Electrochem. 9: 448-456.

35)   DeVries, W.T.; van Dalen, E. 1967. Linear Potential Sweep
      Voltammetry at a Plane Mercury Film Electrode. J. Electro-
      anal. Interfac. Electrochem. 14: 315-327.

36)   DeVries, W.T. 1968. Potential Step Electroanalysis followed
      by Linear Sweep Voltammetry at a Plane Mercury Film
      Electrode. J.Electroanal.Interfac.Electrochem. 16: 295-312.

37)   Elving, P.J. 1974. Voltammetry in Organic Analysis. In
      Electroanalytical Chemistry, ed. H.W. Nürnberg, Vol. 10,
      pp. 197-286, Advances in Analytical Chemistry and Instru-
      mentation, eds. C.N. Reilles, R.W. Murray. London: J. Wiley.

38)   Engelsman, J.J.; Classens A.M.J.M. 1961. Nature 191: 240.

39)   Erikson, L. 1953. Acta chem. scand. 7: 1146-1154.

40)   Flato, J.B. 1972. The Renaissance in Polarographic and
      Voltammetric Analysis. Anal. Chem. 44: 75A-87A.

41)   Florence, T.M. 1970. Anodic Stripping Voltammetry with a
      Glassy Carbon Electrode Mercury-Plated in situ.
      J. Electroanal. Interfac. Electrochem. 27: 273-281.

42)+) Florence, T.M. 1972. J. Electroanal. Interfac. Electrochem.
      35: 237-245.

43)+) Florence, T.M. 1974. J. Electroanal. Interfac. Electrochem.
      49: 255-264.

44)+) Gilbert, T.R.; Hume, D.N. 1973. Anal. Chim. Acta 65: 451-459.

45)   Glietenberg, D.; van Riesenbeck, G.; and Nürnberg, H.W.
      1962. Z. Anal. Chem. 186: 102-114.

46)+) Goldberg, E.D.; Broecker, W.S.; Gross, M.G.; and
      Turekian, K.K. 1971. Marine Chemistry. In Radioactivity
      in the Marine Environment, Chap. 5, pp. 137-146.
      Washington: National Academy of Sciences.

47)   Heyrovský J.; Kuta J. 1965. Grundlagen der Polarographie,
       562 p. Berlin: Akademie-Verlag. Engl.ed.1966. Principles
       of Polarography, 581 p. New York: Academic Press.

48)+) Hume, D.N.; Carter, J.N. 1972. Chemia Analytyczna
       17: 747-759.

49)+) Interlaboratory Lead Analyses of Standardized Samples
       of Sea Water 1973. Report NSF Office Internat.Decade of
       Ocean Exploration. Pasadena, Calif.

50)   Irving, H. 1960. The Stability of Metal Complexes and
       their Measurement Polarographically. In Advances in
       Polarography 1, ed. I.S.Longmuir, pp. 42-67.
       Oxford: Pergamon Press.

51)   Kastening, B.; Holleck, L. 1965. Die Bedeutung der
       Adsorption in der Polarographie. Talenta 12: 1259-1288.

52)   Kemula, W.; Kublik, Z. 1958. Anal. Chim. Acta 18: 104-111.

53)   Kemula, W. 1960. Voltammetry with the HMDE. In Advances
       in Polarography 1, ed. I.S.Longmuir, pp. 105-143.
       Oxford: Pergamon Press.

54)   Kemula, W.; Kublik, Z. 1963. In Advances in Analytical
       Chemistry and Instrumentation 2, ed. C.N. Reilley,
       pp. 123-177. New York: J. Wiley.

55)+) King, W.J.; Rodriguez, J.M.; and Wai, C.M. 1974.
       Anal. Chem. 46: 771-773.

56)   Kozlovsky, M.; Zebreva, A. 1972. Intermetallic Compounds
       in Amalgams. In Progress in Polarography 3, eds. P.Zuman,
       L. Meites, I.M. Kolthoff, pp. 157-194. New York: Wiley-
       Interscience.

57)   Koryta, J. 1967. Electrochemical Kinetics of Metal
       Complexes. In Advances in Electrochemistry and Electro-
       chemical Engineering 6, ed. P.Delahay, pp. 289-327.
       New York: Interscience.

58)+) Kozar, S.; Sipos, L.; and Branica, M. 1957. Determination
       of Traces of Heavy Metals by Differential Stripping
       Voltammetry. Abstracts Meeting of Chemists of Croatia,
       Zagreb, pp. 232-233.

59)+) Kremling, K. 1973. Kieler Meeresforschungen XXIX: 77-84.

60)   Leden, I. 1940. Z. phys. Chem. 188A: 160.

61)+) Macchi, G. 1965. J. Electroanal. Interfac. Electrochem.
       9: 290-298.

62)   Mairanovskii, S.G. 1972. Double Layer and Related Effects
       in Polarography. In Progress in Polarography 3, ed.
       P. Zuman, L. Meites, I.M. Kolthoff, pp. 287-369. New York:
       Wiley-Interscience.

63)+) Maljković, D.; Branica, M. 1971. Limnol.and Oceanogr.
      16: 779-785.

64)+) Matson, W.R.; Roe, D.K.; and Carritt, D.E. 1965.
      Anal. Chem. 37: 1594-1595.

65)   Meites, L. 1965. Polarographic Techniques, 2nd edit.,
      752 p. New York: Interscience.

66)   Milner, G.W.C. 1957. The Principles and Applications
      of Polarography, 729 p. London: Longmans, Green & Co.

67)+) Milner, G.W.C.; Wilson, J.D.; Barnett, G.A.; and
      Smales, A.A. 1961. J. Electroanal.Interfac.Electrochem.
      2: 25-38.

68)   Monien, H. 1970. Fortschritte der inversen Voltammetrie.
      I.Methodik und bestimmbare Elemente. Chem.Ing.Techn.
      42: 857-866.

69)   Monien, H. 1971. Fortschritte der inversen Voltammetrie.
      II.Analysenverfahren. Chem.Ing.Techn. 43: 666-676.

70)   Monien, H.; Jacob, P. 1971. Z.Anal.Chem. 255: 33-34.

71)+) Muzzarelli, R.A.A.; Sipos, L. 1971. Talanta 18: 853-858.

72)   Neeb, R. 1963. Neuere polarographische und voltammetrische
      Verfahren zur Spurenanalyse. Fortschr.chem.Forschg.
      4: 335-458.

73)   Neeb, R. 1965. Doppeltonpolarographie. Z. Anal.Chem.
      208: 168-187.

74)   Neeb, R. 1969. Inverse Polarographie und Voltammetrie.
      256 p. Weinheim/Bergstr.: Verlag Chemie.

75)   Nürnberg, H.W. 1960. Die Anwendungen der Polarographie
      in der Organischen Chemie. Angew.Chem. 72: 433-449.

76)   Nürnberg, H.W.; v.Stackelberg, M. 1961. Arbeitsmethoden
      und Anwendungen der Gleichspannungspolarographie.
      a) I.Apparatives, Methoden und Elektroden; II. Theorie
         der Polarographischen Kurve. J. Electroanal.Interfac.
         Electrochem. 2: 181-229;
      b) III. Reaktionskinetische Messungen. ibid. 2: 350-387;
      c) IV. Doppelschicht-, Adsorptions- und Inhibitionseffekte.
         1962. ibid. 4: 1-47.

77)   Nürnberg, H.W. 1962. Moderne Methoden der Gleichspannungs-
      polarographie. Z.Anal.Chem. 186: 1-53.

78)   Nürnberg, H.W.; Wolff, G. Stand der polarographischen
      Methoden und ihre Instrumentation.
      a) 1965, Teil I Gleichspannungsverfahren, Chem.Ing.Techn.
         37: 977-993;
      b) 1966, Teil II Wechselspannungsverfahren, ibid. 38: 160-18C

79)   Nürnberg, H.W. 1967. Untersuchung von Protonen-Transfer-
      vorgängen mit der High Level Faradaic Rectification-Technik.
      Fortschr.chem.Forschg. 8:241-308.

80)   Nürnberg, H.W.; Wolff, G. 1969. Influences on Homogeneous
      Chemical Reactions in the Diffuse Double Layer.
      J.Electroanal.Interfac.Electrochem. 21: 99-122.

81)   Nürnberg, H.W. 1971. Studies on the Kinetics and Thermo-
      dynamics of Acid-Base-Systems by Spectrophotometric and
      Advanced Voltammetric Methods. Cronache di Chimica 31: 6-16.

82)   Nürnberg, H.W.; Kastening, G. German Ed. 1973;
      Engl.Ed. 1974. Polarographic and Voltammetric Techniques.
      In Methodicum Chimicum, Vol. 1/1, ed.F.Korte,
      German Ed.pp.606-630. Stuttgart: G.Thieme,
      Engl.Ed.pp.584-607. New York: Academic Press.

83)   Nürnberg, H.W. 1974. The Influence of Double Layer
      Effects on Chemical Reactions at Charged Interfaces.
      In Membrane Transport in Plants, eds. U. Zimmermann,
      J. Dainty, pp. 48-53. Berlin: Springer.

84)   Nürnberg, H,W. ed. 1974. Electroanalytical Chemistry,
      Vol. 10, Advances Analytical Chemistry and Instrumentation,
      C.N. Reilley, L. Gordon eds. 609 p. London, New York:
      J. Wiley.

85)   Nürnberg, H.W. 1975. Anwendung polarographischer und
      voltammetrischer Verfahren in der Strukturanalyse.
      Z. Anal. Chem 273: 432-448

86)+) Odier, M.; Plichon, V. 1971. Anal.Chim.Acta. 55: 209-220.

87)   Princeton Applied Research 1969. Electrochemical
      Instrumentation, Models 170 and 171. Technical Note
      T-211-M-3, pp.1-33 and T-211A-20M-11, pp.1-28. Princeton,N.J:
      Princeton Applied Research Corp..

88)   Piljac, J.; Grabarić, B.; and Filipoviĉ, J. 1973.
      J. Electroanal. Interfac. Electrochem. 42: 433-442.

89)+) Piro , A. 1970. Rev.Intern.Océanogr.Med. XX: 1-17.

90)+) Piro, A.; Bernhard, M.; Branica.; and Verzi, M. 1973.
      Incomplete Exchange Reaction between Radioactive Ionic
      Zinc and Stable Natural Zinc in Seawater. In Radioactive
      Contamination of the Marine Environment, pp. 29-45.
      Vienna: IAEA.

91)+) Prochorova, G.V.; Vinogradova, E.N.; Grebneva, I.S.; and
      Skobelkina, E.V. 1973. Z.analit.Chimii 28: 123-126.

92)   Prozt, G.; Cieleszky, V.; and Györbiro, K. 1967.
      Polarographie, 587 p., Budapest: Akádémiai Kiadó.

93)+) Pytkowicz, R.M.; Kester, D.R. 1971. The Physical Chemistry
      of Sea Water. In Oceanographic Marine Biology Annual Reviews
      9, ed. H. Barnes, pp.11-60. London: G. Allen and Unwin Ltd..

94)+) Raspor, B.; Branica, M. 1975. J. Electroanal.Interfac.Electro-
      chem. 59: 99-109.

95)+) Raspor, B.; Valenta, P.; Nürnberg, H.W.; and Branica, M.;
      unpublished results.

96)   Ringbom, A.;. Erikson, L. 1953. Acta chem.scand.
      7: 1105-1111.

97)+) Robertson, D.E. 1968. Anal.Chim.Acta. 42: 537-539.

98)+) Rojahn, T. 1972. Anal. Chim. Acta. 62: 438-441.

99)   Schmidt, H.; v.Stackelberg, M. 1962. Neuartige polaro-
      graphische Methoden. 97 p. Weinheim/Bergstr.: Verlag
      Chemie.

100)+) Sillen, L.G. 1961. The Physical Chemistry of Sea Water.
       In Proc. 1st Internat.Congress Oceanography, New York 1959,
       ed.M.Sears, Publ.67, pp. 549-581. Washington: American
       Assoc.Adv.Science.

101)+) Sipos, L.; Magjer, T.; and Branica, M. 1974. A
       Universal Voltammetrie Cell.Croat.Chim.Acta 46: 35-37.

102)+) Sipos, L.; Kontusić, I.; and Branica, M. 1975. Differential
       Stripping Voltammetry with Two Rotating Glassy Carbon
       Electrodes. Abstracts Meeting of Chemists of Croatia,
       Zagreb, pp. 268-269.

103)+) Sipos, L.; Valenta, P. unpublished results.

104)+) Smith, J.D.; Redmond, J.D. 1971. J. Electroanal. Interfac.
       Electrochem. 33: 169-175.

105)   v.Stackelberg, M. 1951. Polarographische Maxima.
       Fortschr.chem.Forschg. 2: 229-272.

106)   v.Stackelberg, M.; Doppelfeld, R. 1960. Polarographische
       Maxima. In Advances in Polarography 1, ed. I.S.Longmuir,
       pp. 68-104. Oxford: Pergamon Press.

107)+) Struempler, A.W. 1973. Anal. Chem. 45: 2251-2254.

108)+) Stumm, W.; Bilinski, H. 1973. Trace Metals in Natural
       Waters. In Advances in Water Pollution Research, ed.
       S.K. Jenkins, pp. 39-49. Oxford: Pergamon Press.

109)   v.Sturm, F.; Ressel, M. 1962. Z.Anal.Chem. 186: 63-78.

110)   Struck, B.D.; Nürnberg, H.W.; and Heckner, H.N. 1973.
       J. Electroanal.Interfac.Electrochem. 48: 171-174.

111)   Struck, B.D.; Nürnberg, H.W. 1973. J. Electroanal.
        Interfac. Electrochem. 48: 175-182.

112)   van Swaay, M.; Deelder, R.S. 1961. Nature 191: 241.

113)   Tacussel, J. 1974. The 'VOCTAN', an Apparatus for
        Electrochemical Techniques involving Voltage/Current-Time
        Relationships. Proc. 25th ISE-Meeting, Brighton.

114)   Tamamushi, R.; Sato, G.P. 1972. Application of Polaro-
        graphy and Related Electrochemical Methods to the Study
        of Labile Complexes in Solution. In Progress in Polaro-
        graphy 3, eds. P.Zuman, L.Meites, I.M.Kolthoff,
        pp. 1-72. New York: Wiley - Interscience.

115)   Underkofler, W.L.; Shain, I. 1961. Anal.Chem. 33: 1966-1967.

116)   United Kingdom Atomic Energy Authority, London, AERE
        Harwell 1969. The Modulation Polarograph.

117)   Valenta, P. 1954. Registration of the Time Dependence
        of the Polarographic Curves. Czechoslov.Pat.Nr.92357.

118)+) Whitnack, G.C. 1961. J. Electroanal.Interfac.Electro-
        chem. 2: 110-115.

119)+) Whitnack, G.C. 1966. In Polarography 1964, Vol.1,
        ed.G.J.Hills, pp.641-651. London: MacMillan.

120)+) Whitnack, G.C.; Sasselli, R. 1969 Anal. Chim. Acta.
        47: 267-2774.

121)   Wolff, G.; Nürnberg, H.W. 1967. Z.Anal.Chem.
        224: 332-345.

122)+) Zirino, A.; Healy, M. 1971. Limnol.and Oceanogr.
        16: 773-778.

123)+) Zirino, A. Healy, M. 1972. Environm.Sci.and Technol.
        6: 243-249.

124)+) Zirino, A.; Lieberman, St.H. 1972. Anodic Stripping
        Voltammetry of Trace Metals in Sea Water. Proc. Sympos.
        Marine Electrochemistry, Miami Beach, Fla..

125)   Zuman, P. 1964. Organic Polarographic Analysis.
        In Internat. Series Monographs Analytical Chemistry,
        12, eds. R. Belcher, L. Gordon, 313 p.. London: Pergamon
        Press.

126)   Zuman, P. 1967. Substituent Effects in Organic Polaro-
        graphy. 384 p.. New York: Plenum Press.

127)   Zuman, P. 1969. Polarography in Organic Chemistry.
        Fortschr.chem.Forschg. 12: 1-76.

128)   Zuman, P. 1972. Effects of Acidity in the Elucidation
        of Organic Electrode Processes. In Progress in Polaro-
        graphy 3, eds. P.Zuman, L.Meites and I.M.Kolthoff,
        pp. 73-156. New York: Wiley - Interscience.

129)+) Zvonarić, T.; Zutić, V.; and Branica, M. 1973.
        Thalassia Jugoslavica 9: 65-73.

130)+) Zvonarić, T.; Kozarac, Z.; Zutić, V.; Cosović, B.;
        and Branica, M. 1974. Electroanalytical Estimation
        of Sea Water Pollution by Organic Substance. Analysis
        of North Adriatic Samples. XXIV. Congrès Assemblée
        plénière C.I.E.S.M., Monaco.

131)+) Zvonarić, T.; Zutić, V.; and Branica, M. 1975. Use of
        Polarographic Maximum of Mercury (II) for Estimation
        of Sea Water Pollution by Surfactants. Abstracts
        Meeting of Chemists of Croatia, Zagreb, pp. 292-293.

132)   Barker, G.C.; Nürnberg, H.W. 1962. Largely unpublished
        results; Abstracts Meeting Recent Development in Polaro-
        graphy. London: Society for Analytical Chemistry.

133)   Wolff, G.; Nürnberg, H.W. 1966. Z. Anal. Chem. 216: 169-183.

134)   Nürnberg, H.W. 1966. In Polarography 1964, Vol. 1,
        ed. G.J. Hills, pp. 149-186. London: MacMillan.

135)   Barić, A.; Branica, M. 1967. J. polarograph. Soc. 13,
        No. 1.: 4-8.

Addendum:

        Barker, G.C. 1975. Modern polarographic techniques.
        Proc. Anal. Div. Chem. Soc. 12: 179.

The Effects of Temperature and Pressure on Speciation

Michael Whitfield
The Laboratory, Citadel Hill,
Plymouth, PL1 2PB, England.

Abstract: The influence of temperature and pressure on chemical speciation can be determined either by the direct measurement of the appropriate stability constants or by measurement of the relevant standard partial molal thermodynamic functions. The experimental techniques are reviewed with particular emphasis on recent developments. Consideration is then given to theoretical correlations that can guide the interpretation of the experimental data and assist in estimating temperature and pressure effects where experimental values are not available.

1. Definitions

The chemical speciation of a solution may be defined by a series of molal stability constants (K_m^O). For the reaction

$$M + A \rightleftharpoons MA$$

$$\ln K_m^O = \ln(\gamma_{MA}/\gamma_M \gamma_A) + \ln([MA]/[M][A])$$

$$= \ln \Gamma_m + \ln K_m^* \qquad (1)$$

γ_X is the activity coefficient of component X and [X] is its concentration. K_m^* is the stoichiometric stability constant, and Γ_m describes the deviation of the reacting system from ideal behaviour. The influence of temperature and pressure on K_m^O can be described in terms of standard partial molal quantities ($\Delta \overline{Y}^O$, TABLE 1).

TABLE 1 – Standard partial molal functions of speciation reactions

Y	$(\partial Y/\partial P)_T$	$(\partial^2 Y/\partial P^2)_T$	$(\partial Y/\partial T)_p^{*}$	$(\partial^2 Y/\partial T^2)_p^{*}$	$-(\partial^2 Y/\partial P\partial T)$
$\ln K_m^o$	$-\Delta\bar{V}^o/RT$ [51]••	$\Delta\bar{\kappa}^o/RT$	$\Delta\bar{H}^o/RT^2$ [14]	$(\Delta\bar{C}_p^o - 2\Delta\bar{H}^o/T)/RT^2$	$(\Delta\bar{E}^o - \Delta\bar{V}^o/T)RT$
$-\ln\gamma_i^{\dagger\dagger}$	$-\bar{V}/RT$ [87,89]••	$\bar{\kappa}/RT$	$\bar{H}/RT^2$ [76,106]	$(\bar{C}_p - 2\bar{H}/T)/RT^2$	$(\bar{E}-\bar{V}/T)RT$

Subsidiary relationships:

$$\Delta\bar{G}^o = -RT\ln K_m^o; \qquad \Delta\bar{G}^o = \Delta\bar{H}^o - T\Delta\bar{S}^o$$

$$\Delta\bar{S}^o = (\partial\Delta\bar{G}^o/\partial T)_p = R\ln K_m^o + \Delta\bar{H}^o/T$$

$$\partial\Delta\bar{S}^o/\partial P = -\Delta\bar{E}^o; \qquad \partial\Delta\bar{S}^o/\partial T = -\Delta\bar{C}_p^o/T$$

• See [80] for corresponding isochoric coefficients

•• Numbers in square brackets indicate sources of data

[†] $\Delta\bar{E}^o = (\partial\Delta\bar{V}^o/\partial T)_p$ = standard partial molal expansibility

[††] Expressed as <u>relative</u> partial molal quantities where $\bar{Y} = \bar{Y}_i - \bar{Y}_i^o$

The standard state to which these functions refer is a hypothetical ideal solution of unit concentration (i.e. $[X] = \gamma_x = 1$, $\Gamma_m = 1$) with the same temperature as the experimental solution. Its pressure can either be fixed at some reference value or it can be identified with the ambient pressure of the solution [131]. An experimentally approachable reference state is required where $\Gamma_m \rightarrow 1$ so that ΔY^o values (TABLE 1) can be estimated. Γ_m can be factorised so that:

$$\Gamma_m = \Gamma_i \cdot \Gamma_s \qquad (2)$$

The self-medium effect (Γ_i) refers to interactions between the reacting components themselves and can be removed by measuring K• over a range of reactant concentrations and extrapolating to zero reactant concentration to give K^o/Γ_s. The ionic medium effect (Γ_s) refers to interactions between the reacting components and the other solutes present. Γ_s can be eliminated by estimating K• in a series of solutions with different medium ion concentrations and extrapolating to infinite dilution. To

avoid successive extrapolation an 'ionic medium method' can be used where
the reference state is infinite dilution of the reacting components in a
solution containing an indifferent electrolyte at a high and constant
ionic strength. By definition $\Gamma_s = 1$. For small concentrations of the
reacting components $\Gamma_i = 1$. If the results in two different media are
to be compared it is necessary to calculate Γ_s in each case. Relationships analogous to equation (1) can be defined for the other $\Delta \overline{Y}^o$ values
(TABLE 1) e.g. [111]

$$\Delta \overline{H}^o = \Delta \overline{H}^\bullet + RT^2 (\partial \ln \Gamma_m / \partial T) \qquad (3)$$

The relevant functions of γ_x are listed in TABLE 1 (see also [131]).
The discussion here will centre on the estimation of the stability
constant K_m (either as K_m^o or $K_m^\bullet$) as a function of temperature and pressure.
These constants can either be estimated directly or they can be calculated
by integration of the relevant thermodynamic parameters (Table 1, Fig. 1).
The latter procedure will yield the most precise results. A number of
pathways are available depending on the ionic medium used in the
measurements. With few exceptions stability constants have been measured
or estimated in simplified ionic media rather than in natural sea water.

2. Direct Determination of K_m

Stability constants are usually estimated from measurements of the
concentration of a single component made over a wide range of solution
composition [5, 17, 73, 81, 117, 118]. Such measurements will define the
system unequivocally if only a single, strong mononuclear complex is
formed [17, 73]. In all other cases there is some flexibility in the
interpretation of the data, and the pattern of complexes and stability
constants must be selected that shows the greatest compatibility with the
experimental evidence [119]. The various experimental methods look at
different aspects of speciation in solution and will not necessarily
produce comparable values for K_m [108].

Since most techniques can be modified without difficulty to cover the
oceanographic temperature range (0° to 35°C), the discussion of hardware
will be confined to high pressure techniques. Recent examples of precise
potentiometric [36, 44, 69], spectrophotometric [46, 81] and conductometric

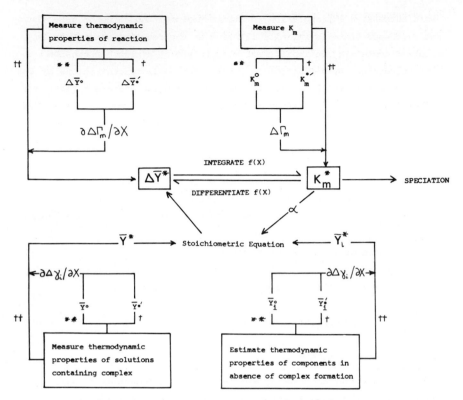

Symbols: $\Delta\Gamma_m$ – activity coefficient quotient required to correct data to natural ionic medium scale.

$\partial/\partial X$ – differentiation with respect to temperature and/or pressure.

α – degree of complex formation K_m^*, Γ_m and γ_i refer to the natural ionic medium. Primes indicate corresponding properties in a simplified ionic medium.

Notes: ** Extrapolated to infinite dilution of reactant and medium.

$$K_m^* = K_m^o / \Delta\Gamma_m; \quad \Delta\gamma_i = \gamma_i; \quad \Delta\Gamma_m = \Gamma_m.$$

† In simplified medium or at finite concentration of reactants.

$$K_m^* = K_m^{o\prime} / \Delta\Gamma_m; \quad \Delta\gamma_i = \gamma_i - \gamma_i^{\prime} \quad ; \quad \Delta\Gamma_m = \Gamma_m - \Gamma_m^{\prime}.$$

†† In natural ionic medium.

FIG. 1.   Summary of pathways used in the determination of stability constants as a function of temperature and pressure.

[68] measurements over a range of temperatures may be consulted for details [see also 3, 17, 63, 73]. Technical problems at high pressure have so far restricted equilibrium studies to solutions dominated by a single reaction yielding a mononuclear complex.

Potentiometric procedures are most widely used for determining K_m and give the most precise results since they can be tailored to respond fairly directly to the concentrations of individual components [116-118]. At normal temperatures and pressures a cell in which the reference electrode is isolated from the solution compartment by a salt bridge is preferred [44, 116, 117, see also 8]. However, high pressure measurements have been largely confined to pH cells without a liquid junction [19, 24-28, 50, 51, 128-130]. The experimental procedure is tedious since no high pressure titration systems are available, and long equilibration times are usually required following changes in temperature and pressure. Multicell assemblies [128, 130] reduce this problem but high pressure studies are characterised by a sparsity of data points. Long equilibration times also aggravate problems associated with the drift in asymmetry potential of the glass electrode [24, 50, 129]. The measurements are consequently less precise ($\pm$ 0.2 mV) than those made at atmospheric pressure and only merit interpretation as estimates of shifts in the stability constants of clearly defined systems as a function of pressure [25]. (TABLE 2). Few systems have been studied by potentiometric methods over a range of temperature and pressure [19, 55, 130].

Sodium selective glass [26, 72, 128] and metal amalgam [15] electrodes can also be used at high pressure. The poor response of liquid ion-exchange electrodes to changes in calcium ion activity at high pressures [72, 128] is greatly improved if the ion-exchanger is fixed in a PVC matrix. Mercury based electrodes [128] have been studied for the determination of chloride [30] and sulphate [29] ions. Solid state membrane electrodes could also be incorporated in high pressure cells without difficulty. The newer ion-selective electrodes can extend the range of systems studied at atmospheric pressure [4] provided that rigorous procedures are used to assess their performance [10]. The problems of calibrating these electrodes over a range of temperatures have been considered in detail [18, 99].

TABLE 2 - Pressure effects measured by direct determination of K_m at high pressure

Acceptor	Donor	T (°C)	P (Kb)	$\Delta \overline{v}^o$ ($cm^3 mole^{-1}$)	Method	Ref.
H+	OH^-	25	2	20.4	pot.	[50,130]
H+	HCO_3^-	22	2	26.6	pot.	[19,27,28]
H+	CO_3^{2-}	22	2	25.6	pot.	
H+	$B(OH)_4^-$	25	1	32.1	pot.	[19]
H+	H_2PO_4-	22	1	16.6	pot.	[24,27]
H+	HPO_4-	22	1	24.0	pot.	
H+	CH_3COO-	22	1	11.6	pot.	[24]
Na+	SO_4^{2-}	2,22	1	15.8*,**	pot.	[72]
H+	$Cr(H_2O)_5OH^{2+}$	5,25	3	3.8*	abs. spectr.	[124]
Eu^{3+}	SO_4^{2-}	25	2	25.6	abs. spectr.	[47]
H+	HPO_4-	20	6.5	23.8	abs. spectr.	[100]
H+	CH_3COO-	20	6.5	11.2	abs. spectr.	
H+	SO_4^{2-}	8-27	1	—	Raman spectr.	[22]
Mg^{2+}	SO_4^{2-}	7-25	1	20.3*	Raman spectr.	[13]
NH_4^+	OH^-	25,45	3	28.9*	cond.	[12]
Mg^{2+}	SO_4^{2-}	25	2	7.3	cond.	[37]
La^{3+}	SO_4^{2-}	25	2	22.5	cond.	[39]
Mn^{2+}	SO_4^{2-}	25	2	7.4	cond.	[38]
$Co(NH_3)_6^{2+}$	SO_4^{2-}	15-40	5	6.8*	cond.	[96]
La^{3+}	$Fe(CN)_6^{3-}$	25	2	8.0	cond.	[53]
H^+	CH_3COO^-	25-225	3	11.2	cond.	[65,79]
H^+	HS^-	25	2	15	cond.	[32]
H^+	HCO_3^-	25-65	2.5	26.5*	cond.	[31]

* 25°C values   ** sea water ionic medium scale

Spectrophotometric techniques [81] are normally less precise than potentiometric methods [117], particularly if the absorbence of the solution is the sum of the absorptivities of several chemical species. Technical difficulties have restricted most high pressure measurements (TABLE 2) to single beam instruments [1, 47, 51, 115] and the absorbence of the reference solutions must be substracted manually from those of the sample solutions, thus doubling the experimental work. Precisions of $\pm$ 0.001 [124] to $\pm$ 0.005 [47] absorbency units can be attained. The concentrations of both reactants and products can be monitored if their absorption peaks are sufficiently well separated [52, 124]. The observed optical densities must be corrected for alterations in the absorptivities of the various components (several per cent per Kb) and allowance must be made for shifts in the position of the absorbence peak [52, 124]. Indicator species can be used if the reactants and products themselves do not provide suitable absorbence peaks [100], but the precision is correspondingly lower. Laser Raman spectroscopy [67, 77] has been adapted for high pressure measurements [1, 20] of vibrational spectra from polyatomic ions in aqueous solution (TABLE 2). The procedure is restricted to high solute concentrations ($>$ 0.1 M) because of the low intensity of the scattered radiation. In magnesium sulphate solutions at a concentration of 2M, the ion pair produces a slight asymmetric perturbation of the sulphate stretching band. The large value calculated for $\Delta \overline{V}^{\circ}$ (TABLE 2) suggests that the Raman technique is sensitive only to the formation of contact ion pairs. Measurements have also been reported on concentrated aqueous CO_2 solutions [1].

Conductometry is necessarily dependent on the concentration of more than one species in solution and is generally a less precise procedure for determining K_m than potentiometry [117]. Because of its instrumental simplicity, however, it has been widely used in high pressure studies [1, 11, 64, 66] (TABLE 2). Initial difficulties in cell construction [11] have been overcome by several simple and effective designs [71, 104]. Since the limiting conductances of the ionic components must be estimated

via Kohlrausch's Law [49, 51, 80], a large number of individual
measurements are required and groups of cells are packed into a single
pressure vessel [71, 104].

The relevant thermodynamic parameters (TABLE 1) can be obtained by
differentiation of empirical relationships describing the dependence of
K_m on temperature or pressure. Each differentiation results in a decrease
in the precision of the parameter estimated [63, 73]. Consequently,
direct measurements of K_m, particularly at high pressure, are rarely
sufficiently precise to yield meaningful information on the second
derivatives ($\Delta \bar{C}_p^{\,o}$, $\Delta \bar{\kappa}^{\,o}$, $\Delta \bar{E}^{\,o}$, TABLE 1, [125] see also [45, 68, 69,
80]). These parameters are best determined by direct calorimetric or
densimetric measurements [63]. The application of a rigorous error
analysis [63, 73] provides a salutory lesson to those tempted to draw too
detailed conclusions from experimental data. The accuracy of the
thermodynamic data deduced will depend largely on the accuracy with which
the empirical equations fit the experimental data. The choice of a
fitting function for K_m is somewhat arbitrary [54, 73, 125]. King [73]
selected the equation

$$-R \ln K_m^o = (A/T) - B + CT \tag{4}$$

as adequate for the temperature variation of most acid/base equilibria.
A more flexible equation [16] is obtained by expressing $\Delta \bar{H}^{\,o}$ as a
Taylor series expansion in temperature. $\ln K_m$ is then represented by a
regression equation

$$R \ln K_m = b_o + b_1 t_1 + b_2 t_2 + b_3 t_3 \ \ldots\ldots \tag{5}$$

where $t_i = x^i \sum_{n=1}^{\infty} n(-x)^{n-1}/(n-2)$ and $x = (T - \Theta)/\Theta$.
T is the experimental temperature and Θ is the reference temperature for
which the thermodynamic parameters are to be calculated. These parameters
are determined by a multiple least squares regression analysis of equation
(5) [9, 16, 125]. Detailed consideration has been given to error
propagation [16] and the use of small computers [9] in the application of
equation (5).

If $\Delta \bar{\kappa}_1^{\,o}$ is assumed to be independent of pressure, the stability
constant at pressure P (K_p^o) may be related to that at 1 atmosphere

$(K_1^{\,o})$ by [73, 79],

$$RT\ (P-1)^{-1}\ \ln(K_p^{\,o}/K_1^{\,o}) = -\Delta\bar{V}_1^{\,o} + 0.5\ \Delta\bar{\kappa}_1^{\,o}\ (P-1) \qquad (6)$$

Plotting the left hand side against (P-1) gives a good straight line from which $\Delta\bar{V}_1^{\,o}$ and $\Delta\bar{\kappa}_1^{\,o}$ (the standard partial molal quantities at 1 atmosphere pressure) can be estimated. Equation (6) has been developed further to express $\Delta\bar{\kappa}_1^{\,o}$ as a function of pressure [65, 79, 103]. Many acid-base equilibria obey the simpler equation [33, 51, 52],

$$RT\ \ln(K_p/K_1) = -c\,\Delta\bar{V}_1^{\,o} \qquad (7)$$

where $c = (P-1)/[1+b(P-1)]$ and $b = 9.2 \times 10^{-5}\ bar^{-1}$

This relationship is consistent with the linear correlation observed between $\Delta\bar{V}^{\,o}$ and $\Delta\bar{\kappa}^{\,o}$ [79, 80].

3. Direct Measurement of Thermodynamic Parameters

The heat and volume changes accompanying the reaction may be measured directly or they may be estimated from data on the individual reactants and products (Fig. 1). $\Delta\bar{H}^{\,o}$ and $\Delta\bar{C}_p^{\,o}$ can be estimated directly by measuring the heat change accompanying the reaction over a range of temperatures [35, 56, 105]. (TABLE 3). The reaction can be followed over a range of solution composition using titration calorimetry [6, 45, 74]. The standard deviation in the heat equivalent measured is usually no more than a few tenths of a per cent. The calorimetric data can be processed by appropriate generalised least squares programmes [6, 74]. K_m values can also be estimated from these data (entropy titration, [35, 111, 123]) provided that a simple mononuclear complex is formed with a small stability constant ($0 < \log K_m < 4$, [74]). The accompanying $\Delta\bar{H}^{\,o}$ value should result in a heat equivalent that is several orders of magnitude greater than the sensitivity of the apparatus [98]. Most measurements have yielded $\overset{\bullet}{K}_m$ values in perchlorate media [6, 74] but Powell [111, 112] discusses in detail the problems involved in extrapolation to determine $K_m^{\,o}$. Where a number of complexes are formed, titration calorimetry is more convenient than conventional batch calorimetry [56, 94, 97, 98, 126], since each titration curve is equivalent to a large number of conventional measurements. Highly sensitive flow calorimeters [34, 41, 56] enable enthalpy changes accompanying the dilution [42] and mixing [70] of electrolyte solutions to be measured quite simply [94]. These data make useful contributions

TABLE 3 - Thermodynamic data for complex formation obtained
          calorimetrically*

Acceptor	Donor	$\Delta \bar{G}^{\circ}$ (Kcal mole^{-1})	$\Delta \bar{H}^{\circ}$ (Kcal mole^{-1})	$T \Delta \bar{S}^{\circ}$ (Kcal mole^{-1})	I	Ref.
Be^{2+}	F^-	- 6.7	- 0.4	6.3	1	[120]
Al^{3+}	F^-	- 8.4	1.1	9.5	0.5	[120]
Mg^{2+}	F^-	- 1.8	3.2	5.0	1	[98]
UO_2^{2+}	F^-	-25.89	1.7	27.6	1	[74]
UO_2F^+	F^-	-19.65	0.4	20.0	1	[74]
UO_2F_2	F^-	-13.9	0.25	14.2	1	[74]
$UO_2F_3^-$	F^-	- 8.4	- 2.1	6.3	1	[74]
UO_2^{2+}	SO_4^{2-}	-10.3	18.2	28.5	1	[74]
UO_2SO_4	SO_4^{2-}	- 5.4	16.9	22.4	1	[74]
$\underline{Ag}^+$	$\underline{Cl}^-$	- 4.5	- 2.7	1.8	0	[120]
$\underline{Hg}^{2+}$	$\underline{Cl}^-$	- 9.2	- 5.5	3.7	0.5	[120]
$\underline{Hg}^{2+}$	$\underline{I}^-$	-17.5	-18.0	-0.5	0.5	[120]
$\underline{Tl}^+$	$\underline{Br}^-$	- 1.2	- 2.45	-1.25	0	[98]
$\underline{Ch_2Hg}^+$	$\underline{CN}^-$	-18.8	-22.1	-3.3	0.1	[98]
$\underline{Ag}^+$	$\underline{CN}^-$	-27.9	-33.0	-5.1	0	[98]
$\underline{Cd}^{2+}$	$\underline{S_2O_3}^{2-}$	-15.5	0	15.5	1	[74]
$\underline{CdS_2O_3}$	$\underline{S_2O_3}^{2-}$	-14.4	- 6.3	7.9	1	[74]
$\underline{Cd(S_2O_3)_2}^{2-}$	$\underline{S_2O_3}^{2-}$	- 6.2	- 8.0	-1.8	1	[74]

Soft donors and acceptors are underlined

* For further data see references cited and [6, 7, 14, 75]

to the estimation of $\partial \ln \Gamma_m / \partial T$, equation (2). Heat of dilution
measurements provide a particularly sensitive method for obtaining $\Delta \bar{H}^o$
for ion-pair formation [75]. The flow technique can be modified to
measure, simply and precisely, the heat capacity of a solution relative
to that of a reference liquid [93, 109]. These techniques could be
applied to study chemical speciation, possibly in conjunction with some
form of gradient titrimetry [40].

$\Delta \bar{V}^o$ values can be measured directly [122] or they can be calculated
from solution densities [78, 87, 89, 122] (TABLE 4, Fig. 1). $\Delta \bar{R}^o$ can
be estimated if the solution densities are measured over a reasonable
pressure range [95]. Simple and precise density measurements can be made
using magnetic float [86, 91] or continuous flow [110] densimeters. In
the former the buoyancy of an immersed float is counterbalanced by an
electromagnet. The current required to hold down the float is related
to the solution density [86] with a precision of $\pm$ 2 ppm. The high
pressure version of this densimeter [91] is capable of a precision
($\pm$ 5 ppm) comparable to that of the more cumbersome volumometric and
dilatometric methods used hitherto. With the continuous flow densimeter
[110] the solution flows through a V-shaped steel tube which is vibrated
like a tuning fork. Changes in the resonant frequency of vibration are
related to the mass of the tube and hence to the density ($\pm$ 2 ppm) of
the solution flowing within it. So far the system has been used to study
single electrolyte solutions [42, 107] and hence to provide data for the
estimation of $\partial \ln \Gamma_m / \partial P$. Here, too, the concept of gradient
titrimetry [40] might prove useful for the study of chemical speciation.

K_m^o may be calculated from the thermodynamic parameters using integrated
forms of the equations listed in TABLE 1 (e.g. equation 6), see also [59].
It is normally sufficient to assume that $\partial \Delta \bar{R}^o / \partial P = 0$ and
$\partial \Delta \bar{C}_p^o / \partial T = 0$ for the rather small oceanographic temperature and
pressure range. $\Delta \bar{C}_p^o$ data are rarely available and Helgeson [58] has
developed a semi-empirical equation enabling K_m^o at a temperature T to be
calculated from $\Delta \bar{H}^o$ and $\Delta \bar{S}^o$ measured at some reference temperature T^o
(see [58] for tabulated $\Delta \bar{H}^o$ and $\Delta \bar{S}^o$ values);

TABLE 4 – $\Delta \overline{V}^{\circ}$ values calculated from density measurements

Acceptor	Donor	T (°C)	$\Delta \overline{V}^{\circ}$ ($cm^3\ mole^{-1}$)	Method	Ref.
H^+	$B(OH)_4^-$	0	38.68		
		15	36.59	Hydrostatic	
		25	35.45	balance	[127]
		50	35.90		
H^+	OH^-	0	25.75		
		10	23.71		
		20	22.43	Magnetic float	
		25	22.07	densimeter	[92, see also 130]
		30	21.89		
		35	21.91		
Mg^{2+}	SO_4^{2-}	0	10.0		
		25	7 to 5.6	Via densities of	
		50	7.1 to 5.7	component salts	[90]
Rb^+	NO_3^-	25	5.2•	Magnetic float	
Tl^+	NO_3^-	25	12.2•	densimeter	[84]

• Apparent molal volume changes at a concentration of 0.1M.

$$-RT \ln K_m^{\circ} (T) = \Delta \overline{H}^{\circ} - \Delta \overline{S}^{\circ} [T^{\circ} - 218.3 (1-\exp (\exp 0.01875 T - 12.741)$$
$$- 7.84 \times 10^{-4} + (T - T^{\circ})/219)] \tag{8}$$

Similar equations can be used to calculate $\Delta \overline{Cp}^{\circ}$ and $\Delta \overline{S}^{\circ}$ over a range of temperatures [58].

4. Theoretical Correlations

Thermodynamic data, especially for complex ionic media such as sea water, are still rather sparse and it is worthwhile to consider briefly methods for extrapolating the available information beyond its present confines.

The _electrostatic theory_ [57, 73, 114] assumes that environmental
contributions, involving interactions between the ions and the solvent,
dominate the thermodynamics of reactions in which charged particles are
involved [23]. In the simplest model the ions are treated as charged
spheres in a dielectric continuum. The electrostatic free energy change
($\Delta \overline{G}^{o}_{e}$) accompanying a reaction is then given by [49, 73]:

$$\Delta \overline{G}^{o}_{e} = (Ne^2/2) \ (\underset{PROD}{\sum} z^2/r - \underset{REACT}{\sum} z^2/r)(1 - \varepsilon^{-1})$$

$$= (Ne^2 \phi /2)(1 - \varepsilon^{-1}) \qquad\qquad (9)$$

where N is Avagadro's number, e is the electronic charge and ε is the
dielectric constant of water. Z and r are respectively the charge and
the effective radius of the reaction components. $\Delta \overline{G}^{o}$ values for the
formation of fluoride complexes show a good correlation with ϕ [57].
Equations for the other thermodynamic parameters can be obtained from
equation (9) using the relationships in TABLE 1 [51, 73, 80, 113]. For
reactions involving a net reduction in charge, $\Delta \overline{C}^{o}_{p,e}$, $\Delta \overline{S}^{o}_{e}$ and $\Delta \overline{V}^{o}_{e}$
will be positive, suggesting that such complexes may be stabilised by an
increase in temperature and broken down by an increase in pressure. If
there is no change in net charge these properties will have small values
and could be negative or positive. The predictions for pressure effects
are generally confirmed [51], but the story for temperature effects is
somewhat more complex [57]. The numerical predictions are rarely correct
because water is a highly structured solvent, not a continuum, and
because there is no simple way of defining the effective radius (r, [57]).
If the charge on the complex is delocalised [49, 73, 124], unusually small
$\Delta \overline{V}^{o}$ values will be observed. Similar effects are noted if the combining
ions form solvent-separated ion pairs so that their hydration sheaths are
only slightly altered. Unusually large $\Delta \overline{V}^{o}$ values may be observed if a
water molecule is actually covalently bonded to an ion (e.g. formation of
HCO_3^{-}, [31, 51]). The electrostatic theory has been elaborated to give an
account of the formation of solvent-separated ion pairs. The model
devised by Fuoss [31, 54, 108, 114] gives

$$\Delta \overline{V}^{o} = RT \ \beta \ [(b A' \varepsilon /d^{o}) - 1] \qquad\qquad (10)$$

where $b = |z_1 z_2| \ e^2/a \varepsilon kT$, A' is a constant and β and d^{o} are
respectively the compressibility and density of water. The interionic
distance defining the ion pair, represented by a, is determined from the

corresponding equation defining K_m^o [31, 60]. Equation (10) gives a
reasonable account of $\Delta \bar{V}^o$ values (TABLE 5, see also [75]). The
electrostatic model is less accurate for $\Delta \bar{S}^o$ and $\Delta \bar{C_p}^o$ since these
parameters are sensitive to intramolecular motions that may be influenced
by complex formation [107]. The electrostatic theory also gives a poor
account of $\Delta \bar{H}^o$. Even in simple electrolyte solutions at high dilutions,
the analogous Debye-Hückel theory provides a poor guide to the
extrapolation of heats of dilution [54, 94]. The simple electrostatic
theories are also unable to give an adequate account of the maximum in
K_m^o that is observed in many systems studied over a range of temperatures
[73, 90, 97, 98].

If ϕ (equation (9)) is treated as a constant, a number of linear
correlations can be deduced between the electrostatic contributions to
the thermodynamic parameters (TABLE 6, [73]). Correlations between the
corresponding experimental parameters provide a useful means of
extending the available data. The relationship between $\Delta \bar{V}^o$ and $\Delta \bar{K}^o$
is particularly useful since it gives the simple equation

$$RT \ln (K_p/K_1) = - P \Delta \bar{V}_1^o (1 - AP) \qquad (11)$$

The correlations hold whether the parameters are compared for different
solutes at the same temperature and pressure [62, 79, 95, 121] or for
a single solute over a range of temperature and pressure [80]. General
patterns in the behaviour of $\Delta \bar{H}^o$ and $\Delta \bar{S}^o$ may be related to the degree
of covalency observed in the bond between the electron donor and the

TABLE 5 - Comparison of observed and calculated values of $\bar{V}^o$.[*]

Ion pair	$\Delta \bar{V}^o$ (calculated)		$\Delta \bar{V}^o$ (experimental)
	Fuoss[**]	Bjerrum[‡]	
La Fe $(CN)_6$	8.98	6.89	8.0
$MgSO_4$	7.42	4.86	7.3
$MnSO_4$	8.3	5.0	7.4

[*] Values taken from [51, 60].

[**] Equation (9). Some calculations give a value for $MnSO_4$ in exact
     agreement with experimental values [38].

[‡] Values calculated from electrostatic theory of Bjerrum [54,60,108,114].

electron acceptor when the complex is formed [3, 7, 74, 98, 120]. Highly
polarizable acceptors with a large number of d electrons (class b or soft
acceptors, [2, 3, 132]) tend to form stable complexes with polarizable
(soft) donors with a low electro-negativity and the resulting bond is
predominantly covalent. Soft acceptors are generally not heavily hydrated
and soft donors often reduce the structural organisation of water in their
vicinity. The complex formation reaction therefore has a minimal effect
on the organisation of the water structure. $\Delta \overline{G}^O$ for soft-soft
interactions is consequently dominated by a large negative value of
$\Delta \overline{H}^O$. (TABLE 3). $\Delta \overline{S}^O$ is small and often negative after allowance for
the cratic term associated with the change in the number of solute
particles [7, 120].

Small highly charged acceptors (a-class or hard acceptors) have a low
polarizability and form strong complexes with highly electronegative
ligands which have a low polarizability and are difficult to oxidise (hard
donors). The bond is largely electrostatic and results in a considerable
disturbance of the hydration sheaths that surround such hard ions. The
resulting donor-acceptor bond is not sufficiently energetic to counter-
balance the energy absorbed in breaking down the metal-water bonds so
that the reactions are endothermic or only slightly exothermic. $\Delta \overline{G}^O$ is
therefore dominated by the accompanying large positive value of $\Delta \overline{S}^O$
[114] (TABLE 3). $\Delta \overline{S}^O$ will be slightly less positive for reactions
involving neutral ligands and for solvent separated ion pairs. The
difference between hard-hard and soft-soft interactions is emphasized
when stepwise formation constants are considered (TABLE 3, [74]). Nieboer
and McBryde [101] have discussed the restrictions that $\Delta \overline{H}^O$ and $\Delta \overline{S}^O$
place on the validity of linear correlations observed for K_m for a wide
range of complexes [102]. The correlations between $\Delta \overline{S}^O$ and $\Delta \overline{V}^O$ and
between $\Delta \overline{V}^O$ and $\Delta \overline{K}^O$ (TABLE 6) suggest that hard-hard interactions
will in general be associated with large positive values of $\Delta \overline{V}^O$ and
$- \Delta \overline{K}^O$ and soft-soft interactions with small values.

So far the donor and acceptor molecules have been treated as the sole
reactants. Marshall [82, 83 see also 103] suggests that the water
molecules themselves should also be treated as reactants, i.e. the reaction

TABLE 6 - Cross correlations between thermodynamic functions*

Y	X	m		Notes	Ref.
		Theoretical	Experimental		
$\Delta \overline{S}^o$	$\Delta \overline{V}^o$	2.39 cal cm^3 deg^{-1}			[73]
			1.05 cal cm^3 deg^{-1}	acid-base equilibria	[62]
			0.8 cal cm^3 deg^{-1}	Acetic acid only	[80,72]
$\Delta \overline{S}^o$	$\Delta \overline{C}_p{}^o$	0.718			[73]
$\Delta \overline{H}^o$	$\Delta \overline{S}^o$	80 deg			[73]
			258 deg	hard-hard complexes	[121,61]
$\Delta \overline{C}_p{}^o$	$\Delta \overline{V}^o$	3.32 cal cm^3 deg^{-1}			[73]
$\Delta \overline{\kappa}^o$	$\Delta \overline{V}^o$	1.99 x 10^{-4} bar^{-1}		acid-base equilibria	[51]
		1.47 x 10^{-4} bar^{-1}			[80]
			2.14 x 10^{-4} bar^{-1}	acid-base equilibria	[79]
		3.6 x 10^{-4} bar^{-1}	3.6 x 10^{-4} bar^{-1}	ion-pair formation	[95]

* Parameters for the equation $Y = mX$. The theoretical equations refer to
the electrostatic contributions only. The experimental values include
detailed structural effects not considered in the electrostatic model.

should be written

$$M\,(H_2O)_m + A(H_2O)_n \rightleftharpoons MA\,(H_2O)_j + kH_2O$$

and
$$K_o = K_c^o\,[H_2O]^k \tag{12}$$

if the standard state of water is chosen so that $\gamma_{H_2O} = 1$ [85]. K_o
is the <u>complete equilibrium constant</u> and all concentrations are on the
molar scale. In many instances [82,83] a plot of $- \ln K_c^o$ versus
$\ln [H_2O]$ gives a good straight line fit whether $[H_2O]$ is altered by
varying the pressure and temperature or by the addition of a second
solvent. One conclusion is that K_o is independent of pressure so that
the volume change for the complete equilibrium is zero. However [51, 85]
differentiation of equation (12) gives

$$\partial \ln K_o / \partial P = \Delta \bar{V}^o + (1 - k) RT\beta \qquad (13)$$

From a consideration of the standard states Matheson [85] concludes that there is no a priori reason why the right hand side of this equation should be zero, suggesting that k is not necessarily a hydration number. Certainly the hydration numbers obtained by this procedure are very large (e.g. k = 29 for the ionization of ammonia) and do not seem to fit a coherent pattern [85]. The k values obtained by varying the temperature and pressure and by varying the solvent are not necessarily in agreement. Consequently it is preferable to treat equation (12) as an empirical correlation. If $\partial K_o / \partial P = 0$ then, on the molar scale (see also equation 10),

$$(\partial \ln K_c^o / \partial P)_T = -k \, (\partial \ln d^o / \partial P) = - k\beta \qquad (14)$$

The pressure coefficient of a reaction can then be predicted from the compressibility of water (β) once the value of k has been determined in one experimental system. $\Delta \bar{V}^o$ can then be calculated at any pressure and temperature thus providing a means of estimating $\Delta \bar{\kappa}^o$ and $\Delta \bar{E}^o$. The approach is seductive in its simplicity and it certainly results in some startling correlations over a wide temperature and pressure range.

References

[1] Adams, W.A., and Davis, A.R. 1973. Survey of techniques to study aqueous systems at pressures of 1 - 3 kbar. In Marine Electrochemistry. eds. J.B. Berkowitz, R.A. Horne, M. Banus, P.L. Howard, M.J. Pryor and G.C. Whitnack, pp. 53 - 75. Princeton: Electrochemical Society.

[2] Ahrland, S. 1966. Factors contributing to (b) - behaviour in acceptors. Struct. Bonding $\underline{1}$: 207 - 220.

[3] Ahrland, S. 1968. Thermodynamics of complex formation between hard and soft acceptors and donors. Struct. Bonding $\underline{5}$: 118 - 149.

[4] Ainsworth, R.G. 1974. Dissociation constant of calcium sulphate from 25° to 50°C. J.C.S. Faraday Trans. I. $\underline{69}$: 1028 - 1032.

[5] Albert, A., and Sergeant, E.P. 1971. 'The determination of ionisation constants' 2nd Edition. London : Chapman and Hall.

[6] Arnek, R. 1970. On the thermodynamics of some aqueous hydrolytic species. Arkiv för Kemi $\underline{32}$: 55 - 80.

[7] Beech, G. 1969. Some recent studies in the Thermodynamics of metal complex formation. Quart. Rev. $\underline{23}$: 410 - 429.

[8] Ben-Yaakov, S., and Kaplan, I.R. 1968. High pressure pH sensor for oceanographic application. Rev. Sci. Instr. $\underline{39}$: 1133 - 1138.

[9] Bolton, P.D. 1970. Calculation of thermodynamic functions from equilibrium data. J. Chem. Ed. $\underline{47}$: 638 - 641.

[10] Briggs, C.C., and Lilley, T.H. 1974. A rigorous test of a calcium ion-exchange membrane electrode. J. Chem. Thermodynamics. $\underline{6}$: 599.

[11] Brummer, S.B., and Gancy, A.B. 1972. In 'Water and Aqueous Solutions : Structure, Thermodynamics and Transport Processes.' ed. R.A. Horne, p. 745. New York : Wiley Interscience.

[12] Buchanan, J., and Hamann, S.D. 1953. The chemical effects of pressure. Part I. Trans. Faraday Soc. $\underline{49}$: 1425 - 1433.

[13] Chatterjee, R.M., Adams, W.A., and Davis, A.R. 1974. A high pressure laser raman spectroscopic investigation of aqueous magnesium sulfate solutions. J. Phys. Chem. $\underline{78}$: 246 - 250.

[14] Christensen, J., and Izatt, R.M. 1970. Handbook of metal ligand heats. New York : Marcel Dekker.

[15]   Churagulov, B.R., Kalashnikov, Ya.A., Feklichov, E.M., and
       Khokhlova, G.I. 1967. The emf of voltaic cells at high pressures.
       Russ. J. Phys. Chem. 41 : 816 - 817.

[16]   Clarke, E.C.W., and Glew, D.N. 1966. Evaluation of thermodynamic
       functions from equilibrium constants. Trans Faraday. Soc. 62 :
       539 - 547.

[17]   Cookson, R.F. 1974. The determination of acidity constants.
       Chem. Rev. 74 : 5 - 28.

[18]   Covington, A.K. 1974. Ion selective electrodes. CRC Crit. Rev.
       Anal. Chem. 1974 : 355 - 406.

[19]   Culberson, C.,and Pytkowicz, R.M. 1968. Effects of pressure on
       carbonic acid, boric acid and the pH of seawater. Limnol.
       Oceanogr. 13 : 403 - 417.

[20]   Davis, A.R., and Adams, W.A. 1972. A technique for obtaining the
       raman spectra of liquids and solutions under high pressure.
       Spectrochim. Acta. 27A : 2401 - 2405.

[21]   Davis, A.R., and Oliver, B.G. 1973. Raman spectroscopic evidence
       for contact ion pairing in aqueous magnesium sulphate solutions.
       J. Phys. Chem. 77, 1315 - 1316.

[22]   Davis, A.R., Adams, W.A., and McGuire, M.J. 1974. High pressure
       laser raman study of the dissociation of aqueous bisulphate ion.
       J. Chem. Phys. 60 : 1751 - 1753.

[23]   Degischer, G., and Nancollas, G.N. 1970. Thermodynamics of ion
       association. Part XX. Interpretation of the enthalpy changes.
       J. Chem. Soc. (A) 1970 : 1125 - 1128.

[24]   Distèche, A. 1962. Electrochemical measurements at high
       pressures. J. Electrochem. Soc. 109 : 1084 - 1092.

[25]   Distèche, A. 1972. Effects of pressure on dissociation of weak
       acids. Symp. Soc. Exp. Biol. 26 : 27 - 60.

[26]   Distèche, A. 1972. Electrochemical devices for in-situ or
       simulated deep sea measurements. In 'Barobiology'. ed. R.W.
       Bauer. pp. 234 - 265. Proc. 1st Symp. on High Pressure Aquarium
       Systems.

[27]   Distèche, A., and Distèche, S. 1965. The effect of pressure on
         pH and dissociation constants from measurements with buffered and
         unbuffered glass electrode cells. J. Electrochem. Soc. $\underline{112}$:
         350 - 354.

[28]   Distèche, A., and Distèche, S. 1967. The effect of pressure on
         the dissociation of carbonic acid from measurements with buffered
         glass electrode cells. The effect of NaCl, KCl, Mg^{2+}, Ca^{2+}, SO_4^{2-}
         and boric acid with special reference to sea water. J. Electro-
         chem. Soc. $\underline{114}$: 330 - 340.

[29]   Dobson, J.V., and Firman, R.E. 1972. The behaviour of cells
         using silver-silver sulphate and the skin-mercurous sulphate
         electrodes at temperatures between 25° and 200°C and 1 bar to 2kbar
         pressure. J. Electroanal. Chem. $\underline{40}$: 283 - 293.

[30]   Dobson, J.V., Firman, R.E., and Thirsk, H.R. 1971. The behaviour
         of cells using silver-silver chloride and skin calomel electrodes
         at temperatures from 25° to 200°C and 1bar to 1kbar pressure.
         Electrochim. Acta. $\underline{16}$: 793 - 809.

[31]   Ellis, A.J. 1959. The effect of pressure on the first
         dissociation constant of "carbonic acid". J. Chem. Soc. (London)
         $\underline{1959}$: 3689 - 3699.

[32]   Ellis, A.J. 1961. The first dissociation constant of hydrogen
         sulphide at high pressures. J. Chem. Soc. (London) $\underline{1961}$: 4678 -
         4680.

[33]   El'yanov, B.S., and Gonikberg, M.G. 1972. Calculation of the
         dissociation constants of weak electrolytes at high pressures.
         Russ. J. Phys. Chem. $\underline{46}$: 856 - 858.

[34]   Falk, B., and Sunner, S. 1973. A stepwise scanning flow micro-
         calorimeter system for the determination of enthalpies of mixing
         of liquids. Enthalpy of dilution of hydrochloric acid. J. Chem.
         Thermodyn. $\underline{5}$: 533.

[35]   Fenby, D.V., and Hepler, L.G. 1974. Calorimetric investigation
         of hydrogen-bond and charge-transfer complexes. Chem. Soc. Rev.
         $\underline{3}$: 193 - 207.

[36]   Ferroni, G., Antonetti, G., Romanetti, R., and Galea, J. 1973.
        Potentiometric study of the dissociation and association of
        $H_2 PO_4$ - ion in 3MKCl at 5 - 65°C. Bull. Soc. Chim. (France)
        <u>1973</u> : 3269 - 3273.

[37]   Fisher, F.H. 1962. The effect of pressure on the equilibrium of
        magnesium sulphate. J. Phys. Chem. <u>66</u> : 1607 - 1611.

[38]   Fisher, F.H., and Davies, D.F. 1965. The effect of pressure on
        the dissociation of manganese sulphate ion pairs in water. J. Phys.
        Chem. <u>69</u> : 2595 - 2598.

[39]   Fisher, F.H., and Davies, D.F. 1967. Effect of pressure on the
        dissociation of the La $SO4^+$ complex ion. J. Phys. Chem. <u>71</u>
        819 - 822.

[40]   Fleet, B., and Ho, A.Y.W. 1974. Gradient titration - a novel
        approach to continuous monitoring using ion-selective electrodes.
        Anal. Chem. <u>46</u> : 9 - 11.

[41]   Fortier, J-L., Leduc, P.-A., Picker, P., and Desnoyers, J.E. 1973.
        Enthalpies of dilution of electrolyte solutions by flow calorimetry.
        J. Solution Chem. <u>2</u> : 467 - 475.

[42]   Fortier, J-L., Leduc P-A., and Desnoyers, J.E. 1974. Thermodynamic
        Properties of alkali halides.II.Enthalpies of dilution and heat
        capacities in water at 25°C. J. Solution Chem. <u>3</u> : 323 - 349.

[43]   Fortier, J-L., Philip, P.R., and Desnoyers, J.E. 1974. Thermodynamic
        properties of alkali halides.III. Volumes and heat capacities of
        transfer from H_2O to D_2O at 25°C. J. Solution Chem. <u>3</u> : 523 -
        538.

[44]   Grenthe, I., and Ots, H. 1972. Thermodynamic properties of rare
        earth complexes.XI.stability constants and free energy changes for
        the formation of rare earth diglycolate complexes at 5, 20, 35 and
        50°C. Acta. Chem Scand. <u>26</u> : 1217 - 1228.

[45]   Grenthe, I., Ots, H., and Ginstrup, O. 1970. A calorimetric
        determination of the enthalpy of ionisation of water and the
        enthalpy of the protonation of THAM at 5, 20, 25, 35 and 50°C.
        Acta. Chem. Scand. <u>24</u> : 1067 - 1080.

[46]   Hale, C.F., and Spedding, F.H. 1972. Thermodynamics of the
        association of aqueous Europium (III) and sulphate ions. J. Phys.
        Chem. 76 : 1887 - 1894.

[47]   Hale, C.F., and Spedding, F.H. 1972. Effect of high pressure on
        the formation of aqueous Eu SO_4^+ at 25°C. J. Phys. Chem. 76 :
        2925 - 2929.

[48]   Hamann, S.D. 1957. Physicochemical effects of pressure. pp 246.
        London : Butterworths.

[49]   Hamann, S.D. 1963. Chemical equilibria in condensed systems.
        In 'High Pressure Physics and Chemistry'. Vol. 2. eds.
        R.S. Bradley and D.C. Munro, pp. 131 - 162. New York : Academic
        Press.

[50]   Hamann, S.D. 1963. The ionisation of water at high pressures.
        J. Phys. Chem. 67 : 2233 - 2235.

[51]   Hamann, S.D. 1974. Electrolyte solutions at high pressure. In
        Modern aspects of electrochemistry No 9 eds. B.E. Conway and
        J. O'M Bockris. pp. 47 - 158. New York : Plenum Press.

[52]   Hamann, S.D., and Linton, M. 1975. Influence of pressure on the
        ionisation of substituted phenols J.C.S. Faraday I., (in press).

[53]   Hamann, S.D., Pearce, P.J., and Strauss, W. 1964. The effect of
        pressure on the dissociation of Lanthanum ferricyanide ion pairs
        in water. J. Phys. Chem. 68 : 375 - 380.

[54]   Harned, H.S., and Owen, B.B. 1958. The physical chemistry of
        electrolytic solutions. pp 803. New York : Reinhold.

[55]   Hawley, J., and Pytkowicz, R.M. 1969. Solubility of calcium
        carbonate in sea water at high pressures and 2°C. Geochim.
        Cosmochim. Acta. 33 : 1557 - 1561.

[56]   Head, A.J. 1973. Combustion and reaction calorimetry In
        Chemical Thermodynamics, pp. 95 - 132. Vol. I. Specialist
        Periodical Reports, Chem. Soc. (London).

[57]   Hefter, G. 1974. Simple electrostatic correlations of fluoride
        complexes in aqueous solution. Coord. Chem. Rev. 12 : 221 - 239.

[58]   Helgeson, H.C. 1967. Thermodynamics of complex dissociation in
        aqueous solution at elevated temperatures. J. Phys. Chem. 71 :
        3121 - 3136.

[59]   Helgeson, H.C. 1969. Thermodynamics of hydrothermal systems at
        elevated temperatures and pressures. Am. J. Sci. 267 : 729 - 804.

[60]   Hemmes, P. 1972. The volume changes of ionic association
        reactions. J. Phys. Chem. 76 : 895 - 900.

[61]   Hepler, L.G. 1963. Effects of substitutes on acidities of organic
        acids in water: Thermodynamic theory of Hammett equation. J. Am.
        Chem. Soc. 85 : 3089 - 3092.

[62]   Hepler, L.G. 1965. Entropy and volume changes on ionisation of
        aqueous acids. J. Phys. Chem. 69 : 965 - 967.

[63]   Hepler, L.G., and Woolley, E.M. 1973. Hydration effects and acid-
        base equilibria. In Water, A Comprehensive Treatise, ed. F.
        Franks, pp. 145 - 172. New York : Plenum Press.

[64]   Hills, G.J., and Ovenden, P.J. 1966. Electrochemistry at high
        pressures. Adv. Electrochem. Electrochem. Engng. 4 : 185 - 247.

[65]   Høiland, H. 1974. Pressure dependence of the volumes of ionisation
        of carboxylic acids at 25, 35 and 45°C and 1 - 1200 bar. J.C.S.
        Faraday I. 70 : 1180 - 1185.

[66]   Horne, R.A. 1969. The effect of pressure on the electrical
        conductivity of aqueous solutions. In 'Advances in High Pressure
        Research', ed. R.S. Bradley, Vol. 2. New York : Academic Press.

[67]   Irish, D.E. 1971. In 'Ionic Interactions'. Vol. II, ed.
        S. Petrucci, p. 187. New York : Academic Press.

[68]   Ives, D.J.G., and Moseley, P.G.N. 1970. The ionisation functions
        of some cyanoacetic acids. J. Chem. Soc. (B) 1970 : 1655 - 1658.

[69]   Ives, D.J.G. and Prasad, D. 1970. Free energies and heats of
        ionisation of some malonic acids. J. Chem. Soc. (B) 1970 :
        1652 - 1654.

[70]   Joliceour, C., Picker, P., and Desnoyers, J.E. 1969. The
        concentration dependence of the enthalpies of mixing of some
        aqueous electrolytes at 25°C. A test of Young's rule. J. Chem.
        Thermodyn. 1 : 485 - 493.

[71]   Kay, R.L. 1973. Ionic transport in water and mixed aqueous
        solvents. In 'Water, A comprehensive treatise' Vol. 3, ed.
        F. Franks. New York : Plenum Press.

[72] Kester, D.R., and Pytkowicz, R.M. 1970. Effect of temperature
      and pressure on sulphate ion association in sea water. Geochim.
      Cosmochim. Acta 34 : 1039 - 1051.

[73] King, E.J. 1965. Acid-base equilibria, pp. 341. New York :
      Pergamon Press.

[74] Kullberg, L. 1974. Thermodynamics of metal complex formation
      in aqueous solution. Ph.D. Thesis. University of Lund, Sweden.

[75] Larson, J.W. 1970. Thermodynamics of divalent metal sulphate
      dissociation and the structure of the solvated metal sulphate ion
      pair. J. Phys. Chem. 74 : 3392.

[76] Lewis, G.N., and Randall, M. 1961. 'Thermodynamics' (revised
      by K.S. Pitzer and L. Brewer) pp 723. New York : McGraw-Hill.

[77] Lilley, T.H. 1973. Raman spectroscopy of aqueous electrolyte
      solutions. In 'Water, a comprehensive treatise' Vol. 3. ed.
      F. Franks, pp. 265 - 299. New York : Plenum Press.

[78] Lindstrom, R.E., and Wirth, H.E. 1969. Estimation of bisulphate
      ion dissociation in solutions of sulphuric acid and sodium
      bisulphate. J. Phys. Chem. 73 : 218 - 223.

[79] Lown, D.A., Thirsk, H.R., and Lord Wynne-Jones. 1968. Effect
      of pressure on ionisation equilibria in water at 25°C. Trans.
      Faraday. Soc. 64 : 2073 - 2080.

[80] Lown, D.A., Thirsk, H.R., and Lord Wynne-Jones. 1970.
      Temperature and pressure dependence of the volume of ionization of
      acetic acid in water from 25 to 225°C and 1 - 3000 bar. Trans.
      Faraday Soc. 66 : 51 - 73.

[81] McBryde, W.A.E. 1974. Spectrophotometric determination of
      equilibrium constants in solution. Talanta 21 : 979 - 1004.

[82] Marshall, W.L. 1970. Complete equilibrium constants, electrolyte
      equilibria and reaction rates. J. Phys. Chem. 74 : 346 - 355.

[83] Marshall, W.L. 1972. A further description of complete
      equilibrium constants. J. Phys. Chem. 76, 720 - 731.

[84] Masterton, W.L., Welles, H., Knox, J.H., and Millero, F.J. 1974.
      Volume change of ion pair formation: rubidium nitrate and
      Thallium (I) nitrate in water. J. Solution Chem. 3 : 91 - 102.

[85] Matheson, R.A. 1969. The thermodynamics of electrolyte equilibria in media of variable water concentrations. J. Phys. Chem. $\underline{73}$: 3635 - 3642.

[86] Millero, F.J. 1967. A high precision magnetic float densimeter. Rev. Sci. Instr. $\underline{38}$: 1441 - 1444.

[87] Millero, F.J. 1971. Molal volumes of electrolytes. Chem. Rev. $\underline{71}$: 147 - 169.

[88] Millero, F.J. 1971. Effect of pressure on sulphate ion association in sea water. Geochim. Cosmochim. Acta. $\underline{35}$: 1089 - 1098

[89] Millero, F.J. 1972. The partial molal volumes of electrolytes in aqueous solution. In 'Water and Aqueous Solutions' ed. R.A. Horne, pp. 519 - 595. New York : Wiley-Interscience.

[90] Millero, F.J., and Masterton, W.L. 1974. Volume change for the formation of magnesium sulphate ion pairs at various temperatures. J. Phys. Chem. $\underline{78}$: 1287 - 1294.

[91] Millero, F.J., Knox, J.H., and Emmet, R.T. 1972. A high-precision, variable-pressure magnetic float densimeter. J. Solution Chem. 1 : 173 - 186.

[92] Millero, F.J., Hoff, E.V., and Kahn, L. 1972. The effect of pressure on the ionisation of water at various temperatures from molal-volume data. J. Solution Chem. $\underline{1}$: 309 - 327.

[93] Millero, F.J., Perron, G., and Desnoyers, J.E. 1973. Heat capacity of seawater solutions from 5° to 35°C and 0.5 to 22%$_o$ chlorinity. J. Geophys. Res. $\underline{78}$: 4499 - 4507.

[94] Millero, F.J., Hansen, L.D., and Hoff, E.V. 1973. The enthalpy of seawater from 0 to 30°C and 0 to 40%$_o$ salinity. J. Mar. Res. $\underline{31}$: 21 - 39.

[95] Millero, F.J., Ward, G.K., Lepple, F.K., and Hoff, E.V. 1974. Isothermal compressibility of aqueous sodium chloride, magnesium chloride, sodium sulphate and magnesium sulphate solutions from 0° - 45°C at 1 atm. J. Phys. Chem. $\underline{78}$: 1636 - 1643.

[96] Nakahara, M., Shimizu, K., and Osugi, J. 1970. Ionic solutions under pressure II. Pressure and temperature effects on the dissociation of the Co $(NH_3)_6^{3+} SO_4^{2-}$ Ion pair. Rev. Phys. Chem. Japan. $\underline{40}$: 12 - 20.

162   M. Whitfield

[97]   Nancollas, G.H. 1966. Interactions in electrolyte solutions. Amsterdam : Elsevier.

[98]   Nancollas, G.H. 1970. The thermodynamics of metal-complex and ion-pair formation. Coord. Chem. Rev. $\underline{5}$: 379 - 415.

[99]   Negus, L.E., and Light, T.S. 1972. Temperature coefficients and their compensation in ion-selective systems. Instr. Technol. $\underline{19}$: 23 - 29.

[100] Neuman, R.C., Kauzmann, W., and Zipp, A. 1973. Pressure dependence of weak acid ionisation in aqueous buffers. J. Phys. Chem. $\underline{77}$: 2687 - 2691.

[101] Nieboer, E., and McBryde, W.A.E. 1970. Free energy relationships in coordination chemistry. I linear relationships among equilibria constants. Can. J. Chem. $\underline{48}$: 2549 - 2564.

[102] Nieboer, E., and McBryde, W.A.E. 1970. Free energy relationships in coordination chemistry. II Requirements for linear relationships. Can. J. Chem. $\underline{48}$: 2565 - 2573.

[103] North, N.A. 1973. Pressure dependence of equilibrium constants in aqueous solution. J. Phys. Chem. $\underline{77}$: 931 - 934.

[104] Oliver, B.G., and Adams, W.A. 1972. An improved high pressure conductivity cell. Rev. Sci. Instr. $\underline{43}$: 830 - 831.

[105] Ots, H. 1973. Thermodynamic properties of rare earth complexes. XV. Enthalpy and heat capacity changes for the formation of rare earth EDTA complexes from Mg EDTA^{2-} at 10°, 20°, 30° and 40°C. Acta. Chem. Scand. $\underline{27}$: 2344 - 2351.

[106] Parker, V.B. 1965. Thermal properties of aqueous univalent electrolytes. National Standard Reference Data Series -- NBS. Washington D.C. : U.S. Government Printing Office.

[107] Perron, G., Desnoyers, J.E. and Millero, F.J. 1974. Apparent molal volumes and heat capacities of alkaline earth chlorides in water at 25°C. Can. J. Chem. $\underline{52}$: 3738 - 3741.

[108] Petrucci, S. 1971. Statistical thermodynamics of ionic association and complexation in dilute solutions of electrolytes. In 'Ionic interactions from dilute solutions to fused salts' Vol. I. ed. S. Petrucci, pp. 117 - 177. London : Academic Press.

[109]   Picker, P., Leduc, P-A., Phillip, P.R. and Desnoyers, J.E. 1971.
        Heat capacity of solutions by flow microcalorimetry. J. Chem.
        Thermodyn. 3 : 631 - 642.

[110]   Picker, P., Tremblay, E. and Joliceour, C. 1974. A high-precision
        digital readout flow densimeter for liquids. J. Solution Chem. 3:
        377 - 384.

[111]   Powell, K.H.J. 1973. Entropy titrations : a reassessment of data
        for the reaction of the sulphate ion with protons and bivalent
        metal ions. J.C.S. Dalton Trans. 1973 : 1947 - 1951.

[112]   Powell, K.K.J. Entropy titrations : a reassessment of data for the
        reaction of the sulphate ion with trivalent lanthanoid ions.
        J.C.S. Dalton Trans. 1974 : 1108 - 1112.

[113]   Prue, J.E. 1966. Ion-association and solvation In 'Chemical
        Physics of Ionic Solutions' eds. B.E. Conway and R.G. Barradas.
        pp. 163 - 173. New York : Wiley.

[114]   Prue, J.E. 1969. Ion pairs and complexes : Free energies,
        Enthalpies and Entropies. J. Chem. Educ. 46 : 12 - 16.

[115]   Robertson, W.W. 1963. Spectral measurements in high pressure
        systems. In 'Technique of Inorganic Chemistry' eds. H.B. Jonassen
        and A. Weisserberger. Vol I, pp. 157 - 172. New York :
        Interscience.

[116]   Rossotti, H.S. 1969. Chemical Applications of Potentiometry.
        London : Van Nostrand.

[117]   Rossotti, H.S. 1974. Design and publication of work on stability
        constants. Talanta 21 : 809 - 829.

[118]   Rossotti, H., and Rossotti, F.J.C. 1961. The determination of
        stability constants. McGraw-Hill : New York.

[119]   Rossotti, F.J.C., Rossotti, H. and Whewell, R.J. 1971. The use
        of electronic computing techniques in the calculation of
        stability constants. J. Inorg. Nucl. Chem. 33 : 2051 - 2065.

[120]   Schwarzenbach, G. 1970. Electrostatic and non-electrostatic
        contributions to ion association in solution. Rev. Pure Appl.
        Chem. 24 : 307 - 334.

[121]   Simeon, V.L. and Ivcic, N. 1971. ΔH - ΔS relationships in
        metal complex formation. Nature Phys. Sci. 232 : 88 - 90.

[122]   Spiro, T.G., Revesz, A., and Lee, J.   1968.   Volume changes in
        Ion Association Reactions.   Inner and outer-sphere complexes.
        J. Am. Chem. Soc. $\underline{90}$: 4000 - 4006.

[123]   Struck, B.D., Nurnberg, N.W., and Heckner, H.N.   1973.   Temperature
        dependence of the ionisation constants and evaluation of related
        thermodynamic parameters for acetic acid and propionic acid in
        aqueous 1M LiCl.   J. Electroanal. Chem. $\underline{46}$: 171 - 179.

[124]   Swaddle, T.W., and Kong, P-C.   1970.   The effect of pressure on
        the hydrolysis equilibria of aqueous metal ions.   Can. J. Chem.
        $\underline{48}$: 3223 - 3228.

[125]   Timimi, B.A.   1974.   The evaluation of ΔC_p^o for acid-base
        equilibria from pK measurements.   Electrochim. Act. $\underline{19}$: 149 -
        158.

[126]   Vanderzee, C.E., King, D.L., Wadsö, I.   1972.   The enthalpy of
        ionisation of aqueous ammonia.   J. Chem. Thermodyn. $\underline{4}$: 685 - 689.

[127]   Ward, G.K., and Millero, F.J.   1974.   The effect of pressure on
        the ionization of boric acid in aqueous solutions from molal-
        volume data.   J. Solution Chem. $\underline{3}$: 417 - 430.

[128]   Whitfield, M.   1969.   Multicell assemblies for studying ion-
        selective electrodes at high pressures.   J. Electrochem. Soc.
        $\underline{116}$: 1042 - 1046.

[129]   Whitfield, M.   1970.   Effect of membrane geometry on the
        performance of glass electrode cells.   Electrochim. Acta. $\underline{15}$:
        83 - 96.

[130]   Whitfield, M.   1972.   Self-ionisation of water in dilute sodium
        chloride solutions from 5° - 35°C and 1 - 2000 bars.   J. Chem.
        Eng. Data. $\underline{17}$: 124 - 128.

[131]   Whitfield, M.   1975.   Sea Water as an electrolyte solution. $\underline{In}$
        Chemical Oceanography, Vol. 1 (2nd Edition) eds. J.P. Riley and
        G. Skirrow.   New York : Academic Press.

[132]   Williams, R.J.P., and Hale, J.D.   1966.   The classification of
        acceptors and donors in inorganic reactions.   Struct. Bonding.
        $\underline{1}$: 249 - 281.

[133]   Wirth, H.E.   1967.   Equilibria in solutions of tetraalkylammonium
        bromides.   J. Phys. Chem. $\underline{71}$: 2922 - 2929.

Application of Physical Methods to the Determination of Structure in Solution

I. D. Campbell and R. A. Dwek
Department of Biochemistry, University of Oxford,
South Parks Road, Oxford OX1 3QU, Great Britain.

Abstract: Spectroscopic techniques which are suitable for the determination of structure in solution are briefly described. Particular emphasis has been placed on problems relating to macromolecules. Applications of these techniques are summarised for two particular systems, namely, the enzyme carbonic anhydrase and antibody-antigen complexes.

Introduction:

Many techniques for the detection and analysis of the elements in sea water are now available (see paper by Nürnberg, this volume and ref.[20]). Chromatography and mass spectrometry have been shown to be useful in the identification of small molecules in marine species, (see papers by Hager and Rinehart, this volume). The spectroscopic techniques described here can also be used to identify compounds, but their main strength is in giving information about other aspects of structure in solution; for example, the ionization state of a molecule, the geometry and kinetics of metal coordination spheres, and the shapes and conformations of large molecules.

Spectroscopy is the study of the interaction of electromagnetic radiation with matter. A molecule possesses a large number of energy levels between which transitions can take place, and the study of the energy involved in such transitions gives information about the state of the molecule. The energy of the transition may arise from any one of a number of sources, but the most important are nuclear orientation, electronic vibration, and rotation. Many of the spectroscopic techniques described are very well established, although several important technical improvements have increased the power of these methods in recent years

e.g. the use of the laser and the mini computer in the fields of light
scattering, i.r. and n.m.r. We omit from our discussion the structure
of the solvent itself [17] and some of the techniques which measure
transport and hydrodynamic properties, e.g. tracer techniques (see paper
by Harris, this volume), sedimentation 6 , viscosity [44] and conductivity [41]. Since we are dealing with a liquid the structure of a
molecule in solution is related to its dynamic properties. Some methods
which give information about molecular dynamics are indicated in Fig. 1.
We also omit discussion, of, fast reaction kinetic methods [23],
ultrasonics [4] and dielectric relaxation [5].

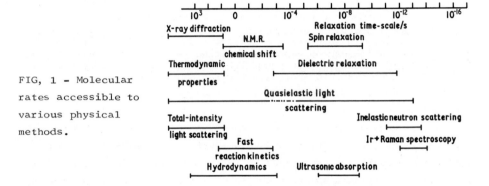

FIG, 1 - Molecular
rates accessible to
various physical
methods.

We conclude the article by describing, how some spectroscopic methods
have been applied to two systems which we are currently studying. One
system is the enzyme carbonic anhydrase which catalyses the interconversion
of HCO_3^- and CO_2 in a large variety of living systems. The other system
is more complex, consisting of proteins which make up part of the immune
response system in mammals. Our understanding of the way these
biological systems operate depends critically on methods which give
us information about their conformation in solution.

Nuclear Magnetic Resonance (n.m.r.) [16, 12]

This is a method in which the nuclear orientation effects of nuclei
which possess a spin are studied. Among the many important nuclei
which are accessible to the method are ^1H, ^2H, ^{13}C, ^{14}N, ^{17}O, ^{19}F,
^{33}Na, ^{31}P, ^{35}Cl and ^{37}Cl. In the modern n.m.r. spectrometer a radio
frequency pulse (in the range 4-400 MHz) is applied to a sample ($\sim$1 ml)

which is in a magnetic field (1-10 tesla). The response to this pulse
contains information about the energy involved in a transition between
nuclear orientations. This energy is reflected in a resonance
position on a frequency scale measured with respect to some standard,
usually in units of parts per million (p.p.m.). This is known as a
chemical shift scale.

The chemical shift of a particular nucleus depends on its chemical
environment e.g. a ^{1}H attached to a carbon in an aromatic ring
resonates in a different position from a methyl ^{1}H. More important for
our discussion here is that changes in chemical shift occur as a
result of changes in local environment, e.g. a change in ionization
state of a neighbouring group. The chemical shift may also be greatly
influenced by the proximity of a paramagnetic centre, e.g. Eu(III) or a
haem group and this paramagnetic shift can be directly related to the
distance between the observed nucleus and the paramagnetic centre.

Another feature of an n.m.r. spectrum is that some resonances are
multiplets e.g. a 1:2:1 triplet. This is the result of spin-spin
coupling to neighbouring nuclei by a through bond mechanism. The
magnitude of the spin-spin coupling (J) depends on the nature of the
chemical bonding between the coupled nuclei and their relative
geometries. In some cases J can be semi-empirically related to bond
angles and conformational analyses of molecules in solution performed.

In addition to being characterised by a chemical shift and a certain
multiplicity, a resonance has two relaxation rates associated with it.
The spin-spin relaxation rate ($^1/T_2$) is related to the linewidth of
the resonance and its origin is similar to the 'uncertainty broadening'
observed in other forms of spectroscopy. The spin lattice relaxation
rate ($^1/T_1$) characterises the rate at which the nuclear spin system
returns to its equilibrium state after it has been perturbed. These
relaxation rates depend principally on the time scale and magnitude
of dipolar interactions with other nuclei. The measured values of T_1
and T_2 thus make it possible to obtain information about rotational
motion. In a system in which chemical exchange is going on, e.g.
water exchanging in and out of a metal ion coordination sphere, T_2 may
also depend on this rate of exchange. T_1 and T_2 are also very
sensitive to the presence of a paramagnetic centre which of course

has a magnetic dipole some 700 times larger than the nuclei. The
influence of a paramagnetic centre is related to the sixth power of the
distance between the centre and the observed nucleus.

N.m.r. can be used to obtain detailed information about all the components in an aqueous solution, e.g. the study of the water itself has
been extensively used to obtain information about the binding of metal
ions to macromolecules [16] and to obtain information about the structure of the solvent itself [17]. A study of the n.m.r. signals from
dissolved ions also gives information about ion-solvent and ion-ion
interactions [7] and the binding of such ions to macromolecules [16],
although the interpretation of the results is not always unambiguous.
The study of the solute molecule itself is potentially the most informative. As the molecule of interest becomes larger, the n.m.r.
method lacks sensitivity and it becomes increasingly difficult to
resolve single resonances and assign observed resonances to
particular groups [16]. Modern techniques which include the use of
computers and very high fields have helped to overcome the first two
of these problems and the assignment difficulties are being reduced by
using methods such as site specific paramagnetic probes, and the
application of several frequencies simultaneously to a sample to
perform double resonance experiments and solvent suppression [9].

Electron Spin Resonance (e.s.r.)[1,12]

This method can only be applied to systems which are paramagnetic, i.e.
possess an unpaired electron. Signals can thus be observed from
compounds containing transition metals, rare earth and transuranic
elements, and stable free radicals. Many of the principles of e.s.r.
are similar to n.m.r. although some of the terminology is changed.
The resonance frequency for a modest applied magnetic field is in the
microwave range and because of the larger transition the technique is
more sensitive than n.m.r.

The important parameters in an e.s.r. spectrum are the g values and the
hyperfine coupling. g is a proportionality constant between the
resonant frequency and the applied magnetic field (i.e. is related to
the chemical shift in n.m.r.). The value of g for a free electron is
2.0023, and observed deviations from this value can give information

about the geometry and distortions of complexes in the solid state, since there the g values for various orientations of the observed molecule can be observed.   In solution, molecular rotation tends to average out this information.

The hyperfine coupling arises from interaction of the electron magnetic moment with nuclear magnetic moments (i.e. is related to spin-spin coupling in n.m.r.).   Like g values the hyperfine coupling is in general anisotropic and the anisotropy can be used to give detailed information about ligand bond angles and binding parameters. Again, however, this usually requires observation in frozen solution, or single crystals.   The isotropic hyperfine coupling which can still be observed in a rapidly tumbling molecule in solution can give information about the unpaired electron density at the nucleus, which is observed to decrease with the amount of covalent character in the bonds.

As in n.m.r., an e.s.r. resonance is characterised by two electron spin relaxation rates.   In many paramagnetic species, e.g. Co(II), Ni(II) and Eu(III) the electron spin relaxation rate is so fast that signals are only observable at very low temperatures.

Stable free radicals in the form of 'spin labels' are being increasingly used in biology [14].   These are mainly nitroxide radicals which give a triplet resonance as a result of coupling with the ^{14}N nucleus.   The anisotropic hyperfine coupling in these radicals broadens the spectrum if the tumbling rate is less than about 2×10^9 sec^{-1}.   These probes can therefore be used to measure the degree of flexibility in certain parts of membranes or large proteins by incorporating them using established chemical methods.

Electron Nuclear Double Resonance (e.n.d.r.)[1,12]

This is a method which involves the simultaneous irradiation of electron and nuclear transitions.   The technique defines rather precisely the interactions of the paramagnetic centre with nuclei in the surrounding ligands.   For example, in frozen solutions of haem proteins, the interactions of the ^{57}Fe with ^{14}N and ^1H nuclei in the porphyrin ring have been observed [19a] and quantified.

Mössbauer Spectroscopy [32]

This method has been found particularly useful in studying iron-protein interactions. The nuclear energy levels of [57]Fe can be monitored in frozen solutions by irradiating with gamma rays from a [57]Co source. The nuclear energy levels depend on the electronic configuration of the iron and this method, together with endor, e.s.r. and n.m.r. measurements has given a detailed picture of the iron-sulphur complexes in several two iron ferredoxins [40].

Infrared and Raman Absorption [3,10,42,45]

The energy of most molecular vibrations corresponds to that of the infrared region of the spectrum. These vibrations may be detected and measured either directly in an infrared spectrum or indirectly in a Raman spectrum. A complex molecule has a large number of vibrational modes which involve the whole molecule. Some of these, to a good approximation, are localized and can be associated with vibrations of individual bonds or functional groups. However the large number of vibrations, the possibility of overtones from these vibrations and of interacting vibrations mean that the spectra are exceedingly complex,. Unscrambling is possible in certain cases because certain groups have characteristic vibrational frequencies, e.g. - C = O has a fundamental stretching frequency of 1700 cm^{-1}. This position will shift if, say, the - C = O group is involved in hydrogen bonding, and such shifts can be used to identify certain structures empirically. The most useful range for most common organic compounds is from 1500 - 5000 cm^{-1} but in aqueous solution much of this range is obscured by solvent absorption bands.

The information obtained by <u>laser Raman spectroscopy</u> is similar and complementary to that obtained from infrared spectroscopy. Irradiating a transparent medium with monochromatic photons of frequency v_o results in most of them passing unchanged through the sample. A small proportion however is scattered by solute and solvent molecules. The bulk of the scattered photons have the same frequency as the incident light (Rayleigh line - see below) but a small number have frequencies $v_o - v_1$, $v_o - v_2$, etc. different from that of the incident light. These are the Raman scattering bands whose frequency shifts are characteristic of the bonds within the molecule producing the scattering. The frequency

shift of covalent bonds in organic substances lie in the range
1500– 4000 cm^{-1} and are in general close to the infrared absorption
frequency of these bonds. Both Raman and infrared spectroscopy therefore give information about intramolecular vibrational and rotational
frequencies but the symmetry selection rules which tell us whether a
particular mode will appear in the spectrum are different for the two
techniques. The most important consequence of these different
selection rules is that in a molecule with a centre of symmetry,
those vibrations symmetrical about the centre of symmetry are allowed
or active in the Raman but not in the infrared and vice versa. This
means the Raman spectroscopy of dilute aqueous solutions is possible in
frequency regions inaccessible to infrared measurements because the
O – H binding vibration which results in very intense infrared bands
produces only weak Raman scattering. Laser Raman spectroscopy has
been applied to studies of aqueous solutions of $SO_4^=$ ions (see paper by
Whitfield, this volume).

A recent technique which may provide a sensitive method for probing
site structure in solution as well as in the solid state is <u>resonance
Raman spectroscopy</u>. Resonance Raman scattering involves an interaction
of vibrational and electronic transitions with the result that certain
vibrational modes are greatly enhanced in intensity. An essential
point is that the wavelength of the exciting light must lie in one of
the electronic absorption bands of material of interest. When applied
to coloured ligands which are bound to proteins, Raman spectra of the
ligand are obtained without interference from that of the protein, a
poor Raman scatterer.

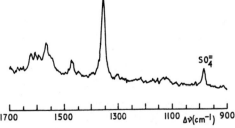

FIG.2. Resonance Raman spectra of 0.34mM deoxyhemoglobin
obtained by irradiating in the Soret absorption band (ν_o=458nm)
The solution also contained 0.4M $(NH_4)_2SO_4$ and the high sensitivity   of the method is illustrated by the difference in
concentration between the heme and the SO_4^{2-} ion. (from [42]).

Visible and Ultra Violet Absorption [24]

The visible and ultra violet spectra of compounds are associated with
electronic excitations usually coupled with vibrational and rotational
changes. Wave mechanical considerations show that the absorption of
energy is only highly probable when certain symmetry relationships hold
between the ground and excited states. These relationships are
expressed as selection rules and while these are relatively straightforward for the hydrogen atom or for atoms containing several electrons,
they become exceedingly complex in dealing with molecules. This usually
means that interpretations of molecular spectra are based largely on
empirical correlations with extensive compilations of data.

Even in those molecules that we can treat to a first approximation as
containing discrete central atoms, e.g. a complex of a transition metal,
the vibrations of the ligands are coupled (albeit weakly at times) to
the electronic transitions. This so called "vibronic" coupling inter-
feres with the simplicity of the atomic selection rules but results in
a net practical result. Transitions forbidden in atoms become partially
allowed in a complex ion. (The area of the absorption peak is a direct
measure of this probability.) For the inorganic chemist, the most
interesting "forbidden" transitions are those involving the f or d
electrons. The energies of d-d or f-f transitions are such that they
lie in or near to the visible region of the spectrum.

The spectra of transition metal complexes are dependent upon the nature
and the stereochemical relationships of the ligands. For instance, the
Co^{2+} ion exists as the pink hydrated complex $[Co(H_2O)_6]^{2+}$ which has an
octohedral arrangement of H_2O molecules about the central cation. The
intensity of the transitions in the spectrum is very weak. On the other
hand the spectrum of $[Co(Cl_4)]^{2-}$ in which the ligands are arranged
tetrahedrally is exceedingly intense, and the solutions appear very blue.
Thus in contrast to infrared spectroscopy, the actual _intensity_ of the
peak as well as the position is usually measured.

In dealing with molecules, the spectra cannot be interpreted in terms
of transitions centred on individual atoms. Instead one considers
electronic transitions between molecular orbitals. These transitions
generally obey selection rules and give rise to intense bands, (with
the weaker bands in the spectrum usually arising from forbidden
transitions). However the energy separation between these orbitals is

only small enough to result in a visible spectrum (i.e. a colour) if
the molecules are very large and unsaturated, e.g. dye-stuffs or if the
molecules contain heavy atoms (e.g. iodine). There is one further
class which ought to be mentioned, that of coloured complex ions and
molecules in which the ligand or cation is either strongly reducing or
oxidizing and its partner has the opposite oxidation-reduction
characteristic e.g. $[Fe(III)(SCN)]^{2+}$ is intensely red. Fe(III) is an
oxidizing agent and thiocyanate a reducing agent. The absorption
process arises from electron transfer from reducing to oxidizing agent.
Such spectra are called <u>charge-transfer</u> spectra. They are often
extremely intense and form the basis for many colorimetric methods for
the detection and analysis of metals.

The word <u>chromophore</u> is used to describe the system containing the
electrons giving rise to the selective absorption in question. Most
unconjugated chromophores such as $C = C$ (isolated) $- \overset{''}{S} -, - \overset{''}{N},$
$- \overset{''}{O} -$ require transitions between molecular orbitals of such high energy
that they occur in the inaccessible range below 200 nm. Above 200 nm,
excitation of electrons from p- and d-orbitals, π-orbitals and
particular π-conjugated systems gives rise to easily measured and
informative spectra. In a large molecule such as a protein, the
absorption from the aromatic chromophores provides a method of
estimating the concentration, and it is in such analytical uses that
many of the applications are to be found. The method of <u>difference
spectroscopy</u> is widely used in biochemistry where the optical density
difference between two samples is measured directly with a double beam
spectrophotometer. This allows very small changes in one of the samples
to be monitored.

A related physical method which has been found useful in structural
determination is that of <u>optical rotatory dispersion</u>. This measures
the change of the rotatory power of an optically active compound with
the change of wavelength used to observe the rotation. Near an ultra
violet absorption maximum the rotation may change sign dramatically;
this phenomenon is termed the <u>Cotton effect</u>. The sign and magnitude
of a Cotton effect can be used to compare the configuration of a
molecule with that of a known absolute configuration of a model compound.
A related technique is <u>circular dichroism</u> which gives similar information but is easier to interpret when Cotton effects occur close
together. Circular dichroism (CD) has been used as a probe for

analysing the three dimensional structure of proteins [26]. In addition
distinct CD bonds may arise upon interaction between a protein and a
ligand. If the induced optical activity is a consequence of the binding
of an optically inactive ligand in the asymmetric environment of the
protein combining site, this is known as an <u>extrinsic</u> Cotton effect.
These extrinsic Cotton effects, of course, are in addition to any
intrinsic Cotton effects in the region of optical absorption of the
protein itself. In proteins too there is an advantage of carrying out
CD studies in high <u>magnetic fields</u> for this may be particularly useful
in the identification of tryptophan residues [25] (which absorb between
290 and 300 nm).

Fluorescence [36]

In discussing absorption we have concentrated on the excitation of a
molecule from a ground state to an excited (higher) energy level and
have given little thought to the subsequent fate of the excited molecule.
In many cases the energy is lost as heat to the surroundings but in some
cases re-radiation (i.e. emission) occurs, usually at a different
wavelength from that of the exciting radiation. This process is called
<u>fluorescence</u>. Absorption of a photon of the correct energy (usually
u.v. or visible light) takes place in about 10^{-15} s to produce the
higher excited state. This process is so fast that significant motion
of the nuclei of the molecule does not occur; moreover, the configuration of the solvation shell remains constant. In the excited
state this may not be the equilibrium configuration and so rearrangement
of the solvation shell will then occur typically in 10^{-12} s, followed,
in the case of fluorescence, by emission of light to give a nonequilibrium ground electronic state.

The result of this is that the emitted radiation is usually of lower
energy (longer wavelength) than the exciting radiation. The separation
of absorption and emission bands reflect the extent of the charge
reorganisation in the excited state and the consequential changes in
geometry and solvation of the chromophores. However, the fluorescence
spectrum is generally independent of the wavelength of the exciting
light. This is because the time scale for rearrangements in the
excited state is 10^{-12} s, much shorter than the life times of the
excited state 10^{-9} s. The fluorescence spectrum, like the absorption
spectrum, can thus be used as a specific finger print for a compound.

The parameters of fluorescence are the excitation spectrum, the emission spectrum, the quantum yield, lifetime and polarization.

The possibility of excitation energy being transferred from one chromophore to another occurs if there is an appreciable overlap of the fluorescence spectrum of the donor and the absorption spectrum of the acceptor. This energy transfer operates via a dipole-dipole interaction and can occur typically over ranges of 1 - 5 nm. This is a powerful means of investigating spatial properties of macromolecules such as conformational changes or distances between specific sites [33]. In most proteins the fluorescence arises mainly from tryptophan residues (those of tyrosine and phenyl-alanine being largely quenched).

If the exciting light is plane polarized, absorption will be most likely for those molecules that have their chromophores suitably oriented to the direction of polarization of the light. If these molecules do not rotate before emission, the emitted light will also be polarized. Thus the measured polarization will report on the relaxation processes, and so provides a further probe for monitoring changes in molecule structure. A recent development is nanosecond fluorescence depolarization [43] involving excitation by a pulse of polarized light of nanosecond duration. The decay of each of the components of polarization (parallel and perpendicular) can be followed separately on the nanosecond scale yielding more information about molecular motion than is obtained from steady state methods.

We have discussed in the previous section how ligands which are optically inactive may acquire optical activity on binding to asymmetric macromolecules. The bound molecules thus contribute to the optical rotatory dispersions of the system and exhibit circular dichroism (CD) in their absorption bands. However, if the molecule is also luminescent the light emitted by asymmetric molecules will be circularly polarized to some extent. This is so termed circular polarization of the luminescence (or fluorescence) [21], C.P.L., and is related to the conformation of the molecule and its environment in the electronically excited state in much the same way as C.D. is related to those properties in the ground state. This is of particular importance if the induced C.D. of the ligand is too small to be measured or because it is masked by the C.D. of other components present (in the former case magnetic C.D. may also be of use). The C.P.L. is expressed by the emission anisotropy factor, defined as twice

the ratio between the intensity of the circularly polarized component
in the fluorescence and the total fluorescence intensity at the same
wavelength. If there is no change in environment or conformation of
the chromophore in the excited state, the value of g_{em} should be the
same as the absorption anisotropy factor g_{ab} which expresses the C.D.
In proteins several chromophores can contribute to the observed C.D.
spectrum, but C.P.L. only probes for tryptophans or tyrosines which are
both fluorescent and situated in an asymmetric environment in their
excited state.

Scattering

We have discussed above the way in which information can be obtained
from radiation which is absorbed or emitted by transitions between
molecular energy levels. Even in a region of the spectrum where no
such transitions take place, radiation can still interact with
inhomogeneous matter. This causes scattering of the incident radiation
in all directions. The angular distribution of the scattered radiation
gives information about the dimensions and dynamics of a molecule in
solution provided the wavelength of the radiation is less than the
molecular dimensions. Unfortunately a large range of wavelengths is
not available due to absorption by the molecules of interest or the
solvent; the shortest wavelength available in the light scattering
region is about 250 nm. The next suitable radiation is that from
neutrons and X-rays which usually have a wavelength of the order of
0.1 nm.

Light Scattering

a. Total intensity scattering [44]

The oldest and still the most common method is to irradiate the sample
of interest with unpolarised light at about 400 nm. The angular
dependence of the scattering at all wavelengths can be described by a
parameter P(Θ) which is proportional to the intensity of scattered
light observed at an angle Θ to the incident beam

$$P(\Theta) = 1 - \frac{h^2 R_G^2}{3} + - - - - e^{-h^2 R_G^2 /3} \qquad - - \qquad (i)$$

where $h = \frac{4\pi}{\lambda} \sin \Theta/2$ and R_G is the radius of gyration, which is
related to the dimensions of the scatterer in a simple manner, e.g.

for a sphere of radius r, $R_G^2 = \frac{3r^2}{5}$. By performing a graphical double
extrapolation, a Zimm plot, to zero concentration and zero scattering
angle Θ, R_G can be evaluated. It is also possible to obtain the
molecular weight of the scattering molecule provided that the
difference between the refractive index of the solvent and the solution
is measured using, for example, a differential diffractometer.

This method gives very little information about the dynamics of a
molecule, is rather laborious and is very sensitive to extraneous
particles such as dust. However changes in R_G caused by, for example,
denaturation of nucleic acids have been detected.

b. <u>Quasielastic light scattering</u> [28]

If the scattered light is analysed in more detail than above it
contains a great deal more information. For example, the
frequency of the scattered light contains components at frequencies
other than that of the incident light. These frequency shifts may be
as small as a few parts in 10^{14} and it is only in the last few years
that it has been possible to study this spectrum as a result of greatly
improved technology e.g. lasers. The spectrum consists of a narrow
central component called the Rayleigh line at the same frequency as the
incident light and two broader components symmetrically placed about
this line called the Brillouin doublet (not to be confused with similar
but larger shifts arising from Raman effects). Because of the
relatively narrow range of this spectrum the scattering can be assumed
elastic for theoretical treatments, hence the term quasielastic.

The width of the central Rayleigh line contains information about the
translational diffusion coefficient of the scattering molecule. This
coefficient can be related to the molecular weight and the radius of
the particle by certain empirical relationships. The method
principally used to study the linewidth is <u>optical mixing</u> spectroscopy,
where the information is extracted by beating the scattered light
spectrum with a suitable reference to produce a low frequency spectrum.

The Brillouin doublet can be measured using interferometric techniques.
The frequency separation of this doublet contains information about
sound velocities and absorption coefficients similar to that obtained
with ultrasonic methods, and it is possible to measure accoustical parameters at frequencies as high as 10^9 Hz. The measurement of Rayleigh-

Brillouin intensity ratios can give accurate values for activity
coefficients, specific heats and compressibilities of solutions.

Small Angle X-ray Scattering [31]

This method is very similar to total light scattering except that the
irradiation wavelength is now usually .15 nm (the Cu K_α wavelength).
The $P(\Theta)$ function is as described above in equation (i) but in this
field it is customary to use a Guinier plot which arises from the
relationship $\ln P(\Theta) \simeq h^2 R_G^2/3$ i.e. a plot of $\ln i(\Theta)$ against $\sin^2 \Theta/2$
gives a straight line and R_G can be determined from the slope. Like the
light scattering methods it is necessary to extrapolate to zero concentration: In most molecules of biological interest $R_G \gg \lambda$, thus the
scattering is very small except at low values of Θ. In some cases
however, it is possible to collect information at relatively large
angles and thus obtain information about the shape of the molecule as
well as R_G. For example, if a macromolecule is composed of a large
number of identical or similar subunits a perodicity can be observed
in the scattering curve at large angles.

Neutron Scattering

Unlike X-rays which are scattered by electrons, neutrons are scattered
by atomic nuclei. Thus neutrons are significantly scattered by H atoms
whereas X-rays are scattered very little. The information obtained
from neutron scattering is often complementary to that obtained from
X-ray work. The scattering amplitude of a molecule in solution is the
sum of the scattering amplitude per unit volume of its component atoms
minus that in the same volume of solvent. Since the neutron scattering
amplitude of H_2O and D_2O are of opposite sign, the contrast between the
aqueous medium and the solute molecules can be varied by changing the
ratio of H_2O to D_2O. The use of this variable contrast technique
together with recent improvements in neutron sources makes this a
rather promising technique for information about structure and dynamics
of simple aqueous salt solutions [18] and large biological systems [48].
The method is expensive and, in spite of improvements in detectors,
laborious.

Carbonic Anhydrase

The reaction $CO_2 + H_2O \rightleftharpoons HCO_3^{\ominus} + H^{\oplus}$ proceeds quite rapidly at room temperature $\sim 10^{-1}$ sec^{-1} in the forward direction. This is, however, not rapid enough for most biological systems. In mammals, for example, a large quantity of CO_2 is transported in the blood as $HCO_3^{\ominus}$ and this must be converted very rapidly in the lungs to allow efficient exhalation of CO_2. The result is that a very efficient catalyst has evolved to speed up the reaction by up to the remarkable factor of 10^7 times. This catalyst, or enzyme is a protein of about 30,000 Mol.wt. which contains one zinc atom per molecule. The biosynthesis of the enzyme in unicellular algae appears to be repressed at increased concentrations of CO_2. This evidence has been used to support the idea that carbonic anhydrase is involved in the photosynthetic fixation of CO_2 [35a].

This enzyme, especially the human species, has been extensively studied [34], and a great deal is known about its structure in solution, much of it gleaned by inference from studies on the amino acid sequence and X-ray studies of the crystal form. However, some of the finer points of the structure which are probably unique to the solution form remain obscure. For example, the reactants or substrates are rather small and little information about the enzyme-substrate complexes is obtained from X-ray diffraction of the crystals. This sort of information is of course vital if we are to find out how the enzyme works. We wish to illustrate some of the spectroscopic techniques outlined above by discussing their application to carbonic anhydrase. In particular we will discuss the geometry in the immediate vicinity of the zinc atom. It is known that the zinc is coordinated to 3 imidazole rings of histidine residues, and it has been proposed that the other coordination position contains a water molecule at low pH which ionises to become $OH^{\ominus}$ above pH 7. This is consistent with activity measurements where the enzyme is shown to be inactive for the hydration reaction at low Ph and active at high pH. There is, however, considerable speculation about this proposal since the pK_a of the water must be lowered by a factor of 8 pH units by the local environment of the enzyme.

Visible Spectra - The enzyme is also active when the zinc atom is replaced by cobalt. This makes an excellent chromophore and visible spectra of the various states of the enzyme can be readily obtained.

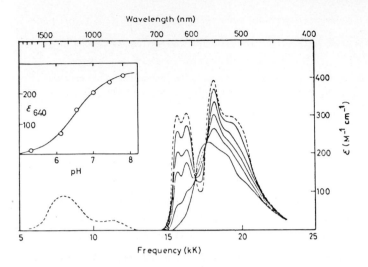

FIG.3. Visible spectrum of Co(II) carbonic anhydrase at several values of pH. Enzyme concentration 6×10^{-5}M, from [34].

Fig. 3 shows the changes in the cobalt spectrum as a function of pH. The inset shows how the absorption at 640 nm can be used to monitor the extent of acid and basic forms.

This pH curve matches precisely the pH dependence of the activity thus showing that the cobalt is intimately linked to the group whose ionization is vital for activity. Moreover the spectra show that the coordination geometry of the zinc ion is not a regular tetrahedron but is either distorted or even 5 coordinate, similar conclusions have been obtained from <u>magnetic circular dichroism</u> experiments [29].

<u>Infrared</u> - Even in aqueous solution where infrared methods are limited by strong aqueous absorption bands, there is a region between 2000 to 2800 cm^{-1} which is accessible. CO_2 has a strong absorption peak at 2343.5 cm^{-1} and by studying this CO_2 absorption in a solution containing carbonic anhydrase us ing difference spectroscopy, Riepe and Wang [39] concluded that CO_2 was loosely bound to a hydrophobic surface of the enzyme in the vicinity of, but not coordinated to, the zinc atom.

E.S.R. - Cobalt has a short electron spin relaxation time, and therefore
e.s.r. spectra can only be observed at low temperature. The enzyme
is inhibited by cyanide and studies of the inhibited coenzyme at 77° C
have shown that up to two cyanide molecules can coordinate to the cobalt
through the carbon of the CN. This was shown using ^{13}CN and by
analyzing the hyperfine coupling resulting from the nuclear spin of
the ^{13}C [13]. Another application of e.s.r. is illustrated by the
work of Fitzgerald and Chasteen [20a], where the zinc ion was replaced
by the vanadyl ion. It was shown that an ionisable group with a pK_a
of about 7 is in the vicinity of the vanadyl ion by studying enzyme
concentrations of 4×10^{-4} M in aqueous solution.

N.M.R.

This method has been used extensively to study this enzyme and has
given particularly useful information about the coordination sphere of
the metal ion. The chemical shift of resonances from the liganded

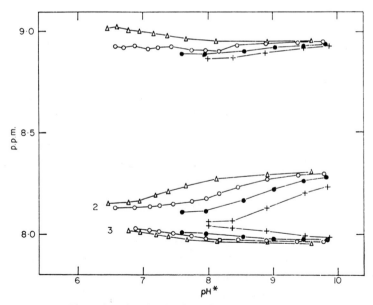

FIG. 4 - The chemical shift of the three ligand histidine C2
proton resonance of carbonic anhydrase as a function of pH[9].
Δ : no I^- added. +: 16 mM I^- added. Enzyme concentration 3×10^{-3} M.

histidines and the relaxation rates of H_2O, inhibitory halide ions and $^{13}CO_2$ have been measured as a function of pH. The water relaxation measurements, for example, have shown that a water molecule or OH^- is in rapid exchange between bulk solvent and a coordination position of the cobalt only at high pH [19]. The linewidths of ^{35}Cl resonances have shown that Cl^- binds in the active site at low pH with an exchange rate of about 10^6 sec^{-1} [47]. These results are consistent with OH^- and Cl^- competing for a metal coordination position, but not consistent with a simple ionization of H_2O to OH^-. The simplest explanation is a change in coordination number between low and high pH, e.g. from 4 to 5. This model is consistent with the results of high resolution n.m.r. where the ligand histidines have been shown to reflect the presence of the essential group (presumably OH^-) and the presence of I^- [9]. This is illustrated in Fig. 4.

Recognition and the Immune Response

The immune response in mammals is triggered   by the specific binding of a globular protein, known as an antibody, to specific groups on an intruding molecule, known as haptens. The binding properties of these antibodies are obviously of enormous importance and this has resulted in a large research effort to investigate their structure and the nature of the binding site. We use this system to illustrate how spectroscopy can be used to investigate binding sites and binding properties of haptens and metal ions.

N.M.R. Measurements [14,15] - The smallest fragment of a homogeneous antibody that has the native binding site intact is the Fv fragment from the mouse myeloma protein MOPC 315. This myeloma protein binds dinitrophenyl derivatives. The addition of such a diamagnetic hapten (similar to that shown in Fig. 5) to the Fv fragment causes changes in certain resonances in the n.m.r. spectrum of the Fv which are most clearly observed in a difference spectrum. By using a paramagnetic analogue which broadens resonances close to it, this difference spectrum will contain only those resonances arising from residues near to the hapten. The analysis of this difference spectrum enables the residues in the combining site to be identified.

Fluorescence [15] - The binding of dinitrophenyl derivatives to the Fv is easily monitored by measuring the fluorescent quenching on addition of the hapten. The fluorescent quenching is often 90% and suggests that the dinitrophenyl group and a tryptophan group (or groups) in the Fv may be involved in energy transfer.

The binding of lanthanides to Fv also affects the protein fluorescence. The observed kinetics of this reaction, as monitored by fluorescence, have been used to argue that the Fv molecule exists in at least two different conformations one of which the hapten favours while the metal binds preferentially to the other [13]. This may imply that there are hapten induced conformational changes.

The binding of lanthanides can also be monitored by using the fluorescence of Tb(III) which is enhanced on addition of Fv.

E.S.R. Measurements [14,15] - Using a variety of dinitrophenyl spin labels as shown in Fig. 5, the e.s.r. spectra of the labels bound to the Fv have been analyzed. The results show that the combining site is rigid and has dimensions of approximately 12 x 9 x 6 Å.

Circular Polarisation of Luminescence (C.P.L.) [37] - Using a series of dinitrophenyl-NH-$(CH_2)_n$-acridine derivatives, a circularly polarized component of the fluorescence was only observed when n = 2. This means that only when the 9-aminoacridine group is as close as 7.5 Å to the centre of the dinitrophenyl anchoring point ($\sim$9 Å from the 4-nitro group end) does it begin to sense the asymmetric environment caused by the contact residues of the site. This gives an independent criterion for the dimensions of the site as approximately 6 x 9 x 11 Å.

Nuclear Solvent Water Relaxation Measurements [14] - Another technique to monitor metal binding is provided by measuring the solvent water proton relaxation rates or solutions of Fv containing Gd(III). Use has been made of the enhancement caused by interaction of Gd(III) with the Fv to show that there is a unique, tight metal binding site on the Fv.

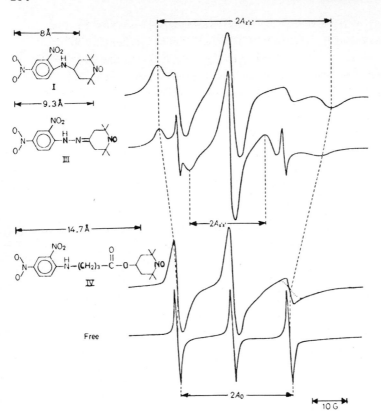

FIG.5- E.s.r. spectra of hapten spin labels bound to the Fv
fragment of an antibody protein. The 'free' spectrum is
characteristic of a freely tumbling spin label in aqueous
solution. The protein concentration was 3×10^{-4} M.

Other techniques for studying Antibody Complexes

<u>Circular Dichroism</u> (C.D.) studies [27] have been used to show that the
Fv fragment from MOPC 315 has almost the same conformation as the
intact protein on binding the dinitrophenyl lysine hapten. <u>M.C.D.</u>
studies in this laboratory have also shown that there are no significant changes in the spectrum of the tryptophan residues on hapten
binding.

<u>Small angle X-ray studies</u> [38] of two anti-poly-D-adenyl antibodies
before or after interaction with hapten showed decrease**s** ($\sim$10%) in the

radius of gyration and volume on hapten binding. Light scattering
studies [35] on the formation of aggregates in mixtures of antigen
and antibody have led to the suggestion that aggregation is accelerated
on combination with hapten. Measurements of rotational relaxation
times of an antibody molecule (after complex formation with a fluorescent specific dansyl hapten [46]), using polarisation of fluorescence,
show that the rotational time of the whole antibody molecule increases
on addition of the small hapten. Resonance Raman studies of rabbit
anti-dinitrophenyl-antibodies and their haptens [11] have shown that
the geometry of the hapten molecule may alter on combination. The
changes observed by Givol et al. [22] in the circular polarisation of
luminescence of various antibodies and fragments in the presence of
their haptens suggest that a conformational change occurs on hapten
binding but that there is a critical size of hapten required to produce
this change.

Conclusions

The application of the above methods will almost always require higher
concentrations and better defined systems than occur in natural sea
water. This means that concentration and purification will have to be
carried out, or model systems used. Such procedures could be justified
in at least three cases: (i) in the investigation of important reactions
such as the hydration rate of CO_2 (which could be followed using ^{13}C
n.m.r. in model systems [30]); (ii) in the identification of organic
ligands of trace metals; and (iii) in the investigation of biosynthetic
and biodegradation processes. The last of these three examples could
be particularly important; a structural change with time, namely the
racemization of amino-acids has already been exploited [2] to give
useful information. Many of the spectroscopic techniques described in
this paper are sensitive to even more subtle structural changes than
racemization. Our experience from biochemistry also tells us that it
is often necessary to apply more than one technique to a problem to
obtain detailed information about the properties of a molecule in
solution.

REFERENCES

(1) Abragam, A. and Bleaney, B.   1970.   EPR of Transition Ions
     Oxford University Press, London.

(2) Bada, J. L., Schroeder, R. A., Protsch, R. and Berger, R.   1974.
     Age determination by aspartic acid racemization.   Proc. Nat.
     Acad. Sci. U.S.A. $\underline{71}$: 914-917.

(3) Bellamy, L. J.   1968.   In Advances in Infrared Group Frequencies
     London: Methuen.   And references therein.

(4) Blandamer, M. J.   1973.   Introduction to Ultrasonics.   Academic
     Press, London.

(5) Block, H. and North, A. M.   1970.   Dielectric Relaxation in
     Polymer Solutions.   Adv. in Relaxation Process $\underline{1}$: 309

(6) Bowen, T. J.   1970.   An Introduction to Ultracentrifugation.
     Wiley (Interscience), New York.

(7) Burgess, J. and Symons, M. C. R.   1968.   The Study of Ion-Solvent
     and Ion-Ion Interactions by Magnetic Resonance Techniques.   Quart.
     Rev. Chem. Soc. $\underline{22}$: 276-301.

(8) Campbell, I. D., Lindskog, S. and White, A. I.   1974.   A Study of
     the Histidine Residues of Human Carbonic Anhydrase B using 270
     MHz Proton Magnetic Resonance.   J. Mol. Biol. $\underline{90}$: 469-489.

(9) Campbell, I. D., Dobson, C. M., Jeminet, G. and Williams, R. J. P.
     1974.   Pulsed N.M.R. Methods for the Observation and Assignment
     of Exchangeable Hydrogens: Application to Bacitracin.   FEBS
     Letters $\underline{49}$: 115-119.

(10) Carey, P. R., Schneider, H. and Bernstein, M. J.   1972.   Raman
     Spectroscopic Studies of Ligand-Protein Interactions: The Binding
     of Methyl Orange by Bovine Serum Albumin.   Biochem. Biophys. Res.
     Commun. $\underline{47}$: 588-595.

(11) Carey, P. R., Froese, A. and Scheider, H.   1973.   Resonance Raman
     Spectroscopic Studies of 2,4,Dinitrophenyl Hapten-Antibody
     Interactions.   Biochemistry $\underline{12}$: 2198-2208.

(12) Carrington, A. and McLachlan, A. D.   1967.   Introduction to
     Magnetic Resonance.   Harper and Row, New York.

(13) Cockle, S. A.   1974.   Electron Paramagnetic Resonance Studies on
     Cobalt (II) carbonic Anhydrase.   Biochem. J. $\underline{137}$: 587-596.

(14) Dwek, R. A., Jones, R., Marsh, D., McLaughlin, A. C., Press, E. M.,
     Price, N. C. and White, A. I.   1975.   Antibody Hapten Interactions
     in Solutions.   Proc. Roy. Soc. $\underline{B}$ - in press.

(15)   Dwek, R. A., Knott, J. C. A., Marsh, D., McLaughlin, A. C.,
       Press, E. M. and White, A. I. 1975. Structural Studies on
       the Combining Site of the Myeloma Protein MOPC 315. Eur. J.
       Biochem. 53, 25-39.

(16)   Dwek, R. A. 1973. Nuclear Magnetic Resonance in Biochemistry
       Applications to Enzyme Systems. Clarendon Press, Oxford,
       England.

(17)   Eisenberg, D. and Kauzmann, W. 1969. The Structure and
       Properties of Water. Oxford University Press.

(18)   Enderby, J. E., Howells, W. S. and Howe, R. A. 1973. The
       Structure of Aqueous Solutions. Chem. Phys. Lett. 21: 109-112.

(19)   Fabry, M. E., Koenig, S. H. and Schillinger, W. E. 1970. Nuclear
       Magnetic Relaxation Dispersion in Protein Solutions. J. Biol.
       Chem. 245: 4256-4262.

(19a) Feher, G., Isaacson, R. A., Scholes, C. P. and Nagel, R. E.n.d.o.r.
       investigation of myoglobin and hemoglobin. Ann. N.Y. Acad. Sci.
       222, 86-101.

(20)   Fishman, M. J. and Erdmann, D. E. 1973. Water Analysis.Analyti-
       cal Chemistry, 361-403R.

(20a) Fitzgerald, J. J. and Chasteen, N. D. EPR of vanadyl (IV) car-
       bonic anhydrase. Biochemistry 13: 4338-4347.

(21)   Gafni, A. and Steinberg, I. Z. 1972. Circular Polarization of
       Fluorescence Emitted by an Optically Active Compound. Photochem.
       Photobiol. 15: 93-96.

(22)   Givol, D., Pecht, I., Hochman, J. Schlissinger, J. and Steinberg,
       I. Z. 1974. Conformation Changes in the Fab and Fc of the
       Antibody as a Consequence of Antigen Binding - in Progress in
       Immunology - in press.

(23)   Hague, D. N. 1971. Fast Reactions. Wiley, New York.

(24)   Hirs, C. W. and Timasheff, S. N. 1973. Ed. Methods in Enzymology
       27: Part D. Sections IV and V and references therein.

(25)   Holmquist, B. and Valee, B. L. 1973. Tryptophan Quantitation by
       Magnetic Circular Dichroism in Native and Modified Proteins.
       Biochemistry 12: 4409-4417.

(26)   Hooker, Jr., T. M. and Schellman, J. A. 1970. Optical Activity
       of Aromatic Chromophores I, o, m and p-tyrosine. Biopolymers
       9: 1319-1347.

(27)   Inbar, D., Givol, D. and Hochman, J. 1973. Circular Dichroism
       Study of the antibody Combining Site. Eur. J. Biochem. 12:
       4541-4543.

(28)   Jamieson, A. M. and Maret, A. R. 1973. Quasielectric Laser
       Light Scattering. Chem. Soc. Reviews 2: 325-353.

(29)   Kaden, T. A., Holmquist, B. and Vallee, B. L. 1972. Magnetic
       Circular Dichroism of Cobalt Metalloenzyme Derivatives. Biochem.
       Biophys. Res. Comm. 46: 1654-1659.

(30)   Koenig, S. H. and Brown, R. D. 1973. Kinetic parameters of
       carbonic anhydrase from n.m.r. linewidths of ^{13}C in CO_2 and
       HCO_3^-. Biochem. Biophys. Res. Comm. 53: 624-630.

(31)   Kratky, O. and Pilz, I. 1972. X-ray small-angle Scattering of
       Biopolymers. Quart. Rev. of Biophys. 5: 481-537.

(32)   Lang, G. 1970. Mössbauer spectroscopy of heme proteins. Q. Rev.
       Biophys. 3: 1-

(33)   Latt, S. A., Auld, D. S. and Vallee, B. L. 1972. Distance
       Measurements at the Active Site of Carboxypeptidase A during
       Catalysis. Biochemistry 11: 3015-3022.

(34)   Lindskog, S., Henderson, L. E., Kannan, K. K., Liljas, A., Nymann,
       P. O. and Strandberg, B. 1971. Carbonic Anhydrase. In The
       Enzymes Vol. V 3rd ed. (Boyer, P. D. ed.) Academic Press, New York.

(35)   Marrack, J. R. and Richards, C. B. 1971. Light-Scattering Studies
       of the Formation of Aggregates in Mixtures of Antigen and Anti-
       body Immunology 20: 1019-1040.

(35a) Nelson, E. B., Candella, A. and Tolbert, N. E. 1969. Carbonic
       anhydrase levels in chlamydomonas. Phytochemistry 8: 2305-

(36)   Parker, C. A. Photoluminescence of Solutions - Elsevier, Amsterdam.

(37)   Pecht, I. 1974. Antibody Combining Sites as a Model for
       Molecular Recognition, In Symposium on Protein Ligand Interactions
       (Konstang) - in press.

(38)   Pilz, I., Kratky, O. and Karush, F. 1974. Changes of the Con-
       formation of Rabbit IgG Antibody Caused by Specific Binding as a
       Hapten. Eur. J. Biochem. 41: 91-96.

(39)   Riepe, M. E. and Wang, J. H. 1968. Infrared Studies on the
       Mechanism of Action of Carbonic Anhydrase. J. Biol. Chem. 243:
       2779-2787.

(40)   Sands, R. H. and Dunham, W. R. 1975. Spectroscopic studies on
       two iron ferridoxins. Q. Rev. Biophys. 7: 443-504.

(41)   Sophianopoulos, A. H.   1974.   Differential Conductimetry.   In
       Methods in Enzymology Vol. XXVII D (Hirs, C. H. W. and
       Timasheff, S. N., eds.).   Academic Press pp. 557-589.

(42)   Spiro, T. G.   1974.   Resonance Raman Spectroscopy: A new
       structure probe for biological chromophores.   Accounts of Chemical
       Research 7 339-344.

(43)   Stryer, L.   1968.   Fluorescence Spectroscopy of Proteins.
       Science 162: 526-533.

(44)   Tanford, C.   1961.   Physical Chemistry of Macromolecules.   Wiley,
       New York.

(45)   Tobin, M. C.   1971.   In Laser Raman Spectroscopy.   New York:
       Wiley, Interscience - and references therein.

(46)   Tummerman, L. A., Nezlin, R. A. and Zagyonsky, Y. A.   1972.
       Increase of the Rotational Relaxation Time of Antibody Molecule
       After Complex Formation with Dansyl-Hapten.   FEBS Lett. 19:
       290-292.

(47)   Ward, R. L.   1970.   Zinc Environmental Differences in Carbonic
       Anhydrase Isozymes.   Biochemistry 9, 2447-2454.

(48)   White, J. W.   1974.   Neutron Scattering Spectroscopy and the
       Structure of Disordered Crystals.   Spectrochim. Acta 30A:
       1665-1707.

Ion-Selective Electrodes in Thermodynamic Studies

Theodore B. Warner
Ocean Sciences Division, Naval Research Laboratory
Washington, D. C. 20375

Abstract: Ion electrodes directly measure free ion activity and discriminate clearly against related ion pairs. Many appear to have perfect theoretical responses. A number of recent studies are described which demonstrate the kinds of measurements that are possible and also show how various electrode-measurement problems have been solved. Practical considerations are emphasized, particularly regarding how reference electrodes are chosen and how effects due to liquid junction potentials can be minimized. Single-ion activity coefficients are briefly discussed along with a number of studies that have eliminated the need for using them. The present state of high-pressure work, both in the laboratory and directly in the sea, is reviewed.

Introduction

Ion-selective electrodes have a number of properties that make them attractive for speciation studies. They have been successfully used in a variety of solutions, including seawater. The purpose of this paper is to describe some of the major advantages and disadvantages of ion electrodes for such investigations and to emphasize some of the experimental realities. The importance of these practical considerations are so well-understood by workers active in the field that they are often mentioned only in passing in the primary literature. For those with different backgrounds, some reemphasis may be useful.

This study does not attempt to survey the rapidly expanding
literature of the field. Buck's review [14, over 1200 refs.]
gives good coverage of the most recent work, conveniently
grouped by different topics. Instead, relatively few studies
are discussed here only when they illustrate important points
or seem most directly related to speciation studies in seawater.

For basic information on the properties and uses of ion-selective electrodes, the monographs of Eisenman [26], Durst [24],
and Moody and Thomas [61] may be consulted. Warner [78] discussed the use of ion electrodes in seawater, and Koryta [45]
gives a comprehensive review of both theory and present
practice (713 references). At the International Symposium on
Selective Ion-Sensitive Electrodes, held in Cardiff in April,
1973, five papers dealt with the most recent developments in
specific areas [60]. The very recent review by Covington
[21] is particularly helpful. It surveys critically the principles of the subject in a way that should be most accessible
to the non-specialist. The earlier monograph by Whitfield
[84] is also very good in this regard.

Advantages

Ion electrodes measure free ion activity. This is their
greatest advantage in speciation studies. Yet they can also
measure the analytical concentration of a given chemical substance, even if distributed among several forms. The activity
measured is of one well-defined ionic species. Ample evidence exists showing that these electrodes clearly discriminate against most related ion pairs and respond only to the
species of interest. For example, the sulfide electrode responds theoretically to S^{--} ion activity and is totally un-
influenced by HS^- ion activity. The speciation studies discussed later have shown repeatedly that this high specificity
is the general rule. (This kind of specificity should not be
confused with poor selectivity, wherein other ions, e.g., Na^+

in the case of the potassium electrode, can also influence
electrode potential.)

Because the activity measurement is direct and in real time,
kinetic studies can be convenient and simple. The kinetic
data obtained can be continuous rather than being sampled
only at specific times. Electrode response times vary
considerably with conditions of use. However, even slow response can give useful information about rapid reactions by
using rapid-mixing flow techniques [28, 72].

Another substantial advantage is that ion electrodes appear
to be perfect theoretical devices. This is a somewhat controversial statement and is proposed only tentatively at the
present time. The possibility of true theoretical behavior
has not been widely appreciated to date, and a more common
viewpoint is that ion electrodes exhibit close to theoretical
response, but must be used empirically. This view probably
arose because the first ion electrode extensively studied was
the glass pH electrode. The complexity of the glass membrane
and its high electrical impedance made it particularly difficult to use in well-controlled ways. However, evidence cited
below is accumulating which suggests that when proper experimental precautions are taken, the response can be theoretical,
even for the glass membrane electrodes.

The conceptual importance of being able to assume, at least
tentatively, that an ion electrode is responding theoretically
should be stressed. If, in fact, nontheoretical behavior is
observed, it cannot then be attributed to the nature of the
sensor, but must be presumed due to some uncontrolled variable
in the experimental design. Experience in our laboratory and
in others [39, 70] indicates that this can help identify previously unrecognized sources of error.

A final advantage of particular importance to marine chemists
is that ion electrodes can be used at high pressure, both

directly in the ocean and in the laboratory.

Disadvantages

The most important difficulty in using an ion electrode is
that it must always be coupled with a second electrode - a
reference electrode. Electrochemists are well aware that the
choice of a reference electrode and the way that it is used
are critically important in any electrode measurement. Difficulties with apparent nontheoretical response of the working
electrode (i.e., the nonreference electrode) very often arise
because the reference electrode is not the convenient and
stable reference point it is assumed to be. This will be discussed in more detail in a later section. The point emphasized here is that in 99 cases out of 100, experimental difficulties will be traced to reference electrodes. Fortunately,
the unusually stable and predictable behavior of ion electrodes offers promise that they will increasingly be used to
great advantage as reference cells without a liquid junction.
Recent advances in electronic technology now make a truly
differential measurement of the potential between two high-
impedance sources a straightforward procedure.

A second difficulty is the substantial theoretical and practical uncertainty about what single-ion activities are and how
they may be used. This is a highly controversial subject and
often leads to experimental designs where the problem can be
avoided or where nonthermodynamic "constants" are obtained for
the actual system of interest. Yet the very real problems
that exist suggest that this will be an increasingly fruitful
area of research in the future. The ocean system is thermodynamically difficult, being a very complex high-ionic-
strength solution. Furthermore, wide variations in temperature and pressure are encountered. Yet speciation studies
often require that these problems be addressed.

Fortunately, our understanding of the physical chemistry of

seawater has been substantially increased in the last decade.
New experimental results, using a variety of techniques and
coupled with useful theoretical generalizations, are leading
to internally self-consistent models. Millero [56, 57]
summarizes and critically reviews the most recent work.
Dyrssen and Wedborg [25] describe the speciation of the major
and some minor constituents of seawater, and Disteche [23]
has discussed the effects of temperature and pressure on
various equilibria in seawater. Kester [40] has compiled the
extensive data now available for describing chemical processes
in the marine environment in terms of their equilibria and
kinetics. The compilation includes gas-liquid exchanges, homogeneous solution reactions, and solid-solution phase reactions. These sources provide a good point of entry to
the present state of knowledge. It appears that evidence from
many kinds of studies can now be usefully directed towards
the theoretical problems surrounding ion activities in seawater [48, 49].

A practical disadvantage in using electrodes is that they are
quite sensitive to temperature changes. However, with good
temperature control, accurate results are possible. Also, for
most electrodes, ions other than the ion of interest can influence potential. Since selectivity is not perfect, experiments must be arranged to avoid error from this source. The
studies cited later demonstrate a number of ways that this
can be done.

The other disadvantages sometimes cited for electrode
studies, i.e., poor precision, slow response, limited sensitivity, and inaccuracy, are perhaps more apparent than real.
For example, measurements are generally reproducible to 0.1
to 0.2 mV. But a number of investigators have routinely made
useful measurements to the nearest 0.01 mV even with glass
electrodes, which are the most difficult to control [29, 34,
41, 42]. Similar remarks may be made concerning sensitivity
[7, 79], accuracy [80], and response speed [66] although with

regard to this last the discussion and cautionary comments of
Müller [63] and Rechnitz [65] give good perspective.

Reference Electrodes and Liquid Junction Potentials

The potential developed across the junction between two dis-
similar liquids can be quite large. Even worse, it can only
be calculated approximately. Under the best conditions a
residual uncertainty of around 1 to 2 mV must be assumed [2,
37 (p. 55)]. Most commonly used and convenient laboratory reference electrodes include such a junction; its potential is
influenced by solution changes, stirring, and a number of other
factors. Various ingenious methods have been used to minimize
this potential or to infer what it is, and in certain cases
the observed value can be close to that predicted [37]. But
a far more attractive option is to arrange a cell without a
liquid junction and avoid this source of uncertainty.

The effect of a cell without liquid junction was obtained by
Miller [54, 55] by inserting three electrodes into the test
solution. In one case, two electrodes were ion-selective
electrodes for Cl^- and F^-, and one was a calomel reference
electrode with flowing junction. By measuring the potentials
of the Cl^- and F^- electrodes relative to the calomel electrode
and then subtracting, he obtained the potential between the
F/Cl pair and algebraically removed the common liquid junction
potential. This technique may have been partially responsible
for the closely theoretical electrode response observed. The
Nernst slopes observed in various standards were within 0.15 mV
of the predicted value at all temperatures studied.

Similar arrangements were discussed by Covington [20] and used
by Whitfield and Leyendekkers [86] and by Leyendekkers [47].
The latter was a study of single ion activities in the aqueous
systems NaCl-NaF and KCl-NaF. Values found experimentally
agreed well with those predicted theoretically. The residual
liquid junction potentials of the "Thalamid" and calomel ref-

erence electrodes were found to be an approximately linear
function of ionic strength over the range from 0.1 to 2.0.

A simpler experimental set-up involves measuring the potential
directly across two ion-selective electrodes, using a differential amplifier.   One electrode can be used as a reference
by adding a small amount of the proper ion to all test solutions [52, 71].   The possibility of using a pH electrode as
the reference electrode in a well buffered solution should not
be overlooked.   Another option is to measure the ratio between
two ion activities [55].   Several circuits for differential
amplifiers with two high-impedance inputs have been described
by Ben-Yaakov and Ruth [9], by Brand and Rechnitz [13], by
Conti and Wilde [19], and most recently, a simple and inexpen-
sive circuit was discussed by Wilde [87].   This last is of interest also because of the possibility of measuring the activities of a number of different ions in the same solution at
the same time.   The study of Wawro and Rechnitz [81] using a
split crystal ion-selective membrane electrode as both working
and reference electrodes shows the considerable advantages
gained by using a "double beam" system with closely matched
electrodes, and at the same time offers the possibility of
minimizing liquid junction potentials when reference and test
solutions are very similar.

Hansson [31] described a cell which involved a liquid junction
between test and reference solutions; however, the liquid
junction potential was kept small by making the test and reference cell solutions almost identical.   The design used is
shown in Fig. 1.   The reference solution was the same as the
test solution, except saturated with AgCl.   The junction could
be renewed by pressing down slightly on the movable inner reference electrode section.   Both in principle and in practice
this approach offers promise for careful speciation studies
[32-34].   Similar geometries have often been used in the past;
the general discussion of reference electrodes by Covington
[20] gives good perspective.

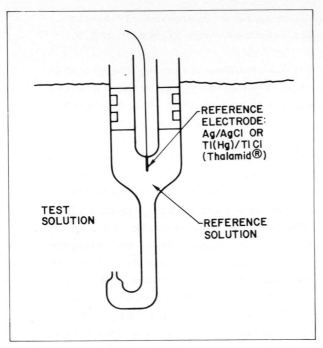

FIG.1 - The reference electrode used by Hansson to
minimize liquid junction potentials [31].

Theoretical Response of Membrane Electrodes

Evidence is accumulating which indicates that many ion electrodes can be depended upon to give true theoretical response
[15]. Whether this is true for electrodes with liquid membranes is uncertain. A corollary of this is that when response is not quite theoretical, the causes most likely lie in
some other part of the cell design. The studies of Miller and
Kester cited earlier [54, 55] showed that when liquid junction
potentials were algebraically removed, Na-Cl and F-Cl electrode pairs showed response slopes within 0.15 mV of the

predicted Nernst slope at temperatures of 15, 25, and $35^{\circ}C$.
Hansson [31] examined the emf of pH electrodes against hydrogen electrodes and found the value constant to within 0.1 mV
over a pH range of 2.1 to 8.5. Similar studies by Mehrbach,
et al. [53] gave glass/hydrogen potentials constant to 0.10 mV
from pH 2.4 to 8.9 in seawater, and constant to 0.13 mV from
pH 2.1 to 9.0 in buffered NaCl.

Baumann [7] demonstrated that the potential developed by a
fluoride electrode is a valid measure of free fluoride activity down to levels near 10^{-10} M, when the activity was controlled by various complexing cations (Zr^{4+}, Th^{4+}, La^{3+}, H^{+}).
Previously, 10^{-6} M was commonly accepted as the lower limit
of sensitivity and was believed inherent to the electrode due
to dissolution of the LaF_3 membrane. Our studies with fluoride indicated that no deviation from Nernst response could
be detected in NaF and NaF + NaCl solutions from 10^{-1} to 10^{-6} M
[76], and that even in delicately poised solutions containing less than 1 ppb fluoride, the potentials observed appeared
to be a valid indication of the fluoride activity very close
to the membrane [79]. Müller and co-workers [62] noted theoretical response for a silver electrode over a wide range.

Many other such studies could be cited. It may be time to
adopt, at least tentatively, a somewhat less conservative view
concerning the probability of theoretical response from membrane electrodes. However, if asymmetry potentials are significant in non-glass electrodes, as they are known to be in
glass electrodes [2(p. 310)], then the effect of solution composition on this potential might be one source of nontheoretical behavior. Little is known about this for the nonglass
electrodes. But experience to date suggests that under carefully controlled conditions, influences from this source can
be small.

Individual Ionic Activity Coefficients

Both Garrels [29] and Bates [2] have clearly underscored the
fact that what is measured with an ion electrode is an operational emf difference between some standard solution and the
test solution. Any attempt to interpret such measurements in
terms of activity depends upon some estimate of individual
ionic activity coefficients. These estimates must always include nonthermodynamic assumptions and must be regarded as
conventional, not real. In general, the concept is probably
best avoided except in certain theoretical analyses when in
the end the single ion activity coefficients are again combined to give activity coefficients of the actual solution
components.

The conventional or assumed activities for a given set of
standards need not bear any known relation to the true activities, assuming that different workers use the same convention.
However, the fact that the conventional activities adopted
seem reasonable should not lead to the implicit assumption
that they are real, as Garrels and many others have emphasized.

Nevertheless, these conventional activity scales can be operationally useful, and much effort has been applied to the question of how best to estimate individual activity coefficients
and how to establish a consistent set of activity standards
[4]. For seawater, Bates discusses pH scales elsewhere in
this volume. For other ion-sensitive electrodes, the problem
of estimating activity coefficients and establishing reference standards is made even more difficult because measurements are normally made in unbuffered media exhibiting wide
changes in total ionic strength as pIon changes. It is thus
necessary to estimate pIon even into regions of high total
ionic strength. It is obvious that wide differences in ionic
strength from solution to solution will also intensify the
experimental uncertainties due to liquid junction potential
changes [69].

Garrels [29] made estimates of single ion activities of Na^+, Ca^{2+}, Mg^{2+}, HCO_3^-, and CO_3^{2-} based on electrode measurements in solutions up to an ionic strength of 4.0, and compared them with values estimated using the Debye-Hückel theory and also using the MacInnes assumption. He concluded that while there is no way to estimate the error in any one of the methods, "a comparison of the results obtained leads one to the conclusion that the 'best values' are probably good to within ±5% of the number given at ionic strengths up to 1.0."

Scales of ionic activity at ionic strengths above 0.1 have been developed based on considerations of the degree of hydration of the ions involved [3, 6, 69]. Bates and Robinson [5] have suggested that the ion activities reproduced in Table 1 be adopted as standard reference values, and this was endorsed by the Commission of Electroanalytical Chemistry of the International Union of Pure and Applied Chemistry at its meeting in Munich in 1973. The single-ion activity convention suggested by Bates, et al. [6] was tested by Bagg and Rechnitz [1] and found to fit the data up to 6m NaCl, 4m KCl, 4m KBr, 3m KF, and 1m LiCl. Another portion of this study examined the theoretical potentiometric response of ion electrodes in chloride, bromide, and fluoride solutions using a cell whose emf is independent of the way the liquid junction is formed. No use of extra-thermodynamic assumptions was needed to calculate the theoretical emf and response was shown to be nearly theoretical up to 4-5 molal.

Electrode Determination of Ion-Pairing in Seawater and in Other High-Ionic-Strength Solutions

Some studies have been selected for emphasis here because they illustrate useful solutions to important problems. No attempt is made to survey all of the recent work in this area.

TABLE 1 - Reference values of ionic activity for the standard-
         ization of ion-selective electrodes at 25°C [3]

| molality/ | NaCl | | KCl | |
mol kg⁻¹	pNa	pCl	pK	pCl
0.01	2.044	2.045	2.045	2.045
0.1	1.106	1.112	1.112	1.115
0.2	0.827	0.838	0.840	0.845
0.5	0.455	0.481	0.482	0.496
1.0	0.157	0.208	0.206	0.232
2.0	-0.180	-0.072	-0.086	-0.032

| | NH$_4$Cl | | KF | |
	pNH$_4$	pCl	pK	pF
0.01	2.045	2.045	2.044	2.044
0.1	1.112	1.115	1.111	1.111
0.2	0.840	0.845	0.837	0.837
0.5	0.483	0.494	0.475	0.475
1.0	0.208	0.231	0.190	0.190
2.0	-0.080	-0.034	-0.119	-0.119

| | CaCl$_2$ | |
	pCa	pCl
0.01	2.273	1.768
0.1	1.570	0.842
0.2	1.349	0.562
0.5	0.991	0.177
1.0	0.580	-0.140

Sodium fluoride ion pairing in 0.7m NaCl.

Miller [54] and Miller and Kester [55] studied NaF ion-pairing
at the ionic strength of seawater using Na^+, Cl^-, and F^- ion-
selective electrodes. Three aspects of this study are emphasized: effective elimination of liquid junction potentials
(discussed earlier), elimination of single-ion activity coefficients by measuring ion activity ratios, and determination
of formation constants by two separate routes to give an over-
determined system, and hence greater confidence in the re-

sulting values for association constants.

In inferring free ion concentrations from electrode measurements two options are available:
1) Hold total ionic strength (TIS) constant and assume γ_{ion}, the individual ion activity coefficient, does not vary with solution composition changes.
2) Assume γ_{mean} is known from other experimental data, and allows TIS to vary.
Most previous work has preferred option 1, yet at high ionic strengths differing amounts of hydration in different solutions probably do influence γ_{ion}. One must also assume that other ions in the solution do not change their complexing with composition changes. In the NaF study both approaches were used, although since ratios were determined, the much less restrictive assumption regarding option 1 was that the γ_F/γ_{Cl} activity <u>ratio</u> did not change in various KF/KCl mixtures at constant TIS.

One set of measurements involved standardizing the F/Cl electrode pair in mixtures of 0.7m KCl and 0.7m KF. KF was assumed to be completely dissociated. The concentration of free [F$^-$] in mixtures of NaCl and NaF was measured, and the amount of NaF^O inferred from the difference between total and free fluoride.

A second set of measurements obtained [NaF^O] from the difference between total and free sodium in the same solutions. Here, the Na/Cl electrode pair was standardized in NaCl solutions ranging from 0.1 to 0.7m, and the assumption made was that the mean activity coefficient, $\gamma_\pm$, of NaCl was known from other data and that it was essentially the same in NaCl and in NaCl-NaF solutions of the same ionic strength. Thus, from the measured ΔE_{NaCl} in the test solutions could be inferred ($\gamma_{\pm\ NaCl}^2$ [Na$^+$][Cl$^-$]), and assuming none of the chloride was ion-paired by Na$^+$ or K$^+$, free [Na$^+$] could be found. Note that no assumptions about individual ion activity coefficients are required here.

Experimentally, the estimates for $[NaF°]$ obtained using each
method agreed fairly well when this value exceeded 0.010m, and
showed increasing scatter as the ion-paired amount decreased.
Since in each case differences between large values were being
used, this is not surprising. The agreement obtained using
two different techniques strengthens confidence in the resulting values, and hence in the assumptions made and in the
computed association constants.

Ion-pairing in seawater and other high-ionic-strength solutions.

A number of previous studies have been carried out using different ion electrodes coupled with conventional reference
electrodes. In synthetic seawater, Kester and Pytkowicz [42,
43, 64] determined $MgSO_4$ association using a magnesium electrode, and sodium, magnesium, and calcium sulfate ion pairs
using appropriate cation-sensitive electrodes. Earlier,
Thompson [73] and Thompson and Ross [74] investigated the
fraction of Mg^{++} and Ca^{++} existing as free ions in real seawater. Kester and Pytkowicz [44] measured $NaSO_4^-$ and $MgSO_4°$
ion pairing at 2°C. $NaSO_4^-$ ion-pairing was also studied at
pressures up to 1000 atm. Elgquist [27] examined the stability constants of MgF^+ and CaF^+ in NaCl at ionic strengths from
0.1 to 1.0, and Warner [77] estimated the fraction of free
fluoride in seawater.

Mean activity coefficients in high ionic-strength solutions.

In a series of carefully designed experiments, Butler and
Huston studied the activity coefficients of NaCl, KCl, and
NaF in concentrated aqueous mixed electrolytes [16-18, 36].
Similar studies for $CaCl_2$ were attempted but were not possible
because the Ca^{++} electrode is much less selective for Ca^{++}
over Na^+ in concentrated solutions [35]. These measurements
were made in cells without liquid junctions. Leyendekkers and
Whitfield [50] studied changes in the activity coefficient of

calcium chloride in the aqueous systems $CaCl_2$-$MgCl_2$ and $CaCl_2$-$SrCl_2$ over the ionic strength range 0.1 to 6 molal at $25^{\circ}C$ and found good comparison with isopiestic data. Here the measurements were made between Cl^- and Ca^{++} electrodes, and one conclusion of the study was that liquid ion exchange electrodes can indeed be useful tools for measuring such activities up to rather high ionic strengths.

Thermodynamic Studies in Other Media

Much of the work prior to 1969 was discussed in some detail by Butler [15] and Rechnitz [65]. Butler also discusses the general questions of single-ion activity coefficients, of liquid junction potentials, and of electrode selectivity, stability, and kinetic response.

As new ion electrodes have become available, systems have been studied directly that had previously only been approached in-directly. Association constants so derived often differed substantially from those previously estimated, thus pointing up the need for direct studies [54, 58, 59, 67].

Little data is available regarding the stability constants of sparingly soluble salts, primarily because of the difficulties of measuring the very low concentrations of the uncomplexed species. Ion electrodes have good sensitivity at low levels and hence are well-suited to such studies. Bond and Hefter [10] studied the lead (II)-fluoride system using the fluoride electrode. They found good agreement with polarographic results (Table 2), and clear evidence that an earlier indirect

TABLE 2 - Stability constants of the PbF^+ complex β_1 at $15^{\circ}C$

ionic strength	β_1 by polarography	β_1 by electrode
1.00	34 ± 5	42 ± 3
0.10		54 ± 5

determination $\beta_1 < 2$ was incorrect. Of interest here is that
the actual free fluoride measurements were made at concentra-
tions between 6×10^{-6} M and 6×10^{-5} M, and also that calibration
graphs were strictly linear with slopes of 57 mV (theoretical
value = 57.2 mV/decade). The cell included a conventional
reference electrode with a liquid junction.

Subsequently, Bond and Hefter [11] studied formation constants
for Mg(II), Ca(II), Sr(II), and Ba(II)-fluoride complexes at
ionic strength of 1.0 and at temperatures from 2^O to 35^OC.
Bond and O'Donnell [12] examined the stability constants of
CdF^+, MgF^+, ZnF^+, NiF^+, and AgF at 16° and 0.5 ionic strength.
In all cases, their results were in good agreement with values
found by other methods. The mononuclear fluoroborate complexes were studied by Grassino and Hume [30] at 25° and an
ionic strength of 1.0, and Roberson and Hem [68] determined
the activity product constant of cryolyte at 25^OC.

Exchange Studies Between Solids and Liquids

The partition of chemical species between solid and liquid
phases is of particular interest to marine chemists and geochemists because particulate matter is everywhere a part of
the systems studied, and because many active ion exchangers
occur naturally. Suspended particulate matter does not affect
ion electrode response. It is thus possible to examine ion
exchange between clays and solutions, or even to measure ion
activity directly in the interstitial fluids of sediments
without prior separation.

An important caution should be mentioned here. Although
particulate matter will not affect the ion-selective electrode
response, it can cause problems at a reference electrode if a
liquid junction is present in the cell. Whenever measurements
are made in a sol or suspension, or in a solution likely to
deposit a gel or polymeric material at the liquid junction,
potentials can be generated. Very large potentials can be

developed in sufficiently unfavorable cases. For example,
Jenny and coworkers [38] set up systems using bentonite or
cation exchange resins to demonstrate the phenomenon and measured junction potentials of tens of millivolts in many cases,
and as high as 100 mV in the most extreme case. This effect,
the suspension effect, as well as membrane potentials (created
when two electrolyte solutions of different concentrations are
separated by a porous medium or gel in which the pore walls
carry an electric double layer) are discussed in some detail
by van Olphen [75]. It should be noted, however, that some
investigators report that the suspension effect does not always affect potentials even under conditions where an effect
is expected, i.e., a reference electrode immersed in an
oceanic sediment sample. In general, when dealing with such
media, avoid flowing junctions unless this effect is negligible.

Wood [88] used electrodes for five different ions and studied
the rate of ion transfer between clay and water. Four reactions were followed simultaneously in the same sample after
mixing clay with the water. The fifth was followed separately, due to the number of meters available. The laboratory experiment simulated the conditions that would be created by
ion exchange and mineral solution during artificial recharge
of ground waters through surface spreading of river water.
His goal was to predict the quality of the recharge water with
time and space after interaction with the local clay. The
ions studied were Ca^{+2}, $(Ca^{+2} + Mg^{+2})$, F^-, H^+, and Na^+. A
major finding was that at least the first reaction steps were
rapid. Nearly all were faster than the response times of the
electrodes, i.e., 90% of full response in about 40 seconds
under the conditions used.

Wood's study shows one way that many parameters can be simultaneously and nondestructively monitored in a single sample.
Note that the samples were stirred mixtures of clay and water,
opaque and full of particles. His technique yielded not only

final steady-state values, but also kinetic data.

A compact probe suitable for in situ determination of pH, pS^{--}, and Eh in water or in sediments was developed by Whitfield [83], and a probe suitable for use by a SCUBA diver in water or in bottom sediment was described by Conti and Wilde [19]. The probe included electrodes for pH, for Na^+, Cl^-, and CO_3^{--}.

In Situ Measurements and Speciation Studies at High Pressure

The real possibility exists that certain speciation studies may be feasible directly in the ocean. While the actual difficulties of performing the measurements in the environment should not be minimized, there are a number of reasons why this may be desirable. Both temperature and pressure can be known and controlled very precisely in the sea, and the solution can be truly representative, including traces of organic matter and particulates. The ocean is such a complex solution that it can be difficult to prepare and keep uncontaminated suitable synthetic solutions. For the less abundant ions, in particular, complexation by small amounts of dissolved organic species is highly possible. Perhaps the only way to be sure that laboratory studies adequately describe the real system is to check predictions against measurements in the sea.

Progress in this area was summarized by Warner [78]. More recent advances include the in situ devices of Whitfield, and Conti and Wilde discussed in the previous section. Whitfield's sensor includes a platinum electrode for measuring Eh. This parameter has long been of great interest in evaluating the ionic forms occurring in redox systems [46], yet the practical difficulties in making meaningful measurements are great. Whitfield [85] has discussed this in some detail.

The in situ pH sensor of Ben-Yaakov and Kaplan has been im-

proved in a number of ways [9]. It is of interest for several
reasons. First, the design considerations apply directly to
similar sensors using other ion electrodes. Second, the way
that they have used this sensor with a pumped system to evaluate $CaCO_3$ solubility in real seawater [8] demonstrates the
multiple possibilities of conducting various kinds of thermodynamic studies in the ocean. This is an area that will undoubtedly receive greater attention in the future [48].

Because ion electrodes can be used directly at high pressures,
they are particularly well-adapted to laboratory examination
of speciation as a function of depth. The study of $NaSO_4^-$
and $NaSO_4^o$ ion-pairing as a function of temperature and pressure has already been mentioned [44]. Earlier work by
Disteche [22] examined the pH changes resulting from dissociation constant shifts caused by pressure in acid and buffer
solutions. He found good agreement with the theoretically
expected values for HCl, acetic acid, carbonic acid, and
acetate buffer. No agreement was found for bicarbonate
buffer. Recently, Disteche [23] discussed in detail the present state of knowledge concerning the effects of temperature
and pressure on speciation. Whitfield [82] described pressure
vessels allowing the simultaneous study of several electrodes
at pressures up to 3000 bars. His design, which had a number
of interesting features, enclosed the electrode system in a
syringe vessel within the pressure vessel itself to avoid
difficulties with contamination of the cell solution or with
gas exchange. He studied assymetry potentials and the reproducibility of a number of different kinds of pH membranes, of
sodium glass, and of calcium liquid-ion exchanger electrodes.
The hydrogen and sodium electrodes showed good theoretical
response. The calcium electrode performed well at atomspheric
pressure but not at high pressure.

Most recent studies of the effect of temperature and pressure
on speciation have used other techniques. This has been discussed in some detail by Millero [56]. In general, such ther-

modynamic data have not agreed well. It may be fruitful to
make direct electrode measurements as a check on existing
data. When suitable data are lacking, a simple equation has
been proposed by Lown, et al. [51] and shown to be satisfactory for the calculation of the pressure dependence of the
dissociation constants of weak electrolytes to 2000 bars from
density and compressibility measurements.

Summary

Ion electrodes are useful for speciation studies because they
measure free ionic activity. Many of them appear to have perfect theoretical response. Since the measurement is direct,
and. since suspended solids need not interfere, kinetic solu-
tion-clay exchange studies are possible and have been carried
out. Electrodes can be used directly at high pressure.

Major difficulties in electrode studies are caused by reference electrodes having liquid junction potentials. Another
problem is that single-ion activity coefficients are, in principle, unknowable. Recent work has centered around eliminating or minimizing liquid junction potentials either by design
or, even better, by using cells without a liquid junction.
Several workers have achieved the effect of a cell without
liquid junction by referencing several working electrodes to
a third electrode, which does have a liquid junction, and then
obtaining the difference in potential. A true differential
measurement between two ion electrodes may be a good way to
avoid the problem.

Recent investigations of association constants and of activity
coefficients in seawater and in other high-ionic-strength solutions show the kinds of measurements that are now possible.
Many studies confirm data obtained previously. Others show
that when stability constants can be measured directly, they
often differ substantially from those previously inferred from
indirect determinations. The need for direct measurements is

clear. Ion electrodes appear well-suited to many such studies.

Acknowledgements

I thank R. G. Bates, S. Ben-Yaakov, C. H. Cheek, M. S. Frant, M. M. Jones, D. R. Kester, K. A. Kraus, F. J. Millero, J. W. Ross, Jr., and M. Whitfield for helpful and stimulating discussions about various topics covered in this chapter and in many instances for sharing their most recent results prior to publication.

References

(1) Bagg, J., and Rechnitz, G. A. 1973. Activity measurements at high ionic strengths using halide-selective membrane electrodes. Anal. Chem. 45: 271-276.

(2) Bates, R. G. 1964. Determination of pH: Theory and practice. New York: John Wiley and Sons.

(3) Bates, R. G. 1973. Ion activity scales for use with selective ion-sensitive electrodes. Pure and Appl. Chem. 36: 407-420.

(4) Bates, R. G., and Alfenaar, M. 1969. Activity standards for ion-selective electrodes. In Ion-Selective Electrodes, ed. R. A. Durst, pp. 191-214. Washington, D. C.: National Bureau of Standards Special Publication 314.

(5) Bates, R. G., and Robinson, R. A. 1974. An approach to conventional scales of ionic activity for the standardization of ion-selective electrodes. Pure and Appl. Chem. 37: 575-577.

(6) Bates, R. G.; Staples, B. R.; and Robinson, R. A. 1970. Ionic hydration and single ion activities in unassociated chlorides at high ionic strengths. Anal. Chem. 42: 867-871.

(7) Baumann, E. W. 1971. Sensitivity of the fluoride-selective electrode below the micromolar range. Anal. Chim. Acta. 54: 189-197.

(8) Ben-Yaakov, S., and Kaplan, I. R. 1971. Deep sea in situ calcium carbonate saturometry. J. Geophys. Res. 76: 722-731.

(9) Ben-Yaakov, S., and Ruth, E. 1974. An improved in situ
    pH sensor for oceanographic and limnological applica-
    tions. Limnol. and Oceanog. 19: 144-151.

(10) Bond, A. M., and Hefter, G. 1970. Use of ion-selective
     electrodes in the evaluation of stability constants of
     sparingly soluble salts. Application to the lead (II)-
     fluoride system in aqueous solution. Inorg. Chem. 9:
     1021-1023.

(11) Bond, A. M., and Hefter, G. 1971. Use of the fluoride
     ion-selective electrode for the detection of weak
     fluoride complexes. J. Inorg. Nucl. Chem. 33: 429-
     434.

(12) Bond, A. M., and O'Donnell, T. A. 1970. Evaluation of
     the stability constants of metal ion-fluoride complexes
     by the specific fluoride ion electrode. J. Electro-
     anal. Chem. 26: 137-154.

(13) Brand, M. J. D., and Rechnitz, G. A. 1970. Fast-response
     differential amplifier for use with ion-selective elec-
     trodes. Anal. Chem. 42: 1659-1661.

(14) Buck, R. P. 1974. Ion selective electrodes, potentio-
     metry, and potentiometric titrations. Anal. Chem. 46:
     28R-51R.

(15) Butler, J. N. 1969. Thermodynamic Studies. In Ion-
     Selective Electrodes, ed. R. A. Durst, pp. 143-189.
     Washington, D. C.: National Bureau of Standards Special
     Publication 314.

(16) Butler, J. N., and Huston, R. 1970. Activity measure-
     ments using a potassium-selective liquid ion-exchange
     electrode. Anal. Chem. 42: 676-679.

(17) Butler, J. N., and Huston, R. 1970. Potentiometric
     studies of multicomponent activity coefficients using
     the lanthanum fluoride membrane electrode. Anal. Chem.
     42: 1308-1311.

(18) Butler, J. N.; Huston, R.; and Hsu, P. T. 1967. Activity
     coefficient measurements in aqueous NaCl-LiCl and NaCl-
     KCl electrolytes using sodium amalgam electrodes. J.
     Phys. Chem. 71: 3294-3300.

(19) Conti, U., and Wilde, P. 1972. Diver-operated in situ
     electrochemical measurements. Mar. Technol. Soc. Jour.
     6(2): 17-23.

(20) Covington, A. K. 1969. Reference Electrodes. In Ion-
     Selective Electrodes, ed. R. A. Durst, pp. 107-141.
     Washington, D. C.: National Bureau of Standards Special
     Publication 314.

(21) Covington, A. K. 1974.   Ion-selective electrodes.   CRC
     Crit. Rev. in Anal. Chem. $\underline{4}(1)$: 355-406.

(22) Distèche, A. 1959.   pH measurements with a glass elec-
     trode withstanding 1500 Kg/cm^2 hydrostatic pressure.
     Rev. Sci. Inst. $\underline{30}$: 474-478.

(23) Distèche, A. 1974.   The effect of pressure on dissocia-
     tion constants and its temperature dependency. $\underline{In}$ The
     Sea, Vol. 5, ed. E. D. Goldberg, pp. 81-121.   New York:
     John Wiley and Sons.

(24) Durst, R. A., editor. 1969.   Ion-Selective Electrodes.
     Washington, D. C.: National Bureau of Standards Special
     Publication 314.

(25) Dyrssen, D., and Wedborg, M. 1974.   Equilibrium calcula-
     tions of the speciation of elements in seawater. $\underline{In}$
     The Sea, Vol. 5, ed. E. D. Goldberg, pp. 181-195.
     New York: John Wiley and Sons.

(26) Eisenman, G., editor. 1967.   Glass Electrodes for Hydro-
     gen and Other Cations: Principles and Practice.
     New York: Marcel Dekker, Inc.

(27) Elgquist, B. 1970.   Determination of the stability con-
     stants of MgF^+ and CaF^+ using a fluoride ion selective
     electrode.   J. Inorg. Nucl. Chem. $\underline{32}$: 937-944.

(28) Fleet, B., and Rechnitz, G. A. 1970.   Fast flow studies
     of biological reactions with ion-selective electrodes.
     Anal. Chem. $\underline{42}$: 690-693.

(29) Garrels, R. M. 1967.   Ion-sensitive electrodes and indi-
     vidual ion activity coefficients. $\underline{In}$ Glass Electrodes
     for Hydrogen and Other Cations, ed. G. Eisenman,
     pp. 344-361.   New York: Marcel Dekker, Inc.

(30) Grassino, S. L., and Hume, D. N. 1971.   Stability con-
     stants of mononuclear fluoborate complexes in aqueous
     solution.   J. Inorg. Nucl. Chem. $\underline{33}$: 421-428.

(31) Hansson, I. 1973.   The determination of dissociation con-
     stants of carbonic acid in synthetic sea water in the
     salinity range of 20-40 $\%_o$ and temperature range of
     5-30°C.   Acta Chem. Scand. $\underline{27}$: 931-944.

(32) Hansson, I. 1973.   A new set of acidity constants for
     carbonic acid and boric acid in sea water.   Deep-Sea
     Res. $\underline{20}$: 461-478.

(33) Hansson, I. 1973.   Determination of the acidity constant
     of boric acid in synthetic sea water media.   Acta Chem.
     Scand. $\underline{27}$: 924-930.

(34) Hansson, I. 1973. A new set of pH-scales and standard
     buffers for sea water. Deep-Sea Res. 20: 479-491.

(35) Huston, R., and Butler, J. N. 1969. Calcium activity
     measurements using a liquid ion exchange electrode in
     concentrated aqueous solutions. Anal. Chem. 41:
     200-202.

(36) Huston, R., and Butler, J. N. 1969. Activity measure-
     ments in concentrated sodium chloride-potassium
     chloride electrolytes using cation-sensitive glass
     electrodes. Anal. Chem. 41: 1695-1698.

(37) Ives, D. J. G., and Janz, G. J., editors. 1961. Refer-
     ence Electrodes, Theory and Practice. New York:
     Academic Press.

(38) Jenny, H.; Nielsen, T. R.; Coleman, N. T.; and Williams,
     D. E. 1950. Concerning the measurement of pH, ion
     activities, and membrane potentials in colloidal
     systems. Science 112: 164-167.

(39) Kester, D. R. 1974. Personal communication.

(40) Kester, D. R. In press. Marine chemical equilibria and
     kinetics. In The Oceans Handbook, ed. R. A. Horne.
     New York: Marcel Dekker, Inc.

(41) Kester, D. R., and Pytkowicz, R. M. 1967. Determination
     of the apparent dissociation constants of phosphoric
     acid. Limnol. Oceanog. 12: 243-252.

(42) Kester, D. R., and Pytkowicz, R. M. 1968. Magnesium
     sulfate association at 25C in synthetic seawater.
     Limnol. Oceanog. 13: 670-674.

(43) Kester, D. R., and Pytkowicz, R. M. 1969. Sodium, mag-
     nesium, and calcium sulfate ion-pairs in seawater at
     25C. Limnol. and Oceanog. 14: 686-692.

(44) Kester, D. R., and Pytkowicz, R. M. 1970. Effect of
     temperature and pressure on sulfate ion association in
     sea water. Geochim. et Cosmochim. Acta 34: 1039-1051.

(45) Koryta, J. 1972. Theory and applications of ion-
     selective electrodes. Anal. Chim. Acta 61: 329-411.

(46) Krauskopf, K. B. 1967. Introduction to Geochemistry.
     New York: McGraw Hill.

(47) Leyendekkers, J. V. 1971. Single ion activities in
     multicomponent systems. Anal. Chem. 43: 1835-1843.

(48) Leyendekkers, J. V. 1972-73. The chemical potentials of
     seawater components. Mar. Chem. 1: 75-88.

(49) Leyendekkers, J. V. 1974. Prediction of the partial
     molal volumes of electrolytes in seawater. Mar. Chem.
     2: 89-110.

(50) Leyendekkers, J. V., and Whitfield, M. 1971. Liquid ion
     exchange electrodes in mixed electrolyte solutions.
     Anal. Chem. 43: 322-327.

(51) Lown, D. A.; Thirsk, H. R.; and Wynne-Jones, L. 1968.
     Effect of pressure on ionization equilibria in water
     at 25°C. Faraday Soc. Trans. 64: 2073-2080.

(52) Manahan, S. E. 1970. Fluoride electrode as a reference
     in the determination of nitrate ion. Anal. Chem.
     42: 128-129.

(53) Mehrbach, C.; Culberson, C. H.; Hawley, J. E.; and
     Pytkowicz, R. M. 1973. Measurement of the apparent
     dissociation constants of carbonic acid in seawater at
     atmospheric pressure. Limnol. Oceanog. 18: 897-907.

(54) Miller, G. R., Jr. 1974. Fluoride in seawater: distri-
     bution in the North Atlantic Ocean and formation of
     ion pairs with sodium. Ph.D. thesis, University of
     Rhode Island, U.S.A.

(55) Miller, G. R., Jr., and Kester, D. R. 1975. Sodium
     fluoride ion-pairs in seawater. Submitted for publi-
     cation.

(56) Millero, F. J. 1974. The physical chemistry of seawater.
     Ann. Rev. Earth and Planetary Sciences 2: 101-150.

(57) Millero, F. J. 1974. Seawater as a multicomponent elec-
     trolyte solution. In The Sea, Vol. 5, ed. E. D.
     Goldberg, pp. 3-80. New York: John Wiley and Sons.

(58) Mohan, M. S., and Rechnitz, G. A. 1970. Ion-electrode
     study of alkali metal adenosine triphosphate complexes.
     J.A.C.S. 92: 5839-5842.

(59) Mohan, M. S., and Rechnitz, G. A. 1972. Ion-electrode
     study of the calcium-adenosine triphosphate system.
     J.A.C.S. 94: 1714-1716.

(60) Moody, G. J., editor. 1973. Selective ion-sensitive
     electrodes. Plenary lectures presented at the Inter-
     national Symposium on Selective Ion-Sensitive
     Electrodes. Pure and Appl. Chem. 36: 407-487.

(61) Moody, G. J., and Thomas, J. D. R. 1971. Selective Ion
     Sensitive Electrodes. Watford, Herts.: Merrow.

(62) Müller, D. C.; West, P. W.; and Müller, R. H. 1969.
     Determination of silver ion in parts per billion range
     with a selective ion electrode. Anal. Chem. 41: 2038-2040.

(63) Müller, R. H. 1969. Commentary. Anal. Chem. 41: 113A-
     116A.

(64) Pytkowicz, R. M., and Kester, D. R. 1969. Harned's rule
     behavior of NaCl-Na$_2$SO$_4$ solutions explained by an ion
     association model. Am. J. Sci. 267: 217-229.

(65) Rechnitz, G. A. 1969. Analytical studies on ion-
     selective membrane electrodes. In Ion-Selective
     Electrodes, ed. R. A. Durst, pp. 313-348. Washington,
     D. C.: National Bureau of Standards Special Publication
     314.

(66) Rechnitz, G. A., and Kugler, G. C. 1967. Transient
     phenomena at glass electrodes. Anal. Chem. 39: 1682-
     1688.

(67) Rechnitz, G. A., and Mohan, M. S. 1970. Potassium-
     adenosine triphosphate complex: formation constant
     measured with ion-selective electrodes. Science 168:
     1460.

(68) Roberson, C. E., and Hem, J. D. 1968. Activity product
     constant of cryolite at 25°C and one atmosphere using
     selective-ion electrodes to estimate sodium and fluo-
     ride activities. Geochim. et cosmochim. Acta 32:
     1343-1351.

(69) Robinson, R. A.; Duer, W. C.; and Bates, R. G. 1971.
     Potassium fluoride--reference standard for fluoride
     ion activity. Anal. Chem. 43: 1862-1865.

(70) Ross, J. W., Jr., and Frant, M. S. 1974. Personal
     communication.

(71) Stelting, K. M., and Manahan, S. E. 1974. Change in
     potential of reference fluoride electrode without
     liquid junction in mixed solvents. Anal. Chem. 46:
     592-594.

(72) Thompson, H. I., and Rechnitz, G. A. 1972. Fast reaction
     flow system using crystal-membrane ion-selective
     electrodes. Anal. Chem. 44: 300-305.

(73) Thompson, M. E. 1966. Magnesium in seawater: an elec-
     trode measurement. Science 153: 866.

(74) Thompson, M. E., and Ross, J. W., Jr. 1966. Calcium in
     sea water by electrode measurement. Science 154:
     1643-1644.

(75) van Olphen, H. 1963. An Introduction to Clay Colloid
     Chemistry, pp. 196-209. New York: Interscience.

(76) Warner, T. B. 1969. Lanthanum fluoride electrode response
     in water and in sodium chloride. Anal. Chem. 41: 527-529.

(77) Warner, T. B. 1971. Normal fluoride content of seawater. Deep-Sea Res. $\underline{18}$: 1255-1263.

(78) Warner, T. B. 1972. Ion selective electrodes--Properties and uses in seawater. Mar. Technol. Soc. Jour. $\underline{6}$(2): 24-33.

(79) Warner, T. B., and Bressan, D. J. 1973. Direct measurement of less than 1 part-per-billion fluoride in rain, fog, and aerosols with an ion-selective electrode. Anal. Chim. Acta $\underline{63}$: 165-173.

(80) Warner, T. B.; Jones, M. M.; Miller, G. R., Jr.; and Kester, D. R. 1975. Fluoride in sea water: intercalibration study using electrometric and spectrophotometric methods. Anal. Chim. Acta, in press.

(81) Wawro, R., and Rechnitz, G. A. 1974. Split crystal ion selective membrane electrodes. Anal. Chem. $\underline{46}$: 806-808.

(82) Whitfield, M. 1969. Multicell assemblies for studying ion-selective electrodes at high pressures. J. Electrochem. Soc. $\underline{116}$: 1042-1046.

(83) Whitfield, M. 1971. A compact potentiometric sensor of novel design. In situ determination of pH, pS^{2-}, and Eh. Limnol. and Oceanog. $\underline{16}$: 829-837.

(84) Whitfield, M. 1971. Ion selective electrodes for the analysis of natural waters. AMSA Handbook No. 2. Sidney, Australia: Australian Marine Sciences Association, Australian Museum.

(85) Whitfield, M. 1974. Thermodynamic limitations on the use of the platinum electrode in Eh measurements. Limnol. and Oceanog. $\underline{19}$: 857-865.

(86) Whitfield, M., and Leyendekkers, J. V. 1970. Selectivity characteristics of a calcium-selective ion-exchange electrode in the system calcium(II)-sodium(I)-chloride (I)-water. Anal. Chem. $\underline{42}$: 444-448.

(87) Wilde, P. 1974. Activity coefficients of Na^+, Cl^-, Mg^{++}, Ca^{++}, and K^+ in sea water from the Gulf of California by shipboard electrode measurements. (abstract) EOS $\underline{55}$: 310.

(88) Wood, W. W. 1973. Rapid reaction rates between water and calcareous clay as observed by specific-ion electrodes. Jour. Research U.S. Geol. Survey $\underline{1}$: 237-241.

Metal Complexes Present in Seawater

Sten Ahrland
Inorganic Chemistry 1, Chemical Center,
University of Lund, Box 740, S-220 07 Lund, Sweden

Abstract: The speciation of metal ions in seawater is considered primarily under aerobic conditions. The major constituents Na^+, Mg^{2+}, Ca^{2+}, and K^+ are mainly present as simple hydrates, but also to a certain extent as complexes of ligands coordinating via oxygen, primarily sulfate and carbonate. The same is true for many of the minor constituents, namely other alkali and alkaline earth ions, lanthanides, and several divalent transition metal ions, such as Co^{2+}, Ni^{2+}, and Zn^{2+}. Traces of other transition metals, e.g., Fe, Mn, Cr, V, are present in high oxidation states and are strongly hydrolyzed at the prevailing pH = 8. In all these cases, the complexes formed with chloride and bromide ions are quite weak. However, for the so-called (b), or soft, acceptors the opposite is true. The chloride and bromide complexes are strong while the affinity to ligands coordinating via oxygen is less marked. Typical (b) acceptors are among others several ions formed by elements at the end of the transition series, e.g. Ag^+, Au^+, Hg^{2+}. Finally, some aspects are discussed of the very different speciation occurring under anoxic conditions where the formation of sulfide complexes becomes especially important.

Components of Seawater

In standard seawater, alkali and alkaline earth ions are by far the most abundant metal ions present. The concentrations of the four main ones, namely $Na(I)$, $Mg(II)$, $Ca(II)$, and $K(I)$, are 479, 54.4, 10.53, and 10.45 mM, respectively [9]. Also, the concentrations of $Sr(II)$, $Li(I)$, and $Rb(I)$ are relatively high, 95, 25, and 1.4 μM, respectively. All other metals are present in concentrations < 1 μM. For the first row transition metals, from Ti to Zn, the concentrations are between 10^{-7} and 10^{-8} M. For heavier metals, they are generally lower, between 10^{-8} and 10^{-9} M for Ag, Cd, and Hg, presumably around 10^{-10} M for Au, Tl, Pb, and Bi. In some cases, comparatively high concentrations are found for heavy metals however, e.g. 10^{-7} M for

Mo, and 10^{-8} M for U [17]. The latter figure has even encouraged experiments aimed at the utilization of the uranium content of the sea.

The ligands present in seawater that are able to form complexes with
the various metal ion acceptors may be divided into two groups [9,25].
The first consists of inorganic anions which are main constituents
of seawater. Among these, Cl^- strongly predominates with a concentration of 559 mM, followed by SO_4^{2-}, 28.9 mM. The halide ions Br^-
and F^- occur in much lower concentrations, 0.86 and 0.075 mM, respectively, but their strong affinities to particular metal ions still
make them important. The total carbonate and borate concentrations,
on the average 2.35 and 0.4 mM respectively, are present as ions of
different degrees of protolysis, as will be further discussed below.
The second group of ligands are those which are present in very low
and often widely varying concentrations. Such ligands are often of
organic origin, stemming from the life processes going on in the
ocean. In spite of their low concentrations, some of these may be
significant because of their high affinity for certain metals. If
the latter are present only in trace amounts, they may become more
or less completely sequestered by such highly selective ligands, at
least locally. Such effects are naturally very difficult to account
for in quantitative terms. In the present review, some probable, or
at least possible effects that such ligands may bring about will be
discussed. For certain trace metals, a considerable part of their
total concentration may even be incorporated in various organisms if
these are abundant. This is especially likely to occur with metals
vital to life which may be taken up even in very minute concentrations by highly efficient mechanisms.

Oxidation potential and pH of seawater

If certain basins with very poor circulation and mixing are excepted,
the oxidation potential of the seawater should be determined essen-
tially by the oxygen water redox system $\frac{1}{2}O_2 + 2H^+ + 2e^- \rightleftharpoons H_2O$, of a
standard potential $E^o = 1229$ mV. The system is not reversible, how-
ever, so that true equilibria are not necessarily established with
other redox systems present. The practical oxidation potential of
seawater has therefore been the subject of dispute ([16], see also

R. Parsons , this volume). Its true value might well be considerably lower than the value calculated from the oxygen system according to

$$E = E^o + \frac{RT}{2F} \ln p(O_2)^{\frac{1}{2}} [H^+]^2 \tag{1}$$

with the oxygen pressure $p(O_2) = 0.21$ atm and a value of pH = 8.0, E = 746 mV. The corresponding value of $pE = -\log[e^-] = 12.6$ is calculated from

$$pE = E(\frac{RT}{F} \ln 10)^{-1} \tag{2}$$

and yields another measure of the oxidative power, often more convenient to use than E in equilibrium calculations. The equilibrium constant $K = 10^{41.55} M^{-4} atm^{-\frac{1}{2}}$ is found from

$$K = p(O_2)^{-\frac{1}{2}} [H^+]^{-2} \{e^-\}^{-2} \tag{3}$$

and may also be calculated directly from

$$\log K = E^o(\frac{RT}{2F} \ln 10)^{-1} \tag{4}$$

Values based on the iodide and nitrogen systems result in the distinctly lower values of pE = 10.6 and 10.5, respectively [16].

Generally, the pH of seawater is close to the value of 8.0 quoted above. Remarkably enough, this value is not far from one of the buffer capacity minima of the carbonate system, the only acid-base system present in any sizable concentration in seawater. It has therefore been argued [22] that the stable value of pH characteristic of seawater cannot be due to this system, but rather to heterogenous equilibria involving ion exchanging silicates in the bottom sediments. However, most of the water has very little contact with the sediment. The silicate suspended in water corresponds to < 10 μg Si/l [7] which in fact is much less than the concentration of carbonate. Moreover, from the amount of upwelling in the oceans it may be calculated that a direct contact between the bottom sediments and any small volume of ocean water occurs only once in about 1600 years. If such processes are to keep the value of pH virtually constant, all other protolytic reactions must indeed be either very slow or occur on a rather small scale. It seems, therefore, that even this approach so far does not provide a quite satisfactory explanation of the constancy of pH observed.

In areas where strong upwelling occurs, the concentration of oxygen
stays practically constant with increasing depth. Generally, however,
the concentration decreases until a minimum is reached at around
500 m and then increases again as the decay of organic material causing the oxygen consumption is completed. The minimum concentration
is often < 10 % of the surface concentration. To the oxidative power
at equilibrium, such a decrease does not mean very much, however. The
value of pE decreases only to 12.1 even for a drastic reduction of
the oxygen to 1 % of the initial value. However, the near depletion
of the oxidized form of this redox system implies a severe decrease
of the redox buffering capacity of the solution. Consequently, a
further consumption of oxygen by reducing substances might rather
easily bring about a drastic lowering of the oxidation potential.
This has indeed happened in the so-called anoxic zones existing in
the Baltic and Black Seas, and in the Scandinavian and British Co-
lumbian fjords. In these waters, an impeded circulation combined
with a fairly high oxygen consumption results in a complete depletion of oxygen. Under such extreme conditions, the oxidation potential may be determined by the sulfide system, present due to the
activity of sulfate reducing bacteria. The reaction
$S(s) + 2H^+ + 2e^- \rightleftharpoons H_2S(aq)$ has a very low value of E^o = 141 mV, corresponding to log K = 4.77. In anoxic waters, the sulfide concentra-
tion may reach values $\simeq$ 0.5 mM, while the value of pH drops to $\simeq$ 7.5
[8]. Assuming that $K_1 = 10^{6.9}$ M^{-1} for the reaction $SH^- + H^+ \rightleftharpoons H_2S(aq)$,
this would mean the very low value of pE = -3.1.

The mutual affinities between different classes of metal ions and ligands

Metal ions can be divided in two classes, (a) or hard and (b) or
soft, characterized by their differing affinity to various ligands
[2, 18]. Metal ion acceptors of the first class, (a), strongly prefer ligands coordinating via the light donor atoms F, O,and N, while
acceptors of the second class, (b), prefer ligands coordinating via
 the heavier donor atoms of each group. The donors preferred by the
hard and soft acceptors are termed hard and soft donors, respectively. The (a)-acceptors have the same affinity sequence towards the

TABLE 1. Characteristic affinity sequences of acceptors of the two classes (a) or hard, and (b) or soft, for various donor groups.

Donor group	Oxidation state	(a) or hard	(b) or soft
7 B	-I	$F \gg Cl > Br > I$	$F \ll Cl < Br < I$
6 B	-II	$O \gg S > Se > Te$	$O \ll S < Se \simeq Te$
5 B	-III	$N \gg P > As > Sb$	$N \ll P > As > Sb$

various groups of donor atoms, while the sequences of the (b)-acceptors differ between the various groups, as shown in Table 1. A very important common feature is, however, that the affinity difference between the first and second donor atom is always large, though in the opposite sense for (a)- and (b)-acceptors.

The (a)-sequences are those expected if the complex formation is mainly due to electrostatic interaction. In concordance with this, the complexes formed by (a)-acceptors are invariably stronger, the higher the charge and the smaller the radius of the acceptor. The most typical (a)-acceptors are therefore small multivalent cations.

The (b)-sequences are, on the other hand, evidently not compatible with a mainly electrostatic interaction. In these cases, the bonds formed must be of an essentially covalent character. This conclusion is further corroborated by the observations that complexes formed by (b)-acceptors are generally stronger the larger the radius of the acceptor involved, and that strong complexes are formed also by acceptors of low charge, or even by elements in their zerovalent oxidation state. In most cases, the (b)-character of an element, in fact, increases as the oxidation state decreases.

This classification of acceptors represents a systematization of a large mass of experimental facts. It is purely empirical and per se independent of any interpretation in terms of bonding. The model suggested seems to cover the facts quite well, however. The affinity sequences must of course also depend upon the dielectric and solvating properties of the solvent. The present discussion naturally refers to the conditions in aqueous solution.

1	2	3	4	5	6	7	8			1	2	3	4	5	6	7	0
1 H																	2 He
3 Li	4 Be											5 B	6 C	7 N	8 O	9 F	10 Ne
11 Na	12 Mg											13 Al	14 Si	15 P	16 S	17 Cl	18 Ar
19 K	20 Ca	21 Sc	22 Ti	23 V	24 Cr	25 Mn	26 Fe	27 Co	28 Ni	29 Cu I,II	30 Zn	31 Ga	32 Ge	33 As	34 Se	35 Br	36 Kr
37 Rb	38 Sr	39 Y	40 Zr	41 Nb	42 Mo	43 Tc	44 Ru	45 Rh	46 Pd	47 Ag	48 Cd	49 In	50 Sn	51 Sb	52 Te	53 I	54 Xe
55 Cs	56 Ba	57 La t.o.m. 71 Lu	72 Hf	73 Ta	74 W	75 Re	76 Os	77 Ir	78 Pt	79 Au	80 Hg	81 Tl	82 Pb	83 Bi	84 Po	85 At	86 Rn
87 Fr	88 Ra	89 Ac t.o.m. 103 Lw															

FIG 1 - The distribution of (a)- and (b)-acceptors in the periodic system. Elements forming typical (b)-acceptors are crossed over. Elements forming acceptors on the border-line between (a) and (b) are marked by a diagonal line. Elements forming (a)-acceptors surround the (b)-area. In the case of copper, Cu(I) is a typical (b)-acceptor while Cu(II) is an (a)-acceptor tending towards (b).

The two types of acceptors are distributed in the Periodic System in a most striking manner (Fig. 1). The (b)-acceptors are all situated within two roughly triangular areas. The left triangle, which is the more well-chartered one, has its apex at copper(I). The extension of the right triangle is less well-known, as the investigation of complex equilibria in this area has been much hampered by experimental difficulties. Presumably, the apex is to be found at arsenic or antimony. The bases of the triangles stretch along the highest period at least as far to the left as osmium. The (b)-area comprises acceptors which combine many d-electrons with a high polarizability. Both these features are necessary in order to constitute a (b)-acceptor. The lack of either destroys the (b)-character, i.e., the ability to form essentially covalent bonds in aqueous solution [1]. The most typical (b)-acceptors are in fact the monovalent oxidation states of the noble metals: Cu(I), Ag(I), Au(I). These have the outer electron configuration d^{10}, i.e., filled d-shells, and the low charge brings about a very high polarizability which, moreover, increases with the radius. As a consequence, these acceptors are all able to form markedly covalent bonds increasing in strength from $Cu(I)$ to $Au(I)$.

The (a)-acceptors are situated around the (b)-area of the Periodic System (Fig. 1). The transition from (a)- to (b)-character along the border lines between the two areas is rather sudden, though acceptors of a transitional behavior do exist. Rather typical cases are Cu^{2+} which is mainly (a) but tends towards (b), and Cd^{2+} which is mainly (b) but tends towards (a).

Complexes formed by the main metal ion constituents

All the main metal ions of seawater are typical (a)-acceptors. Among the ligands present in fair concentrations, they therefore much prefer the hard oxygen donors water and sulfate to the soft halide donors chloride and bromide. As the sulfate complexes are not very strong, especially not in the ionic medium offered by seawater where the activity coefficients of divalent ions are quite low, $\simeq 0.1$, (and the concentration of sulfate is very low compared with that of water),the predominant species are in fact the hydrated ions Na^+, K^+, Mg^{2+}, and Ca^{2+}. These hydrates are also very weak acids, so no hydrolysis occurs at the prevailing value of pH.

As it is a difficult task to determine equilibrium constants for complexes as weak as these sulfates, the distribution between the different species present has been much debated. According to the most realiable recent calculations [9], however, the share of the sulfate complexes would be $\leq$ 10 %, for Na^+ and for K^+ even $\leq$ 2 % (Table 2).

TABLE 2. Distribution (%) of the main metal(M) components of seawater on various species.

	Na(I)	K(I)	Mg(II)	Ca(II)
M^{n+}	98	99	92	92
MSO_4^{n-2}	2.4	1.2	7.9	7.9
MF^+	–	–	0.07	0.015
$MHCO_3^+$	–	–	0.18	0.06
MCO_3	–	–	0.15	0.05
$MB(OH)_4^+$	–	–	0.02	0.01

The very hard fluoride ion forms complexes especially with Mg^{2+}. On account of the low fluoride concentration, this complex represents only a negligible fraction, 0.07 %, of the total concentration of magnesium despite the fact that half of the fluoride is present as MgF^+. Only $\simeq$ 2 % is present as CaF^+, corresponding to $\simeq$ 0.015 % of the total concentration of calcium. For the other main metal ion constituents, no fluoride complexes can be discerned.

The metal ions and ligands so far discussed do not participate in any protolytic reactions at the pH of seawater. Some ligands prone to form complexes with the main metal ion constituents are also strong bases, however. Most important of these are the carbonate and borate ions which both are extensively protolyzed at pH = 8. The value of the constant $K_2 = [HCO_3^-]/[H^+][CO_3^{2-}]$ in seawater is $K_2 = 10^{9.54}M^{-1}$, which means a ratio $[HCO_3^-]/[CO_3^{2-}] = 35$ at pH = 8. The stability constants of the metal carbonate complexes are not known with accuracy. Presumably, the values of K_1 for $MgCO_3$ and $CaCO_3$ are $\simeq$ 30 M^{-1} and 10 M^{-1}, respectively [9,24]. The constants of the hydrogen carbonate equilibria are much lower in any case e.g. $\simeq$ 1 M^{-1} for $MgHCO_3$. Consequently, the protonated and unprotonated complexes are present in about the same amounts, in spite of the high value of the ratio $[HCO_3^-]/[CO_3^{2-}]$ (Table 2). This is a generally observed phenomenon, evidently due to the repellant action of the metal ion on the coordinated proton. In the case of borate, no complexes are formed with the uncharged protonated form $B(OH)_3$.

In carbonate solutions, several slightly soluble solid phases containing magnesium and/or calcium may be formed, $MgCO_3(H_2O)_3$ (nesquehonite), $MgCO_3$ (magnesite), $CaCO_3$ (aragonite and calcite), and $MgCa(CO_3)_2$ (dolomite). The solubility products, K_{so}, of these in pure water are listed in Table 3. In seawater, where the mean activity coefficients of 2-2 electrolytes are $f_\pm \simeq$ 0.1, an increase of the values of log K_{so} with 2 and 4 units, respectively, for phases of the compositions MCO_3 and $MM'(CO_3)_2$ would be expected. In fact, direct determinations of K_{so} for calcite and dolomite indicate an increase of 2.01 and 4.29 units respectively, very much as expected. To obtain the values of log K_{so} valid in seawater from those found at I = 0 for the other phases of the composition MCO_3 listed in Table 4, 2.0 units have therefore been added (2.01 in the case of aragonite, see footnote to

TABLE 3. The concentration of CO_3^{2-} in equilibrium with the various slightly soluble carbonate phases that can be precipitated from sea-water. The values of $[Mg^{2+}]$ and $[Ca^{2+}]$ have been taken as 0.05 M and 0.01 M, respectively. Values of pK_{so} from [24, 14].

Solid	Composition	pK_{so} I = 0	$[CO_3^{2-}] \times 10^5$ M Seawater
Nesquehonite	$MgCO_3(H_2O)_3$	4.67	2.7	4000
Magnesite	$MgCO_3$	7.46	5.5	6
Aragonite	$CaCO_3$	8.22	6.21	6.2
Calcite	$CaCO_3$	8.35*	6.34	4.6
Dolomite	$MgCa(CO_3)_2$	16.82**	12.53	2.5

*The difference $pK_{so(calcite)} - pK_{so(aragonite)} = 0.13$ found by Garrels and Thompson [24] agrees very well with Bäckströms [4, 24] mean value of 0.14. This difference should be the same in seawater, hence $pK_{so(aragonite)} = 6.21$ in this medium, from the directly measured $pK_{so(calcite)} = 6.34$ [14].

**For dolomite, Kramer's [24] values have been listed. The value for I = 0 agrees well with that preferred by Halla, $pK_{so} = 16.90$ [24].

Table 3). The concentrations of CO_3^{2-} in equilibrium with the various phases under the prevailing concentrations of Mg^{2+} (= 0.05 M) and Ca^{2+} (= 0.01 M) can then be calculated, (Table 3). If the rather soluble nesquehonite is excepted, these equilibrium concentrations differ very little, especially in view of the uncertainties involved in the calculation of the values of K_{so}. The difference found between dolomite and the rest is presumably significant, however, and would indicate that dolomite is the thermodynamically solid phase in equilibrium with seawater. Nevertheless, dolomite is not found in the sea, nor is magnesite. This is the more remarkable as both compounds are present in huge amounts in sedimentary rocks. The solid carbonate phases immediately precipitated from seawater are invariably calcite and aragonite, and these are almost always of biogenic origin.

Generally, the surface water is even somewhat supersaturated with
respect to these phases. As their values of K_{so} increase considerably with increasing pressure and decreasing temperature, this supersaturation disappears with increasing depth [12]. Calcium carbonates precipitated in the surface water therefore tend to dissolve
on sinking in deep water.

Among organic ligands [4] with sizable affinities to the major metal
ion constituents, carboxylates and aminoacid zwitterions have been
found in seawater. The former are oxygen donors which do not compete
very seriously with the hydrate water of the metal ions. The latter
are potentially chelating oxygen-nitrogen donors. Their affinity depends very much upon whether chelates are formed or not and may thus
vary considerably between, e.g., Mg^{2+} and Ca^{2+} , and between different
acids. Thus, the difference is large for glycin: $K_1 = 1000$ M^{-1} and
10 M^{-1}, respectively, [9], but much smaller for α-alanine [24]. The
total concentrations of these ligands are very low, however, namely
$\simeq 10^{-6}$ M for carboxylates and $\simeq 10^{-7}$ M for amino acids, so the
amounts of calcium and magnesium present as complexes of these ligands are extremely low.

Trace metals of class (a): oxidation states, hydrolysis and complexes under aerobic conditions

Many of the trace elements in seawater are also typical (a)-accep-
tors. This applies not only to the alkali and alkaline earth ions
not discussed so far, but also to rare earth and actinide ions as
well as to aluminium. In addition, the first row transition metals
in the oxidation states stable under aerobic conditions clearly behave as (a)-acceptors. For many of these elements, however, variations of pE within the limits observed in seawater may cause a complete change of the oxidation state, and hence of the chemical behavior, which is not the case for the other elements so far discussed. For some of them, even the oxidation states under the aerobic
conditions normally prevailing in seawater have been in doubt. It
seems appropriate therefore to discuss this question first.

There is no doubt that the last four metals, cobalt, nickel, copper,
and zinc are all present in the divalent state. The hydrolysis of
Co^{2+} and Ni^{2+} is practically negligible at pH = 8, as is that of

Zn^{2+}. The hydrolysis of Cu^{2+}, on the other hand, is fairly extensive though the evidence is somewhat conflicting [5]. In no case, however, are there any reliable indications that the hydrolysis extends beyond the first mononuclear complex MOH^+. In particular, the formation of polynuclear hydrolytic complexes is certainly negligible at the extremely low concentrations present, $\simeq 10^{-7}M$. Even for copper, the concentration of the most prominent polynuclear complex (the dimer $Cu_2(OH)_2^{2+}$, participating in the equilibrium $2Cu^{2+} + 2H_2O \rightleftharpoons Cu_2(OH)_2^{2+} + 2H^+$, with a constant $\beta_{22}^* \simeq 10^{11}$ M [5, 24]) is negligible, probably $\simeq 10^{-11}M$.

With regard to iron, the extensive hydrolysis of iron(III) at the prevailing pH strongly stabilizes this oxidation state relative to iron(II). Quantitatively, this stabilization can be expressed by the standard potential of the system $FeO(OH)(s) + 3H^+ + e^- \rightleftharpoons Fe^{2+} + 2H_2O$, which is $E^o = 908$ mV. At pE = 12.6 and pH = 8.0 this means a concentration $[Fe^{2+}] = 10^{-15.8}$ M in equilibrium with $FeO(OH)(s)$. Because Fe^{2+} is not hydrolyzed, this extremely minute concentration represents practically all iron(II) present in seawater, except the varying amounts bonded to organic matter. Some information about the amounts of various iron(III) species can be obtained from the constants of the equilibria $FeO(OH(s) + 3H^+ \rightleftharpoons Fe^{3+} + 3H_2O$, $Fe^{3+} + H_2O \rightleftharpoons Fe(OH)^{2+} + H^+$, $Fe^{3+} + 2H_2O \rightleftharpoons Fe(OH)_2^+ + 2H^+$ and $2Fe^{3+} + 2H_2O \rightleftharpoons Fe_2(OH)_2^{4+} + 2H^+$. In seawater, these constants are approximately

$$K_{so}^* = [Fe^{3+}]/[H^+]^3 = 10^{4.3} \ M^{-2} \tag{5}$$

$$K_1^* = [Fe(OH)^{2+}][H^+]/[Fe^{3+}] = 10^{-2.8} \ M \tag{6}$$

$$\beta_2^* = [Fe(OH)_2^+][H^+]^2/[Fe^{3+}] = 10^{-6.0} \ M^2 \tag{7}$$

$$\beta_{22}^* = [Fe_2(OH)_2^{4+}][H^+]^2/[Fe^{3+}]^2 = 10^{-2.7} \tag{8}$$

From (5), $[Fe^{3+}] = 10^{-19.7}$ M at pH = 8. With (6), (7), and (8) this yields $Fe(OH)^{2+} = 10^{-14.5}$ M, $Fe(OH)_2^+ = 10^{-9.7}$ M, and $[Fe_2(OH)_2^{4+}] = 10^{-26.1}$. Even the complex present in the highest concentration, $Fe(OH)_2^+$, accounts for only a small fraction of the total amount of iron in seawater, which is between 10^{-6} and 10^{-8} M according to various estimates. To what extent an uncharged soluble complex $Fe(OH)_3$ exists is not known. At present, the most reasonable inference seems to be that most of the iron exists as finely dispersed hydrous oxide. At the prevailing low concentration, the dispersion may be at least partly colloidal, despite the high concentration of ions present.

For manganese an even higher (and more strongly oxidized) oxidation state is preferred, namely $Mn(IV)$. The system $MnO_2(s,\beta) + 4H^+ + 2e^- \rightleftharpoons Mn^{2+} + 2H_2O$ has $E^o = 1230$ mV which in seawater means a concentration $[Mn^{2+}] = 10^{-15.7}$ M in equilibrium with the solid β-phase pyrolusite. The hydroxide of manganese(III) is not stable relative to $MnO_2(\beta)$ under the present conditions either. On the other hand, the higher oxidation states of manganese are reduced. It may thus be concluded that once equilibrium has been reached, manganese is present in seawater only in the form of dispersed $MnO_2(s)$.

Eventually,the iron(III) hydrous oxide as well as the manganese(IV) oxide reach the bottom sediments, often coprecipitated in the form of the much discussed iron-manganese nodules.

For chromium as well, the rather high value of pH in seawater strongly favors a high oxidation state, namely chromium(VI). Contrary to iron(III) and manganese(IV), however, chromium(VI) is present as a soluble species, i.e., the chromate ion, CrO_4^{2-}. Though this ion is a fairly strong base, with a corresponding acid of pK $\simeq 5.7$ in the present medium, practically no $HCrO_4^-$ is evidently formed at the prevailing pH = 8. At this pH, no cationic hydrolytic complexes of chromium(III) exist. The equilibrium $CrO_4^{2-} + 4H_2O + 3e^- \rightleftharpoons Cr(OH)_3(s) + 5OH^-$ is only slowly established,and the standard potential is therefore very difficult to measure. A value of $E^o = -130$ mV has been calculated, however, which corresponds to a concentration of chromate $[CrO_4^{2-}] = 10^{14.5}$ M (!) in equilibrium with $Cr(OH)_3(s)$ at pE = 12.6 and pH = 8. Evidently,chromium(III) is not thermodynamically stable in seawater. At equilibrium, all chromium will be in the form of CrO_4^{2-}. For vanadium, oxidation potentials valid in alkaline solutions are not available. Nevertheless,it is certain that in this case also the highest oxidation state, vanadium(V), is the stable one in seawater. The species present are most probably the mononuclear ions $H_2VO_4^-$ and HVO_4^{2-} (often written as $VO_2(OH)_2^-$ and $VO_2(OH)_3^{2-}$, respectively). With a probable value of pK $\simeq$ 7.8 [24], the latter should be the slightly predominating form. No polyvanadates are formed at the very low concentrations present.

Under aerobic conditions, the last four elements, Fe, Mn, Cr, and V, thus do not exist in equilibrium as metal cations. As the oxidation processes leading to equilibrium are generally slow, however, this does not exclude that their lower oxidation states when added to seawater may survive for some time. In marine organisms, the speciation is quite different of course, and other oxidation states are also likely to prevail.

Complexes with the anions present are not formed by these elements. On the contrary, the chromate and vanadate ions are themselves potential metal coordinating ligands. But because their concentrations are very low in comparison with that of the sulfate ion, a ligand of the same type and charge, they are not of much consequence in this respect. Nor are their concentrations high enough for the precipitation of slightly soluble salts, though some of these have quite low solubility products, e.g., $PbCrO_4$ with the value of K_{so} = = $10^{-12.5}$ M^2. This value is not reached, however, the product $[Pb^{2+}][CrO_4^{2-}]$ only amounting to at most $\simeq 10^{-19}$ M^2.

In contrast the divalent ions of zinc, copper, nickel, and cobalt form complexes with the anions present. Among these, the doubly charged oxygen donor CO_3^{2-} is certainly most strongly coordinated, though no very accurate values are known for the stability constants. The values of log β_1 entered in Table 4 must be considered as approximate. In fact, constants have been experimentally determined only for Cu^{2+} and Zn^{2+}, and only at I = 0 [20]. These constants have been recalculated to the actual medium by subtracting 2.0 from the values of log β_1 at I = 0, a reasonable procedure considering what has been found for the alkaline earth carbonates (Table 3). The constants for Ni^{2+} and Co^{2+} are estimates arrived at with the aid of Irving-Williams order, an affinity trend characteristic for complexes of the divalent first row transition metal ions. This trend has been found valid for so many different ligands that it certainly applies also to the present systems.

TABLE 4. Distribution on various species (α, %) of divalent first row transition metal ions of class (a).

	MOH^+	MCO_3	M^{2+}	MOH^+	MCO_3	MSO_4	MCl^+
	pK_1^*	$\log \beta_1$			α		
Co	9.85	3.4	54	1	7	7	31
Ni	9.76	3.5	53	1	9	6	31
Cu	7.9	4.7	17	22	49	2	10
Zn	9.5	3.3	55	2	6	6	31

$\log \beta_1(SO_4^{2-}) = 1$, $\log \beta_1(Cl^-) = 0$
$pH = 8.0$, $p[CO_3^{2-}] = 4.25$, $p[SO_4^{2-}] = 1.90$, $p[Cl^-] = 0.25$

TABLE 5. Slightly soluble carbonate phases of divalent cobalt, copper, and zinc. The values K_{so} and the ionic products refer to the conditions in seawater at a total concentration of each metal $= 10^{-7}$ M, $p[CO_3^{2-}] = 4.25$, and $p[OH^-] = 5.8$ [20, 24].

Solid	$\log K_{so}$	$\log$ ionic product
$CoCO_3$	-7.0	-11.5
$CuCO_3$	-7.6	-12.0
$ZnCO_3$	-8.8	-11.5
$Cu_2(OH)_2CO_3$ *	-30.6	-31.2
$Cu_3(OH)_2(CO_3)_2$ **	-40.8	-43.2

* Malachite   ** Azurite

These constants are not better known due to the easy formation of slightly soluble carbonate phases. Some of these are listed in Table 5. For the simple carbonates, the values of $\log K_{so}$ have been estimated by adding 2.0 to the values determined at $I = 0$. For malachite and azurite, a reasonable estimate for seawater should be obtained by adding 0.3 and 0.5, respectively, to the values deter-

mined for $I = 0.2$ M [20]. With a total metal concentration $C_M =$
$= 10^{-7}$ M, values of [M] can be found from Table 4. Hence the ionic
products, $[M^{2+}][CO_3{}^{2-}]$, can be calculated for the simple carbonates as well as the corresponding expressions for malachite and
azurite. The solubility products for the simple carbonates are not
closely approached. Rather it seems as if the solubility of copper
(II) in seawater might in fact be controlled by the solubility
product of malachite.

In addition, protonated carbonate complexes may conceivably be formed but, as pointed out above, their stability constants are much
lower than those of the unprotonated complexes (for the present
acceptors at least by a factor $\simeq 1000$). As the ratio $[HCO_3]/[CO_3^{2-}]$
is $\simeq 35$, this means that the complexes $MHCO_3^+$ are present only in
small amounts. Only in the case of Cu^{2+} might its share be as high
as $\simeq 1$ %, while for the other ions it must be negligible.

The sulfate complexes are much weaker than the carbonate ones. Their
equilibrium constants are generally not known for the actual medium,
but a value of $\log \beta_1 = 1$ for all of them seems to be a very reasonable estimate. The chloride complexes are weaker still, with
$\log \beta_1 = 0$ for all as the best estimate [24].

The result of the calculations is presented in Table 4. For cobalt,
nickel, and zinc, the hydrated ions predominate. Due to the high
chloride concentration, the chloride complexes come next, in spite
of their low value of β_1. They account for about one third of the
total. Part of this might be in the form of the second complex
MCl_2, but the data available do not warrant any partition between
consecutive chloride complexes. The higher affinity of the sulfate
ion, and especially the carbonate ion, to the metal ions cannot
compensate their lower concentrations, the part present as sulfate
and carbonate complexes amounting only to about 6 % and 8 %, respectively. For all the three metals mentioned the hydrolysis is
practically negligible.

Copper, on the other hand, shows a pattern distinctly different from
the one common to the other metals. For this metal, the hydroxide
and especially the carbonate complexes are the predominating species, with the hydrated ion next. The chloride and particularly

the sulfate complexes are only of minor importance.

Among the other elements of (a)-character present as traces in seawater, aluminium, thorium, and uranium will be briefly treated here.
The fate of a possible plutonium pollution will also be discussed
in this connection.

At pH = 8, the hydrolysis of the small and highly charged Al^{3+} has
already proceeded beyond the slightly soluble $Al(OH)_3$ into the formation of mononuclear aluminate ions. In seawater, the constant of
the equilibrium $Al(OH)_3(s) + H_2O \rightleftharpoons Al(OH)_4^- + H^+$ can be estimated to
$*K_{s4} = [Al(OH)_4^-] \cdot h = 10^{-12.7}$ M^2 which would mean an equilibrium concentration of $Al(OH)_4^-$ of $10^{-4.7}$ M. The actual aluminium concentration, $\simeq 10^{-7.4}$ M, is thus easily accomodated in the form of $Al(OH)_4^-$.
The existence of a soluble neutral complex $Al(OH)_3$ has not been
proved beyond doubt [5, 6, 24].

The even more highly charged and much larger Th^{4+} is an acid of
about the same strength as Al^{3+}, but it does not form small soluble
anionic species at high values of pH. Instead, highly polynuclear
aggregates of very low solubility are formed which are also easily
sorbed on other solid phases. As a consequence, the concentration
of thorium in seawater is in fact too low to be reliably determined,
in any case $< 10^{-12}$ M [17].

Uranium(VI) is the stable oxidation state of this element. A partial hydrolysis to uranyl(VI), UO_2^{2+}, always takes place in water.
The ion UO_2^{2+} is a fairly strong acid, though considerably weaker
than Th^{4+}. A most remarkable property of UO_2^{2+} is its ability to form
strong and soluble complexes with CO_3^{2-}. This is due to the peculiar
build of UO_2^{2+} which allows the coordination of CO_3^{2-} as a chelate. For
ions of spherical symmetry, CO_3^{2-} which generally acts as a bridging
ligand causes the formation of large aggregates which account for
the low solubility of most metal carbonates. In excess carbonate,
the final uranyl complex formed is no doubt $UO_2(CO_3)_3^{4-}$ [24]. It is
not certain, however, whether this complex is the predominating
one at the fairly low concentration of CO_3^{2-} in seawater. The constant
K_3 for the equilibrium $UO_2(CO_3)_2^{2-} + CO_3^{2-} \rightleftharpoons UO_2(CO_3)_3^{4-}$ is not very
accurately known, least of all in the present medium. A reasonable
estimate is $K_3 \simeq 10^5$ M^{-1} which would mean a preponderance of the

third complex at the actual $p[CO_3^{2-}] = 4.25$. Due to the existence of
these strong and soluble complexes, the concentration of uranium in
seawater, $\simeq 10^{-8}$ M, is much higher than that of thorium.
Plutonium has perhaps more complicated redox properties than any
other element, illustrated by the fact that no less than four oxidation states, from trivalent to hexavalent, might coexist in perceptible amounts in aqueous solution [3]. In strongly acid solutions
containing no strong complexing agents, these are present as the
hydrated ions Pu^{3+}, Pu^{4+}, PuO_2^+, and PuO_2^{2+}, respectively, which all
have their analogues for other actinides, cf. the species Th^{4+} and
UO_2^{2+} discussed above. Among these, Pu^{4+}, like Th^{4+}, is completely
hydrolyzed at the pH of seawater to large insoluble aggregates
while PuO_2^{2+}, like UO_2^{2+}, would stay in solution as carbonate complexes. The ions Pu^{3+} and PuO_2^+ are little hydrolyzed and do not
form any strong complexes in seawater. Consequently, relative to
acidic aqueous solutions, the redox equilibria in seawater are very
much displaced in favor of the tetra- and hexavalent states. Due to
the high oxidation potential of the plutonium(VI)/plutonium(IV) couple, the tetravalent state will probably prevail at the pH of seawater, though no quantitative data are available to prove this de-
finitively. In this most plausible case, a plutonium pollution
would follow the path of thorium and not of uranium, i.e., it would
finally sink into the bottom sediments as insoluble aggregates of
plutonium(IV) hydroxide, or hydrous oxide.

Trace elements of class (b): oxidation states, hydrolysis, and complexes under aerobic conditions

Among the (b)-acceptors present as traces in seawater under aerobic
conditions, the d^{10}-acceptors cadmium(II), mercury(II), silver(I),
and gold(I) possess an interesting solution chemistry which is fairly well known. Therefore it seems suitable to discuss these acceptors primarily.

Cd^{2+} is an acceptor of mild (b)-character, with a chemistry intermediate between that of the rather marked (a)-acceptor Zn^{2+} and the
very marked (b)-acceptor Hg^{2+}. Though the chloride complexes of
Cd^{2+} are only moderately strong, they still completely dominate its
chemistry in seawater, with the second complex $CdCl_2$ as the major
species (Table 6). The bromide complexes are somewhat stronger, but

due to the low bromide concentration even the most abundant of them, the statistically favored mixed complex CdClBr, still makes up only $\simeq 0.2$ % of the total. The hydrolysis is negligible, $\simeq 0.1$ %, as well as the formation of carbonate and sulfate complexes.

TABLE 6. Stability constants for complexes formed by cadmium(II) and mercury(II) in seawater, and the distribution of the metals on the various species (α, %) [9, 11, 24].

	Cadmium(II)		Mercury(II)	
Species	log β	α	log β	α
M^{2+}	–	3	–	–
MOH^+	4.3	0.1	10.1	–
MCO_3	3.4	0.4	–	–
MCl^+	1.36	34	6.74	–
MCl_2	1.79	51	13.22	3
MCl_3^-	1.44	12	14.07	12
MCl_4^{2-}	–	–	15.07	66
MBr^+	1.56	0.1	9.05	–
$MClBr$	2.25	0.2	15.88	2
MCl_2Br^-	2.14	–	16.44	4
MCl_3Br^{2-}	–	–	17.15	12
$MClOH$	–	–	17.43	0.2
MSO_4	1	0.3	1.3	–

$p[OH^-] = 5.8$, $p[CO_3^{2-}] = 4.25$, $p[Cl^-] = 0.25$, $p[Br^-] = 3.07$
$p[SO_4^{2-}] = 1.90$

Hg^{2+} is a very marked (b)-acceptor, forming very strong halide complexes. The bromide complexes are, moreover, much stronger than the chloride ones. Consequently, though the final chloride complex $HgCl_4^{2-}$ is the predominating species, considerable amounts not only of $HgCl_3^-$ but also of the mixed complex $HgCl_3Br^{2-}$ are also present (Table 6). The complexes $HgCl_2Br^-$, $HgClBr$, and $HgCl_2$ also presumably exist in perceptible amounts. Hydrolytic, carbonate, and sulphate complexes are virtually absent, however [9]. A typical (b)-acceptor, mercury(II), has, on the other hand, a very strong affinity to ligands coordinating via sulphur. Such ligands are present in

living organisms, and they may at least temporarily and locally
completely sequester the low concentrations of mercury present,
10^{-9} to 10^{-10} M. Once the organic matter has been degraded, however,
such ligands presumably succumb fairly rapidly to oxidation under
aerobic conditions. In any case, no such ligands seem to have been
identified beyond doubt as a dissolved species in normal seawater.
Presumably, their concentration is therefore $\lesssim 10^{-10}$ M, which would
mean that they would have to have extremely high stability constants
in order to compete seriously with the halide ions for the mercury.
It should be remembered that even the bromide ion, at the comparatively high $[Br^-] \simeq 10^{-3}$ M, still plays only a modest part in the
complex formation, in spite of its strong affinity for mercury(II).
It should also be remembered, however, that preformed organic mercury complexes may be kinetically inert and hence survive for a long
time in seawater, as is the case with the alkylmercury compounds.

Ag^+ is also a typical (b)-acceptor, with a strong affinity for chloride and bromide ions. The neutral complexes are slightly soluble,
which is not the case for mercury and even less for cadmium. At the
halide concentration of seawater, however, silver exists almost
exclusively as anionic species which do not form slightly soluble
phases. The solubility products of AgCl and AgBr are not exceeded.
The bromide complexes are stronger than the chloride ones but the
difference is less than for mercury(II). Consequently, the mixed
chloride-bromide complexes are much less important. The distribution between various complexes calculated with stability constants
corrected to the actual medium are given in Table 7. The predomi-
nant complex is $AgCl_4^{3-}$, but $AgCl_3^{2-}$ and $AgCl_2^-$ are also important. The
distribution between $AgCl_4^{3-}$ and $AgCl_3^{2-}$ is somewhat in doubt, however,as
the correction of the constants β_3 and β_4 to the present medium is
a little uncertain. The share of the most prominent mixed complex,
$AgCl_3Br^{3-}$, is only $\simeq 2$ %, as against 12 % for its mercury(II) analogue $HgCl_3Br^{2-}$. The hydrolysis of silver(I) is negligible, as well
as the formation of other complexes coordinating via oxygen.

Both gold(I) and gold(III) are certainly even more marked (b)-accep-
tors than any of the acceptors discussed previously. The predominating complex of gold(I) at the actual $[Cl^-]$ is certainly $AuCl_2^-$,

TABLE 7. Stability constants for complexes formed by silver(I) and gold(I) and the distribution of the metals on the various species $(\alpha, \%)$ [10, 13, 19, 24].

	silver(I)		gold(I)	
Species	$\log \beta$	α	$\log \beta^{*}$	α
MCl	2.7	0.4		
MCl_2^-	4.6	17	9.8, 11.9	94
MCl_3^{2-}	5.0	24		
MCl_4^{3-}	5.6	54		
MBr	4.0	–		
MBr_2^-	7.0	–	13.0, 15.1	0.3
MBr_3^{2-}	8.0	–		
MBr_4^{3-}	9.0	–		
$MClBr^-$	6.1	0.8	11.7, 13.8	6
MCl_2Br^{2-}	6.5	1.2		
MCl_3Br^{3-}	7.1	2.3		

*Calculated with the two different values of $\beta_2(Cl)$ that are found from $E^o_{01} = 1.73$ and 1.85 V, respectively.

though the value of its stability constant β_2 is not exactly known. An approximate value can be found from the standard potentials of the redox systems $AuCl_2^- + e^- \rightleftharpoons Au(s) + 2Cl^-$ and $Au^+ + e^- \rightleftharpoons Au(s)$, however. At $I = 0$, the former system has $E^o_{10}(Cl) = 1148$ mV [19] while the most recent estimates of the latter system are $E^o_{10}(aq) = 1730$ mV [13] and 1850 mV [10], corresponding to values of $\beta_2 = 10^{9.8}$ M^{-2} and $10^{11.9}$ M^{-2}, respectively. In any case, the lower complex AuCl is not likely to be present in any perceptible amounts. On the other hand, no higher complex than $AuCl_2^-$ has ever been found; this is in striking contrast to silver(I). Consequently, $AuCl_2^-$ must be the only complex present of the formula $AuCl_n^{(n-1)-}$. Like the analogous silver(I) complex, $AuCl_2^-$ is not perceptibly hydrolyzed. For gold(III), on the other hand, the hydrolysis is quite extensive at pH = 8.0, as is evident from the constants of the equilibria $Au(OH)_{5-n}Cl_{n-1}^- + H^+ + Cl^- \rightleftharpoons Au(OH)_{4-n}Cl_n^-$. These have been determined for $I = 0$, partly also in 3 M $NaClO_4$ [24]. Together with the values obtained for the present medium by applying $f_\pm = 0.77$ for hydrochloric acid, these constants are listed in Table 8. Among the gold(III) species, $Au(OH)_3Cl^-$ predominates while only a very small part, $\simeq 10^{-4}$, is present as the unhydrolyzed $AuCl_4^-$ (Table 8).

TABLE 8. Constants for the equilibria $Au(OH)_{5-n}Cl_{n-1}^- + H^+ + Cl^- \rightleftharpoons$ $\rightleftharpoons Au(OH)_{4-n}Cl_n^- + H_2O$, and the distribution between different species of gold(III) at pH = 8 and $p[Cl^-] = 0.25$.

Species	n	I=0	I=3	Seawater	Seawater
		K_n	K_n		α
$Au(OH)_4^-$					23
$Au(OH)_3Cl^-$	1	8.7		8.6	52
$Au(OH)_2Cl_2^-$	2	8.0		7.9	23
$Au(OH)Cl_3^-$	3	7.15	7.04	7.04	2
$AuCl_4^-$	4	6.15	6.22	6.04	0.01

The distribution between gold(I) and gold(III) can be found from the standard potential E_{13}^o of the redox system $AuCl_4^- + 2e \rightleftharpoons AuCl_2^- +$ $+ 2Cl^-$. In seawater, the best value of E_{13}^o is probably close to 935 mV [26] which gives, with pE = 12.6 and $p[Cl] = 0.25$, a ratio $[AuCl_4^-]/[AuCl_2^-] = 10^{-6.9}$, i.e., a ratio gold(III)/gold(I) $\simeq 10^{-2.9}$. The gold(I) complexes thus predominate strongly.

Further, for the equilibrium between gold(I) and metal $AuCl_2^- + e^- \rightleftharpoons$ $\rightleftharpoons Au(s) + 2Cl^-$, the formal standard potential in the present medium is $E_{01}^o = 1113$ mV [26], implying that a concentration $[AuCl_2^-] = 10^{-6.7}$ M must be exceeded before $Au(s)$ is precipitated at pE = 12.6. With a total concentration of gold in seawater $\simeq 10^{-10}$ M, no gold is evidently present in the metallic state at equilibrium under these conditions. For values of $pE \lesssim 9.3$ reduction would occur, however.

From the difference between the standard potentials of the couples [19] $AuCl_2^- + e^- \rightleftharpoons Au(s) + 2Cl^-$ and $AuBr_2^- + e^- \rightleftharpoons Au(s) + 2Br^-$ under the same conditions, $E_{01}^o(Cl^-) = 1148$ mV and $E_{01}^o(Br) = 960$ at I = 0, the constant

$$K = \frac{[AuBr_2^-][Cl^-]^2}{[AuCl_2^-][Br^-]^2} = \frac{\beta_2(Br)}{\beta_2(Cl)} = 10^{3.18} \qquad (9)$$

of the equilibrium $AuCl_2^- + 2Br^- \rightleftharpoons AuBr_2^- + 2Cl^-$ can be calculated. On the usual assumption that the mixed complex $AuClBr^-$ is stabilized by the statistical factor 2 relative to $AuCl_2^-$ and $AuBr_2^-$ it is further possible to calculate the constant

$$K' = \frac{[AuBrCl^-][Cl^-]}{[AuCl_2^-][Br^-]} = 2\sqrt{\frac{\beta_2(Br)}{\beta_2(Cl)}} = 10^{1.89} \qquad (10)$$

Hence the distribution on the various complexes can be calculated (Table 7). Very little of the bromide complex $AuBr_2^-$ is present, whereas the mixed complex $AuClBr^-$ exists in fair amounts. Still, by far the largest part of the gold is present as $AuCl_2^-$.

Oxidation states and complexes formed under anoxic conditions

As already mentioned, the oxidation states of the major metal ions of seawater are not changed by any reasonable change of pE or pH. On the other hand, many trace metals are profoundly affected. The reactions taking place under various conditions of lower pE are so far not very extensively or accurately known. The subject will therefore only be dealt with briefly here, in the form of a few selected examples.

The oxidation states and solid phases of iron and manganese stable for various values of pE have been thoroughly discussed [23]. Though many of the fundamental data are very uncertain, there is no doubt that the stable iron phase under aerobic conditions is $FeO(OH)$, as stated above. As pE decreases, Fe_3O_4 presumably becomes the stable phase, possibly followed by $FeCO_3$, until finally pyrite, FeS_2, comes to the fore at the low value of pE reached in sulfide solutions. For manganese, MnO_2 is seemingly the stable phase over a rather wide range of pE, perhaps down to pE $\simeq 8$. It is not certain whether $MnO(OH)$ and/or Mn_3O_4 appear as stable phases. At lower values of pE, $MnCO_3$ is most probably the stable solid phase. Only at very low values of pE, $\simeq -10$, would the sulfide phase MnS be stable.

While copper(II) is stable under aerobic conditions, copper(I) becomes stable as the value of pE decreases. With E_{01}^o = 158.6 mV for the redox system $Cu^{2+} + e^- \rightleftharpoons Cu^+$ and the constants $\beta_2 = 10^{5.0}$ M^{-2} and $K_3^{\ *} = 10^{-0.35}$ M^{-1} for the equilibria $Cu^+ + 2Cl^- \rightleftharpoons CuCl_2^-$ and $CuCl_2^- + Cl^- \rightleftharpoons CuCl_3^{2-}$, respectively, the amount of monovalent copper is larger than that of divalent for pE < 6.7. On the other hand, copper(I) is so highly stabilized by the high $[Cl^-]$ that, assuming a value of E_{01}^o = 518.2 mV for the system $Cu^+ + e^- \rightleftharpoons Cu(s)$, a reduction of a 10^{-7} M solution of copper(I) to the metallic state takes place only for pE < -2.7. It is then assumed that no further ligands occur in the solution. Under typically anoxic conditions sulfide is also present, however. At the lowest value of $pE \simeq 7$ where $[Cu^{2+}]$ still might be of the order 10^{-7} M, a concentration of $[S^{2-}] \gtrsim 10^{-29}$ M has to be reached in order to bring about a precipitation of CuS(s), with $K_{so} = 10^{-36.1}$ M^2. The highest value of $[S^{2-}]$ possible at pE = 7 can be calculated from the E_s^o = 141 mV of the redox system $S(s) + 2H^+ + 2e^- \rightleftharpoons H_2S(aq)$ [15] and the constant $K_1 \cdot K_2 = 10^{21}$ M^{-2} [27] of the equilibrium $2H^+ + S^{2-} \rightleftharpoons H_2S(aq)$. It turns out to be $[S^{2-}] = 10^{-30.3}$ M. A precipitation of CuS(s) will therefore hardly take place. In order that $Cu_2S(s)$ might precipitate, $K_{so} = 10^{-48.9}$ M^3 has to be exceeded [15]. A total concentration of copper (I) $\simeq 10^{-7}$ M means at the present $[Cl^-]$ a $[Cu^+] \simeq 10^{-11.5}$ M, and hence a value of $[S^{2-}] > 10^{-25.9}$ M in order to bring about precipitation. This value can be reached as soon as $pE \simeq 4.8$. At higher values of $[S^{2-}]$ which are possible at lower values of pE, soluble sulfide complexes may also be formed. To what extent such a complex formation takes place is presently unknown, but certain inferences are possible from the analogous silver(I) complexes which have been thoroughly investigated.

At the value of $pH \simeq 7.5$ often found under anoxic conditions, the soluble silver sulfide complex mainly formed is $Ag(SH)_2^-$ [21]. The constant of the equilibrium $Ag_2S(s) + H_2S + 2HS^- \rightleftharpoons 2Ag(SH)_2^-$ is $K_{s2} = 10^{-8.05}$ M^{-1}. At a total sulfide concentration = 0.5 mM, implying $[H_2S] = 10^{-4}$ M and $[HS^-] = 4 \cdot 10^{-4}$ M, this means an equilibrium concentration $[Ag(SH)_2^-] = 10^{-9.4}$ M, which is not much less than the total concentration of silver generally found in seawater. Already a fourfold increase of the sulfide concentration to 2 mM would mean an

$[Ag(SH)_2^-] = 10^{-8.5}$ M, i.e, probably the whole amount of silver present. The chloride complexes are not strong enough to compete with this sulfide complex, the stability constant β_2 of which is $\beta_2(S) = 10^{17.2}$ M^{-2} [18]. Hence,

$$\frac{[AgCl_2^-]}{[Ag(SH)_2^-]} = \frac{\beta_2(Cl)[Cl-]^2}{\beta_2(S)[SH^-]^2} = 10^{-9.5} \tag{11}$$

i.e., a negligible fraction. At lower sulfide concentrations, silver will be present as $Ag_2S(s)$ with $K_{so} = 10^{-49.7}$ M^3 which is not very different from K_{so} of $Cu_2S(s)$. It may be inferred that though part of the copper may be present at soluble copper(I) sulfide complexes under anoxic conditions, it is unlikely that this will be the case for the whole concentration of $\simeq 10^{-7}$ M, except for very extreme concentrations of sulfide.

Concluding remarks

It should be emphasized once more that the considerations above refer to equilibrium conditions and that several of the reactions discussed reach equilibrium only slowly. This applies especially when gases or solids are involved. It should also be remembered that the equilibria change considerably with temperature and pressure and that these changes are not well understood at present. Also, the identities and concentrations of strongly sequestering organic ligands are virtually unknown, and their influence cannot, therefore, be accounted for. Finally, fairly large volumes of seawater do not have the standard salinity of 35 ‰ presumed in the reasonings above, but are more saline, like the Mediterranean, or more or less brackish, as the Baltic. The discussion conducted here should therefore be regarded as no more than a fairly rough sketch, which nevertheless ought to give a true picture of the main features of metal complexation in seawater.

References

(1) Ahrland, S. 1966. Factors contributing to (b)-behaviour in accep-
     tors. Structure and Bonding 1: 207-220.

(2) Ahrland, S. 1968. Thermodynamics of complex formation between
     hard and soft acceptors and donors. Structure and Bonding 5:
     118-149.

(3) Ahrland, S., Liljenzin, J.O., and Rydberg, J. 1973. The actini-
     des: Solution chemistry. In Comprehensive Inorganic Chemistry,
     5, pp. 465-635. Oxford and New York. Pergamon Press.

(4) Bäckström, H.L.J. 1921. Über die Affinität der Aragonit-Calcit-
     Umvandlung. Z. physik. Chem. 97: 179-228.

(5) Baes, C.F.J. and Mesmer, R.E. 1974. The hydrolysis of cations,
     ORNL - NSF - EATC-3, Oak Ridge National Laboratory, Oak Ridge,
     Tennessee.

(6) Brosset, C., Biedermann, G., and Sillén, L.G. 1954. Studies on
     the hydrolysis of metal ions XI. The aluminium ion, Al^{3+}. Acta
     Chem. Scand. 8: 1917-1926.

(7) Chesselet, R. 1974. Proc. III. Intern. Symposium on the Chemist-
     ry of the Mediterranean, Rovinj, Yugoslavia.

(8) Dyrssen, D. Private communication.

(9) Dyrssen, D.,and Wedborg, M. 1974. Equilibrium calculations of
     the speciation of elements in seawater. In The Sea 5, ed. E.D.
     Goldberg, pp. 181-195. John Wiley and Sons.

(10) Erenburg, A.M. and Peshchevitskii, B.I. 1969. Standard poten-
     tials of the aquogold(I) ion. Russ. J. Inorg. Chem. 14: 1429-
     1431.

(11) Gerding, P. and Jönsson, I. 1968. Thermochemical studies on me-
     tal complexes VII. Acta Chem. Scand. 22: 2247-2254.

(12) Hawley, J. and Pytkowicz, R.M. 1969. Solubility of calcium carbon-
     ate in seawater at high pressures and 2^oC. Geochim. Cosmochim. Acta
     33: 1557-1561.

(13) Hancock, R.D. and Finkelstein, N.P. 1971. π- and σ-bonding in
     the stabilities of d^{10} metal-ion complexes in aqueous solution.
     Inorg. Nucl. Chem. Lett. 7: 477-484.

(14) Ingle, S.E., Culberson, C.H., Hawley, J.E.,and Pytkowicz, R.M.
     1973. The solubility of calcite in seawater at atmospheric pres-
     sure and 35 ‰ salinity. Marine Chem. 1: 295-307.

(15) Latimer, W.M. 1952. Oxidation Potentials, 2 ed., Englewood
     Cliffs, N.J.: Prentice Hall.

(16) Liss, P.S., Hering, J.R., and Goldberg, E.D. 1973. The iodide/
     iodate system in seawater as a possible measure of redox poten-
     tial. Nature Phys. Sci. 242: 108-109.

(17) Marine Chemistry. A report of the Marine Chemistry Panel of the
     Committee on Oceanography 1971. Washington D.C.: National Aca-
     demy of Sciences.

(18)   Pearson, R.G. 1968. Hard and soft acids and bases. J. Chem.
       Educ. 45: 581-587, 643-648.

(19)   Poaradier, J., Gadet, M.-C., and Chateau, H. 1965. Electrochi-
       mie de sels d'or, I and II. J. Chim. Phys. 62: 203-216, 1181-
       1186.

(20)   Schindler, P., Reinert, M., and Gamsjäger, H. 1968. Löslich-
       keitskonstanten und Freie Bildungsenthalpien von $Cu_2(OH)_2CO_3$
       (Malachit) und $Cu_3(OH)_2(CO_3)_2$(Azurit) bei $25^{\circ}C$. Helv. Chim.
       Acta 51: 1845-1856.

(21)   Schwarzenbach, G., and Widmer, M. 1966. Die Löslichkeit von
       Metallsulfiden II. Silbersulfid. Helv. Chim. Acta 49: 111-123.

(22)   Sillén, L.G. 1961. The physical chemistry of seawater. In
       Oceanography, ed. M. Sears, pp. 549-581. Amer. Assoc. Advanc.
       Science.

(23)   Sillén, L.G. 1966. Oxidation state of Earth's ocean and atmos-
       phere. Arkiv Kemi 25: 159-176.

(24)   Sillén, L.G. and Martell, A.E. 1964, 1971. Stability Constants
       of Metal Ion Complexes. London. The Chemical Society, special
       publications No 17 and 25.

(25)   Stumm, W. and Brauner, P.A. 1973. Chemical Speciation. In
       Chemical Oceanography, 2. ed., ed. J.P. Riley and G. Skirrow,
       Acedemic Press.

(26)   Tschappat, C., and Robert, E. 1954. Contribution a l'étude du
       potential de l'or. Helv. Chim. Acta 37: 333-344.

(27)   Widmer, M. and Schwarzenbach, G. 1964. Die Acidität des Hydro-
       gensulfidions HS^-. Helv. Chim. Acta 47: 266-271.

Organic Ligands in Natural Systems

Gunther L. Eichhorn
National Institutes of Health, Gerontology Research Center,
Laboratory of Molecular Aging, Baltimore City Hospitals,
Baltimore, Maryland 21224

Abstract: Since metal ions play an important role in biological processes, living organisms contain a large number of organic ligands specifically designed for metal binding. Many other biological molecules possess functional groups that can serve as potential ligands.

Introduction

It is of course obvious that the composition of ocean water is affected by the composition of the living organisms that are found within it. One of the ways in which living organisms can affect the chemistry of the water is through control of the chemical form of metal ions by ligands contained in the organisms. Very little is known at present about the nature of such interactions between living organisms and sea water. To provide a basis for such studies it is of some use to consider the nature of the organic ligands that can be found in living organisms.

It would certainly not fit the purposes of this symposium to discuss this topic either comprehensively, or with any degree of depth, or to deal very much with the biological significance of the substances. Rather an attempt will be made to illustrate the types of ligands characteristic of living organisms. The reader is referred to the literature for broader and deeper expositions [9, 36].

Many biological ligands for metal ions can be found in a wide

variety of   species, with little or no difference in structure.
Some ligands nevertheless are characteristic of certain species.
For this brief discussion of ligand types species differences
will not be considered; instead the presentation will be concerned with those species for which the best information is
available, whether or not the species are from the marine environment.

Biological ligands exist in part because metal binding is important to living organisms. Therefore some ligands are designed for metal binding. Other biological molecules contain functional groups that are not designed for metal binding but that
nevertheless will bind metal ions when the latter come in contact with them. Both types of ligands must be considered.

Nucleic Acids and Their Constituents as Ligands

Since the nucleic acids are the bearers of genetic information,
they are constituents of all living matter. They consist of a
backbone in which phosphate groups alternate with sugar moieties;
the latter are attached to heterocyclic bases, the sequence of
which determines the genetic code. Two types of nucleic acid,
RNA and DNA, are differentiated by the nature of the sugar,
which is ribose in RNA (ribonucleic acid) and 2'-deoxyribose in
DNA (deoxynucleic acid).

The monomeric constituents of these nucleic acids are the nucle-
otides (with phosphate) or nucleosides (without phosphate). Nu-
cleoside diphosphates and triphosphates are also essential for
life processes; the latter are involved in a multitude of enzymatic reactions. The structure of a nucleotide is shown in Fig. 1.
Three general types of metal binding sites can be observed
in these molecules: the phosphate groups, the ribose hydroxyls,
and the oxygen and nitrogen atoms on the bases.

Metal ions will bind to all three of these sites [10, 11]. The
ribose site is perhaps least important for marine studies, since
it is favored only at high pH in aqueous solution, or in non-aqueous solution, or in non-aqueous solvents. The phosphate

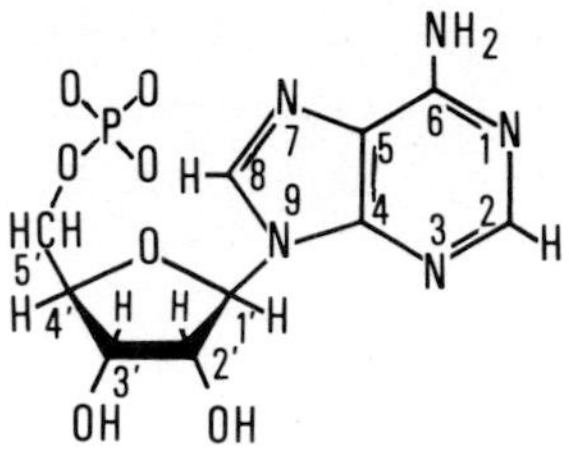

FIG. 1 - Nucleotide

groups and the bases form stable complexes in aqueous solution
at lower pH. Some metals, such as the alkalis and alkaline
earths, bind almost exclusively to phosphate, whereas others,
such as Ag^+, Hg^{2+}, and Pt^{4+}, bind to the bases. These metals
can be classified as hard, class (a), or soft, class (b), respectively [1, 29, 34]. Other metal ions, such as Cu^{2+}, Co^{2+},
and Ni^{2+}, bind to both phosphate and base groups. Although the
stability of the metal complexes of monomers is different from
that of the polymeric nucleic acids, the relative tendency to
bind these sites is approximately the same.

Amino Acids and Peptides as Ligands

Many structural and functional requirements of cells are fulfilled by proteins, which are polymers of amino acids that are joined together by peptide bonds. Amino acids and small oligopeptides occur in living matter as a result of a variety of biochemical processes. Metal ions bind to amino acids through the carboxyl and amino groups, as well as through the functional groups
that characterize specific amino acids, e.g. SH in cysteine,
CH_3S in methionine, OH in serine, imidazole in histidine, and
NH_2 in lysine. Peptide groups by themselves are poor electron
donors, but in conjunction with another electron donor atom four
or five atoms away, the peptide group can produce an effective
chelating agent (Fig. 2) [12]. Such chelation of peptide link-
ages can occur also when metal ions bind to proteins [4].

Low molecular weight oligopeptides have been designed in nature
for the purpose of complexing metal ions.

M = Ni(II), Co(III)   FIG. 2 - Glycylglycine Complex [12]

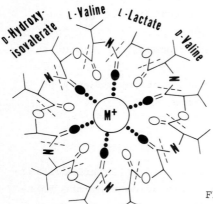

FIG. 3 - Valinomycin [31]

Among such oligopeptides are the "ionophores", a group of substances that bind alkali metals and can carry them across lipid
barriers [31]. These substances are illustrated by valinomycin
in Fig. 3. They generally form rings in which the metal ions are
contained. Not all of these substances are peptides, but the
peptide and non-peptide ligands have somewhat similar structures.

Another group of substances, some of them oligopeptides produced by micro-organisms, are the siderochromes, which are

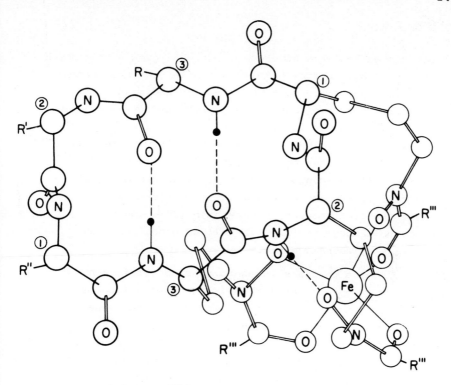

FIG. 4 - Ferrichrome [26]

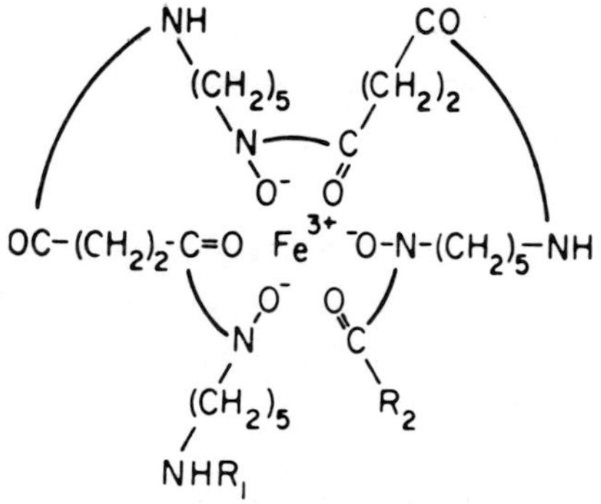

FIG. 5 - Ferrioxamine B [30]
R_1 = H
R_2 = CH_3

designed to transport iron [26]. Figure 4 demonstrates the
structure of ferrichrome, a peptide siderochrome and Fig. 5 de-
picts ferrioxamine, a non-peptide type [30]. These ligands form
extremely strong complexes with iron(III), and have been commercially produced as iron ligands [30].

Proteins as Ligands

It has been noted that the numerous functional groups contained
in proteins are able to form complexes similar to those obtained
from amino acids and small peptides [4]. In addition to this
general capacity for complexation many proteins contain sites
specifically designed for binding metal ions. Some of these
proteins exhibit an ability to store or to transport metals,
e.g. ferritin [16] and the transferrins [2] for iron, and
ceruloplasmin [33] for copper. Other proteins are designed
to bind a metal ion which in turn binds molecular oxygen;
examples are the iron protein, hemerythrin [27], and the
copper protein, hemocyanin [22], as well as hemoglobin and
myoglobin, to be discussed below.

Many of the proteins that are intended to bind metals are enzymes that require metal ions for their function, often as part
of the catalytic site. Some of these enzymes contain the metal
ion strongly bound and are isolated in association with it.
These are sometimes called metalloenzymes. Others are isolated
without a metal ion but require the addition of metal ions for
activity. These may be called metal activated enzymes.

One of the most thoroughly studied of the metal enzymes is bovine pancreatic carboxypeptidase [23]. We shall consider some
of its characteristics to illustrate the binding properties of
such a protein. The bovine enzyme is incidentally very similar
to the much less understood dogfish enzyme [23].

Carboxypeptidase contains one atom of zinc per molecule. The
zinc is on the active site, where it is attached to the protein
through three nitrogen atoms, two from histidines and one from
a lysine. Figure 6 is a diagram of the carboxypeptidase
structure [21]. One coordination position on the zinc is free
to bind to the substrate.

It is possible to remove the zinc, and replace it with other
metal ions, e.g. Ni^{2+}, Co^{2+}, Mn^{2+}, Cd^{2+}, Hg^{2+}, and Cu^{2+}. Some
of these substituted enzymes retain activity; apparently the
active site is not damaged by this displacement [7].

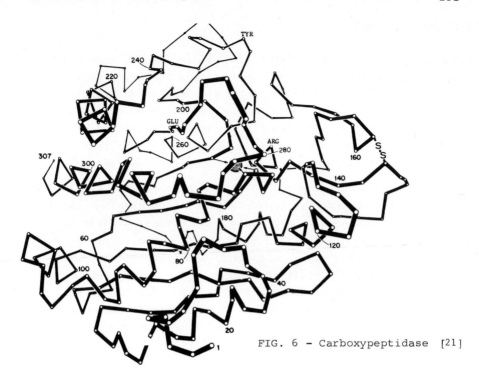

FIG. 6 - Carboxypeptidase [21]

A number of other metalloenzymes from which it has been possible
to replace the native metal by other metal ions have the common
characteristic that they are zinc enzymes. They are carbonic
anhydrase [6], alkaline phosphatase [37], and alcohol dehydro-
genase [35]. Metal activated enzymes frequently work best with
a specific metal ion, which may however be replaced. The metal
enzymes that can function with a variety of metal ions are generally the hydrolytic enzymes. Oxidation-reduction enzymes are
very specifically constructed for a given metal, generally iron
or copper, and in this instance the metal cannot be displaced.
Examples of such enzymes that are specifically constructed for
copper binding are ascorbate oxidase [25], tryrosinase, laccase,
and galaxtose oxidase [24].

Iron – Sulfur Proteins

One of the more interesting types of protein ligands is a class
of compounds, important in electron transfer reaction, in which
iron atoms are surrounded by sulfur [28]. The sulfur donor
atoms are supplied either by sulfhydryl groups from cysteines or
as free sulfide ion that is readily removable by acid treatment.
Many of these ligands contain both labile and non-labile sulfur.
These proteins are also known by other names such as ferredoxins.

These ligands have been classified on the basis of the number of
iron atoms that they contain [28]. Most of them have one labile
sulfur atom associated with each iron. Structural studies on
some of these compounds indicate that the iron and labile sulfur
atoms occupy alternate edges of a cube, and that cysteine sulfhydryl groups are additionally bonded to the irons to produce
iron tetrahedra. Such structures are feasible for the four
and eight-iron containing molecules. Other ligands bind one
and two atoms of iron; the structure of a one-iron containing
substance, rubredoxin, is shown in Fig. 7 [18].

Two iron-sulfur proteins make up nitrogenase [15], the enzyme
that can convert molecular nitrogen (dinitrogen) into ammonia.
One of the proteins contains molybdenum as well as iron.

Porphyrins and Hemoproteins

So far we have discussed protein ligands in which the electron
donor atoms are derived from functional groups of the amino
acids. (In the iron-sulfur proteins some of the donor groups
are sulfur atoms not attached to protein but these sulfur atoms
are not a part of an organic ligand.) A number of very important iron proteins contain the iron liganded to porphyrin [5],
which is a macrocycle that furnishes four nitrogen atoms for coordination. Figure 8 shows iron coordinated to protoporphyrin,
the most common of these substances [5]. The iron porphyrin
complex is called heme, and proteins containing heme are hemoproteins.

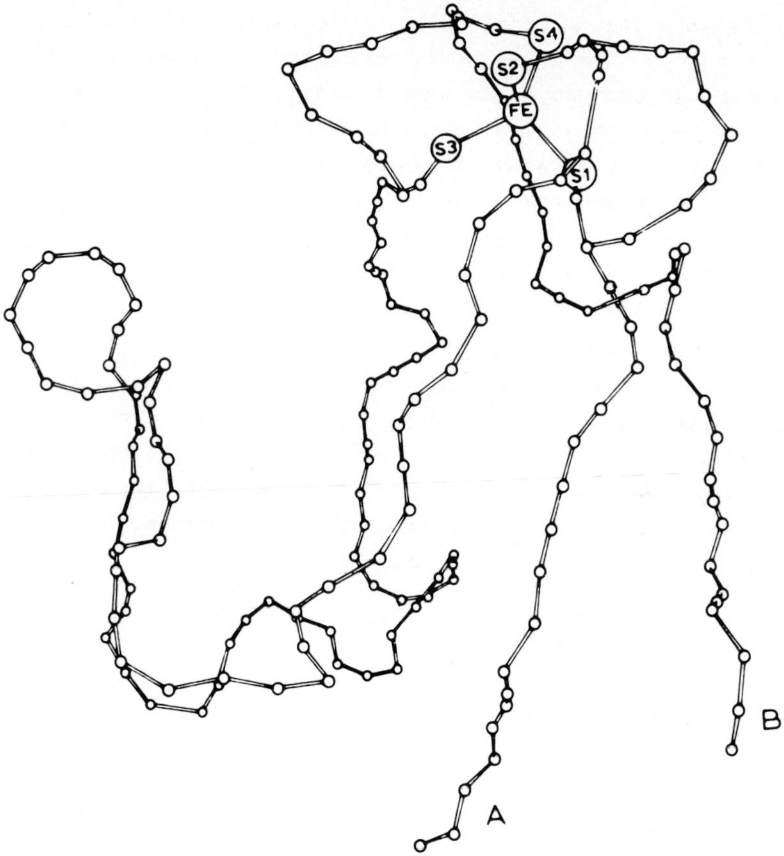

FIG. 7 - Rubredoxin [18]

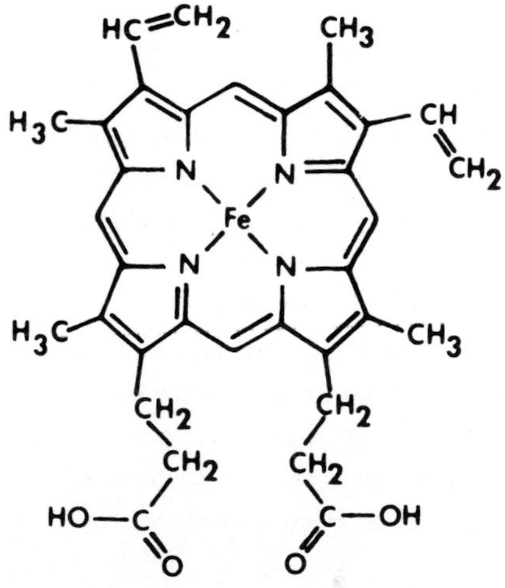

FIG. 8 - Heme

Heme is attached to proteins by coordination of amino acid side
chains through the axial position of the iron, and sometimes
also through the porphyrin side chains. Figure 9 demonstrates
the structural arrangement in cytochrome c [8, 14]. In this
molecule the two axial positions of iron are coordinated to a
histidine nitrogen and a methionine sulfur. Additionally, sulfhydryl groups from cysteines have added across the double bonds
of the vinyl side chains to form rigid covalent attachments
between porphyrin and protein.

Hemoproteins are not generally covalently bound to porphyrin
side chains, so that the only attachment is through coordination.
In hemoglobin and myoglobin only one coordination position is
used for protein binding. In the unoxygenated proteins the iron
has a coordination number of 5. When, in fulfillment of biological function, oxygen is bound to these molecules, the oxygen
occupies the sixth coordination position [32].

Catalase, peroxidase, and the various cytochromes are all hemoproteins.

Chlorophyll

The chlorophylls [20] are constituents of photosynthetic plants
and they are closely related to porphyrin. As Fig. 10 reveals,
chlorophyll a is essentially a porphyrin with one extra carbon
ring condensed to one of the pyrrole rings; another pyrrole ring
is partly reduced. Chlorophyll is a ligand for magnesium in its
natural state. The magnesium can be displaced by a variety of
other metal ions, but these do not confer biological activity.

Coenzyme B_{12}

Another structural relative of the porphyrins is coenzyme B_{12}
(Fig. 11). This substance, which is a component of a variety of
enzymatic reactions, can be considered a porphyrin derivative in
which all the pyrroles are reduced and one of the bridging carbon atoms has been eliminated [19]. The coenzyme metal ion is
cobalt(III).

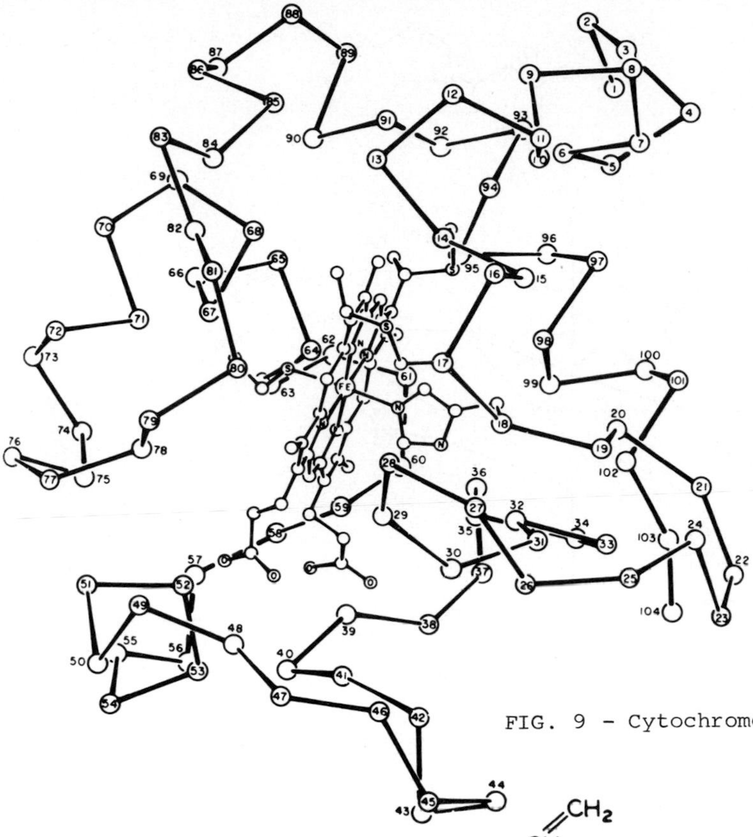

FIG. 9 - Cytochrome c [8]

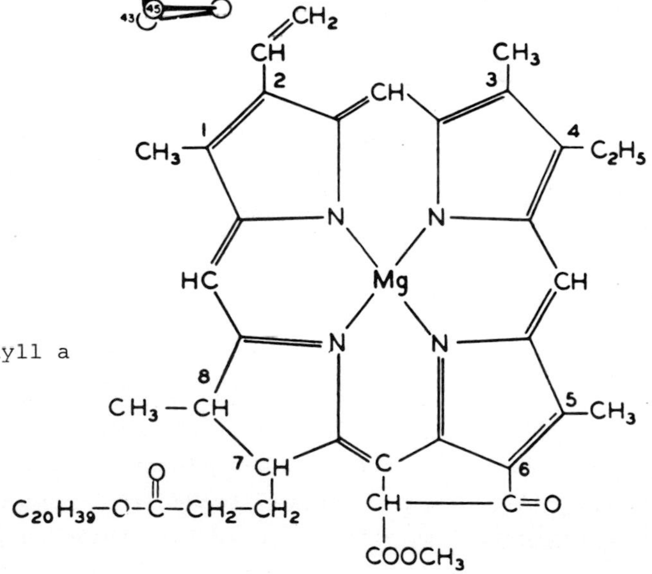

FIG. 10 - Chlorophyll a

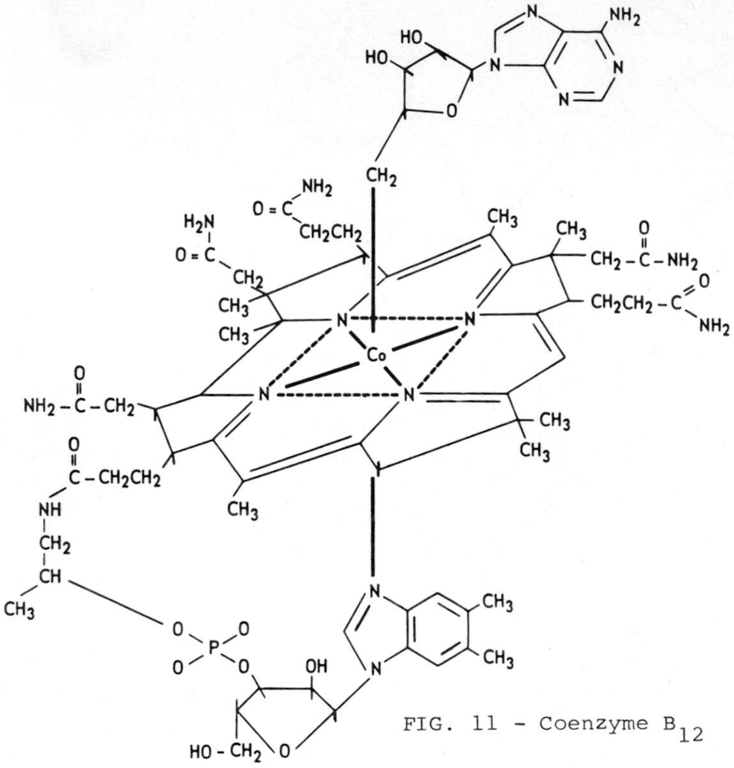

FIG. 11 - Coenzyme B$_{12}$

Other Coenzymes

Coenzymes are small molecules that are required as adjuncts to
the enzymatic proteins to produce enzyme action. Whereas coenzyme B$_{12}$ is a metal-containing coenzyme, many other coenzymes
have functional groups that make them potential ligands for
metal ions. Vitamin B$_6$ exists in a variety of forms, one of
which is pyridoxal phosphate [13]. The reaction of this molecule with amino acids produces a Schiff base which is an active
intermediate in a variety of biochemical reactions. Both the
vitamin (Fig. 12) and the Schiff base derivative form metal complexes (Fig. 13) [3].

Flavins (Fig. 14) form a number of different types of metal complexes [17]. Other coenzyme ligands are coenzyme A (Fig. 15),
the tripeptide glutathione (Fig. 16), thiamine pyrophosphate,

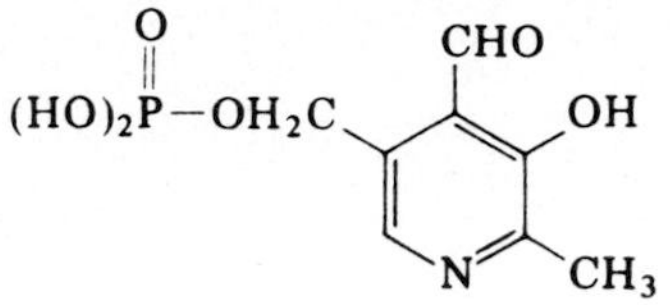

FIG. 12 – Pyridoxal Phosphate

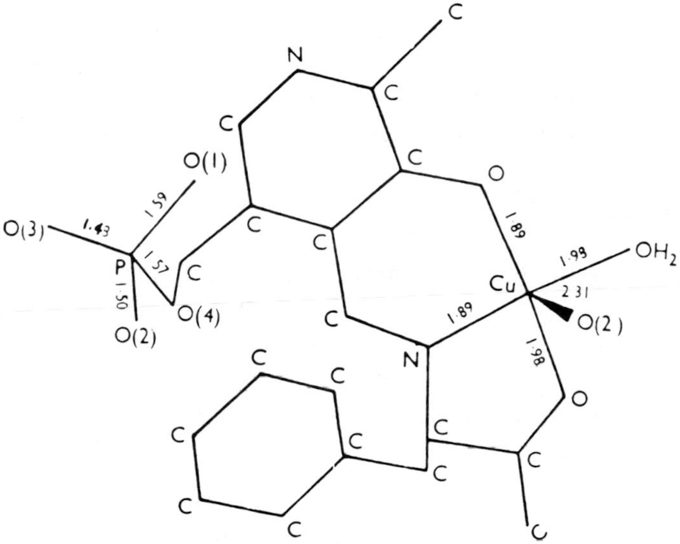

FIG. 13 – Copper Complex of Pyridoxal Phosphate –
Phenylalanine Schiff Base [3]

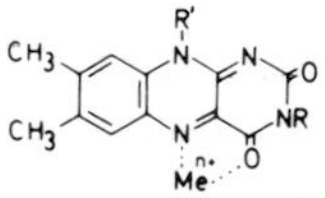

FIG. 14 – Flavin Complex [17]

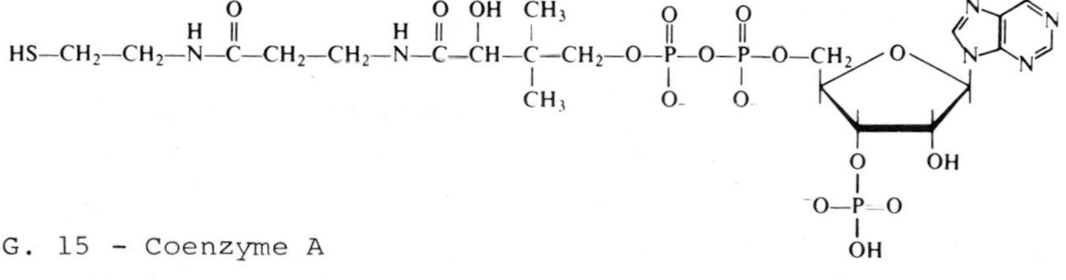

FIG. 15 – Coenzyme A

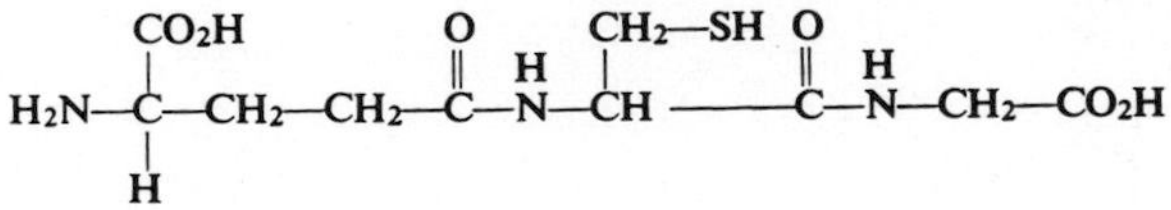

$$H_2N-\overset{\displaystyle CO_2H}{\underset{\displaystyle H}{C}}-CH_2-CH_2-\overset{O}{C}-\overset{H}{N}-\overset{CH_2-SH}{CH}-\overset{O}{C}-\overset{H}{N}-CH_2-CO_2H$$

FIG. 16 - Glutathione

tetrahydrofolic acid, nicotinamide adenine dinucleotide (NAD^+)
(Fig. 17) and the corresponding triphosphate ($NADP^+$).

Other Types of Ligands

Carbohydrates contain hydroxyl groups that are potential metal
binding agents. Phospholipids also contain electron donors;
these substances are generally derivatives of phosphatidic acids,
such as lecithin (Fig. 18). Some of these ligands bind metal
ions in biological processes, though little is known about
the structure of the resulting complexes.

Much remains to be learned about ligands designed for the transport of metal ions within the cell as well as about those that
are required for other biological processes. The present list
is illustrative of known and potential ligands, but is far from
exhaustive even of biological ligands that are known at this
time.

It must be recognized, of course, that many organic compounds
in the sea are not directly derived from living organisms,
but may be reaction products that have accumulated over long
periods of time. No consideration has been given here to such
poorly defined substances as the humic acids or to products
introduced into the sea through the activities of man. Biological ligands must be very important in a consideration of
organic ligands in the sea, and it is hoped that this chapter
can be useful to marine chemists for this reason. However, it
should be understood that biologically derived marine substances may have undergone numerous chemical changes before
attaining their present forms.

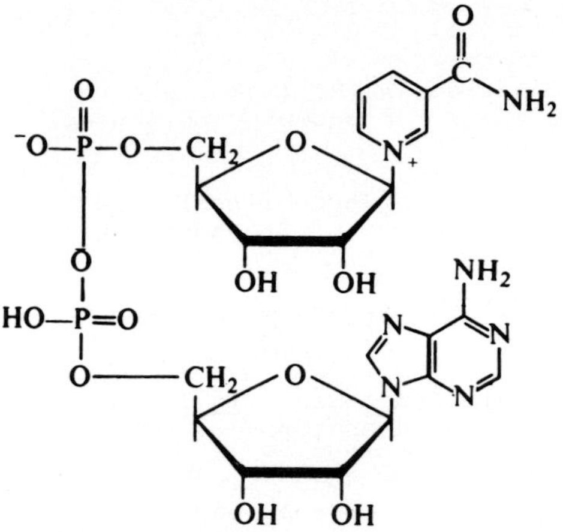

FIG. 17 - Nicotine Adenine Dinucleotide (NAD$^+$)

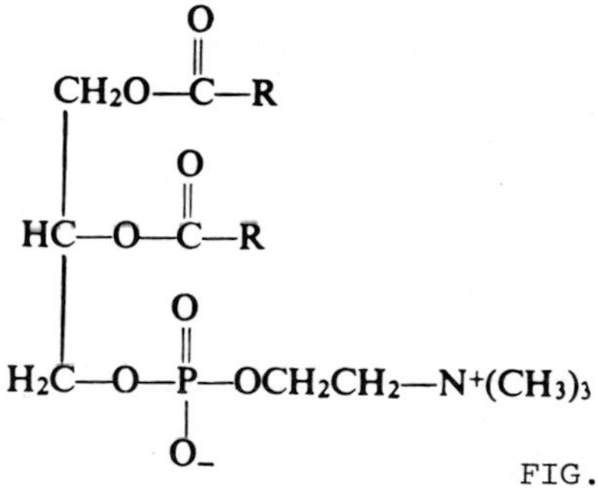

FIG. 18 - Lecithin (R is hydrocarbon)

References

(1)   Ahrland, S.; Chatt, J.; and Davies, N. R. 1958. The re-
      lative affinities of ligand atoms for acceptor molecules
      and ions. Quart. Rev. 12: 265-276.

(2)   Aisen, P. 1973. The Transferrins (Siderophilins). In
      Inorganic Biochemistry, Vol. 1, ed. G. L. Eichhorn, pp.
      280-305. Amsterdam: Elsevier.

(3)   Bentley, G. A.; Waters, J. M.; and Waters, T. N. 1968.
      Chem. Commun. 988.

(4)   Breslow, E. 1973. Metal-Protein Complexes. In Inorganic
      Biochemistry, Vol. 1, ed. G. L. Eichhorn, pp. 227-249.
      Amsterdam: Elsevier.

(5)   Caughey, W. S. 1973. Iron Porphyrins--Hemes and Hemins.
      In Inorganic Biochemistry, Vol. 2, ed. G. L. Eichhorn, pp.
      797-831. Amsterdam: Elsevier.

(6)   Coleman, J. E. 1973. Carbonic Anhydrase. In Inorganic
      Biochemistry, Vol. 1, ed. G. L. Eichhorn, pp. 488-548.
      Amsterdam: Elsevier.

(7)   Coleman, J. E., and Vallee, B. L. 1964. Metallocarboxy-
      peptidase--inhibitor complexes. Biochemistry 3: 1874-1879.

(8)   Dickerson, R. E.; Takano, T.; Eisenberg, D.; Kallai, O. B.;
      Samson, L.; Cooper, A.; and Margoliash, E. 1971. Ferri-
      cytochrome c. I. General features of the horse and bonito
      proteins at 2.8 A resolution. J. Biol. Chem. 246: 1511-
      1535.

(9)   Eichhorn, G. L., ed. 1973. Inorganic Biochemistry, 2 Vols.
      Amsterdam: Elsevier.

(10) Eichhorn, G. L. 1973. Complexes of Nucleosides and
      Nucleotides. Complexes of Polynucleotides and Nucleic
      Acids. In Inorganic Biochemistry, Vol. 2, ed. G. L.
      Eichhorn, pp. 1191-1209, 1210-1243. Amsterdam: Elsevier.

(11) Eichhorn, G. L. 1973. Some Effects of Metal Ions on the
      Structure and Function of Nucleic Acids. In Metal Ions in
      Biological Systems, ed. S. K. Dhar, pp. 43-66. New York:
      Plenum Press.

(12) Freeman, H. C. 1973. Metal Complexes of Amino Acids and
      Peptides. In Inorganic Biochemistry, Vol. 1, ed. G. L.
      Eichhorn, pp. 121-166. Amsterdam: Elsevier.

(13) Holm, R. H. 1973. Vitamin B_6 Complexes. In Inorganic
      Biochemistry, Vol. 2, ed. G. L. Eichhorn, pp. 1137-1167.
      Amsterdam: Elsevier.

(14)   Harbury, H. A., and Marks, R. H. L. 1973.   Cytochromes b
       and a. In Inorganic Biochemistry, Vol. 2, ed. G. L.
       Eichhorn, pp. 902-954. Amsterdam: Elsevier.

(15)   Hardy, R. W. F.; Burns, R. C.; and Parshall, G. W. 1973.
       Bioinorganic Chemistry of Dinitrogen Fixation. In
       Inorganic Biochemistry, Vol. 2, ed. G. L. Eichhorn, pp.
       745-793. Amsterdam: Elsevier.

(16)   Harrison, P. M., and Hoy, T. G. 1973.   Ferritin. In
       Inorganic Biochemistry, Vol. 1, ed. G. L. Eichhorn, pp.
       253-279. Amsterdam: Elsevier.

(17)   Hemmerich, P., and Lauterwein, J. 1973.   The Structure and
       Reactivity of Flavin-Metal Complexes. In Inorganic Bio-
       chemistry, Vol. 2, ed. G. L. Eichhorn, pp. 1168-1190.
       Amsterdam: Elsevier.

(18)   Herriott, J. R.; Sieker, L. C.; and Jensen, L. H. 1970.
       Structure of rubredoxin: an X-ray study to 2.5 Å resolu-
       tion. J. Mol. Biol. 50: 391-406.

(19)   Hill, H. A. O. 1973.   Corrinoids. In Inorganic Biochemis-
       try, Vol. 2, ed. G. L. Eichhorn, pp. 1067-1133. Amsterdam:
       Elsevier.

(20)   Katz, J. J. 1973.   Chlorophyll. In Inorganic Biochemistry,
       Vol. 2, ed. G. L. Eichhorn, pp. 1022-1066. Amsterdam:
       Elsevier.

(21)   Lipscomb, W. N.; Hartsuck, J. A.; Reeke, G. N., Jr.; and
       Quiocho, F. A. 1968.   The Structure of Carboxypeptidase A.
       VII.   The 2.0-Angstrom Resolution Studies of the Enzyme
       and Its Complex with Glycltyrosine, and Mechanistic
       Deductions. Brookhaven Symposium Biol. 21: 24-90.

(22)   Lontie, R., and Witters, R. 1973.   Hemocyanin. In Inor-
       ganic Biochemistry, Vol. 1, ed. G. L. Eichhorn, pp. 244-
       358. Amsterdam: Elsevier.

(23). Ludwig, M. L., and Lipscomb, W. N. 1973.   Carboxypeptidase
       A and Other Peptidases. In Inorganic Biochemistry, Vol. 1,
       ed. G. L. Eichhorn, pp. 438-487. Amsterdam: Elsevier.

(24)   Malkin, R. 1973.   The Copper-Containing Oxidases. In
       Inorganic Biochemistry, Vol. 2, ed. G. L. Eichhorn, pp.
       687-709. Amsterdam: Elsevier.

(25)   Martell, A. E., and Khan, M. M. T. 1973.   Metal Ion Catal-
       ysis of Reactions of Molecular Oxygen. In Inorganic Bio-
       chemistry, Vol. 2, ed. G. L. Eichhorn, pp. 654-688.
       Amsterdam: Elsevier.

(26) Neilands, J. B. 1973. Microbial Iron Transport Compounds
      (Siderochromes). *In* Inorganic Biochemistry, Vol. 1, ed.
      G. L. Eichhorn, pp. 167-202. Amsterdam: Elsevier.

(27) Okamura, M. Y., and Klotz, I. M. 1973. Hemerythrin. *In*
      Inorganic Biochemistry, Vol. 1, ed. G. L. Eichhorn, pp.
      320-343. Amsterdam: Elsevier.

(28) Orme-Johnson, W. H. 1973. Ferredoxins and Other Iron-Sul-
      fur Proteins. *In* Inorganic Biochemistry, Vol. 2, ed. G.
      L. Eichhorn, pp. 710-744. Amsterdam: Elsevier.

(29) Pearson, R. G. 1968. J. Chem. Educ. **45**: 581, 643.

(30) Prelog, V. 1964. Iron-Containing Compounds in Micro-organ-
      isms. *In* Iron Metabolism, ed. E. Gross, pp. 73-83.
      Berlin: Springer.

(31) Pressman, B. C. 1973. Alkali Metal Chelators--The Iono-
      phores. *In* Inorganic Biochemistry, Vol. 1, ed. G. L.
      Eichhorn, pp. 203-226. Amsterdam: Elsevier.

(32) Rifkind, J. M. 1973. Hemoglobin and Myoglobin. *In* Inor-
      ganic Biochemistry, Vol. 2, ed. G. L. Eichhorn, pp. 832-
      901. Amsterdam: Elsevier.

(33) Scheinberg, I. H., and Morell, A. G. 1973. Ceruloplasmin.
      In Inorganic Biochemistry, Vol. 1, ed. G. L. Eichhorn, pp.
      306-319. Amsterdam: Elsevier.

(34) Schwarzenbach, G. 1956. Experentia, Suppl. **5**: 162.

(35) Scrutton, M. C. 1973. Metal Enzymes. *In* Inorganic Bio-
      chemistry, Vol. 1, ed. G. L. Eichhorn, pp. 381-437.
      Amsterdam: Elsevier.

(36) Sigel, H. 1973. Function of Metal Ions in Biological
      Systems, Series. New York: Mercel Dekker.

(37) Spiro, T. G. 1973. Phosphate Transfer and Its Activation
      by Metal Ions; Alkaline Phosphatase. *In* Inorganic Bio-
      chemistry, Vol. 1, ed. G. L. Eichhorn, pp. 549-581.
      Amsterdam: Elsevier.

Conventions for Seawater Equilibria
Group Report

I. Hansson, Rapporteur
S. Ahrland   A. E. Martell
R. G. Bates   J. J. Morgan
G. Biedermann   P. W. Schindler
D. Dyrssen   T. B. Warner
E. Högfeldt   M. Whitfield

INTRODUCTION

Although acid-base and metal complexation equilibria are of primary importance in understanding chemical reactions in seawater,
nearly all of the thermodynamically well-defined stability constants have been measured in quite different media. The most
common reference states employed for these reactions are zero
ionic strength (infinite dilution), 0.10 M ionic strength (usually a KNO_3 solution), and 1.0-3.0 M ionic strength (adjusted
with sodium perchlorate). Application of such data to seawater
requires calculation of the medium effect through the use of
semi-empirical relationships. Because of the approximate nature
of the mathematical relationships currently available, such calculations give us only approximate equilibrium constants which
nevertheless may be sufficient for many purposes. For more accurate determinations and for further work on new systems, it is
desirable to use seawater itself, or a closely similar artificial
seawater, as the reference solution.

It is the purpose of this chapter to describe and compare the
available conventions for describing and measuring pH and ionic
equilibrium constants in seawater. The use of an accepted, uniform set of conventions will make it possible to develop a body
of self-consistent data for seawater reactions. Suggestions will

also be made concerning the most convenient and accurate techniques of measuring hydrogen ion and metal ion concentrations
and their equilibria in marine systems. Since there is interest
in saline solutions that have higher or lower concentrations
than normal seawater (e.g., estuarine waters), conventions and
methods of calibration of electrode systems will also be suggested for such systems. Finally, two simple procedures are described that enable an estimation of the activity coefficients
required for the conversion of equilibrium constants related to
other reference states into the seawater scale.

It is recommended that wherever practical, the standard state of
solutes in seawater should be defined on the ionic medium scale
so that thermodynamically rigorous stability constants can be
defined in terms of the concentrations of the reacting components.

CONCENTRATION SCALES

The following scales have been used in connection with studies
on ionic media and equilibrium speciation in aqueous solutions.

Unit	Symbol	Principal field
mole fraction	X or N(n)	activity shifts vs. ionic composition
molal (moles per kg water)	m	physico-chemical treatments of mixed electrolyte solutions
mol/l	M	equilibrium speciation studies
moles per kg seawater	M_w	high precision deter-minations of weighed seawater samples

The group recommends the molality scale for physico-chemical
studies of mixed electrolyte solutions related to problems in
marine chemistry as well as for studies of equilibrium speciation.
Equilibrium constants should be reported with units (e.g.,
m^{-1} for $K_1 = m_{AB}\, m_A^{-1}\, m_B^{-1}$) together with method, temperature, pressure, and medium composition.

The group accepts analytical arguments for the p, T independent
M_w scale, but recommends that concentration data be supplemented

by density data to allow conversion between the different units.
The molality scale should be used wherever possible. The p, T,
salinity dependence of the density must be considered thereby.

Weight units such as parts-per-million (ppm) should be avoided.

Two conventions have been used for defining the activity of water
in salt solutions: ·

    (a) $a_{H_2O} = 1$ in the ionic medium

    (b) $a_{H_2O} = 1$ when the $X_{H_2O} = 1$;

where X_{H_2O} is the mole fraction of water in the solution.

Convention (a) is recommended for presenting equilibrium constants related to seawater as an ionic medium, particularly in
cases where the reaction under consideration involves the transfer of an unknown number of water molecules.

Convention (b) is recommended for presenting other physico-
chemical properties of seawater, since it avoids the necessity
of defining a separate standard state for water at each salinity
and it preserves the concept, used in calculations such as osmo-
regulation and desalination, that the activity of water depends
on salinity.

pH MEASUREMENTS

Definition of pH

It is recommended that a new scale should be formulated with the
pH in seawater defined by the relationship

$$pm_H \equiv -\log (m_H)_X \qquad\qquad\qquad\qquad (1)$$

where m_H is the molality of "free" hydrogen ion, in the seawater (X).

Experimental values of pH on this scale in <u>media of fixed salinity</u>
can be obtained with reference to a standard of known pH $(pm_H)_S$

by measurement of the emf (E_X or E_S) of a cell with the liquid junction

glass electrode │ seawater (X) or ‖ artificial sea- │ AgCl,Ag (A)
                │ standard (S)   ‖ water saturated │
                │   ‖ with AgCl   │

or with a cell with the liquid junction

glass electrode │ seawater (X) or ‖ 3.5 M KCl, Hg_2Cl_2, Hg   (B)
                │ standard (S)   ‖

Although the commercially available reference electrodes at present make use of the calomel electrode, the future use of cell (A) is strongly recommended (see "Suggestions Regarding Reference Electrodes" section).

In both cases, $(pm_H)_X$ is calculated from $(pm_H)_S$ by the relationship

$$(pm_H)_X \equiv (pm_H)_S + \frac{E_X - E_S}{(RT\ln 10)/F} \qquad (2)$$

It is recommended that reference standards for pm_H in seawater should be formulated and characterized. These standards should have the same ionic strength as seawater (X) and should match the seawater as closely as possible with respect to composition. These solutions should be prepared in artificial seawater composed of NaCl, Na_2SO_4, and $MgCl_2$ (KCl being replaced by NaCl, and $CaCl_2$ by $MgCl_2$) with ionic ratios as close as possible to natural seawater. Buffer substances suitable for adjustment of the pH in the range of 7.5 to 8.8 (at $25^{\circ}C$) should be added. One such material that has been found stable and useful is TRIS plus TRIS-HCl.

The procedure of standardizing these buffers by potentiometric measurements involves calibration of the cell in seawater media of known m_H where the sulfate has been replaced by chloride followed by measurement of the $(pm_H)_S$ values of the buffer solutions based on artificial seawater containing sulfate. The emf cell should be without liquid junction.

The pH scale suggested by Hansson includes H^+ bound to sulfate ($[H^+]_{tot}$), and thus the two scales are related by the conditional constant for the protonization of sulfate (K_1) together with the sulfate concentration:

$$[H^+]_{tot} \ (M_w \ scale) = m_H + K_1 m_H [SO_4^{2-}] \tag{3}$$

As a consequence of buffer composition the (pm_H)-scale applies only when the salinity concept (constant ratio of major constituents) applies.

Techniques of pH Measurement

An instrument capable of converting $E_X - E_S$ into a difference of pH with an accuracy of 0.003 pH unit is desirable. Manual or automatic adjustment of the slope factor $(RTln10)/F$ should be incorporated. This adjustment only applies, however, if the electrode system is allowed to reach the solution temperature. If the calculation is made by eq. (2), an electrometer capable of an accuracy of $\pm$ 0.1 mV with an input impedance of at least 500 MΩ is needed. The temperature of solutions X and S should be known and should be equal within 2^oC. The cell should be standardized with two buffer solutions, preferably bracketing the pH of seawater. The standardization should be repeated at frequent intervals, and it is recommended that the electrodes be kept in artificial seawater when they are not in use.

The surface of the glass electrode should be kept clean and free from deposits. It can be washed with water and dried with soft tissue. From time to time, it may be necessary to immerse it in 6 M HCl for a few minutes to remove accumulations of inorganic substances. After this treatment, it should be reconditioned for several hours in seawater. Several reference electrodes should be available. They should be intercompared occasionally in order to detect irreversible changes characteristic of electrodes that have outlived their usefulness.

It is often convenient when studying the carbonate system to standardize the pH cell in the manner described by Hansson (1973)

by a potentiometric titration which simultaneously yields values
of alkalinity, total carbonate content, and pH. This method
furnishes $-\log (m_H + m_{HSO_4} + m_{HF})$ values which can be converted
readily to $pm_H = -\log m_H$.

Suggestions Regarding Reference Electrodes

As a consequence of the decision to recommend a procedure for pH
measurement involving standardization by buffer solutions based
on seawater, the group suggests that the cell (A)

| glass electrode | solution ‖ | artificial seawater saturated with AgCl | AgCl, Ag |

be used. The bridge solution should be as free from bromide as
possible, and the saturation with AgCl is necessary, since it pre-
vents dissolution of the AgCl(s)-layer of the electrode. The
reference half-cell designed by Hansson (see Warner, Fig. 1, this
volume) is recommended, since it offers the possibility of a well-
defined diffusion layer in the junction. The salinity of the
bridge solution should be 35 $^{o}/oo$ to match the mean salinity of
seawater. However, if extensive measurements are performed in
another salinity range, it is recommended that the inner solution match the mean salinity of that range.

If the calomel half-cell is used, the bridge solution may be
3.5 M KCl, and the junction must be designed to allow a well-
defined diffusion layer to be set up. A possibly attractive alternative may be to use a calomel reference cell containing a
0.7 M NaCl to reduce junction effects. Saturated KCl should be
avoided, since temperature changes may cause crystallization in
the junction, thereby disturbing the diffusion layer.

Liquid Junction Potentials

At the present level of experience in handling hydrogen and alkali ion-sensitive membranes as half-cells, the exhortation to
build cells without liquid junctions to study ionic equilibria
is no longer an empty phrase but practical advice. For reactions

in which hydrogen ions do not participate, the choice is obvious:
The familiar glass electrode may be employed as the reference
half-cell, provided the pH does not exceed the value of 10.
When only one single charged cation is present in the test solution and the pH range of 3 to 10 need not be exceeded, the alka-
li-sensitive glass electrode may be taken as a reference. Most
ionic equilibria must, however, still be investigated using a
liquid junction. This situation is not likely to change until
new types of alkali ion-sensitive glass electrodes employable at
high acidities and alkalinities are available.

Liquid junction potentials arise from the transfer of ionic species through the <u>transition region</u> that divides test solution
from bridge solution. To take the liquid junction potential into account, we must know the concentration distribution in this
region. In practice, this distribution is determined mainly by
prevailing hydrodynamic conditions, which may vary greatly from
one experiment to another, due to variations in stirring rate
or composition of the test solution. When the transition region
has formed, the enthalpy of mixing gives rise to temperature
changes and hence to changes in density.

The key to successful emf measurments with liquid junctions is
to choose a junction type which minimizes the influence of inci-
dental experimental conditions. This influence can be kept at
a very low level by setting up the junction in a thin channel to
confine the transition region. In channels of this type, concentration distribution is one-dimensional, depending only on height.

The most important practical question is choosing an appropriate
channel width. A too narrow channel gives rise to a great and
undesirable increase in cell resistance. Moreover, a thin channel is easily blocked by suspended particles and/or stopcock
grease. If it is too wide, the channel is likely to permit a
multidimensional concentration distribution in the transition
region. Channels of about 0.5 mm width have proved optimal.

To simplify matters further, solutions of the same total molality
should be employed throughout the cell. Using this precaution,
emf values obtained with different types of junction were found
to agree closely. They have also invariably shown only negligible
drift with time; upon renewal of the junction, the initial value
was resumed within a few minutes. The junctions compared were of
three types: (1) free diffusion, (2) constrained diffusion (another boundary condition), and (3) linear concentration distribution built up from thin layers. The familiar sintered glass junctions are difficult to use. They are hard to clean and unless
evacuated repeatedly, will retain much air, which confines the
real contact area to a fraction of the geometric surface.

The close agreement of emf values found for the different junctions (thin channels in solutions of identical total concentration) makes a theoretical estimation of liquid junction potentials possible (Biedermann, this volume). A practical junction-
cell design has been in use in Stockholm now for decades. The
junction has a U-shaped, narrow channel of 0.5 mm width. The
bent channel allows the use of test solutions of a higher density than that of the bridge solution. The density difference
serves only to replace bridge with test solution in the U of the
channel.

This cell, called a Wilhelm cell (Fig. 1), is not very well suited
to work at temperatures far above or below room temperature. A
new version has been constructed to meet these needs with a U-
shaped channel built into a stopcock. Here the solutions can be
brought into contact at will, when pressure and temperature equilibrium have been established. This junction is also renewable
at any time (Fig. 2).

pH Measurements at Various Salinities

For accurate determination of pm_H in a seawater sample of a salinity different from 35 ^{o}/oo S, the cell should be standardized
with a buffer solution based on synthetic seawater of the same

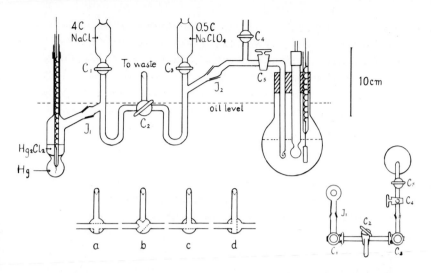

Fig. 1.   Cell arrangement for room temperature ("Wilhelm type").
cf. W. Forsling, S. Hietanen, and L.G. Sillén.   1952.   Acta Chem. Scand. 6: 901.

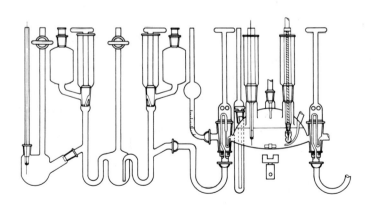

Fig. 2.   Cell arrangement for arbitrary temperature, provided with renewable liquid junctions.
A full description of the arrangement will be given in a publication submitted to Chemica Scripta (1975) by G. Biedermann and G. Douherét.

salinity. However, for most oceanic measurements (ranging between 32 - 38 ^{O}/oo S), a 35 ^{O}/oo S synthetic seawater buffer
suffices, provided that a linear calibration has been performed
using measurements in buffers prepared at 30 and 40 ^{O}/oo S. The
same liquid junction should be used for calibration and routine
measurements. The experimental uncertainty introduced by this
procedure is on the order of 0.01 pH units if a seawater-like
medium is used in the reference bridge solution.

Estuarine studies will involve the use of several buffers covering different salinity ranges with the composition of dilute
seawater. The number of such reference solutions chosen will be
dictated by the measurement accuracy required. Below about
1 - 3 ^{O}/oo salinity, for measurements in river or estuarine systems, the dilute NBS buffers and the corresponding conventional
activity scale of pH should be used.

The NBS pH Scale and the System of Apparent Constants

The NBS pH scale, based on conventional single-ion activities,
has been extensively used for measurements of pH in seawater.
This scale is fixed by dilute standard reference solutions with
ionic strengths of 0.1 m or less; consequently, pH measurements
with cells of type B will involve an appreciable residual liquid
junction potential when standardized with NBS buffers and used
subsequently to measure the pH of seawater.

This procedure is widely used for studying protolytic equilibria
in marine chemistry, and it gives an operationally consistent
scheme of pH values and "apparent" stability constants. It is
recommended that it should be gradually replaced by the hydrogen
ion molality scale (pm_H scale) for the following reasons:
1. The pm_H scale is thermodynamically well-defined and can be
    interconnected with pH scales defined in a similar way in
    other media.
2. The pm_H scale contains no assumptions about the activity
    coefficient of single ions.

3. The experimental procedure on the pm_H scale minimizes the
    influence of liquid junction potentials on pH measurements
    and enables calibrations to be made simply in terms of hydro-
    gen ion concentration.

The NBS scale is likely to remain in use for some time - at least
until suitable reference electrodes and buffer solutions for the
pm_H scale become commercially available. The following recommen-
dations are made for the practical use of this scale:

1. To minimize the influence of shifts in ionic environment on
    the glass electrode, secondary standard buffers should be
    prepared in artificial seawater and related to the primary
    dilute standards by measurements with the hydrogen electrode
    and a capillary junction where steady-state cylindrical sym-
    metry is achieved. These secondary standards should be used
    in all seawater measurements.
2. To avoid artifacts due to erratic liquid junction potentials,
    reference electrodes should be carefully selected by taking
    those that show low bias potentials (<0.1 mV) when a group
    of four or five electrodes are compared in a sample of the
    secondary buffer solution. Combination electrodes should not
    be used because of their poor liquid junction characteristics.
3. The same reference electrode type should be used in the deter-
    mination of the apparent constant and in the measurement of
    pH.

It is recommended that some attention be paid to the calculation
of conversion factors that will enable the approximate adjustment of measured pH values from the NBS scale to the pm_H scale.
Also, a central laboratory should prepare the seawater buffers
to avoid systematic errors.

CONCENTRATION MEASUREMENTS WITH ION-SELECTIVE ELECTRODES

Ionic Medium Method

In determining equilibrium constants in artificial seawater as
well as in the preparation of standard reference solutions for

measurements in seawater, "foreign" solutes (buffer materials,
ions of special interest, etc.) must be added to the medium.
When this is done, the composition of the solution and consequently the applicable activity coefficients and liquid junction
potentials are unavoidably changed. It is important to determine what amounts of these substances can be added without alterations that are too large to be tolerated. With simple solutes such as HCl, weak acids of low molecular weight, and inorganic salts, alterations of the activity coefficients caused by
changes as much as 6% in composition appear to be very small,
provided the ionic strength is kept constant. The change in the
logarithm of the activity coefficient is linear with the fractional change in composition. For highest accuracy, this slope
should be determined experimentally and corrections applied.

For example, in a study of the change in activity coefficient
of HCl in a medium of ionic strength 0.66 m and constant molality of chloride ion (0.5577 mol kg^{-1}), the following relationship was found:

$$\log \gamma_{HCl} = 0.016 \, m_{HCl} - 0.136 \tag{4}$$

Thus, when m_{HCl} is 0.05 mol kg^{-1}, or contributes 7.6% of the
total ionic strength, $\log \gamma_{HCl}$ differs by only 0.001 m from its
value in the synthetic seawater of ionic strength 0.66 m.   The
extrapolation is readily made from experimental data obtained
in the range m_{HCl} = 0.05 to 0.01 mol kg^{-1}. It is likely that
the addition of other unassociated electrolytes will yield relationships similar to eq. (4) with slopes of the same order, in
accordance with known rules for mixtures. At a molality of 0.01
mol kg^{-1} of different added solutes, it seems safe to expect
$\log \gamma_{HCl}$ to be the same within 0.004 units.

Calibration Procedure

Just as it will be frequently most useful to calibrate a glass
electrode in terms of hydrogen ion molality, it may often be
desirable to calibrate ion electrodes in terms of ion concentration in the desired medium, thus avoiding the use of troublesome

single-ion activity coefficients. This should be done in synthetic seawater. It should be stressed that when this standard
state is adopted, the concentration of "free" metals defined includes all complexes formed with the medium ions, e.g.,

$$m_{Zn(II)tot} = m_{Zn^{2+}} + m_{ZnSO_4} + m_{ZnCl^+}$$

$$m_{SO_4 tot} = m_{SO_4^{2-}} + m_{MgSO_4} + m_{NaSO_4^-}$$

For the purpose of speciation studies involving medium ions, a
possible alternative would be to calibrate the ion-selective
electrodes in $NaClO_4$ solutions of the same ionic strength. It
is easy to prepare solutions containing defined concentrations
of the nonhydrolyzable species, but for hydrolyzable species
one requires knowledge of protonation constants. Since such
constants (e.g., for SO_4^{2-}, PO_4^{3-}, etc.) can be studied by measuring   pH only, it is possible to standardize ion-selective
electrodes responsive to these ions using the measured pH value
and the appropriate protonation constant. The replacement of
medium ions with others might be of some concern if it is large.
Here, however, activity coefficient variations can be estimated
using interaction coefficients.

For species such as S^{2-}, it may be difficult to obtain well-
defined concentrations at convenient pH levels. In this instance
it may be better to calibrate the electrode in terms of SH^-
rather than S^{2-}, even though electrode response probably devel-
ops via the equilibrium

$$SH^- + H_2O \rightleftharpoons H_3O^+ + S^{2-}$$

It may be useful to determine the pK value of the reaction

$$H_2S(aq) + H_2O \rightleftharpoons H_3O^+ + SH^-$$

in the medium used (data for NaCl and seawater are available
from D. Dyrssen) if one wishes to work at a pH close to that of
seawater. Here, about 10% of all sulfide will be in the form
of H_2S. A possible method would be to do a Gran titration of
Na_2S with HCl in oxygen-free 0.7 m NaCl, or to titrate H_2S
coulometrically in the same medium over a suitable pH range.

THE REDOX SCALE IN SEAWATER

Even if the redox potential in seawater at present is difficult
to measure or even to estimate because of the problem of mixed
potentials and time for reaching true equilibrium, as stressed
by Parsons (this volume), it may be worthwhile to emphasize that
the present redox scale refers to infinite dilution in pure water
by using the SHE (standard hydrogen electrode) as the reference
half-cell in defining redox potential. When applying standard
potentials taken from the literature an error is introduced, because the reference states of the activity coefficients of the
species involved are given as infinite dilution in pure water
instead of infinite dilution in the solvent seawater, as has been
suggested at this conference. Potential differences on the order
of a few mV should be anticipated because of the change in the
medium. Methods for estimating the actual differences are summarized in the next section and details are given by Biedermann
(this volume).

Moreover, the whole pE scale should be changed by changing from
SHE to a hydrogen electrode in the solvent seawater, again with
infinite dilution in seawater as the reference state for H^+, as
suggested in the definition of a pH scale for seawater. Differences of the order of perhaps 10 mV might be involved for multivalent ion redox reactions. If the state of the art is to proceed satisfactorily, this difference has to be taken into account.

CALCULATION OF ACTIVITY COEFFICIENTS

Purpose

Since few constants are available for the seawater ionic medium
in activity terms, simple procedures are required for calculating Γ_S (Whitfield, this volume) so that equilibrium data can be
transferred to the seawater scale from the infinite dilution
scale or from other salt media. The simplest procedures assume
that only specific interactions between ions of opposite charge
are responsible for deviations from simple ionic strength behavior.

Two simple approaches have been applied to marine chemistry.

Methods

Ion pair model

Input data required: Stability constants for the various ion
pair formation reactions on the infinite dilution scale; estimates of the activity coefficients of the free ions and of the
ion pairs in the medium of interest. An iterative procedure is
then used to calculate the total single-ion activity coefficients
(Garrels and Thompson, 1962).

Assumptions: Salt solutions are defined where ion pair formation
is negligible. For the major seawater components, the alkali and
alkaline earth metal chloride solutions are used as unassociated
reference electrolytes. For the minor components for which unassociated salts cannot be identified, a simple electrostatic equation (e.g., the Davies equation) is used to identify the unasscoci-
ated ions. Any deviation of the measured activity coefficients
form the behavior of these reference salts is attributed to ion
pair formation. To apply the model to electrolyte mixtures, it
is also necessary to assume values for the activity coefficients
of the ion pairs. The calculations are not very sensitive to the
values assumed here. Finally, it is necessary to divide the mean-
ion activity coefficients of the unassociated reference solutes
into conventional single-ion activities.

Advantages: The model is conceptually simple and provides a
smooth transition between weak interactions (e.g., $Mg^{2+} - SO_4^{2-}$),
and strong interactions (e.g., $H^+ - CO_3^{2-}$).

Disadvantages: As formulated at present, the ion pair model requires that ion association occur in mixtures of chlorides which
obey Harned's rule or its quadratic extension. The procedure of
necessity involves the use of single-ion activity coefficients,
and the MacInnes convention normally used to calculate these

values is ambiguous at ionic strengths above 0.1 m. At higher
ionic strengths, single-ion activity coefficients derived from
mean-ion activity coefficients by use of an ion hydration model
have proved useful (Bates and Robinson, 1974).

Specific interaction model

Input data required: Mean-ion activity coefficients of component
single electrolyte solutions at the same total ionic strength
as the mixture (Whitfield, 1973) or indirectly derived interaction coefficients using constants or formal potentials for specified ionic media (Biedermann, this volume).

Assumptions: Mean-ion activity coefficients are split into two
factors (i.e., $\gamma_\pm = \gamma_{DH}\,\gamma_\varepsilon$)

$$\log \gamma_{DH} = -A\,z_+z_-\ I^{1/2}/(1 + B\overset{\circ}{a}I^{1/2}) \tag{5}$$

A and B are the familiar Debye-Hückel parameters. The parameter
$\overset{\circ}{a}$ can be set at some convenient arbitrary value. It is most practical to choose a value for the adjustable parameter $B\overset{\circ}{a}$ so that
the concentration dependence of the interaction parameter (β,
below) will become a minimum. This seems to be the case by set-
ting $B\overset{\circ}{a}$ equal to 1.5 $(mol^{-1}\,kg)^{1/2}$. If osmotic coefficients are
to be calculated, it is simpler to weight these according to the
molalities of the components of the component salts rather than
to attempt more elaborate calculations of $\overset{\circ}{a}$.

$$\log \gamma_\varepsilon = \underline{\nu}\,\beta\,m \tag{6}$$

where m is the molality of the salt in the single electrolyte
solution and $\underline{\nu}^{-1} = 0.5\ (\nu_M^{-1} + \nu_X^{-1})$. ν_M and ν_X are the stoichiometric numbers of the cation and anion respectively in the salt.
As a first approximation, β can be considered as a constant and
values can be calculated from $\gamma_\pm$ for the single electrolyte solution. β is assumed to be independent of the solution composition
at constant total ionic strength. The β values of the component
salts are combined on molality weighting to give $\gamma_\pm$ in the mixture. Analogous procedures can be used for calculating conventional single-ion activity coefficients.

Advantages: Little computational effort is needed. One has only to sum the interaction parameters. This procedure gives values for $\gamma_\pm$ accurate to better than $\pm$ 10% for a wide range of ionic media including seawater up to ionic strength levels of 3-4 m. A self-consistent picture is provided for all mixtures of electrolytes generally considered to be completely dissociated without the need to introduce on an ad hoc basis new solute species.

Disadvantages: The required $\gamma_\pm$ values of the component electrolytes are not always available either because measurements have not been made (e.g., MgF_2, $MgCO_3$), because slightly soluble salts are formed (e.g., $CaSO_4$ or $SrSO_4$), or because the ion in question can exist only in mixtures due to hydrolysis or complex formation (e.g., Bi^{3+} or NbO_4^{3-}). In such cases, values of the β-parameters must be estimated by considering equilibrium measurements in an appropriate medium (Biedermann, this volume).

SUMMARY

The specific interaction method appears to provide the simplest procedures for estimating, with moderate precision, activity coefficients in electrolyte mixtures by employing a minimum of assumptions.

REFERENCES

Bates, R.G. 1973. Determination of pH, Theory and Practice, 2nd ed. New York: John Wiley and Sons.

Bates, R.G., and Macaskill, J.B. 1975. Acid-base measurements in sea water. In Analytical Methods in Oceanography, Advances in Chemistry Series, American Chemical Society. Washington, D.C., in press.

Bates, R.G., and Robinson, R.A. 1974. An approach to conventional scales of ionic activities for the standardization of ion-selective electrodes. Pure Appl.Chem. 37: 575-577.

Biedermann, G. 1975. Ionic Media. In Dahlem Workshop on the Nature of Seawater, ed. E.D. Goldberg. Berlin: Dahlem Konferenzen.

Garrels, R.M, and Thompson, M.E. 1962. A chemical model for
    sea water at 25°C and 1 atmosphere total pressure.
    Am.J.Science 260: 57-66.

Hansson, I. 1973. A new set of acidity constants for carbonic
    acid and boric acid in sea water. Deep-Sea Res. 20: 461-478.

Hansson, I. 1973. A new set of pH-scales and standard buffers
    for seawater. Deep-Sea Res. 20: 479-491.

Hansson, I., and Jagner, D. 1973. Evaluation of the accuracy
    of Gran plots by means of computer calculations. Applica-
    tion to the potentiometric titration of the total alkalinity
    and carbonate content in sea water. Anal.Chim.Acta 65:
    363-373.

Harned, H.S., and Owen, B.B. 1958. The Physical Chemistry of
    Electrolyte Solutions. New York: Reinhold Publishing
    Corp.

Martell, A.E., and Smith, R. 1974. Critical Stability Constants.
    Vol. I. New York: Plenum Publ. Co.

Parsons, R. 1975. The role of oxygen in redox processes in
    aqueous solutions. In Dahlem Workshop on the Nature of
    Seawater, ed. E.D. Goldberg. Berlin, Dahlem Konferenzen.

Robinson, R.A., and Stokes, R.H. 1959. Electrolyte Solutions,
    2nd ed. London: Butterworths.

Sillén, L.G., and Martell, A.E. 1964, 1971. Stability Constants
    of Metal Ion Complexes. Special publications no. 17 and 25.
    The Chemical Society, London.

Warner, T.B. 1975. Ion selective electrodes in thermodynamic
    studies. In Dahelm Workshop on the Nature os Seawater,
    ed. E.D. Goldberg. Berlin: Dahlem Konferenzen.

Whitfield, M. 1973. A chemical model for the major electrolyte
    components of sea water based on the Brønsted–Guggenheim
    hypothesis. Mar.Chem. 1: 251-266.

Whitfield, M. 1975. The effects of temperature and pressure
    on speciation. In Dahlem Workshop on the Nature of Sea-
    Water, ed. E.D. Goldberg. Berlin: Dahlem Konferenzen.

On the Construction of Single-Ion Activity Functions and Some Comments on the Formulation of Conventions to Describe Sea Water Equilibria.

Erik Högfeldt

Department of Inorganic Chemistry, Royal Institute of
Technology, S-100 44 Stockholm 70, Sweden.

Abstract: Some problems in connection with the construction of
single-ion activity functions are reviewed. A new approach to
the evaluation of ionic hydration is described, and its implications for the construction of single-ion activities discussed. The formulation of activity scales in sea water is briefly discussed with emphasis on the principles of the ionic
medium method.

Introduction

In systems with many coexisting equilibria it is most difficult to get a good idea of what the important species are
without the help of carefully selected master variables [1,2].
The important master variables for the description of seawater equilibria are

$$pH = -\log\{H^+\} \tag{1a}$$

$$pE = -\log\{e^-\} \tag{1b}$$

$$pCl = -\log\{Cl^-\} \tag{1c}$$

where $\{\ \}$ stands for activity. The importance of the three
master variables is related to the problem of speciation in
sea water. Many equilibria in sea water are pH-dependent, some
of the most important ones being the carbonate and borate
equilibria. Many redox equilibria exist in sea water, and here
pE or the electron activity is a most useful quantity for
relating different oxidation states of solutes such as
manganese, iron etc. The chloride content of sea water is high
enough to allow many solutes to be present as chloride complexes such as Cd(II), Zn(II), Hg(II), etc.

As seen from eq. (1) all master variables are single-ion
activities, and it is well-known that single-ion activities
cannot be measured. Only combinations such as single-ion
activity products or quotients are experimentally accessible.
The problem is thus to find useful extrathermodynamic assumptions or a useful design of the experiments permitting the
evaluation of pH, etc., to the desired level of accuracy.
In the following, most of the discussion will be devoted to
the concept of pH, where much effort has been spent on the
design of useful pH-scales.

The pH-concept

Hydrogen ion concentration. The simplest approach to an
approximation of pH is to use the concentration of free hydro-

gen ion in the solution under consideration. It is well known
that free protons do not exist to any appreciable degree in
aqueous solution, and what is usually termed $[H^+] = h$ is
rather

$$h = [H^+] = \Sigma[H(H_2O)_n^+] \tag{2}$$

i.e., the sum of all hydrates present in solution. We shall
have more to say about proton hydration below. If we have a
mixture of salts of rather high total concentration and practically constant composition, such as sea water, and some of
the medium ions are protolytes such as SO_4^{2-}, we have

$$H = h + [HSO_4^-] + \ldots \tag{3}$$

where now H is proportional to h. The equilibrium condition
applied to the reaction

$$H^+ + SO_4^{2-} \rightleftarrows HSO_4^- \tag{4}$$

gives

$$[HSO_4^-] = K_a h[SO_4^{2-}] \frac{y_H + y_{SO_4^{2-}}}{y_{HSO_4^-}} = K_a' h[SO_4^{2-}] \tag{5}$$

where K_a' contains the activity coefficient quotient $\dfrac{y_H + y_{SO_4^{2-}}}{y_{HSO_4^-}}$,

which presumably is held constant by the ionic medium used.
Eq. (5) inserted in (3) gives

$$H = h(1 + K_a'[SO_4^{2-}]) \tag{6}$$

With knowledge of K_a' and other such constants it is possible
to proceed from H to h provided all acid-base equilibria involving medium ions have been determined (or estimated) at
the composition of the medium. However, this is not necessary,
H being as useful a quantity as h in making the speciation in
the solution under study.

In systems with variable composition the quantity

$$pH = pl = -\log h \tag{7}$$

is consistent with the original one given by Sörensen [3,4].
Sörensen designed a cell for measuring h which failed,
however, to give h because of neglect of activity coefficient
variations and liquid junction corrections (cf. ref. 3a).
On the other hand, in ionic media it is possible to design
cells that will give h or H (depending upon the system) and
pH obtained from eq. (7) or

$$pH_c = -\log H \tag{8}$$

The problem of proceeding from (7) or (8) to (1a) is connected with the possibility to estimate y_{H^+}, the stoichiometric
activity coefficient of the hydrated protons. Before we proceed to do so, the two most commonly used conventions for
the definition of activity scales must be briefly mentioned.

Activity scales

Two activity scales have been in common use for treating
solution equilibria in water. The first is the traditional
infinite dilution scale, where the activity coefficient of a
species A has a reference state such that

$$\lim y_A = \lim\{A\}/[A] = 1 \tag{9}$$
$$[A] \to 0 \qquad [A] \to 0$$
$$\{H_2O\} \to 1 \quad \{H_2O\} \to 0$$

With this scale, activity approaches concentration with increasing dilution and for H^+ pH as defined by (7) and (1a)

approach each other with increasing dilution.

In contrast, the ionic medium scale has the pure medium as
the reference state. Thus, the activity coefficient approaches
unity at infinite dilution in the pure medium for all species
except water and the medium ions, given by the equation:

$$\lim_{\substack{[A] \to 0 \\ \{H_2O\} \to a_m}} y_A = \lim_{\substack{[A] \to 0 \\ \{H_2O\} \to a_m}} \{A\}/[A] = 1 \tag{10}$$

where a_m is the water activity in the pure medium. Since the
activity coefficient of H^+ in pure ionic medium differs from
that of infinite dilution in pure water, a transformation
from the ionic medium scale to the infinite dilution scale
requires an estimate of y_{H^+} at infinite dilution in the ionic
medium used.

Hydrogen ion activity

Several suggestions have been made as to how to approach a
useful definition of pH. From (1a) we get

$$pH = -\log h - \log y_{H^+} \tag{11}$$

or

$$pH = -\log m_h - \log \gamma_h \tag{12}$$

where h,y refer to the molarity scale ($moles \cdot liter^{-1}$) and m_h,
γ_h to the molality ($moles \cdot kg^{-1}$). The two scales differ by the
density of pure solvent, which is small for water at room
temperature but can be appreciable for other solvents. In
the following the molarity scale will be adhered to when not

otherwise stated. The difficulties of obtaining pH from (12)
are of two kinds. If one uses a cell without transference, an
activity product is measured. For instance, for $\{H^+\}\{Cl^-\}$ the
degree of certainty in pH will depend upon how well $\{Cl^-\}$ can
be estimated from available theories. If one uses a cell with
transference, the measurement is a ratio of two proton activities whose accuracy is dependent on the estimation of the
diffusion potential involved. Since computations of diffussion
potentials most often involve estimates of single-ion activities, the level of definition of pH will again be dependent on
the accuracy of these estimates. A third possibility, strongly
favored by Bates [3a] involves an operational definition of pH.
By measuring on a suitable cell such as

$$Pt,H_2 \mid soln\ X \mid\mid 0.1\ M\ Calomel\ electrode \qquad (13)$$

using in one case a buffer solution with pH estimated in a
suitable manner (soln S) and the solution of interest (soln X)
pH_X is defined by

$$pH_X - pH_S = F(E_X - E_S)/RTln10 \qquad (14)$$

where E has been corrected to unit pressure.

For cell (13) the relation between pH and other quantities is

$$pH = \frac{F(E - E_o - E_j)}{RTln10} + log\{Cl^-\}_{0.1} \qquad (15)$$

and the relation between pH_X and pH_S becomes

$$pH_X - pH_S = F(E_X - E_S)/RTln10 - F(E_j^X - E_j^S)/RTln10 \qquad (16)$$

While the measurement on cell (13) and the definition according
to eq. (14) will always give a reproducible number, the interpretation is not as straightforward as implied by eq. (15), as
seen from eq. (16). As soon as one changes from composition S
to X the quantity $E_j^X - E_j^S$ may not be zero or may be impossible
to estimate to the desired certainty. When large changes in
composition are made, the pH measured may differ considerably
from the definition (1a).

From (15) it is evident that an estimate of pH is connected
with both estimates of diffusion potentials and single-ion
activities, which also are involved in estimates of diffusion
potentials.

Since the proton activity is often coupled with an anion activity, many attempts have been made to estimate the latter
quantity. One definition of pH by Bates denoted by ptH is the
following
$$ptH = -\log m_h \cdot \gamma_\pm \qquad\qquad (17)$$
This definition will coincide with (1a) as long as
$$\gamma_+ = \gamma_-$$
which is true in range of the validity of the Debye-Hückel
theory but not in more concentrated solutions. Similarly,
Guggenheim and Hitchcock [3a] used the definition
$$paH = -\log m_h \gamma_h \gamma_{Cl} \qquad\qquad (18)$$
Simplifying assumptions like $\gamma_+ = \gamma_-$ are also used in estimates of liquid junction potentials. McInnes [3b] assumed
that
$$\gamma_{K^+} = \gamma_{Cl^-} \qquad\qquad (19)$$

in KCl-solutions. Valensi and Maronny [3b] used instead

$$\gamma_{Cl^-} = \gamma_{\pm(KCl)} \tag{20}$$

Bates and Guggenheim [4] suggested the following expression
for the activity coefficient of Cl^- in dilute solutions

$$\log \gamma_{Cl} = - \frac{A\sqrt{I}}{1+1.5\sqrt{I}} \tag{21}$$

This has been used in solutions up to 0.1 M when setting the
activity scale (cf. ref. 3c), where A is the Debye-Hückel
slope and I the ionic strength. It would be of interest to
get some idea of how useful conventions like (19) - (21)
really are in more concentrated solutions. In eqs. like (19)
and (20) the individual characteristics of the anion and
cation are neglected. It is often assumed that anions are
unhydrated or practically unhydrated. An attempt to evaluate
single-ion activities in rather concentrated solutions contains the assumption that Cl^- is unhydrated [5]. Recently, this
author developed a useful though admittedly oversimplified
approach to ionic hydration [6], which, in contrast to existing approaches, (with the exception of a recent attempt by
Stokes and Robinson [7]) takes into account the possibility of
several coexisting hydrates. With this approach some idea
about the influence of hydration on activity coefficients and
the usefulness of conventions like (19) - (21) might be gained.
Together with some information from Hammett acidity function
data, an attempt will also be made to obtain information about
the possible hydration of the proton and chloride ion as well,
the latter being of importance with reference to conventions
(19) - (21).

A simple semiempirical approach to ionic hydration

Consider a simple 1:1 electrolyte A^+B^- dissolved in water.
The ions A^+ and B^- react with water according to the reactions

$$A^+ + n+H_2O \rightleftharpoons A(H_2O)_{n+}^+ \qquad (22a)$$

$$B^- + n-H_2O \rightleftharpoons B(H_2O)_{n-}^- \qquad (22b)$$

Application of the equilibrium condition to reactions (22a)
and (22b) gives

$$[A(H_2O)_{n+}^+] = \frac{K+}{y+} a^{n+}\{A^+\} \qquad (23a)$$

$$[B(H_2O)_{n-}^-] = \frac{K-}{y-} a^{n-}\{B^-\} \qquad (23b)$$

where a is the water activity and $[A(H_2O)_{n+}^+]$ is the concentration of $A(H_2O)_{n+}^+$ in M (moles·liter^{-1}), i.e. the molarity scale.
This concentration scale is preferred to the molality scale
because it is independent of the amount of water that is free
or bound to ions in the form of hydrates. If we sum up the
concentrations of all cation and all anion hydrates we get for
the stoichiometric molarity of the salt

$$C = \Sigma \frac{K_i}{y_i} a^i\{A^+\} \qquad (24a)$$

$$C = \Sigma \frac{K_j}{y_j} a^j\{B^-\} \qquad (24b)$$

We now make the simplifying assumption that the activity
coefficient of all hydrated cations is the same, and similarly for all hydrated anions. The expressions (24a) and
(24b) are multiplied with each other giving

$$C^2 = \frac{\{A^+\}\{B^-\}}{y+y-} \Sigma K_i a^i \Sigma K_j a^j = \frac{\{A^+\}\{B^-\}}{y+y-} \Sigma K_n a^n \qquad (25)$$

where K_n now is the sum of the products of the equilibrium constants for all pairs, i,j such that i+j = n. By rearrangement of eq.(25) we get

$$\frac{c^2}{\{A^+\}\{B^-\}} = \frac{1}{y_A y_B} = \frac{1}{y_\pm^2} = \frac{1}{y+y-} \Sigma K_n a^n = \frac{1}{y+y-} S \qquad (26)$$

where the complexity sum S is defined by

$$S = \Sigma K_n a^n \qquad (27)$$

The function S has a property such that

$$\frac{d\log S}{d\log a} = \bar{n} = \Sigma n K_n a^n / \Sigma K_n a^n \qquad (28)$$

From eq. (26) it is obvious that if we can determine or assign values to y+y-, i.e. the activity coefficient product of the hydrated salt, we can obtain information through (28) about the average degree of hydration, because $y_\pm$ is easily computed from tabulated activity coefficients in the literature. This is a most difficult problem with the present knowledge of aqueous solutions and here some simplifying assumptions are necessary. This writer started with a Debye-Hückel type equation

$$\log y_A y_B = - \frac{1.023\sqrt{C}}{1+Bg\sqrt{C}} - 2\log \frac{1}{d_o}[d+10^{-3}(36.02-M_{AB})C] -$$
$$- \log S \qquad (29)$$

where d and d_o are the densities of the salt solution and pure solvent, while M_{AB} is the molecular weight of the solute. The second term in eq. (29) is a scale factor connecting the mole fraction and molarity scales, because the Debye-Hückel theory is derived from the mole fraction scale (cf. ref. 8). In using eq. (29) it is tacitly assumed that the bulk dielectric constant can be used, which is another simplifying as-

sumption. With that assumption only one problem remains and
that is to assign values to the distance of closest approach,
g. In order to get some idea about the importance of this
quantity $\bar{n}$ was computed from eqs. (26), (29), and (28) for
some different choices of g for the system NaCl-H$_2$O. The results are shown in FIG.1.

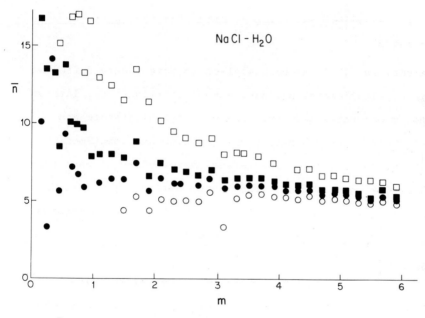

FIG. 1 $\bar{n}$ plotted against m for the system NaCl-H$_2$O

    o g = 6.06 Å ; ●   g = Bjerrum´s q-value ; □   g = 1.55 Å

    ■ g = 2.76 Å

The choices of g range from half the sum of the crystallogra-
phic radii (a completely unrealistic value) to a rough estimate of g for a pentahydrate. As seen from FIG. 1, all curves
$\bar{n}(m)$ converge towards a constant value $\bar{n} \sim 5$ independent of
the assignment of g. This indicates that it may be possible

to evaluate primary hydration numbers independent of the
choice of g as long as an expression like eq. (29) fairly well
simulates the electrostatic part of the excess free energy.
Following a suggestion by Pitzer [9], the Bjerrum q-value was
selected as a suitable compromise (FIG. 1). With this value
for the distance of closest approach we get

$$\log y_A \ y_B \ = -\frac{1.023\sqrt{C}}{1+1.176\sqrt{C}} - 2\log \frac{1}{d_o} \ d+10^{-3}(36.03-M_{AB}) -$$
$$- \log S \tag{30}$$

At present, eq. (30) has been applied to some twenty different
salts, the alkali metal halides, except the fluorides, lithium
and sodium chlorates and perchlorates, lithium nitrate and
several others. Surprisingly simple results are sometimes
found. Especially interesting is the system $KCl-H_2O$. When evaluating $\bar{n}$ for this system in the manner outlined above, it was
found that $\bar{n} \sim 4$. For $\bar{n} = n = 4$, eq. (30) for $KCl-H_2O$ becomes

$$\log y_{K^+}y_{Cl^-} \ = -\frac{1.023\sqrt{C}}{1+1.176\sqrt{C}} - 2\log[\frac{1}{0.99707}(d-0.3853C)] -$$
$$- 4\log a \tag{31}$$

TABLE 1 gives a comparison between experimental activity
coefficients and those computed from eq. (31). The transformation from the molar to the molal scale is performed by

$$y_\pm \ = \sqrt{y_{K^+}y_{Cl^-}} \ = \frac{m\gamma_\pm d_o}{C} \tag{32}$$

where m is the stoichiometric molality in the system.

TABLE 1

Comparison of Experimental Activity Coefficients for $KCl-H_2O$
with those calculated from eqs. (31) and (32)

m	γ_{exp}	γ_{calc}	m	γ_{exp}	γ_{calc}
0.1	0.7698	0.7651	3.2	0.5698	0.5711
0.2	0.7181	0.7130	3.4	0.5711	0.5725
0.3	0.6875	0.6824	3.6	0.5725	0.5743
0.4	0.6657	0.6611	3.8	0.5745	0.5764
0.5	0.6492	0.6453	4.0	0.5768	0.5789
0.6	0.6365	0.6329	4.2	0.5793	0.5817
0.7	0.6262	0.6228	4.4	0.5820	0.5848
0.8	0.6176	0.6145	4.6	0.5848	0.5881
0.9	0.6101	0.6075	4.8	0.5879	0.5918
1.0	0.6038	0.6016			
1.2	0.5933	0.5921			
1.4	0.5856	0.5852			
1.6	0.5800	0.5800			
1.8	0.5758	0.5761			
2.0	0.5728	0.5732			
2.2	0.5707	0.5713			
2.4	0.5694	0.5702			
2.6	0.5687	0.5696			
2.8	0.5686	0.5696			
3.0	0.5689	0.5702			

As seen in TABLE 1, the fit to the experimental values is to within ±0.75% with an equation that is essentially parameter-free once the value of n has been found [13]. This result might be fortuitous but nevertheless of some interest. A slight improvement was obtained by adding a small amount of a dihydrate to the tetrahydrate [10]. Since KCl is a very important electrolyte when defining pH, this result is of interest in the assignment of values to $\{Cl^-\}$. Before we do so, it is of interest to learn how eq. (30) works in concentrated solutions. As an illustration we will use the system $LiClO_3-H_2O$ studied by Campbell and Oliver [14] all the way up to saturation (43.76 m). The following relations were found to fit the data fairly well

$$\log y_{Li^+}y_{ClO_3^-} = -\frac{1.023\sqrt{C}}{1+1.176\sqrt{C}} - 2\log\frac{(d-0.05436\cdot\text{C})}{0.99707} -\log S \quad (33)$$

with the following expression for S

$$S = 0.0018a + 0.0005a^2 + 0.0831a^4 + 0.360^{10} + \frac{0.02756a^{17}}{1-0.9503a} \quad (34)$$

Observe that according to convention (9), $\lim\limits_{a\to1} S = 1$, is putting a restriction on the K_n-values.

According to (34) the system can be described by the formation of a mono-, a di-, a tetra- and a decahydrate together with secondary hydrates starting as a seventeen hydrate with an equilibrium constant equal to 0.02756. For the sake of simplicity the ratio between two consecutive constants is taken as 0.9503 and the summation made from 17 to infinity. It must be remembered that what is here called secondary hydration may in part be an artifact due to the simplification introduced

in using the Bjerrum q-value for the distance of closest
approach of all hydrates.

TABLE 2

Comparison of various approaches to compute activity coefficients in the system $LiClO_3-H_2O$

m	$\gamma_\pm$ exp	$\gamma_\pm$ Högfeldt	$\gamma_\pm$ S-R	$\gamma_\pm$ Glueckauf	m	$\gamma_\pm$ exp	$\gamma_\pm$ Hög-feldt
1	0.809	0.812	0.806	0.808	12	5.501	5.478
1.2	0.837	0.843	0.834	0.836	14	6.838	6.813
1.4	0.868	0.876	0.866	0.868	16	8.234	8.273
1.6	0.905	0.908	0.903	0.904	18	9.657	9.699
1.8	0.946	0.943	0.943	0.942	20	11.05	11.02
2	0.988	0.980	0.988	0.983	22	12.20	11.75
2.5	1.088	1.079	1.118	1.102	24	13.03	12.38
3	1.193	1.186	1.279	1.242	26	13.40	12.95
3.5	1.306	1.304	1.478	1.408	28	13.68	13.35
4	1.428	1.438	1.727	1.605	30	13.94	13.81
5	1.711	1.761	2.440	2.119	33	14.25	14.08.
6	2.104	2.118	3.614	2.865	36	14.41	14.42
7	2.472	2.606	5.660	3.992	39	14.95	14.95
8	2.990	3.052	9.534	5.788	42	15.75	15.76
9	3.562	3.560	17.39	8.851	43.7577	16.25	16.42
10	4.161	4.153	36.34	14.66			

TABLE 2 gives $\gamma_\pm$-values computed from (33), (34),and (32) together with the experimental $\gamma_\pm$-values. As seen, a rather good
fit is obtained over the whole range of concentration even if
some points may be off as much as ±5%. The TABLE also contains
$\gamma_\pm$ computed from the equations by Stokes and Robinson [15]
(eq. (35)) and that of Glueckauf [16] (eq. (36)).

$$\log \gamma_\pm = -\frac{1.023\sqrt{C}}{1+Ba\sqrt{C}} - \frac{n}{2} \log a - \log(1+10^{-3} \cdot 18.015 \cdot (2-n)m) \quad (35)$$
$$\text{(Stokes and Robinson)}$$

$$\log \gamma_\pm = -\frac{1.023\sqrt{C}}{1+Ba\sqrt{C}} + \frac{0.018 \ mr}{2.3 \cdot 2}(r+n-2)+\frac{n-2}{2} \log(1+0.018mr) -$$
$$- \frac{n}{2} \log(1-0.018mn) \qquad \text{(Glueckauf)} \qquad\qquad (36)$$

n is the constant hydration number obtained by curve-fitting
and $r = \emptyset/v^o$ where $\emptyset$ is the apparent molar volume of the unhydrated electrolyte and v^o the mole volume of pure water. As
seen previously, the latter two equations break down already
in rather dilute solutions, mainly due to the fact that the
hydration number is assumed to be a constant in eqs. (35) and
(36).

Assuming acknowledge of the amount of water tied up in hydrates, it is possible to compute the concentration of free water
(in M) from

$$C_{H_2O} = (\frac{55.51}{m})- \bar{n})C \qquad\qquad (37)$$

In FIG. 2, C_{H_2O} is plotted against a in the range $26 \leq m \leq 43.76$.
A straight line can be fitted to the data indicating that the
activity coefficient of water is constant at these high electrolyte concentrations. By using the relation

$$\bar{n} = \Sigma i K_i a^i / \Sigma K_i a^i = \frac{d\log \ C_{H_2O}}{d\log \ a} \qquad\qquad (38)$$

it is inferred that the water structure is broken down to monomers already at m ∿ 10.

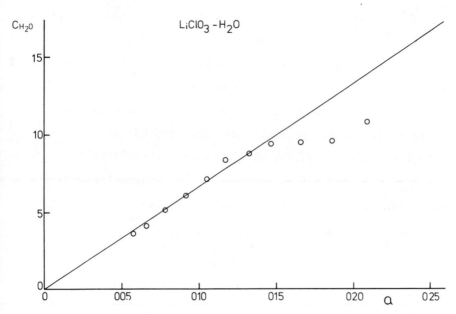

FIG. 2 C_{H_2O} plotted against a for the system $LiClO_3-H_2O$ in
concentration range $26 \leq m \leq 43.76$

These results give support to the finding in FIG. 1, namely
that the approach outlined here becomes better the more the
solutions are concentrated, because here the choice of the
value for the distance of closest approach becomes unimportant. The results also imply the possibility that $\log y_{el}$
approaches a constant limit with increasing concentration; so,
practically all the variation in excess free energy is due to
hydration.

On the hydration of the chloride ion

When extending the use of eq. (1) to higher concentrations [5], it was assumed that the chloride ion is practically unhydrated. If this is so, most of the water of hydration in KCl should belong to the potassium ion. It is now possible to obtain some information on that possibility by combining the approach developed with another one developed some fifteen years ago by the author [15]. In this approach, one uses the Hammett acidity function H_o to split an activity product like $\{H^+\}\{Cl^-\}$ in two terms, one for the cation and one for the anion. From the definition of the Hammett acidity function we have

$$-\log\{H^+\} \frac{y_B}{y_{BH^+}} = -\log\{H^+\}\varphi_o \equiv H_o = pK_{BH^+} + \log\frac{[B]}{[BH^+]} \qquad (39)$$

where y_B/y_{BH^+} is the activity coefficient ratio for the base and acid forms of the indicators used for the determination of H_o, and K_{BH^+} the acidity constant of the acid form. As seen from (39) H_o is proportional to the proton activity when φ_o is practically constant. With knowledge of C_{H^+} the stoichiometric concentration of H^+ in the solution we get from (39)

$$-\log y_{H^+}\varphi_o = H_o + \log C_{H^+} \qquad (40)$$

If necessary, C_{H^+} can be substituted by αC, where C is the stoichiometric molarity of the acid and α the degree of dissociation as determined by, for example, Raman measurements, etc.

It can be shown that

$$-d\log y_{H^+}/d\log a = \bar{n}_{H^+} \qquad (41)$$

From

$$-\text{dlog } \varphi_o y_{H+}/\text{dlog } a = \bar{n}'_{H+} \tag{42}$$

an approximation to $\bar{n}_{H+}$ is obtained [15]. In the first attempts
to evaluate hydration numbers for the proton, the possible hydration of the indicator species was neglected [15,16,17].
Recently, Essig and Marinsky [18] measured the solubilities
of Hammett indicators, both the base form and the pentacyanopropenide (PCP⁻) salt as well as the solubility of the tetra-
ethylammonium (TEA⁺) pentacyanopropenide salt. By using the
extrathermodynamic assumption that

$$y_{TEA+} = y_{PCP-} \tag{43}$$

estimates could be made of the indicator hydration [19] and
φ_o could be estimated. FIG. 3 now gives $\bar{n}$ for H^+ in $HClO_4-H_2O$
(o) as computed from (41) after correcting for variations in
φ_o with water activity.

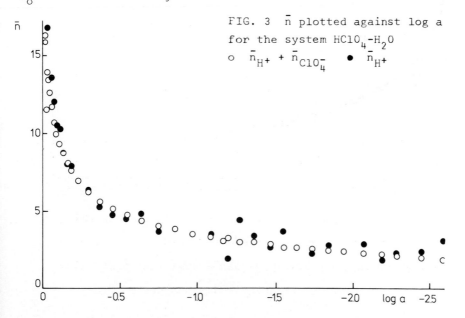

FIG. 3 $\bar{n}$ plotted against log a
for the system $HClO_4-H_2O$
o $\bar{n}_{H+} + \bar{n}_{ClO_4^-}$ • $\bar{n}_{H+}$

In FIG. 3 $\bar{n}$ for $HClO_4$ (o) is also given. This latter quantity
was computed from eq. (30) using the data of Yates et al.
[20,21], also used above. It is rather striking to find that
the curves practically coincide over the whole concentration
range studied, $0.1 \leq m \leq 29.5$. This indicates that all hydration can be assigned to H^+ with ClO_4^- being practically unhydrated. Furthermore, in FIG. 4, $\bar{n}$ for HCl in $HCl-H_2O$ is compared with that of $HClO_4-H_2O$. The thermodynamic data for HCl
derives from the compilation of Robinson and Stokes [22] and
density data from international Critical Tables [23].

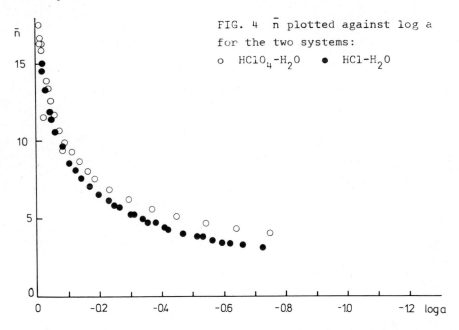

FIG. 4 $\bar{n}$ plotted against log a
for the two systems:

o $HClO_4-H_2O$ • $HCl-H_2O$

As seen from FIG. 4 the two curves coincide in the beginning
but at high concentrations the curve for $HClO_4$ lies slightly
above. In the range of overlap we can assume that $\bar{n}_{H+}(HCl) =$
$= \bar{n}_{H+}(HClO_4)$ and that Cl^- is practically unhydrated. This

should extend to even higher concentrations, leaving the reason for the difference open for the time being. We can conclude that to a first approximation, both ClO_4^- and Cl^- are practically unhydrated. These recent results thus give some support to the assumption used by Bates et al. [5]. We can now use this result together with the description of the system $KCl-H_2O$ given above to get some idea of the range of usefulness of conventions (19 - 21).

The convention $\gamma_{Cl^-} = \gamma_{K^+} = \gamma_\pm$

We assume for the sake of argument that we can use equation (31) for the activity coefficient of KCl, together with the assumption that Cl^- is unhydrated. This gives for Cl^-

$$\log y_{Cl^-} = -\frac{0.5115\sqrt{C}}{1+1.176\sqrt{C}} - \log\frac{(d-0.3853C)}{0.99707} \qquad (44)$$

With the aid of eq. (32) y_{Cl^-} is transformed into γ_{Cl^-}. The results are collected in TABLE 3. For the sake of comparison γ_{K^+} computed from

$$\gamma_\pm^2 / \gamma_{Cl^-} \qquad (45)$$

is also given. The last column gives the difference $\log \gamma_\pm - \log \gamma_{Cl^-}$. At 0.1 m KCl the difference is already larger than the precision in pH-measurements, and at ionic strengths close to sea water (I ∿ 0.7) the difference is about 0.02. These results should discourage people from using $\gamma_\pm$ as an estimate of γ_{Cl^-} . Unfortunately, many people, especially in the field of extraction, use this approximation even at very high concentrations. It deserves to be mentioned that eq. (44) for y_{Cl^-} has recently been found to fit data in our

laboratory for the extraction of $HgCl_2$ by benzene in the range
1-10 M HCl using only one unknown quantity, the distribution
coefficient of $HgCl_2$.

TABLE 3

Estimates of individual activity coefficients in $KCl-H_2O$ mixtures using eqs.(44) and (32) for computing γ_{Cl^-} comp   with
$\gamma_{\pm}$.

m	$\gamma_{\pm}$	γ_{Cl^-}	γ_{K^+}	$\log\gamma_{\pm}$	$\log\gamma_{Cl^-}$	$\Delta\log\gamma$
0.1	0.7698	0.7600	0.7797	-0.1136	-0.1192	-0.0056
0.2	0.7181	0.7037	0.7328	-0.1438	-0.1526	-0.0088
0.3	0.6875	0.6691	0.7069	-0.1627	-0.1745	-0.0118
0.4	0.6657	0.6442	0.6879	-0.1767	-0.1960	-0.0143
0.5	0.6492	0.6247	0.6747	-0.1876	-0.2043	-0.0167
0.6	0.6365	0.6088	0.6655	-0.1962	-0.2155	-0.0193
0.7	0.6262	0.5953	0.6587	-0.2033	-0.2253	-0.0220
0.8	0.6176	0.5835	0.6537	-0.2093	-0.2340	-0.0247
0.9	0.6101	0.5732	0.6494	-0.2146	-0.2417	-0.0271
1.0	0.6038	0.5640	0.6464	-0.2191	-0.2487	-0.0296

Some other attempts to evaluate γ_{Cl^-}

Eq. (44) bears great resemblance to eq. (21),and it would be
of interest to compare the two. However, Bates et al. [5]
preferred not to extend the use of eq. (21) beyond I = 0.1
but made use of the Stokes and Robinson approach (cf. eq.(35))
and derived for 1:1 chlorides

$$\log \gamma_{Cl^-} = \log \gamma_{\pm} - 0.00782 \, n \, m \, \varphi \qquad (46)$$

where n is the hydration number and φ the osmotic coefficient. As mentioned earlier in the derivation, cf. eq. (46),
it is assumed that Cl^- is unhydrated and that the hydration
n = 1.9 belongs to K^+.

From eq. (21) we have

$$\log \gamma_{Cl^-} = -\frac{0.5108\sqrt{m}}{1+1.5\sqrt{m}} \qquad (47)$$

TABLE 4 gives a comparison of $\log \gamma_{Cl^-}$ computed from eqs.(44), (46), and (47) for the system $KCl-H_2O$.

TABLE 4

Estimates of γ_{Cl^-} from eqs. (44), (46), and (47)

m	$\log \gamma_{Cl^-}$ eq. (44)	$\log \gamma_{Cl^-}$ eq. (46)	$\log \gamma_{Cl^-}$ eq. (47)
0.1	−0.1192	−0.1150	−0.1096
0.2	−0.1526	−0.1465	−0.1367
0.3	−0.1745	−0.1667	−0.1536
0.4	−0.1910	−0.1821	−0.1658
0.5	−0.2043	−0.1943	−0.1753
0.6	−0.2155	−0.2042	−0.1830
0.7	−0.2253	−0.2126	−0.1895
0.8	−0.2340	−0.2200	−0.1951
0.9	−0.2147	−0.2266	−0.2000
1.0	−0.2487	−0.2324	−0.2043

As seen from TABLE 4, rather different estimates of γ_{Cl^-} are obtained with the three equations. While all three contain the assumption that Cl^- is practically unhydrated, a comparison of the results from eqs. (44) and (47) shows that the distance of the closest approach influences γ_{Cl^-} considerably. From a comparison of the results from eqs. (44) and (46), it is seen that a difference of two in the estimate of the hydration also has a profound influence. Both the Högfeldt and the Stokes-Robinson approaches for the evaluation of hydration numbers from thermodynamic data assume for simplification that a

Debye-Hückel type expression fairly well describes the electrostatic part of the excess free energy. The Högfeldt approach
allows the resolution of the average degree of hydration obtained into several coexisting hydrates. This is much more
satisfactory, at least to a solution chemist, than an average
like 1.9 presumed to be valid over a large range in concentration. In terms of complex chemistry such a value must indicate
the coexistence of several different hydrates, the proportion
of the various species being a function of ligand activity as
indicated by eq. (28). Although the various estimates of ionic
hydration vary considerably [24], it should be mentioned that
a recent near-infrared study gives $\bar{n}_{KCl}$ = 3.46 [25] in 3 M KCl,
as compared to 3.89 found by taking into account the formation
of a dihydrate besides the tetrahydrate in KCl [10]. Another
estimate is 4.25 in 1 M KCl [26] from compressibility measurements, as compared to 3.90 obtained from the approach mentioned
above.

As seen from TABLE 4, however, it is obvious that we are far
from defining chloride ion activities in simple electrolytes
to a certainty comparable to the precision of experimental experiments. Further examples of estimates of γ_{Cl^-} are given by
Leyendekkers [27] who attempted to predict single-ion activities
in multicomponent systems from interaction theory with some
success. Since sea water is a multicomponent mixture, the results for simple mixtures have to be transferred to such systems. Unfortunately, the simple approach given above has not
been extended yet to such systems.

Millero [28] has recently reviewed attempts to predict properties of sea water from the main components, and it is interesting to note that Leyendekkers and Robinson and Wood
have been able to predict the activity coefficients of the
main components in sea water (cf. TABLE XXXI in ref. 28) with
considerable success. The split to single-ion activity coefficients was made by using the assumption that $\gamma_{Na^+} = \gamma_{Cl^-}$
which may be a poor assumption at the high ionic strength of
sea water. From FIG. 1 we find $\bar{n}_{NaCl} \sim 5$. In accord with this
are the assumptions that (1) Cl^- is unhydrated, (2) that the
true value of the hydration number of Na^+ is larger than that
of K^+ and the observation that the discrepency between γ_{Na^+}
and γ_{Cl^-} is higher than that between K^+ and Cl^- .

From the discussion above it is evident that, at present, it
is impossible to split an activity coefficient product into
its two terms with any degree of certainty. This means that
attempts to estimate $\{Cl^-\}$ as well as $\{H^+\}$ in sea water should
be regarded with caution.

The pH-concept in sea water

The difficulties encountered above with estimates of $\{Cl^-\}$
also relate to the problem of defining pH in sea water. At
present three different scales seem to have been suggested:
Hansson [29] recently discussed the pH-scales used by Buch
[30], who adhered to the Sörensen scale, and that of Lyman
[31], who used a cell with a considerable diffusion potential because standard solutions with a defined pH are mostly
prepared in dilute solutions. Such a procedure creates a large

diffusion potential which is difficult to estimate, and the
procedure used by Lyman makes it difficult to interpret the
pH measured. The Sörensen scale has been criticized by Bates
[3a].

It deserves also to be mentioned that assignment of pH-values
to buffer solutions on the NBS scale involves the use of eq.
(47) for estimating the activity coefficient of chloride. As
seen in TABLE 4, there is some uncertainty with this definition in addition to the difficulty of estimating a diffusion
potential between a standard buffer of low ionic strength and
sea water (I $\sim$ 0.7).

In order to eliminate the diffusion potential as much as
possible, Hansson [29] prepared buffer solutions in synthetic sea water. This is an important step towards a definition
of pH with some physical significance. Hansson gives detailed
instructions on how to prepare buffer solutions, perform the
measurements and to treat the data. The pH-definition used by
Hansson is close to H as defined by eq. (3), i.e. the total
concentration of H^+ in the solution and the convention

$$\lim_{\substack{h \to 0 \\ [HSO_4^-] \to 0}} y_{H^+} = \{H^+\}/(h+[HSO_4^-]) = \{H^+\}/(h+\beta_{HSO_4}[SO_4^{2-}]) \quad (48)$$

This is equivalent to the definition given by eq. (10). Since
H^+ is always a minor species in sea water, y_{H^+} can be expected
to be constant over a large concentration range, provided the
sulfate ion concentration is kept constant. Experience in this
department shows that activity coefficients remain practically
constant as long as the concentration is less than 10% of the

total medium concentration. Critical studies of the effect of
medium changes on activity coefficients were recently made by
Ginstrup [32] as well as Ohtaki and Biedermann [33]. For this
reason it would be easy to define the pH-scale according to
the definition

$$pH = -\log H \tag{49}$$

and remove all uncertainties involved in estimating single-ion
activity coefficients. With this definition calibration of the
system could be performed without the use of buffer solutions.
By using the high precision coulometric technique developed by
Ciavatta [34], it should be possible to calibrate the system
with a satisfactory precision in synthetic sea water. A coulo
metric titration of 1 mM HCl in synthetic sea water should
also give some information on the possible influence of
complex formation between trisbuffer and sea water components.
It should also be worthwhile to try a sodium sensitive electrode as reference electrode, since Biedermann et al. [35]
have recently had some success in the use of this electrode.
It is believed that such measurements should prove the ade-
quacy of the method outlined by Hansson. Some titrations should
be performed at various sulfate levels in the synthetic sea
water to obtain information on the influence of the formation
of HSO_4^- on the measurements and the possibility of defining
pH in terms of h. The variation of the activity coefficient of
SO_4^{2-} with composition creates a problem here. However, studies
are presently in progress on the influence of medium changes
on activity coefficients [36], and hopefully good estimates of
the variation of $y_{SO_4^{2-}}$ can be made in the near future.

It deserves to be mentioned that according to the operational definition of pH, many methods to measure pH will do as long as calibration etc., is done in a consistent and reproducible way. It is only when the physical meaning of pH is involved that not all methods are equally useful.

The approach made by Hansson and initiated by Dyrssen and Sillén appears to the present writer to be the only sensible one at the present state of our knowledge. To take advantage of the ionic medium principle and evaluate equilibria in terms of concentration, as started for the carbonate and borate equilibria by Hansson, will permit a higher precision in speciation than using equilibrium constants determined in media other than sea water. This is a formidable task, which may be greatly reduced in the future by the formulation of rules for predicting the influence of medium changes. The problem of sampling which has some bearing on the pressure and temperature dependence of pH, will not be dealt with. The use of the Gran method for alkalinity and total carbonate in sea water suggested by Dyrssen and Sillén [37] gives information independent of p, T, which must be a considerable advantage in finding useful properties to characterize sea water.

The pE-scale

The pE-scale used by Sillén [1] is connected to the redox potential E by

$$pE = -\log\{e^-\} = \frac{FE}{2.30302T} = \frac{E}{0.05916} \quad \text{at } 25^{\circ}C \quad (50)$$

This is a convenient transformation from the experimental quantity to the electron activity $\{e^-\}$. With the definition of redox potential, the emf of the cell

$$- Pt \mid H_2(1 \text{ atm})/\{H^+\} = 1 \mid\mid \text{redox couple} \mid Pt + E \qquad (51)$$

is really a measure of the ratio of the electron activities
in the two half-cells, the electron activity being unity by
definition in the hydrogen half-cell. At present, the redox
scale is related to the infinite dilution scale. As seen from
(51) diffusion potentials are sometimes involved in redox
measurements, and some of the problems are common with those
involved in the estimation of pH.

While acid-base equilibria are fast, redox equilibria are
often slow and sometimes not reached within a reasonable time
scale. Moreover, mixed potentials might appear, making interpretation difficult. For this reason, analytical methods
capable of identification of various oxidation states are
more useful. Some of the problems involved in redox measurements were recently reviewed by Breck [38]. He warns against
the use of platinum electrodes and discusses other electrode
systems for measuring redox potentials. It is interesting to
note that Breck suggests the reaction

$$O_2(g) + 2H^+ + 2e^- \rightleftarrows H_2O_2 \qquad \log K = 23.0$$

where H_2O_2 is in a steady state and the concentration $\sim 10^{-11}$
rather than the reaction

$$\frac{1}{2}O_2(g) + 2H^+ + 2e^- \rightleftarrows 2H_2O(l) \quad \log K = 41.55$$

suggested by Sillén [1].

It is possible to study redox reactions in synthetic sea
water using the conventions given by eq. (10) and to establish a redox scale consistent with the pH-scale introduced

by Hansson. With the establishment of such a scale, log K-values for redox reactions could be added to log K-values for
acid-base and solubility equilibria determined on the sea
water scale, making the estimate of Δlog K for a change from
one scale to the other unnecessary.

Concluding remarks

The problem of activity scales in sea water is both complicated and intriguing, and the aspects treated here have been
limited to those of the author's experience. It is hoped that
the notes above will be considered as a contribution to the
discussion of the problem already started by Pytkowicz [39]
and Dyrssen [40].

Acknowledgement

The research presented in this paper is part of a program
supported by the Swedish Natural Science Research Council
(NFR) as well as the National Swedish Environment Protection
Board.

References

(1)   Sillén, L.G., 1967. Advances in Chemistry Series No. 67:
      45-56.

(2)   Sillén, L.G. 1959. Treatise on analytical chemistry Part I
      Section B (I.M.Kolthoff-P.J.Elving Eds) pp. 277-317.

(3)   Bates, R.G. 1973. Determination of pH, Theory and Practice
      Second Ed., Wiley, New York a) Chap. 2   b) Chap. 3
      c) Chap. 4.

(4)   Bates, R.G., and Guggenheim, E.A. 1960. Pure Appl.Chem. 1:
      163.

(5)   Bates, R.G., Staples, B.R., and Robinson, R.A. 1970. Anal.
      Chem. 48: 867.

(6)   Högfeldt, E. Chemica Scripts. In print.

(7)   Stokes, R.H., and Robinsson, R.A. 1973. J. Solution Chem.
      2: 173.

(8)   Bahe, L. 1972. J. Phys. Chem. 76: 1062.

(9)   Pitzer, K.S. 1968. Faraday Transactions II: 101.

(10) Högfeldt, E., and Leifer, L., Chemica Scripts, In print.

(11) Högfeldt, E., Barone, J.P., and Ficner, S.A. To be pub-
      lished.

(12) Högfeldt, E., Chemica Scripta, In print.

(13) Högfeldt, L. 1974. Acta Chem. Scand. 28A: 930.

(14) Campbell, A.N., and Oliver, B.G. 1969. Canad.J.Chem. 47:
      2681.

(15) Högfeldt, E. 1960. Acta Chem.Scand. 14: 1627.

(16) Wyatt, P.A.H. 1957. Faraday Discussion 24: 162.

(17) Bascombe, K.N., and Bell, R.P. 1957. Faraday Discussion 24:
      158.

(18) Essig, T.R., and Marinsky, J. 1972. Canad.J.Chem. 50: 2254.

(19) Marinsky, J.A., Högfeldt, E., and Leifer, L., to be pub-
      lished.

(20) Yates, K., and Wai, H., 1964. J.Amer.Chem.Soc. 86: 5408.

(21) Wai, H., and Yates, K. 1969. Canad.J.Chem. 47: 2326.

(22)   Robinson, R.A. and Stokes, R.H. 1959. Electrolyte
       Solutions, 2nd Ed. Butterworths, London, Appendix 8.

(23)   International Critical Tables. 1928. Vol. III.
       E.W. Washburn Ed. McGraw-Hill, New York pp. 51-95.

(24)   Hinton, J.F., and Amis, E.S. 1971. Chem.Revs. 71: 627.

(25)   McCabe, W.C., and Fisher, H.F. 1970. J.Phys.Chem. 74:
       2990.

(26)   Isemura, T., and Goto, S., 1964. Bull.Chem.Soc. Japan
       37: 1690.

(27)   Leyendekkers, J.V. 1971. Anal.Chem. 43: 1835.

(28)   Millero, F.J. 1974. The Sea 5: 1.

(29)   Hansson, I. 1972. Thesis, Anal.Chem., Univ. Göteborg.

(30)   Buch, K., Harvey, H.W., Wallenberg, H., and Gripenberg,S.
       1932. Con.Explor.Mer. 79: 1 (as quoted by Hansson,
       ref. 29).

(31)   Lyman, J. 1957. Thesis, Univ.California, Los Angeles
       (as quoted by Hansson, ref. 29).

(32)   Ginstrup, O., 1970. Acta Chem.Scand. 24: 875.

(33)   Ohtaki, H., and Biedermann, G., 1971. Bull.Chem.Soc.
       Japan 44: 1515.

(34)   Ciavatta, L. 1963. Arkiv Kemi 20: 417.

(35)   Biedermann, G., Lagrange, J., and Lagrange, P. 1974.
       Chemica Scripta 5: 153.

(36)   Biedermann, G. 1975. Personal comm. January 1975.

(37)   Dyrssen, D., and Sillén, L.G. 1967. Tellus 19: 113.

(38)   Breck, W.G. 1974. The Sea 5: 153.

(39)   Pytkowicz, R.M. Manuscripts: a) Sept. 9, 1974
       b) November 25, 1974.

(40)   Dyrssen, D. and Hansson,I. Report on the chemistry of
       sea water XIII, Göteborg, 1974.

pH Scales for Sea Water

Roger G. Bates
Department of Chemistry, University of Florida, Gainesville,
Florida 32611, USA

Abstract: The several possible numerical scales for expressing the acid-base level of sea water are considered in the
light of their convenience and their validity in terms of the
electrometric methods on which they are based. The international operational pH scale, which embodies the concept of a
conventional hydrogen ion activity, is convenient to use for
routine measurements. In conjunction with the corresponding
apparent equilibrium constants, it is capable of furnishing
correct values for species concentrations. Its disadvantages
are largely conceptual; they may limit the straightforward
application of acid-base measurements in kinetic and steady-
state systems.

As a constant ionic medium, sea water is effective in stabilizing the activity coefficients of solutes present at low
concentrations as well as the liquid-junction potential of
the pH cell. The possibility therefore exists of setting up
an experimental scale based on the hydrogen ion concentration,
a concept free from the uncertainties attendant on the use of
the single ion activity. Means for establishing standards
for such a scale are considered. It is of primary importance
that a single scale for measurements of the pH of sea water
be adopted universally.

Introduction

Sea water is a complex system the properties of which are the

result of the interplay of numerous processes of a chemical

and biological nature. These processes involve both homo-

geneous and heterogeneous systems. Some of them are at equil-

ibrium or quasiequilibrium, some are characterized by a steady-
state condition, and others are progressing toward equilibrium
at rates that vary from very fast to very slow.

The state of some of these equilibrium and kinetic processes
in sea water is regulated by proton transfer reactions. Equilibria involving soluble bases and solid silicates combine to
control the pH of natural sea water in the weakly alkaline
region. The pH is altered to some extent by changes of temperature and pressure as well as by changes in the concentration of acidic and basic ·species. Consequently, the accurate
measurement of pH is of critical importance in assessing the
acid-base balance of the sea water medium.

About 95% of the total ionic strength of an average sample of
sea water is contributed by sea salts whose ions are neither
acids nor bases, that is, are incapable of either accepting or
donating protons. Minor constituents are largely responsible
for the buffer capacity and pH of sea water. Of these, carbonates, borates, and phosphates are of prime importance
(9,10,22,32,39,48), while reactions of sea water with silicate minerals make a significant contribution (19,34,52). It
is not surprising that ion-ion interactions are important in
a medium of 35‰ salinity and ionic strength approaching 0.7
mol kg^{-1} (16,20,38,58). Ion pairing occurs among the cations
and anions present in sea water and may influence the pH of
the medium (18,31,39,40,44,45,48,56,58).

Techniques by which pH values can be measured at elevated
pressures (1,9,11,12) or in situ at depths of several thousand

meters (1,14,15,42,43,55) have been developed. Measurements
of this sort have been used to determine directly the change
of acid-base equilibrium constants with pressure and temperature. The partial molar volumes of the species participating
in the equilibrium process also reveal the effect of changes
in pressure on the position of equilibrium (37,57).

It is therefore clear that an accurate assessment of the thermodynamic properties of sea water depends to a considerable extent on measurements of pH - on the techniques used and on the
meaning of the pH numbers assigned to the reference solutions
with which the pH equipment is standardized. Furthermore,
these factors acquire an even greater importance when experimental pH numbers are used to elucidate the kinetic condition
or equilibrium state of other biological and chemical processes
in which acidic or basic species take part.

At the present time, there is no general agreement on a single
standard pH scale for sea water. This contribution has as its
purpose to review the state-of-the-art and to examine in detail
the advantages and disadvantages of various approaches to this
problem, in the hope that the most suitable pH scale can be
chosen for universal adoption.

The International pH Scale

It was recognized many years ago (33) that reproducibility of
pH measurements is the prime consideration, and that interpretation of 95% of pH measurements in terms of hydrogen ion concentration or activity is neither possible nor necessary. Considerations such as these led to the operational definition of
pH:

$$pH(X) = pH(S) + \frac{(E_X - E_S)F}{RT \ln 10} \qquad (1)$$

In this equation, X and S refer respectively to a medium of unknown pH and a standard reference solution of known or assigned pH; E represents the emf of a pH cell consisting of a pH-responsive electrode and a reference electrode of constant potential at a given temperature and pressure. Most commonly the cell is of the type

Glass electrode $|$ Solution X $||$ Conc. KCl $|$ Hg$_2$Cl$_2$;Hg $\quad$ (A)
$\qquad\qquad\qquad$ or S $\qquad$ solution

although the hydrogen gas electrode is occasionally used instead of the glass electrode, and the silver-silver chloride electrode and the thallium amalgam-thallous chloride electrode often find use as reference electrodes. If the pH response of the glass electrode departs from the theoretical Nernst slope, (RT ln 10)/F volts per pH unit, corrections must be applied to $E_X - E_S$.

The seven primary standard solutions have been assigned pH(S) values on what is termed the NBS conventional activity scale (3). These values are defined by

$$pH(S) \equiv pa_H = -\log(a_H \gamma_{Cl}) - \frac{AI^{1/2}}{1 + 1.5I^{1/2}} \qquad (2)$$

where a_H is the activity of hydrogen ion, γ is an activity coefficient (scale of molality), $-\log(a_H \gamma_{Cl})$ is a thermodynamically defined acidity function, and I is the ionic strength, which, for all of the standard reference solutions, is kept less than 0.1. The term on the right of equation 2

represents a conventional definition of log γ_{Cl} to be applied
at ionic strengths of 0.1 or below (4). Details of the establishment of the primary standard scale are given elsewhere
(3). This scale has been adopted for international use (35);
the standard values at temperatures from 0 to 40 $^{\circ}$C are listed
in Table 1.

Cell A contains a liquid-liquid boundary at the interface
marked by a double vertical line. Consequently, the measured
values of E_X and E_S include a liquid-junction potential E_j,
the magnitude of which depends on the concentrations and
mobilities of the ionic species on the two sides of the boundary. There is reason to believe that a 3.5M or saturated KCl
solution on the reference side of the boundary reduces E_j to
a small constant value when solutions X and S are both dilute
aqueous solutions (I between 0.01 and 0.1 mol l^{-1}) and both
pH(X) and pH(S) lie between 3 and 11. If these requirements
are not met, the residual liquid-junction potential $\bar{E}_j$ expressed in pH units

$$\bar{E}_j \equiv \frac{E_j(S)-E_j(X)}{(RT \ln 10/F)} \tag{3}$$

will not be zero. Under these conditions, experimental values
of pH(X) could be brought closer to the standard scale defined
by equation 2 if equation 1 were modified to include $\bar{E}_j$:

$$pa_H = pH(S) + \frac{E_X-E_S}{(RT \ln 10)/F} + \bar{E}_j \tag{4}$$

TABLE 1.

pH(S) of the NBS Primary Standards from 0 to 40 °C [3]

(m = molality in moles per kilogram of water)

t/°C	KH-tartrate, satd. at 25 °C	KH$_2$-citrate (m=0.05)	KH-phthalate (m=0.05)	KH$_2$PO$_4$(m=0.025), Na$_2$HPO$_4$(m=0.025)	KH$_2$PO$_4$ (m=0.008695), Na$_2$HPO$_4$ (m=0.03043)	Borax (m=0.01)	NaHCO$_3$ (m=0.025) Na$_2$CO$_3$ (m=0.025)
0	-	3.863	4.003	6.984	7.534	9.464	10.317
5	-	3.840	3.999	6.951	7.500	9.395	10.245
10	-	3.820	3.998	6.923	7.472	9.332	10.179
15	-	3.802	3.999	6.900	7.448	9.276	10.118
20	-	3.788	4.002	6.881	7.429	9.225	10.062
25	3.557	3.776	4.008	6.865	7.413	9.180	10.012
30	3.552	3.766	4.015	6.853	7.400	9.139	9.966
35	3.549	3.759	4.024	6.844	7.389	9.102	9.925
40	3.547	3.753	4.035	6.838	7.380	9.068	9.889

Properties of Concentrated Saline Solvent Media

For most routine pH measurements, the estimation of $\bar{E}_j$ is not feasible. Because its ionic composition is relatively fixed and its ionic strength is high, sea water is a possible exception. Hawley and Pytkowicz (28), for example, have estimated that $E_j(S)-E_j(X)$ is about 3.2 mV when S is a dilute NBS buffer solution and X is 0.725 molal NaCl, saturated KCl forming the reference side of the boundary. From equation 4, therefore, $\bar{E}_j$ is about 0.054 pH unit under conditions closely approximating pH measurements in sea water.

The simplifications afforded by "constant ionic media" in the measurements of equilibrium constants have long been known to coordination chemists (50,51). When the solute species under study contributes only a small fraction of the total salt content of the medium, changes in the concentration of reactants and products in an equilibrium or kinetic process may occur without appreciable change in activity coefficients of the species concerned. In addition, constant ionic media also "swamp out" changes in the liquid-junction potential, such as $\bar{E}_j$ in cell A (7). There is ample evidence (6,16,24,46,49,53) that sea water of a fixed salinity also displays these favorable properties to a considerable degree and thus may be regarded as a constant ionic medium. It may be possible to take advantage of this fact to design a standard pH scale especially for sea water in a manner that will be outlined in a later section.

Equilibrium Properties of Sea Water

The pH is a parameter useful in characterizing and comparing samples of sea water, in much the same way as salinity, density, and temperature are used. More importantly, the pH value serves as an index of acid-base balance and speciation. When combined with the appropriate equilibrium constants, the pH permits the actual concentrations of acidic and basic species in sea water to be derived.

Equilibria in sea water have often been expressed by "apparent" acid-base equilibrium constants K' for the process $HA = H^+ + A$,

$$pK' \equiv pH(X) - \log \frac{[A]}{[HA]} \simeq pa_H - \log \frac{[A]}{[HA]} \tag{5}$$

where the square brackets signify concentrations in moles per liter. The constant K', termed the "unvollständige Dissoziationskonstante" by Bjerrum (8), was favored by Buch (9,10) and by Lyman (32) for measurements in sea water and more recently also by Pytkowicz and his co-workers (11,12,30,36,46). In a constant ionic medium, one may expect that $\bar{E}_j$, γ_A, and γ_{HA} will remain substantially unchanged even though the degree of protonation of the base A is altered. Consequently, from equations 1 and 4, it is seen that

$$a_H = k_1 a_H' \tag{6}$$

where a_H' is antilog $[-pH(X)]$ and k_1 is a constant. Thus,

$$k' = \frac{k_1 a_H' [A]}{[HA]} \tag{7}$$

As a consequence of these relationships, speciation in sea
water is accounted for as successfully by pH(X) as by pa_H
(see equation 5), provided that the apparent equilibrium constants are also based on measurements of pH(X), for then the constant k_1 disappears in the combination of equations 6 and 7
(46). Likewise, the differences in the operational pH based
on the NBS scale yield correct values for the total alkalinity
of sea water (13).

It is evident, however, that the role of the apparent equilibrium constant K' in the thermodynamic description of the sea
water system is somewhat more restricted than that of the
thermodynamic constant K. Furthermore, pH(X) and a_H' are not
exactly related to either the hydrogen ion concentration or
the conventional hydrogen ion activity. Although this limitation does not preclude an exact assessment of equilibrium
relationships, it may detract from the utility of pH measurements in the characterization of other sea water processes of
a kinetic or biologic nature.

The standard solutions for the measurement of pH(X) upon which
apparent equilibrium constants are based are the dilute
(I < 0.1) NBS buffer solutions. Although this procedure has
been found to be capable of high reproducibility, the possibility of transient errors remains when the solution in contact with the glass electrode is subjected to an abrupt increase in salt concentration, as is encountered in the transfer from the dilute reference solutions to sea water (24,49).

For this reason, secondary buffer standards prepared in natural or synthetic sea water are to be recommended. The pH
values of these reference solutions should be related to the
NBS scale with the use of the hydrogen gas electrode.

Thermodynamic Equilibrium Constants

The thermodynamic equilibrium constant K for the dissociation
of an acidic species HA is defined, on the scale of molality
(m) in moles per kilogram of pure water, by

$$K \equiv \frac{m_H \, m_A}{m_{HA}} \frac{\gamma_H \, \gamma_A}{\gamma_{HA}} \tag{8}$$

A corresponding expression can be written in terms of concentrations in moles per liter and activity coefficients y_i.

The choice of standard state is arbitrary; for aqueous solutions, it is usual to choose a standard state such that the
activity coefficients become unity at infinite dilution in
pure water. If sea water of a fixed salinity qualifies as a
constant ionic medium, however, the activity coefficients in
equation 8 remain substantially constant for different degrees of dissociation of HA, provided that the acid-base
system is present at a concentration much smaller than the
total sea salt concentration. According to Sillén (53), this
constancy is maintained when the concentration of solute substances amounts to less than 10% of the concentration of the
saline medium.

There are advantages, then, in shifting the standard state of reference, making the activity coefficients γ_i^* become unity in pure sea water instead of in the infinitely dilute aqueous solution (6,16,17,24,53). The corresponding value of the equilibrium constant K* is

$$K^* \equiv \frac{K}{_m\gamma} = \frac{m_H \; m_A}{m_{HA}} \; \frac{\gamma_H^* \; \gamma_A^*}{\gamma_{HA}^*} \tag{9}$$

where $_m\gamma$ is known as the "medium effect" for the dissociation of HA (2). Hansson (23,25,26) has based a redetermination of the dissociation constants of carbonic acid and boric acid in sea water on this thermodynamic scale.

Hydrogen Ion Concentrations in Sea Water

Inasmuch as the NBS pH scale is based on the infinitely dilute aqueous standard state, pH(X) is less directly applicable to a determination of K* than to a measurement of K' or K. An experimental measure of the hydrogen ion molality m_H in sea water, however, would lead directly to the thermodynamically defined constants K*. Furthermore, the hydrogen ion concentration or molality in sea water is a clearly defined concept, free from the uncertainties attached to the use of single ion activities. The possibility of establishing an experimental method for the measurement of m_H in sea water will now be explored.

Equation 9 shows that the value of K* can be obtained by extrapolation of data for the dissociation of HA in sea water of

a given salinity to zero cencentration of solute species in
the pure saline medium. In this limit, K* is equal to the
"concentration dissociation constant" $m_H m_A / m_{HA}$, since the
activity coefficients γ_i^* all become unity. A knowledge of
m_H is then the key to a calculation of the acid-base ratio.

Hansson has proposed (24) that the standard state for hydrogen ion in sea water be chosen such that $\gamma_H = a_H / (m_H + m_{HSO_4})$
approaches unity as $(m_H + m_{HSO_4})$ approaches zero in the sea
water medium, where m_H represents the molality of "free" hydrogen ion. If the concentration of "free" sulfate ion in
the medium does not change,

$$m_H + m_{HSO_4} = \text{const} \cdot (m_H) \tag{10}$$

where the constant is determined by the stability constant of
the HSO_4^- species. As a consequence of this choice of standard state, values of pH(SWS) in Hansson's terminology are
somewhat lower than pm_H. From data given by Hansson (24) it
can easily be shown that the relationship in mildly alkaline
sea water at 25 $^\circ$C should be

$$\text{pH(SWS)} = \text{pM}_H - 0.149 \tag{11}$$

when M_H is moles of hydrogen ion per kilogram of sea water.

A standard buffer solution in artificial sea water, composed
of 0.005 moles of tris(hydroxymethyl)aminomethane ("tris")
and 0.005 moles of tris hydrochloride in 1000 g of sea water,
was recommended by Hansson. Protonated tris has a pK value
of 8.076 at 25 $^\circ$C (5); the advantages of tris buffers as pH

standards in sea water were recognized earlier by Smith and
Hood (54). The values of the standards for the measurement
of pH(SWS) were obtained by measurements of cells of type A
and also those of the type

Glass electrode | solution || Artificial sea |AgCl;Ag   (B)
water satd. with|
AgCl

To standardize the cell and to determine the Nernst slope of
the glass electrode, the buffer solution was titrated with a
solution of HCl in sea water of the same salinity as that in
which the buffer was prepared. Hansson's standard values for
the tris buffer at salinities from 10 to 40‰ and temperatures
of 5, 15, and 25 $^{\circ}$C are given in Table 2. The values are expressed as pM_H, where M_H is in moles of $(H^+ + HSO_4^-)$ per kilogram of sea water.

Hansson's study shows that cells A and B give results in close
agreement when referred to the same standard. This discovery,
which is consistent with data obtained in the author's laboratory (6), confirms the belief that sea water is effective
in stabilizing the liquid-junction potential in cell A.

The demonstrated constancy of the liquid-junction potential
and the activity coefficient of the hydrogen ion in sea water
led Bates and Macaskill (6) to suggest that values of pM_H,
where M_H is in moles of _free_ hydrogen ion per kilogram of sea
water, might be obtained from measurements of cell A by the
relationship (compare equation 1)

$$pM_H(X) = pM_H(S) + \frac{E_X-E_s}{(RT \ln 10)/F} \qquad (12)$$

TABLE 2.

Standards for the Measurement of pH(SWS)

in Sea Water [Hansson (24)]

(Composition of buffer solution: 0.005 moles of tris and 0.005
moles of tris·HCl in 1000g artificial sea water)

Salinity ($^o/oo$)	5 ^{o}C	15 ^{o}C	25 ^{o}C
10	8.675	8.347	8.047
20	8.695	8.362	8.055
25	8.710	8.367	8.060
30	8.720	8.378	8.068
35	8.735	8.390	8.074
40	8.743	8.404	8.083

They proposed that standards for pm_H and pM_H in artificial sea
water be established by measurements of the emf of the cell
without liquid junction

$$Pt;H_2(g, 1 \text{ atm}) \mid \text{soln. in artificial} \mid AgCl;Ag \qquad (C)$$
$$\text{sea water}$$

For this purpose, they studied cells of type C containing artificial sea water, a small part of the sea salt having been replaced by an equivalent amount of HCl or one of the following
buffer systems: tris, "bis-tris", or "bis".* The ionic

---

* Bis-tris (pK_a=6.483 at 25 ^{o}C [41]) is the N-bis(hydroxymethyl) derivative of tris; bis (pK_a=8.801 at 25 ^{o}C [29] is
2-amino-2-methyl-1,3-propanediol. Each buffer contained the
base B and its hydrochloride BHCl in equal molal amounts.

strength of the cell solutions was always 0.66 and the salinity about 35‰ . Measurements of the emf were made at 5, 15, 25, and 35 ^{O}C. As m_{Cl} and the standard emf E^{O} (aqueous standard state) were known, it was possible to calculate the acidity function $p(m_H\gamma_{\pm}^2)$ in each of the solutions studied:

$$p(m_H\gamma_{\pm}^2) \equiv pm_H - 2 \log \gamma_{\pm} = \frac{(E-E^{O})F}{RT \ln 10} + \log m_{Cl} \qquad (13)$$

The symbol $\gamma_{\pm}$ represents the mean activity coefficient of hydrochloric acid.

For the measurements with added HCl, Bates and Macaskill used an artificial sea water without sulfate, in order to avoid the complications of HSO_4^- formation. By addition of $NaClO_4$ and small adjustments in the amounts of NaCl and $MgCl_2$, the ionic strength and the concentrations of Na^+ and Cl^- were kept the same as in the sea water containing sulfate used in the preparation of the buffer solutions. Addition of HCl in the molality range 0.01 to 0.05 was not without effect on $\gamma_{\pm}$, but the change was small. For a solute contribution (I_s) to the total ionic strength (I_s between 0.01 and 0.05)

$$\log \gamma_{\pm} = 0.016 I_s - 0.136 \qquad (14)$$

This linear variation is consistent with the change of $\gamma_{\pm}$ in sodium chloride solutions and with "Harned's rule" (21,27,47). For solutions of HCl, $I_s = m_{HCl}$; hence, if the molality of HCl is 0.05, equations 13 and 14 show that the term $-2 \log \gamma_{\pm}$ is altered by only 0.0016 from its value in the pure sea water.

This observation led Bates and Macaskill to conclude that
a) $\gamma_\pm$ is nearly constant in sea water of 0.66 ionic strength
(salinity about 35‰.)when the molality of "foreign" solutes
does not exceed 0.05, and b) that the value of log $\gamma_\pm$ in sea
water (I=0.66) containing solutes (buffer substances) other
than HCl can also be approximated by equation 14. Furthermore, it was noted that -log $\gamma_\pm$ in 0.66 molal NaCl is 0.137
(27), as compared with 0.136 in the artificial sea water of
the same ionic strength. As NaCl contributes only 65% of the
total ionic strength of the sea water, it seems likely that
-log $\gamma_\pm$ in the sulfate-free sea water is close to that in the
sea water with sulfate used for the preparation of the base-
salt buffer solutions, the ionic strength being the same in
all cases.

The calculation of pm_H for buffer standards containing small
amounts (m=0.01 to 0.05 mol kg^{-1}) of buffer substances in
artificial sea water from the emf of cells of type C by equation 13 was therefore regarded as justifiable. In this way,
the standard reference values of pM_H given in Table 3 were
obtained; the units of M_H are moles of free hydrogen ion per
kilogram of sea water. If $pM_H(X)$ and E_X refer to a buffer
solution while $pM_H(S)$ and E_S refer to the HCl solution of the
same I_s, it is seen that the calculation can also be made by
equation 12, since the molality of chloride ion was the
same in all of the solutions. The value of 8.224 for the
0.02m tris buffer at 25 $^\circ$C can be converted to 8.075 on
Hansson's scale (compare equation 11). The result is in ex-

TABLE 3.

Standards for the Measurement of pM_H in
Sea Water (Bates and Macaskill [6])

(M_H = moles free hydrogen ion per kilogram sea water)

----

t/°C	Bis-tris (m=0.02)*	Tris (m=0.02)*	Bis (m=0.02)*
5	6.953	8.835	9.598
15	6.766	8.517	9.265
25	6.593	8.224	8.958
35	6.431	7.953	8.673

----

* $m = m_B = m_{BHCl}$. Units: moles per kilogram H_2O.
Artificial sea water containing sulfate; salinity
34.2‰ chlorinity 19.1‰ , I = 0.66.

cellent agreement with 8.074 found by Hansson and listed in
Table 2. The difference in buffer concentration is unimportant at this pH.

Routine Measurements

For routine measurements of sea water pH, cell A with a
glass electrode, salt bridge of 3.5M KCl, and a reference
electrode of the calomel, Ag;AgCl, or Tl(Hg);TlCl types is
doubtless the most convenient. Care is needed in the selection of electrodes (49). If the assembly is standardized
with two reference buffer solutions prepared with sea water

and closely matching the pH of the "unknown" samples, de-
fects in the response of the glass electrode (Nernst slope)
will not be of concern.

It now seems well established that the liquid junction
potential of cell A is effectively stabilized by the high
salt concentration of sea water. For this reason, and to
obviate drifts due to changes in the condition of the surface of the glass electrode, standards prepared in artificial or natural sea water should be used. If it is desired to base pH on the NBS scale and speciation on apparent
dissociation constants K', these will be secondary standards
related to the dilute NBS primary standards by careful independent measurements with the hydrogen electrode. It
must be borne in mind that some evidence exists (24) that
the measured difference of pH between the dilute buffers and
the standards in sea water is a function of the design of
the liquid junction.

Alternatively, an experimental scale of pH can be based on
the total molality of hydrogen ion $(M_H + M_{HSO_4})$ or on the
molality of free hydrogen ion (M_H) (16,24). Accordingly,
speciation will then be expressed in terms of the thermodynamic equilibrium constants K and K*. The latter approach
offers a welcome means of avoiding that bête noire of solution
chemistry, the single ion activity. Nevertheless, the choice
of a standard pH scale must ultimately rest on considerations
of convenience and simplicity in the application of pH measurements to all of the acid-base processes on which the nature of
sea water depends.

Acknowledgement. The author gratefully acknowledges partial support of this work by the National Science Foundation under Grant GP-40869X

References

(1)   Almgren, T., Dyrssen, D., and Strandberg, J.   1974. Determination of pH on the moles per kilogram sea water scale (M_w). Deep-sea Res., in press.

(2)   Bates, R. G. 1969. Medium effects and pH in nonaqueous solvents. In Solute-Solvent Interactions, ed. J. F. Coetzee and C. D. Ritchie, pp. 45-96. New York: Marcel Dekker.

(3)   Bates, R. G. 1973. Determination of pH, 2nd ed., chap. 4. New York: John Wiley and Sons.

(4)   Bates, R. G., and Guggenheim, E. A. 1960. Report on the standardization of pH and related terminology. Pure Appl. Chem. 1: 163-168.

(5)   Bates, R. G., and Hetzer, H. B. 1961. Dissociation constant of the protonated acid form of 2-amino-2-(hy-droxymethyl)-1,3-propanediol [tris(hydroxymethyl)amin-omethane] and related thermodynamic quantities from 0 to 50°. J. Phys. Chem. 65: 667-671.

(6) Bates, R. G., and Macaskill, J. B. 1975. Acid-base measurements in sea water. In Analytical Methods in Oceanography, Advances in Chemistry Series, American Chemical Society. Washington, D. C., in press.

(7) Biedermann, G., and Sillén, L. G. 1953. Studies on the hydrolysis of metal ions. IV. Liquid-junction potentials and constancy of activity factors in $NaClO_4$-$HClO_4$ ionic medium. Ark. Kemi 5: 425-455.

(8) Bjerrum, N., and Unmack, A. 1929. Electrometric measurements with the hydrogen electrode on mixtures of acids and bases with salts. The dissociation constants of water, phosphoric acid, citric acid, and glycine. Kgl. Danske Videnskab. Selskab, Math.-fys. Medd. 9: 5-206.

(9) Buch, K., and Gripenberg, S. 1932. Über den Einfluss des Wasserdruckes auf pH und das Kohlensäuregleichgewicht in grosseren Meerstiefen. J. Conseil Perm. Int. Exploration Mer 7: 233-245.

(10) Buch, K., Harvey, H. W., Wattenberg, H., and Gripenberg, S. 1932. Über das Kohlensäuresystem in Meerwasser. Rapp. P.-V. Reunion, Conseil Perm. Int. Exploration Mer 79: 1-70.

(11) Culberson, C., Kester, D. R., and Pytkowicz, R. M. 1967. High-pressure dissociation of carbonic and boric acids in seawater. Science 157: 59-61.

(12)   Culberson, C., and Pytkowicz, R. M. 1968. Effect of
        pressure on carbonic acid, boric acid, and the pH in
        seawater. Limnol. Oceanogr. 13: 403-417.

(13)   Culberson, C., Pytkowicz, R. M., and Hawley, J. E. 1970.
        Seawater alkalinity determination by the pH method.
        J. Mar. Res. 28: 15-21.

(14)   Distèche, A. 1959. pH measurements with a glass elec-
        trode withstanding 1500 kg/cm^2 hydrostatic pressure.
        Rev. Sci. Instr. 30: 474-478.

(15)   Distèche, A., and Distèche, S. 1967. The effect of
        pressure on the dissociation of carbonic acid from
        measurements with buffered glass electrode cells. J.
        Electrochem. Soc. 114: 330-340.

(16)   Dyrssen, D., and Hansson, I. 1973. Ionic medium effects
        in sea water - a comparison of acidity constants of car-
        bonic acid and boric acid in sodium chloride and syn-
        thetic sea water. Mar. Chem. 1: 137-149.

(17)   Dyrssen, D., and Sillén, L. G. 1967. Alkalinity and
        total carbonate in sea water. A plea for p-t indepen-
        dent data. Tellus 19: 113-121.

(18)   Dyrssen, D., and Wedborg, M. 1974. Equilibrium calcula-
        tions of the speciation of elements in seawater. In The
        Sea, Vol. 5, ed. E. D. Goldberg, pp. 181-195. New York:
        Wiley-Interscience.

(19)   Garrels, R. M. 1965. Silica: role in buffering of
        natural waters. Science 148: 69.

(20)   Garrels, R. M., and Thompson, M. E.   1962.   A chemical
       model for seawater at 25 $^{\circ}$C and one atmosphere total
       pressure.   Am. J. Sci. $\underline{260}$, 57-66.

(21)   Gieskes, J. M. T. M. 1966.   The activity coefficients
       of sodium chloride in mixed electrolyte solutions at
       25 $^{\circ}$C.   Z. Physik. Chem., N. F. $\underline{50}$: 78-90.

(22)   Gieskes, J. M. 1974.   The alkalinity-total carbon diox-
       ide system in seawater. $\underline{In}$ The Sea, Vol. 5, ed. E. D.
       Goldberg, pp. 123-151. New York: Wiley-Interscience.

(23)   Hansson, I. 1973.   A new set of acidity constants of
       carbonic acid and boric acid in sea water. Deep-sea
       Res. $\underline{20}$: 461-478.

(24)   Hansson, I. 1973.   A new pH scale and set of standard
       buffers for sea water. Deep-Sea Res. $\underline{20}$:   479-491.

(25)   Hansson, I. 1973.   Determination of the acidity cons-
       tant of boric acid in synthetic sea water media.   Acta
       Chem.   Scand. $\underline{27}$: 924-930.

(26)   Hansson, I. 1973.   The determination of dissociation
       constants of carbonic acid in synthetic sea water in
       the salinity range of 20-40‰ and temperature range 5-
       30 $^{\circ}$C. Acta Chem. Scand. $\underline{27}$: 931-944.

(27)   Harned, H. S., and Owen, B. B.   1958.   The Physical
       Chemistry of Electrolytic Solutions, 3rd ed., chap. 14.
       New York: Reinhold Publishing Corp.

(28)   Hawley, J. E., and Pytkowicz, R. M. 1973.   Interpreta-
       tion of pH measurements in concentrated electrolyte sol-
       utions. Mar. Chem. $\underline{1}$.: 245-250.

(29) Hetzer, H. B., and Bates, R. G. 1962. Dissociation constant of 2-ammonium-2-methyl-1,3-propanediol in water from 0 to 50° and related thermodynamic quantities. J. Phys. Chem. <u>66</u>: 308-311.

(30) Kester, D. R., and Pytkowicz, R. M. 1967. Determination of the apparent dissociation constants of phosphoric acid in seawater. Limnol. Oceanogr. <u>12</u>: 243-252.

(31) Kester, D. R., and Pytkowicz, R. M. 1969. Sodium, magnesium, and calcium sulfate ion-pairs in sea water at 25 ^{O}C. Limnol. Oceanogr. <u>14</u>: 686-692.

(32) Lyman, J. 1956. Buffer mechanism of sea water. Ph.D. thesis, University of California at Los Angeles.

(33) MacInnes, D. A. 1948. Criticism of a definition of pH. Science <u>108</u>: 693.

(34) Mackenzie, F. T., and Garrels, R. M. 1965. Silicates: reactivity with sea water. Science <u>150</u>: 57-58.

(35) Manual of Symbols and Terminology for Physicochemical Quantities and Units, Int. Union Pure Appl. Chem., pp. 33-34. London: Butterworths. 1970.

(36) Mehrbach, Culberson, C. H., Hawley, J. E. and Pytkowicz, R. M. 1973. Measurement of the apparent dissociation constants of carbonic acid in seawater at atmospheric pressure. Limnol. Oceanogr. <u>18</u>: 897-907.

(37) Millero, F. J. 1971. Effect of pressure on sulfate ion association in sea water. Geochim. Cosmochim. Acta <u>35</u>: 1089-1098.

(38)   Millero, F. J. 1973. Sea water - a test of multicom-
       ponent electrolyte solution theories.   I. The apparent
       equivalent volume, expansibility, and compressibility
       of artificial sea water. J. Solution Chem. $\underline{2}$: 1-22.

(39)   Millero, F. J. 1974. The physical chemistry of sea
       water. Ann. Rev. Earth Planet Sci. $\underline{2}$: 101-150.

(40)   Millero, F. J. 1975. Thermodynamic models for the state
       of metal ions in sea water. $\underline{In}$ The Sea, Vol. 6, ed.
       E. D. Goldberg, chap. 34. New York: Wiley-Interscience
       (in press).

(41)   Paabo, M., and Bates, R. G. 1970. Dissociation con-
       stant of protonated 2,2-bis(hydroxymethyl)-2,2',2"-
       nitrilotriethanol (bis-tris) and related thermodynamic
       functions from 0 to 50°. J. Phys. Chem. $\underline{74}$: 702-705.

(42)   Park, K. 1966. Deep-sea pH. Science $\underline{154}$: 1540-1542.

(43)   Park, K. P. 1969. Oceanic CO_2 system: an evaluation of
       ten methods of investigation. Limnol. Oceanogr. $\underline{14}$:
       179-186.

(44)   Pytkowicz, R. M. 1972. Comments on "The control of sea
       water pH by ion pairing" (P. J. Wangersky). Limnol.
       Oceanogr. $\underline{17}$: 958-959.

(45)   Pytkowicz, R. M., and Hawley, J. E. 1974. Bicarbonate
       and carbonate ion-pairs and a model of seawater at 25 $^\circ$C.
       Limnol. Oceanogr. $\underline{19}$: 223-234.

(46)   Pytkowicz, R. M., Ingle, S. E., and Mehrbach, C. 1974.
       Invariance of apparent equilibrium constants with pH.
       Limnol. Oceanogr. $\underline{19}$: 665-669.

(47) Pytkowicz, R. M., and Kester, D. R. 1969. Harned's rule
      behavior of $NaCl-Na_2SO_4$ solutions explained by an ion
      association model. Am. J. Sci. 267: 217-229.

(48) Pytkowicz, R. M., and Kester, D. R. 1971. The physical
      chemistry of sea water. Oceanogr. Mar. Biol. Ann. Rev.
      9: 11-60.

(49) Pytkowicz, R. M., Kester, D. R., and Burgener, B. C.
      1966. Reproducibility of pH measurements in seawater.
      Limnol. Oceanogr. 11: 417-419.

(50) Rossotti, F. J. C., and Rossotti, H. 1961. The Deter-
      mination of Stability Constants. New York: McGraw-
      Hill Book Co.

(51) Schwarzenbach, G. 1950. Metallkomplexe mit Polyaminen.
      I. Allgemeines. Helv. Chim. Acta 33: 947-962.

(52) Sillén, L. G. 1961. The physical chemistry of sea water.
      In Oceanography, ed. M. Sears, pp. 549-581. Washington:
      Amer. Assn. Adv. Sci.

(53) Sillén, L. G. 1967. Master variables and activity scales.
      In Equilibrium Concepts in Natural Water Systems, ed.
      W. Stumm, Adv. in Chem. Series No. 67, pp. 45-56.
      Washington: American Chemical Society.

(54) Smith, W. H. Jr., and Hood, D. W. 1964. pH measurements
      in the ocean: a sea water secondary buffer system. In
      Recent Researches in the Fields of Hydrosphere, Atmos-
      phere, and Nuclear Geochemistry, pp. 186-202. Tokyo:
      Maruzen Co. Ltd.

(55) Strickland, J. D. H., and Parsons, R. R. 1965. A
      Manual of Sea Water Analysis, pp. 31-33. Fisheries Re-
      search Board of Canada, Bull. No. 125. Ottawa.

(56) Wangersky, P. J. 1972. The control of seawater pH by
      ion pairing. Limnol. Oceanogr. $\underline{17}$: 1-6.

(57) Ward, G. K., and Millero, F. J. 1974. The effect of
      pressure on the ionization of boric acid in aqueous sol-
      lutions from molal-volume data. J. Solution Chem. $\underline{3}$:
      417-430.

(58) Whitfield, M. 1973. A chemical model for the major
      electrolyte component of sea water based on the Brønsted-
      Guggenheim hypothesis. Mar. Chem. $\underline{1}$: 251-266.

Ionic Media

Georg Biedermann
Department of Inorganic Chemistry, The Royal Institute of
Technology, S-100 44 Stockholm, Sweden

Abstract: The great practical value of the specific interaction theory is demonstrated for (1) the construction of a
consistent thermodynamics of aqueous solutions, (2) the estimation of the medium effect on magnitude of equilibrium
constants and of formal potentials, (3) equilibrium analysis,
and (4) the choice of optimum experimental conditions in
solution chemistry.

Exposition of the problem and definition of the terms

Salt solutions are employed as solvents partly by necessity
and partly by deliberation.

As quantitative analyses are performed almost without exception in a salt environment which is made to change but little,
it is natural that the practical utility of equilibrium constants and half-cell potentials expressed in concentration terms,
which are valid only in the specified media, was first recognized by analytical chemists. Today the indispensability of
these "conditional constants" is universally appreciated in
all fields of chemistry for the evaluation of the concentrations of coexistent species at equilibrium.

The principles for the correct experimental determination of
the medium bound constants were developed in 1928 by Güntelberg
and Schiödt [4], who studied the protolysis of carbonic acid

and of some acid-base indicators in sodium chloride and potassium chloride media. The main point is to relate only data
belonging to the same medium which is considered to be the
solvent.

So when redox reactions are studied, the half-cell potential
of the H^+/H_2 couple is expressed by the equation

$$e = RT\ln 10F^{-1}\log hp_{H_2}^{-\frac{1}{2}}$$

where h denotes a hydrogen ion concentration value which is negligible compared with the magnitude of the solvent salt concentration. A particular reference has thus to be introduced which
is defined so that the activity factors for all the reacting species tend to unity as the concentration of the test solution con-
verges to the pure medium composition.

This practical standard differs from the classical reference
state by the trace activity factor of the reacting species. It
is perhaps worthwhile to recall that the idea of medium applies
only as long as an electrolyte or an ion is present at a concentration exceeding by far that of all the other solutes which
are termed the reacting species. When this condition is no
longer valid, we enter the field of electrolyte mixtures. For
the treatment of equilibria occurring in mixtures, the specific
interaction theory, discussed in the next section, provides a
first approximation.

The consistent use of solutions adjusted by the addition of an
indifferent salt, e.g., an alkali perchlorate, to a <u>high total
molarity level</u> has opened the way for the quantitative study of
complicated ionic equilibria. By maintaining an ionic medium
higher than 1 M, the concentration of the reacting species may
be increased to about 0.1 M without the need to introduce correction terms for the activity factor changes, and under these
conditions the liquid junction potential arising from the replacement of the inert by the reacting ions becomes much suppressed as well.

The remarkable effectiveness of an ionic medium for the mini-
mization of the activity factor variations is illustrated in
FIG. 1. This shows $29.58 \log \gamma_H^2 + \gamma_{Cd^{2+}}^{-1}$, where γ denotes an activity factor, as a function of $[Cd^{2+}]$ in a 3 M $LiClO_4$ medium at
the 0.01 M acidity level; the other set of data represents
$19.72 \log \gamma_H^3 + \gamma_{In^{3+}}^{-1}$ versus $[In^{3+}]$ in 3 M $NaClO_4$ at the hydrogen
ion concentration level 100 mM. The measurements were done with
cells consisting of a glass and a cadmium- and indium amalgam
electrode, respectively; the uncertainty is around 0.05 mV.

Thirty years experience has demonstrated that formation constants
exceeding in magnitude 10^2 can be reliably determined by the
ionic medium method, and the great progress achieved in this
field is documented in Sillén's and Martell's monumental work:
The Stability Constants [17].

Complications arise when the formation constant has a low value,
as, e.g., $\beta(TlCl)$ or $\beta(CdSO_4)$, and when a polynuclear mechanism
has to be investigated, since in both cases a large portion of
the solvent ions must be replaced by the reacting species. In
the following discussion these problems will be considered in
some detail together with the estimation of the medium effect
on the equilibrium constants. The practical importance of the
latter question is obviously great.

Extension of solution chemistry to multiply charged cations and
anions inevitably entails an encounter with ionic media if we
agree to generalize this term a little. The great majority of
the highly charged aquo cations represent acids of considerable
strength which on the addition of alkali give rise to slightly
soluble solid phases. Consequently, these ions, of which Fe^{3+}
and Bi^{3+} are the classical examples, can only be studied in solutions containing a sufficiently high concentration of hydrogen ions. Thus they are capable of existing in appreciable
amounts in mixtures of electrolytes.

A similar situation arises with the anions of high charge. All
of them are weak bases, and most of them are transformed by
acid to oxide phases of a low solubility. Hence, the greatest

part of the multiply charged anions can be studied only in the
presence of a high hydroxide ion concentration; the silicates
and niobates may serve as illustrations.

As a consequence, equilibria involving species of this type must
have been studied in acid and alkaline media, respectively, of
a high ionic strength.

We are then confronted with two main problems: (1) to find a
common reference state suitable for all the ionic species of
the periodic table; and (2) to develop methods for the estimation of the magnitude of the equilibrium constant in an arbitrary medium on the basis of minimal experimental data.

A glance at a table of <u>standard electrode potentials</u> may con-
vince anyone that the data are not quite consistent and that we
are still far from the goal set by the founders of chemical
thermodynamics, Nernst, Lewis, and Abegg.

The standard potentials evaluated by Latimer [7], whose comprehensive work represents the only authoritative treatise on this
subject, are based on four different sources. For the inert
couples, the third law had to be used, and the combination of calorimetric data, often from widely different sources, cannot be
expected to furnish more than a first approximation. For the uncommon species which have as yet not been studied quantitatively,
such as Ga(I), the standard potential estimates were deduced by
considering their reactions with familiar couples, e.g., H^+/H_2;
the results represent, of course, maximum or minimum values. To
the third group belong the ions which are acids or bases of negligible strength and do not form strong halide or sulfate complexes. The standard potential values for the third group are derived
from accurate emf data obtained with dilute solutions and can be
regarded to possess an uncertainty not exceeding a few tenths of
a mV.

The last group consists of the hydrolyzing and/or complex species
accessible for study in the presence of an ionic medium. The formal potentials valid in the particular solvent chosen by the

author had to be accepted by Latimer, who justly mistrusted
the ad hoc extrapolation methods often proposed, and he inserted the values of the author with a caveat in the final
table, which thus contains estimates of widely different validity.

To relieve us from the burden of the experimental determination
of equilibrium constants and of formal potentials in each
of the media encountered, except when the highest precision
is required, will be recognized by all to be an urgent
task. Development of a method for the estimation of the medium effect is also important,as prediction of the influence of
a certain medium on the magnitude of an equilibrium constant
and of a half-cell potential would enable us to choose the
conditions most appropriate to achieve a high yield in a synthesis and to enhance the concentration of a species sought
for study.

We intend to demonstrate in the following discussion, which
forms a part of a greater project, that on the basis of the
specific interaction theory the main problems raised in this
introduction:

(1) the estimation of the medium effect;
(2) the evaluation of standard potentials; and
(3) the assessment of the activity factor changes likely to
occur in equilibrium analysis may receive in many cases an
approximate solution. The approximations may then serve as
a starting point for the development of a more comprehensive
model for electrolyte mixtures.

Terminology of the specific interaction theory

This theory was introduced in 1922 by Brønsted with the purpose of making possible the calculation of the thermodynamic
properties of electrolyte mixtures by employing data relevant
to single electrolytes. The most recent version of the theory
developed by Scatchard [16] and Guggenheim [3] may be con-
cisely formulated by the following postulate: The activity factor, γ_j, of an ion of the charge z_j in a solution of the ionic

strength I may be expressed by the equation

$$\log \gamma_j = -z_j^2 D + \sum_k \varepsilon(j,k,I)m_k \qquad (1)$$

where $D = \dfrac{A\sqrt{I}}{1+1.5\sqrt{I}}$ represents the Debye-Hückel term (thus at $25°C$, $A = 0.5107\ m^{-1/2}$), and the summation extends over all the ions k present in the solution at the weight molarity, m_k. The basic hypothesis is that the ε terms, called interaction coefficients, are set equal to zero when the ion k has the same sign charge as ion j. Otherwise, the definition of the mean activity factor yields that

$$\varepsilon(k,j,I) = \frac{(z_j+z_k)^2}{4I} (\log \gamma_{kj}^o + z_k z_j D) \qquad (2)$$

where z_j and z_k denote the magnitudes of the charges of the ions k and j, and γ_{kj}^o is the symbol for the activity factor of the electrolyte jk in its own solution at the ionic strength I.

In order to minimize the concentration dependence of the interaction coefficients, Scatchard suggested choosing the value of 1.5 for the factor of $\sqrt{I}$ appearing in the denominator of the D term. Guggenheim found up to I = 3 m such a small variation in ε for the great majority of 1:1 electrolytes that he suggested accepting, as a first approximation, a mean value of ε which is to be calculated on the basis of the data covering the range 0.1 to 3 m. Guggenheim goes as far as to consider a substantial trend in ε, which occurs, e.g., with $AgNO_3$, as an indication for incomplete dissociation.

Only two of the 1:1 electrolytes discussed in this work, $TlClO_4$ and NH_4ClO_4, were found to show a serious trend in their interaction coefficients. Both functions $\varepsilon(Tl^+,ClO_4^-,I)$ and $\varepsilon(NH_4^+,ClO_4^-,I)$ have proved to be a linear function of $\log I$, so an equation of the form $\varepsilon(I) = \varepsilon(0.1)+C(\log I+1)$, where C stands for a graphically evaluated constant, could be employed for inter- and extrapolation. The latter was required, as at $25°C$ the solubility of $TlClO_4$ is 0.53 m and that of NH_4ClO_4 is 2.1 m, while we had to consider ionic strength levels as high as 3.5.

For the electrolytes of higher charge type, which entered
our calculations, the concentration dependence for ε was found
to be small, so that an average value covering the I range 0.5
to 3.5 m could be used.

No serious error is likely to arise from this rough treatment.
In each case - both for the 1:1 and for the multiple charged
electrolytes - $\frac{d\varepsilon}{dI}$ was found to be monotonically decreasing. In
consequence, the fit at high I is satisfactory; at the low ionic
strengths, however, where the high concentration average devi-
ates considerably from the true ε value, the D term predominates.

Obviously equation (2) cannot be used for the evaluation of the
interaction coefficients of ions capable of existing at appreciable concentrations only in mixtures, as e.g. Fe^{3+} and $AgNH_3^+$.
In these cases the ε values were estimated by considering an
equilibrium or a cell reaction in which the species whose ε is
sought participates together with other ions of known interaction coefficients, e.g., the magnitude of $\varepsilon(Fe^{3+},ClO_4^-)$ was deduced by considering the equilibrium

$$Fe^{3+} + Ag \rightleftharpoons Fe^{2+} + Ag^+ \tag{3}$$

which was studied by chemical analysis by Schumb and Sweetzer
in perchloric acid media ranging from 0.1 to 1.2 m. Application
of equation (1) yields the relationship

$$\log K_3 + 4D = \log K_3^o + m_{ClO_4^-} \cdot \{\varepsilon(Fe^{3+},ClO_4^-) - \varepsilon(Fe^{2+},ClO_4^-) -$$
$$- \varepsilon(Ag^+,ClO_4^-)\} \tag{4}$$

Here K_3 is the symbol for the concentration constant, and K_3^o
stands for its limiting value in dilute solutions. A plot of
$\log K_3 + 4D$ versus $m_{ClO_4^-}$ could be easily approximated by a
straight line. Its intercept furnished a value for $\log K_o$ (and
hence also that $e^o(Fe^{3+},Fe^{2+}) = 779.6 \pm 1$ mV), and its slope
yielded the estimate $\varepsilon(Fe^{3+},ClO_4^-) = 0.56$ m^{-1}, as the interaction coefficients $\varepsilon(Fe^{2+},ClO_4^-)$ and $\varepsilon(Ag^+,ClO_4^-)$ were known
from other sources.

On the medium effect on standard potentials

Our interest in this problem originated mainly from the desire

to test the validity of the interaction theory in some simple
but still realistic cases. Moreover, we also would like to
gain some idea on the feasibility of interaction coefficient
-based predictions concerning the regulation of redox potentials by medium adjustment.

We first turn to couples in which the standard potentials
could have been evaluated straightforwardly by emf measurements in dilute solutions.

The formal potentials of the half-cells shown in TABLE 1 were
determined in a series of $NaClO_4$ media by the investigators
referenced in the legend of this TABLE. The formal potentials
represent standard potentials in a specified medium. We will
denote them by the symbol η^0. They are evaluated by extrapolation, on the basis of emf data measured with low reacting
species concentrations. The extrapolation is required to eliminate the liquid junction potential.

For cations Me^{p+} we have the relationship between the standard
potential e^0, and η^0:

$$\eta^0 = e^0 + p^{-1}RT\ln10F^{-1}\log\frac{\gamma_{Me^{p+}}^{trace}}{(\gamma_{H^+}^{trace})^p}$$

and for the silver halides $\eta^0 = e^0 - RT\ln10F^{-1}\log\gamma_{H^+}^{trace}\gamma_{X^-}^{trace}$.

As the interaction coefficients $\varepsilon(H^+,ClO_4^-)$, $\varepsilon(Na^+,Cl^-)$,
$\varepsilon(Na^+,I^-)$, and $\varepsilon(Tl^+,ClO_4^-)$ are accessible from the isopiestic
measurements of Robinson and Stokes [14], the $\eta^0(Cl^-/AgCl)$,
$\eta^0(I^-/AgI)$, and $\eta^0(Tl^+,Tl)$ functions may be evaluated directly.
Since the osmotic coefficients of $Cd(ClO_4)_2$ and $AgClO_4$ solutions do not seem to have been made the subject of an experimental study, additional assumptions were needed to deduce the
$\eta^0(Ag^+/Ag)$ and $\eta^0(Cd^{2+},Cd)$ functions. The interaction coefficients $\varepsilon(Ag^+,ClO_4^-)$ and $\varepsilon(Cd^{2+},ClO_4^-)$ were calculated from the
relevant η^0 and e^0 data; the latter were taken from the
Stability Constants [17]. For the Cd^{2+}/Cd half-cell the assump-
tion that $\varepsilon(Cd^{2+},ClO_4^-) = \varepsilon(Zn^{2+},ClO_4^-)$ was tested as well. This
attempt was prompted by Libuś´ and Sadowska´s results, who
have shown [8] that the osmotic coefficients of the doubly

charged transition metal perchlorate solutions up to 3 m practically coincide with those of the corresponding magnesium perchlorate solutions.

The η^0 values of TABLE 1 are recalculated for the sake of consistency to the weight molarity scale; they differ therefore
somewhat from the data of the authors. This convention is maintained throughout this discussion. Thus, the equilibrium constants are also given in weight molarity units. The recalculations were made by utilizing published density data.

The deviations in TABLE 1 are seen not to exceed 0.1 units in
log γ. This degree of discrepancy may often be tolerated for
practical purposes.

We now consider couples which cannot be studied in dilute solutions because of hydrolysis. As a consequence, the standard potentials for these half-cells could not be determined with a desirable accuracy.

In 1916, Linhart [9] developed the most reliable experimental
approach for ascertaining the e° values for this type of couple.
He studied with the intention to find $e^\circ(Hg_2^{2+},Hg)$ the emf of
the cell

$$H_2 \mid HClO_4H \mid HClO_4H,Hg_2(ClO_4)_2B \mid Hg \qquad BH^{-1} \ll 1 \qquad (5)$$

as a function of H. Later, in 1926, this cell was investigated
comprehensively by Fenwick [2].

Inserting into the cell equation the expressions for the relevant activity factors according to equation (1) we obtain

$$E_5 + 29.58 \log \frac{H^2}{B} + 59.16D = 29.58\{\varepsilon(Hg_2^{2+},ClO_4^-) -$$
$$-2\varepsilon(H^+,ClO_4^-)\}m_{ClO_4^-} + e^\circ(Hg_2^{2+},Hg) \qquad (5a)$$

As long as the ionic strength dependence of the interaction
coefficients remains negligible compared with the experimental
precision, the data of equation (5a) should be fitted to a
straight line. As FIG. 2 demonstrates, this condition is satisfied up to I = 2.4. We may therefore with some confidence con-

clude that $e^o(Hg_2^{2+},Hg) = 796.0 \pm 0.5$ mV and $\varepsilon(Hg_2^{2+},ClO_4^-) =$
$= 0.09 \pm 0.01$ mV. These results are supported by the analo-
gous evaluation of Bonner's and Unietis' glass electrode data
in nitric acid media [1]. Covering the I range 0.05 to 0.7 m,
the evaluation affords $e^o(Hg_2^{2+},Hg) = 795.5 \pm 0.3$ mV. Previous estimates for this standard potential varied between 789
and 799 mV. The difficulties were caused by the special assumptions introduced to take the activity factors into account.
The assumptions necessitated the consideration of emf data obtained in dilute solutions where the redox buffer capacity becomes quite low.

A similar treatment of the data of Popoff et al. [13], who studied the Hg^{2+}/Hg_2^{2+} couple in $HClO_4$ media, is graphically represented in FIG. 3. The treatment leaves little doubt that the
data for I < 0.1 m are less reliable. The deviations cannot be
explained by the hydrolysis of Hg^{2+}.

The result $e^o(Hg^{2+},Hg_2^{2+}) = 914.0 \pm 0.5$ mV differs considerably
from earlier estimates which for reasons just mentioned were
based on the uncertain emf data.

We can calculate with this e^o value and with $\varepsilon(Hg^{2+},ClO_4^-) = 0.34$
that $\eta^o(Hg^{2+},Hg_2^{2+}, 2.2$ m $ClO_4^-) = 923.7$ mV. Zielen and Sullivan
[18] obtained in 2.2 m $HClO_4$ 921.6 mV and in 2.2 m $NaClO_4$ medium
916.7 mV. If the interaction theory were strictly valid, the
formal potentials in these two media would be identical.

On the basis of these evaluations we can deduce for the perchlo-
rate medium dependence of the equilibrium $Hg^{2+} + Hg \rightleftharpoons Hg_2^{2+}$, the
equation

$$\log K_6 = 1.99 + 0.25\ m_{ClO_4^-} \tag{6}$$

which according to the theory should be independent of the nature
of the cation present.

In FIG. 4 equation (6) is compared with Hietanen's and Sillén's
data [6]. The deviations are seen to become serious for ionic

strength values exceeding 1 m. A recent determination of log K_6 in 3.5 m $NaClO_4$ in this laboratory furnished the value of 2.66; equation (6) gives 2.86.

Another application is to estimate the medium influence on the magnitude of the solubility product of HgO, $K_s = [Hg^{2+}][H^+]^{-2}$. Again in 3.5 m $NaClO_4$ we obtained in this laboratory that log K_s(3.5 m) = 2.70 ± 0.01. The theory indicates 2.6.

Finally, we would like to comment on some problems associated with the determination of $e^{\circ}(Fe^{3+},Fe^{2+})$. The approach based on equilibrium (3) was discussed briefly in the preceding section. A few additional remarks are needed. The value for $\varepsilon(Ag^+,ClO_4^-)$ was taken from the data of TABLE 1; moreover it was assumed, for reasons discussed in connection with the estimation of $\eta^{\circ}(Cd^{2+},Cd)$, that $\varepsilon(Fe^{2+},ClO_4^-) = \varepsilon(Mg^{2+},ClO_4^-)$. I am unable to propose a method to overcome the experimental difficulties involved in the determination of the activity factor of iron(II)-perchlorate.

With $e^{\circ}(Fe^{3+},Fe^{2+})$ 779.6 and the pertinent interaction coefficients, we can derive for $\eta^{\circ}(Fe^{3+},Fe^{2+})$ the equation

$$\eta^{\circ} = 779.6 + 59.16(0.09I-4D) \tag{7}$$

for the ionic strength dependence of the formal potential in perchlorate media. Equation (7) is compared with the data of the investigators referenced in the legend in FIG. 5. The measurements at $m_{HClO_4} \le 0.1$ m were corrected for hydrolysis. The medium effect for the formation constant of $FeOH^{2+}$ was estimated with the data obtained in 3.5 and 1 m $NaClO_4$.

An analogous data treatment afforded for $e^{\circ}(Tl^{3+},Tl^+)$ the value of 1286 ± 1 mV.

TABLE 1

Estimation of formal potential values in $NaClO_4$ media

m_{NaClO_4}	Ag⁺ + e⁻ ⇌ Ag(s) η^0 mV *	Δ mV	Tl⁺ + e⁻ ⇌ Tl(s) η^0 mV	Δ mV	Cd²⁺ + 2e⁻ ⇌ Cd(s) η^0 mV	Δ mV	Δ_1 mV	AgCl(s) + e⁻ ⇌ Ag + Cl⁻ η^0 mV	Δ mV	m_{NaClO_4}	AgI(s) + e⁻ ⇌ Ag + I⁻ η^0 mV	Δ mV
1.05	792.4	−	−357.2	−2.8	−410.6	− ※	+1.4	234.9	−3.3	1	−142(2)	−3
2.21	784.0	+1.8	−374.8	−2.5	−409.5	−1.8	+1.7	225.6	−4.2	3	−164(2)	−3
3.50	775.3	+3.0	−393.0	−0.7	−409.1	−5.2	0.0	211.4	−4.6	3.5	−166.8(1)	+0.5
					−407.0(1)	−3.1	+2.1	214.7(1)	−1.3	6	−201(2)	+3

(1): Leden, I. 1943. Thesis, Lund.

(2): Schwabe, K.; Ferse, E.; and Reetz, T. 1967. Berichte Bunseng. $\underline{71}$: 101.

All the other η^0 data are taken from the work of Kraft, W. 1967. Monatshefte $\underline{98}$: 1978.

Δ = measured formal potential minus estimated formal potential

Δ_1 = estimate based on the assumption that $\varepsilon(Cd^{2+}, ClO_4^-) = \varepsilon(Zn^{2+}, ClO_4^-) = 0.34$

* : $\varepsilon(Ag^+, ClO_4^-) = 0.0$

※ : $\varepsilon(Cd^{2+}, ClO_4^-) = 0.363$

On the medium effect on equilibrium constants

Two illustrative examples only from this very wide field will be considered due to space limitations.

The interaction coefficients deduced in the preceding section may be employed to estimate in perchlorate media the magnitude of various equilibrium constants involving Hg_2^{2+} and Hg^{2+}. The results of these calculations are presented in TABLE 2.

The procedure for $\log K_s$ is straightforward. To estimate the value of $\log \beta_1$, the measurements in the two perchloric acid media were used to derive the interaction coefficient $\varepsilon(HgCl^+, ClO_4^-)$ and the logarithm of the equilibrium constant in activity terms, $\log \beta_1^0$.

For the prediction of $\log \beta_2$ (I), the activity factor of the uncharged species $HgCl_2$ is needed in perchlorate media. This was determined by Marcus [12] who found his distribution equilibrium data to be explained by the simple equation given in TABLE 2. The validity of the interaction theory was tested by calculating from each $\log \beta_2$ (I) value the logarithm of the activity constant, $\log \beta_2^0$. If the theory were exact, the variation of the computed $\log \beta_2^0$ values would not exceed the experimental uncertainty.

Estimates for the medium effect on the protolysis equilibrium of the NH_4^+ ion are summarized in TABLE 3. The remarkably large medium effect is due to the great difference between the activity factors of perchloric, hydrochloric, and nitric acid and the corresponding ammonium salts. Harned´s and Robinson´s hydroxide ion concentration data in alkali chloride solutions were converted to pK_a values, by taking into account the relevant autoprotolysis constants which had been evaluated by Harned and his coworkers [5].

TABLE 2

Estimation of the magnitude of equilibrium constants involving Hg_2^{2+} and Hg^{2+} ions

		3 M NaClO$_4$	3 M HClO$_4$	1 M NaClO$_4$	0.5 M NaClO$_4$	0.5 M HClO$_4$	Comments
$Hg_2Cl_2(s) \rightleftharpoons$	$-\log K_s$ meas	$17.12^{(1)}$	$17.67^{(2)}$	–	$16.88^{(3)}$	$16.95^{(2)}$	$-\log K_s^0 =$ $= 17.88$
$Hg_2^{2+} + 2Cl^-$	$-\log K_s$ est	16.9_0	17.5_3	16.8_0	16.8_9	16.9_9	
$Hg^{2+} + Cl^-$	$\log \beta_1$ meas	$7.00^{(1)}$	$7.45^{(2)}$	$7.70^{(4)}$	$6.74^{(3)}$	$6.94^{(2)}$	$\varepsilon(HgCl^+, ClO_4^-)$ $= 0.20$
$\rightleftharpoons HgCl^+$	$\log \beta_1$ est	7.1_3	–	6.8_8	6.8_9		$\log \beta_1^0 = 7.50$
$Hg^{2+} + 2Cl^-$	$\log \beta_2$ meas	$13.8_5 \pm 0.2^{(1)}$	$14.6 \pm 0.2^{(2)}$	$13.19^{(4)}$	$13.22^{(3)}$	$13.32^{(2)}$	$\log \gamma_{HgCl_2} =$ $= 0.14\ I^2$
$\rightleftharpoons HgCl_2$	$\log \beta_2^0$ est	14.3_4	14.4	14.1_4	14.1_4	14.1	

(1) : Arnek, R. 1965. Arkiv Kemi 24: 231.

(2) : Neumann, G., Unpublished work in the Stockholm laboratory.

(3) : Sillén, L.G. 1949. Acta Chem. Scand. 3: 539.

(4) : Ciavatta, L., and Grimaldi, M. 1968. J. Inorg. Nuclear Chem. 30: 197.

TABLE 3

Estimates of pK_a (I) for NH_4^+ in various media

I	NaCl pK_a	Δ	KCl pK_a	Δ	LiCl pK_a	Δ
0.1	9.37	0.1_0	9.37	0.1_1	9.35	0.0_9
0.2	.39	0.1_1	.37	0.0_9	.36	0.0_9
0.5	.44	0.1_1	.38	0.0_5	.39	0.0_9
1	.53	0.1_3	.46	0.0_5	.47	0.1_2
2	.67	0.1_2	.62	0.0_6	.63	0.20
3	.82	0.10	.74	0.0_2	.79	0.2_4

Medium	pK_a	Δ	
0.1 M KCl	9.29	0.0_3	(2)
1 M NH_4Cl	9.38	0.0_1	(3)
0.5 M NH_4NO_3	9.27	-0.0_8	(3)
2 M NH_4NO_3	9.45	-0.1_3	(4)
1 M $NaClO_4$	9.45	-0.0_5	(5)
3 M $LiClO_4$	9.88	0.10	(6)
3 M $NaNO_3$	9.78	0.0_1	(6)

(1)   Harned, H.S., and Robinson, R.A. 1928. JACS 50: 3157.
(2)   Paoletti, P.; Stern, J.H.; and Vacca, A. 1965. J.Phys. Chem. 69: 3759.
(3)   Bjerrum, J. 1941. Diss., Copenhagen.
(4)   Spike, C.G. 1953. Thesis, University of Michigan.
(5)   Wirth, T.H., and Davidson, N. 1964. JACS 86: 4325.
(6)   Unpublished work of the Stockholm laboratory.

Δ : pK_a measured minus pK_a estimated.

According to Bates, G., and Pinching, G.D. 1949. (J.Res. NBS 42: 419.)

pK_a^o was assumed to equal 9.245.

Applications to equilibrium analysis

We choose for illustration the problem of finding an approach for the study of the complex formation equilibria between the cadmium and sulfate ions. These equilibria were made the subject of a comprehensive investigation by Leden, first in 1941 and then in 1952 [10]. In the latter work Leden, on the basis of the measurement of the influence of the cadmium ions on the Ag^+/Ag half-cell potential, reached the conclusion that up to 0.75 M sulfate ion concentration a single complex species of the composition $CdSO_4$ is formed. He estimated that at the 3 M ionic strength level the logarithm of the formation constant, log β_1, equals $0.8_5 \pm 0.1$. On the other hand, Leden recognized that for the interpretation of his extensive cadmium amalgam data in concentration terms, a correction for the activity factor changes arising by the replacement of the ClO_4^- by SO_4^{2-} ions has to be introduced.

An attempt will be presented here for the estimation of these activity factor changes.

The amalgam cells studied by Leden had the general composition

$$\text{Cd-Hg(sat)} \left| \begin{array}{l} \text{B Cd(II),(3 M-B-3A)}ClO_4^- \\ \text{A } SO_4^{2-},\text{(3 M-A-3B)}Na^+ \end{array} \right| \begin{array}{l} \text{B } Cd^{2+},\text{(3 M-3B)}Na^+ \\ \text{(3 M-B)}ClO_4^- \end{array} \left| \text{Cd-Hg(sat) +} \right.$$

Thus, in all test solutions the ionic strength was maintained at 3 M. In each series the value of B was kept constant while A was increased stepwise to 0.7 M. The B range 3.33 to 100 mM was studied.

By assuming that no appreciable complex formation occurs between Cd^{2+} and SO_4^{2-}, the emf of this cell may be expressed at $25^\circ C$ by the equation

$$E_h = E_1 + E_2 + E_3$$

where

$$\frac{E_1}{29.58} = \log \frac{(a_{Cd^{2+}}\ a_{ClO_4^-}^2)\text{I}}{(a_{Cd^{2+}}\ a_{ClO_4^-}^2)\text{II}}$$

$$\frac{E_2}{59.16} = \int_{II}^{I} t_{SO_4^{2-}} \, d\log \frac{[SO_4^{2-}]^{\frac{1}{2}}}{[ClO_4^-]} - \int_{II}^{I} t_{Na^+} \, d\log[Na^+][ClO_4^-]$$

and

$$\frac{E_3}{59.16} = \int_{II}^{I} t_{SO_4^{2-}} \, d\log \frac{\gamma_{Na_2SO_4}^{3/2}}{\gamma_{NaClO_4}^2} - 2 \int_{II}^{I} t_{Na^+} \, d\log \gamma_{NaClO_4}$$

In these equations the symbol I denotes the sulfate-free solution in the positive half-cell, while II denotes that containing A SO_4^{2-}. The transport numbers are represented by t. The transport number of the cadmium ions was neglected in these calculations; the equation $t_{Na^+} + t_{ClO_4^-} + t_{SO_4^{2-}} = 1$ was thus assumed to be valid. As B was kept below 0.04 I, no significant error is likely to arise from this neglect.

The interaction coefficient between Cd^{2+} and ClO_4^- was evaluated previously in connection with the discussion of the formal potential of the Cd^{2+}/Cd half-cell. The magnitudes of $\varepsilon(Na^+,ClO_4^-)$ and of $\varepsilon(Na^+,SO_4^{2-})$ were evaluated from the isopiestic data of Robinson and Stokes [14].

The crucial point has been to estimate the hypothetical interaction coefficient $\varepsilon(Cd^{2+},SO_4^{2-})$ which would prevail in the absence of complex formation. It was assumed that $\varepsilon(Cd^{2+},SO_4^{2-},3.5) = \varepsilon(Mg^{2+},SO_4^{2-},3.5)$. Consequently, we take as reference $MgSO_4$-$NaClO_4$ solutions of I = 3.5 m. Hence we can detect only complex formation exceeding that occurring between Mg^{2+} and SO_4^{2-} ions.

The integrals were evaluated by the hypothesis that in the transition region, which is formed between solution I and II, the ionic strength remains constant throughout, and that the $[ClO_4^-]$ varies continuously between (3 M-B) and (3 M-3B-A). Furthermore, the mobilities of SO_4^{2-} and ClO_4^- were assumed to equal their values in 1.5 M Na_2SO_4 and 3 M $NaClO_4$ solutions, while the mobility of the Na^+ ion was taken to vary linearly between the values valid in 1 M Na_2SO_4 and 3 M $NaClO_4$. The transport number and conductance of 3 M $NaClO_4$ solutions were recently measured in

this laboratory. The transport number of the sulfate ion was
assumed to equal $t_{SO_4^{2-}}$ in 0.2 M Na_2SO_4 which was determined
by Longsworth [11]. The specific conductance of 1 M Na_2SO_4
was estimated to 0.0927 $\Omega^{-1}cm^{-1}$ by interpolating the data compiled in Gmelins Handbuch (Natrium, Ergänzungsband, Lieferung
3, 1966, page 1137). The relevant values for log γ_{NaClO_4} and
log $\gamma_{Na_2SO_4}$ were calculated in each of the transition layers
by the specific interaction theory.

To enable us to gain some idea of the complex formation equilibria the difference between the measured (E) and calculated
(E_h) emf value was assumed to satisfy the equation

$$E - E_h = 29.58 \log \frac{B}{[Cd^{2+}]}$$

The results of these calculations are illustrated in FIG. 5
where the average number of cadmium ions bound per sulfate,
$R = \frac{B-[Cd^{2+}]}{A}$, is plotted as a function of $\log[Cd^{2+}]$. The data
$R(\log[Cd^{2+}])$ are seen to be satisfactorily explained by the
hypothesis that log β_1 = $\log([CdSO_4][Cd^{2+}]^{-1}[SO_4^{2-}]^{-1})$ = 0.6±0.1.

The small discrepancy between the present result and Leden's
conclusion, which is based on a method that virtually eliminates
the influence of the activity factor variations, inspires
confidence in the data evaluation treatment proposed.

Our estimate for E_h represents only a first approximation, and
it should be refined. With the help of the β_1 value obtained,
$\log(\gamma_{Cd^{2+}})_{II}$ had to be recalculated with the actual $[SO_4^{2-}]$ instead of the A data which were employed. The error arising
from this source is greatest for the highest B level. In view
of the uncertainties involved in the evaluation of the liquid
junction potential, the second approximation was not undertaken.

Some conclusions of general interest for research planning may
be gained on the basis of our calculations.

First, we can recognize that the largest variation in log $\gamma_{Cd^{2+}}$
arises because of the great difference between $\varepsilon(Cd^{2+}, ClO_4^-)$ and
$\varepsilon(Mg^{2+}, SO_4^{2-})$ which at I = 3.5 m amounts to 0.55 m^{-1}. If, instead

of keeping I constant, the $[ClO_4^-]$ would have been maintained
at the 3.5 m level, $\log \gamma_{Cd}2+$ would have shown a much smaller
variation with the sulfate ion concentration.

At the high ionic strength values in question the magnitude of
the D(I) term variation becomes almost insignificant; an increase in I from 3.5 to 5.6 m, corresponding to the passage
from 3.5 m $NaClO_4$ to a solution containing in addition 0.7 m
Na_2SO_4, entails a change in D(I) affecting E by 1.7 mV only.
Indeed, besides the suppression of the magnitude of the liquid
junction potential, the main reason for the success of the
ionic medium method is that it employs solutions of such a high
ionic strength that the change in the D term due to ligand replacement and complex formation may be neglected.

It is perhaps appropriate now to call attention to the great
practical value of the specific interaction theory to estimate
the integrals occurring in the expression for the liquid junction potentials. In highly acidic and highly alkaline solutions
they are often difficult to avoid and represent a serious
source of uncertainty. In a project now being conducted in cooperation with Dr. Gerard Douhéret, much evidence has been obtained for the usefulness of the specific interaction theory in
evaluating liquid junction potentials.

In the intermediate pH range they can be entirely eliminated by
employing a sodium (alkali) ion sensitive glass electrode as the
reference half-cell (cf. Biedermann, G.; Lagrange, J.; and
Lagrange, P. 1974. Chemica Scripta, 5: 153). Emf values obtained
with the sodium ion sensitive glass electrode using cadmium perchlorate-sodium perchlorate-sodium chloride mixtures are now being assessed by a treatment similar to that presented for the
cadmium sulfate solutions.

The weak complex formation between Tl^+ and Cl^-, which was also
studied by liquid junction potential-free cells, is being re-exam-
ined on the basis of the specific interaction theory as well.

In each case the most problematical step is to guess the experi-

mentally inaccessible interaction coefficients as $\varepsilon(Cd^{2+},Cl^-)$
and $\varepsilon(Tl^+,Cl^-)$. The former was set in our calculations equal to
$\varepsilon(Mg^{2+},Cl^-)$ and the latter to $\varepsilon(NH_4^+,Cl^-)$. Another difficulty
arises in connection with the estimate of the medium effect on
neutral species, as $CdCl_2$ and $TlCl$. The value of γ_{CdCl_2} was
approximated with $HgCl_2$. No model species could, however, be
found for $TlCl$.

Conclusions

The calculations of this discussion appear to show that for I
levels up to 3 to 4 m activity coefficients can be estimated by
the ionic interaction theory with an uncertainty not likely to
exceed 20%, corresponding to 0.1 unit in log γ.

The next step in developing a more reliable theory for electrolyte mixtures is to introduce interaction coefficients between
ions of the same sign charge. Such coefficients were evaluated
by Guggenheim [3] for a few 1:1 electrolyte mixtures and by
Rush [15] for many mixtures of different charge type.

A systematic extension of their pioneer investigation would en-
tail, however, an enormous effort. Further progress requires
methods which would enable us to estimate interaction coefficients on the basis of the molecular properties of ionic species.

REFERENCES

(1)   Bonner, O.D., and Unietis, F.A. 1953. JACS 75: 5111.

(2)   Fenwick, F. 1926. JACS 48: 860.

(3)   Guggenheim, E.A. 1966. Applications of Statistical
      Mechanics, Oxford, Clarendon Press.

(4)   Güntelberg, E., and Schiödt, E. 1928. Z.ph.Chem. 135:
      393.

(5)   Harned, H.S. , and Owen, B.B. 1958. The Physical
      Chemistry of Electrolytic Solutions, New York,
      Reinhold Publishing Corporation.

(6)   Hietanen, S., and Sillén, L.G. 1956. Arkiv Kemi 10:
      103.

(7) Latimer, W.M. 1952. The Oxidation State of the
     Elements, New York, Prentice-Hall, Inc.

(8) Libus, Z., and Sadowska, T. 1969. J.Phys.Chem. $\underline{73}$:
     3229.

(9) Linhart, G.A. 1916. JACS $\underline{38}$: 2356.

(10) Leden, I. 1952. Acta Chem.Scand. $\underline{6}$: 971.

(11) Longsworth, L.G. 1935. JACS $\underline{57}$: 1185.

(12) Marcus, Y. 1957. Acta Chem.Scand. $\underline{11}$: 329.

(13) Popoff, S.; Riddick, J.A.; Wirth, V.I.; and Ough, L.D.
     1931. JACS $\underline{55}$: 1195.

(14) Robinson, R.A., and Stokes, R.H. 1959. Electrolyte
     Solutions, London, Butterworth.

(15) Rush, R.M. 1969. Parameters for the Calculation of
     Osmotic and Activity Coefficients. ORNL, Oak Ridge,
     Tennessee.

(16) Scatchard, G. 1936. Chem.Revs. $\underline{19}$: 309. An especially
     lucid description is given in his lecture notes. Equi-
     librium in solutions, 1956. MIT, Cambridge, Massachu-
     setts.

(17) Sillén, L.G., and Martell, A.E. 1964 and 1971. Stability
     Constants of Metal Ion Complexes, London, The Chemical
     Society, Spec.Publ. No. 17 and 25.

(18) Zielen, A.J., and Sullivan, J.C. 1962. J.Phys.Chem.
     $\underline{66}$: 1065.

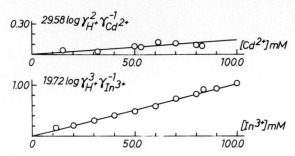

Figure 1. Variation of activity factor ratios at 3 M $[ClO_4^-]$
level. Upper half: 29.58 log $\gamma_{H^+}^2\gamma_{Cd^{2+}}^{-1}$ versus $[Cd^{2+}]$, 3 M
$LiClO_4$. The line represents the equation log $\gamma_{H^+}^2\gamma_{Cd^{2+}}^{-1}$ =
= $1.2[Cd^{2+}]$, the interaction theory yields 0.06 mV for the
value of this function at 100 mM $[Cd^{2+}]$.

Lower half: 19.72 log $\gamma_{H^+}^3\gamma_{In^{3+}}^{-1}$ versus $[In^{3+}]$, 3 M $NaClO_4$. The
line shows the equation 19.72 log $\gamma_{H^+}^3\gamma_{In^{3+}}^{-1}$ = $10.2[In^{3+}]$, the
theory gives 0.37 mV for the value of this function at 100 mM
$[In^{3+}]$.

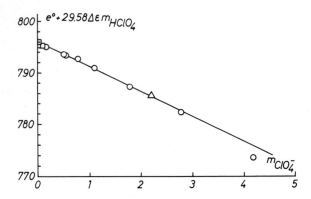

Figure 2. Determination of $e^o(Hg_2^{2+},Hg)$. Data: o Fenwick, F.
1928. JACS 48: 860, □ Linhart, G.A. 1916. JACS 38: 2356,
Δ Zielen, A.J., and Sullivan, J.C. 1962. J.Phys.Chem. 66:1065.
The line represents the equation 796.0-29.58(0.162) m_{HClO_4}.

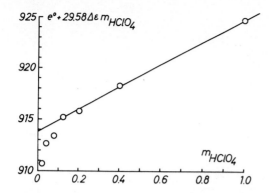

Figure 3.   Determination of $e^{\circ}(Hg^{2+},Hg_2^{2+})$. Data: Popoff, S. et al. 1931. JACS $\underline{53}$: 1195. The line represents the equation $913.9 + 29.58(0.365)\ m_{HClO_4}$.

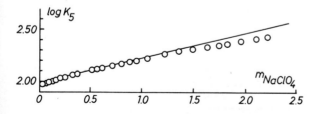

Figure 4. $\log K_5 = \log[Hg_2^{2+}][Hg^{2+}]^{-1}$ as a function of m_{NaClO_4} Data: Hietanen, S., and Sillén, L.G. 1956. Arkiv Kemi $\underline{10}$: 103. The line shows the equation $\log K_5 = 1.99 + 0.25\ m_{HClO_4}$.

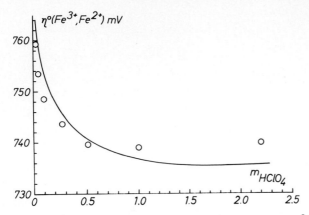

Figure 5. The formal potential of the Fe^{3+},Fe^{2+} couple in perchloric acid media. Data: Schumb, W.C.; Sherill, S.M.; and Sweetzer, S.B. 1937. JACS 59: 2360; Connick, R.E., and Mc Vey, W.H. 1951. JACS 73: 1798; Magnusson, L.B., and Huizenga, J.R. 1953. JACS 75: 2242; Zielen, A.J., and Sullivan, J.C. 1962. J.Phys.Chem. 66: 1065. The curve represents the equation $\eta_o = 779.6 + 59.16(-4D+0.09 \, m \, HClO_4)$.

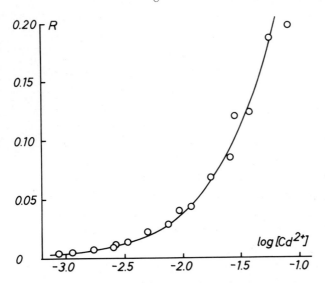

Figure 6. The average number of cadmium ions bound by sulfate, $R = (B-[Cd^{2+}])A^{-1}$, as a function of $\log [Cd^{2+}]$. The curve represents the hypothesis that $\log \beta_1 = 0.60$.

Kinetic Problems in Seawater
Group Report

J. M. Edmond, Rapporteur
N. R. Andersen   W. Schneider
R. A. Berner   K. Wagener
E. D. Goldberg   R. G. Wilkins
G. R. Harris   J. M. Wood

INTRODUCTION

Why is it important to study the kinetics of chemical reactions
in seawater? In order to provide a background to answer this
question, it is instructive to consider a simple outline of
marine circulation and chemistry. Over most of its area the
ocean has a relatively simple two-layer structure. The upper
layer, of average depth about 75 m, is well-mixed vertically
by the wind and shows latitudinal gradients in properties determined by the climatic gradients. Thus, in low latitudes it
is warm (>20°C) and, because of evaporation, relatively salty
(>3.5% total dissolved salts, by weight); at higher latitudes
it becomes progressively cooler but also more dilute (<3.4%)
because of the increase of precipitation relative to evaporation. Since the effect on the density of seawater of a one
degree decrease in temperature is about the same as an increase
in the salinity of 0.01%, the effects of the climatic gradients
on temperature and salinity cancel approximately, the mixed
layer being of relatively low density. At certain specific
high latitude locations, however, cold and salty water is produced by evaporative and radiative cooling to the freezing
point (~-1.8°C) and by the subsequent freezing out of pack ice.
Such waters form almost solely at the opposite ends of the

Atlantic in the Norwegian and Weddell Seas. They cascade down
into the deep sea and propagate through the ocean basins, the
water mixing slowly upwards along its path to complete the
cycle. The ocean is therefore ventilated continuously and maintained at an average temperature of about 4°C.

The circulation of the Atlantic can be represented as two large
convection cells driven by intense cooling and freezing at high
latitudes and dissipating by vertical mixing with warmer waters
at low latitudes. Because there are no dense waters formed in
the northern Indian Ocean (the temperature is too high) or in
the north Pacific (the rainfall is too high) these oceans consist of single cells both driven from the Weddell Sea. The ven-
tilation time for the Atlantic is around 700 years. For the
Pacific it is about 1500 years.

The surface mixed layer floats on these dense waters, and the
sharp vertical gradient in the density which marks their interface (the pycnocline) acts as a strong barrier to vertical fluid
mixing. The photic zone - the layer illuminated by sunlight -
coincides in general with the mixed layer and the uppermost
part of the pycnocline. Hence, primary productivity and the
base of the food chain are confined to the upper layers of the
ocean. Organisms absorb from the water the dissolved constituents necessary for life and fix them as particles - tissues and
hard parts. Upon the death or grazing of these organisms their
remains sink across the pycnocline mixing barrier into the deep
sea. The photic zone is continually being stripped of the chemicals essential for life processes.

The cycle is closed in the deep interior of the oceans, where
the particles are regenerated in soluble form by metabolic and
inorganic processes. The deep water column is enriched in all
the elements of biochemical importance relative to surface
waters. Over most of the ocean the slow upward diffusion of
water resupplies these to the photic zone. However, biological
productivity is, in general, nutrient limited. Commonly, in the

central oceans the concentrations of phosphate and nitrate in
the mixed layer are below 10^{-7} molar. In certain localized
places, due to hydrodynamic processes in the wind-driven shallow
water circulation, the pycnocline is eroded down and nutrient-
rich waters mixed up to the surface. Well-known examples are
the large fishing grounds off Peru and Southwest Africa, and
in the Antarctic Ocean and the North Pacific and Bering Sea.

The overall cycle is not completely closed but "leaks" to the
extent of a few percent. Biogenous sediments accumulate in certain regions of the ocean floor where the rate of decomposition
of organisms at the sediment surface is slower than their pre-
servation by burial under the continuing rain of material. As
a result of this, the concentration level of most of the biologically important elements in seawater is controlled by the
balance between the river input rate from the continents and
the removal rate to these biogenous sediments. It is a reasonable assumption that the composition of the ocean is quite close
to steady state. However, our understanding of the processes
maintaining this balance is almost entirely descriptive. There
have been very few studies of the kinetics and mechanisms of
the actual reactions controlling regeneration and of their
responses to differing oceanographic environments.

The situation is similar for the inorganic processes going on
in seawater. The exchange of dissolved gases between the atmosphere and ocean serves as the primary control on their concentrations in the gas phase. Other processes complicate the
situation. Two are hydrodynamic; the large scale ocean circulation, expressed as the residence time of water in the mixed
layer relative to the deep sea (about 20 years) determines the
rate at which, for instance, anthropogenic CO_2 can be mixed
into the oceanic reservoir; within the laminar boundary layer
molecular diffusion occurs, slowing the exchange rate. For
CO_2, slow kinetics of the hydration reaction further inhibits
exchange. Thus, the transfer of CO_2 between the sea and the

atmosphere is much slower than for oxygen or the other non-hydrated gases.

Crystalline phases form inorganically at the sediment-water interface and within the sediment itself. The best known examples are the ferromanganese nodules. These grow at an average rate of several millimeters per million years in the deep sea. They show a diverse compositional and crystalline chemistry and interesting systematic relationships between the ratios of the minor and major constituents, Mn, Fe, Ni, Cu, Co, Cr, etc. The formation and growth processes, the reactions and mechanisms, are not understood; neither are the factors controlling the incorporation of the trace transition metals or the oxidation states. It can be said in general that almost nothing is known about the chemistry of transition metals at trace concentration ($\sim 10^{-9}$ molar) in mixed electrolytes at intermediate pH.

PROBLEM AREAS

The composition of seawater can be expected to change continuously as a consequence of the activities of human society. These alterations in composition will perturb the geochemistry of the marine environment and may conceivably affect life processes, especially in enclosed seas and coastal areas. The largest contemporary anthropogenic effect results from the burning of fossil fuel. The CO_2 produced is presently increasing the atmospheric concentration (320ppm) by over 0.7% per year. The sulfur, introduced as SO_2, reacts with the atmosphere to form sulfuric acid. The resulting "acid rain" of pH<4 (and even, on occasion, <3) has resulted in severe ecological problems in soft water lakes in Scandinavia and the eastern United States. The river-borne load of sulfate is presently about double the natural one. Although difficult to quantify given the strongly perturbed nature of the system, it is likely that the generally increased acidity of precipitation in the Northern Hemisphere will increase the weathering rate of rocks and soils

and hence,"accelerate" the geochemical cycle. The kinetics of
oxidation of SO_2 are not well understood. The heterogeneous
reactions involved in the weathering of rocks are only beginning
to be studied. While the existence of acid rain and of increased atmospheric CO_2 is well documented, their effects cannot
be understood without the link of chemical kinetics.

The effects of society's influence on the geochemical environment will be recorded in marine sediments. Increased levels of
lead, silver, and other exotic industrial metals have already
been reported in coastal deposits. Predictive understanding
of the response of the global chemical system to stress can
perhaps be gained from an understanding of the record of past
environments which is contained in deep sea sediments. A large
amount of kinetic information will be required in the decoding
of this record. Trace metals are of particular interest in this
context since they are essential to living organisms, are potentially dangerous as pollutants, and occur as important components of marine sediments (especially ferromanganese nodules).
The sedimentary occurrence is known to be complex, indicating
a rich and varied chemistry. The reaction kinetics of trace
metals in a seawater-type medium at intermediate pH and in the
presence of solid phases are at present unexplored by experimental chemists.

APPROACHES

Approaches used at the present time by biologists to study environmental problems include the holistic approach (systems
analysis) versus the reductionist approach (the study of processes). In the sea, we can separate our efforts into these
two categories: model systems analysis including both theoretical and laboratory models; process analysis through the study
of (a) geochemical processes; (b) the biological perturbations
upon these; and (c) the environmental perturbations upon both
geological and biological processes.

Typical Problems

The CO_2 equilibration in the ocean involves three factors:
(1) The interfacial exchange between atmosphere and ocean;
(2) The homogeneous chemical reaction within the ocean;
(3) The vertical transport of CO_2 within the ocean.

Most further effort should be devoted to items (2) and (3).
The most important homogeneous reaction is the hydration reaction of dissolved carbon dioxide and its subsequent dissociation according to equation (1):

$$CO_2 + H_2O \rightleftharpoons H_2CO_3 \rightleftharpoons H^+ + HCO_3^- \rightleftharpoons H^+ + CO_3^{2-} \tag{1}$$

This equilibration acts as the instantaneous local control of
the pH of seawater. It has been thoroughly studied in aqueous
solution, both from a thermodynamic and kinetic viewpoint. The
first step is the rate controlling one and will be sensitive
to biological materials such as carbonic anhydrase if present
in appreciable quantities.

Inorganic Reactions

It should be stressed that some inorganic reactions occurring in
the upper level of the sea (100 meters) may be heterogeneous
rather than homogeneous in character. However, these are unlikely to alter the characteristics of the fast ionic reactions.
A number of these have been studied in aqueous solution. The
chemistry of transition metals at very low concentrations in a
seawater-type medium is a new and important field of great potential in marine chemistry. Perhaps concentrated effort towards
one transition metal may be most rewarding. Iron may be a
suitable candidate for input studies because of its abundance,
variable oxidation states, and involvements in biological and
sedimentary systems. Cobalt also appears attractive because of
the availability of a tracer isotope (Co-60), its biological
importance, multiple oxidation states, and its enrichment in

ferromanganese minerals.   Chromium is also worthy of consideration for similar reasons.

Heterogeneous Chemical System

Many of the chemical reactions which affect the composition of
seawater take place within the uppermost meter of the bottom
sediments; that is, we have a heterogeneous chemical system.
Active transport of dissolved species between sediment and water
takes place. The sediments are altered by compaction (advec-
tion of water) and by diffusion. These physical processes can
be modelled explicitly. Within the context of such models,
variations in the concentrations of solutes and solids can be
interpreted kinetically. This approach is crude and lumps together all processes affecting the species under consideration.
Laboratory studies are needed which both duplicate the natural
environment as closely as possible, and which enable the elucidation of rate laws and mechanisms. Reaction in sediment is
largely heterogeneous, and invariably influenced by biological
activity, both directly (e.g., bacterial sulfate reduction) and
indirectly (precipitation of $CaCO_3$ from HCO_3^- formed by sulfate
reduction). A major problem in duplicating natural sediment
reactions in the laboratory is the time scale. Many sedimentary reactions in the top meter take place within times of the
order of 10^2 to 10^6 years. The simulation of such reactions in
the laboratory and their concurrent study pose a challenge to
the experimentalist.

"Box Models"

"Box models" are a good basis for a preliminary understanding
of a system. In terms of systems analysis, we have to define
proper compartments which may be identified with different chemical states of the element (including organisms), and also
sources and sinks (if existing). The next step is to analyze
the physical properties of each compartment, whether they fit
the characteristics of one box, or a series of boxes, or have

to be represented by a continuous <u>diffusive phase</u>. In order
to keep the number of boxes small, only long-lived intermediates
can be taken into account. Such an engineering approach to the
understanding of an elementary cycle offers the best opportunity
to check all data for consistency and to identify important
areas of ignorance. Continuous models require maximum information on the physics and chemistry of the system for their application and bring in the whole range of oceanographic experience.

Box modeling of the global sulfur cycle appears promising. Recent work has greatly clarified the mechanisms of bacterial formation of H_2S. It is of great importance to extend this work
to the determination of kinetic parameters applicable to marine
and terrestrial systems. This will involve detailed work on
the nature of the $SO_4^=/SO_2/H_2S/$ organic sulfur interconversions
and of the rate-limiting processes involved. Isotopic measurements of sulfur may help to determine the fluxes of the natural
and anthropogenic components.

TECHNIQUES

Isotopic Procedures

Isotopes can be used both to identify reactants by labeling and
to study reactions through fractionation effects. Both techniques are still in the early stages of application to seawater
chemistry.

The study of diffusion using radioisotopes has been reported
for a few instances. Given the importance of diffusion in the
study and interpretation of reactions in pore waters, systematic work should be undertaken in this area. The number of
available radioisotopes suitable for such studies is large.
Diffusion in heterogeneous media is controlled not only by the
molecular and ionic processes in the fluid, but also by interactions with the solid phases present. Experimental studies are
required to unravel these interactions.

In cases where important diagenetic reactions can be reproduced
in the laboratory (for example, the redox reactions of sulfur
and nitrogen), isotopic trace experiments would be very useful
in establishing reaction paths. Such experiments are common-
place in biochemistry but have not been used extensively in
marine problems.

Fractionation of naturally occurring isotopes during reaction
is recognized as a powerful tool in the identification of
chemical phenomena in the natural environment. An extensive
literature exists on the observed ranges of isotopic composition of the light elements and their interpretation. There is
considerable uncertainty, however, regarding the temperature
dependence of fractionation coefficients and of their variation
with species. Systematic work is required in this area.

The Study of Rapid Reactions

There are now a large number of techniques available to the experimentalist for studying rapid reactions. The approximate
time range for reactions covered by the most utilized methods
is indicated below:

flow	$1 \ - \ 10^{-4}$ sec.	
pressure jump	$1 \ - \ 10^{-6}$ sec.	
temperature jump	$1 \ - \ 10^{-8}$ sec.	
electric-field jump	$10^{-2} - 10^{-9}$ sec.	
sound absorption	$10^{-3} - 10^{-11}$ sec.	
NMR	$1 \ - \ 10^{-6}$ sec.	

In the flow method, which is now over 50 years old, reactants
are rapidly mixed in specially designed mixers, and the emerging
(reacting) solution is examined by a variety of methods, of
which spectrophotometry is by far the most convenient and popular. Reactions with half-life as short as one millisecond can
be examined fairly easily by the flow method. Use of flow techniques also enables one to examine the properties of labile
intermediates before they proceed to further products. Hohl and

Geier (1971) have, for example, determined the pK_a (=11.0) for
the deprotonation of $Ni(H_2O)_6^{2+}$ before slower condensation to
polynuclear hydroxo species can occur.

In the relaxation method, a chemical system at equilibrium is
perturbed by some external agency, and the change to the new
equilibrium (relaxation) is monitored. The rate at which the
new equilibrium is attained is a measure of the values of the
rate constants linking the equilibrium or equilibria. There
are three ways for perturbing the equilibrium: pressure, temperature, and electric field changes. These can be rapidly
imposed in one abrupt change. The time limitations inherent
in the mixing (flow) method are thus circumvented, and these
perturbations can be imposed in times much less than a micro-
second. The time range and power, particularly in the temperature-jump method, have been extended in recent technical
developments. Oscillatory perturbations can also be used to
obtain relaxation data, and this is the basis of the important
ultrasonic method which has been used to measure the rate of
complexing of many metal ions with sulfate ion. This is discussed in more detail in the paper of R.G. Wilkins (this volume)
and in a recent review by Purdie and Farrow (1973). The reaction times which can be covered by relaxation methods are indicated above.

NMR and EPR are also useful methods. The broadening of spectral
lines in certain solutions may arise from chemical exchange
processes occurring in the solution. The extent of the line
broadening can then be related to exchange rates.

Finally, a number of other methods, both electrochemical and
those such as flash photolysis and pulse radiolysis, can be
used to study the dynamics of certain chemical processes. Although somewhat restrictive in their application, they are
nevertheless important techniques for understanding the detailed
course of a reaction.

CONCLUSION

To date, time parameters have been used in environmental systems primarily in the study of physical processes. Future progress depends on the investigation of the kinetics of biogeochemistry and the interpretation of natural systems in terms of chemical dynamics.

REFERENCES

Descriptive Oceanography:

Pickard, G.L. 1964. Descriptive Physical Oceanography.
    New York: Pergamon Press.

Turekian, K.K. 1968. Oceans, Foundations of Earth Science
    Series. Englewood Cliffs: Prentice-Hall, Inc.

The CO_2 System:

Hall, C.A.S.; Ekdahl, C.A.; and Wartenberg, D.E. 1975. A Fifteen Year Record of Biotic Metabolism in the Northern
    Hemisphere. Nature 255: 136-138.

Machta, L. 1972. The Role of the Oceans and Biosphere in the
    Carbon Dioxide Cycle. In The Changing Chemistry of the
    Oceans, Nobel Symposium 20, eds. D. Dyrssen and D. Jagner,
    pp. 121-145. New York: Wiley Interscience.

The Sulphur System:

Berner, R.A. 1972. Sulfate Reduction, Pyrite Formation and
    the Oceanic Sulfur Budget. In The Changing Chemistry of
    the Oceans. Nobel Symposium 20, eds. D. Dyrssen and D.
    Jagner, pp. 347-361. New York: Wiley Interscience.

Goldhaber, M.B., and Kaplan, I.R. 1974. The Sulfur Cycle in
    the Sea. In The Sea, vol. 5, Marine Chemistry, ed.
    E.D. Goldberg, pp. 569-655. New York: Wiley Interscience.

Isotopic Studies:

Goldberg, E.D., and Bruland, K. 1974. Radioactive Geochronologies.
    In The Sea, vol. 5, Marine Chemistry, ed. E.D. Goldberg,
    pp. 457-468. New York: Wiley Interscience.

Hoefs, J. 1973. Stable Isotope Geochemistry. Berlin/New York:
    Springer.

Study of Rapid Reactions:

Caldin, E.F. 1964. Fast Reactions in Solution. Oxford: Blackwell.

Hague, D.N. 1971. Fast Reactions. New York: Wiley Interscience.

Hohl, H., and Geier, G. 1971. Die Deprotonierung des Ni(II)-
    Aquoions (Stopped Flow Methode). Chimia 25: 401-403.

Purdie, N., and Farrow, M.M. 1973. The Application of Ultra-
    sound Absorption to Reaction Kinetics. Coordin. Chem.
    Revs. 11: 189-226.

Wilkins, R.G. 1974. The Study of Kinetics and Mechanisms of
    Reactions of Transition Metal Complexes. Boston:
    Allyn and Bacon.

Kinetics and Mechanism of Metalloporphyrin Formation

W. Schneider
Laboratorium für Anorganische Chemie
Eidgenössische Technische Hochschule, Universitätsstr. 6,
8006 Zürich, Switzerland

Abstract: Metalloporphyrins are generally formed at rates which are much smaller than those of the formation of complexes with monodentate, or open chain chelating ligands. Rate constants for the reaction of hydrated metal ions $M^{z+} = Mn^{2+}$, Fe^{2+}, Fe^{3+}, Co^{2+}, Ni^{2+}, Cu^{2+}, Zn^{2+} with water soluble porphyrins are some 8 to 9 order of magnitudes smaller than normal substitution reactions of M^{z+}. Appropriate variation of the coordination sphere of metal ions produces considerable accelerations of metalloporphyrin formation. Limiting rates are reached with mononuclear hydroxo complexes, or with ooordinated ligands which are approaching properties of hydroxide. Cu(II) forms the most stable porphyrins and can displace iron from pyramidal ironporphyrins.

Introduction:

Ferric haems, and chlorophylls are spectacular cases of very stable complexes which are formed much more slowly than the usual complexes of iron and magnesium. In this review, metals are considered which are essential components of natural water systems and which, consequently, participate in biologically relevant functions. In this context, Mn(II, III, IV), Fe(II, III), Co(II, III), Cu(II) and Zn(II) are important central atoms. Although porphyrin complexes of practically all transition metals have been prepared in a variety of oxidation states [17], kine-

tic studies have so far been restricted to reactions of porphyrins with complexes of Mn(II), Fe(II, III), Co(II), Ni(II),
Cu(I, II) and Zn(II) in homogenous solutions. The present review primarly deals with results obtained in aqueous solutions
under comparable conditions. It will be shown that the rates of
formation of metalloporphyrins are strongly dependent on the
inner coordination sphere of the metal ion. The title subject
has recently been reviewed elsewhere [19], whereas a variety of
aspects of the coordination chemistry of metalloporphyrins have
been summarized by Hambright [10].

Porphyrins and Metalloporphyrins [6]

Metal free porphyrins exhibit the skeleton (I) which is practically planar [7]. Native porphyrins differ by the substituents
in the positions 1 to 8, but contain only hydrogen in the meso-
positions α to γ.

I

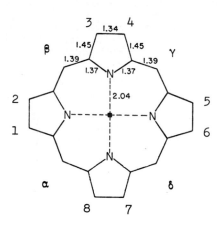

"Best" set of parameters for porphyrin skeleton from Ref. [7].

In Table 1 the substituents of some native porphyrins are listed.

TABLE 1

		1	2	3	4	5	6	7	8
Proto-	IX	me	v	me	v	me	P	P	me
Meso-	IX	me	et	me	et	me	P	P	me
Deutero-	IX	me	H	me	H	me	P	P	me
Hemato-	IX	me	et-OH	me	et-OH	me	P	P	me
Copro-	I	me	P	me	P	me	P	me	P
Uro-	I	A	P	A	P	A	P	A	P

me: CH_3; et: C_2H_5; v: $CH=CH_2$; et-OH: $CHOHCH_3$;
A: CH_2CO_2H; P: $CH_2CH_2CO_2H$

The first four porphyrins are roughly equivalent with respect to kinetics of metal insertion. However, due to the lack of solubility (→ aggregation) they cannot be studied in aqueous solutions.

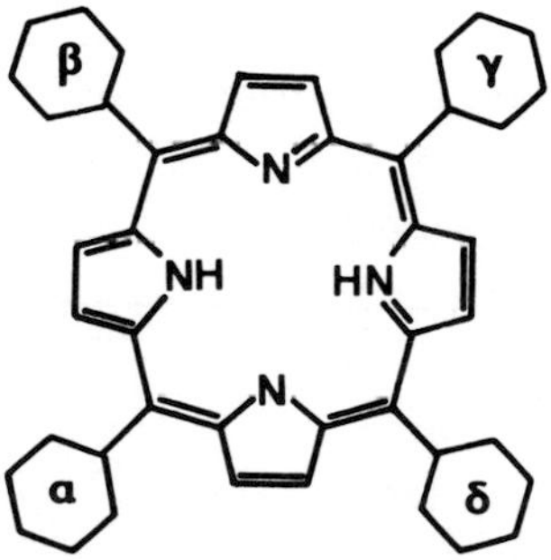

II - V

II   α, β, γ, δ :   [N-methylpyridyl group] N-CH₃(+)
      Tetra-(N-methylpyridyl)-porphin
      TMPyP (+4)

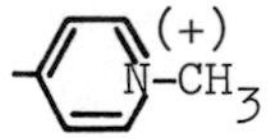

III   α, β, γ, δ :   [pyridyl group] NH(+)
      Tetrapyridylporphin
      TPyP(+4); pH ≤ 3

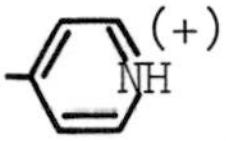

IV   α, β, γ :   [phenyl group] SO_3^-
      Tetraphenylporphintrisulfonate
      TPPS₃ (-3)

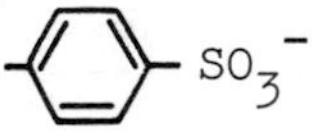

V   α, β, γ, δ :   [phenyl group] SO_3^-
      Tetraphenylporphintetrasulfonate
      TPPS₄ (-4)

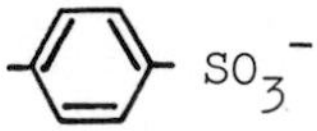

VI   α, β, γ, δ :   [phenyl group] CO_2^-
      Tetracarboxyphenylporphin
      TCPP

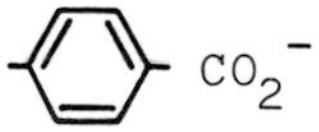

Consequently, water soluble synthetic porphyrins have received
more attention recently [11,18,19]. It can be shown that the conclusions derived from kinetic studies involving meso-substituted
porphyrins such as (II, III, V) are relevant to all other porphyrins because the mechanisms of metalloporphyrin formation depend mainly on the properties of the skeleton (I). In the so
called free bases, two protons are distributed on the four pyrrole nitrogens. In an instantaneous picture they are opposite to
each other as indicated in (I). Free bases H_2P (general short
notation) can be protonated to mono acids H_3P^+, and to diacids
H_4P^{2+}, or deprotonated to mono anions HP^- and dianions P^{2-} (charges refer to central part only). HP^- and P^{2-} are very strong
nitrogen bases, whereas the H_2P forms are weak bases and very

$$
\begin{array}{lll}
H_4P^{2+}, & H_3P^+ & pK_4 \quad 1 \text{ to } 4 \\
H_3P^+, & H_2P & pK_3 \quad 2 \text{ to } 6 \\
H_2P, & HP^- & pK_2 \geq 13 \\
HP^-, & P^{2-} & pK_4 > 14
\end{array}
\Bigg\} \quad \text{depending on substituents}
$$

weak acids. The remarkable stability of porphyrin complexes emer-
ges from the chelate effect of the macrocyclic structure and the
high basicity of the pyrrole nitrogens. Tetra(N-methylpyridyl)-
porphin(II) is the most suitable derivative for studies in aqueous solutions. The free base TMPyP, having charge +4, prevails in
the interval 3 < pH < 12 at R.T. and ionic strength 0.1 < I < 1
[11,15,19]. The peripheral charges and the hydration of these
groups prevent TMPyP(+4) from selfassociation [18]. In native
porphyrins, hydration is weaker than pi-interactions which produce aggregation. Even water soluble porphyrins can dimerize as
has been shown for $TPPS_3(-3)$ and TCPP(-4) at pH 7.5 in 0.1 M
KNO_3 [18]. The stability of these dimers $(H_2P)_2$ is considerable
$(K_D \sim 10^{+8} M^{-1})$. Pronounced pi-interactions can also operate
between porphyrins and other aromatic molecules [16]. For example,
it has been found that TMPyP associates with paratoluenesulfonate
(Ts^-), sulfosalicylate $(ssal^{2-})$, and tiron (1,2-dihydroxybenze-
ne-3,5-disulfonate, H_2tir^{2-}) [19,20]. The association with NH_4^+

and carboxylic acids stems from other types of interactions.
Quite generally, the solvation/association behaviour of porphyrins is complex because

(i)   the pyrrole nitrogens provide weakly basic sites
(ii)   the region of the pyrrole rings is hydrophobic
(iii) peripheral alkyl and vinyl groups are hydrophobic
(iv)   carboxylate and other charged groups are strongly hydra-
       ted. Opposite to $\geqslant\overset{+}{N}-CH_3$ and $-SO_3^-$, the groups $-CO_2^-$ may
       even bind metal ions.

As a rule, the composition of the solvation shell of a porphyrin
does not reflect the bulk composition of the solution.
The planar conformation of the skeleton (I) is not strictly in-
flexible [7]. The positions of the protons switch quickly possibly coupled to out-of-plane vibrations of the skeleton. In the
diacids H_4P^{2+}, the skeleton is frozen in a non-planar conformation (symmetry of N-positions approx. S_4), and pyrrole planes
are tilted with respect to the average plane of C_α-carbons. The
results of kinetic studies are compatible with the idea that the
dynamic loss of planar conformation of H_2P enables a stepwise
substitution of ligands of the metal complex which reacts with
H_2P to give metalloporphyrin MP. Formally, two protons are replaced in this process (1; z: oxidation number).

$$M(z) + H_2P \rightarrow MP^{z-2} + 2\,H^+ \qquad\qquad (1)$$

The coordination shell of M(z) is stripped off rather completely
when MP is formed. The stability constants K of eq. (2) cannot be

$$M_{aq}^{z+} + P^{2-} \rightleftarrows MP^{z-2} \qquad\qquad K \qquad\qquad (2)$$

$$M_{aq}^{z+} + H_2P \rightleftarrows MP^{z-2} + 2\,H^+ \qquad K^* \qquad (3)$$

measured, but may be estimated from the constants K^* (3) to be
higher than for any other ligand known. Table 2 gives some data
on M(TMPyP) [21].

TABLE 2

Stability of metalloporphyrins M(TMPyP) in aqueous solutions;
25° C. a: I = 1.0 (HCl,NaCl); b: I = 0.1 (HCl,NaCl). From Ref.
[21].

$M(H_2O)_n^{z+}$	$\log K^*$	$\log K$ (est.)	
Cu^{2+}	$\geq$ 10; $\leq$ 16	$\geq$ 38; $\leq$ 44	a)
Fe^{3+}	8.8 ($\pm$ 0.3)	37	a)
Zn^{2+}	2.1 ($\pm$ 0.05)	30	b)
Fe^{2+}	$-$ 0.9 ($\pm$ 0.2)	27	b)
Mg^{2+}	$\leq -$ 8	$\leq$ 20	b)

Hence, it is safe to postulate the following order of stability
of metalloporphyrins:

Cu(II)>Fe(III)>Ni(II)>Zn(II)>Co(II)>Fe(II)>Mn(II)$\geq$Mg(II)

These data are significant to possible metal exchange
reactions (4). In (4), Λ is the symbol for the coordination

$$MP + M'\Lambda \;\rightarrow\; M'P + M\Lambda \tag{4}$$

shell. The equilibrium constant of (4) depends on Λ. It has been
shown that the following substitutions can be realized for a variety of Λ [21]:

Fe(III)P + Cu(II) $\rightarrow$ Cu(II)P + Fe(III)
     (if some Fe(II)P is in equilibrium with Fe(III)P)
Fe(II)P + Cu(II) $\rightarrow$ Cu(II)P + Fe(II)
Zn(II)P + Cu(II) $\rightarrow$ Cu(II)P + Zn(II)

     (H_2P = TMPyP)

On the other hand, it has never been possible to replace Cu(II)
by Fe(III), or Ni(II) by Cu(II). At medium pH values, Cu(II) can
be displaced from Cu(II)P only by sulfide within some days.

Metalloporphyrins are either planar, pyramidal, or nearly
octahedral [7,13].

Cu(II), Ni(II)   Fe(II),Fe(III),Co(III)   Zn(II), Mg(II)

                          low spin   high spin Fe(III)

The porphyrins of Mn(II), Fe(II) and Co(II) have remarkable reducing properties which depend strongly on other ligands L. In
air, all these M(II)P are easily oxidized. The redox properties
of metalloporphyrins have recently been reviewed by Fuhrhop [8].

Metalloporphyrin Formation vs. Usual Complex Formation

In order to understand the time scale relevant to reactions
$M\Lambda + H_2P \rightarrow MP + (\Lambda, 2 H^+)$, it is useful to compare the latter
with normal substitution reactions.

$$k_2 \ (M^{-1}sec^{-1}) \ ^{*)}$$

$Cu^{2+} + dip \rightarrow Cu(dip)^{2+}$ $4 \cdot 10^{+7}$ (5)

$Cu^{2+} + Hdip^+ \rightarrow Cu(dip) + H^+$ $3 \cdot 10^{+5}$ (6)

$Cu^{2+} + TMPyP \rightarrow Cu(TMPyP) + 2 H^+$ 2 (7)

dip =

$^{*)}$ 25° C, I = 0.3

(5,6: $NaClO_4$; 7: NaCl)

The open chain 2,2'-bipyridyl replaces water of hydrated Cu^{2+}
in a very fast reaction [5]. For reaction (6), the second order rate constant k_2 is smaller by two orders of magnitude [5].
Previous studies [19] assert that (7) is smaller by another
factor 10^{-5} mainly for two reasons:

(i) the barrier created by the protons of H_2P is very effecti-
     ve in preventing bonding of pyrrole nitrogen of H_2P to the
     metal ion. Hence, it is understood that H_3P^+ and H_4P^{2+} are
     kinetically irrelevant compared to H_2P.

(ii) a small fraction of all configurations of encounter com-
     plexes $(Cu(H_2O)_n, H_2P)$, or $(M\Lambda, H_2P)$ respectively, are ap-
     propriate to enable concerted dissociation of water and
     association of pyrrole nitrogen.

It will not be discussed here in detail that scheme (8) is a good
approximation for reactions (5), (6) and particularly (7)[1].

$$Cu(H_2O)_n^{2+} + H_iL \underset{}{\overset{K_o}{\rightleftharpoons}} [Cu(H_2O)_n, H_iL] \overset{k_z}{\longrightarrow} CuL + i\ H^+ \qquad (8)$$

$$k_2 = K_o \cdot k_z$$

For normal substitution reactions, the pre-equilibrium constant
K_o has frequently been estimated by the Fuoss theory [9] which
is appropriate for association of spherical ions (including uncharged spheres). Hence, the coefficient $\varkappa$ in (9) has been
assurred equal to one. (K_{os}: from the Fuoss equation).

$$K_o = \varkappa \cdot K_{os} \qquad (9)$$

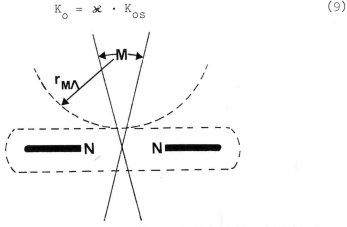

FIG. 1 - Configuration of outer sphere complex $(M\Lambda, H_2P)$ prece-
         ding the insertion of the metal. Space angle indicated
         ca. $4\pi/50$.

Fig. 1 visualizes the argument that $\varkappa$ may be as small as 10^{-2} if the same statistical weight is given to all configurations of encounter complexes. However, if specific site interactions operate, $\varkappa$ may increase to values beyond one. For example, $K_o \sim$ $3 \cdot 10^{+3}$ M^{-1} has been determined for $(Fe(tir)^{5-}, TMPyP^{4+})$ which forms Fe(III)TMPyP at moderate rates, $t_{1/2} \sim 3$ h at $40°$ C. On the other hand, Fe_{aq}^{3+} ($K_o < 3$, $I \sim 0.1$) does not react with the same porphyrin at measurable rates. (Fe^{3+} 10^{-3} M, TMPyP 10^{-4} M: $t_{1/2} \geq 1$ y).

The limiting rates of Cu(II) insertion have been reached with ligands which are able to accept protons from H_2P in the intermediates (see Table 4). Corresponding second order rate constants are smaller than k_2 of (6) by less than two orders of magnitude only. Hence, the factors (i) and (ii), are more severe than the restricted flexibility of the porphyrin skeleton in lowering the rates of substitution by H_2P compared to open chain chelating ligands. In Fig. 2, ranges of rate constants are given for normal substitution reactions of Fe^{3+}, Ni^{2+}, Fe^{2+} and Cu^{2+}.

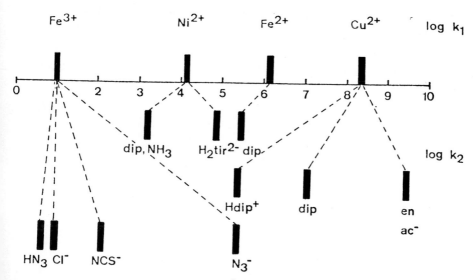

FIG. 2 - Rate constants k_1 (sec^{-1}) for water exchange of hydrated metal ions, and for the formation of complexes ML (k_2, $M^{-1}sec^{-1}$).

Kinetic Data for Reactions in Aqueous Solution

Significant studies in well defined solutions mostly refer to the water soluble porphyrins TMPyP(II), TPPS$_4$(V) and to native porphyrins with peripheral carboxylic groups such as hemato-, copro- and uroporphyrin (Table 1). Obviously, salt effects have to be considered if charged porphyrins are used. Although salt effects are not well understood at present, available data show that specific effects are more important than general salt effects. Therefore , systems to which the data of Tables 4 to 8 refer are well specified. Whenever a constant medium is preserved (including constant temperature, pH and constant mole fractions of components within narrow limits), the formation of MP from a complex MΛ and a free base H$_2$P is a second order reaction. Within

$$\frac{d[MP]}{dt} = k_2 \cdot [M\Lambda]\,[H_2P]$$

scheme (8), second order rate constants k$_2$ are products K$_o$ · k$_z$. In all but one case, K$_o$ is too small to be determined from kinetic experiments. In Table 3 to 7, the temperature is 25° if not stated otherwise; rate constants k$_2$ are in the unit M^{-1}sec^{-1}; error limits are generally about ± 10 %. Ions M^{z+} refer to aquo complexes.

Symbols used in Table 3 to 7:

ac$^-$	:	acetate	im :	imidazole
dip	:	2,2'-bipyridyl	py :	pyridine
tir^{2-}	:	tiron	HGG :	glycylglycine
hoq	:	8-hydroxyquinoline	HGlS :	glycylsarcosine

TABLE 3 <u>Cu(II)</u>

M	H_2P	Medium [M]	pH (Acid/Base)	k_2 ($M^{-1}sec^{-1}$)	Ref.
Cu^{2+}	TMPyP(+4)	0.1 KNO_3	3 (HNO_3)	0.2	[11]
Cu^{2+}	TMPyP(+4)	0.1 NaCl	3 (HCl)	0.6	[11]
Cu^{2+}	TMPyP(+4)	0.1 NaTs	3 (HTs)	0.006	[19]
$Cu(OH)^+$	TMPyP(+4)	0.1 NaCl	~ 5 (unbuffered)	$\geq 10^{+3}$ (est.)	[19]
$Cu(ac)_2$	TMPyP(+4)	0.1 < I < 1.0	4.6 (Hac, Naac)	50	[19]
$Cu(NH_3)$	TMPyP(+4)	1.0 NH_4NO_3	4–6 (NH_4^+, NH_3)	5	[19]
$Cu(NH_3)_4^{2+}$	TMPyP(+4)	0.1 NH_4Cl	9 (NH_4^+, NH_3)	20	[19]
$Cu(N_3)^+$	TMPyP(+4)	0.1 KNO_3	4.6 (Hac, Naac)	~ 10^{+2} (est.)	[19]
$Cu(dip)^{2+}$	TMPyP(+4)	0.1 KNO_3	3 (HNO_3)	0.1	[19]
$Cu(dip)(OH)^+$	TMPyP(+4)	0.1 KNO_3	9–10	~ 2 · 10^{+3}	[19]
$Cu(tir)^{2-}$	TMPyP(+4)	0.1 KNO_3	3.3–3.9	1.6 · 10^{+3}	[19]
$Cu(oq)^+$	TMPyP(+4)	0.1 Na_2SO_4	4 (H_2SO_4)	0.7 · 10^{+3}	[15]

TABLE 4 Cu(II) (continued), Cu(I), Zn(II)

M_A	H_2P	Medium [M]	pH (Acid/Base)	k_2 ($M^{-1} sec^{-1}$)	Ref.
$Cu(ac)_{1,2}$	Deutero(−2)	I 0.5	4.6 (Hac, Naac)	3.2	[3]
$Cu(OH)_3^-(?)$	Hemato(−2)	I 0.5	0.5 M NaOH	0.02	[3]
Cu(I)					
$Cu(NCCH_3)_n^+$ $\leq 5\cdot10^{-4}$ M	TMPyP(+4)	5 M CH_3CN	~ 7 (Veronal buffer)	~ $3\cdot10^{+2}$($\bar{n} > 2$)	[19]
$Cu(im)_2^+$	TMPyP(+4)	5 M CH_3CN	~ 7 (Him^+, im)	$5\cdot10^{+2}$	[19]
Zn(II)					
Zn^{2+}	TMPyP(+4)	0.1 $NaNO_3$	3 (HNO_3)	$5\cdot10^{-3}$ (22°C)	[11]
Zn^{2+}	TMPyP(+4)	1.0 $NaNO_3$	6.7 (Lutidine buffer)	0.5 (22°C)	[11]
$Zn(ac)_2$	TMPyP(+4)	I var ($NaNO_3$)	~ 4 (Hac, Naac)	3 (22°C)	[11]
Zn^{2+}	$TPPS_4(−4)$	I var ($NaNO_3$)	6–7 (PIPES)	0.8	[11]
$Zn(OH)^+$	$TPPS_4(−4)$	I var ($NaNO_3$)	6–7 (PIPES)	~ 40	[11]

TABLE 5 Ni(II)

MA	H_2P	Medium	pH (Acid/Base)	Rate Constant	Ref.
Ni^{2+}	TMPyP(+4)	0.1 NaNO$_3$	3 (HNO$_3$)	k_2 5 · 10^{-5}	[11]
$Ni(ac)_n^{2-n}$	TMPyP(+4)	$\bar{n} \approx 1$ 0.1<I<1.0	~ 5 (Hac, Naac)	$k_e/[Ni]_t \leq 10^{-3}$	[19]
$Ni(NH_3)_n^{2+}$	TMPyP(+4)	$3 \leq \bar{n} \leq 4$ n = 1,2,3	8-9 (NH$_4^+$, NH$_3$)		[19]
$Ni(GG)_n^{2-n}$	TMPyP(+4)	0.05<I<0.5	7-10 (HGG, GG$^-$)	k_2 < 10^{-3}	[19]
$Ni(GGH\_)(OH)^-$	TMPyP(+4)	0.05<I<0.5	7-10 (HGG, GG$^-$)	k_2 ~ 10	[19]
$Ni(GlS)(OH)$	TMPyP(+4)	0.05<I<0.1	7-9 (HGlS, GlS$^-$)	k_2 6	[19]

GG^-

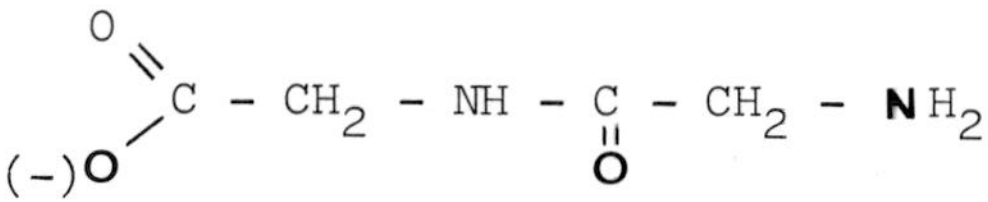

$$O=C(-O^-)-CH_2-NH-C(=O)-CH_2-NH_2$$

GlS^-

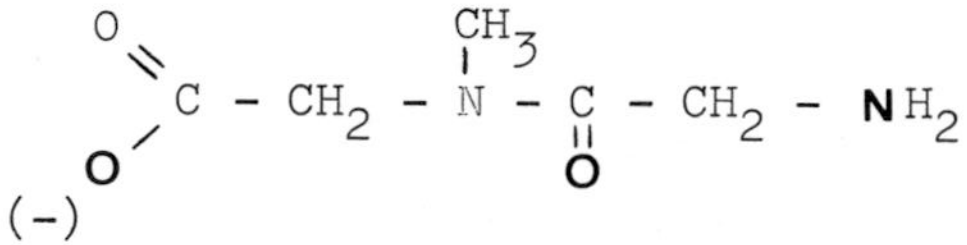

$$O=C(-O^-)-CH_2-\underset{\underset{CH_3}{|}}{N}-C(=O)-CH_2-NH_2$$

$(GGH\_)^{2-}$

$$O=C(-O^-)-CH_2-\underset{(-)}{N}-COCH_2-NH_2$$

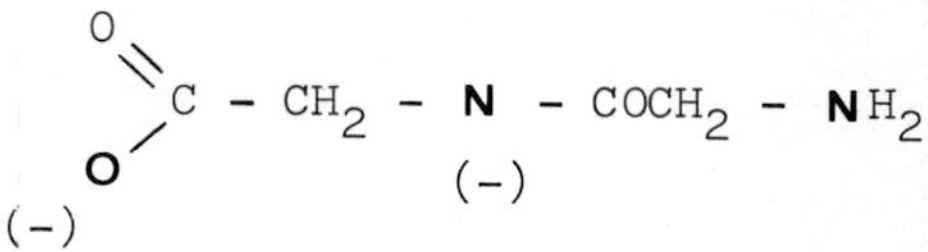

TABLE 6 Fe(II) and Fe(III)

M_Λ	H_2P	Medium	pH (Acid/Base)	k_2 ($M^{-1}sec^{-1}$)	Ref.
			Fe(II)		
Fe^{2+}	Hemato(-2)	10% v/v py $I \leq 0.001$	8.2 (Hpy$^+$, py)	0.22	[14]
Fe^{2+}	Copro(-4)	"	"	8.2	[14]
Fe^{2+}	Uro(-8)	"	"	84	[14]
Fe^{2+}	TMPyP(+4)	0.5 NaCl	3.2 (Hac, Naac)	$0.2 \cdot 10^{-2}$ (40°C)	[19]
			Fe(III) (40°C)		
Fe^{3+}	TMPyP(+4)	0.1 NaCl	1-2 (HCl)	$< 10^{-8}$	[19]
$Fe(tir)^-$	TMPyP(+4)	0.1 < I < 0.5 (NaCl)	3.2 (Hac, Naac)	$2.2 \cdot 10^{-2}$	[19]
$Fe(tir)_2^{5-}$	TMPyP(+4)	"	5 (Hac, Naac)	0.2 (K_o $3 \cdot 10^{+3}$)	[19]
$Fe(tir)_3^{9-}$	TMPyP(+4)	"	> 5 (Hac, Naac)	inhibition (K $6 \cdot 10^{+5}$)	[19]

TABLE 7 <u>Mg(II), Mn(II), Co(II)</u>

MΛ	H$_2$P	Medium	pH (Acid/Base)	k$_2$ (M^{-1}sec^{-1})	Ref.
Mg^{2+}	TMPyP	0.1 NaNO$_3$	5	< 10^{-6} (40°C)	[20]
Mg(ac)$_2$	TMPyP	1.0 Naac	8 (Hac, Naac)	ca. 10^{-3} (40°C)	[19]
MgCO$_3$ aq.	TMPyP	0.4 NaNO$_3$	8-9 (HCO$_3^-$, CO$_3^{2-}$)	ca. 10^{-2} (40°C)	[19]
Mg(tir)$^{2-}$	TMPyP	1.0 NaNO$_3$	~ 11 (NaOH)	ca. 3 · 10^{-2} (40°C)	[19]
Mn^{2+}	TMPyP	0.1 KNO$_3$	4	2.5 · 10^{-4} (22°C)	[11]
Mn(II)	TPyP	Hac (glac.)	–	0.006 (Cu(II): 0.4)	[4]
Co^{2+}	TMPyP	0.1 KNO$_3$	4	2.2 · 10^{-4} (22°C)	[11]
Co(II)	TPyP	Hac (glac.)	–	0.09	[4]

Time Scales for Metalloporphyrin Formation

a) Hydrated Metal Ions

Rate constants which have been determined for the formation
of M(z) (TMPyP) show pronounced differences between hydrated
metal ions [11, 19]. The values indicated in Fig. 3 are
valid for acid solutions. At pH-values around 7 the formation of hydroxocomplexes has to be taken into account. Hence, rates of reactions of aquo complexes are mainly relevant
as a reference to the reactivity of other complexes. In addition to the rate constants k_2, two further types of numerical
values are given in Figs. 3, 4 and 5:

(i)   the half time $\tau = (k_2 \cdot c_o)^{-1}$ of the second order reac-
      tion $M\Lambda + H_2P \rightarrow MP + (\Lambda, 2\ H^+)$ for initial concentrations
      $c_o = [M\Lambda]_o = [H_2P]_o = 10^{-6}$ M; unit of τ: h.

(ii) the rate of formation ρ of MP for steady state concentra-
      tions $[M\Lambda] = [H_2P] = 10^{-6}$ M in the unit $[\text{mole} \cdot m^{-3} \cdot y^{-1}]$.

Relative rates are

$$Cu^{2+} > Zn^{2+} > Mn^{2+} \geq Co^{2+} \geq Fe^{2+} > Ni^{2+}\ (> Fe^{3+})$$

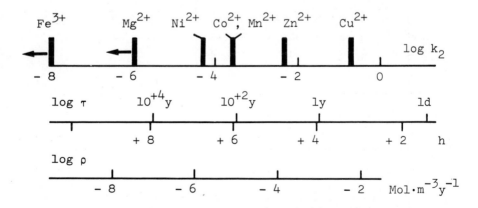

FIG. 3 - Rates of insertion of hydrated metal ions into TMPyP
25° C; ionic strength 0.1 M (Na, KNO$_3$).

b) <u>Effects of Chemical Variation</u>

The data on the insertion of Cu(II) from a variety of complexes show that the association of TMPyP(+4) with tosylate
on one hand, and the variation of Λ on the other hand, can
cause a spread of rate constants over many orders of magnitude. A limiting rate appears to be reached with ligands containing phenolate ligand groups. The mononuclear complex
$Cu(OH)^+_{aq}$ is about equally reactive as $Cu(tir)^{2-}$ and $Cu(oq)^+$
(Fig. 4). The data on Ni(II) clearly show that aminoacetates
and oligopeptides do not provide optimum ligand spheres. However, mononuclear hydroxocomplexes of Ni(II), and $Ni(tir)^{2-}$,
react with TMPyP even slightly faster than Cu^{2+}. Polynuclear
hydroxocomplexes of Fe(III) are unreactive [19], in contrast
to the mononuclear tiron complexes $Fe(tir)^-$ and $Fe(tir)_2^{5-}$
which react with TMPyP even faster than Fe^{2+} (Fig. 5). Hence,
it is not strictly required that Fe(III) be reduced to Fe(II)
prior to the incorporation of iron into a porphyrin.

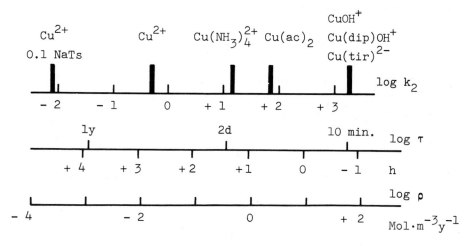

FIG. 4 - Insertion of Cu(II) into TMPyP in various systems at
        25° C; ionic strength 0.1 (Na, KNO_3).

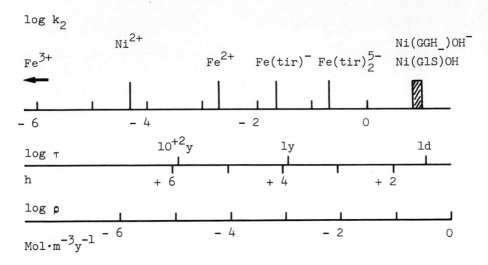

FIG. 5 - Ligand catalysis of the insertion of Ni(II) and Fe(III)
into TMPy; Ni(II): 25° C; Fe(II), Fe(III): 40° C.

Metal Exchange Reactions [21]

It is not surprising that the insertion of a metal ion into a
porphyrin free base H_2P is a faster reaction than the formation
of the same MP by an exchange of the metal ion. For example, k_2
for reaction (11) is smaller by five orders of magnitude than it
is for the insertion (10).

$$Cu^{2+} + H_2P \rightarrow CuP + 2\,H^+ \qquad k_2 = 0.6 \qquad M^{-1}sec^{-1} \qquad (10)$$

$$Cu^{2+} + ZnP \rightarrow CuP + Zn^{2+} \qquad k_2 = 1.3\cdot10^{-5} \; M^{-1}sec^{-1} \qquad (11)$$

$(H_2P = TMPyP; 25° C; I\ 0.1, NaCl)$

However, it is possible to increase the rates by ligand catalysis.
Thus, the complex $Cu(ssal)^-$ associates with Zn(TMPyP) to form
$Cu(ssal)\cdot ZnP$ which exchanges Zn(II) for Cu(II) in a subsequent
reaction (13) with another $Cu(ssal)^-$, $(ssal^{3-} = 5\text{-sulfosalicylate})$.

$$Cu(ssal)^- + ZnP \rightleftarrows Cu(ssal) \cdot ZnP \quad K = 30 \ (\pm 10) \tag{12}$$

$$Cu(ssal)ZnP + Cu(ssal) \rightarrow CuP + Cu(ssal)^- + Zn(ssal)^- \tag{13}$$

$$k_2 = 0.8 \ (\pm 2) \ M^{-1}sec^{-1}$$
$$40° \ C, \ I \ 0.1 \ (NaCl)$$

The corresponding exchange Fe(II) → Cu(II) occurs in a second order reaction (14) which means that, compared to (Cu(ssal)·ZnP), the exchange in the outer sphere complex (Cu(ssal)·Fe(II)P) proceeds easier.

$$Cu(ssal)^- + Fe(II)P + H^+ \rightarrow CuP + (Fe(II), Hssal^{2-}) \tag{14}$$

$$k_2 = 0.8 \ M^{-1}sec^{-1}$$
$$40° \ C, \ I \ 0.1 \ (NaCl)$$

It is important to note that Fe(II)P is strongly reducing. Hence, the intimate mechanisms of (13) and (14) are rather different. In air, the reaction (14) is inhibited because of the oxidation of Fe(II)P to Fe(III)P. Actually, the reaction (14) is possible only under reducing conditions in which case both Fe(II)P and Fe(III)P are present. The redox potential E_o (vs. NHE) of the pair Fe(III)P, Fe(II)P (TMPyP) is + 0.19 V [21]. Fig. 6 summarizes some results on metal exchange reactions.

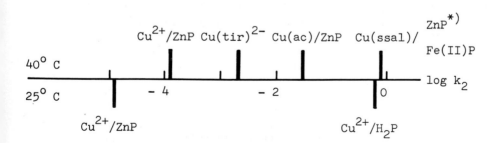

FIG. 6 - Metal exchange reactions; I = 0.1 (NaCl), H_2P = TMPyP; *) eq. (13); $ssal^{3-}$ = 5-sulfosalicylate.

Native Porphyrins in Aqueous Solutions

Native Porphyrins are only soluble in aqueous solutions when the
aggregation is prevented either by acid solutions (pH < 1), or
by association with other molecules. Consequently, kinetic studies on native porphyrins have usually been carried out in organic solvents such as ethanol, acetone or others [2]. In their
study on the insertion of Fe^{2+}, Kassner and Wang [14] used wa-
ter-pyridine (10 % v/v) to overcome the aggregation of hemato-,
copro- and uroporphyrine. Molecules which associate with porphyrins may either inhibit or catalyze the insertion. It seems
that catalytic effects require molecules which are able to bind
metals. Moreover, the admission of the metal to the central part
of H_2P should not be restricted. So far, no systematic studies
have been reported on metalloporphyrin formation in systems
where H_2P is either adsorbed on a solid, or kept monomeric by
suitable molecules containing ligating groups. Very recently,
it has been shown that Fe(III)P is formed by the reaction of
Fe^{3+} with TMPyP if both are adsorbed on silica [22].

Literature

(1)   Basolo, F., and Pearson, R.G. 1967. Mechanisms on Inorga-
      nic Reactions. New York: J. Wiley.

(2)   Berezin, B.D. 1973. The Formation and Dissociation of
      Chlorophylls and Similar Compounds in Solution. Uspekhi
      Khimii: 42: 2007; and references quoted therein.

(3)   Cabbiness, D.K., and Margerum, D.W. 1970. Effect of Macro-
      cyclic Structures on the Rate of Formation and Dissociation
      of Cu(II)-Complexes. J. Amer. Chem. Soc. 92: 2151.

(4)   Choi, E.I., and Fleischer, E.B. 1963. Kinetics of the Re-
      action of Some Divalent Transition Metal Ions with Tetra-
      (4-pyridyl)-porphin. Inorg. Chem. 2: 94.

(5)   Diebler, H. 1970. Gleichgewichte und Kinetik der Bildung
      der Monodipyridyl-Komplexe des Cr(II) und Cu(II). Ber. Bun-
      senges. 74: 268.

(6)   Falk, J.E. 1964. Porphyrins and Metalloporphyrins. Amster-
      dam: Elsevier Publ. Co.

(7)   Fleischer, E.B. 1970. The Structure of Porphyrins and Me-
      talloporphyrins. Accounts Chem. Res. $\underline{3}$: 105.

(8)   Fuhrhop, J.-H. 1974. Redox Reactions of Metalloporphyrins.
      In Structure and Bonding $\underline{18}$: 1. Berlin: Springer-Verlag.

(9)   Fuoss, R.M. 1958. Ionic Association III. The Equilibrium
      between Ion Pairs and Free Ions. J. Amer. Chem. Soc. $\underline{80}$:
      5059.

(10) Hambright, P. 1971. The Coordination Chemistry of Metallo-
      porphyrins. Coordin. Chem. Rev. $\underline{6}$: 247.

(11) Hambright, P., and Chock, P.B. 1974. Metal-Porphyrin Inter-
      actions III. J. Amer. Chem. Soc. $\underline{96}$: 3123.

(12) Hambright, P., and Fleischer, E.B. 1970. The Water-Soluble
      Porphyrin Tetra(N-methylpyridyl)porphin. Inorg. Chem. $\underline{9}$:
      1757.

(13) Hoard, J.L. 1971. Stereochemistry of Hemes and other Me-
      talloporphyrins. Science $\underline{174}$: 1295.

(14) Kassner, R.J., and Wang, J.H. 1966. Kinetic Studies on the
      Incorporation of Iron(II) into Porphyrins. J. Amer. Chem.
      Soc. $\underline{88}$: 5170.

(15) Lowe, M.B., and Phillips, J.N. 1968. Chelate Catalysis of
      Metalloporphyrin Formation. Proc. 11 ICCC: 16.

(16) Mauzerall, D. 1965. Spectra of Molecular Complexes of Por-
      phyrins in Aqueous Solution. Biochemistry $\underline{4}$: 1801.

(17) Ostfeld, D., and Tsutsui, M. 1974. Novel Metalloporphyrins-
      Syntheses and Implications. Accounts Chem. Res. $\underline{7}$: 52.

(18) Pasternack, R.F. 1973. Aggregation Properties of Water-
      Soluble Porphyrins. Ann. N.Y. Acad. Sci. $\underline{206}$: 614.

(19) Schneider, W. 1975. Kinetics and Mechanism of Metallopor-
      phyrin Formation. In Structure and Bonding. Berlin: Spin-
      ger-Verlag.

(20) Schneider, W., and Schoder, A. 1975. The Incorporation of
      Mg(II) into Porphyrins. Unpublished work.

(21) Schoder, A., and Schneider, W. 1975. Metal Exchange Reac-
      tions of Metalloporphyrins. To be published. Schoder, A.
      ETH-Zürich: Dissertation.

(22) Schoder, A., Schneider, W., and Berner, R. 1975. Unpub-
      lished work on metalloporphyrin formation in heterogeneous
      systems.

The Kinetics of Complex Formation in Aqueous Solution

Ralph G. Wilkins
Department of Chemistry
New Mexico State University
Las Cruces, New Mexico 88003

Abstract. The kinetics of formation of complexes from aquated metal ions and a variety of ligands is surveyed. Likely mechanisms are discussed, and further evidence for them detailed. The factors influencing the rates of formation of complexes are briefly discussed.

Introduction and General Features of Complex Formation. Solvent molecules coordinated to a metal ion have lost their translational degrees of freedom and move as one entity with the metal ion in solution. This coordinated solvent can be replaced by other ligands, which may occupy one (unidentate ligand) or more than one (multidentate ligand) of the solvent positions. Such a replacement is referred to as a formation reaction. In the simple case of a neutral unidentate ligand L replacing H_2O from $M(H_2O)_n^{m+}$ this will be stepwise and lead eventually to the formation of ML_n^{n+}

$$M(H_2O)_n^{m+} \xrightarrow[\text{+H}_2\text{O}]{+L} M(H_2O)_{n-1}L^{m+} \xrightarrow[\text{+(n-1)H}_2\text{O}]{+(n-1)L} ML_n^{m+} \qquad (1)$$

If L is anionic, the reaction is termed anation. The reverse process, in which H_2O replaces L from the metal complex, is variously referred to as solvolysis (or hydrolysis) or dissociation.

For the vast majority of metal ions these are rapid processes, normally occurring in times as short as a second, and in a number of cases shorter than milli- or even micro-seconds.

Most of the metal ions have a coordination number of six, so
we are mainly concerned with octahedral complexes. The examination of a restricted number of slowly reacting metal ions
gave way in the early 1960's to investigations of all the metal
ions. This was made possible with the development of techniques for measuring the rates of even the very fastest possible
reactions in solution, i.e., those which are controlled by the
diffusion of reactants together.

The observation of the excess sound absorption which occurs in
seawater, over that in pure water, was the event which heralded
the vigorous interest in labile complex ion formation. After
an extended discussion of its origins, the excess sound absorption was finally linked to an equilibrium occurring in seawater
involving formation of a complex between Mg^{2+} and SO_4^{2-} ions.[27]
This rationalization, in turn, has led to the use of sound absorption to investigate the kinetics and mechanistic details of
the formation of complexes of a large number of metal ions with
SO_4^{2-} and other ions -- and thence to the general concepts
which prevail at the present time.

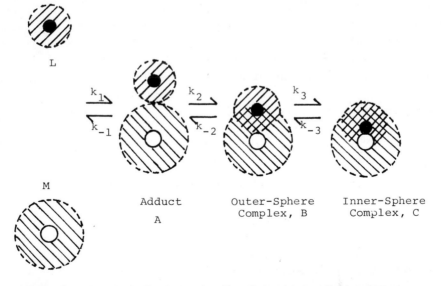

FIGURE 1.   Suggested steps in the formation of the inner-
            sphere complex from constituents.

Let us examine the finer detail which must form part of equation (1). The solvated metal ion M and the solvated ligand L are shown in Figure 1 with the solvation shells shaded.[27] These might be expected to interact in a diffusion-controlled reaction to form an adduct A in which the primary solvation shells are still intact. Release of one solvent molecule from the ligand shell in A leads to B, in which the metal ion and the ligand have only one solvent molecule located between them. B is usually termed an outer-sphere complex (or ion pair when charged reactants are involved). In the final stage yet another solvent molecule, which originated with the metal ion, is lost with the formation of C, an inner-sphere complex (or contact ion pair). In C there is, of course, direct contact between metal ion and ligand, and thus C represents $M(H_2O)_{n-1}L^{m+}$ of equation (1). Transferring this notion to the interaction of metal ions M^{2+} with SO_4^{2-} anions we can abbreviate the scheme as in (2) - (4):

$$M_{aq}^{2+} + SO_{4aq}^{2-} \rightleftharpoons M_{aq}^{2+}{}_{aq}SO_4^{2-} \qquad\qquad k_1, k_{-1}, K_1 \qquad (2)$$
$$\text{(A)}$$

$$M_{aq}^{2+}{}_{aq}SO_4^{2-} \rightleftharpoons M_{aq}^{2+}SO_4^{2-} \qquad\qquad k_2, k_{-2}, K_2 \qquad (3)$$
$$\text{(B) outer ion pair}$$

$$M_{aq}^{2+}SO_4^{2-} \rightleftharpoons MSO_{4aq} \qquad\qquad k_3, k_{-3}, K_3 \qquad (4)$$
$$\text{(C) contact ion pair}$$

Each equilibrium can "interact" with sound waves and contribute to the excess sound absorption by affecting the amplitude and frequency range of the incident sound waves. Sound absorption techniques for studying the dynamics of equilibria have been well described.[15,24,27] For a single step

$$A \rightleftharpoons B \qquad\qquad k_f, k_r \qquad\qquad (5)$$

the absorption of power from the sound wave will be a maximum at a frequency f (cycles/sec = Hz) where

$$k = k_f + k_r = 2\pi f \qquad\qquad (6)$$

and

$$\{B\}/\{A\} = k_f/k_r \qquad\qquad (7)$$

For a reaction

$$A + B \xrightleftharpoons{} C \qquad\qquad k_f, k_r \qquad\qquad (8)$$

which occurs commonly in complex ion chemistry, the corresponding resonance frequency f is given by

$$k = k_f(\{A\} + \{B\}) + k_r = 2\pi f \qquad\qquad (9)$$

where $\{A\}$ and $\{B\}$ represent the equilibrium concentrations of A and B.[15] A plot of sound absorption vs. frequency of sound waves will thus yield a maximum at a relaxation frequency f. If the concentrations of A and B are known at equilibrium, then individual values for k_f and k_r may be determined.

If each of the steps (2) - (4) were separable kinetically (i.e., associated with quite different time scales), one would expect three associated frequency maxima. For a number of metal ion-sulfate systems, most workers report only <u>two</u> relaxation frequencies and attribute these to (a) formation of B through the combined steps (1) and (2). This occurs at the very highest frequencies and its position is little dependent on the nature of the metal ion. It is possible that this broad high frequency relaxation could consist of two closely coupled relaxations. (b) formation of C from B giving rise to a lower frequency maximum which is strongly dependent on the nature of the metal ion, since the solvation shell of the metal is intimately involved. For the Mn^{2+} - SO_4^{2-} system the frequencies are located at $4 - 6 \times 10^8$ Hz and $3 - 6 \times 10^6$ Hz, corresponding to relaxation rate constants of approximately $3 \times 10^9 sec^{-1}$ and $2 \times 10^7 sec^{-1}$, respectively.[24]

Step (a) can be isolated from subsequent steps by examining

the interaction of an inert complex ion with sulfate ion, e.g.,

$$Co(NH_3)_6^{3+} + SO_4^{2-} \rightleftharpoons Co(NH_3)_6^{3+}{}_{aq}SO_4^{2-} \qquad k_f \quad (10)$$

Erosion of the coordinated ammonia by sulfate would occur extremely slowly, if at all. The rate constant k_f, 2.4×10^{11}
$M^{-1}sec^{-1}$, is similar to that for a diffusion-controlled value
which can be calculated[6] as $1.0 \times 10^{11} M^{-1}sec^{-1}$. The volume
change associated with (10) is ~ 20 cm^3 mol^{-1}, which suggests
that a water molecule loosely attached to the cation may be released in forming the ion pair.[11] This example demonstrates
that thermodynamic as well as kinetic data may be obtained for
the various steps (2) - (4) by ultrasonic measurement. This
information, it must be stressed, is not available from
straightforward kinetic studies of complex formation. The investigation of sulfate and other complexes with similar types
of ligands is important because addition of sulfate to metal
ions produces comparable amounts of all the species in (2) -
(4), whereas more powerful ligands tend to form exclusively C
at the expense of A and B.

From the results of the ultrasonics work it became quickly
apparent that the value of k_3 in (4) was sensibly independent
of the nature of the replacing anion for a specific metal, e.g.,
for Mg^{2+} reacting with SO_4^{2-}, $S_2O_3^{2-}$, or CrO_4^{2-} all yielded
$k_3 \sim 1 \times 10^5 sec^{-1}$. This suggested a dissociative mechanism for
the outer-inner sphere complex transformation, with the entering ligand playing little role in the process.[7] This idea
received strong support when data for the k_3 step involving
$M(H_2O)_6^{2+}$, from ultrasonics measurements, was compared with
the rate constant for the exchange reaction for (11):

$$M(H_2O)_6^{2+} + H_2{}^*O \rightleftharpoons M(H_2O)_5(H_2{}^*O) + H_2O \qquad k_{exch} \quad (11)$$

Values for k_{exch} were becoming available in the early 1960's[28]
as a result of observations of the line broadening of the H_2O
NMR signal by metal ions $M(H_2O)_6^{2+}$. This technique has played

a key role in subsequent investigations.[16,25,31] On the basis
of a dissociative mechanism, values for k_3 and k_{exch} might be
expected to be similar to one another since both represent loss
of water from the aquated metal ion. This was shown to be the
case. (See Table 1, which includes updated rate constants.)

TABLE 1
Log Rate Constants (sec^{-1}) for Reactions (4) and
(11) For Some Bivalent Metal Ions

Metal Ion	Mg^{2+}	Mn^{2+}	Co^{2+}	Ni^{2+}	Cu^{2+}
log k_3 (ultrasonics)	5.2	6.6	5.6	4.0	7.2
log k_{exch} (NMR)	5.6	7.5	6.3	4.3	8.3

It might, further, be anticipated that k_{exch} would be somewhat
greater than k_3. Every event of water loss from $M(H_2O)_6^{2+}$ or
$M(H_2O)_6SO_4$ will lead to exchange since water from the surrounding solvent fills the vacancy. Only when a nearby SO_4^{2-} replaces the vacated H_2O will the step corresponding to k_3 occur.
It appears that $k_{exch}/k_3 \sim 5$,[31] (see Table 1).

In certain circumstances $k_{-1} > k_2$ and $k_{-2} > k_3$ in equations (2) -
(4). The overall rate constants for complex formation, k_f,
and complex dissociation, k_r, will then be given by

$$k_f = K_1K_2k_3 = K_0k_3 \qquad (12)$$

and

$$k_r = k_{-3} \qquad (13)$$

In principle, K_1 and K_2 can be determined from acoustic measurements at high frequency. In practice this is difficult and
theoretical equations are usually resorted to for the calculation of K_0.[6,13] Values for k_3 and k_{-3} can be assigned from
the lower frequency relaxation, for which there appears to be

no ambiguity in interpretation.

A large number of studies of complex formation have now been made using a variety of rapid reaction techniques, as well as ultrasonics and NMR, and flow and perturbation methods.[15,31a] In the perturbation method, temperature, pressure or electric field changes are rapidly imposed on a system at chemical equilibrium. The time lag of the system (relaxation) in reaching the new equilibrium forced by the perturbation is monitored. The relaxation for a simple system is always first-order, and the associated rate constant, k, is defined, for example, by equations (6) or (9) for reactions (5) and (8), respectively. In multistep equilibria, the situation is more complex, and relaxation rate constants may not be simply related to rate constants for the specific steps (see (6) and (9)).[15]

A large variety of ligands, both unidentate and multidentate, containing nitrogen, oxygen, and halide donor atoms have been used.[10,15a,18,22] The transition metal ions particularly have been examined, nickel alone with some 100 different ligands, forming mono and higher complexes.[30] Non-transition metal ions have also been studied, although in a much more limited way.[4] Since the value of k_3 in the scheme (Eq. (4)) is largely independent of the nature of the ligand, then complex formation rate constants k_f in combination with estimated values of K_0 lead to values for k_3 from (12). The constancy of this value for a variety of nickel(II) complexes estimated by a number of methods (Table 2) lends credence to the dissociative mechanism.[30] Eigen[4,8] has developed a chart of characteristic rate constants for the reaction of metal ions, using values of k_{exch} (11), or k_3 from ultrasonics (4), or indirectly from overall formation rate constants (12), depending on what is available. The values of k_{exch} from NMR are mainly used and reflect the approximate lability of coordinated water. Figure 2 includes the most recent information.

TABLE 2

Computed Values for k_3 from Second Order Rate Constants (k_f)

for the Formation of Nickel(II) Complexes from

Unidentate Ligands at 25

L^{n-}	$10^{-3} \times k_f$ $M^{-1} sec^{-1}$	K_O, M^{-1}	$10^{-4} \times k_3$ sec^{-1}
$CH_3PO_4^{2-}$	290	40	0.7
CH_3COO^-	100	3	3
NCS^-	6	1	0.6
F^-	8	1	0.8
HF	3	0.15	2
H_2O	...	...	3
NH_3	5	0.15	3
C_5H_5N	$\sim$4	0.15	$\sim$3
$C_4H_4N_2$ (imidazole)	2.8	0.15	2
$NH_2(CH_2)_2NMe_3^+$	0.4	0.02	2

The specific groups of metal ions will now be discussed.

<u>Alkali Metal Ions</u>. The kinetics of complexing by the alkali metal ions have been surveyed previously.[4,8,10] No reported studies have been conducted on complexing by the simpler ligands since 1968 and little previous to that![4] They are not easily investigated because they only form a limited number of complexes of any stability, with few spectral features. Additionally, the rates approach those for diffusion-controlled processes, and have to be measured by techniques such as ultrasonics and electric-field -- these mainly by Eigen and his associates.[4]

There is a small increase in rate as the ion size becomes larger, a behavior which would be anticipated for a dissociative mechanism. This is shown in sound absorption studies for complexing of alkali metal ions by aminopolycarboxylate ions, and in complexing by murexide using the electric-field

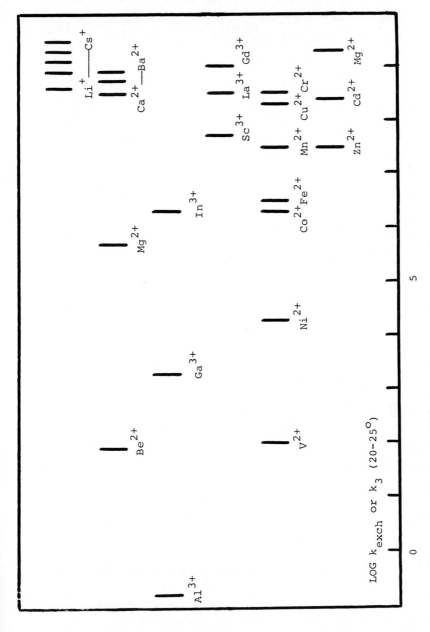

FIGURE 2. Approximate labilities of metal ion coordinated waters.

technique. The formation rates for the latter in methanol
(which will approximate closely the behavior in water) is
$4 \times 10^9 M^{-1} sec^{-1}$ (Li$^+$), $1.4 \times 10^{10} M^{-1} sec^{-1}$ (Na$^+$), $>1.4 \times 10^{10}$
$M^{-1} sec^{-1}$ (K$^+$, Rb$^+$ and Cs$^+$).[4]

Examination of the mechanism of transfer of cations through
cell membranes has occasioned recent interest in the kinetics
of interaction of alkali metal and other ions with bulky, cage-
like ligands, such as the biologically important nonactin and
monactin or the synthetic cryptates such as {1}

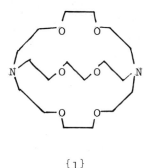

{1}

The reaction of Na$^+$ ion with monactin ($3 \times 10^8 M^{-1} sec^{-1}$) in
MeOH[4] has already been slowed down over that with murexide
(see above), while with {1}in H_2O the estimated value is
several orders of magnitude slower still ($2 \times 10^5 M^{-1} sec^{-1}$ at
$3°$).[20]

Alkaline-Earth Metal Ions. Within this group the reactivity
increases in the order

$$Be^{2+} \ll Mg^{2+} \ll Ca^{2+} < Sr^{2+} < Ba^{2+} \qquad (14)$$

Comparison of all ions having the common electron configuration $1s^2 2s^2 2p^6$ shows that lability increases:[15a]

$$Al^{3+} \ll Mg^{2+} \ll Na^+ \tag{15}$$

This illustrates that with these non-transition elements, the smaller the charge the more loosely held are the coordinated solvent molecules and the faster their substitution rate.

The reactivity of only Mg^{2+} and Ca^{2+} of this group has been examined with a relatively large number of ligands (Table 3).[4,23]

TABLE 3

Rate Constants, k_f, $M^{-1}sec^{-1}$ at 25° for the Formation
of Mg^{2+} and Ca^{2+} complexes with several ligands

Ligand	Mg^{2+} k_f(expl.)	Mg^{2+} k_f(calc.)[a]	Ca^{2+} k_f(expl.)
$P_2O_7^{4-}$	7.1×10^7	4.5×10^7	...
ATP^{4-}	1.8×10^7	9.0×10^6	$\geq 1 \times 10^9$
ADP^{3-}	8.0×10^6	3.0×10^6	$\geq 3 \times 10^8$
IDA^{2-}	9.0×10^5	1.2×10^6	2.5×10^{8b}
Oxine$^-$	3.8×10^5	2.1×10^5	$\geq 1 \times 10^8$
OxineH	1.3×10^4	4.0×10^4	...

[a]Calculated value on basis of estimated K_0 and $k_3 = 1.0 \times 10^5 sec^{-1}$

[b]Value of k_3 from ultrasonics measurements

The formation rate constants for Mg^{2+} reactions can be seen to be in reasonable agreement with (12). They obviously increase as the charge product increases (i.e., K_0 increases). Included in this relationship is the Mg^{2+}-$P_2O_7^{4-}$ system, showing that strong electrostatic interaction in the outer-sphere complex (analogous to B in (3)) does not perceptibly accelerate its water loss when going over to the inner-sphere complex (C in (4)).[23] Since the formation constant ($=k_f/k_r$) of Mg^{2+} and Ca^{2+} ions with a particular ligand is similar, then the differences in k_f amounting to nearly three orders of magnitude must mean

that complex dissociative rate constants (k_r) differ to a similar extent. Their marked differences as enzyme activators
have been proposed to result from this.[9] The rate constants
for reaction of Ca^{2+}, Sr^{2+}, and Ba^{2+} group with {1}(2 x 10^3,
6 x 10^3, and 3 x 10^4 $M^{-1}sec^{-1}$ at 25°, respectively[20,21]) are
surprisingly low and warrant further examination. Reasons
for this slowness have been suggested.[20]

Strehlow and co-workers[26] have concluded that the energy
necessary to remove coordinated water from small polyvalent
cations such as Be^{2+} and Al^{3+}, as might be required in a
mechanism such as shown in Figure 1, is much too high. They
prefer a pathway denoted in the scheme below:

$$(16)$$

They calculate approximate values for $\Delta H^{\ddagger}$ for the process in
reasonable agreement with the experimental ones.

Group 3 and Lanthanide Metal Ions.

The difference in lability between $Al(H_2O)_6^{3+}$ and $Ga(H_2O)_6^{3+}$ is unexpected. Even more surprising are the exchange activation parameters which are $\Delta H^{\ddagger} = +27$ kcal mole^{-1} and $\Delta S^{\ddagger} = 28$ eu for aluminum and $\Delta H^{\ddagger} = 6.3$ kcal mole^{-1} and $\Delta S^{\ddagger} + -22$ eu for gallium.[12] It has been suggested[12] that a dissociative mechanism, D,[19] applies for the reaction of $Al(H_2O)_6^{3+}$ and an associative mechanism, A,[19] for that of $Ga(H_2O)_6^{3+}$. These large differences in activation enthalpies persist in the outer- to inner-sphere complex transformation for the sulfates (21.5 and 12.5 kcal mole^{-1}).[17] However, it is suggested that both these values are expected for a concerted mechanism (Eq. (16)) and that the differences can be rationalized in terms of the different sizes of the cations.[17] More work is obviously required for this group of ions.

The kinetics of complexing by the lanthanide ions have been discussed at length by Kustin and Swinehart[18] and Purdie and Farrow.[24] The lanthanide ions were the last group of metal ions to be studied, and although extensive data are now available, their unambiguous interpretation and an understanding of any trends within the group are still matters of some conjecture.[24] The unexpected lability of this group of ions is ascribed to their having a high coordination number. The lability of coordinated water is strongly dependent on the nature of other ligands coordinated to the lanthanide ion. In the intermediate range of the La series, hydration equilibria

$$LaY(H_2O)_x \;\rightleftharpoons\; LaY(H_2O)_{x-1} + H_2O \tag{17}$$

occur, and the change in hydration number has important consequences on the labilities.[14] As might be anticipated, the trend in rate constants within the group is therefore not a monotonic function of the atomic number, in contrast to the previous groups discussed. Current feeling is that the mechanisms are dissociative in character with NMR exchange data and ultrasonic or temperature-jump formation kinetics in reasonable agreement with each other. Activation enthalpies are in the range 2-5 kcal mole^{-1} from ^{17}O NMR water exchange studies on Gd^{3+}, acoustic measurement on $Sm_2(SO_4)_3$, and temperature-jump studies on Dy^{3+}-anthranilate system.[24]

Transition Metal Ions. This group of metal ions, particularly of the first row, has been thoroughly studied, and the results more than adequately reviewed.[1,10,15a,18,19,22,29,31b] The different parameters which can affect rates have been mostly investigated with the transition metals. It is difficult to distinguish between two dissociative mechanisms for complex formation. In both, metal-water bond breaking is the rate-limiting step, but this occurs either within an outer-sphere complex (an interchange dissociative mechanism, I_d)[19] or apart from the outer-sphere complex (a dissociative mechanism, D). Both lead to extremely similar kinetic characteristics.[31b] In the majority of reactions an I_d mechanism is favored. Evidence for a dissociative mechanism of some kind for substitution in Werner-type octahedral complexes is plentiful.[31b] Since the character of the transition state approximates that of the products in many respects for a dissociative mechanism, linear relationships between activation parameters and the corresponding reaction parameters would be anticipated, and are, in fact, observed. For example, the volumes of activation, $\Delta V^{\ddagger}$, for the reaction of Ni^{2+} with the small NH_3 and with the bulky bidentate ligand PAN are similar, 7.1 and 8.2 $cm^3 mole^{-1}$, respectively. This is consistent with a dissociative mechanism, in which a considerable fraction of the coordinated water is released from Ni^{2+} ion in both cases forming the transition state.[3] We shall consider very briefly several other aspects of the formation of transition metal complexes.

Reaction rates and electron configurations. There has been some success with correlations in this area.[1,2] Crystal field considerations predict for a dissociative or associative mechanism that d^3, low spin d^4, d^5 and d^6, and d^8 systems will generally tend to react slower with ligands than other d-configurations. The relative inertness of the $V^{2+}(d^3)$, Ru^{2+} (low-spin d^6) and $Ni^{2+}(d^8)$ ions, see Figure 2, are striking confirmations of these theories. The marked lability of the Cr^{2+} (high-spin d^4) and $Cu^{2+}(d^9)$ systems, on the other hand, can be ascribed to Jahn-Teller effects, in which substitution takes place at the very labile axial positions. This is followed by rapid inversion of the axial and equatorial ligands, leading then to apparent easy substitution in the equatorial positions.[8] The other bivalent metal ions of the first row -- Mn^{2+}, Fe^{2+}, Co^{2+}, and Zn^{2+} -- react at rates close to, but somewhat slower than, the similarly sized non-transition metal ion (Ca^{2+}). The activation energies, calculated on the basis of removal of a water molecule from the metal ion sufficient to allow the entering ligand to take its place, i.e., a dissociative mechanism, are in reasonable agreement with the experimental values.[1,2] This contrasts with the behavior of $Be(H_2O)_4^{2+}$ and $Al(H_2O)_6^{3+}$ ions, where a concerted mechanism has been suggested.[26]

The d^{10} systems, Zn^{2+}, Cd^{2+}, and Hg^{2+} behave much like the appropriate non-transition metal ions. The Ca^{2+} ion (radius 0.99 A) reacts slightly faster than Zn^{2+} (radius 0.83 A) but at about the same rate as Cd^{2+} ion (radius 1.03 A).

The situation at present is much less clear with tervalent transition metal ions, which do not follow the simpler dissociative pattern established with bivalent metal ions.[5,31] Substitution of $M(H_2O)_6^{3+}$, M = Ti, V, Cr, Mo, and Fe with a variety of anions occurs with rate constants which range over several orders of magnitude. Ligand-assisted substitution is supported.

The effect of bound ligands on reactivity. The effect of ligands within the coordination sphere of a metal on the lability of any remaining coordinated water is rarely drastic. This means that the chart shown of characteristic rate constants (Figure 2) will also apply, within an order of magnitude or two, to higher complex formation, e.g.,

$$ML_5(H_2O)^{n+} + L \rightleftharpoons ML_6^{n+} + H_2O \qquad\qquad (18)$$

Generally, the stronger the ligand L in (18), the weaker the H_2O is coordinated, and the more rapidly it is replaced. Thus carboxylate-O has little effect, whereas NH_3 and (particularly) en and higher polyamines have noticeable labilizing effects on any remaining H_2O. Strong ligands such as phenanthroline or bipyridine have a small effect. Apparently the electron-donor properties of the heterocyclic N are neutralized by back π-bonding effects. For a number of ligands complexing with Ni(II) and Co(II), log k_{exch} (11) increases approximately linearly as the number of H_2O molecules in the complex decreases.[16]

Substitution by multidentate ligands. The similar rate constants for the reaction of the transition metal ions with simple unidentate ligands, e.g., NH_3 and multidentate ligands such as EDTA or polyamines, indicate that the first step of chelation by the multidentate ligand is rate determining, and that this is followed by a rapid sequence of ring closures to give the final chelate. The rate constants for reaction of EDTAH^{3-} with Co^{2+}, Ni^{2+}, Cu^{2+}, Zn^{2+} and Cd^{2+}, in conjunction with known values of k_3 for each metal ion, can all be accommodated with reasonable values of K_0 of $\sim$10. For discussion of this topic see Refs. 1, 18, 24, 30, and 31.

References

1. Basolo, F., and Pearson, R. G. 1967. Mechanisms of Inorganic Reactions. Wiley, New York.

2. Breitschwerdt, K. 1968. Evaluation of Activation Energies for Ligand Exchange in Transition Metal Ions in Solution. Ber. Bunsengesellschaft Phys. Chem., $\underline{72}$: 1046-1051.

3. Caldin, E. F., Grant, M. W., and Hasinoff, B. 1971. Kinetics and Volume of Activation of Reactions of Nickel(II) and Cobalt(II) with some Uncharged Ligands in Water, Studied by a Laser Temperature-Jump Method at High Pressure. Chem. Commun., 1351-1352.

4. Diebler, H., Eigen, M., Ilgenfritz, G., Maass, G., and Winkler, R. 1969. Kinetics and Mechanism of Reactions of Main Group Metal Ions with Biological Carriers. Pure Appl. Chem., $\underline{20}$: 93-115.

5. Diebler, H. 1974. Proceedings 16th International Coordination Chemistry Conference, Dublin, Ireland, August 1974, p. 513.

6. Eigen, M. 1954. Kinetics of Very Fast Ionic Reactions in Aqueous Solution. Z. Physik. Chem. (Frankfurt), $\underline{1}$: 176-200.

7. Eigen, M. 1961. The Kinetics of Fast Solvent Substitution in Metal Complex Formation. In Advances in the Chemistry of the Coordination Compounds, pp. 371-378, ed. S. Kirschner, MacMillan, New York.

8. Eigen, M. 1963. Fast Elementary Steps in Chemical Reaction Mechanisms. Pure Appl. Chem., $\underline{6}$: 97-115.

9. Eigen, M., and Hammes, G. G. 1963. Elementary Steps in Enzyme Reactions. Adv. Enzym., $\underline{25}$: 1-38.

10. Eigen, M., and Wilkins, R. G. 1964. The Kinetics and Mechanism of Formation of Metal Complexes. Adv. Chem., $\underline{49}$: 55-80.

11. Elder, A., and Petrucci, S. 1970. Kinetics of Outer-Sphere Ion-Pair Formation of Aqueous $\{Co(NH_3)_6\}_2(SO_4)_3$ and $\{Co(en)_3\}_2(SO_4)_3$ at $25°$. Inorg. Chem., $\underline{9}$: 19-22.

12. Fiat, D., and Connick, R. E. 1968. Oxygen-17 Magnetic Resonance Studies of Ion Solvation. The Hydration of Aluminum(III) and Gallium(III) Ions. J. Amer. Chem. Soc., $\underline{90}$: 608-615.

13. Fuoss, R. M. 1958. Ionic Association. III. The Equilibrium between Ion Pairs and Free Ions. J. Amer. Chem. Soc., $\underline{80}$: 5059-61.

14. Geier, G. 1973. Kinetics of Water Substitution in Rare Earth Complexes. Dansk Kemi., $\underline{54}$: 129, 161, and previous references.

15. Hammes, G. 1974. Investigations of Rates and Mechanisms of Reaction, 3rd Edit. Part II, Wiley-Interscience, New York.

15a. Hewkin, D. J., and Prince, R. H. 1970. The Mechanism of Octahedral Complex Formation by Labile Metal Ions. Coordn. Chem. Revs., $\underline{5}$: 45-73.

16. Hunt, J. P. 1971. Water Exchange Kinetics in Labile Aquo and Substituted Aquo Transition Metal Ions by Means of ^{17}O NMR Studies. Coordn. Chem. Revs., $\underline{7}$: 1-10.

17. Kalidas, C., Knoche, W., and Papdopoulos, D. 1971. Mechanism of Ligand Substitution in Weak Complexes Part III. Ber. Bunsengesellschaft Phys. Chem., $\underline{75}$: 106-110.

18. Kustin, K., and Swinehart, J. 1970. Fast Metal Complex Reactions. In Inorganic Reaction Mechanisms, ed. J. O. Edwards, pp. 107-158, Wiley, New York.

19. Langford, C. H., and Gray, H. B. 1965. Ligand Substitution Processes, Benjamin, New York.

20. Lehn, J-M. 1973. Design of Organic Complexing Agents. Strategies towards Properties. In Structure and Bonding Vol. 16, Springer-Verlag, Berlin.

21. Loyola, V., and Wilkins, R. G. 1974. Unpublished measurements.

22. McAuley, A., and Hill, J. 1969. Kinetics and Mechanism of Metal-Ion Complex Formation in Solution. Quart Revs., $\underline{23}$: 18-36.

23. Patel, R. C., and Taylor, R. S. 1973. Kinetics of Binding of Pyrophosphate to Magnesium Ions. J. Phys. Chem., $\underline{77}$: 2318-2323.

24. Purdie, N., and Farrow, M. M. 1973. The Application of Ultrasound Absorption to Reaction Kinetics. Coordn. Chem. Revs., $\underline{11}$: 189-226.

25. Stengle, T. R., and Langford, C. H. 1967. The Uses of Nuclear Magnetic Resonance in the Study of Ligand Substitution Processes. Coordn. Chem. Revs., $\underline{2}$: 349-370.

26. Strehlow, H., and Knoche, W. 1969. On the Mechanism of Ligand Substitution in Weak Complexes. Ber. Bunsengesellschaft Phys. Chem., $\underline{73}$, 427-432; $\underline{73}$, 982-986.

27. Stuehr, J., and Yeager, E. 1965. The Propagation of Ultra-
     sonic Waves in Electrolytic Solutions. In Physical Acous-
     tics, Volume 2A, Chapter 6. Academic Press, New York.

28. Swift, T. J., and Connick, R. E. 1962. NMR-Relaxation
     Mechanisms of O^{17} in Aqueous Solutions of Paramagnetic
     Cations and the Lifetime of Water Molecules in the First
     Coordination Sphere. J. Chem. Phys., 37: 307-320.

29. Tobe, M. L. 1972. Inorganic Reaction Mechanisms. Nelson,
     London.

30. Wilkins, R. G. 1970. Mechanisms of Ligand Replacement in
     Octahedral Nickel(II) Complexes. Accs. Chem. Res., 3:
     408-416.

31. Wilkins, R. G. 1974. The Study of Kinetics and Mechanisms
     of Reactions of Transition Metal Complexes. Allyn and
     Bacon, Boston. (a) Chapter 3 (b) Chapter 4.

Applications of Isotopes to Kinetic Studies of Carbonate Systems

G. M. Harris, Larkin Professor of Chemistry
Department of Chemistry
State University of New York at Buffalo
Buffalo, New York 14214, U.S.A.

Abstract: A review is given of the various ways in which isotopes can be used to assist in providing information concerning the kinetics and mechanism of chemical reactions, particularly those involving carbon dioxide or carbonates. Experimental procedures for isotopic composition determination are outlined, and the tracer technique is explained, both as applied to simple studies of the path of a chemical reaction and to the kinetics of isotopic exchange systems. The phenomenon of chemical isotope effect is discussed in terms of three major aspects: equilibrium isotope effects, kinetic isotope effects, and deuterium solvent isotope effects. Examples are given illustrating how these various approaches have been used, and references to some of the major sources of general information are quoted.

Introduction:

Carbonate systems were among the first to be studied by isotopic methods, extending back to the classic stable isotope separation work by H. C. Urey and co-workers in the 1930's. Both carbon and oxygen isotopes are involved in isotopic carbonate chemistry, and since there are three stable (or at

TABLE 1 - Properties of the Long-Lived Isotopes of Carbon and Oxygen

Nuclide	Natural Abundance	Atomic Mass	Other Distinguishing Properties
^{12}C	98.89%	12.00000	
^{13}C	1.11	13.00335	$\mu = 0.702$ (nmr detection is 1.59% of proton sensitivity)
^{14}C	-	14.00	β^- emitter, 0.156 Mev, $t_{1/2} = 5770y.$
^{16}O	99.759	15.99491	
^{17}O	0.037	16.99914	$\mu = -1.89$ (nmr detection is 2.91% of proton sensitivity)
^{18}O	0.204	17.99916	

least long-lived) isotopic species for each element (^{12}C, ^{13}C, ^{14}C and ^{16}O, ^{17}O, ^{18}O), (see TABLE I) the CO_2 molecule can exist in 18 different isotopic forms, while the CO_3 radical has no less than 30 such variations. Actually, since only ^{12}C, ^{13}C, ^{16}O and ^{18}O occur in appreciable amounts in nature, most of the earlier studies of the isotope chemistry of carbonates involved only these and were based entirely on mass spectrometry. Nevertheless, the discovery of practical methods for synthesizing carbon-14 during the Manhattan Project years, its relatively long half-life, and the ease of using its radioactivity in its detection, have resulted in many useful applications of this isotope in all types of carbon chemistry. In recent years, both carbon-13 and oxygen-17 have become more useful as detectable isotopes because of the development of effective nuclear magnetic techniques for these nuclides. In special circumstances, even the very short-lived oxygen isotope ^{15}O ($t_{1/2} = 2.03m$, β^+, 1.73 Mev) has been effectively utilized in carbonate

research, as will be seen. In summary, it can be stated that
isotopic methods have always been and will continue to be
among the most versatile for investigating the chemistry of
carbonates. Our review, as the title indicates, will stress
the reaction rate aspects of such work, but reference will be
made to other complementary approaches as the need arises.

The Determination of Isotopic Composition of Compounds of the Carbonate Type.

In order to utilize isotopic techniques in chemical investigation, one must have rapid, convenient, and accurate detection
procedures. In the case of radioactive species such as ^{14}C
and ^{15}O, the procedure is perhaps most direct, since both of
these emit particles (β^- and β^+, respectively) of sufficient
energy to readily detectable by the Geiger counter.[14] The
classic method for examining radioactive carbonate systems is
to precipitate the separated carbonate at a pH of about 8 as
barium carbonate. The latter can then be spread in plan-
chettes by standardized techniques and the counting done by
means of a thin-window Geiger counter assembly. Alternatively,
the separated carbon-containing residue can be dispersed in a
suitable liquid scintillator and the counting is then accomplished by photomultiplier detection of the scintillations.
A third possibility is to introduce the labelled gaseous
carbon dioxide or methane directly into the Geiger tube.
For the stable isotopes, mass spectrometry offers the only
generally applicable detection procedure.[11] For carbon-13 or
oxygen-18 labelled systems, for example, the carbonate is
volatilized as carbon dioxide, which is then fed directly into
the ionization chamber of the mass spectrometer. The species
which will appear in measurable amounts (assuming little
enrichment of any of the rarer isotopes above their natural
abundances) are $^{12}C^{16}O_2$, $^{13}C^{16}O_2$, $^{12}C^{16}O^{18}O$ and $^{12}C^{18}O^{18}O$,
with masses 44, 45, 46, and 48, respectively. The mass ratios
$R_1 = 45/44$ or $R_2 = 46/44$ are then determined by means of the
mass spectrometer, and simple statistics show that

$$\%^{13}C = 100 \, R_1/(1 + R_1) \qquad (1a)$$

or

$$\%^{18}O = 100 \, R_2/(2 + R_2) \qquad (1b)$$

The <u>nuclear magnetic resonance</u> procedure, as stated earlier, is applicable only to carbon-13 and oxygen-17 (the latter only if sufficiently enriched) and involves much more sensitive instrumentation than the usual proton-detecting models (see TABLE I). However, instruments currently available[19] can generate carbon-13 spectra from samples containing less than 100 mg. of carbon in its natural isotopic composition.

Methods of Using Isotopes in Chemical Kinetics

The Tracer Technique

In this procedure, one is interested merely in determining the chemical path of a given element in a reaction or series of reactions. For example, acidification of an inorganic carbonato complex of the type $[Co(NH_3)_4CO_3]NO_3$, liberates carbon dioxide according to the equation:

$$(2)$$

$$Co(NH_3)_4CO_3^+ + 2H_3O^+ \rightarrow Co(NH_3)_4(OH_2)_2^{3+} + CO_2 + H_2O$$

One of the questions of interest in early studies of this complex was the identity of the oxygen atoms in the aquo complex formed - did they come from the water, or were they the ones originally attached to the cobalt(III) center? The problems is illustrated by the following structural representation:

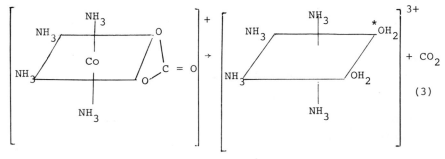

The question posed above was answered[16] by using oxygen-18-
enriched water as the solvent. The experiments showed that
one of the oxygens left on the complex was there originally
while the other came from the labelled solvent, as indicated
in equation (3). The CO_2 itself escapes in unlabelled form,
due to the relatively slow rate of exchange of CO_2 oxygen
atoms with water. The results of these experiments are
readily explainable in terms of later kinetic studies of the
same reaction by stopped-flow techniques. The rate data show[5]
that such reactions occur in two steps according to the scheme

(4)

As can be seen, this mechanistic interpretation is consistent
with the Posey and Taube tracer observation. The mechanism has
been further confirmed by another type of kinetic isotope
application, the deuterium solvent isotope effect, to be discussed later.

Another kind of tracer application is that known as the isotopic exchange technique. Suppose one has the atom or group
X present in either of two compounds, AX and BX, and suppose
further that chemical exchange of these atoms or groups occurs,
such that if one of them is labelled, equilibration takes
place according to the reversible reaction:

$$AX + BX^* \rightleftharpoons AX^* + BX \qquad (5)$$

Since the chemical properties of X and X* are essentially identical,[*] the driving force for the reaction is entirely entro-
pic, its equilibrium constant is unity, and the rates (and
mechanisms) of forward and reverse reactions are identical.
It was shown many years ago[13] that the kinetics of such
systems are relatively simple.

One can assume the constant value R for the rate of both forward and reverse chemical reactions under a specified set of
conditions of concentration (both of the AX and BX type of
compounds), pH, temperature, solvent composition, etc. Then,
if [AX] + [AX*] = a and [BX] + [BX*] = b, and the fraction
of exchange at time t is F, it is readily derived on statistical grounds that:

$$R = \frac{-2.303}{t} \left(\frac{ab}{a+b}\right) \log(1-F)$$

$$= \frac{0.693}{t_{1/2}\ (\text{exchange})} \left(\frac{ab}{a+b}\right) \tag{6}$$

Since R = f(conc., pH, temp., etc.), a series of exchange runs
carried out under various experimental conditions enables the
nature of the function R to be determined, from which conclusions may be drawn concerning the kinetics and mechanism of
the reaction under study.

An example of this type of research as applied to carbonate
systems is afforded by the investigation[7] of the pair of reactions (en = enthylenediamine):

$$\text{\underline{cis} or \underline{trans} } Co(NH_3)_2enCO_3^+ + {}^{14}CO_3^{2-} \rightleftarrows Co(NH_3)_2en\ {}^{14}CO_3^+ + CO_3^{2-} \tag{7}$$

---

[*] The chemical non-identity of isotopic species is discussed
later under the heading of "Chemical Isotope Effects."

The cis and trans isomers are defined by the octahedral
geometry of the complex, as shown below:

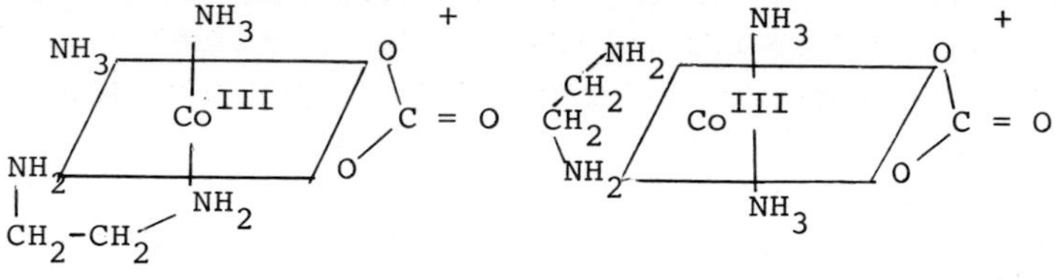

cis   trans

Earlier studies (see listing in reference 7) had indicated
that the nature and relative positioning of the amine ligands
has considerable effect on the kinetics of the carbonate
exchange process, despite the fact that the amine ligands
remain firmly fixed throughout the exchange. The study,[7]
carried out in the range 7.5 < pH < 9.5 at 25°, showed that
in both cis and trans cases the mechanism of the exchange
consisted of a series of reactions involving the solvent
water molecules, proton transfers thereto, and transfer of
carbon dioxide from "free" carbonate ion to that in the complex. The most significant contributions to the reaction were
from the equilibrations:

$$Co(NH_3)_2enCO_3^+ + H_2O \rightleftharpoons Co(NH_3)_2en(OH)(CO_3H)^+ \qquad (9)$$

$$Co(NH_3)_2en(OH)(CO_3H)^+ + H_2O \rightleftharpoons Co(NH_3)_2en(OH)(CO_3) + H_3O^+ \qquad (10)$$

$$Co(NH_3)_2en(OH)(CO_3H)^+ \rightleftharpoons Co(NH_3)_2en(OH)_2^+ + CO_2 \qquad (11)$$

and $Co(NH_3)_2en(OH)(CO_3) + CO_2 \rightleftharpoons Co(NH_3)_2en(CO_3H)(CO_3)$ (12)

together with the well-known carbon dioxide/bicarbonate equilibration:

$$CO_2 + H_2O \rightleftharpoons H_3O^+ + HCO_3^- \qquad (13)$$

The study showed that the trans form of the complex underwent
carbonate exchange about three times more rapidly than did the
cis. It was concluded that the effect is related to the rates
of the water-promoted ring-opening reaction (9), which is
expected to be more facile for the trans congener because of

the strain introduced by the in-plane chelation of both ethy-
lenediamine and carbonate in this isomer (see equation (8)
above). Another modification of the tracer technique is
illustrated by a recent study[23] of the very important aqueous
reactions

$$CO_2 \; + \; H_2O \; \rightarrow \; H_2CO_3 \qquad\qquad (14)$$

$$HCO_3^- \; \rightarrow \; OH^- \; + \; CO_2 \qquad\qquad (15)$$

Here, the short-lived isotope oxygen-15 was used as tracer,
its advantage over oxygen-18 being that, since the radioisotope is so easily detected, very low concentrations of carbon
dioxide could be used. The exchange of oxygen-15 between the
labelled carbon dioxide and the water solvent was followed,
and data were obtained over a wide pH range without addition
of buffers (which are known to interfere with the rates of
reactions(14) and (15)). A temperature dependence study was
also made. The rate constant values obtained agree well with
the commonly accepted values from earlier work using several
other rate determination procedures.[9]

Chemical Isotope Effects

For the purpose of this discussion, we define chemical isotope
effects as those changes in the chemical properties of an atom
or molecule which are directly related to the differences in
the mass of the isotopic nuclei in the species being compared.
In general, most fundamental chemical properties may be dealt
with theoretically in terms of the significant statistical
mechanical partition functions. The latter are themselves
functions of the nature and number of the various electronic,
vibrational, rotational, and translational energy states
accessible to the species under consideration. The most useful isotope effects in relation to mechanistic studies of
chemical reactions in carbonate systems are three in number:
(a) those associated with differences in the thermodynamic
equilibrium constants involving isotopic molecules (equili-

brium isotope effects); (b) those which appear as differences
in the relative rates of specified elementary processes in
chemical reactions, in which the reactants differ only in
terms of isotopic composition (kinetic isotope effects); and
(c) those resulting from the substitution of deuterium for
hydrogen in the solvent water used in an aqueous system
(deuterium solvent isotope effects). The theoretical bases
of these effects are now briefly reviewed and examples are
given of their applications.

Equilibrium isotope effects [10]

For any chemical equilibrium of the type

$$aA + bB + \ldots \rightleftarrows cC + dD + \ldots, \qquad (16)$$

statistical mechanics shows that the calculated equilibrium
constant (neglecting activity corrections) is given by:

$$K_{St} = [Q_C^c \; Q_D^d \ldots / Q_A^a \; Q_B^b \ldots] \; e^{-\Delta E^0/RT} \qquad (17)$$

In this equation, the Q's are the partition functions for a
unit volume system, and are related to the molecular energy
levels of the various species by expressions of the form
$Q = \Sigma g_i e^{-\epsilon_i/kT}$, in which the ϵ_i's are increments of energy of
each state above its ground state and the g_i's are the
degeneracies of each state of a given energy. The term ΔE^0
is the total change per mole in ground-state internal energy
of the system in going from reactants to products.

Consider, for example, the equilibrium constant for a typical
carbonate isotopic exchange system, such as:

$$\qquad (18)$$

$$^{13}CO_2(g) + {}^{12}CO_3^{2-}(aq) \rightleftarrows {}^{12}CO_2(g) + {}^{13}CO_3^{2-}(aq)$$

A number of simplifications are possible, as fully explained
in reports of studies of this system.[21,12] One needs only
detailed information on the vibrational frequencies of the
various molecules involved in order to calculate an accurate
equilibrium constant at any desired temperature. Such equilibrium data are of course widely used by geochemists in discussing the age and the nature of the processes involved in
the formation of various carbonate minerals.[2]

The use of this kind of information as an interpretive aid for kinetic data is illustrated in early studies in our laboratory of the same type of carbonate exchange system discussed above as an example of a tracer application. A comparison was made of the kinetics of several exchange reactions of the type of equation (7):

$$CoN_4CO_3^+ + {}^{14}CO_3^{2-} \rightleftharpoons CoN_4{}^{14}CO_3^+ + CO_3^{2-} \tag{19}$$

in which N_4 symbolizes not only the $(NH_3)_2en$ grouping of equation (7), but also several others, such as en_2 or tn_2 (where tn = 1,3 diaminopropane). It turns out that the rate constants determining the rates of isotopic exchange for the $Cotn_2CO_3^+$ species are about one-tenth as great as for the en_2 analog.[7] A possible explanation is that the chelated carbonato group in the tn_2 species is more firmly attached than it is in the en_2 congener. This is attributed to the greater flexibility of the $Cotn_2CO_3^+$ complex ion as a result of the increased ring size of the chelated amine ligand tn as compared to en. This would suggest that the carbonato grouping in $Cotn_2CO_3^+$ should in fact differ somewhat more from "free" carbonate in its structural and thus vibrational properties than does the carbonato of the en_2 analog. One might therefore expect to get a greater deviation from unity of the isotopic exchange equilibrium constant:

$$K_{20} = \frac{[CoN_4{}^{14}CO_3^+]\ [{}^{12}CO_3^{2-}]}{[CoN_4{}^{12}CO_3^+]\ [{}^{14}CO_3^{2-}]} \tag{20}$$

for the tn_2 species than for the en_2. This is in fact found to be the case, the respective values[3] of K_{20} being 0.93 ±0.01 and 0.99 ±0.01. In support of this argument, it should be mentioned that the corresponding K value for monodentate carbonato exchange in the system involving $Co(NH_3)_5CO_3^+$ and ${}^{14}CO_3^{2-}$ is 1.00, i.e., complexed but non-chelated carbonate is indistinguishable thermodynamically from "free" carbonate.[20] As a second example of the use of equilibrium isotope effects to enable mechanistic deductions to be made, consider the series of equilibrations:

$$CO_2(g) \;\rightleftarrows\; CO_2(aq) \;\rightleftarrows\; HCO_3^-(aq) \tag{21}$$

By using carbon-13-labelled CO_2, it was found possible[6] to evaluate experimentally the two isotopic exchange equilibrium constants:

$$^{13}CO_2(g) \;+\; {}^{12}CO_2(aq) \;\rightleftarrows\; {}^{12}CO_2(g) \;+\; {}^{13}CO_2(aq), K_{22} \tag{22}$$

$$^{13}CO_2(aq) + H^{12}CO_3^-(aq) \;\rightleftarrows\; {}^{12}CO_2(aq) + H^{13}CO_3^-(aq), K_{23} \tag{23}$$

as well as the overall constant $K_{22} \cdot K_{23}$. It turns out that <u>no</u> isotopic fractionation occurs during reaction (22), but there is an appreciable enrichment of carbon-13 in the bicarbonate constituent in reaction (23). Thus if an aquatic plant utilizes CO_2 exclusively in its metabolism, its carbon should be isotopically identical to that of neighboring air-breathing plants, provided that their metabolic paths are similar, and that the dissolved CO_2 is in equilibrium with the atmosphere. However, an aquatic plant which can utilize bicarbonate will have an excess of carbon-13 in its carbon, which should amount to about 0.7% at 25°.

<u>Kinetic isotope effects</u>

According to the most widely accepted theory of chemical kinetics, the transition state theory, an equilibrium is first established between reactants and transition state, followed by rate-determining bond cleavage leading to chemical reaction. For isotopically substituted but otherwise identical molecules A and A_i, one may symbolize reaction with molecule B as follows:

$$A + B \;\underset{K^{\neq}}{\rightleftarrows}\; [AB]^{\neq} \;\overset{k}{\rightarrow}\; Products \tag{24}$$

$$A_i + B \;\underset{K_i^{\neq}}{\rightleftarrows}\; [A_iB]^{\neq} \;\overset{k_i}{\rightarrow}\; Products$$

The statistical mechanical treatment of reaction rates[22] based on this scheme leads to fairly effective theoretical procedures for determining the magnitude of the ratio k_i/k, which defines the kinetic isotope effect for the primary bimolecular process A + B → Products. The effect is negligible for carbon and oxygen isotopes unless the chemical bond reorganization in the rate-determining step directly involves the carbon or oxygen isotope (i.e., it is a primary kinetic isotope effect*). In typical instances, one is looking for effects such that the ratio k_i/k is within a few percent of unity, with the rate constant predicted by theory to be slightly larger for the lighter isotopic species. The net result is that the heavier isotope becomes more and more concentrated in the residual reactant as reaction proceeds. Consider, for example the simple Cannizaro reaction of formaldehyde

$$2CH_2O + OH^- \rightarrow CH_3OH + HCO_2^- \qquad (25)$$

for which it is of interest to determine whether the rate-determining step involves bonds attached to the carbon atom. Provided $[A_i] << [A]$, as is always the case when using trace-level labelling, it may be shown[8] that

$$\ln S_F/S_O = (k_i/k-1) \ln(1-F) \qquad (26)$$

where S_F is the specific activity (a quantity proportional to $[A_i]/[A]$) of the residual reactant after a fraction F has undergone reaction, and S_O is the corresponding initial quantity. Experimentally, it is fairly simple, by using carbon-14-labelled formaldehyde, to follow the change in the specific activity ratio S_F/S_O of the formaldehyde as a function of fraction of reaction F. A plot is then made of $\ln(S_F/S_O)$ vs $\ln(1-F)$, the slope of which should be $(k_i/k-1)$ (see equation 26). When this was carried out it was found[8] that $k_i/k = 0.94$, indicating a 6% reduction in rate for the carbon-14-labelled species, and confirming that the mechanism of the reaction must involve rate-determining bond rupture at the carbon atom.

---

* Secondary kinetic isotope effects refer to those resulting from isotopic substitution on an atom adjacent to but not part of the bond or bonds involved in the reaction. In general, these effects are experimentally inobservable except for deuterated species (see ref. 22, Ch. 3).

The above type of kinetic isotope technique has been widely
applied in   organic chemistry,[17] but has not been used to
any great extent in inorganic carbonate chemistry. There is
however one recent example, in which oxygen-18 isotope fractionation was followed in the acid decomposition of several
metal carbonates[15] of the type MCO_3 where M = Mn, Zn, Cd, Pb,
Ca, Sr, or Ba. Here the interpretation is complicated by the
fact that, with oxygen-18 labelling, there are two different
ways in which the CO_3 radical can undergo reaction to produce
CO_2, depending upon whether $C-^{18}O$ or $C-^{16}O$ bond fission occurs.
However, this possibility can be accounted for statistically
in the treatment of the kinetics, and values for k_i/k for
decarboxylation of $MC^{16}O_2^{18}O$ to produce $C^{16}O_2$ and $C^{16}O^{18}O$,
respectively, were obtained experimentally and calculated
theoretically. The effects are not great, with the experimental deviations from unity of the rate constant ratio at
25° ranging between 1.49% for $MnCO_3$ and 1.68% for $CdCO_3$. The
only appreciable discrepancy between theory and experiment
occurred in the case of $PbCO_3$, and this was ascribed to the
more basic nature of this compound as compared to the others
discussed.

Deuterium solvent isotope effect
Many compounds have readily exchangeable protons, particularly
acids, and thus, when equilibrated with an excess of heavy
water, D_2O, end up with all their labile protons replaced by
deuterons. There are two main kinetic consequences of this
replacement, depending upon the nature of the rate-determining
step in the specified chemical reaction. Consider, for example,
an acid-catalyzed process for which the stoichiometry may be
written:

$$B + H_3O^+ \rightarrow \text{Products}$$

One mechanism for this reaction involves direct transfer of
the proton from the H_3O^+ ion to B in the transition state:

$$B + H_3O^+ \rightleftarrows [B\text{--}H^+\text{---}OH_2]^{\neq} \rightarrow \text{Products} \quad k_H \qquad (27)$$

The corresponding deuterated system may be symbolized:

$$B + D_3O^+ \rightleftarrows [B\text{--}D^+\text{---}OD_2]^{\neq} \rightarrow \text{Products} \quad k_D \qquad (28)$$

It is seen that the bond reorganization may involve breaking H---O or D---O bonds, and making B---H or B---D bonds. This is the pattern for a straightforward kinetic isotope effect of the kind described earlier, and defined in terms of a rate constant ratio k_D/k_H. Since H and D differ in mass by a factor of 2, large isotope effects are to be expected and frequently observed, with a factor k_D/k_H of less than 0.5 not at all uncommon.

Suppose now that the mechanism of the reaction, unlike equations (27) and (28), requires <u>rapid proton</u> (or deuteron) <u>equilibration</u> prior to the rate-determining step, such that the mechanism becomes:

$$B + H_3O^+ \rightleftharpoons BH^+ + H_2O \quad 1/K_H \tag{29}$$

$$BH^+ \rightarrow \text{Products} \quad k_H$$

or

$$B + D_3O^+ \rightleftharpoons BD^+ + D_2O \quad 1/K_D \tag{30}$$

$$BD^+ \rightarrow \text{Products} \quad k_D$$

It is clear that the effective rate-constant ratio now involves also the acid dissociation constants K_H and K_D, so that the isotope effect is defined by the quantity $k_D K_H / k_H K_D$. Frequently, the second (rate-determining) step in the mechanism does <u>not</u> directly involve the bonds formed to H or D in the pre-equilibration step, so that $k_H \sim k_D$. When this is true, the rate of the reaction in D_2O may be considerably greater than in H_2O, since the acid dissociation constants of deuterated acids are in general much smaller than of the corresponding protonated species.[1] One can see, therefore, that a choice between the direct proton transfer mechanism or the proton pre-equilibration mechanism can perhaps be made on the basis of heavy water experiments. Obviously, if the reaction is faster in heavy water than in light, the second possibility is strongly supported. Otherwise, the direct protonation mechanism is most likely.

An application of this kind of approach has been made in our laboratory during studies of the acid-catalyzed decarboxylation of cobalt(III) carbonato complexes of the type $CoN_4CO_3^+$

mentioned earlier. The mechanism shown (equation 4) includes proton transfer, but does not clearly indicate whether the process is of the direct transfer or pre-equilibration type. This question was answered in a study[18] of the acid decomposition of the complex ions $Coen_2CO_3^+$, $Copn_2CO_3^+$ (pn = 1,2 diaminopropane) and $Cotn_2CO_3^+$. In each case, the reaction was found to be about three times more rapid in H_2O than in D_2O, supporting the direct transfer mechanism. Subsequent studies have shown unequivocally that the ring-opened protonated intermediate of the type symbolized in equation 4 is extremely unstable,[4] and so could not be expected to take part in an acid/base equilibrium system in the normal manner.

References

(1) R. P. Bell, "The Proton in Chemistry", Ch. XI.   Cornell University Press, Ithaca, N.Y., 1959.

(2) Some other recent related studies are the following: Y. Bottinga, J. Phys. Chem., 72, 800 (1968); W. G. Deuser and E. T. Degens, Nature, 215, 1033 (1967); Y. Horibe, K. Shigehara, and Y. Takakuwa, J. Geophys. Research, 78, 2625 (1973); I. Wendt, Earth and Planetary Science Letters, 4, 64 (1968).

(3) J. E. Boyle, Ph. D. Dissertation, University of Buffalo, Buffalo, N.Y., 1956.

(4) T. P. Dasgupta and G. M. Harris, J. Am. Chem. Soc., 97, 1733 (1975).

(5) T. P. Dasgupta and G. M. Harris, J. Am. Chem. Soc., 91, 3207 (1969).

(6) W. G. Deuser and E. T. Degens (see ref. 2 for listing).

(7) R. J. Dobbins and G. M. Harris, J. Am. Chem. Soc., 92, 5204 (1970).

(8) A. M. Downes and G. M. Harris, J. Chem. Phys., 20, 196 (1952).

(9) J. T. Edsall, R. E. Forster, A. B. Otis, and F. J. W.
     Roughton, Eds., "CO_2: Chemical, Biochemical and Physio-
     logical Aspects," National Aeronautics and Space Admini-
     stration, Washington, D. C., (U.S. Government Printing
     Office, 1969).

(10) T. Ishida, W. Spindel and J. Bigeleisen, in "Isotope
     Effects in Chemical Processes" p. 192 (Advances in
     Chemistry Series, No. 89, R. F. Gould, Ed., American
     Chemical Society, Washington, D. C., (1969)).

(11) R. W. Kiser, "Introduction to Mass Spectrometry and Its
     Applications," Prentice-Hall, Inc., Englewood Cliffs,
     N.J., 1965.

(12) K. V. Krishnamurty and R. W. Wolfe, Indian J. of Chemistry
     6, 674 (1968).

(13) H. A. C. McKay, J. Am. Chem. Soc., 65, 703 (1943).

(14) R. T. Overman and H. M. Clark, "Radioisotope Techniques,"
     McGraw-Hill Book Co., New York, N.Y., 1960.

(15) G. C. Pandey, N. V. Pillai, and T. Sharma, Z. phys.
     Chemie (Leipzig), 246, 297 (1971).

(16) F. A. Posey and H. Taube, J. Am. Chem. Soc., 75, 4099
     (1953).

(17) H. P. Raaen, V. F. Raaen, and G. A. Ropp, "Carbon-14",
     McGraw-Hill Book Co., New York, N. Y., 1968.

(18) V. S. Sastri and G. M. Harris, J. Am. Chem. Soc., 92,
     2943 (1970).

(19) R. B. Stothers, "Carbon-13 NMR Spectroscopy", Academic
     Press, New York, N.Y., 1972.

(20) D. R. Stranks, Trans. Far. Soc., 51, 492 (1955).

(21) H. G. Thode, M. Shima, C. E. Rees, and K. V. Krishnamurty,
     Can. J. Chem., 43, 582 (1965).

(22) W. A. Van Hook, Ch. 1 in "Isotope Effects in Chemical
     Reactions," C. J. Collins and N. S. Bowman, Eds., ACS
     Monograph No. 167, Van Nostrand and Reinhold Co., New
     York, N.Y., 1970.

(23) M. J. Welch, J. F. Lifton and J. A. Seck, J. Phys. Chem.,
     73, 3351 (1969). For related studies using oxygen-18
     as the tracer isotope, see H. W. Baldwin and D. J.
     Poulton, Can. J. Chem., 45, 1045 (1967), and D. Stas-
     chewski, Chemie-Ing.-Techn., 41, 1111 (1969).

Kinetic Isotope Effects of Oxygen in Photosynthesis and Respiration

Klaus Wagener
Institute of Biophysical Chemistry, Nuclear Research Center
Juelich (KFA), 517 Juelich, F. R. Germany

Abstract: Isotope effects can provide subtle insight into reaction mechanisms, pathways, and rates. For large-scale systems, especially the global system, tracer experiments may be the most advantageous or only method of obtaining such knowledge. This paper reviews the present knowledge of isotope fractionation occurring in the oxygen cycles. Models of the fractionation mechanism in respiratory processes and photosynthesis are discussed. The applicability to some actual problems of biogeochemistry, correlated to the marine oxygen cycle, is pointed out and discussed.

1. Introduction

The cyclical turnover of elements in the biological matter cycles is most commonly described in terms of material fluxes flowing between compartments. In box models, these compartments are considered well-mixed reservoirs, and the flow resistance for each flux is located in the "surface" of the boxes. Examples for well justified box models may be the troposphere or the mixed layer of the oceans. The ocean as a whole cannot be considered as one box, and even the two box model (mixed layer and deep sea) will be proper only under very limited aspects. A se-

quence of boxes, e. g. a series of ocean layers, ultimately
leads to a continuous model, and the material transport in such
a system can be described in terms of diffusion kinetics. Under
constant environmental conditions and for sufficiently long
periods of (averaged) observation, such a compartmental picture of a biome gives a stationary state.

Under these conditions we find, in general, a different isotopic composition in each box for all the lighter elements. This
is a consequence of the so-called isotope effects, i. e.
slightly different physico-chemical properties due to the primary mass difference of isotopes. Isotope effects are well
understood, in most cases, resulting either from kinetic phenomena in transport processes or from quantum effects in chemical equilibria. With few exceptions (F, Na, Al, P), all light
elements are mixtures of at least two stable isotopes, including the main components of organic matter: C, H, O, N, S.

The isotope composition of a reservoir is usually given as
abundance ratio of two isotopes; for the purpose of mass balances it is convenient to use the mole fraction of the rare isotope. The isotope fractionation between natural reservoirs is
generally of the order of 1 %, ranging between a few permill
and several percent. The accuracy of modern mass spectrometry
allows isotope analyses of better than 1/10 of a permill by
routine procedure, so that the effects under consideration can
be studied quite easily. One item, however, deserves special
attention, and that is the procedure of taking, handling,
storing and processing samples, since artifacts are very easily introduced. The necessary precautions are well-known, but
unfortunately not always noted: Therefore many (mainly of the
older) data are suspect.

Isotope effects can provide subtle insight into reaction mechanisms, pathways, and rates as well. Tracer experiments are
sometimes the best or only way to study large-scale systems,
especially the global system. The present knowledge of isotope
fractionation occurring in the oxygen cycles will therefore be

reviewed here, as well as some actual problems of bio-geo-chemistry correlated to the oxygen cycle (e. g. the gas ex-change between atmosphere and ocean).

2. Reservoirs and Reaction Pathways of Oxygen in the Biocycles

All the components involved in photosynthesis and respiration are turned over in stoichiometric proportions according to the gross equation

$$CO_2 + H_2O \; \overset{\rightarrow}{\leftarrow} \; |\; CH_2O \;| \; + \; O_2 \tag{1}$$

They form reservoirs, and the three inorganic components under-go exchange between their reservoirs involved in the land cycle and the marine matter cycle, respectively (see FIG. 1).

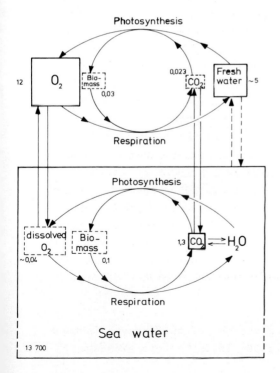

FIG. 1 - Reservoirs and reaction pathways of oxygen in the bio-cycles. The figures at the reservoirs are mass numbers, given in 10^{14} tons.
The oxygen of dissolved CO_2 undergoes rapid isotope exchange with water.
Reservoirs in broken lines are out of scale.
(after WAGENER 1973)

Seawater represents the largest reservoir, with almost constant
isotopic composition. Therefore, the $^{18}O/^{16}O$ ratio of any given
sample is usually compared with the isotope ratio in standard
mean ocean water (SMOW). Deviations against SMOW are given as
δ values (= permill = parts per thousand = ppt). The ^{18}O content of fresh water depends on its meteorological history and,
therefore, on the geographic location; the content decreases,
in general, from the equator to the poles (30° : - 5 ppt;
60° : - 15 ppt; for details see GARLICK 1969; IAEA 1969).

The isotope composition of free atmospheric oxygen has been
found constant all over the world and up to heights of 51 km,
as expected (DOLE et al., 1954). The composition of dissolved
oxygen in the seawater, however, depends strongly on the depth
(RAKESTRAW et al. 1951; VINOGRADOV et al. 1959; KROOPNICK et
al. 1972). Due to the complex pathways of marine O_2, and to the
vertical distribution of O_2 sources and sinks in addition, the
dissolved oxygen cannot be considered as one single reservoir
(see section 3). The euphotic zone produces and consumes oxygen
at the same time; in addition, gas is exchanged with the atmosphere. From this zone, oxygen is transported into deeper layers
by eddy diffusion, while the oxygen supply of the deep sea depends on the large-scale circulation of the deep sea water
masses with a characteristic circulation time of the order of
1000 years. In areas with well established stratigraphy it is
very easy to recognize the depth to which the euphotic zone
contributes to the oxygen content. It is the depth of the
oxygen minimum, which coincides with a maximum in the ^{18}O content
of the dissolved oxygen. This correlation (DOLE et al. 1951;
VINOGRADOV et al. 1959; KROOPNICK et al. 1972) seems to be the
result of a Rayleigh fractionation of isotopic oxygen molecules
during the progressive consumption on the way down by processes
which decompose the dead organic matter. Horizontal convection,
however, must be taken into account, so that samples taken at
different depths of one vertical profile may have a different
history.

CO_2 in equilibrium with water gives one of the largest isotope
effects (+ 41 ppt). Atmospheric CO_2 is in isotope exchange

equilibrium with sea water (CRAIG et al. 1963). This fact, however, has certainly no importance for the ^{18}O budget of atmospheric and marine O_2 as well, since the isotope exchange rate between O_2 and CO_2 must be very small.

In the bio-cycles, free oxygen only travels between the reservoirs of O_2 and water, whereas the oxygen bound to carbon changes between CO_2, organic matter, and water:

$$CO_2 + 2H_2O^* \rightleftarrows \mid CH_2O \mid + O_2^* + H_2O \qquad (2)$$

3. Isotope Fractionation during Respiration

Free oxygen is present, starting from the atmospheric or marine reservoir, respectively, and through more or less numerous intermediate compartments, up to the interior of the cells where it is consumed in the respiration chain. The consumed oxygen is removed from the cells and the organism in the form of water. In the following the oxygen fluxes between compartments are denoted by R; in chemical compounds the R's refer to the portion of oxygen in the compounds. The same applies to the reservoirs. In the case of respiration we differentiate between three compartments:

(1) the reservoir of free oxygen (atmospheric or marine, respectively)

(2) the O_2 content of the single cell

(3) the oxydation products in the cell

Exchange between reservoirs (1) and (2) consists of a sequence of transport processes in condensed phases and depends on the anatomy of the organisms. In any case, the final step will be the diffusion to the enzymes of the respiration chain which are fixed to membranes inside of the cells. All the transport steps are rate-controlled by diffusion, and the result of any net turnover will be a mass fractionation which is given by

$$\alpha_D = D^{34}/D^{32} \tag{3}$$

where D^{32} and D^{34} are the (mean) diffusion coefficients of $^{16}O_2$ and $^{16}O^{18}O$, respectively, in the given matrices.
Between the reservoirs (2) and (3) occur the approximately 30 reaction steps of the respiration chain, but free oxygen only reacts with the cytochrom a/a_3. Enzymes indeed are real catalysts, which can catalyze the forward and reverse reaction as well. The equilibria in the respiration chain, however, are normally quite on the oxydized side, so that the reverse reaction from reservoir (3) into reservoir (2) can be neglected. For the reaction of free oxygen in the cells with the cytochrom a/a_3 an isotope fractionation is to be expected, occurring in the isotope exchange equilibrium between the reaction partners (fractionation factor α_{23}). Following this scheme, there are two groups of reaction steps involved in respirative processes and arranged in a series: the transport processes associated with kinetic mass fractionation of the oxygen molecules, and enzymatically catalyzed reactions in the cells giving an equilibrium isotope effect (see FIG. 2).

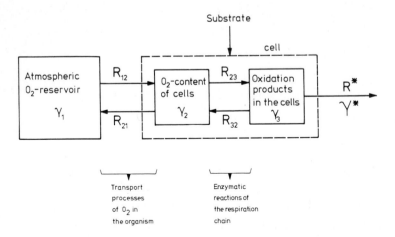

FIG. 2 - Model of the oxygen passage through a respiring organism, for calculating the isotope fractionation. For details see text.

According to this model, the oxygen and the ^{18}O balance, respectively, read as follows:

$$R^* = R_{12} - R_{21} \simeq R_{23} \tag{4}$$

$$R^*\gamma^* = R_{12}\gamma_1\alpha_D - R_{21}\gamma_2\alpha_D \simeq R^*\gamma_2\alpha_{23} \tag{5}$$

Notation: R_{ik} means the oxygen flux running from reservoir i into reservoir k; R^* = respiration rate = net flux of oxygen entering the respiration chain; γ = mole fraction of ^{18}O. The consequence, $R_{32} \ll R_{23}$ as mentioned above, is taken into account in the equations. The maximum oxygen flux, R_{max}, passing through the organism would be reached, if the O_2 concentration in the cells would be zero, and consequently $R_{21} = 0$ which, of course, is physiologically unrealistic. The general dependence of the isotope fractionation as a function of R^* is (due to eq. 5): if $R^* \to R_{max}$, γ^*/γ_1 tends to α_D, for $R^* \to 0$, γ_2 tends to γ_1, and γ^*/γ_1 to α_{23} (see FIG. 3).

Physiologists use the term "respiration intensity", i. e. the oxygen consumption per unit of time and per unit of living biomass. According to the foregoing, the degree of isotope fractionation occurring in respiration processes should depend on the respiration intensity. In higher animals, however, there

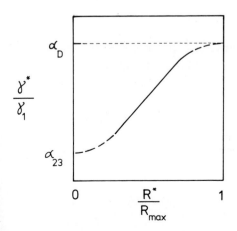

FIG. 3 - Expected isotope fractionation of respiratory processes due to the model given in FIG. 2.
R^* = respiration rate
R_{max} = maximum oxygen flow rate

are always organs of different respiration intensity, so that
these model considerations cannot be applied directly to a
whole organism. Fortunately, phytoplankton, representing the
biggest marine biomass, should be simple enough in its structure
for the discussed respiration model. The few data known from the
literature fit into these model expectations (WAGENER et al.
1969).

The advantage of such a relationship is that it allows an estimate of unknown fractionation factors, which are necessary for
the computation of the global average of the oxygen fractionation factor in respiration. These estimates are possible on the
basis of the abundant data on respiration intensities. The main
contribution to the global respiration is by the soil microorganisms (about 70 % of the land cycle), and respiration and
decay of phytoplankton (about 90 % of the marine cycle).

Using the scarce data presently available on isotope fractionation in respirative processes, and completing them by estimates, the global average of the oxygen fractionation factor
occurring in <u>respiration on land</u> is calculated as:

$$\alpha_{13} = \frac{\gamma_3}{\gamma_1} \approx 0.983$$

which means that the light molecule, $^{16}O_2$, is preferrably consumed by about 1.7 %.

The corresponding fractionation factor in the marine cycle,
α'_{13}, has been derived from vertical profiles of total O_2
dissolved in the sea water and the ^{18}O content in it (cf.
RAYLEIGH fractionation; section 2 of this paper), by following
both variables down to the oxygen minimum. The fractionation
factor is then given by the RAYLEIGH formula

$$\frac{\gamma}{\gamma_o} = (\frac{V_o}{V})^{\alpha'_{13} - 1} \tag{6}$$

where the index $_o$ refers to the initial values (e. g. in the
surface waters), while the second reading (without index) may
be taken at the oxygen minimum. V is the amount of dissolved
oxygen per liter of sea water. The results are shown in
TABLE 1.

TABLE 1

Oxygen isotope fractionation factors, α'_{13}, as derived from the
RAYLEIGH fractionation during the decomposition of marine organic
matter

Authors	Station	Depth of upper and lower point of profile selected for evaluation		α'_{13}	$1 - \alpha'_{13}$
RAKESTRAW, RUDD, DOLE 1951	Pacific Ocean 32° 10' N 120° 19' W (Febr. 1951)	167 m 420	420 m 670	0.998 0.978	0.002 0.022
VINOGRADOW, KUTYURIN, ZADOROZHNYI 1959	South Atlantic ∿ 60° S ∿ 20° E	98	362	0.9875	0.0125
"	Indian Ocean ∿ 45° S ∿ 35° E	100 400	400 939	0.988 0.995	0.012 0.005
KROOPNICK, WEISS, CRAIG 1972	North Atlantic 35° 45' N 68° 00' W (Aug. 1970)	390	950	0.986	0.014

4. Isotope Fractionation in Photosynthesis

A. Marine Environment

The oxygen liberated in photosynthesis originates in the water. This is the result of a number of experiments with ^{18}O labelled water and carbon dioxide (for references see: DONGMANN, FÖRSTEL and WAGENER 1972). The same conclusion has been drawn from the fact that the O_2 production can be obtained in vitro independent of any CO_2 fixation, when using, instead of CO_2, HILL reagents (e. g. chinon) as hydrogen acceptors. The tracer experiments have been criticized with respect to the isotope exchange between H_2O and CO_2 (BROWN & FRENKEL 1953). A critical reconsideration about the commonly accepted concept of a light-induced water oxidation has recently been given by METZNER (1975).

In any case, it is important for our further conclusions that a strict correlation be expected between the isotopic composition of liberated oxygen and the composition of the water in which photosynthesis takes place. This is true, because of the fast isotope exchange between H_2O and CO_2 so that even if the liberated oxygen stems from the carbon dioxide, the isotopic composition of the CO_2 depends strictly on the possibly varying composition of the water.

Several experiments demonstrated that no significant isotopic shift occurs between the composition of the water and the liberated oxygen (VINOGRADOV et al. 1947; KUTYURIN 1969). Small fractionation effects, reported in earlier papers, seem to be due to uncontrolled respiration. Therefore we can conclude that the isotopic composition of oxygen produced in the marine biocycles resembles the composition of sea water. A possible deviation should not exceed the order of 1 ppt.

B. Photosynthesis on Land

Free atmospheric oxygen is (almost) exclusively produced by photosynthesis, mainly on land. The annual turnover on land is approximately $1 \cdot 10^{11}$ t CO_2, in the oceans about $0.5 \cdot 10^{11}$ t (LIETH et al. 1974). The oxygen produced in the marine cycle only partly escapes into the atmosphere, and this in equivalent exchange for atmospheric oxygen, so that no net flux results. This, however, holds true only in those areas with no deposition of unoxidized organic matter, or where organic matter is transported from the continents (brackish water, estuaries).

If free oxygen is contributed to the atmosphere from other sources besides photosynthesis, then other (inorganic) oxidation processes of equal turnover rate must also exist. Otherwise the atmospheric oxygen reservoir would increase very rapidly. The biocycle on land turns the atmospheric oxygen over once in about 10 000 years. The difference between production and consumption rate (in the global average) must be as low as 1/100 of one percent, as result from geochemical material balances (see e. g. WELTE 1970). In the sediments about $(1 - 2) \cdot 10^{16}$ tons of unoxidized organic carbon have accumulated over at least 1 billion years, and the equivalent excess of unrespired oxygen has been consumed in the weathering of igneous rocks or the oxidation of juvenile gases (see HOLLAND 1962). Other processes which produce free oxygen are possible, e. g. photochemically induced water dissociation in the upper regions of the atmosphere and escape of hydrogen into space (see UREY 1959), or sensibilisized water photolysis at the earth's surface. However, in terms of turnover rates, they could have been of importance only in pre-biological times. This is evident, since the biological turnover (at least at the present time) is higher than that of the inorganic oxydation processes by about 4 orders of magnitude, if we calculate the weathering rate by dividing the total oxygen loss of the atmosphere by a period of the order of 1 billion years. Thus, for the matter of isotope fractionation, we only have to account for the photosynthesis of plants as a source of free oxygen.

Photosynthesis on land mainly takes place in transpiring leaves,
and from the foregoing it is clear that the liberated oxygen
will have the same isotopic composition as the water present in
the leaves. The leaf water composition, however, depends on two
items:

(1) the local rain water composition (see section 2);

(2) the $H_2^{18}O$ concentration in transpiring leaves, due to
    the vapor pressure difference between light and heavy
    water ("transpiration effect"; DONGMANN, FÖRSTEL &
    WAGENER 1972).

The degree of $H_2^{18}O$ enrichment after item (2) depends mainly on
the meteorological conditions, but furthermore on the physiolo-
gical properties of the plant. Diurnal variations in the ^{18}O-
content of leaf water of 1 - 2 % in the 24 hour cycle are observed (DONGMANN 1973). This effect can be explained as a pure
transpiration and exchange effect (exchange with atmospheric
water vapor), and can be simulated in model experiments using
filter papers as transpiring leaves. In actual leaves photosynthesis and transpiration are correlated such that in times
of high $H_2^{18}O$ concentration in the leaves the photosynthetic
activity is also high, so that the liberated oxygen is correspondingly rich in ^{18}O. An estimate of the global average of
the ^{18}O excess in oxygen from land photosynthesis gives about
+ 7 ppt relative to SMOW (DONGMANN 1973). For this estimate,
the global distribution pattern of the earth's primary productivity (LIETH et al. 1974) and the ^{18}O distribution in rain
water as well (IAEA 1969) have been taken into account. Since
more than 60 % of the primary productivity on land is concentrated in the tropics, the importance of these regions and the
investigation of their properties under this aspect is evident
(DONGMANN, FÖRSTEL, WAGENER & ZUNDEL 1975).

5. The Steady-State Isotopic Composition of the Reservoirs

As discussed before photosynthesis and respiration are the
only significant processes involved in the oxygen cycle. Therefore, if the isotope fractionation factors of these biochemical processes are known, the steady-state ^{18}O concentration
in the reservoirs can be quantitatively understood.

A steady-state flow sheet of the oxygen cycle includes all the
fluxes between the involved reservoirs and the fractionation
factors between the reservoirs. Thus every complete set of
data can be checked for consistency. Any missing figure (e.g.
any unknown flux or reaction rate) can also be calculated
from the other data. The concept of isotope fractionation in
bio-geochemical matter cycles becomes applicable to pollution
studies at this point. This special procedure of investigating
an environmental system may be applied to a limited region
(e. g., a polluted bay, a stagnant basin etc.), or to the global system as a whole. In the latter case global average values
for the fractionation factors are required. Further discussion
will be restricted here to the global system, because the average data utilized in this system may provide useful guiding
figures for any special system.

As mentioned above (see section 2) the marine reservoir of
free oxygen is very complicated. In order to overcome this
difficulty, the ^{18}O balance is calculated for a surface layer
of the ocean containing 90 % marine biomass. In the open ocean
which contains 75 % of marine primary productivity, this layer
is of the order of 100 m, and will be identical, in general,
with the euphotic zone. This reservoir, defined and limited as
stated, can be considered a well-mixed reservoir with respect
to the O_2 exchange with the atmosphere. This becomes evident
from the fact that the mean life time of an O_2 molecule in
this layer would be about 5 years, if the chance to escape
into the atmosphere is cut off. This figures out for the average, using a mean oxygen concentration of 6 ml O_2/ l of sea-

water and a mean annual productivity of 12.5 ml O_2/cm^2 of ocean-surface. However, the mixing time of this layer is small compared to 5 years, so that this reservoir of free oxygen may be justifiably considered as one box.

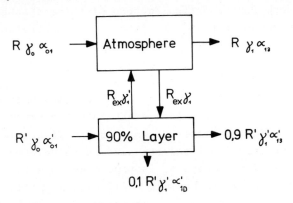

FIG. 4 - Compartment model and flow sheet for the steady-state ^{18}O balance between atmosphere and ocean

Figure 4 shows the flow sheet and compartment model for the ^{18}O balance of the atmosphere and the surface layer of the oceans. For the steady-state follows (see TABLE 2 for notations):

Atmosphere:

$$R(\gamma_0 \alpha_{01} - \gamma_1 \alpha_{13}) + R_{ex}(\gamma_1' - \gamma_1) = 0 \qquad (7)$$

"90 % Layer":

$$R'(\gamma_0 \alpha_{01}' - 0.9 \cdot \gamma_1' \alpha_{13}' - 0.1\gamma_1' \alpha_{1D}') + R_{ex}(\gamma_1 - \gamma_1') = 0 \qquad (8)$$

Comments to the data presented in TABLE 2 and the balance in FIG. 4: the fractionation factor for eddy diffusion, α_{1D}', is 1, since eddy diffusion is not a molecular process. The eddy movement of water masses transports all dissolved species at the same rate. The isotope fractionation in the solubility equilibrium between atmosphere and ocean has been neglected, because it is

TABLE 2

Data used for the ^{18}O balance according to the flow sheet in FIG. 4
(IFF = isotope fractionation factor)

Cycle	Quantity	Symbol	Value	Source
Land cycle	turnover rate	R	$1.16 \cdot 10^{11}$ t O_2/year	LITH et al. 1974
Land cycle	IFF (respir.)	α_{13}	~ 0.983	see section 3 of this paper
Land cycle	IFF (photosynth.)	α_{01}	1.007	see section 4B of this paper
Atmospheric Oxygen	^{18}O content (relative to SMOW)	γ_1/γ_0	1.0235	KROOPNICK & CRAIG 1972
Marine cycle	turnover rate	R'	$0.64 \cdot 10^{11}$ t O_2/year	LITH et al. 1974
Marine cycle	IFF (respir.)	α'_{13}	~ 0.986	see section 3 of this paper
Marine cycle	IFF (photosynth.)	α'_{01}	~ 1.000	see section 4A of this paper
Marine cycle	IFF (eddy diff.)	α'_{1D}	1.000	see section 5 of this paper

smaller than 1 ppt (KROOPNICK & CRAIG 1972). Concerning the
oxygen balance of the "90 % surface layer", we have to keep
in mind that, by definition, 10 % of the total amount of oxygen
produced is not consumed there, but transported into the depth
(together with the equivalent organic matter).

Since all data used in eqs. (7) and (8) have been determined
independently, it is possible to check them for consistency
and, at the same time, to check the compartment model used.
This, however, is not very reasonable at the present time,
since some data are fairly poor. If we calculate the two lacking
figures (that is, the average isotopic composition of dissolved
oxygen in that surface layer (γ_1'), and the oxygen exchange rate
between atmosphere and ocean (R_{ex}), respectively, from the two
independent equations (7) and (8) then these results will be
very unreliable. It is not even known, whether oxygen released
by the oceans into the atmosphere (in exchange for atmospheric
oxygen) is isotopically heavier or lighter than atmospheric
oxygen. The present data are not compatible, indicating either
an error in one figure, or (more probably) our incomplete understanding of the marine oxygen cycle. This may be demonstrated by
the following disagreement.

From eq. (8) follows:

$$\frac{R_{ex}}{R'} \simeq \frac{\gamma_1' \cdot \alpha_{13}' - \gamma_0}{\gamma_1' - \gamma_1} \tag{9}$$

For the two limiting cases ($R_{ex} = 0$ and $R_{ex} \rightarrow \infty$) we obtain from
eq. (9) for the isotopic composition of dissolved oxygen in the
surface layer:

R_{ex}	γ_1'	δ
0	γ_0/α_{13}'	~ 14
∞	γ_1	$23,5$

In the real system, R_{ex} will have any value between 0 and ∞, so that the δ value of dissolved oxygen in the said surface layer should be in the range of

$$14 < \delta \text{ (dissolved oxygen)} < 23,5 \qquad (10)$$

As a matter of fact, however, all the measured δ values of oxygen from the upper 100 meters of ocean water are higher than 23,5 ppt. A conclusive explanation for these unexpected circumstances is not available, but some possible suppositions may be summarized here:

(1) Some oxydation processes may have continued after the water samples were taken, so that the RAYLEIGH fractionation proceeded, too. This has to be checked in very careful new experiments.

(2) The fractionation factor for respirative processes, α'_{13}, derived from profiles below the euphotic zone (see TABLE 1), may be smaller than that which is effective under light conditions (photorespiration).

(3) The measured data mainly refer to areas of higher productivity than the global average, so that the mean life time of an O_2 molecule is considerably smaller than estimated for the average. Under these circumstances, the assumption of a well-mixed reservoir (surface layer) may become questionable.

Thus, it seems worthwhile to reconsider thoroughly some details of the oxygen cycle, mainly for the upper layers of the ocean. The demonstrated disagreement in the isotope budget is certainly more than only a sophisticated peculiarity in a special field, distant from everyday oceanography. The smallness of the effects has nothing to do with the importance of their evidence.

References

(1) Brown & Frenkel 1953
    Ann. Review of Plant Physiol. $\underline{4}$, 23

(2) Craig, H. and Keeling, C. D. 1963
    Geochim. Cosmochim. Acta $\underline{27}$, 549

(3) Dole, M., Lane, G. A., Rudd, D. P. and Zaukelies, D. A. 1954
    Geochim. Cosmochim. Acta $\underline{6}$, 65

(4) Dongmann, G., Förstel, H. and Wagener, K. 1972
    Nature New Biology $\underline{240}$, 127

(5) Dongmann, G. 1973
    Dissertation, RWTH Aachen

(6) Dongmann, G., Förstel, H., Wagener, K. and Zundel, G. 1975
    Acad. Brasileira Sci., in press

(7) Garlick, G. D. 1969
    In: K. H. Wedepohl (ed.): Handbook of Geochemistry,
    Springer-Verlag, Berlin, Bd. II-1, 8-B.

(8) Holland, H. D. 1962
    Geol. Soc. Amer. Buddington, 447

(9) IAEA (Wien) 1969
    Technical Reports Series, Wien $\underline{96}$, No. 1

(10) Kroopnik, Weiss, Craig. 1972.
     Earth and Planetary Science Letters $\underline{16}$, 103-110

(11) Kutyurin, V. W. 1969
     Israel Sci. Transl. Problems of Geochemistry, 661

(12) Lieth, H. and Whittaker, R. W. (eds.) 1974
     The Primary Productivity of the Biosphere
     Springer-Verlag, Berlin, in press

(13) Metzner, H. 1975
     J. Theoret. Biol., in press

(14) Rakestraw, N. M., Rudd, D. P. and Dole, M. 1951
     J. Amer. Soc. $\underline{73}$, 2976

(15) Urey, H. C. 1959
     In: S. Flügge (ed.) Handbuch d. Physik
     Springer-Verlag, Berlin, Bd. 52, 363

(16) Vinogradov, A. P., Kutyurin, V. M., Zadorozhnyi, I. K. 1959
     Geokhimiya $\underline{3}$, 195

(17) Vinogradov, A. P. and Teis, R. V. 1947
     Doklady Acad. Sci. URSS 56, 59

(18) Wagener, K., Förstel, H. and Freyer, H. D. 1969
     CACR-Symp. Heidelberg

(19) Wagener, K. 1973
     Rheinisch-Westf. Akad. Wiss, Vorträge N 233
     Westd. Verlag, Opladen

(20) Welte, D. H. 1970
     Naturwiss. 57, 17

The Colloidal State and Surface Phenomena – Group Report

P. S. Liss, Rapporteur
K. Bertine   G. H. Morrison
A. Clearfield   G. H. Nancollas
J. Kratohvil   R. H. Ottewill
J. Lyklema   R. Parsons
F. MacIntyre   V. Pravdić
R. A. Marcus   H. S. Sherry
J. M. Martin

INTRODUCTION

Seawater contains particles, both inorganic and biologically produced, ranging in size from colloidal to those which will settle
under gravity. The concentration of particulate matter in any
part of the oceans depends on the proximity and magnitude of inputs of solid material. Such sources can be both external (atmosphere, land masses, marine sediments) and internal, which includes particles formed biologically as well as those produced
by bubbling, precipitation, etc. Solid-liquid interfaces provided by the particles are sites for a wide variety of chemical
and biological interactions. Similarly, wind-induced bubbling
near the sea surface gives gas-liquid interfaces which are also
highly reactive. In the absence of interfaces of both sorts,
the types and rates of processes occurring in the marine environment would be very substantially reduced. Of paramount importance to surface chemistry are synergistic effects (a) between
compounds (surface chemical interactions between lipids and proteins); (b) between disciplines (organic coatings on inorganic
particles); and (c) between kingdoms (biota grazing at surfaces).
Such interactions add greatly to the interest (and difficulty)
of marine surface chemistry.

ELECTRON TRANSFER REACTIONS

Electron transfer in aqueous media occurs either homogeneously
or at surfaces. To the marine chemist the surface can be either
a natural solid particle or the "dirty piece of platinum" (Sillén)
sometimes used to measure the oxidation potential of seawater.
Whether the electron exchange is homogeneous or heterogeneous
makes little basic difference in the statistical theory of these
reactions developed by Marcus (this volume), because the surface
may be regarded simply as an additional reagent in the reaction
mixture. There is good agreement between the Marcus model and
results of laboratory experiments on "pure" solutions, except in
the case of Co(III), for which considerable discrepancies occur.

Although the theory is statistical, this should not produce problems in applying it to seawater, where the concentration of many
transition metal ions is of order 10^{-9} M. Even at these low
concentrations, there will be about 10^{14} species per liter, and
since statistical fluctuations are proportional to $N^{-1/2}$ (where
N is the species concentration), such perturbations will be negligible. In the case of a biological system, a single event may
produce a whole chain of reactions, each of which would have to
be treated separately. Rates of electron transfer reactions for
low reactant concentrations are generally not subject to diffusion control, unless the reaction itself is very rapid. For
example, if hydrated electrons can be formed in surface seawater
(see "Photosynthesis" section), then, because they exhibit
extremely fast kinetics, there would probably be diffusion control of the reaction rate. Application of the model to seawater
is complicated somewhat by the large number of competing reactions, but even greater problems are likely to arise because of
the current lack of knowledge concerning the speciation of many
elements in seawater.

TECHNIQUES FOR COUNTING PARTICLES IN SUSPENSIONS AND SCATTERING
PROPERTIES OF SEAWATER

Light-scattering is a technique widely used in oceanography for
the study of particles in suspension (Jerlov, 1968). In seawater,
a light beam will experience scattering from three components:
the water, the dissolved electrolytes, and the particles in suspension. The first two are well understood, but because the particles have widely differing shapes, sizes, refractive indices,
and internal structures, their light-scattering properties are
extremely complex. The applicability of the Mie theory for spherical isotropic particles (Kerker, 1969) to the assemblage of particles found in seawater is of unknown reliability at present. In
spite of this, oceanographers (as well as other scientists) regu-
larly use scattering techniques to look at suspended particles.

Another technique widely used for studying marine solid phases
is the Coulter counter (Strickland and Parsons, 1972) which measures the change in solution conductance produced by the presence
of particles. This instrument suffers from the deficiency that
only a part of the spectrum of particle sizes can be examined at
any one time, and what is really measured is not the particles
themselves, but a complicated function of the relative conduc-
tivities of the particles and the solution.

The most promising novel experimental technique for particle size
analysis, counting of particles, and studies of colloidal stability of particulates is to use single particle scattering counters
(Kratohvil, personal communication). These devices, which use
laser sources, are already applied to various hydrosols and aerosols. Further research should be conducted on model particles,
spherical and nonspherical, of sizes as found in seawater (up to
100 μm) in order to establish the calibration procedure.

Another novel technique worth exploring is the effect of an electric field on light-scattering by suspended particles (Jennings,
1972). In the case of clay suspensions, the quantities derived
from such measurements (dipole moment, rotatory diffusion

coefficients, particle mass, radius of gyration) can help in de-
ducing the possible mode or modes of aggregation of clay particles (Schweitzer and Jennings, 1971).

The exchange of ions on clay particles is known to change their
stability and hence scattering properties, a topic worth pursuing further with seawater clays (Kratohvil, personal communication).

Except for the soluble macromolecular substances, the application
of laser scattering spectroscopy (Chu, 1975) to seawater particulates will probably be limited to the determination of their
electrophoretic mobility from the shift of the broadened Rayleigh
line caused by the applied electric field (Ware, 1974; Uzgiris
and Costaschuk, 1973).

Aggregation-disaggregation of particles at high pressures can
also be followed by light-scattering, and instrumentation for
working at pressures up to 1500 atm has been described (Schulz
and Lechnor, 1970).

In respect to studies of light penetration in the sea, less re-
liance on the theoretical computed Mie scattering functions is
recommended. What is needed are absolute measurements of scattering radiance, as well as polarization and turbidity, in the
single and multiple scattering regimes (Querfeld et al., 1972)
on model suspensions consisting of particles of well-defined geometrical shapes.

ELECTRICAL PROPERTIES OF PARTICLES

A hydrophobic particle immersed in an aqueous solution will generally carry an excess surface charge. This can be acquired by
dissociation of surface groups, uptake of ions such as H^+ or OH^-
from the water or may be a property of the solid structure, e.g.,
isomorphous substitution in clays leading to an excess negative
charge or unsatisfied valencies at the edges of crystal matrices.
Whatever its cause, such surface charge will produce polarization

of the water and electrolyte ions close to the particle. Immediately adjacent to the charged surface there will be a thin
layer of ions of charge opposite to that of the particle, and
further out a more diffuse region of counter ions. Together
these constitute the electrical double layer. The magnitude of
the voltage drop across the outer part of the layer (the ζ potential) is important in determining particle stability. In weak
or dilute electrolytes the number of counter ions in the inner
part of the double layer will be small, leading to a relatively
large ζ potential. If there are nearby particles having similarly large ζ potentials, electrostatic repulsion between them
will inhibit aggregation. In seawater, one would predict that
due to the high electrolyte concentration, most of the excess
charge on particles will be neutralized in the inner part of the
double layer. This will lead to small values for the ζ potential and consequent destabilization by compression of the double
layer and coagulation of unprotected colloidal particles. The
coagulation process should be particularly dramatic in estuaries
where the charged particles experience rapid changes in electrolyte concentration.

Through the above approach it is possible to understand why some
ions are adsorbed by particles more strongly than other ions,
and to explain trends in adsorption within groups of elements
in the periodic table. Such properties can also be thought of
in terms of particular reactions, such as ion exchange and coordinate bonding, in which ions are held at specific sites rather
than by more general electrostatic forces. For instance, using
a coordinate model for the uptake of trace metals by silica particles, it has been possible to account for the observed residence times of these metals in the oceans (Schindler, 1974).
There is no real conflict between the double layer and specific
interaction approaches. The former is more useful in describing
ion adsorption and the latter in explaining ion exchange reactions. Neither theory seems able to explain the changes in composition of marine sediment pore waters found when the water is
squeezed from the sediment at different temperatures. Perhaps

particle-particle interactions (see next section) are important
in explaining such effects.

Application of double layer theory to solids in the real ocean
is made complex because particles in the marine environment are
coated with organic material which will provide steric stabilization and thus greatly alter their electrical properties. For
example, it has been shown that estuarine particles, examined by
the streaming current method, have surprisingly large ζ potentials, and the sign of the charge can reverse with increase in
water salinity (Pravdic, 1970). Organic coatings obviously modify very considerably the predictions of double layer theory and
enable particles to remain discrete in spite of the high salt
content of the water.

The chemical composition of organic coatings on particles in the
ocean is largely unknown, but such coatings are probably reworked
by marine bacteria and other microorganisms. Within the sediments, polychaete worms will also be of great importance both
in coating particles with organic material and in mixing bottom
deposits. Organic layers are difficult to remove by mild chemical treatment (dilute HCl), implying that once coated, a particle
is likely to remain so, except possibly in the sediments where
there is some evidence for degradative breakdown.

CHARACTERIZATION OF SEDIMENTS

The interaction between sediment and solution is important in
determining the composition of seawater. Particle-particle interactions are important in understanding the nature of pore
solutions, mass transport through the sediments, and pore-water
content. The pore structure will also depend on the kind of particle (e.g., silica, kaolinite, montmorillonite), their shape
and size distribution, as well as pressure and the chemical composition of the pore water. For example, at atmospheric pressures montmorillonite particles form a gel, but at higher pressures, ca. 10 atm, the clay platelets become aligned in parallel
arrays. On the other hand, at atmospheric pressures kaolinite

particles can form "card-house" structures because the edges
and faces of the clay platelets are of opposite electrical
charge. The application of high pressures, e.g., about 60 atm,
can crush the "card-houses" and cause the platelets to take on
some degree of alignment.

Little appears to be known about the arrangement of clay particles coated with marine organic matter, and this may be a controlling feature in understanding particle interaction in marine
sediments. Therefore, it is important to study how natural
samples of coated clay particles pack under pressure and to measure pore volumes, surface areas and pressure-volume responses
(packing structure), and electrokinetic properties. Of the various methods available, surface area measurements may be most immediately accessible.

Methods of measuring the surface areas of solid particulate material can be broadly divided into two categories:
(1) examination of the material in the dry state;
(2) examination in the "wet" state, e.g., as far as possible
     that of the natural environment of the particles.

An approach commonly used for dried material is the BET method
in which the adsorption of N_2 or Kr is determined at liquid nitrogen temperatures. In the case of dried sea sediments, this
would include salt crystals formed in the drying process. A further problem is that in the case of clay minerals, only the external surface is detected by N_2 molecules. The adsorption of
water vapor, however, can be used to determine the internal surface of clays. For the "wet" state, the adsorption of dye ions,
surface active ions, and some nonionic molecules can be used.
These methods, however, need to be carefully checked on standard
samples, and the influence of organic matter present on the particles in marine sediments will have to be taken into account.
In some samples, e.g., sands, manganese nodules, the porosity of
the particles will also need to be investigated.

Newly developed flow microcalorimetric methods (Templer, 1972)
offer both the sensitivity and the capability of studying marine
sediments without pretreatment, with respect to determining the
specific surface area and energetics of adsorption of a variety
of naturally occurring and man-made organic compounds.

NATURE AND STRUCTURE OF SOLID PHASES

Zeolites are aluminosilicate minerals having a framework structure whose ion exchange properties are due to the presence of
aluminum. These properties are well characterized and can be understood in terms of crystal structure. Zeolites vary greatly in
internal porosity and in Si/Al atom ratio (from 1/1 to 5/1). Ion
exchange selectivity is a function of both the porosity of the
structure (and therefore water content) and Si/Al atom ratio.
There are only two zeolites or groups of zeolites reported to
be present in marine sediments, namely phillipsite and clinoptilolite. Phillipsite in marine sediments is derived from alteration of basic glass, while clinoptilolite is an alteration product of silicic volcanic ash. Based on general selectivity rules,
phillipsite with Si/Al ratio of about 1.5/1 should prefer alkaline earth to alkali metal cations and potassium over sodium,
and clinoptilolite with a Si/Al atom ratio of 5/1 should prefer
sodium to calcium ions and potassium over sodium. Literature
data indicate that this statement is correct. Most trivalent
cations do not diffuse into the naturally occurring zeolites at
any measurable rate at ambient temperatures because of the necessity of stripping the hydration envelopes from these cations,
and because of the strong interactions that occur with framework oxygen atoms within the zeolite structure. In the case of
hydrolyzed trivalent ions (e.g., polymeric hydrolyzed oxides),
exchange is further inhibited by physical blocking due to their
large size. The rate of ion exchange reactions is either solid
phase or liquid phase diffusion controlled. Which of these two
resistances to mass transfer is rate controlling in the poorly
stirred marine sediments depends on both particle size and the
value of the ionic diffusion coefficient. For those zeolites
with extremely dense structures and very small diffusion

coefficients, diffusion in the solid phase may be rate controlling. In open zeolite structures, liquid film diffusion may become the slow step. Alkali metal and alkaline earth cation exchange in phillipsite and clinoptilolite should fall into the latter category.

The ion exchange properties of clays can be understood and interpreted using the same general principles elucidated for zeolites. There are, however, problems which are specific to clays; for example, their anion exchange properties and kinetic problems arising from close packing of layers in some structures.

Other groups of minerals (and synthetic materials) possessing ion exchange properties are hydrous oxides and phosphates of polyvalent metals. In the case of hydrous oxides, the exchange capacity stems from nonbridging hydroxyl groups on the surface. Both anions and cations are exchanged, and this exchange is pH dependent. The initial exchange reactions are sometimes followed by a second reaction which fixes the ions on the surface. Examples of fixation include phase formation, such as $CaSiO_3$ which may accompany exchange of Ca^{++} on active silica surfaces, and olation and/or oxolation of basic metallic species to the surface. The formation and subsequent surface reactions of hydrous oxides in seawater needs further study. Coprecipitation phenomena accompanying hydrous oxide formation and their effects upon surface properties are still poorly understood. Also, almost nothing is known about the effect of organic coatings on ion exchange reactions.

For phosphates, exchange takes place by an initial surface reaction involving phosphate-OH groups. With some phosphates, such as those of Zr(IV) and Ti(IV), this initial reaction is followed by diffusion into the interior of the structure. In others, i.e., Fe(III) and Al(III), diffusion is not extensive and ion exchange may be considered to be a surface reaction.

In anoxic sediments, insoluble sulfides form and these can exchange or adsorb with dissolved species in the pore water.

Zirconium phosphate may find uses as a separation tool in marine
analytical chemistry due to its ability to take up ions such as
NH_4^+, Ca^{++}, Mg^{++} from solutions rich in sodium chloride. Furthermore, because they exhibit very high selectivities, inorganic
exchangers may be applicable to problems of concentration, separation, and identification of seawater metal species.

THE FORMULATION OF MIXED SOLID PHASES IN THE OCEAN - THE MANGANESE NODULE PROBLEM

The formation of deep sea nodules consisting of layers of manganese oxides and ferric hyroxide colloids appears to be a common phenomenon. Whether this is a true epitaxial growth of one
phase upon another, or heterogeneous nucleation, is not yet
known, and there is a need for model studies of the growth of
synthetic manganese nodules in the laboratory. Various nucle-
ating substrates should be investigated in order to first determine the most efficient heterogeneous nucleation sites for the
growth of $Fe(OH)_3$ and subsequent manganese oxides under simulated
seawater conditions. The determination of the critical supersat-
urations of manganese oxides and $Fe(OH)_3$ in the presence of trace
concentrations of the other components will be particularly important.

It is now possible to study the kinetics of formation of synthetic nodules in the laboratory in order to assess the influence of
trace metal ions on the rate of the process. The conditions under which $Fe(OH)_3$ or manganese oxides will grow on the other substrate will be determined by the results of such studies. Inhibition or initiation of the growth of one phase by traces of
metal ions, organic impurities, and organisms, coupled with minute changes of pH, may account for the rather well-defined
change in the nature of the growing phase (e.g., layered manganese oxide-$Fe(OH)_3$). Available information on the growth of crystals from supersaturated solution shows clearly that it is not
necessary to completely cover the growing surface in order to
modify the rate of the process. The number of active growth

sites may be relatively small. Redox reactions involving Fe(II) and (III) and Mn(II) and (IV) can also be investigated by this method.

A biological model of the interaction of metal hydroxide polymers and organic molecules is ferritin. This substance consists of Fe(III) hydroxide phosphate micelles coated with protein (Harrison and Hoy, 1973). The model is undoubtedly very different from a marine system, but it may furnish some clues to marine chemists.

Natural manganese nodules should be studied by selective dissolution of the surface phase. Not only would kinetics of the process be important (here we should mention that there is considerable electrochemical literature dealing with the dissolution of MnO_2 electrodes, e.g., Kordesch, 1974; Heise and Cahoon, 1971; Malati, 1971) but also the structure and composition of the surface phases. Microscopic studies (SEM, electron microprobes, ion microprobe, etc.) should be made as a function of depth in order to identify the layered structure of the nodules and the presence of trace metal ions. Potentiometric titrations (which will be described later) of the nodules in artificial seawater will yield information on the nature of the surface phases. These potentiometric titrations could be made with metal ions as well as the hydrogen ions.

PARTICLES IN ESTUARIES AND DELTAS

An estuary is the meeting place for waters of very different chemical composition and properties. It is here that seawater of ionic strength approximately 0.7 M mixes with river water of considerably lower salt content and often lower pH. The fresh water, however, may be more concentrated with respect to the plant nutrient elements P, N and Si derived from land drainage, and many of the transition metals. During the mixing process the water will be in contact with solid phases, including sediment on the estuary bed and particles in suspension. These latter are derived from the inflowing river and sea waters, as well

as by resuspension of bottom material under the action of tidal
currents.

Due to the large change in physico-chemical environment experienced by estuarine particles, a wide variety of mineral-water reactions are possible. For example, ion exchange occurs when
riverborne solids encounter saline water in the estuary. Where
the inflowing river water is acidic, elements which form insoluble hydrous oxides at the pH of seawater are removed from the
water. There is field evidence for the importance of such a process for iron, and laboratory results indicate that the removal
is more likely to be by heterogeneous nucleation onto pre-
existing solid particles, rather than by homogeneous floccula-
tion (Aston and Chester, 1973). The formation of such hydrous
oxide phases could lead to the scavenging of other species from
solution, but there is little field evidence for this at the present time. In highly polluted estuaries, the enhanced levels
of dissolved organic molecules may lead to release of some transition metals from particles via formation of soluble organo-
metallic complexes. As well as these chemical interactions, particles also show considerable changes in   potential with water
salinity, as discussed previously.

The above discussion gives some idea of the large variety of
solid-water reactions which are possible in estuaries. From our
present knowledge it is difficult to know the relative importance
of the various interactions and whether they occur in all estuaries. In such circumstances the development of new chemical
techniques does not seem warranted at the present. It may be
possible to get some leads from other environmental areas such
as soil science, but the way ahead is probably to use existing
techniques for field studies and laboratory experiments of various degrees of complexity, aimed at simulating estuarine chemical processes.

THE AIR-SEA INTERFACE

Introduction

Defining the thickness of water constituting the surface layer
of the oceans is a problem on a par with deciding the hydration
number of an ion in solution or the size of a particle suspended
in an aqueous medium. The thickness of the sea surface microlayer can be derived in a number of ways: (a) by harvesting a
sample of water from the interface (methods for doing this are
discussed below); (b) by measuring the level at which some physical property of the water near the interface begins to diverge
from its value in the bulk water; and (c) from conceptual models
of the interface, e.g., assume it is covered by a monolayer or
interpret the kinetics of air-sea gas exchange in terms of a
laminar film model. It is hardly surprising that these various
approaches yield layer thicknesses spanning six orders of magnitude.

Most currently available field data have been obtained using surface samples which collect a slice of water approximately 200 μm
thick. The results show that relative to subsurface water, the
interfacial material is enriched in dissolved and particulate
organics, trace metals bound to dissolved organic and particulate
phases, bacteria and other microorganisms, DDT and PCBs. With
such enrichments the interfacial layer has obvious importance
in the transfer of matter and energy across the air-sea interface.

Sampling Techniques

The available microlayer samplers are categorized in Table 1.
While all of these samplers except the Baier slide may transport
surfactants from underlying water to the surface, this problem
is most serious for the bubbling techniques.

Three identifiable needs with respect to sampling are:

- better definition of the "surface" collected;
- comparison experiments to determine collection efficiencies
  for various classes of surfactant;
- methods for collecting larger quantities of the surfactant
  organic material.

TABLE 1 - Examples of microlayer samplers

Sampler	Thickness sampled	Comments

Screen
  Garret (1965)
  Sieburth (1965)
	$\sim$200 μm	Quantitative for lipids, probably not for proteins. Good for neuston.

Skimmer Harvey (1966)	$\sim$200 μm	Probably as for screen

Bubble-microtome
  MacIntyre (1968)
	$\sim$0.001 bubble
	     diameter
		Collects inner surface of bubble rather than air/sea interface

Germanium slide Baier (1970)	molecular	Allows direct IR analysis of collected material
Foam fractionation Lemlich (1972)	$\sim$2 μm	Prefers most surface-active materials

The use of polytetrafluoroethylene materials (Fluon and Teflon)
should be carefully examined since these are not necessarily
chemically inert. These materials are frequently prepared, prior
to fabrication, by emulsion polymerization and hence the surfaces
can contain chemical groups, e.g., carboxyl, which could bind
metal ions. Bulk polymerized materials, e.g., FEP, are preferable, but again these should be checked for surface groupings.

Foam fractionation is a useful method of rapidly stripping milli-
gram quantities of surfactant from the upper layers. Well known
to surface chemists both as a preparative technique and as a way
of removing surfactant contaminants from water, it has received
little attention from oceanographers and appears to be a most
promising technique. It consists of blowing air or nitrogen

through the system in order to create a foam, i.e. a large interfacial area with a small volume. Removal of the foam from
the surface of the bulk phase thus yields a high concentration
of the most surface-active materials.

Trace Metals

The affinity of certain surfactants for trace metals ensures a
high concentration of these biologically active materials at the
molecular surface of the sea. Metals reach the sea surface either
by atmospheric fallout of terrigenous or anthropogenous material,
or by attachment to rising bubbles and spend appreciable time
at the interface. Since the surface layer represents a high-
energy food source utilized by a special biota, this material is
directly available to the food chain in concentrated form. Since
bubbles selectively eject near surface water, this material is
also available for concentrated re-injection into the atmosphere.

The interfacial chemistry of these metals is largely unknown,
and two identifiable problems with environmental repercussions
are:
(a) the nature of "binding" of trace metals to the interface -
     whether inorganic particulate, biogenic particulate, or
     chemical binding to identifiable organic ligands of sur-
     factant material;
(b) the processes which regulate trace metals in the micro-
     layer. The sources, sinks, and transfer rates are still
     mostly conjectural.

Photochemistry

The surface microlayer is the only region of the ocean in which
ultraviolet photochemistry may be important, and studies exist
for both iodine and hydrocarbons. However, such fundamental information as the wavelength-vs-depth spectrum of actinic light
within the microlayer seems to be unavailable. The possibility
exists of generating, however briefly, a photochemically induced hydrated electron within the microlayer, and thence direct
reduction of an available electron acceptor. It is of some interest to put better limits on microlayer photochemistry.

Physico-Chemical Hydrodynamics

The physico-chemical hydrodynamics of the microlayer dominates
the transfer of particles from sea to air, and affects the transport kinetics of water, gases, heat, and momentum.
Identifiable problems in this area include:

(a)   The chemical nature of organic material in the microlayer.
      Despite considerable work, our understanding is best des-
      cribed as rudimentary, and agreement between methods (of
      collection and analysis) leaves much to be desired.

(b)   Glycoproteins (proteins with sugar sidechains, of which a
      bacterial cell membrane is a typical single-molecule ex-
      ample) may be the most important member of the interfacial
      chemical family. It is important to verify the identifi-
      cation of these compounds and to develop (or import) methods
      for studying them.

(c)   The rheological nature of the microlayer - its viscosity,
      surface tension, elasticity, etc. - is particularly impor-
      tant with respect to interfacial transport, but is largely
      unknown. Part of the problem may be that existing infor-
      mation on the surface chemistry of proteins is underutilized
      by oceanographers. Specific data on the rheology of micro-
      layer constituents is nonexistent, but can be obtained us-
      ing the traditional tools of the surface chemist: static
      and dynamic measurements of surface tension, potential,
      and viscosity.

(d)   Bubble-bursting is demonstrably the most important sea-to-
      air transfer mechanism for both particles and electric
      charge. The dynamics of the process remain elusive, and
      we do not know, for instance, the changes in transfer re-
      sulting from changes in surface tension or viscosity.
      There is evidence that the gas composition of the bubble
      can influence transfer, but no theory to suggest reasons
      for such influence

NOVEL TECHNIQUES FOR USE IN STUDIES OF MARINE INTERFACES

Separation of Particulate and Dissolved Fractions

The most popular method of separation currently in use, namely
that of using a filter membrane having a pore diameter of approximately 0.5 μm, is open to question:

(a)   on the basis that the separation between various particle
      sizes is arbitrary and that colloidal material and macro-
      molecular material will pass through the filter;

(b)   that microorganisms can be damaged by the filtration process and so alter the composition of the aqueous phase.

For collection and partial fractionation of the suspended material prior to examination, the use of centrifugation could prove
valuable in giving fractions as a function of the size and density of the particles. Modifications of the centrifuge technique
are possible in that separations can be achieved by variation
of the centrifugal field. In addition, a continuous flow centrifuge can be used for the treatment of large volumes of material.
This technique has already proved useful in collecting particulate material from seawater (Chester et al., 1974).

For more detailed examination of the colloidal fractions, both
lyophobic (particulate) and lyophilic (macromolecular) dialysis
could be used to remove the seawater electrolytes. While accepting that this could cause long term changes in the system
removal of salts would be necessary for the most advantageous application of some techniques, e.g., electrophoresis. Short term
dialysis, e.g., against 10^{-3} M saline, could be achieved by about
three changes of dialysate of two hours each with the colloidal
fractions contained in the dialysis bag.

Microelectrophoretic Examination

It appears probable that much of the material in the dialysis
bag will be of an organic nature, and this can be used as a
starting point for qualitative investigations of its nature. One
possible approach is to adsorb the material on to carrier particles of known size and surface properties which can then be examined by microelectrophoresis. The reversal of electrophoretic charge by various inorganic ions falls into well-defined patterns depending on the nature of the chemical groups on the surface - the so-called reversal of charge spectra (Kruyt, 1952).
Establishment of the ion-binding sequence for cations with the
organic matter from seawater would give useful clues as to the
nature of its composition.

Potentiometric and Thermometric Titrimetry

Potentiometric titration is a relatively simple technique that
can probably be carried out on board ship. For well-defined
model systems it has been used as a tool to obtain information on
the number of charged groups on the surface, sometimes also on
their nature and ion-binding. Although the situation in seawater
is obviously far more complex, it seems that the expertise available with model systems can be helpful as a tool of characterization in addition to the existing ones.

Titrations can be performed with any dispersed matter, whether
colloidal or suspended. The material may be marine sediments
(crushed or original), particulate matter, manganese nodules,
material taken from the sea surface, both organic and inorganic
materials, or mixtures of them. Fractionation and/or concentration as a first stage is required to obtain a large enough adsorbing area. How much is actually needed depends on the surface area
of the material, or, for that matter, on the amount of available
titratable groups. Perhaps it is of the order of a few hundred
milligrams.

The classical titration is a pH-titration which can be carried out
in situ. It gives the number of groups that at a given pH are
protonated. In the most ideal systems (isolated polyelectrolytes
or proteins) it is sometimes, but not always, possible to distinguish between different groups (carboxyl, ε-amino, etc.). However, in the case of seawater, we might expect to obtain a composite overall curve which would be relatively uninformative. Hence
it seems more appropriate to apply the titration technique in conjunction with dialysis and fractionation so that information can
be obtained on the influence of salts (nature and concentration)
on the various components of the mixture to be investigated. For
this reason, dialysis down to about 10^{-3} M should precede the titration.

Once the material is available in 10^{-3} M electrolyte, preferably
in fractionated form, it can be titrated with H^+ or OH^- ions

(preferably in two directions to analyze the extent of pH reversibility) as a function of the concentration of deliberately added
electrolytes. Electrolytes "screen" any charge on the material
to be titrated, thereby reducing the mutual electrostatic repulsion between adjoining charged groups. Consequently, more groups
become dissociated at given pH and upon titration. This is measured in that more acid or base (depending on the direction of titration) is needed over a particular pH range. It is here that
ion specificity enters; the stronger a given cation binds to a
given negative group, the higher the titratable negative charge.
By the same token, the stronger an anion binds, the higher the
positive charge. By carrying out titrations with different electrolytes (NaCl, LiCl, $CaCl_2$, $MgCl_2$, $MgSO_4$, Na_2SO_4, etc.) it should
be possible to obtain at least a semiquantitative insight into
the relative ion-binding on the various fractions.

Inference of ion binding can also be obtained from the shift of
the point of zero charge, assuming that there is one. The stronger a cation binds, the more it shifts to a lower pH (and con-
versely for anions). This shift is just opposite to that of the
isoelectric point, measured by electrophoresis. In view of this,
it seems feasible to carry out titrations at fixed electrolyte
concentration. Ion-selective electrodes may be useful in this
respect. Information is now available in the literature on various oxidic materials, polyelectrolytes and proteins, so that comparison of the curves obtained against these well-characterized
molecules is possible.

The technique of thermometric titration as applied to seawater
has been described by Millero et al.(1974). It has been used on
suspended natural clay minerals and humic material to distinguish
groups that protonate as well as some of the major functional
groups. Application of this technique is made possible because
of the large differences in the heats of protonation of phenolic
and carboxylic groups.

By combining various separation techniques, thermometric titration may prove to be very useful in studying colloidal material

suspended in seawater, as well as other particulate material.

Approaches to Metal-Organic Binding

The organic-like metal ion binding material in the sea undoubtedly consists of a variety of species, and it would be useful to
have some overall characterization. Direct chemical analysis,
for example, will yield information about the amounts of heavy
metal ions (e.g., Fe, Ni, etc.), but not the nature of their coordination. There are also unbound ligands attached to the organic residues offering potential binding atoms of differing degrees
of polarizability or "hardness". It is well known in coordination chemistry that "hard" and "soft" metal ions preferentially
bind ligand atoms of similar polarizability. To determine the
approximate character of the potential binding sites in the organic residues, potentiometric titration with metal ions can be
utilized. Thus, the "hard" alkaline earth cations will be expected to be taken up by ligand molecules offering oxygen-
coordination sites while the more polarizable transition metal
ions will be bound by -N and other "soft" ligand atoms. In this
manner, it will be possible to compare the nature of the binding
sites in different organic fractions.

Characterizing the material with respect to already bound cations
and with respect to unbound ligands serves the useful purpose of
determining potentially exchanging or reactive sites for heavy
metal ions. Study of the number of and redox potentials of the
bound heavy metal cations (Fe, Co, etc.) should serve to help understand the overall redox processes. Because of the slow diffusion rate toward an electrode of any large organic species containing these ions, it may be desirable to use redox mediators
(dissolved small redox active molecules) to bring the heavy metal
cations into redox equilibrium with the electrode.

To some extent it may be necessary to introduce new concepts in
dealing with this material containing such a wide distribution
of species. In dealing with simple materials, the chemist puri-
fies and provides a detailed characterization. In dealing with

the next stage of complication (a system of polymer molecules of
a variety of sizes), one introduces parameters and measurements
to characterize the distribution of molecular size and weight
rather than measuring each molecule individually. Similarly, in
the present system one may have to introduce the notion of a distribution of redox potentials and of binding sites.

Enzyme Analysis

Enzyme analysis is a potentially valuable technique in characterizing organic coatings on particles. It has been used with success in the study of bacterial cell surfaces and is just beginning to be applied to the study of animal cell surfaces. There
is a large arsenal of enzyme systems which could assist in identifying the nature of these organic coatings.

Ion Microprobe - Ion Microscopy

One of the most exciting techniques for the study of solid surfaces involves ion-sputtering mass spectrometry. It is possible
to determine the compositional distributions of any element on
an inorganic surface with a spatial resolution of 1 μm. It is
also possible to perform compositional depth profiles of various
elements from less than 1 μm down to several tens of microns.
This technique should be applied to the study of the various
phases that can be isolated from the marine environment including
sediment particles, manganese nodules, phosphorites, etc. The
technique greatly extends the amount of information presently
obtained by the electron microprobe technique. It is much more
sensitive and is applicable to all elements (and isotopes) including the elements of low atomic number.

In the ion microscopy mode the technique can be used to study
surface compositional distribution which can then be correlated
with morphological microscopic techniques such as light microscopy, electron microscopy, SEM.

ESCA ("Electron Spectroscopy for Chemical Analysis")

In addition to the ion microprobe, there are a number of surface
techniques that have been used with considerable success for the
study of metals, minerals, airborne particulates, etc. These
obviously should be investigated for their applicability to
marine surfaces. They include ESCA, Auger, and ion-scattering
spectrometry. ESCA has been used to provide information on the
chemical form of inorganic compounds of sulfur, phosphorus, nitrogen, etc. For the most effective characterization of surfaces,
the various techniques should be used in combination.

REFERENCES

Aston, S.R., and Chester, R. 1973. Estuarine and Coastal Marine
      Science 1: 225-231.

Baier, R.E. 1970. Proc. 13th Conf. Great Lakes Res. Internat.
      Assoc. Great Lakes Res.: 114-127.

Chester, R.; Stoner, J.H.; and Johnson, L.R. 1974. Nature 249:
      335-336.

Chu, B. 1975. Laser Scattering Spectroscopy. London: Academic
      Press.

Garrett, W.D. 1965. Limnol.Oceanog. 10: 602-605.

Harrison, P.M., and Hoy, T.G. 1973. In Inorganic Biochemistry,
      ed. G.L. Eichhorn. Vol. 1, pp. 253-279. Amsterdam:
      Elsevier.

Harvey, G.W. 1966. Limnol.Oceanog. 11: 608-613.

Heise, G.W., and Cahoon, N.C. 1971. The Primary Battery,
      Vol 1. New York: Wiley.

Jennings, B.R. 1972. In Light Scattering by Polymer Solutions,
      ed. M. Huglin. pp. 529-579. London: Academic Press.

Jerlov, N.G. 1968. Optical Oceanography. Amsterdam: Elsevier.

Kerker, M. 1969. Scattering of Light. London: Academic Press.

Kordesch, K.V. 1974. Batteries, Vol. 1, Manganese Dioxide.
      New York: Marcel Dekker.

Kruyt, H.R. 1952. Colloid Science, Vol. 2. Amsterdam: Elsevier

Lemlich, R.   1972.   J.Geophys.Res. 77: 5204-5210.

MacIntyre, F.   1968.   J.Phys.Chem. 72: 589-592.

Malati, M.A.   1971.   Chemistry and Industry: 446-452.

Marcus, R.A.   1975.   In Dahlem Workshop on the Nature of Sea-
    water, ed. E.D. Goldberg.   Berlin: Dahlem Konferenzen.

Millero, F.J.; Schrager, S.R.; and Hansen, L.D.   1974.
    Limnol.Oceanog. 19: 711-715.

Pravdic, V.   1970.   Limnol.Oceanog. 15: 230-233.

Querfeld, C.W.; Kerker, M.; and Kratohvil, J.P.   1972.
    J. Colloid Interface Sci. 39: 568-582.

Schindler, P.W.   1974.   Paper presented at the III Internat'l
    Conf. on the Chemistry of the Mediterranean, Rovini.

Schulz, G.V., and Lechnor, M.   1970.   J. Polymer Sci. A-2, 8:
    1885-1896.

Schweitzer, J., and Jennings, B.R.   1971.   J. Colloid Interface
    Sci. 37: 443-457.

Sieburth, J. M.   1965.   Trans. Joint Conf. Ocean Engng.
    Washington, D.C.   pp. 1064-1068.

Strickland, J.D.H., and Parsons, T.H.   1972.   In A Practical
    Handbook of Seawater Analysis.   pp. 251-258.   Ottawa:
    Fisheries Research Board of Canada.

Templer, C.E.   1972.   Nature - Physical Science 235: 158-160.

Uzgiris, E.E., and Costaschuk, F.M.   1973.   Nature - Physical
    Science 242: 77-79.

Ware, B.R.   1974.   Advances in Colloid and Interface Science 4:
    1-44.

Electron Transfer in Homogeneous and Heterogeneous Systems

R. A. Marcus
Department of Chemistry, 174 Noyes Laboratory
University of Illinois
Urbana, Illinois 61801 USA

Abstract: The mechanism of electron transfer in solution and at electrodes is described. A theoretical analysis involving the fluctuations in the chemical bond distances and in the dielectric polarization of the partially oriented solvent molecules about the reactants leads to an expression for the rate constant of these reactions. Relations are obtained between the rate constants of cross reactions k_{12}, self-exchange reactions k_{11}, [e.g., $k_{12} \cong (k_{11}k_{22}K_{12}f_{12})^{1/2}$], and reactions at surfaces (electrodes, both metal and semiconductor type). There are many comparisons between theory and experiment and a survey is given. The effect of standard free energy of reaction and of electrode potential is included, as in the $Co^{+3}(aq)$ anomaly, and the occurrence of chemiluminescence. The discussion is preceded by a brief description of reaction rate theory in general and of atom versus electron transfer mechanisms in particular.

I. Introduction

The rates and mechanism of electron transfer reactions have been extensively studied in solution and, electrochemically, at surfaces. These surface studies have been made primarily with metal electrodes, and in some cases with semiconductor electrodes. In the present survey the extensive relation between theory and experiment in electron transfer reactions is discussed. Most reaction rate studies of electron transfer reactions have involved hydrated or otherwise coordinated inorganic ions. There have also been studies with large organic ions, and some between inorganic ions and organic ions and with molecules of biological interest. The field has been the subject of many useful reviews, e.g., [1,4,8,10,12,18-23,29,37-45,47].

Before applying any of these concepts and results to problems of sea water it is necessary to identify the species involved, the nature of any surfaces present, the extent of adsorption, and the sequence of steps, if any, constituting the mechanism of the overall reaction. Hopefully this Conference may help define some of these features for various systems.

II. Some General Remarks on Reaction Rates

Typically, for reactions of interest here, one may classify reactions as second order, i.e., those with rates given by

$$-dC_a/dt = k_{rate}C_A C_B \tag{2.1}$$

for a reaction between A and B, with the C's denoting concentration, or first order

$$-dC_A/dt = k_{rate}C_A . \tag{2.2}$$

In the case of first order reaction at a surface one would have

$$-dC_A/dt = k_{rate}S C_A , \tag{2.3}$$

where S is the area of the surface and where the rate per unit area of surface is thereby $k_{rate}C_A$. (Analogously, the rate of a second order reaction at a surface could also be written.) In (2.1)-(2.3) k_{rate} is a constant, the "rate constant." Its units are worth noting: If the units of concentration, time and area are moles cc^{-1}, sec^{-1}, and cm^2, respectively, the units of k_{rate} are cc $mole^{-1}$ sec^{-1} in (2.1), sec^{-1} in (2.2), and cm sec^{-1} in (2.3).

A little computation using kinetic theory shows that if every collision in (2.1) and (2.3) were effective in causing reaction, k_{rate} would equal ca. 10^{14} cc $mole^{-1}$ sec^{-1} and ca 10^4 cm sec^{-1}, respectively. If (2.2) occurred at every vibration of A, the use of a typical vibration frequency shows that k_{rate} of (2.2)

would be ca 10^{13} sec^{-1}. These values for the rate constants
in (2.1)-(2.3) thus represent the upper limits. Most observed
values will be far below these, because not every collision,
nor every vibration in (2.2), leads to reaction.

Activated complex theory will be first considered, since it is
the most commonly used approach to reaction rates in general
[11]. The reader mainly interested in the comparison of theory
and experiment in electron transfer reactions, rather than in
the underlying theory, may wish to proceed directly to Sec. V.

III. Activated Complex Theory

The principal theory which has been applied to reaction rates
in general has been activated complex theory. A recent review
is given in [27].

In activated complex theory all the relevant coordinates (say
N) in the reacting system are considered, including the coordinates of the solvent molecules when the reaction occurs
in solution. These coordinates involve the positions of all
the molecules, their orientations, and their internal vibrational coordinates, or various combinations of these. For
each configuration of these coordinates the system has some
potential energy. (The latter is the "Born-Oppenheimer" electronic energy of the system, obtained by solving the Schrö-
dinger equation for each value of the coordinates.)

One can imagine this potential energy to be plotted as a function of all these coordinates in some N-dimensional coordinate
space. In activated complex theory it is assumed that some
surface (of N-1 dimensions) can be located in this space, such
that once the system starting from the reactants' side has
crossed it, reaction has occurred. Activated complexes are
defined as a set of configurations of the system on this
special N-1 dimensional surface. We shall call it an N-1
surface. The rate constant of the reaction equals the probability of finding the system at this N-1 surface, per unit
length perpendicular to the surface, multiplied by the velocity of crossing the surface, and integrated over all pos-

sible configurations on the surface and over all velocities
of crossing.

In the usual form of activated complex theory one first assumes that an N-1 surface with the property just described
actually exists. Secondly, one assumes that the probability
of finding the system at the N-1 surface, per unit length
normal to the N-1 surface, can be calculated from equilibrium
statistical mechanics: A quasi-equilibrium is postulated
between reactants and activated complexes moving from the reactants' region to the products' region in this N-dimensional
space. Finally, when quantum effects are important for tunneling through the activated complex region one makes some
simplifying assumption to permit a calculation of that tunneling.

The net result for an activated complex theory expression for
the rate constant k_{rate} is

$$k_{rate} = \varkappa(kT/h)\exp(-\Delta G^{\ddagger}/kT) \quad , \qquad (3.1)$$

where k, T, h and $\Delta G^{\ddagger}$ denote Boltzmann's constant, absolute
temperature, Planck's constant, and the Gibbs' free energy
difference between the activated complex (i.e., the system
on the N-1 surface) and the reactants. Tunneling effects,
if any, are included in the $\varkappa$ term. Otherwise, $\varkappa$ is usually
taken to be unity. Various tests of (3.1) using actual
dynamic calculations are available. (A summary is given
in [27].)

In bimolecular reactions $\Delta G^{\ddagger}$ depends on the concentration
unit used, and these units in turn determine those of k_{rate}.
For example, if this unit in $\Delta G^{\ddagger}$ is 1 mole/cc and if the
units of kT and of h are ergs/molecule and ergs sec/molecule,
the units of k_{rate} prove to be cc/mole/sec, as in Sec. II.
In unimolecular reactions $\Delta G^{\ddagger}$ does not depend on concentration
units, and the units of k_{rate} are sec^{-1}. In unimolecular
reactions at surfaces, if the surface concentration unit of
the activated complex in $\Delta G^{\ddagger}$ is 1 $mole/cm^2$ and if the concentration unit of reactant in solution is 1 mole cc^{-1}, the
units of k_{rate} are cm sec^{-1}, as in Sec. II.

Typically, reactions occur as a result of a suitable fluctuation of the coordinates which permits the system to cross
the critical set of configurations (the N-1 surface) known
as the activated complex. In reactions where chemical bonds
are broken or formed these fluctuations in coordinates involve in a major way the increase in distance in the breaking bonds or decrease in distance in any bonds being formed.
Sometimes bonds merely rearrange, and the fluctuations then
involve simultaneous changes in several bond distances and
bond angles. In each case the fluctuations leading to reaction are those from a typical configuration of the reactants
to a typical one of the products. We investigate in Sec. IV
the type of fluctuations involved in simple electron transfers.

In the activated complex of electron transfer reactions, H.
Taube pointed out that the coordination shells of the reactants are either separated ("outer sphere" reactions) or share
some atom or group ("inner sphere" reactions), e.g., refs. in
[43-45]. In the latter instance the net reaction will involve
only an electron transfer if the shared atom is restored to
its original owner, or the reaction will involve an atom
transfer, if the shared atom is not so restored. We will consider mainly outer sphere electron transfers, though applications of the theory [23,26] have been made to those of the
inner sphere type, e.g., [38,49], initially by N. Sutin.

Throughout, the references will be limited to review articles
where possible, because of space limitations and the considerable body of studies available.

IV. Electron Transfer Reactions

In some respects electron transfer reactions are the simplest
of all chemical reactions. Simple electron transfers involve
no breaking or formation of chemical bonds. Changes do occur
in stretching or compressing bonds in the reactants themselves and changes occur in the typical orientations of the
solvent molecules around each reactant [23].

Typically, the bond lengths in a reactant are somewhat different when the molecule is in its oxidized form as compared
with the case where an electron has been added, and the species
is in a reduced form. For example, the Fe-O bonds in an hydrated ferric ion are somewhat shorter, possibly as much as
0.15 Å, than those in a hydrated ferrous ion. Sometimes this
bond length change will be large and sometimes, as in MnO_4^- -
$MnO_4^=$, quite small. Again, the degree of orientation of the
solvent molecules around an ion will depend on the charge of
that ion, and so will change when the redox state of the reactant is changed.

To see how the electron transfer occurs, we plot the potential
energy of the reactants plus solvent as a function of the N
coordinates of the system [23]. One profile of this potential energy surface would appear as the curve labelled R in
Fig. 1. If instead an electron (or more than one) has been
transferred, we would have products, and the profile might
appear as the curve labelled P in Fig. 1. The abscissa in
this figure is a "generalized coordinate" involving changes
in bond lengths of both reactants and reorientation of solvent molecules in the vicinity of the reactants, such that
the system proceeds from a configuration appropriate to reactants (any near the bottom of the well in the R curve) to
a configuration appropriate to the products (any near the
bottom of the well in the P curve).

When the reactants are far apart the R and P curves merely
cross at the intersection (as with the dotted line curves).
When the reactants are a small enough distance apart, their
electronic interaction perturbs the dotted line curves in
Fig. 1 particularly near their point of intersection. At
that point the two unperturbed electronic quantum states R
and P are degenerate and the degeneracy is broken by the interaction. The new curves are the solid ones, and the energy
of the maximum of the lower solid curve is less than that at
the intersection by an electronic interaction energy V_{12}, the
so-called "resonance energy." The intersection point, con-

tinued into the N-1 dimensions perpendicular to the profile, i.e., perpendicular to the plane of the paper, constitutes the N-1 surface referred to in Sec. III.

When V_{12} is zero, a system on the R curve undergoing thermal fluctuations and passing the crossing point in Fig. 1 as a result, will remain on the R curve and eventually recross the N-1 surface and return to a stable R configuration. No reaction has occurred even though the system crossed the N-1 surface. When V_{12} is no longer zero there is a finite probability that a system starting on the R curve and crossing the N-1 surface as a result of a fluctuation will proceed on the P curve, and the reaction will thereby have occurred. An approximate simple formula is available for calculating this probability that a system which is known to cross the N-1 surface ends up on the P curve. V_{12} and the slopes of the R and P curves at the crossing point are used (Landau-Zener-Stueckelberg formula).

When this electron transfer probability per crossing, $\varkappa$, is about unity, the reaction is said to proceed adiabatically on the lower surface in Fig. 1. When $\varkappa \ll 1$ the reaction is said to proceed nonadiabatically. If the electronic interaction between the reactants is strong enough in the activated complex, V_{12} will be large and the reaction will be adiabatic, while in the case of a small electronic interaction energy V_{12},,the reaction is nonadiabatic.

One can rephrase some of the above discussion of Fig. 1 in terms of the Franck-Condon principle: In the case of small V_{12} the only place where the system can move from the R curve to the P curve without emitting or absorbing light is at the crossing point. Here, there is no change in the momentum or position when the system "jumps" from the R to the P curve. It thereby obeys the Franck-Condon Principle, a point first discussed by W. F. Libby (Ref. 9 in [23]).

The problem of calculating the rate constant k_{rate} involves the calculation of $\Delta G^{\ddagger}$ in (3.1), which in turn is related to

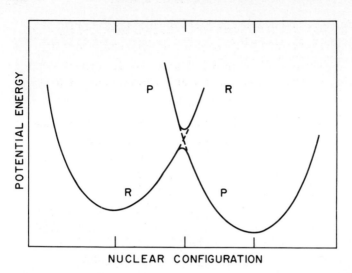

FIG. 1 - Profile of a plot of the potential energy of the
         system (R) consisting of reactants plus solvent
         and (P) products plus solvent, as a function of a
         change in vibrational bond lengths and angles and
         solvent molecules' orientations [23].

the probability of finding the system as an activated com-
plex, and the calculation of $\varkappa$. We consider next $\Delta G^{\ddagger}$.

If the potential energy curves R and P were merely quadratic
(parabolas), and if one knew the relevant force constants
(curvature of the R and P curves), the difference in position of the minima in Fig. 1, and the difference in heights
of the minima, the calculation of $\Delta G^{\ddagger}$ would be straightforward; only simple vibrational analysis would be necessary. However, a major problem arises, since the interactions of the solvent molecules with each other and with the
reactants are strongly anharmonic. Only in a macroscopic
sense can the interaction be approximated by some quadratic
approximation, namely, one for the free energy of solvation.
Furthermore, this solvation has a peculiarity not considered
previously in more conventional reactions, a peculiarity to
which we shall turn in a moment. Finally, when the reactants are far apart, a major additional fluctuation is

needed to bring them closer together. Along that coordinate, which is roughly at right angles to the plane of the
paper in Fig. 1, the potential energy profile is almost
flat at large separation distance rather than being para-
bolic.

We now consider the major peculiarity of the polarized solvent in these reactions. Typically, for a given charge distribution of the reacting species there is an averaged orientation of the solvent molecules at each point in the solvent,
i.e., a dielectric polarization which is a function of position with respect to the reacting ions. Frequently, dielectric continuum theory has been used to calculate this equilibrium position-dependent dielectric polarization and to
calculate, approximately, its contribution to the free energy
of solvation of ions or of pairs of ions. Standard textbook
electrostatics are used. The configurations of the solvent
which contribute most are the stabler ones, namely, those
corresponding to the configurations near the minimum of the
R curve in Fig. 1. Instead, when the reacting species have
a different charge distribution, namely the charges of the
products, and so when the system is on curve P, the equilibrium dielectric polarization function of the solvent is also
different. (Most of the contribution to the latter arise
from configurations near the minimum of the P curve.)

In the case of a system located at the intersection in Fig. 1
(the N-1 surface), neither of these polarization functions is
appropriate, since the configurations which occur at the
intersection are quite different from those which occur at
either minimum in Fig. 1. To calculate the polarization
function appropriate to the intersection region, it was
therefore useful to derive an expression for the free energy
of the entire system as a function of fluctuations in the
solvent dielectric polarization (Ref. 16 in [23]). To do
this, a reversible path was found for producing this nonequilibrium polarization (Ref. 47 in [23]).

The value of the polarization function occurring at the intersection was then found by minimizing this free energy of formation of the activated complex, subject to the condition that the system was at the intersection. This condition was imposed by showing that it was equivalent to one in which an R system and a P system, which had R charges and P charges, respectively, had the same dielectric polarization function and the same total free energy.

The contribution of the vibrations of the reactants to $\Delta G^{\ddagger}$ was included in a straightforward way [23,24], as was the free energy change arising from the formation of a collision pair. (The latter proves to be -kT ℓn Zh/kT, where Z is a collision frequency.) One obtains Eq. (4.1) for bimolecular reactions in solution or for a unimolecular reaction at a surface. (A minor factor ρ is omitted; $\rho \cong 1$.)

$$k_{rate} = \varkappa Z \exp(-\Delta G^{\ddagger}/kT) \qquad (4.1)$$

$\varkappa$ is an electron tunneling probability factor; Z is about 10^{14} cc mole^{-1} sec^{-1} for bimolecular reactions and about 10^4 cm sec^{-1} for surface reactions; ΔG^* is the contribution to $\Delta G^{\ddagger}$ arising from the solvent polarization and vibrational contributions described above and from the work w^r required to bring the reactants together. This work may arise from both ionic and nonpolar interactions between the reactants. One finds [23,24]

$$\Delta G^* = w^r + \frac{\lambda}{4} + \frac{\Delta G^{o\prime}(R)}{2} + \frac{\Delta G^{o\prime}(R)^2}{4\lambda} , \qquad (4.2)$$

where R is the most probable separation distance of the reactants in the activated complex; λ is a reorganization property which depends on the polar properties of the solvent and on the differences in equilibrium bond lengths (and angles) of the R and P systems. Expressions are given in the Appendix of this paper. $\Delta G^{o\prime}(R)$ is given by

$$\Delta G^{o\prime}(R) = \Delta G^{o\prime} + w^p - w^r , \qquad (4.3)$$

where $\Delta G^{o\prime}$ is the "standard" Gibbs free energy of reaction in the prevailing medium, i.e., it is the free energy of reaction for unit concentrations of reactants and products at the prevailing temperature and pressure and in the prevailing solvent environment; w^p is the work required to bring the products together to the separation distance R. $\Delta G^{o\prime}(R)$ is seen from (4.3) to be the Gibbs free energy of reaction at a distance of separation R between the reactants.

The quantity λ in (4.2) has a very useful additivity property: In the cross-reaction

$$A_1(ox) + A_2(red) \rightarrow A_1(red) + A_2(ox) \qquad (4.4)$$

and in the self-exchange reactions

$$A_1(ox) + A_1(red) \rightarrow A_1(red) + A_1(ox) \qquad (4.5)$$

$$A_2(ox) + A_2(red) \rightarrow A_2(red) + A_2(ox) , \qquad (4.6)$$

with λ written as λ_{12}, λ_{11}, and λ_{22}, respectively, we have [22,24]

$$\lambda_{12} \cong \frac{1}{2}(\lambda_{11} + \lambda_{22}) , \qquad (4.7)$$

a relation with far reaching consequences, as we shall see. (Rates of self-exchange reactions (4.5) and (4.6) have been measured by isotopic tracer techniques, and by broadening of electron spin resonance and nuclear magnetic resonance absorption lines.)

The additivity relation (4.7) can be given a simple physical interpretation, arising from the fact that solvent's and coordination shell reorganizations in (4.4) occur around an A ion and a B ion in (4.4) and around two A ions in (4.5) and two B ions in (4.6).

The preceding remarks, up to and including (4.1), apply both to reactions at metal electrodes as well as to homogeneous reactions, Z now denoting the collision frequency with unit area of the surface

$$A(ox) + ne(M) \rightarrow A(red) + M , \qquad (4.8)$$

where M denotes the electrode and n is the number of electrons transferred. Now, reaction occurs upon suitable close

approach of A to M, plus a suitable fluctuation in bond
lengths (angles) of A and in the dielectric polarization of
the solvent near A and M.

One difference which does exist is that when the surface is
a metal electrode there are numerous electronic states present, corresponding to different distributions of the electrons in the metal.   Thereby, there is not merely one R curve
and one P curve in Fig. 1, but numerous curves, one for each
different electronic state   (cf. Fig. 2 of [23]).   This modification presents no major difficulty, since most of the
transfers are to and from the Fermi energy level in the metal
(the level below which the metal's electron states are largely
occupied by electrons and above which they are largely unoc-
cupied) [4,18,23,24].   With this modification Eq. (4.1) is
still applicable but now ΛG^* is given by [23]

$$\Lambda G^* = w^r + \frac{\lambda_e}{4} + \frac{\Delta G_e^{o\prime}(R)}{2} + \frac{\Delta G_e^{o\prime\, 2}(R)}{4\lambda_e} \quad , \qquad (4.9)$$

where

$$\Delta G_e^{o\prime}(R) = \Lambda G_e^{o\prime} + w_e^p - w_e^r \qquad\qquad (4.10)$$

and

$$\Delta G_e^{o\prime} = -nF(E-E^{o\prime}) \qquad\qquad (4.11)$$

In these equations w_e^r is the work required to bring the reactant from the bulk of the solution to a position R from the
electrode, R being the most probable separation distance in
the activated complex (it is also weighted in accordance with
the distance-dependent electron transfer probability, as in
the homogeneous reaction case); w_e^p is the corresponding
property for the product; E is the electrode potential; $E_o{}'$
is the value the latter would have under equilibrium conditions
if the reactant and product concentrations were equal ($E_o{}'$
is thereby the "standard potential," but for the prevailing
medium); λ_e is a reorganization parameter (Appendix), which
is approximately related to the λ_{11} of reaction (4.5) by

$$\lambda_e \geqq \frac{1}{2} \lambda_{11} \quad , \qquad\qquad (4.12)$$

where the equality applies when the distance between reactant and electrode is one-half that between the two reactants in (4.5), and the inequality applies when, because of an extra adsorbed solvent layer in the electrode case, R_e is larger than $R/2$. Eq. (4.12) has a simple physical interpretation: there is only one A in (4.8) but two in (4.5). We note, too, that $-ne(E-E_o')$ has replaced $\Delta G_o'$ as the driving force for the reaction.

V.   Predictions from the Theoretical Relations

A number of theoretical predictions result from these equations [22]. They can be tested experimentally and are listed below.

(1) One immediate consequence of (4.1)-(4.7) is the cross-relation (5.1), which obtains when the work terms either cancel or can be neglected

$$k_{12} \cong (k_{11}k_{22}K_{12}f_{12})^{1/2}, \qquad\qquad (5.1)$$

where

$$f_{12} = (\ln K_{12})^2/4 \, \ln(k_{11}k_{22}/Z^2) \quad . \qquad (5.2)$$

Here, k_{12}, k_{11} and k_{22} are the rate constants of (4.4)-(4.6), K_{12} is the equilibrium constant of (4.4) (in that $-kT \ln K_{12}$ equals $\Delta G^{o'}$); f_{12} arises from the $\Delta G^{o'2}/4\lambda$ term in (4.2). The relation (5.1) has also been used to predict and interpret k_{12}'s or k_{11}'s or in some cases K_{12}, depending on which of the quantities in (4.8) have been measured experimentally. Sometimes the self-exchange rate constants k_{11} and k_{22} may not be known, and then (5.1) has found use in calculating relative values of k_{12} for various λ_e's, for a series in which k_{22} is approximately constant.

(2) A second consequence, and actually a corollary of (1) has been the dependence of $-kT \ln k_{rate}$ on $\Delta G^{o'}$ for a series of reactions of similar λ_{12}. The slope decreases to zero at larger $-\Delta G^{o'}$ and increases to unity at larger $+\Delta G^{o'}$, in the range $|\Delta G^{o'}| < \lambda$. It is 0.5 when $|\Delta G^{o'}| < \lambda$.

(3) Similarly, if in an electrode reaction the electrode
     potential E is systematically varied, the slope α of
the plot of $-kT \ln k_{rate}$ vs. $-neE$ is 0.5 when $|ne(E-E_o^{O'})/\lambda|$
is small. α approaches zero when $-ne(E-E^{O'})$ becomes quite
negative, and it approaches unity when $-ne(E-E^{O'})$ becomes
quite positive, in the range $|ne(E-E^{O'})|/\lambda < 1$.

(4) One consequence of (4.1)-(4.12) is a relation between
     the rate constant of an self-exchange reaction k_{11} and
that for the electrode redox reaction (4.8) k_e at $E = E^{O'}$.

$$k_e/Z_e \cong (k_{11}/Z)^{1/2} \quad , \tag{5.3}$$

when the work terms can be neglected and when the condition
regarding the R's $(R_e \approx \frac{1}{2} R_{11})$ is fulfilled. Here, Z_e is
the collision frequency per unit area of the electrode sur-
face, and Z is the collision frequency for (4.5).

(5) From (4.1)-(4.12) it also follows that when a series of
     homogeneous reactions (4.4) are studied, varying A but
keeping B fixed, and when the rates are compared with those
of a series of electrode reactions (4.8) at a given E but
varying E_o', one expects

$$k_{12}/k_e \cong \text{constant} \quad , \tag{5.4}$$

provided both series are in the range of ΔG^* vs. $\Delta G^{O'}$ [ΔG^*
vs. $-ne(E-E_o')$ in (4.8)] slopes of 1/2, and provided work
terms either cancel or are negligible.

(6) From the dependence of λ_{12}, λ_{11} and λ_e on the properties
     of the system (Appendix), one expects that (i) λ_{12},
λ_{11} and λ_e should increase with increasing difference in
equilibrium bond lengths (bond angles) of corresponding
bonds in A_{ox} and A_{red}, other things being equal; thereby
k_{rate} decreases; (ii) when the dielectric reorganization
can be treated by a dielectric continuum approximation and
when specific solvent effects are absent each λ increases
linearly with $(1/D_{op})-(1/D_s)$, where D_s is the usual dielectric constant of the medium, and D_{op} is the square of the
refractive index (the "optical dielectric constant"); the

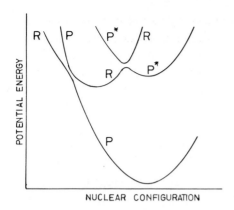

FIG. 2 - Plot similar to Fig. 1 but for a reaction so exothermic that an electronically-excited state of the
products also becomes accessible [25].

dependence of λ on this difference reflects the fact that
only fluctuations in orientation and vibrational polarization of the solvent occur along the abscissa in Fig. 1; the
electronic polarization has a value dictated by the local
field; (iii) each λ increases with the square of the charge
transferred, ne.

(7) Since $\varkappa$ in Eq. (4.1) is closer to unity the greater the
     probability of an electron transfer, when the system is
in the vicinity of the intersection region in Fig. 1, a weak
electronic interaction between the two reactants leads to a
small k_{rate}.

(8) In the case of highly exothermic reactions, as in
     Fig. 2, the electron transfer may occur to form
an electronically excited state of the system (P^* in Fig. 2).
The electronically excited product can then emit light,
either directly or after a sequence of reactions, and one
thereby has an electron transfer chemiluminescent reaction
[25,8].

(9) An apparent possibility, evident from (4.2), is that
     ΔG^* will first decrease with increasingly negative
$\Delta G^{o\prime}$ and then, when $-\Delta G^{o\prime}(R) > \lambda$, increase as $\Delta G^{o\prime}$ is made

still more negative. The same effect is evident by displacing
the P curve in Fig. 2 increasingly downward, and following
the position of the "intersection" point of the R and P curves.

However, tunneling of the nuclei from an R to a P curve (instead of passing to a P curve at the "intersection") might
reduce the extent of this upturn in ΔG^* when $-\Delta G^{o\prime}(R) > \lambda$
[6,14,46]. Quantum effects related to nuclear tunneling were
first discussed by Levich and Dogonadze, refs. in [4,18].

(10) From the definition of the activation energy E_a of a
      reaction as the slope of a $-k \ln k_{rate}$ versus $1/T$ plot,

$$E_a = - k \, \partial \ln k_{rate} / \partial (1/T) \quad , \tag{5.5}$$

and the pre-exponential factor A as

$$k_{rate} = A \exp(-E_a/kT) \quad , \tag{5.6}$$

use of Eq. (4.1) and neglect of the minor temperature dependence of κZ yields

$$A = Z\kappa \exp(\Delta S^*/k) \quad , \tag{5.7}$$

where

$$\Delta S^* = - \partial \Delta G^*/\partial T \quad . \tag{5.8}$$

ΔS^* is the entropy of formation of the activated complex
(apart from the portion included in k $\ln$ Zh/kT). Its main
contribution comes from $\partial w^r/\partial T$, $\partial w^p/\partial T$, and $\Delta S^{o\prime}$, the entropy
of reaction (= $- \partial \Delta G^{o\prime}/\partial T$). When $\Delta S^{o\prime}$ is very negative or
very positive, it tends to make ΔS^* very negative or very
positive, respectively [28]. When there is extensive coulombic repulsion between the reactants, the contribution to
ΔS^* (via the dw/dT terms) is a very negative one. The pre-
exponential factor A in (5.6) is small (e.g., $\ll 10^{14}$ cc
mole^{-1} sec^{-1} for bimolecular homogeneous reactions or $\ll 10^4$
cm sec^{-1} for first order surface reactions) when $\kappa \ll 1$ or
when ΔS^* is very negative.

VI. Tests of the Theoretical Equations

Most of the tests have been of Eq. (5.1). These tests include comparison of k_{12}(calc) and k_{12}(expt) of reactions
involving metal ion hexacyanide and octacyanide complexes,
hexaquo and hexammine ones, complexes with EDTA and related
compounds, phenanthroline and related complexes, reactions
of tri-p-anisylamine with various ferrocenes, reactions of
various ferrocenes with various ferrocinium cations, reactions
of various aromatic anions with aromatic molecules, among
others [1,7,10a,34,35,37-41,48]. A number of examples are given
in Table I [1,7,35]. In these and other studies Eq. (5.1)
has permitted an extensive correlation of the data, and on
the whole the agreement has been quite reasonable. There are
a few major exceptions, mostly involving hexaquo cobaltic
ion, and we shall return to the latter later. Frequently,
Eq. (5.1) has also been used to calculate a value of an unknown self-exchange rate constant k_{11} when the remaining constants are known.

A related test is that of the dependence of ΔG^* on $\Delta G^{o\prime}$ in
Eq. (4.2). Tests of this relation have been made with reactions
such as the oxidation of a series of substituted ferrophen-
anthroline complexes by ceric ion, by manganic ion, and by
cobaltic ion, and a series of substituted ferriphenanthro-
lines reduced by cobaltic ion, by Sutin and his coworkers
(ref. 34 in [38]), and the reactions of various actinide ions
with each other [31]. In each case good agreement was found
between theory and experiment. Similar remarks apply, in the
regime $|\Delta G^{o\prime}| < \lambda$, to a study of the quenching of fluorescence
of various aromatic-type compounds by organic reactants which
quench by electron transfer [36]. In the latter study the
reactions were also studied at extremely negative $\Delta G^{o\prime}$'s
$(|\Delta G^{o\prime}| > \lambda)$, a point to which we return later.

Several comparisons have been made between homogeneous redox
reactions and reactions at electrodes, including that of Eq.
(5.3) and that of (5.4), the former involving various inorganic complex ions [22], and the latter involving the reduc-

TABLE I.   Comparison of Calculated and Experimental k_{12}'s

Reaction	k_{12}, M^{-1} sec^{-1}	
	Observed	Calculated
$Fe(CN)_6^{4-} + MnO_4^-$	1.3×10^4	5×10^3
$V(H_2O)_6^{2+} + Ru(NH_3)_6^{3+}$	1.5×10^3	4.2×10^3
$Ru(en)_3^{2+} + Fe(H_2O)_6^{3+}$	8.4×10^4	4.2×10^5
$Ru(NH_3)_6^{2+} + Fe(H_2O)_6^{3+}$	3.4×10^5	7.5×10^6
$Fe(H_2O)_6^{2+} + Mn(H_2O)_6^{3+}$	1.5×10^4	3×10^4
$IrCl_6^{2-} + W(CN)_8^{4-}$	6.1×10^7	6.1×10^7
$IrCl_6^{2-} + Fe(CN)_6^{4-}$	3.8×10^5	7×10^5
$IrCl_6^{2-} + Mo(CN)_8^{4-}$	1.9×10^6	9×10^5
$Mo(CN)_8^{3-} + W(CN)_8^{4-}$	5.0×10^6	4.8×10^6
$Mo(CN)_8^{3-} + Fe(CN)_6^{4-}$	3.0×10^4	2.9×10^4
$Fe(CN)_6^{3-} + W(CN)_8^{4-}$	4.3×10^4	6.3×10^4
$Ce^{IV} + W(CN)_8^{4-}$	1.9×10^8	4×10^8
$Ce^{IV} + Fe(CN)_6^{4-}$	1.9×10^6	8×10^6
$Ce^{IV} + Mo(CN)_6^{4-}$	1.4×10^7	1.3×10^7
$Co(PDTA)^{2-} + Fe(bipy)_3^{3+}$	8.1×10^4	$> 10^5$
$Fe(PDTA)^{2-} + Co(EDTA)^-$	1.3×10^1	1.3×10^1
$Fe(PDTA)^{2-} + Co(ox)_3^{3-}$	2.2×10^2	1.0×10^1
$Cr(EDTA)^{2-} + Fe(EDTA)^-$	$> 10^6$	10^9
$Cr(EDTA)^{2-} + Co(EDTA)^-$	$\cong 3 \times 10^5$	4×10^7
$Fe(EDTA)^{2-} + Mn(CyDTA)^-$	$\cong 4 \times 10^5$	6×10^6
$Co(EDTA)^{2-} + Mn(CyDTA)^-$	0.9	2.1
$Fe(PDTA)^{2-} + Co(CyDTA)^-$	1.2×10^1	1.8×10^1
$Co(terpy)_2^{2+} + Co(bipy)_3^{3+}$	6.4×10	3.2×10
$Co(terpy)_2^{2+} + Co(phen)_3^{3+}$	2.8×10^2	1.1×10^2
$Co(terpy)_2^{2+} + Co(bipy)(H_2O)_4^{3+}$	6.8×10^2	6.4×10^4
$Co(terpy)_2^{2+} + Co(phen)(H_2O)_4^{3+}$	1.4×10^3	6.4×10^4
$Co(terpy)_2^{2+} + Co(H_2O)_6^{3+}$	7.4×10^4	2×10^{10}[a]
$Fe(phen)_3^{2+} + MnO_4^-$	6×10^3	4×10^3
$Co(phen)_3^{2+} - Fe^{3+}$	1.5×10^3	5.3×10^2
$Cr^{2+} - Co(NH_3)_6^{3+}$	$\leq 1.6 \times 10^{-3}$	1.0×10^{-3}
$Cr^{2+} - Co(en)_3^{3+}$	$\leq 5.1 \times 10^{-4}$	3.4×10^{-4}
$Cr^{2+} - Co(phen)_3^{3+}$	$\leq 1.1 \times 10^4$	3.0×10^1
$V^{2+} - Co(NH_3)_6^{3+}$	$\leq 2.3 \times 10^{-3}$	1.0×10^{-2}
$V^{2+} - Co(en)_3^{3+}$	5.8×10^{-4}	7.2×10^{-4}
$V^{2+} - Co(phen)_3^{3+}$	2.3×10^4	3.8×10^3
$V^{2+} - Co(bipy)_3^{3+}$	7.6×10^3	1.1×10^3

(a) See Table III.

tion of a series of cobaltic pentammino ions $Co^{III}(NH_3)_5X$ by inorganic reductants and by reduction at an electrode (cf. refs. 61, 62 and 74 in [23]). In various studies involving the effect of electrode potential on the reaction rate at an electrode the relation (4.9) has been tested, e.g., refs. in [22]. (In each case the last term in (4.9) was negligible.) The slope α also depends on whether or not an oxide layer is present.

Solvent effects can be quite varied, even including cause of a change in the coordination shell of a reactant. When this effect and other specific solvent effects are absent, and when the solvent orientation contribution to λ can be approximated using dielectric continuum theory, the expression for λ in the Appendix obtains. It has been applied to electron transfers between aromatic anions and aromatic molecules [3] with reasonable agreement between calculated and observed solvent effects, and to reduction of various nitro aromatic anions at an electrode [32], again with reasonable agreement.

Comparison between theory and experiment has also been made via studies of electron transfers at semiconductor electrodes, [29,30] and refs. cited therein. In this case one includes expressions for the electric fields existing within the electrode itself [10].

Rate constants of electron transfer self-exchange reactions can differ by many orders of magnitude, reflecting differences in λ and perhaps in κ. A principal factor influencing λ is the change in bond lengths Δq of corresponding bonds in the two redox forms of a species (Appendix). In the case of the systems in Table I the transfers involve the d-orbitals of the central metal cation, and for reasons which are now understood a change in occupation of an e_g d-orbital (which points along the ligand bonds in hexa-coordinated systems) causes a larger Δq than that by a change in occupation of a t_{2g} d-orbital (which points between the ligands): The loss of an e_g electron from a reductant tends to make the metal-ligand bond become even shorter than it would other-

wise be, as compared with the loss of a t_{2g} electron. Thereby, Δq and λ are larger, and so k_{rate} is smaller. Examples
are given in Table II, where the rate constants of several
reactions at electrodes at $E=E^{0}{}'$ are compared with the loss
of an e_g or a t_{2g} electron. Again, when the lost electron
had been delocalized throughout the complex ion, as in
$Fe(CN)_6^{-4}$ and MnO_4^{-2}, Δq should be smaller, and k_{rate} larger
than otherwise (cf. Table II). An example of the fact that
the metal-ligand bond length depends on whether the extra
electron occupies an e_g orbital of the metal ion or a t_{2g}
orbital is found in cis-$Fe(bipy)_2(NCS)_2$ (Table II), where the
$(t_{2g})^6$ and $(t_{2g})^4(e_g)^2$ states of Fe are compared [17]. (Discussions of electronic structure effects are given in [5,13,
33,40,45,47].

Table II. Effect of Electronic Structure on k_{rate}

System	k_{rate} (cm sec^{-1})^a	Comment
$Co^{+3,+2}$	2×10^{-7}	} e_g involved
$Co(NH_3)_6^{+3,+2}$	5×10^{-6}	
$Fe^{+3,+2}$	5×10^{-3}	} t_{2g} involved
$V^{+3,+2}$	4×10^{-3}	
$Ru(NH_3)_6^{+3,+2}$	ca. 10^{-2}	
$Fe(CN)_6^{-3,-4}$	10^{-1}	} delocalized
$MnO_4^{-1,-2}$	$> 10^{-2}$	
$q_{Fe-N}(e_g)^2 - q_{Fe-N}(t_{2g})^2 = 0.12$ Å		

a. e.g., [12], p. 246, for α's of 0.5; Ru est.
    from Fe and rel. k_{11}'s.

The pre-exponential factor in the rate constants for self-
exchange electron transfers, given by (5.6), is in principle
of considerable interest. However, while many have been
measured, the relative contributions of $\varkappa$ and of the entropy
change associated with bringing two highly charged reacting
ions together in a high ionic strength medium have not been
adequately disentangled in the majority of instances (cf.
[23]). Salt effects are marked when the ionic charges are
large, as expected.

Pre-exponential factors (usually reported indirectly as an "entropy of activation" $\Delta S^{\ddagger}$) for cross-reactions are also influenced by $\Delta S^{0\prime}$, which is no longer zero. The magnitude and sign of $\Delta S^{0\prime}$ can have a major effect on $\Delta S^{\ddagger}$ (and A), as can that of $\Delta H^{0\prime}$ have on $\Delta H^{\ddagger}$ (and E_a). A negative heat of activation $\Delta H^{\ddagger}$ can even occur when $\Lambda H^{0\prime}$ is sufficiently negative [2,28].

The expressions given in Secs. IV and V for k_{rate} for the homogeneous bimolecular reactions refer to the case where the reaction rate is not controlled by diffusion. When the collision efficiency of the reaction becomes high, e.g., in water when it approaches ca. 0.01 or higher, the slow step in the reaction is the diffusion of the two species towards each other. In this case, when the diffusion is followed by reaction, with no back reaction, the rate constant k_{rate} for a homogeneous reaction is given by [26]

$$\frac{1}{k_{rate}} = \frac{1}{k_{act}} + \frac{1}{k_{diff}} \quad , \tag{6.1}$$

where k_{act} is the "activation controlled rate constant, and is given by the expressions in Sec. III-V, and k_{diff} represents the well-known expression for the rate constant of a purely diffusion controlled reaction. It is sometimes necessary to make use of (6.1) for very fast reactions. According as $k_{act} \gg k_{diff}$ or $k_{diff} \gg k_{act}$, we have $k_{rate} \cong k_{diff}$ or $k_{rate} \cong k_{act}$, respectively. (For an application see [13a].)

Thus far, we have considered outer sphere electron transfers. A variety of interesting and specific effects occur in inner sphere electron transfers. The cross-relation (5.1) has been applied to a number of inner sphere electron transfers [38, 49]. Applications have also been made to biological systems involving electron transfer [21,39,40].Other interesting effects in redox systems which have been studied are the effect of pressure on the spin state and on the oxidation state [5] and the spectral properties of intervalency compounds [15].

We return, finally, to two apparent anomalies mentioned earlier: (a) In the main experiment available a very large negative $\Delta G^{o\prime}$ $(-\Delta G^{o\prime} > \lambda)$ did not ultimately cause the k_{rate} to become smaller [36]. This discrepancy has been attributed, in part and in one form or another, to a nuclear tunneling   from the R to the P curve in Fig. 2 [6,14,46] and/or to the occurrence of alternate pathways for k_{rate}, such as formation of electronically excited states of one of the reactants. (b) A large discrepancy occurs for (5.1) in the case of reactions of $Co^{+3}(aq)$ (cf. Table III given later). It was found that an increasingly negative $\Delta G^{o\prime}$ does not reduce to zero or nearly zero the effective barrier to reaction [16]. Two explanations, both consistent with this observation and with the fact that there is an extensive difference in electronic configuration between $Co^{+3}(aq)(t_{2g}^{6})$ and $Co^{+2}(aq)$ $(t_{2g}^{5}e_{g2})$, are (A) $\varkappa$ may be very small or (B) there is a preequilibrium (6.2), unaffected by $\Delta G^{o\prime}$, and followed by (6.3).

$$Co^{+3}(aq)(t_{2g}^{6}) \underset{k_{-1}}{\overset{k_{1}}{\rightleftharpoons}} Co^{+3}(aq)^{*} \qquad\qquad (6.2)$$

$$Co^{+3}(aq)^{*} + A_2(red) \xrightarrow{k_{12}^{\prime}} Co^{+2}(aq)(t_{2g}^{5}e_{g}^{2})+A_2(ox) . \quad (6.3)$$

$Co^{+3}(aq)^{*}$ may be an electronically excited state[†] or a very transient form of the ground state (existing for no more than a vibration) in which the metal-ligand bond angles are bent so as to mix the e_g and t_{2g} orbitals. (In contrast, reaction (6.3) probably involves mainly stretching of the metal-ligand bonds.) The self-exchange reaction would be (6.2) followed by

$$Co^{+3}(aq)^{*} + Co^{+2}(t_{2g}^{5}e_{g}^{2}) \xrightarrow{k_{11}^{\prime}} Co^{+2}(t_{2g}^{5}e_{g}^{2}) + Co^{+3}(aq)^{*}, \quad (6.4)$$

and the latter by $Co^{+3}(aq)^{*} \rightarrow Co^{+3}(aq)(t_{2g})^{6}$. By assuming an equilibrium constant $K \cong 10^{-5}$ for (6.2) in explanation B, stipulating $k_{-1} > k_{12}^{\prime}A_2$, and assuming $\varkappa \cong 10^{-5}$ for explanation A, the results in Table III were obtained. (Details are given in Appendix B.) The large discrepancies are reduced.

[†]The state would be $Co^{+3}(t_{2g}^{4}e_{g}^{2})$ [N. Sutin, private communication], and then (6.3) and (6.4) would involve the transfer of a t_{2g} electron. A possible shortcoming of B for the two phenanthrolines (Table III) is its result for the ratio of k's in the footnote.

Table III. Values of k_{12} for Reactions of $Co^{+3}(aq)(M^{-1} sec^{-1})$

Reagent	k_{obs}	k_{calc} (new,A)[a]	k_{calc} (old)
Fe(II)	2.5×10^2	4×10^4	4×10^7
V(II)	$(\sim 10^6)$	10^6	10^{10}
Cr(II)	1.3×10^4	$<7 \times 10^5$	$<10^{10}$
Co(terpy)$_2^{+2}$	7.4×10^4	5×10^3	$\sim 10^{10}$
Fe(5-NO$_2$-phen)$_3^{+2}$	1.5×10^3	10^3	3×10^8
Fe(5-Me-phen)$_3^{+2}$	1.5×10^4	4×10^3	3×10^9

[a] In B, $k_{calc} \cong 10^5$, 10^5, 10^5, 5×10^3, 4×10^3, 5×10^3, respectively.

Appendix A. Expressions for λ's

The λ's in Eqs. (4.2) and (4.9) can be written as the sum of two terms [22-24]

$$\lambda = \lambda_i + \lambda_o \quad , \qquad (A1)$$

where λ_i is the vibrational contribution from the bonds in each reactant. It is given approximately by

$$\lambda_i = \frac{1}{2} \sum_j k_j (\Delta q_j)^2 \quad , \qquad (A2)$$

when stretching motions of the bonds are principally involved. Δq_j is the difference of equilibrium lengths of the corresponding j'th bond on both sides of reaction (4.4), k_j is the bond force constant, and the sum is over all bonds. In the case that the fluctuations in solvent polarization are treated by dielectric continuum theory, λ_o is given by

$$\lambda_o = (ne)^2 (\frac{1}{2a_1} = \frac{1}{2a_2} - \frac{1}{R})(\frac{1}{D_{op}} - \frac{1}{D_s}) \qquad (A3)$$

in the homogeneous reaction and by

$$\lambda_{o,e} = \frac{1}{2}(ne)^2 (\frac{1}{a} - \frac{1}{R_e})(\frac{1}{D_{op}} - \frac{1}{D_s}) \qquad (A4)$$

in the electrode reaction case. Here, the a's are the radii of the reactants (including coordination shells), and ne is the charge transferred. Data in [9,17] may indicate the $1/R_e$ term to be small.

Appendix B.   Calculations for Table III

For explanation B the reaction rate constant is $k_{calc} = K k_{12}' = K(k_{11}' k_{22} K_{12}' f_{12}')^{1/2}$, with $k_{11}' = k_{11}/K$, $K_{12}' = K_{12}/K$ and f_{12}' calculated from k_{11}', k_{22}, K_{12}'. For explanation A k_{calc} $[= \varkappa k_{12}''] = \varkappa(k_{11}'' k_{22} K_{12}'' f_{12}'')^{1/2}$, with $k_{11}'' = k_{11}/\varkappa$ and $K_{12}'' = K_{12}$. When the relevant $|\Delta G/\lambda|$ in these highly exothermic reactions, namely $|\ln K_{12}'/2 \ln(k_{11}' k_{22}/Z^2)|$ for case B and with double primes for A, exceeded unity, k_{12}' and k_{12}'' were replaced by their maximum, Z, because of the data in [36] referred to in the text. In the case of reactions between an inorganic ion, here $Co^{+3}(aq)$, and the three organiclike ions in Table III a noncancelled work term w has been used in the past [22] to account for other cross-relation results, with $\exp(-w/kT) \sim 0.005$, and so the above k_{12}' and k_{12}'' were multiplied by 0.005 for these three ions. Finally, the maximum value of any k_{12}' is k_{diff}, by (6.1), i.e., ca 10^{10} M^{-1} sec^{-1}. Therefore, since $K = 10^{-5}$, the maximum k_{calc} for case B in Table III is 10^5 M^{-1} sec^{-1}.

References

(1)   Bennett, L. E. 1973. Metalloprotein Redox Reactions.
      In Current Research Topics in Bioinorganic Chemistry,
      ed. S. J. Lippard, pp. 1-176. New York: Wiley and Sons.

(2)   Braddock, J. N., Cramer, J. L., and Meyer T. J. 1975.
      Application of the Marcus Theory for Outer Sphere
      Electron Transfer to Reactions Involving Mixed Ammine-
      Pyridine and Polypyridine Complexes of Ruthenium. (To
      be published).

(3)   Brandon, J. R., and Dorfman, L. M. 1970. Pulse Radiolysis Studies. XIX. Solvent Effects in Electron Transfer and Proton Transfer Reactions of Aromatic Ions.
      J. Chem. Phys. 53: 3849-3856.

(4)   Dogonadze, R. R. 1971. Theory of Molecular Electrode
      Kinetics. In Reactions of Molecules at Electrodes,
      ed. N.S. Hush, pp. 135-227. New York: Wiley and Sons.

(5)   Drickamer, H. G., and Frank, C. W. 1973. Electronic
      Transitions and the High Pressure Chemistry and Physics
      of Solids. London: Chapman and Hall.

(6)   Efrima, S., and Bixon, M. 1974. On the Role of Vibra-
      tional Excitation in Electron Transfer Reactions with
      Large Negative Free Energies. Chem. Phys. Lett. $\underline{25}$:
      34-37.

(7)   Farina, R., and Wilkins, R. G. 1968. Electron-
      Transfer Rate Studies of a Number of Cobalt(II)-
      Cobalt(III) Systems. Inorg. Chem. $\underline{7}$: 514-518.

(8)   Faulkner, L. R. 1975. Models for Chemiluminescence
      in the Liquid Phase. In MTP International Review of
      Science, Physical Chemistry (Chemical Kinetics), ed.
      D. R. Herschbach. Lancaster, Great Britain: Medical
      and Technical Publishing Co. (To be published.)

(9)   Forno, A. E. J., Peover, M. E., and Wilson, R. 1970.
      Homogeneous and Heterogeneous Electron Exchange in the
      Reduction of Aromatic Hydrocarbons. Trans. Faraday
      Soc. $\underline{66}$: 1322-33.

(10) Gerischer, H. 1970. Semiconductor Electrochemistry.
      In Physical Chemistry, An Advanced Treatise $\underline{9A}$. Elec-
      trochemistry, ed. Eyring, H. New York: Academic Press.
      pp. 463-542.

(10a) Gerischer, H., Holzwarth, J., Seifert, D. and Stroh-
      maier, L. 1969. Flow Method with Integrating Obser-
      vation for very fast Irreversible Reactions. Ber.
      Bunsenges. Phys. Chem. $\underline{73}$: 952-955.

(11) Glasstone, S., Laidler, K. J., and Eyring, H. 1941.
      The Theory of Rate Processes. New York: McGraw-Hill.

(12) Hale, J. M. 1971. The Rates of Reactions Involving
      Only Electron Transfer, At Metal Electrodes. In Re-
      actions of Molecules at Electrodes, ed. N. S. Hush,
      pp. 229-257. New York: Wiley and Sons.

(13) Halpern, J. and Orgel, L. E. 1960. The Theory of
      Electron-Transfer Between Metal Ions in Bridged Sys-
      tems. Discussions Faraday Soc. $\underline{29}$: 32-41.

(13a) Holzwarth, J. and Strohmaier, L. 1973. Einfluss der
      Konzentration von Kationen auf die Geschwindigkeit der
      Elektroneniibertragung zurischen Metallkomplexionen.
      Ber. Bunsenges. Phys. Chem. $\underline{72}$: 1145-1151.

(14) Hoytink, G. J. 1973. Cation-Anion Annihilation of
      Naphthalene, Anthracene, and Tetracene. In Chemi-
      luminescence and Bioluminescence, eds. M. J. Cormier,
      D. M. Hercules, and J. Lee, pp. 147-168. New York:
      Plenum Publishing Corporation.

(15) Hush, N.S. 1967. Intervalence-Transfer Adsorption.
      Part 2. Theoretical Considerations and Spectroscopic
      Data. Progr. Inorg. Chem. $\underline{8}$: 391-444.

(16) Hyde, M. R., Davies, R., and Sykes, A. B. 1972.
      Chromium(II) and Vanadium(II) Reductions of Hexa-
      aquocobalt(III) in Aqueous Perchlorate Media. J.
      Chem. Soc., Dalton Trans: 1838-1843.

(17) Konig, E., and Watson, K. J. 1970. The Fe-N Bond
      Lengths, the "Ionic Radii" of Iron(II) and the Crystal
      Field Parameters (10 Dq) in a High-Spin and Low-Spin
      [Fe^{II}-N$_6$] Complex. Chem. Phys. Lett. $\underline{6}$: 457-459.

(18) Levich, V. G. 1966. Present State of the Theory of
      Oxidation-Reduction in Solution (Bulk and Electrode
      Reactions). Adv. Electrochem. Electrochem. Eng. $\underline{4}$:
      249-371.

(19) Linck, R. G. 1972. Rates and Mechanisms of Oxidation-
      Reduction Reactions of Metal Ion Complexes. $\underline{In}$ MTP
      International Review of Science, Reaction Mechanisms in
      Inorganic Chemistry, Series I. $\underline{9}$, ed. M. L. Tobe.
      Baltimore: University Park Press. pp. 303-352.

(20) Lumry, R. W., and Reynolds, W. L. 1966. Mechanisms
      of Electron Transfer. New York: Ronald Press.

(21) McArdle, J. V., Gray, H. B., Creutz, C. and Sutin, N.
      1974. Kinetic Studies of the Oxidation of Ferrocyto-
      chrome C from Horse Heart and Candida krusei by Tris
      (1,10-phenanthroline) Cobalt(III). J. Am. Chem. Soc.
      $\underline{96}$: 5737-5741.

(22) Marcus, R. A. 1963. On the Theory of Oxidation-Reduc-
      tion Reactions Involving Electron Transfer. V. Compari-
      son and Properties of Electrochemical and Chemical Rate
      Constants. J. Phys. Chem. $\underline{67}$: 853-857, 2889.

(23) Marcus, R. A. 1964. Chemical and Electrochemical
      Electron-Transfer Theory. Annu. Rev. Phys. Chem. $\underline{15}$:
      155-196.

(24) Marcus, R. A. 1965. On the Theory of Electron Trans-
      fer Reactions. VI. Unified Treatment for Homogeneous
      and Electrode Reactions. J. Chem. Phys. $\underline{43}$: 679-701.

(25) Marcus, R. A. 1965. On the Theory of Chemiluminescent
      Electron-Transfer Reactions. J. Chem. Phys. $\underline{43}$:
      2654-2657; $\underline{ibid}$. 1970 $\underline{52}$, 2803.

(26) Marcus, R. A. 1968. Theoretical Relations Among Rate
      Constants, Barriers, and Brønsted Slopes of Chemical
      Reactions, J. Phys. Chem. $\underline{72}$: 891-899.

(27) Marcus, R. A. 1974. Activated-Complex Theory: Cur-
      rent Status, Extensions and Applications. $\underline{In}$ Techni-
      ques of Chemistry. 6. Pt. 1, ed. E. S. Lewis, pp. 13-
      46. New York: John Wiley and Sons.

(28) Marcus, R. A. and Sutin, N. 1975. Electron-Transfer Reactions with Unusual Activation Parameters. A Treatment of Reactions Accompanied by Large Entropy Decreases. Inorg. Chem. 14: 213-216.

(29) Mehl, W. 1971. Reactions at Organic Semiconductor Electrodes. In Reactions of Molecules at Electrodes, ed. N. S. Hush, pp. 306-345.

(30) Memming, R., and Mollers, F. 1972. Two-Step Redox Processes with Quinones at Semiconductor Electrodes. Ber. Bunsenges. Phys. Chem. 76: 609-616; cf. 475-481.

(31) Newton, T. W. and Baker, F. B. 1967. Aqueous Oxidation-Reduction Reactions of Uranium, Neptunium, Plutonium and Americium. Advan. Chem. Ser. 71: 268-295.

(32) Peover, M. E., and Powell, J. S. 1969. Dependence of Electrode Kinetics on Molecular Structure. Nitro-Compounds in Dimethylformamide. J. Electroanal. Chem. 20: 427-433.

(33) Piro, J. 1972. Le Comportement Polarographique des Ions Metalliques Complexes et Leur Structure Electronique. Ann. Chim. 7: 351-358.

(34) Pladziewicz, J. R., and Espenson, J. H. 1971. Electron Transfer Reactions of Ferrocenes. J. Phys. Chem. 75: 3381-3382.

(35) Przystas, T. J. and Sutin, N. 1973. Kinetic Studies of Anion-Assisted Outer-Sphere Electron Transfer Reactions. J. Am. Chem. Soc. 95: 5545-5555.

(36) Rehm, D., and Weller, A. 1970. Kinetics of Fluorescent Quenching by Electron and H. Atom Transfer. Israel. J. Chem. 8: 259-271.

(37) Sutin, N. 1966. The Kinetics of Inorganic Reactions in Solution. Annu. Rev. Phys. Chem. 17: 119-142.

(38) Sutin, N. 1968. Free Energies, Barriers and Reactivity Patterns in Oxidation-Reduction Reactions. Accounts Chem. Res. 1: 225-231.

(39) Sutin, N. 1972. Electron Transfer in Chemical and Biological Systems. Chem. Brit. 8: 148-151.

(40) Sutin, N. 1973. Oxidation-Reduction in Coordination Compounds. In Inorganic Biochemistry, 2, ed., G. L. Eichhorn, pp. 611-653. Amsterdam: Elsevier Scientific Publ. Co.

(41) Sykes, A. G. 1967. Further Advances in the Study of Mechanisms of Redox Reactions. Advan. Inorg. Chem. Radiochem. 10: 153-245.

(42)   Sykes, A. G. 1970. Metal-ion Complexes and their
       Redox Properties. Chem. Brit. 6: 159-166.

(43)   Taube, H., and Gould, E. S. 1969. Organic Molecules
       as Bridging Groups in Electron Transfer Reactions.
       Accounts Chem. Res. 2: 321-329.

(44)   Taube, H. 1970. Recent Progress in the Study of
       Inner-Sphere Electron Transfer Reactions. Pure Appl.
       Chem. 24: 289-305.

(45)   Taube, H. 1970. Electron Transfer Reactions of Com-
       plex Ions in Solution. New York: Academic Press.

(46)   Van Dyne, R. P., and Fischer, S. F. 1974. Nonadia-
       batic Description of Electron Transfer Reactions In-
       volving Large Free Energy Changes. Chem. Phys. 5:
       183-197.

(47)   Vleck, A. A. 1963. Polarographic Behavior of Coordi-
       nation Compounds. Progr. Inorg. Chem. 5: 211-384
       (see Sec. 7).

(48)   Winograd, N., and Kuwana, T. 1971. Homogeneous
       Electron-Transfer Reactions Studied by Internal Re-
       flection Spectroelectrochemistry. J. Am. Chem. Soc.
       93: 4343-4354.

(49)   Woodruff, W. H., Burke, B. A., and Margerum, D. W.
       1974. Oxidation of Aminopolycarboxylate Complexes of
       Bivalent Transition Metals by Halogens. Mechanism and
       Free Energy Relationships. Inorg. Chem. 13: 2578-2585.

The Rôle of Oxygen in Redox Processes in Aqueous Solutions

Roger Parsons
Department of Physical Chemistry, The University,
Bristol BS8 1TS, England.

Abstract: The types of redox reaction which may play an important rôle in seawater are considered, with particular attention being paid to the reactions of oxygen. Estimates are made of the rate at which these reactions could occur under natural conditions in an attempt to assess the redox properties of sea water. It is probable that a key rôle is played by hydrogen peroxide at very low concentrations, in both heterogenous and homogeneous reactions. In the framework of these estimates the significance of the direct measurement of the redox potential of seawater is considered. This is most likely to be a mixed potential but further experimental work seems necessary to confirm its true nature.

Introduction

Oxidation - reduction processes in the ocean were surveyed comprehensively by Sillen[33] in two detailed papers. His conclusions were summarized and to some extent modified in a recent article by Breck[7]. In all this work it was assumed that the system was at equilibrium with respect to redox processes, although in situations where this led to unrealistic conclusions, it was remarked that lack of equilibrium may well be due to kinetic factors. Equilibrium calculations are of great importance because they provide a boundary condition for the behaviour of a system which is in principle precise. High

precision may, however, not be obtainable in a system as complex
as natural seawater; nevertheless, true equilibrium with
respect to redox processes is characterized by a single value
of the redox potential. The problem is similar, but not as
difficult as the problems encountered in biological systems[24].
If an inert electrode can be brought to equilibrium with the
system without perturbing it, then the potential of that
electrode gives the redox potential of the system. This
potential must be measured with respect to some other electrode
in contact with the system and is usually expressed with respect
to the standard hydrogen electrode. It is then frequently
referred to by the symbol E_h.

The activities of species forming a redox couple

$$aA + bB \ldots + ne \rightarrow mM + pP \ldots \qquad (1)$$

which is in equilibrium with the electrode are then related to
E_h via the Nernst Equation,

$$E_h = E^{\ominus} - (RT/nF) \ln \; (a_M^m \; a_P^p \ldots / \; a_A^a \; a_B^b \ldots) \qquad (2)$$

where $E^{\ominus}$ is the standard potential (on the hydrogen scale) of
the redox couple and a_A etc. are activities. It is convenient
to cast equation (2) in a dimensionless form

$$pE = E_h \; F/2.3 \; RT = E^{\ominus} \; F/2.3 \; RT - \log_{10}(a_M^m \; a_P^p \ldots / a_A^a \; a_B^b \ldots) \qquad (3)$$

If the activities of the species in a redox couple are
known, for example by measuring their concentrations and calculating their activity coefficients in the environment under
consideration, then pE for the couple may be calculated knowing

the standard potential $E^{\ominus}$ which is directly related to the

standard free energy change $\Delta G^{\ominus}$ in the reaction:

$$aA + bB \ldots + (n/2) H_2 \rightarrow mM + pP \ldots + nH^+ \tag{4}$$

If the system is at equilibrium, pE is the same for all redox

couples in it, and this value is measured by the inert electrode.

However, if the system is not at equilibrium, each reaction i

may have a different value of pE_i and the potential measured

by an inert electrode is a complex function, not only of the

pE_i, but also of the kinetics of the individual redox processes.

If there is a redox couple present in high concentration whose

electron exchange process is fast (a mobile couple) then the

electrode will tend to register the pE_i of that couple.

The nature of a measuring electrode may also be important

when the redox couples are present in very low concentration

because no electrode is truly inert. For example, the oxida-

tion or reduction of species on the electrode surface may also

contribute to the recorded potential. Thus the observed electrode

potential is likely to be a mixed potential depending on the

kinetics of several reactions.

In this paper attention will be focussed upon the reaction

that is likely to be most important in the determination of

redox levels in the ocean: the oxygen/water couple. This will

be considered as a heterogeneous reaction and also as a homo-

geneous process in which a second couple is oxidized. This

reaction is relatively complex and preliminary consideration will

be given to a simpler electron transfer process to provide a

basis for comparison.

A Simple Electron Transfer Reaction

The simplest system likely to occur in seawater at a reasonable concentration is Mn^{2+}/Mn^{3+}. Vetter and Manecke[36] showed that the elementary reaction

$$Mn^{3+} + e \;\rightleftarrows\; Mn^{2+} \tag{5}$$

occurred at Pt in concentrated sulphuric acid with a standard rate constant at the equilibrium potential $k^{\ominus}$ of 10^{-7} m s^{-1} (10^{-5} cm s^{-1}) at 25°C. They did not investigate the possibility that complexes participate in the reaction, although this seems very probable. Chloride and sulphate are likely to form such complexes in seawater. Reactions whose rate is controlled by simple rearrangement of the solvation shell in the electrostatic field of the ion[22,30] usually have rate constants of about 10^{-5} m s^{-1} (10^{-3} cm s^{-1}) at a metal surface[32]. This rate constant may be converted into a time characterising the rate of exchange of the oxidized and reduced forms of the species if the area of interface at which the reaction can occur is known.

The amount of suspended matter[21] in seawater varies about a value of 1 mg ℓ^{-1}, or if it is assumed to consist of mineral matter of density about 10 g cm^{-3}, the volume is 10^{-4} cm^3 ℓ^{-1} = 10^{-10} m^3 ℓ^{-1}. If this matter were subdivided into particles of diameter 0.1 μm assumed to be spherical, then the interfacial area would be $6 \times 10^{-10}/10^{-7} = 6 \times 10^{-3}$ m^2 ℓ^{-1} or 6 m^{-1}. Thus the characteristic exchange time would be $1/6 \times 10^{-5} = 1.7 \times 10^{4}$s, or about 5 hours. This is a lower limit of the exchange time in seawater, since it depends on the assumption that all the particles are metallic, which is highly improbable.

It is more likely that they are at best semiconductors which
are much poorer catalysts and that only a small proportion are
active at all. Hence an exchange time of at least a hundred
times this value is more realistic. There are further
complications in that in a system of this type, a single redox
reaction cannot occur in isolation, but must be coupled with
a second redox reaction and also that mass transport problems
have been ignored. Both of these factors will tend to retard
the reaction. Thus the times involved in setting up equilibrium
even for a "fast" reaction under these conditions are substantial.

The Oxygen Electrode and the Reduction of Oxygen

A very large amount of effort has been expended on studying the oxygen electrode[12,19], but the solution of this difficult
problem remains incomplete. This is partly because the electrode
reaction is slow and partly because it occurs at potentials at
which most metals can oxidize, so that the condition of the
electrode surface may be difficult to control.

The standard potential of the reaction

$$O_2 + 4H^+ + 4e \rightarrow 2 H_2O \tag{6}$$

is obtained as $E^{\ominus} = 1.229$ V by thermodynamic calculation. In
seawater of pH 8 in equilibrium with atmospheric oxygen, an
electrode at which reaction (6) was in equilibrium, would exhibit
a potential of + 0.745 V against a standard hydrogen electrode
or + 0.465 V against a 1 M calomel electrode. However, such an
equilibrium electrode can be achieved only under very special
conditions[5]. This is because the reaction must occur in a
number of steps, several of which are very slow, because they

involve the formation of very unstable intermediates.
Also there is an intermediate of fair stability H_2O_2 which
can lead to the process being divided into two separate
reactions :

$$O_2 + 2H^+ + 2e = H_2O_2 \qquad\qquad (7)$$

$$H_2O_2 + 2H^+ + 2e = 2H_2O \qquad\qquad (8)$$

The standard potentials[28] of these reactions are $E^{\ominus}$ = 0.682 V
and 1.776 V.   In seawater of pH 8 containing unit activity
of H_2O_2, the corresponding potentials would be 0.198 V and
1.303 V against a standard hydrogen electrode or -0.082 V and
1.023 V against a 1 M calomel electrode.

Experimental evidence on metal electrodes shows that there
are some electrodes like mercury at which reaction (6) is clearly
broken up into the two separate stages (7) and (8), while on
other metals like Pt, it probably occurs without the necessity
for intermediate formation of H_2O_2. The distinction between
the two types of mechanism probably depends on the availability
of d-orbitals in the metal surface[12] and it appears that
blocking of these by adventitious impurity can lead to a change-
over of the mechanism to the intermediate formation of H_2O_2.
In seawater, it seems unlikely that any such d-orbitals would
remain available because of the high chloride[4,26] ion concentration, as well as the presence of a variety of organic material;
hence it is most improbable that an interfacial oxidation by
oxygen would occur by overall reaction (6).

On mercury electrode where the interaction between the

reacting species and the metal surface is a minimum, reactions
(7) and (8) occur in two clearly separated polarographic
waves[25] with half wave potentials vs the 1 M calomel electrode
= -0.05 V and -0.94 V in neutral chloride solutions. Thus
reaction (7) is a relatively fast reaction since its $E_{\frac{1}{2}}$ is
almost equal to the equilibrium potential, while reaction (8) is
a very slow reaction, the overpotential at the half-wave potential being of the order of 2 V. The kinetics of reaction (7)
have been thoroughly studied[2,27] on mercury electrodes with the
result that its standard rate constant is of the order of 10^{-5}
$m \ s^{-1}$ and therefore very similar to that of the simple redox
system discussed in the previous section, in spite of the much
greater complexity of the process. The detailed mechanism of
reaction (7) has been thoroughly studied at mercury electrodes,
the most convincing result being obtained by Gierst et al[9] on
the basis of their own results, together with evidence from
pulse radiolysis[10,11]. The rate determining step is the first
electron transfer.

$$e + O_2 \rightarrow O_2^- \tag{9}$$

this is followed by protonation of the superoxide ion, but the
ordinary proton transfer in bulk solution is relatively slow,
since the O_2^- ion has a lifetime of the order of 1 s in alkaline
solution (increasing with pH). Hence it is suggested that proton
transfer occurs from a water molecule activated by adsorption at
the electrode since adsorption of surfactants inhibits the
protonation.

$$O_2^- + H_2O(ads) \rightarrow HO_2 + OH^- \tag{10}$$

The second electron transfer is fast

$$HO_2 + e \rightarrow HO_2^- \tag{11}$$

as is the second proton transfer which occurs only in less alkaline solutions.

The mechanism of reduction of H_2O_2 is less studied[23] and at present very incompletely understood. It seems reasonably certain that the first electron transfer is rate determining but the products of the reaction are not known. Either

$$H_2O_2 + e \rightarrow H_2O_2^- \tag{12}$$

or

$$H_2O_2 + e \rightarrow HO + HO^- \tag{13}$$

result in products of high energy and it is essentially this fact that causes the slowness of (8). Reaction (13) would be readily succeeded by an electron transfer to the OH radical

$$OH^- + e \rightarrow OH^- \tag{14}$$

with protonation of the OH^- ions in acid solution.

The contrast between the rates of (7) and (8) may be considered to be primarily due to the necessity for breaking the O - O bond in (8) which, of course, does not occur in (7). Consequently at all potentials at which O_2 is spontaneously transformed into H_2O via H_2O_2, the mechanism must consist of reaction (7) occurring rapidly in both directions and therefore virtually at equilibrium, while the rate is controlled by (8). In such a system the potential of an electrode is determined by the concentrations of O_2 and H_2O_2 and is unrelated to reaction (6).

In an isolated system of an electrode in a solution of given pH and oxygen pressure, the potential taken up by the electrode (and hence the H_2O_2 concentration) depends on the charging of the electrode by reaction (8), the result being dependent on the size and shape of the electrode and having no fundamental significance. In a real system, this reaction is probably coupled to a second redox reaction. The electrode potential is then a mixed potential controlled by the reduction of H_2O_2 and the oxidation of some other species. Since the former reaction is slow, if it is coupled with a rapid reaction, for example Mn^{2+}/Mn^{3+}, the mixed potential will deviate little from the equilibrium potential of the latter. Of course, the Mn^{2+}/Mn^{3+} couple itself is an improbable candidate for this function as it has a very high redox potential (1.51 V) and there appears to be no likely candidate in seawater for a simple electron transfer reaction[7,20]. The most probable reactions appear to be the heterogeneous couples MnO_2/Mn^{2+}, $FeOOH/Fe_3O_4$ or SO_4^{2-}/FeS_2. Such reactions are generally slower than simple electron-transfer reactions because they involve bond rearrangements or breaking. The rate is also strongly dependent on surface structure and contamination. Hence it is difficult to predict the rate to be observed in a seawater system. Under such conditions the effective redox potential of the system is likely to be very irreproducible, though necessarily greater than the equilibrium potential of the system coupled to oxygen reduction.

Homogeneous Processes

The homogeneous reaction of dissolved oxygen with both

inorganic[31] and organic[35] solutes has been widely studied[13]
although the mechanism is still incompletely understood. The
process is usually described as autoxidation. The best known
reactions with inorganic solutes are those with transition
metal ions such as U^{4+}(ref.18), Fe^{2+}(ref.14), Pu^{3+}(ref.3), V^{2+}(ref.34
Such ions are strongly complexed in solution and in aqueous
solutions, except at low pH, strongly hydrolyzed. Haber and Weiss[17]
proposed a mechanism which accounts for many of the experimental
facts.

$$MOH^{(n-1)+} + O_2 + H^+ \rightarrow MOH^{n+} + HO_2 \qquad (15)$$

$$M^{n+} + HO_2 + H_2O \rightarrow MOH^{n+} + H_2O_2 \qquad (16)$$

$$MOH^{(n-1)+} + H_2O_2 \rightarrow MOH^{n+} + OH^- + OH \quad (17)$$

$$M^{n+} + OH \rightarrow MOH^{n-1} \qquad (18)$$

This mechanism has close analogies with the mechanism proposed
for the reduction of oxygen at mercury electrodes, as may be
seen by comparing (9), (10) and (11) with (15) and (16) and
(13) and (14) with (17) and (18). However it differs from the
latter in that homogeneously the first step (15) must be
assumed to be rate-determining to get a simple explanation of
the observed kinetics which are first order in O_2 and in the
metal. The following reaction with H_2O_2 is much faster in
contrast with the electrode reaction. However, in concentrated
acid solution and in the presence of complexing anions, a second
order dependence on metal ion concentration is observed and this
has led to the suggestion[1] that O_2 is involved with a binuclear
complex, which suggests a plausible mechanism for the reaction to
H_2O_2.

$$(H_2O)_5 \ Fe(II) \cdots O \underset{H \cdots O \cdots H}{\overset{H \cdots O \cdots H}{\diagup \ \ \ \diagdown}} O \cdots Fe(II)(H_2O)_5$$

or

$$(H_2O)_4 \ Fe(II) \diagdown \underset{\overset{OH}{\underset{H}{|}}}{\overset{OH}{}} O \!-\! O \cdots \overset{H \diagdown O \diagup H}{\underset{H \diagup O}{}} Fe(II)(H_2O)_4$$

$$(H_2O)_4 \ Fe(III) \diagdown \underset{\overset{O \cdots H}{\underset{H}{|}}}{\overset{OH}{}} O \!-\! O \diagup \overset{H \cdots O \diagup H}{\underset{H \!-\! O}{}} Fe(III)(H_2O)_4$$

This type of reaction avoids the formation of the free radical
HO_2 and probably facilitates the reaction thereby. However,
the occurrence of reactions of this type in seawater may be doubt-
ful owing to their low rate constants and the small concentration
of ions able to participate. Work in neutral solution[16] has
suggested a second order dependence on [OH⁻].

The reaction of H_2O_2 with transition metal ions can be
studied independently and is found[37] to be first order in H_2O_2
and in the metal ion in agreement with a rate determining
reaction (17). Again, in agreement with the Haber-Weiss
mechanism, this reaction is fast compared with the oxidation by
oxygen. The reaction is accelerated by complexation by halide
ions and the limiting rate constant in the presence of chloride
ion[37] is 68 ℓ mol^{-1} s^{-1}. The total iron concentration in seawater is about 3.6×10^{-7} mol ℓ^{-1} so that if this were entirely
in the form of ferrous ions and the above rate constant remained
valid at pH 8, the rate of removal of H_2O_2 by this reaction would

be about 2.4×10^{-5} $[H_2O_2]$ mol ℓ^{-1} s^{-1}, or the half-life time
of H_2O_2 under these conditions is 4×10^4 s which is comparable
to the characteristic time of a simple electron exchange
reaction mentioned above, and much shorter than the times
involved in heterogeneous removal of H_2O_2. However, it is
extremely unlikely that the whole of the iron in seawater is
present as Fe^{2+} and, in fact, it is probably present entirely
in oxidized forms like FeOOH and Fe_3O_4. Hence this rate is
unreasonably fast probably by many orders of magnitude and the
existence of this type of H_2O_2 removal depends on the presence
of other ions capable of similar reactions, perhaps U or Mo
present in lower concentrations.

It is conceivable that the chloride ion itself could react
with H_2O_2 since this reaction is known to occur at moderate
rates[29]. In acid solutions, the mechanism suggested is

$$H_2O_2 \; + \; Cl^- \; + \; H^+ \; \rightarrow \; HClO \; + \; H_2O \tag{19}$$

$$H_2O_2 \; + \; HClO \; \rightarrow \; O_2 \; + \; Cl^- \; + \; H^+ \; + \; H_2O \tag{20}$$

the first step being rate-determining in agreement with the
observed third order kinetics.

$$-d[H_2O_2]/dt \; = \; k[H_2O_2][H^+][Cl^-] \tag{21}$$

At 25°C and not too strong acid k is about 10^{-4} ℓ^2 mol^{-2} s^{-1}.
If this rate is extrapolated to pH 8 and the chloride content
of seawater, the rate of removal of H_2O_2 would be about 10^{-12}
$[H_2O_2]$ mol ℓ^{-1} s^{-1}. This half-life time of 10^{12} s is very much
longer than those discussed above. However, it provides a lower
limit for the rate of removal of H_2O_2 in the absence of other
mechanisms.

The reaction of organic molecules with oxygen is an autocatalytic chain reaction[13,35] which appears to require initiation by radiation or an impurity which can readily form radicals. Such a radical X reacts with a hydrocarbon alcohol or aldehyde to produce a radical which can react with oxygen:

$$X^{\bullet} + RH \rightarrow R^{\bullet} + XH \qquad\qquad (22)$$

$$R^{\bullet} + O_2 \rightarrow RO_2^{\bullet} \qquad\qquad (23)$$

$$RO_2^{\bullet} + RH \rightarrow ROOH + R^{\bullet} \qquad\qquad (24)$$

leading to a branching chain reaction. Such reactions are extremely sensitive to impurities, especially traces of transition metal ions and consequently may play a rôle in seawater, although the development of a chain reaction is improbable.

Finally, it is well known that enzymic catalysis of oxidation is a highly efficient process and consequently it may play a rôle in the reactions of oxygen in seawater.

The Interpretation of a Redox Potential Measurement

As mentioned above, the measurement of the redox potential of a solution is carried out with an "inert" electrode which can exchange electrons with components of the solution. Breck has rightly pointed out[8] that platinum cannot be considered as a truly inert electrode and has proposed the use of graphite. Although this may be an improvement, the only satisfactory solution is to show that a number of different types of electrode lead to the same result and to understand the processes occurring at each. It may be noted in passing that the use of an intermediate cell in Breck's work makes no contribution to solving this problem since the prerequisite for this method is that the graphite equilibrates with the seawater. There seems, therefore, no reason to avoid a direct measurement of the potential of the graphite with respect to the reference electrode.

In considering the potential taken up in seawater by a graphite, or rather inactive platinum electrode, some of the above proposals for reactions occurring in sea water may be incorporated in a rate-potential diagram (FIG. 1). This is equivalent to a corrosion diagram in which the full lines indicate the rate of reactions (7) and (8) estimated from data on a mercury electrode. The effect of concentration of hydrogen peroxide is indicated by the numbers close to each line. As mentioned above in the presence of these two reactions, the electrode would take up a potential close to the reversible potential of reaction (7). This mixed potential is indicated by the circular points at the appropriate intersections. However, as the hydrogen peroxide concentration decreases, the effect of processes removing H_2O_2 homogeneously must also be considered. The limits for such reactions are shown in the diagram by the triangular points which have been estimated for the Fe^{2+} catalyzed decomposition of H_2O_2 as being the probable maximum rate and the Cl^- catalyzed decomposition and representing the minimum rate. It is evident that homogeneous decomposition may become important as the H_2O_2 concentration decreases below 10^{-10} mol ℓ^{-1}. It may therefore be concluded that an electrode of this type probably responds essentially to the ratio of concentrations of O_2 and H_2O_2 and that these are in equilibrium with the rapid redox reactions in the seawater, provided no redox disturbance has occurred within a period of some days.

The above discussion of the redox electrode is essentially similar though simpler than the proposal of Gerischer and Gerischer[15] for the behaviour of platinum electrodes in solution

containing hydrogen peroxide. It should be noted that an
alternative explanation was given by Bockris and Oldfield[6]
who described this behaviour in terms of the equilibrium of
adsorbed hydroxyl radicals and hydroxyl ions in solution.
The potential they observed at pH 8 is indicated with an
arrow on the Figure. At the time this work was done,
techniques for examining surface radical concentration were
undeveloped and evidence was not available for a clear
distinction between these two viewpoints.   Further experimental work on this is desirable. It would also be useful
to study the effect of hydrogen peroxide additions to seawater on the potential of a redox electrode, as well as to
attempt to detect hydrogen peroxide in seawater and perhaps
to estimate its concentration.

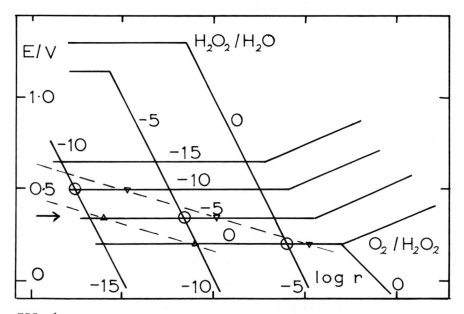

FIG. 1

References

1. Astanina, A.N. and Rudenko, A.P. 1971, Zhur.Fiz.Khim.
    45, 345.

2. Bagotskii, V.S. and Yablokova, I.E., 1953, Zhur.Fiz.Khim.
    27, 1663.

3. Baker, F.B. and Newton, T.W., 1956/7, J.Physical Chem.,
    60, 1417, 61, 38.

4. Bianchi, G. and Mussini, T. 1965, Electrochim.Acta
    10, 445.

5. Bockris, J.O'M. and Huq, A.K.M.S., 1956, Proc.Roy.Soc.,
    A 237, 277.

6. Bockris, J.O'M. and Oldfield, L.F., 1955, Trans.Faraday Soc.,
    51, 249.

7. Breck, W.G., 1974, In The Sea Vol.5 Marine Chemistry,
    ed. E.D. Goldberg, pp.153-179.

8. Breck, W.G., 1972, J.Marine Res. 30, 121.

9. Chevalet, J., Rouille, F., Gierst, L. and Lambert, J.P.
    1972, J.Electroanal.Chem., 39, 201.

10. Czapski, G. and Dorfman, L.M., 1964, J.Physical Chem.,
    68, 1169.

11. Czapski, G., 1967, J.Physical Chem., 71, 1683.

12. Damjanovic, A., 1969, In Modern Aspects of Electrochemistry
    Vol.5, ed. J.O'M. Bockris and B.E. Conway, Plenum,
    New York, Chap.5.

13. Fallab, S., 1967, Angew.Chem.Internat.Ed., 6, 496.

14. George, P. 1954, J.Chem.Soc., 4349.

15. Gerischer, R. and Gerischer, H., 1956, Z.physikal Chem.,
    N.F. 6, 178.

16. Goto, K., Tamura, H. and Nagayama, M., 1970,
      Inorg.Chem., $\underline{9}$, 963.

17. Haber, F. and Weiss, J., 1934, Proc.Roy.Soc., A
      $\underline{147}$, 332.

18. Halpern, J. and Smith, J.G., 1956, Can.J.Chem., $\underline{34}$, 1419.

19. Hoare, J.P., 1968, The Electrochemistry of Oxygen,
      Wiley-Interscience, New York.

20. Horne, R.A., 1969, Marine Chemistry, Wiley Interscience,
      New York, Chapter 5.

21. Idem., ibid, Chapter 8.

22. Hush, N.S., 1958, J.Chem.Physics, $\underline{28}$, 962.

23. Iofa, Z.A., Shimshelovich, Ya.B. and Andreeva, E.P. 1949,
      Zhur.Fiz.Khim., $\underline{23}$, 828.

24. Ives, D.J.G. and Janz, G.J., 1961, Reference Electrodes,
      Academic Press, New York, Chapter 11.

25. Kolthoff, I.M. and Lingane, J.J., 1941, Polarography,
      Interscience, New York. Chapter 22.

26. Kuhn, A.T. and Wright, P.M., 1973, J.Electroanal.Chem.,
      $\underline{41}$, 329.

27. Kuta, J. and Koryta, J., 1965, Coll.Czech.Chem.Comm.,
      $\underline{30}$, 4095.

28. Latimer, W.L., 1952, Oxidation Potentials, 2nd Edn.
      Prentice-Hall Inc., New York. Chapter 4.

29. Livingston, R.S. and Bray, W.C., 1925, J.Amer.Chem.Soc.,
      $\underline{47}$, 2069.

30. Marcus, R.A., 1959, Can.J.Chem., $\underline{37}$, 155.

31. McAuley, A., 1971/2 Specialist Periodical Reports, Inorganic
      Reaction Mechanisms, $\underline{1}$, 88, $\underline{2}$, 90.

32. Randles, J.E.B. and Somerton, K.W., 1952, Trans.Faraday
         Soc., 48, 937.

33. Sillén, L.G., 1965, Arkiv.Kemi, 24, 431, 25, 159.

34. Swinehart, J.H., 1965, Inorg.Chem., 4, 1069.

35. Turney, T.A., 1965, Oxidation Mechanisms, Butterworths,
         London.

36. Vetter, K.J. and Manecke, G., 1950, Z.physikal Chem.,
         195, 270.

37. Wells, C.F. and Salam, M.A., 1967, Trans.Faraday Soc.,
         63, 620.

Ion Exchange Reactions Involving Crystalline Aluminosilicate Zeolites

Howard S. Sherry
Mobil Research and Development Corporation,
Billingsport Road, Paulsboro, New Jersey 08066 USA

Abstract: Zeolites vary greatly in their porosity. This variation results in a wide range of ionic mobility. Some zeolite crystals consist of a region with very open structure and one with a dense structure. Siting of exchange cations in both regions can lead to partial ion exchange, slow exchange reactions, and to hysteresis. The last is sometimes caused by exsolution of a new solid phase that is rich in the entering exchange cation.

Zeolites exhibit ion exchange selectivity that correlates well with structural properties and chemical composition. Dense, aluminous ones prefer alkali metal cations in the order Na > Li > K > Rb > Cs and alkaline earth cations to alkali metal cations. Open, siliceous zeolites prefer alkali-metal cations in the order Cs > Rb > K > Na > Li and prefer some alkali metal cations to alkaline earth cation. Siting of cations in large and small cages in the same crystal structure cause selectivity reversals because the different types of cation sites conform to different selectivity rules.

Introduction

An understanding of ion exchange equilibria between seawater and mineral exchangers present in bottom sediments is an important part of marine geochemistry. The mineral exchangers upon which we will focus our attention are crystalline alumino-silicate zeolites. In a marine environment the most important feature of these zeolites is their ability to undergo ion exchange. In many ways these materials are model ion exchangers because the exchangeable cations are usually located in crystallographically distinct positions, and the use of x-ray crystallography often allows us to describe the ion exchange site in great detail. This information can be used to obtain a very fundamental insight into the ion exchange process.

Zeolite Framework Structure

A zeolite has been defined by Smith [46] as a "crystalline aluminosilicate with a tetrahedral framework structure enclosing cavities occupied by cations and water molecules, both of which have enough freedom of movement to permit cation exchange and reversible dehydration." The term zeolite was originally used to describe just such a material. Later, however, the term was broadened to include all ion exchangers - naturally occurring and synthetic inorganic materials as well as organic ones. Because of the widespread use of crystalline aluminosilicate zeolites in industry today [16] the name zeolite is now fairly well restricted to materials that fit the definition given above by Smith. The name zeolite will be used here in the narrow sense. There are other natural and synthetic crystalline aluminosilicates that are three dimensional framework structures with ion exchange properties that contain salt molecules or other molecules irreversibly occluded in the interstices of the framework structure. These materials are called felspathoids. In some cases the same framework structure can be synthesized without occluding molecules and is therefore truly a zeolite [3]. Because the felspathoids are so closely related to zeolites the ion exchange properties of one of them will be described later. Zeolites can be thought of as crystalline, crosslinked, polymeric macromolecules having repeating units given by the formula

$$M_{1/x} \, AlO_2 \, (SiO_2)_y \cdot n \, H_2O$$

where x is the valence of the metal ion M^{x+} and y ranges from
1 to 5 for natural and most synthetic zeolites. The framework
structure is composed of chains of $Si(O/2)_4$ and $Al(O/2)_4^-$
tetrahedra in which O/2 represents shared oxygen atoms [21].
Because the formal charge of oxygen is -2, and of aluminum is
+3, each $Al(O/2)_4^-$ tetrahedra bears one unit of excess negative
charge that is neutralized by other metal cations. These metal
cations, which neutralize the excess anionic charge on the
aluminosilicate framework, are usually alkali metal and
alkaline earth metal cations and at least some of them must be
able to undergo reversible ion exchange if the material is to
be classed as a zeolite. Water molecules fill the remaining
volume in the interstices of the zeolite.

The seven structural classes of zeolites [28] can be ordered
according to the openness of their frameworks as measured by
their water sorption [3].

Analcite group	0.18 $(cm^3$ per $cm^3)$	
Natrolite group	0.21 to	0.33
Mordenite group	0.27 to	0.33
Heulandite group	0.33 to	0.37
Phillipsite group	0.34 to	0.49
Chabazite group	0.36 to	0.46
Faujasite group	0.46 to	0.54

Stereoscopic drawings of 27 well established framework structures have been published by Meier and Olson [29].

The structures of many zeolites can be built by simple arrangements of polyhedra in a three-dimensional array. Each polyhedra
is built up out of $Si(O/2)_4$ and $Al(O/2)_4$ groups. Zeolite
framework structures can also be classified according to the
kinds of polyhedra that make up the structure. Rather than
review the many types of polyhedra and rings that are the
building blocks of zeolite structures the reader is referred

to other reviews on zeolites [3, 15, 16, 42]. This discussion
will select certain zeolites that are sufficiently well
characterized to permit interpretation of their ion exchange
properties in terms of structure. Generalizations will proceed
from these examples. In order to relate ion exchange to
zeolite structure it is not only necessary to know the positions
of all the framework atoms, but also the positions of the cations
and water molecules.

Three zeolites which range from the most dense to the most
open, can be built by stacking the cubooctahedral building
units called sodalite cages shown in Figure 1. They are
sodalite (really a felspathoid, however the synthetic zeolite
sodalite hydrate can be made), the synthetic zeolite A and the
natural zeolite faujasite. Siliceous synthetic varieties of
faujasite are called zeolite Y and aluminous synthetic varieties
are called zeolite X. The structures of these zeolites are
shown in Figures 1, 2 and 3. In these skeletal representations
the center of an Al or Si atom is at each apex, and the
centers of oxygen atoms are near the midpoints of the lines
connecting apices.

Sodalite is a cubic array of sodalite cages [27, 35] that are
linked together by sharing rings of four tetrahedra. The
interstice formed by this cubic array is another sodalite
cage. Cations are perforce located in the sodalite cages.
This framework structure has a diffusion path for exchanging
cations that is restricted by rings of six tetrahedra that
have a free diameter of 2.6Å. This structure is extremely
dense and sorbs no water. The unit cell composition is:

$$Na_6 \left[(AlO_2)_6 (SiO_2)_6 \right] 2NaCl$$

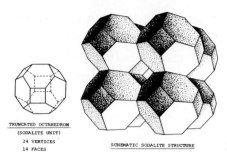

TRUNCATED OCTAHEDRON
(SODALITE UNIT)
24 VERTICES
14 FACES

SCHEMATIC SODALITE STRUCTURE

FIG. 1 - The sodalite unit and the sodalite structure.

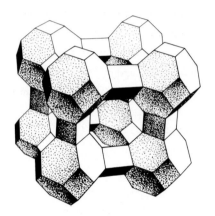

FIG. 2 - The zeolite A structure.

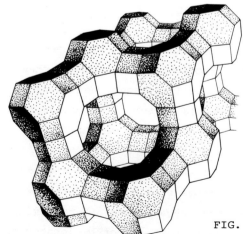

FIG. 3 - The faujasite structure.

The zeolite A framework is also cubic with sodalite cages at
each corner of the cube [17, 37]. The cages are linked by
sharing rings of four oxygen atoms, thus forming square
prisms between adjacent sodalite cages. The volume enclosed
by the cubic array of sodalite cages in zeolite A is a much
larger cage, sometimes called a supercage. These large cages
are interconnected by sharing rings of eight tetrahedra
having a free diameter of 4 Å to form a three-dimensional
diffusion path for ions (FIG. 2). An alternate way to form
the zeolite A framework is to stack the supercages in a cubic
array by sharing rings of eight tetrahedra. The voids in this
array are then sodalite cages. In the A type structure the
diffusion path for ions from the large cage into the sodalite
cage is through a ring of six tetrahedra having about the same
free diameter of 2.6 Å as do the rings in sodalite. The unit
cell contents of NaA, the sodium form of zeolite A (this
zeolite is synthesized in the Na form), is:

$$Na_{96} \left[(AlO_2)_{96} (SiO_2)_{96} \right] \cdot 216 \ H_2O$$

This structure is much more open than sodalite, containing over
two water molecules per cation, and has a water sorption of
0.30 grams per gram of bone dry zeolite.

The Na^+ ions in NaA are all in the large cages [17]. Two-
thirds of them are sited in the rings of six tetrahedra that
separate the supercages from the sodalite cages, one in each
ring, and slightly displaced from the center of the rings into
the supercages. The other 1/3 of the cations cannot be
located by x-ray diffraction and are presumed to be "dissolved"
in the occluded water in the large cavities. The counterions
that are near the center of the rings of six tetrahedra are
partially coordinated to framework oxygen atoms and partially
to water molecules. The counterions that cannot be located are
probably completely coordinated to water molecules.

In the faujasite structure sodalite cages are linked together
via six bridging oxygen atoms to form a tetrahedral array --
each sodalite cage linked to four others, just as each carbon
atom is linked to four others in the diamond structure [17, 36]
(FIG. 3). The resulting face centered cubic structure is very
open. The interstices of the tetrahedral array of sodalite
cages are very large cages, or supercages, having a free
diameter of about 11.8Å. These supercages form an independent
three-dimensional network. The three-dimensional diffusion
path for ions through this network of very large cages is
restricted by the ring of twelve tetrahedra that forms the 7.4Å
window between them. The sodalite cages and the hexagonal
prisms, formed where they link together, make an independent
three-dimensional network. A diffusion path through this network
is created via double rings of six tetrahedra. Alternatively,
cations can diffuse between sodalite cages and supercages through
the rings of six tetrahedra that are the windows between them.

The unit cell contents of a typical synthetic near faujasite,
NaX, is:

$$Na_{85} [(AlO_2)_{85} (SiO_2)_{107}] \cdot 256\ H_2O$$

There are about three water molecules per cation and the water
adsorption is 0.35 grams per gram of bone dry zeolite -- the
highest value for any known zeolite. The unit cell contents of
a typical NaY, a more siliceous variety of synthetic faujasite, is

$$Na_{50} [(AlO_2)_{50} (SiO_2)_{142}] \cdot 256\ H_2O$$

The water sorption is about the same as that for NaX.

In an x-ray structure analysis of a single crystal of NaX,
Olson [31] found that in a unit cell nine Na^+ ions occupy a
site in the hexagonal prisms called S_I and eight occupy a site

just outside of the hexagonal prisms in the sodalite cage at a
site called $S_I{'}$. Thus, he found seventeen cations per unit
cell in the network of sodalite cages and hexagonal prisms.
The remaining cations are in the network of supercages -- 24
of them near the center of the windows between the supercages
and sodalite cages displaced slightly into the supercages in a
site called S_{II} and 44 of them unlocatable by x-ray diffraction
techniques. These latter cations are presumed to be mobile,
highly hydrated ions. Another x-ray study using powder
diffraction techniques [30] showed that in a series of
hydrated synthetic potassium near faujasites varying in
potassium and aluminum content from 48.2 to 86.5 per unit cell,
the number of potassium ions per unit cell in the network of
hexagonal prisms and sodalite cages varied from 14 to 16.

Analysis of Ion Exchange Data

In this section the usual method for expressing and analyzing
ion exchange data is briefly reviewed.

The replacement of ion B^{b+} initially present in an exchanger by
ion A^{a+} is expressed by the following chemical reaction and
equations:

$$bA_S^{a+} + aB_Z^{b+} \rightleftharpoons bA_Z^{a+} + aB_S^{b+}$$

$$K = \frac{f_A^b \, Z_A^b \, \gamma_B^a \, M_A^b}{f_B^a \, Z_B^a \, \gamma_A^b \, M_A^b} = {}_N K_B^A \, \frac{f_A^b \, \gamma_B^a}{f_B^a \, \gamma_A^b} \tag{1}$$

where a and b are the ionic charges of ions A^{a+} and B^{b+}, f_A
and f_B are the rational single ion activity coefficients in
the zeolite phase, γ_A and γ_B the molal single ion activity
coefficients in the solution phase, Z_A and Z_B the equivalent

fraction in the zeolite phase, M_A and M_B the molalities of
ions A and B in the solution phase, K the thermodynamic
equilibrium constant for the ion-exchange reaction, S and Z
the subscripts which identify the solution and zeolite phases,
and $^N K_B^A$ the rational selectivity coefficient or concentration
quotient. The corrected rational selectivity coefficient, K_C
is defined as

$$K_C = {}^N K_B^A \frac{a_B^a}{b_A^b} = K \frac{f_B^a}{f_A^b} \tag{2}$$

$$K_C = {}^N K_B^A \frac{\left[\dfrac{\gamma_{\pm\ BY}^{b+1}}{b} \right]^a}{\left[\dfrac{\gamma_{\pm\ AY}^{a+1}}{a} \right]^b} \tag{3}$$

In equation 3 mean molal activity coefficients have been
substituted for single ion activity coefficients because the
exchanging ions are derived from salts having a common anion.

Ion exchange data are normally graphically presented in the
form of isotherms. The ordinate of these graphs, Z_A, is the
equivalent fraction of the ion A^{a+} in the zeolite phase,
defined as

$$Z_A = \frac{\text{milliequivalents } A^{a+}/\text{gram zeolite}}{\text{milliequivalents } (A^{a+} + B^{b+})/\text{gram zeolite}}$$

and the abscissa, S_A, is the equivalent fraction of the ion, A^{a+},
in the solution phase, defined as

$$S_A = \frac{\text{normality of } A^{a+}}{\text{total normality}}$$

The exchange reaction by nature takes place at constant normality,
though if the exchanging ions have different charges, not at
constant ionic strength.

It is convenient for zeolite ion exchange to use the thermodynamic analysis of Gaines and Thomas [23] to calculate
equilibrium constants and therefore free energies of complete
ion exchange.

$$\log K = -\frac{a-b}{2.303} + \int_0^1 \log K_C \, dZ_A \qquad (4)$$

This working equation neglects salt imbibement by the zeolite
and changes in water activity -- in effect, it is assumed the
reaction takes place at about 0.1 total normality or lower.
Evaluation of Equation 4 simply requires graphical integration
of a plot of $\log K_C$ versus Z_A. The corrected selectivity
coefficient K_C can be evaluated from the experimental data and
literature values for the mean molal activity coefficients in
solution.

If not all of the B ions are exchangeable, the variable Z_A in
equations 1-4 is replaced by

$$Z_A' = \frac{Z_A}{Z_A^{Max}}$$

where Z_A^{Max} is the total fractional loading of the zeolite with
A ions. The curve of Z_A' vs S_A terminates at the point (1,1);
thus the isotherm is normalized and the free energy is
calculated for the complete replacement of all of the
exchangeable B ions by A ions.

Cation Mobility and Irreversible Ion Exchange Phenomena

In dense zeolites the water molecules and exchangeable cations
interact strongly with the framework oxygen atoms and are sited
in positions that can be located by x-ray diffraction techniques.
In the more open zeolites, which have a high water content, the

cations and water molecules in the large cavities or cages resemble a concentrated electrolyte solution. In support of this picture is the variation in self-diffusion coefficients of water and exchangeable cations with pore size shown in Tables 1 and 2. The self-diffusion coefficients vary over many orders of magnitude depending on the porosity of the framework structure. It will be seen later that ion exchange equilibria also depend on the porosity or water content of the structure. Moreover, in complex crystal structures that have both large and small cavities, with cations located in both kinds, different ionic mobilities as well as different kinds of equilibria are observed.

TABLE 1 - Water Mobility in Zeolites

Zeolite	Pore Dimensions [16] (Å)	Self-Diffusion Coefficient (cm^2/sec)	Temperature (°C)	Ref.
Na-Analcite	2.3-2.4	1.97×10^{-13}	46	9
		1.46×10^{-12}	75	9
Ca-Heulandite	2.4-6.1	2.07×10^{-8}	45	8
Ca-Chabazite	3.7-4.2	1.26×10^{-7}	45	8
NaX	10	2.11×10^{-5}	40	34
CaX	8	2.41×10^{-5}	40	34
Liquid Water		3.87×10^{-5}	45	34

TABLE 2 - Cation Mobility in Zeolites

Zeolite	Dimensions [16] (Å)	Self-Diffusion Coefficient (cm^2/sec)	Temperature (°C)	Ref.
Na-Analcite	2.3-2.4	10^{-13}	25	11
Cs-Analcite	2.3-2.4	10^{-24}	25	11
Na-Chabazite	3.7-4.2	6.2×10^{-12}	25	4
Cs-Chabazite	3.7-4.2	4.9×10^{-13}	25	4
Ca-Chabazite	3.7-4.2	4.2×10^{-16}	25	4
Ba-Chabazite	3.7-4.2	1.3×10^{-13}	25	4
NaA	4.0	7.3×10^{-8}	25.8	18
NaX	10	7×10^{-8}	26.1	18
NaCl in H$_2$O		1.61×10^{-5} (Infinite Dilution)	25	

Because some zeolites have very dense structures, or some parts
of the structure are dense, there are systems in which the
exchange reaction cannot be completed within a reasonable time
in the temperature range of interest. Thus, when exchanging
ion A for the ion B initially present in the zeolite, it is not
always possible to produce the homoionic A form of the exchanger.
Three limiting situations leading to partial exchange can be
envisaged:

Case 1. The low temperature ion exchange reaction may appear
to reach a pseudo equilibrium on the time scale employed.
However, a very large increase in reaction time shows the
level of ion exchange to be drifting towards completion and
time dependent hysteresis appears between the path of forward
and reverse reactions. No thermodynamic treatment is
justifiable.

Case 2. The reaction equilibrium is independent of the time
scale at low temperature, but the exchange cannot be made to go
to completion. The maximum exchange level that is attained is,
however, independent of temperature.

Case 3. As in Case 2 the low temperature ion exchange
reaction is independent of the time scale and reversible, and
exchange cannot go to completion. However, the maximum degree
of exchange changes with the temperature.

One example of Case 1 is the Ca-Na-X system [12, 41] shown in
Figure 4. The solid line in this figure represents data
obtained by equilibrating NaY zeolite and aqueous $CaCl_2$
solution for 24 hours. The data points represented by circles
were obtained by equilibrating phases for three to seven days.

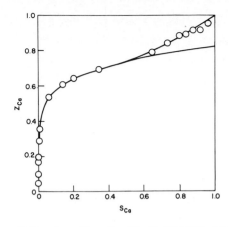

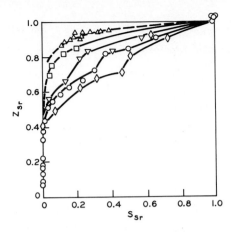

FIG. 4 - The Ca-Na-X system at 25°C and 0.1 total normality.

FIG. 5 - Hysteresis in the Sr-Na-X system at 25°C and 0.1 total normality.

The one day isotherm terminates at a point corresponding to about 82% exchange. Thus 18% of the 85 Na$^+$ ions, or 16, per unit cell are involved in a slow ion exchange process. Another example of a Case 1 is the Sr-Na-X system [32] for which time dependent hysteresis loops were obtained at 25°C (FIG. 5). In the composition region of the hysteresis loops the zeolite separates into two solid phases -- one strontium rich with an expanded lattice, and one strontium poorer with a contracted lattice.

There are many examples of Case 2. For instance ion exchange of NaY by Cs$^+$ and Rb$^+$ ions is not complete at 25°C [6, 39] and is probably incomplete at much higher temperatures. The reversible isotherm for the Rb-Na-Y system is shown in Figure 6. This isotherm, as well as the one for the Cs-Na-Y system, shows that 32% of the Na$^+$ ions, or 16 per unit cell, cannot be replaced. Again we see a slow, in this case infinitely slow, step involving 16 cations per unit cell

in the faujasite type of structure. The maximum Cs^+ and Rb^+
ion exchange that can be achieved in NaX is 68% [12, 39, 44].
The isotherm at 25°C for the Cs-NA-X system, shown in Figure 7,
is similar to the Rb-Na-X isotherm. Thus it appears that 32
of the 85 cations per unit cell of NaX cannot be replaced by
large univalent cations. Incomplete replacement has also been
obtained in the Cs- and Rb-Na-A systems [13]. Other examples
of Case 2 are Ca^{2+}, Sr^{2+} and Ba^{2+} ion exchange of NaY [6, 41]
at 5 to 50°C (see for example the Ba-Na-Y system at 25°C in
Figure 8). In Figure 9 we see the isotherms for the
La-Na-X and -Y systems at 25°C and 82.2°C. At 25°C, or
lower, the isotherms are reversible and terminate at points
corresponding to the inability of La^{3+} to replace 16 Na^+
per unit cell. They are examples of Case 2. At 82°C the
isotherms are not reversible and revert to instances of the
first kind. It is understood that all Case 2 types might revert
to Case 1 types if infinite reaction time were allowed.

It is interesting to note that most of the examples of slow
or incomplete ion exchange in zeolites X and Y involve about
16 cations per unit cell and that all of the x-ray investigations of zeolites X and Y place about 14 to 17 cations per
unit cell in the network of small cavities [30, 31]. It is
likely that the correct number is 16.

The exchange systems discussed above illustrate that in a
zeolite that has cations in both dense and open regions of the
structure both slow and fast ion exchange reactions occur. In
the case of faujasite and its synthetic analogues the slow
reaction is not caused by the inability of Na^+ to diffuse out
of the small cages, but rather by the inability of large
univalent ions or strongly hydrated polyvalent ones to

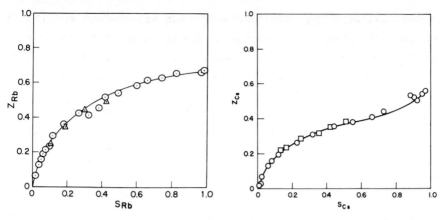

FIG. 6 - The Rb-Na-Y system at
25°C and 0.1 total normality.

FIG. 7 - The Ca-Na-X system at
25°C and 0.1 total normality.

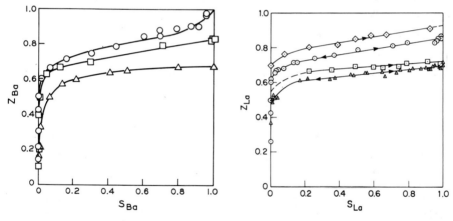

FIG. 8 - -O—O- Ba-Na-X system
at 50°C; -□—□- Ba-Na-X system
at 25°C; -△—△- Ba-Na-Y system
at 25°C;
all at 0.1 total normality

FIG. 9 - -◇—◇-La-Na-X system
at 82°C; -O—O-La-Na-X system
at 25°C; -□—□-La-Na-Y system
at 82°C; -△—△-La-Na-Y system
at 25°C;
all at 0.3 total normality

diffuse into the small cages. This conclusion is reached
because all of the Na^+ ions in Na and NaY can be completely
replaced by Ag^+ and K^+ ions [6, 12, 39].

In view of the above information on slow and rapid ion
exchange steps a model of ion exchange of zeolite X and Y has
been formulated [42]. In this model ingoing ions exchange
rapidly with the ions in the large cages and then slowly with
the ions in the small cages through the windows between the
large and small cages. It is clear that Rb^+ and Cs^+ ions,
with Pauling diameters of 2.96 Å and 3.38 Å [36], should
not diffuse through these 2.6 Å windows between the two kinds
of cages. It is not so evident that Ca^{2+}, Ba^{2+} and La^{3+}
ions, with Pauling diameters of 1.98, 2.70 and 2.30 Å should
do so with difficulty. It is postulated that these small,
highly charged, cations with high heats of hydration [38] are
coordinated strongly to water molecules in the large cavities.
The hydrated cation must then be "stripped" of its water in
order to diffuse from the large cage into a small sodalite cage.

The apparent exceptions to the rule that 16 Na^+ per unit cell
of synthetic faujasites exchange more slowly are Rb^+ and Cs^+
exchange in for Na^+ in zeolite X. In these cases it is
probable that the replacement of some of the Na^+ ions in the
supercages by much bulkier ions crowds the remaining ones
into the network of hexagonal prisms and sodalite cages.
This redistribution of ions resulting from partial ion
exchange has been demonstrated by x-ray studies of cation
positions in Sr-Na-X as a function of Sr^{2+} loading [32].

These results for exchange of large alkali metal ions in
synthetic faujasites are consistent with much earlier work on
sodalite itself by Barrer and Falconer [7]. They showed that
at 85 °C complete exchange could be achieved with Li and Ag^+
ions but not with K^+, Rb^+ and Cs^+ ions.

A more quantitative treatment of the fast and slow ion
exchange reactions in synthetic faujasite has been made by

Hoinkis and Levi [26] in a kinetic study of the Ba-Na-X
system. They found a fast reaction and a very slow one
involving 16 Na^+ ions per unit cell. The slow reaction took
340 hours at 50°C. This result agrees well with the finding
that at 25°C the equilibrium isotherm for the Ba-Na-X system
terminates with 16 Na^+ ions remaining in a unit cell whereas
at 50° with two weeks equilibration time the isotherm
terminates at 100% exchange (FIG. 8). In a kinetic study of Na^+
isotopic exchange in Na-X Brown and Sherry [18] found a slow
step involving 16 Na^+ per unit cell. However, in this case
the slow step only took minutes whereas the fast step took
seconds.

In other important zeolites, such as zeolite T [43], offretite
[1], and zeolite L [14], only a fraction of the total cations
participate in ion exchange reactions at low temperatures because
the remainder are tightly trapped in certain small cavities. No
doubt at sufficiently high temperatures these trapped ions would
also begin to participate and Case 2 would become Case 1. Finally
at still higher temperatures complete exchange might become
possible. Even in such dense frameworks as the felspars, Na^+ and
K^+ can completely exchange at very high temperatures [33].

Other examples of Case 2, which will not be discussed in detail
here, are encountered when large organic cations are exchanged
into zeolites. When the ions are exchanged into NaX and NaY,
complete exchange of all of the Na^+ in the supercages does not
occur because of the large volume occupied by these organic
cations. It has been found [48] that the degree of exchange
varies uniformly with the volume of the organic cation.

Very few examples of Case 3 have been reported. In these
instances tests of isotherm reversibility should be made to
determine if they are really examples of Case 3, or Cases 1 and
2. One apparent example of Case 3 is the study in La^{3+} ion

exchange of NaX and NaY [40] in which the apparent maximum
La^{3+} loading increased with temperature. However, the high
temperature isotherms were not reversible. The low
temperature isotherms are examples of Case 2 and the high
temperature isotherms are examples of Case 1.

It is not inconceivable that the maximum degree of exchange is
temperature dependent in some systems. The migration of B ion
into sites inaccessible to the A ion as a result of A ion
exchange could be temperature dependent.

The dimensions of the rings, channels and cavities in zeolites
are so close to ionic dimensions that changes in the dimensions
of the unit cell almost always occur. Sometimes these changes
result in a new symmetry of the unit cell [5, 47]. Sometimes
the dimensions of the new, or A, form of the crystal are
sufficiently greater than the old, or B, form that limited
miscibility of the end members is observed. The resulting
solubility gap leads to hysteresis loops in the ion exchange
isotherms. This kind of hysteresis was briefly mentioned above
in discussing the Sr-Na-X system and is discussed in great
detail in reference [32]. In Figure 10 the unit cell
dimension for the cubic unit cell of zeolite X is plotted as
a function of Sr^{2+} loading. The edge of the unit cell
decreases linearly with decreasing Sr^{2+} loading up to about
71% loading. At this point the lattice begins to expand and
the expansion is so great with further Sr^{2+} loading that a
new phase that is 87% Sr^{2+} exchanged separates out of the solid.
It is the slow exsolution of the Sr-richer phase that is
responsible for ion exchange hysteresis. Equilibrium takes
about two weeks to be reached and an equilibrium isotherm
can be obtained (FIG. 11).

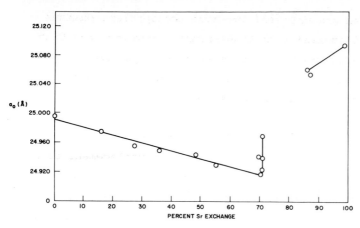

FIG. 10 - Sr-Na-X system. Size of cubic unit cell as a function of ionic content.

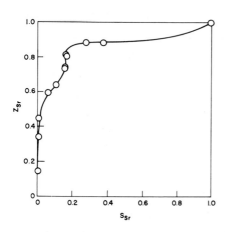

FIG. 11 - Sr-Na-X system at 25°C and 0.1 total normality.

Much earlier, Barrer and coworkers [7, 9] studied ion exchange of analcite and found similar hysteresis effects due to limited miscibility of end members of exchange series. They also attributed hysteresis to slow exsolution of the new solid phase.

Ion Exchange Equilibria

There are broad generalizations that can be made about the equilibrium ion specificity of zeolites and they can be

rationalized using electrostatic arguments. The value of
these generalizations is that they permit qualitative
prediction of equilibrium ion specificity. In the discussion
that follows the difference in the free energy of the
homoionic A and B forms of the exchanger is used as the
measure of ion selectivity or specificity. This free energy
is calculated using the method of Gaines & Thomas [23]
discussed earlier. In cases of incomplete replacement of ion
B by ion A complete exchange means complete replacement of the
exchangeable B ions and the exchange data is normalized as
described earlier. The discussion will be further complicated
by the fact that, during the conversion of the B form of the
exchanger to the A form, selectivity reversals occur in some
systems. Still, the selectivity that will be considered is
based on the free energy change of the system when all of the
exchangeable ions are replaced.

It is instructive to use the approach of Eisenman [20] to
analyze the energetics of ion exchange. Let us consider the
univalent ion exchange reaction

$$A_S^+ + B_Z^+ \rightleftharpoons A_Z^+ + B_S^+ .$$

If we assume the cations interact directly with the anionic
sites in the zeolite to form ion pairs with no interaction
with water molecules and that the entropy of the ions in the
zeolite is negligible, the free energy of ion exchange can be
written as

$$\Delta F_{AB}^{\circ} = \left(\bar{F}_A^{el} - \bar{F}_B^{el} \right) - \left(\bar{F}_A^{hyd} - \bar{F}_B^{hyd} \right) \qquad (5)$$

where $\bar{F}_A^{hyd} - \bar{F}_B^{hyd}$ is the difference between the partial
molar free energy of the ions A^+ and B^+ in aqueous solution
and $\bar{F}_A^{el} - \bar{F}_B^{el}$ is the difference between electrostatic
contribution to the partial molar free energies of ions A^+

and B^+ in the zeolite. In order to estimate the relative
ion specificity of the zeolite it is necessary to evaluate
the electrostatic free energy term $\bar{F}_A^{el} - \bar{F}_B^{el}$ and to use
literature values for free energies of hydration in a
standard salt solution. Eisenman used Coulomb's law to
estimate the electrostatic free energy of ion A in the
exchanger:

$$\bar{F}^{el} = -332/(r_+ + r_-) \qquad (6)$$

The Born-Lande equation for the internal energy of alkali-
metal halide crystals was used for closely spaced sites:

$$\bar{F}^{el} = -1.56\,(332)/(r_+ + r_-) \qquad (7)$$

where $\bar{F}$ is in calories per mole, r_+ is the radius of cation
in angstroms, and r_- is the radius of the anion in angstroms.
The radius of the anion is chosen so that it makes the field
strength of the hypothetical monopolar anion equal to that of
the actual multipole.

The important concept of this greatly over simplified
analysis is that the electrostatic energy term in Equation 5
will depend on the electric field strength in the zeolite
which is assumed to be concentrated in a monopolar anion of
radius r_-. Eisenman varied the field strength of the
exchanger by varying the r_- and showed that at high field
strengths alkali metal cations were selected from salt
solution according to their ionic radii -- the smallest being
most preferred and the largest being least preferred. At low
field strengths the ion with the smallest hydration energy is
most preferred and the ion with the highest is least preferred.
In passing from the one extreme to the other, intermediate
selectivity sequences were predicted. A total of eleven
selectivity series for the five alkali metal cations Li-Cs
were predicted by this approach. These series are shown in
Table 3.

TABLE 3 - Selectivity Series Predicted for Closely Spaced
Sites by Varying Anionic Field Strength.

I.	Cs > Rb > K > Na > Li
II.	Cs > K > Rb > Na > Li
III.	K > Cs > Rb > Na > Li
IV.	K > Cs > Na > Rb > Li
V.	K > Na > Cs > Rb > Li
VI.	K > Na > Rb > Cs > Li
VII.	Na > K > Rb > Cs > Li
VIII.	Na > K > Rb > Li > Cs
IX.	Na > K > Li > Rb > Cs
X.	Na > Li > K > Rb > Cs
XI.	Li > Na > K > Rb > Cs

Some selectivity sequences exhibited by zeolites are shown in
Table 4.

TABLE 4 - Selectivity Patterns Exhibited by Zeolites[a].

I.	Chabazite, mordenite, Norton Zeolon, erionite, phillipsite, clinoptilolite, Linde Y, ZK-4
II.	Mordenite, Norton Zeolon, erionite phillipsite, clinoptilolite, ZK-4
III.	Erionite
IV.	
V.	
VI.	
VII.	Linde 13-X
VIII.	Linde 4-A
IX.	Ultramarine, analcite, NaPt
X.	Basic sodalite, ultramarine
XI.	

[a]In some cases insufficient data are available to differentiate between series I and II or among series I, II,
and III.

Thus, we see that very dense aluminous zeolites or felspathoids,
with high ion exchange capacities, exhibit the selectivity
sequence X predicted for exchangers with high field strength,
and zeolites that are much less aluminous and have high water
sorption capacities and low ion exchange capacity exhibit the
sequence I predicted for exchangers with low field strength.
Comparison of Tables 3 and 4 leads to the conclusion that the
selectivity sequence exhibited by a zeolite depends on the
electric field strength, which in turn depends on its

aluminum content and water content. It is noteworthy that
zeolite NaA with an Si/Al atom ratio of 1 exhibits
selectivity pattern VIII while sodalite which also has a Si/Al
atom ratio of 1 exhibits the selectivity pattern X. NaA has a
much higher water content than sodalite and should have a
lower field strength. Zeolite NaY exhibits the weak field
sequence I and is isostructural with NaX but contains about 40%
fewer anionic sites.

Although we usually think of ion exchange selectivity in terms
of the ability of the exchanger to select ions from solution,
it is more correct to think about water specificity at low
field strengths and zeolite specificity at high field strength.
This conclusion is reached by inspecting Equation 5. When
the zeolite prefers the cations with the lowest hydration
energies, it is because the difference in the free energy of
the ions in the exchanger phase is negligible compared to the
difference in solution free energies. Thus the solution phase
does the selecting and it prefers the most strongly hydrated
cation.

A similar analysis was made for divalent cation exchange [42].
Again, assuming that the total contribution to the energy of an
ion in a zeolite is electrostatic and neglecting entropy terms
we can write that

$$\bar{F}^{el} = - \frac{664}{x} - \frac{664}{d-x} \tag{8}$$

where d is the distance between centers of the fixed anions and
x is the distance between centers of the spherical anion and
cation. The two terms on the right side of Equation 8
represent the energy of interaction between a divalent cation
of radius r_+ and two univalent anions of radius r_-. The
electrostatic force on the cation is zero when $x = \frac{1}{2}d$.
However, differentiating the expression for the energy a second
time indicates that when $x = \frac{1}{2}$, the potential energy is at a
maximum. The lowest potential energy of a system consisting of
a positively charged sphere in the field of two uninegatively

charged spheres is evident when the positively charged sphere is as close as possible to one of the two spheres. Thus Equation 8 becomes:

$$\bar{F}^{el} = -\frac{664}{r_+ + r_-} - \frac{664}{d-(r_+ + r_-)} \qquad (9)$$

For closely spaced sites where the intersite distance is equal to, or less than, $2(r_+ + r_-)$

$$\bar{F}^{el} = -1328/(r_+ + r_-) \qquad (10)$$

When the sites are infinitely far apart

$$\bar{F}^{el} = -664/(r_+ + r_-) \qquad (11)$$

In this analysis the electric field within the zeolite still depends on the aluminum content but an intersite distance must be introduced to properly describe the electrostatics. This approach to zeolite ion exchange predicts [41] only one alkaline earth selectivity series for zeolites:

$$Ba > Sr > Ca > Mg$$

and this is the one that is always observed. However, Equations 6 and 11 do predict that for very widely spaced sites Na^+ ions may be preferred to the larger Ba^{2+} and Sr^{2+} ions. This ion preference has been observed. The selectivity sequence for zeolite T [43] is

$$Ag > K > NH_4 > Ba \gg Na > Ca > Li$$

The sequence observed for chabazite [11] is:

$$TlI > K > Ag > Rb > NH_4 > Pb > Na = Ba > Sr > Ca > Li$$

Both these zeolites are more siliceous than zeolites A or X in which Ca^{2+}, Sr^{2+} and Ba^{2+} ions are preferred to all of the alkali metal cations.

This analysis of divalent ion exchange can be extended to trivalent ion exchange and to other ion exchangers. It should be generally true that ion exchangers with low ion exchange capacity will prefer Na^+ ions to polyvalent ions.

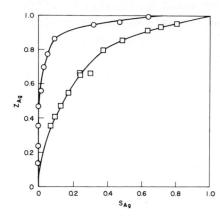

FIG. 12 - -O—O- Ag-Na-X system,
-□—□- Ag-Na-Y system. Both at
25°C and 0.1 total normality.

The influence of the strength of the electric field on ion
selectivity is very marked in the case of silver ion exchange
of zeolites X and Y [39]. In both cases complete exchange
occurs. Two features of silver exchange in these zeolites are
1) that Ag$^+$ ion is very strongly preferred to all the univalent
cations and 2) the selectivity is markedly decreased for
zeolite Y (FIG. 12). Silver does not fit into the alkali
metal ion selectivity series according to its size, which
would place it between sodium and potassium [36]. The
reason for the high Ag$^+$ ion selectivity is its high polarizability.

The generalization concerning ion specificity made above should
qualitatively predict the cation content of a zeolite if the
ion exchange capacity and internal pore volume is known.
However, in most zeolites there are at least two crystallographically distinct sets of cation sites and the electrostatic
field strength at these sites should differ. Indeed, for
zeolites like X and Y with cations in the dense network of
hexagonal prisms and sodalite cages and in the network of
supercages, one would expect to find different selectivity
patterns. The sigmoidal equilibrium isotherm for the Ca-Na-X
system shown in Figure 4 displays just what is expected.

Although there is no selectivity reversal in this system, the
Ca^{2+} selectivity does decrease very rapidly beyond about 60%
Ca^{2+} loading. Some authors have fitted such sigmoidal ion
exchange isotherms with equations requiring two constants
and arrived at values for the equilibrium constant for each of
two sets of sites [10, 24].

A more direct way to determine the equilibrium constants for
two sets of sites is to be able to determine one constant at
low temperature and the other at high temperature. This
approach was used for the Ba-Na-X system [41]. At 5 to 25°C
the equilibrium isotherm terminates at 82% Ba^{2+} loading
(FIG. 8). At 50°C the isotherm is sigmoidal, resembling very
much the Ca^{2+} isotherm, and complete loading of Ba^{2+} is
accomplished. Use of the van't Hoff equation to calculate the
equilibrium constant for large cage exchange at 50°C allows
calculation of the equilibrium constant for small cage
exchange at 50°C from the relationship

$$K_{\alpha\ \beta} = K_{\alpha}^{0.82} \cdot K_{\beta}^{0.18}$$

where α denotes large cages and β denotes small cages. The
values calculated are

$$K_{\alpha} = 72.5$$
$$K_{\beta} = 0.037$$

This approach cannot be completely correct because at 50°C
ions in the β and α sites can equilibrate.

In the case of zeolite A, with cations almost completely in the
large cages, sigmoidal isotherms are still obtained for alkaline
earth ion exchange of Na^+ [45]. The Sr-Na-A isotherm is
shown in Figure 13 as an illustration. The shape of the
alkaline earth-Na^+ isotherms may be accounted for by the
presence of two crystallographically distinct kinds of Na^+
ions in the large cages as discussed in the section on structure.

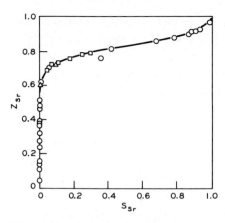

FIG. 13 - Sr-Na-A system at
25°C and 0.1 total normality.

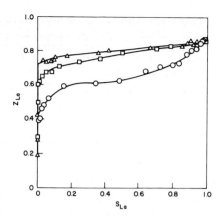

FIG. 14 - Change in La-Na-X
isotherms with total normality
at 25°C, $\triangle\!\!-\!\!\triangle$ 0.1 N_T;
$\square\!\!-\!\!\square$ 0.3 N_T; $\bigcirc\!\!-\!\!\bigcirc$ 3.85 N_T.

Electroselective Effect

When ions of different charge are exchanged against each other,
even in an ideal system, the separation factor is a function of
total normality [25]. Use of dilute salt solution favors
uptake of the ion with the higher charge and use of concentrated
salt solution favors uptake of the one with the lower charge.
See for example the effect of varying total normality on the
La-Na-X system in Figure 14. At constant equivalent fraction
of La^{3+} in solution the La^{3+} content of the zeolite falls
markedly as total normality increases.

References

(1)   Aiello, R., Barrer, R. M., Davies, J. A. and Kerr, I. S.
       1970. Molecular sieving in relation to cation type and
       position in unfaulted offretite. Trans. Far. Soc. 66:
       1610-1617.

(2)   Ames, L. L., Jr. 1965. Zeolite type X equilibria with
       trivalent cerium and yttrium cations. J. Inorg. Nucl.
       Chem. 27: 885-894.

(3)   Barrer, R. M. 1968. Some aspects of molecular sieve
       science and technology. Chemistry and Industry 7 Sept.:
       1203-1213.

(4)   Barrer, R. M., Bartholomew, R. F. and Rees, L. V. C.
      1963. Ion exchange in porous crystals. Part I. Self-
      and exchange diffusion of ions in chabazites. J. Phys.
      Chem. Solids 24: 51-62.

(5)   Barrer, R. M., Bultitude, F. W. and Kerr, I. S. 1959.
      Some properties of, and a structural scheme for, the
      harmotome zeolites. J. Chem. Soc. 1521-1528.

(6)   Barrer, R. M., Davies, J. A., and Rees, L. V. C. 1969.
      Thermochemistry and thermodynamics of cation exchange in
      zeolite Y. J. Inorg. Nucl. Chem. 30: 3333-3349.

(7)   Barrer, R. M. and Falconer, J. D. 1959. Ion exchange
      in felspathoids as a solid state reaction. Proc. Roy.
      Soc. A236: 227-249.

(8)   Barrer, R. M. and Fender, B. E. F. 1961. Diffusion and
      sorption of water in zeolites. II. Intrinsic and self-
      diffusion. J. Phys. Chem. Solids 21: 12-24.

(9)   Barrer, R. M. and Hinds, L. 1953. Ion exchange in
      crystals of analcite and leucite, J. Chem. Soc. 1879-
      1888.

(10) Barrer, R. M. and Meier, W. M. 1959. Exchange equilibria
      in a synthetic crystalline exchanger. Trans. Far. Soc.
      55: 130-141.

(11) Barrer, R. M. and Rees, L. V. C. 1960. Self-diffusion of
      metal cations in analcite. Trans. Far. Soc. 56: 709-721.

(12) Barrer, R. M., Rees, L. V. C., and Shamsuzzoha, M. 1966.
      Thermochemistry and thermodynamics of ion exchange in a
      near faujasite. J. Inorg. Nucl. Chem. 28: 629-643.

(13) Barrer, R. M., Rees, L. V. C., and Ward, D. J. 1963.
      Thermochemistry and thermodynamics of ion exchange in a
      crystalline exchange medium. Proc. Roy. Soc. (London)
      273A: 180-197.

(14) Barrer, R. M. and Villiger, H. 1969. The crystal
      structure of zeolite L. Z. für krist. 128: 352-370.

(15) Breck, D. W. 1964. Crystalline molecular sieves.
      J. Chem. Ed. 41: 678-689.

(16) Breck, D. W. 1974. Zeolite Molecular Sieves. New York:
      John Wiley and Sons.

(17) Broussard, L. and Shoemaker, D. P. 1960. The structure
      of synthetic molecular sieves. J. Am. Chem. Soc. 82:
      1041-1051.

(18) Brown, L. M. and Sherry, H. S. 1971. Mechanism and
      kinetics of isotope exchange in zeolites. II.
      Experimental data. J. Phys. Chem. 75: 3855-3863.

(19)   Dyer, A. and Molyneux, A. 1968. Mobility of water in
       zeolites-I. Self-diffusion of water in analcite.
       J. Inorg. and Nucl. Chem. <u>30</u>: 829-837.

(20)   Eisenman, G. 1962. Cation-selective glass electrodes
       and their mode of operation. Biophys. J. <u>2</u>: 259-323.

(21)   Eitel, W. 1954. Physical Chemistry of the Silicates.
       Chicago: University of Chicago Press.

(22)   Gabuda, S. 1962. Diffusion of water molecules in
       natrolite. Dokl. Akad. Nauk. <u>146</u>: 840-843.

(23)   Gaines, G. L. and Thomas, H. C. 1953. Adsorption
       studies on clay minerals. II. A formalism of the
       thermodynamics of ion exchange. J. Chem. Phys. <u>21</u>:
       714-718.

(24)   Gallei, E., Eisenbach, D. and Ahmed, A. 1974. Ion
       exchange of the transition metal ions Mn^{2+}, Co^{2+}, and Ni^{2+}
       in synthetic zeolites NaX and NaY. J. Cat. <u>33</u>: 62-67.

(25)   Helferrich, F. 1962. Ion Exchange. New York: McGraw-
       Hill Book Company.

(26)   Hoinkis, E. and Levi, H. W. 1970. Cation diffusion
       kinetics in synthetic zeolites of type X and A. In
       Ion Exchange in the Process Industries, papers read at
       the conference, pp 339-351. London: Society of the
       Chemical Industry.

(27)   Loens, J., Schulz, H. 1967. Strukturverfeinerung von
       sodalith. Acta. Cryst. <u>23</u>: 434-436.

(28)   Meier, W. M. 1968. Zeolite Structures. <u>In</u> Molecular
       Sieves, pp. 10-27. London: Society of the Chemical
       Industry.

(29)   Meier, W. M. and Olson, D. H. 1971. Zeolite Frameworks.
       Paper 14 <u>in</u> Molecular Sieve Zeolites. Advances in
       Chemistry Series, No. 101, ed., R. F. Gould, pp 155-170.
       Washington, D. C.: American Chemical Society.

(30)   Mortier, W. J. and Bosmens, H. J. 1971. Location of
       univalent cations in synthetic zeolites of the X and
       Y type with varying silicon to aluminum ratio. I.
       Hydrated potassium exchange forms. J. Phys. Chem.
       <u>75</u>: 3327-3334.

(31)   Olson, D. H. 1970. A reinvestigation of the crystal
       structure of the zeolite' hydrated NaX. J. Phys. Chem.
       <u>74</u>: 2758-2764.

(32)   Olson, D. H. and Sherry, H. S. 1968. An x-ray study of
       strontium-sodium ion exchange in Linde X. An example
       of a two phase system. J. Phys. Chem. <u>72</u>: 4095-4104.

(33) Orville, P. M. 1963. Alkali metal ion exchange between
      vapor and felspar phases. Am. J. Sci. 261: 201-237.

(34) Parravano, C., Baldeschwieler, J. P. and Boudart, M.
      1967. Diffusion of water in zeolites. Science 155:
      1535-1536.

(35) Pauling, L. 1930. Structure of sodalite and Helvite.
      Z. Krist. 74: 213-225.

(36) Pauling, L. 1960. The Nature of the Chemical Bond,
      3rd ed. Ithaca, New York: Cornell University Press.

(37) Reed, T. B. and Breck, D. W. 1956. Crystal structure of
      synthetic zeolite, type A. J. Am. Chem. Soc. 78:
      5972-5977.

(38) Rosseinsky, D. R. 1965. Electrode potentials and
      hydration energies. Theories and correlations. Chem.
      Rev. 65, 467-490.

(39) Sherry, H. S. 1966. The ion exchange properties of
      zeolites. I. Univalent ion exchange in synthetic
      faujasite. J. Phys. Chem. 70: 1158-1168.

(40) Sherry, H. S. 1968. The ion exchange properties of
      zeolites. III. Rare earth ion exchange of synthetic
      faujasites. J. Coll. Inter. Sci. 28: 288-292.

(41) Sherry, H. S. 1968. The ion exchange properties of
      zeolites. IV. Alkaline earth ion exchange in the
      synthetic zeolites X and Y. J. Phys. Chem. 72:
      4068-4094.

(42) Sherry, H. S. 1969. The Ion Exchange Properties of
      Zeolites. In Ion Exchange, Vol. 2, ed. J. A. Marinsky,
      pp. 89-133. New York: Marcel Dekker, Inc.

(43) Sherry, H. S. 1970. Ion exchange properties of the
      synthetic zeolite Linde T. In Ion Exchange in the
      Process Industries, Papers read at the conference,
      pp. 329-338. London: Society of the Chemical
      Industry.

(44) Sherry, H. S. 1971. Ion Exchange in Zeolites.
      Paper 28 in Molecular Sieve Zeolites, Advances in
      Chemistry Series, No. 101, ed. R. F. Gould, pp. 350-379.
      Washington, D. C.: American Chemical Society.

(45) Sherry, H. S. and Walton, H. F. 1967. The ion exchange
      properties of zeolites. II. Ion exchange in the
      synthetic zeolite Linde-4-A. J. Phys. Chem. 71:
      1457-1465.

(46) Smith, J. V. 1963. Special Paper No. 1,
      Mineralogical Society of America.

(47) Taylor, A. M. and Roy R. 1964. Zeolite studies IV:
      Na-P zeolites and the ion-exchanged derivatives of
      Na-P. Amer. Miner. $\underline{49}$: 656-681.

(48) Theng, B. K. G., Vansant, E. and Uytterhoeven, J. B.
      1968. Ion exchange in synthetic zeolites. Part 1.
      Ammonium and some of its alkyl derivatives in Linde
      sieves X and Y. Trans. Far. Soc. $\underline{64}$: 3370-3382.

Ion Exchange Reactions Involving Inorganic Phosphate and Oxide Exchangers

A. Clearfield
Department of Chemistry
Ohio University
Athens, Ohio 45701/USA

Abstract. In the last twenty years interest in inorganic ion exchangers has revived. Two of the major classes of compounds studied are the hydrous oxides and phosphates of polyvalent metals. The hydrous oxides exchange via surface hydroxyl groups, and generally exchange anions in acidic solutions and cations in basic solution. In some cases (where the cation has a high charge to size ratio) anions present in solution are sorbed along with the cation, apparently forming complex species on the surface of the oxide. The phosphates can be prepared as amorphous gels and as crystalline compounds, and certain ones in stages of crystallinity between the two extremes. An enormous range of cation exchange behavior is exhibited by these compounds from organic resin-like exchange for the gels to ion sieving for the crystals. Suggestions for the application of these inorganic exchangers for the concentration, removal, and separation of seawater ionic species are presented.

Introduction

In recent years interest in non-aluminosilicate inorganic ion exchangers has been revived. This revival stemmed from a need for exchangers which could operate at high temperatures and pressures and in highly radioactive media without appreciable degradation. As a result, it is now known that a wider variety of compounds exhibit ion exchange behavior than was previously supposed. A partial list includes salts of heteropoly acids,

metal ferrocyanides, hydrous oxides, acidic salts of polyvalent
cations, polyphosphates and polytitinates, synthetic apatites,
insoluble sulfides, and alkaline earth sulfates. The interested
reader is referred to several review articles [14,33,60,70,71]
for a more complete list of compounds and description of their
ion exchange properties. These compounds represent a vast new
arsenal of materials for the concentration and separation of
cations, anions, and in some instances neutral molecules.
However, it appears that a great deal more knowledge will be
required before they are widely applied. In particular, more
must be learned about their structures and the mechanisms of
the exchange processes, including thermodynamic and rate data.
In many instances sorption (removal of ions from solution)
occurs by mechanisms other than ion exchange such as chemisorption and precipitation in the exchanger. These processes need
further clarification. In this paper the discussion will be
limited to the hydrous oxides and phosphates of polyvalent
metals, not only because a great deal is now known about them
but because they show great promise of near term applications
in several areas of technology.

Hydrous Oxides

The sorption properties of hydrous oxides such as silica, alumina, and ferric oxide have been known for many years. Much of
this work was concerned with attaining a better understanding
of surface properties as they relate to the role of these oxides
as catalysts and catalyst carriers. However, with the impetus
gained from their potential utilization in processing of radioactive materials and in water desalinization processes, the ion
exchange properties of a large number of hydrous oxides have
been examined in recent years [14,21,46,70]. These include the
oxides and/or hydroxides of Be, Mg, Zn, Al, Fe, Ga, Sb(III),
Cr, Si, Sn(IV), Zr, Ti, Th, Mn(IV), Sb(V), V, Ta, Nb, Mo(VI),
W(VI). For specific references to the individual oxides the
reader is referred to the already mentioned reviews [14,21,33,70].

The ion exchange properties of hydrous oxides stem from the presence of surface hydroxyl groups. Many of the oxides exhibit amphoteric behavior, exchanging anions in acidic and cations in basic solution. This is shown in Fig. 1 [46]. The two types of exchange can be represented by the following schematic equations:

In acid solution

$$\Big\}-OH + H^+ \rightleftarrows \Big\}+ + H_2O \tag{1}$$

In basic solution

$$\Big\}-OH + OH^- \rightleftarrows \Big\}-O^- + H_2O \tag{2}$$

where $\Big\}$ represents the surface of the hydrous oxide. The anions or cations then associate with the surface charges. An alternative representation to eq. (1) is

$$\Big\}-OH + H^+ \rightleftarrows \Big\}-O^+_{\substack{H \\ H}} \tag{3}$$

The smooth dependence of capacity (meq. of ion exchanged per gram of dry exchanger) suggests a heterogeneity of active groups within the exchanger. Note also in Fig. 1 that hydrous stannic oxide is a better cation exchanger than zirconium oxide but a poorer anion exchanger and that the crossover points of the two branches of the exchange curves occur at different pH values. These characteristics of the two oxides are largely the result of the differences in basicity of the two metals. For example, the more basic metal, zirconium, would be expected to undergo reaction (1) more readily than tin(IV), as it in fact does. This effect reaches its extreme in silicon which exhibits almost no exchange of anions [57,69].

The crossover points in Fig. 1 correlate well with the isoelectric point of the oxides, and this seems to be general [21,46]. In this region of the isoelectric point both anions and cations are sorbed simultaneously. A total capacity for hydrous zirconia of about 1 meq/g indicates the presence of about one surface hydroxyl group for every eight metal atoms in the

solid. Hydrous thorium oxide was reported to have an exchange
capacity of ~2 meq/g [42] and this requires about one hydroxyl
group for every two thorium atoms. In order to achieve such
high capacities, the oxides must have large surface areas and
this, of course, is the case [10,48].

Hydrous oxides are formed by the hydrolytic polymerization of
low molecular weight species. In the case of silica this polymerizing species is thought to be $Si(OH)_4$ which condenses by
split out of water to form oxo bridges as in eq.(4) [55].
Further condensation can occur to produce chains. In the case

$$2Si(OH)_4 \rightarrow (HO)_3Si \overset{O}{\diagdown} Si(OH)_3 + H_2O \qquad (4)$$

of zirconia the polymerizing species is thought to be the tetramer $[Zr(OH)_2 \cdot 4H_2O]_4^{8+}$ which is known to exist in solutions of
zirconyl halides [53]. The zirconium atoms are arranged in a
square and are linked together by double hydroxo-bridges above
and below the plane of the square. Four water molecules are
also bonded to each metal atom in the crystal making the coordination number eight [22]. However, in solution some of the
water groups hydrolyse to form hydroxyl as shown in eq.(5).

$$[Zr(OH)_2 \cdot 4H_2O]_4^{8+} \rightleftarrows [Zr(OH)_{2+x} \cdot 4-XH_2O]_4^{(8-x)+} + XH^+ \qquad (5)$$

When X becomes sufficiently large, the tetrameric units poly-
merize through olation [24,61]. That is, by formation of double
hydroxo-bridges between tetramer units. Addition of base and/or
boiling causes the equilibrium represented by eq.(5) to shift to
the right with attendant polymerization. The double hydroxo-
bridges constrain the tetramer units to lie in planes so that
sheet-like polymers form [24,40]. In the ultimate sheet the
composition would be $[Zr(OH)_4]_n$. The sheets can thicken into
a three dimensional particle by oxolation between sheets, i.e.,
by condensation of water from two hydroxo groups in adjacent
sheets [24,61]. The resulting three dimensional polymer would
have the composition $[ZrO_b(OH)_{4-2b}]_n$ with the value of b depending upon the degree of condensation which in turn depends
upon the method of preparation. For example, upon addition of

base to a Zr(IV) solution, the hydrolytic polymerization processes described above occur rapidly. Since each tetramer has
four metal sites at which olation can occur, polymerization
takes place in many directions simultaneously. This produces a
random structure of tetramers. Sheets of tetramers so formed
could condense with other sheets only at a few positions, and the
end product would have a small value of b. These features of
the growth mechanism explain why the end product is an amorphous
gel. Of course, there are always a certain number of water
molecules associated with the gel particles.

In contrast, polymerization of tetramer units occurs very slowly
when Zr(IV) solutions are refluxed. Many hours are required
before precipitation occurs and the product is crystalline [23].
Under these conditions orderly growth of the tetramer sheets
can occur [24,61] and oxolation readily achieved. Thus, b would
be large and a ZrO_2 like structure obtained. The crystalline
particles range from 30 - 100 $\overset{o}{A}$ in size. In the interior of
the particle the composition and structure are very nearly those
of ZrO_2. Along the surfaces the zirconium atoms are bonded to
water molecules and unbridged hydroxyl groups. Surface areas
range from 150 - 350 sq. m/g [61] and are roughly those to be
expected from the sizes of the individual particles. However,
these particles agglomerate into much larger ones, and this must
occur by olation and/or oxolation at contact points. The re-
sultant conglomerate contains pores of roughly 20 $\overset{o}{A}$ diameter
for the amorphous preparations and about half this size for the
crystalline form obtained by the boiling procedure. Heating the
solids to progressively higher temperatures increases the sizes
of their pores [62].

The foregoing description of hydrous zirconia can be generalized
to include those of other hydrous oxides. The initial polymerizing species are different and the conditions of polymerization vary, as do the relative amounts of olation and oxolation.
However, the end products consist of small particles agglomerated
together into larger porous particles. A high proportion of the

surface contains non-bridging hydroxyl groups, and these are
available for exchange reactions. The behavior of the hydroxyl
groups depends upon a number of factors. We have already mentioned the relative basicity of the metal, but we must also
consider the different environments available to the hydroxyl.
For example, the following are some of the possibilities:

```
        H                      H                    H          H    H
        O               H      O             H      O   H      O    O
        |               |      |             |      |   |      |    |
  M~O\  M  ~O\  M~       M~O\   M  ~O\  M     M~O\   M  ~O\     M~O\  M
                                                                  
      (a)                    (b)                  (c)           (d)
```

Evidence for the different character of surface hydroxyls is
available from infrared spectral studies. Most hydrous oxides
exhibit a multiplicity of absorption peaks due to the O-H
stretch or a broad band in this region of the spectrum due to
a broad range of O-H types [49]. The more negative the region
surrounding the hydroxyl group the more basic will its character
be.

Several types of reactions other than ion exchange are possible
at hydrous oxide surfaces. These include physical and chemisorption, and complex formation or compound formation. The
possibility that the so-called ion exchange involves these
other phenomena must not be overlooked. However, for alkali
metal ions a one for one ion exchange mechanism has been shown
to hold with silica [10,50,74], titania [47],and zirconia [16].
However, some evidence exists that adsorption and ion exclusion
from small pores may also be operative [67]. Such additional
factors may be necessary to explain the partial irreversibility
of exchange for ions on hydrous oxides.

The mechanism of exchange is much more complicated for polyvalent
cations. In nearly neutral or basic solution many of these ions
exist as basic or polycondensed species so that other than simple exchange reactions occur. Examples for individual hydrous
oxides are given below.

<u>Hydrous Silica</u>. In acid solutions where hydrolysis is not too
severe, it is found that the higher the charge of the cation
the greater the affinity for exchange. Within a group of ions
the ion with smaller radius is the preferred one [37,64]. At
higher pH values the exchange process is followed by an adsorption process. This adsorption may take several forms. With
$Ca(OH)_2$ the calcium ion is exchanged rapidly, and this is
followed by slow formation of a calcium silicate phase [58].
Thorium has been reported as being exchanged in hydrolysed forms
such as $[Th(OH)]^{3+}$, $[Th(OH)_2]^{2+}$ and from acetate buffers as
$[Th(CH_3COO)_3]^+$ and $[Th(OH)(CH_3COO)_2]^+$. Similar complexes of
Al, Cr, Fe [75,76] and Zr [18] have been reported. The irreversibility of some of these reactions [18,56] indicates that
olation or oxolation may have occurred following the initial
exchange.

<u>Titanium Oxide</u>. Plots of log K_d vs. log $[H^+]$ were linear for
several mono and divalent cations with the slope equal to the
charge of the exchanged ion [43]. This is indicative of a
simple ion exchange mechanism. However, species such as $Sr(OH)^+$
were adsorbed from alkaline solution with formation of a crystalline compound [66]. An unusually high level of Fe(III)
absorption was observed and ascribed to the formation of bonds
between the titania surface and a hydrolyzed iron species [63].

<u>Zirconium Oxide</u>. The ion exchange behavior of a large number
of cations in acid solution was examined [65]. Among the transition elements,Cr(III), Fe(III), and Cu(II) were strongly sorbed,
whereas Mn(II), Co(II), and Ni(II) were sorbed to a lesser extent.
For alkaline earth ions it was shown that the larger the radius
of the ion the lower the extent of sorption. Barium exhibited
an anomalous uptake which was attributed to formation of $BaCO_3$.
This result is interesting, since it is known that hydrous zirconia (and thoria) contain appreciable amounts of sorbed CO_2
when prepared without special precautions [35]. It was also
found that the amount of chloride ion exchanged simultaneously
with the cation increased with the increasingly covalent

character of the cation. These results were explained on the
basis of an initial ion exchange reaction followed by the formation of a surface complex of the type

$$\left[\begin{array}{c} Zr - O \\ \backslash \\ OH \quad M \\ / \\ Zr - O \end{array} \begin{array}{c} Cl \\ / \\ \backslash \\ Cl \end{array} \right]^{2-} \quad 2H^{+}$$

Thus, the relative affinity shown by the cations is presumed to
be related to the stability of the complexes. Similarly,
selectivity sequences observed on thorium, titanium, and tin
oxides have been ascribed to the stability order of the respective cation hydroxo- complexes [43,38].

Hydrous zirconia and thoria show unusual selectivity towards
phosphate ion, and this is probably due to compound formation
[72,73].

In spite of our dearth of definitive knowledge concerning the
exchange processes on hydrous oxides, a large number of useful
separations have been effected. The interested reader is referred to references [14,33,60,70,71] for further details. We
will close this section by citing those processes that may be
of potential value in connection with seawater studies. The
most obvious application is for the concentration, removal,
separation, and determination of trace constituents. In this
connection the irreversibility of exchange (as in compound
formation) is a distinct advantage. Thus, by the correct choice
of sorbent it may be possible to selectively remove certain
species of interest. For example, zirconia and/or thoria should
be tried for the removal of phosphates and carbonates. Al^{3+}
and Cr^{3+} are strongly sorbed on hydrous SnO_2 [39], and it is reported that the capacity of ferric oxide for Ni^{+2} is increased
in the presence of strong electrolytes [20]. . A mixture of hydrous MnO_2 and Fe_2O_3 has been used to scavenge ^{60}Co, ^{106}Ru,
and ^{75}Zn from seawater [51], and hydrous titania was reported
to concentrate uranium from seawater [45]. A systematic approach
to the problem can be suggested. It appears that in general the
greater the covalency of a cation as determined by its charge

to size ratio, the greater is the sorption at a given pH.   In
fact, several examples are known where cations were sorbed from
highly acid solutions, most probably as anionic complexes   ·
[19,41].   By starting with highly acidified solutions and slowly
increasing the pH it may be possible to achieve removal and
separation of groups of ions in turn.   Another approach might
involve concentration of trace species by coprecipitation.   This
technique using hydrous oxides has already been demonstrated
with good results [39,54].

Inorganic Phosphates

The discovery that certain transition metal phosphates behaved
as ion exchangers was an outgrowth of the early work on hydrous
oxides [46].   Hydrous zirconia was found to have much enhanced
ability to exchange cations after treatment with phosphate ions.
This led to the synthesis of phosphates of Ti, Th, Sn, Ce, Al,
and Fe and to an examination of their ion exchange properties
[14,33,46,60,70].   In addition, arsenates, antimonates, vanadates,
molybdates, tungstates, tellurates, silicates, etc. of these
metals have also been studied.   The preparations are generally
amorphous gels of indefinite composition whose ion exchange
properties depend upon their method of preparation.   In this
discussion we shall confine ourselves to considering only the
phosphates and, of these, mainly zirconium phosphates.

Zirconium Phosphate.   The first preparations involved addition
of a Zr(IV) solution to a soluble phosphate.   The gelatinous
products resemble hydrous oxides in appearance and filterability.
The ratio of phosphate to zirconium in the solid is variable
but approaches two with increasing acidity, digestion time, and
phosphate to Zr ratio of the reactants [1,14,25].   The amorphous
character and stoichiometric variability of these precipitates
made progress towards understanding the mechanism of the exchange process difficult.   These difficulties were overcome
when it was discovered that a stoichiometric, crystalline compound could be obtained by refluxing the gels in phosphoric

acid [25]. The composition of the crystals was shown to be
$Zr(HPO_4)_2 \cdot H_2O$ [25]. On the basis of this formula, it was predicted that the protons from the monohydrogen phosphate groups
are exchangeable ions, and this gives a calculated exchange
capacity of 6.64 meq/g. Exchange capacities can be determined
by titration of a weighed amount of exchanger with dilute base
usually in the presence of a supporting salt. Such titration
curves are shown in Fig. 2. When NaOH is the titrant, two end
points are exhibited by crystalline zirconium phosphate. These
correspond to the replacement of the two phosphate protons and
give the expected exchange capacity of 6.64 meq/g. No such
regularity was observed with the gelatinous zirconium phosphate.
Furthermore, it was found that Cs^+ did not exchange in acid
solution with the crystals but is known to be strongly sorbed
by the gel [12] under these conditions.

The exchange behavior of crystalline zirconium phosphate, here-
after termed α-ZrP, became clear once its crystal structure was
solved [29]. The structure is a layered one, a portion of which
is shown in Fig. 3. The zirconium atoms lie very nearly in a
plane and are bridged by phosphate groups situated alternately
above and below the plane of the metal atoms. Any three adjacent metal atoms in the same layer form a slightly distorted
equilateral triangle. The phosphate groups are located such
that the phosphorus atoms are near the centers of the triangles
about 1.2 Å above or below the plane. Three oxygen atoms of
each phosphate group are bonded to the three metal atoms com-
posing the triangle. This produces an almost perfect octahedral coordination of oxygen atoms around the zirconium with
an average Zr-O distance of 2.07 Å. The layered arrangement
creates a hexagonal pseudocell with $a_h \cong 5.24$ Å and $c_h \cong 22.6$ Å.
The interlayer distance is 7.6 Å.

The fourth oxygen atom of each phosphate group is not bonded to
zirconium and presumably bears the hydrogen atom. The two
phosphate groups (per α-ZrP formula weight) occupy slightly
different positions relative to the layers. In the one labelled

P(3) (Fig. 4), the P(3) - O(10) bond is directed almost perpendicular to the metal atom plane. The other phosphate group
has the P(2) - O(7) bond tilted away from the perpendicular.
This tilting produces a low tetrahedral bond angle of 102.6°
for the O(7) - P(2) - O(5) bond angle. Almost the same positioning of the arsenate groups is present in α-ZrAs [27].

The layers in α-ZrP are situated relative to each other such
that, if a line is drawn perpendicular to a layer at a metal
atom, it will intersect a phosphorus atom in an adjacent layer.
This arrangement produces cavities of the type shown in Fig. 4
with the water molecule, O(12), situated near the center of
the cavity. There is one such cavity per α-ZrP formula in the
crystal.

The cavity may be thought of as being built up of sides and faces.
A typical side would be $Zr - O_7'' - P_2 - O_5 - Zr - O_7 - P_2 - O_6'$,
and a typical face $Zr - O_6 - P_2 - O_4' - Zr - O_6' - P_2 - O_4$.
The largest free distance in the sides occurs between zirconium
and O_{10} type oxygens, and these distances are large enough to
allow a spherical ion of 2.63 Å diameter to diffuse into the
cavity without obstruction [28]. The largest free distance in
the faces is 2.4 Å.

The positions of the hydrogen atoms in the structure were not
determined from the x-ray data. Thus, the hydrogen bonding
scheme is open to speculation. In any case the forces between
layers are very weak and permit the crystals to expand and contract during exchange.

When Na^+ is exchanged into α-ZrP, the reaction up to the first
end point (curves b and e in Fig. 2) is

$$Zr(HPO_4)_2 \cdot H_2O + 4H_2O + Na^+ \rightleftharpoons ZrNaH(PO_4)_2 \cdot 5H_2O + H^+ \qquad (6)$$

Both the half-exchanged and α-ZrP phases occur together with
the latter decreasing and the former increasing in amount pro-
portionate to loading [28,68]. At higher loadings the

half-exchanged phase is converted to $Zr(NaPO_4)_2 \cdot 3H_2O$. These two exchanged phases have interlayer spacings of 11.8 Å and 9.8 Å, respectively. In the reverse titration, where H^+ replaces Na^+, the first stage is reversible, but in the second step the half-exchanged phase forms the compound $Zr(HPO_4)_2 \cdot 8H_2O$ which has an interlayer spacing 10.4 Å. When this latter phase is removed from contact with the solution, it reverts to α-ZrP with loss of 7 moles of water.

Cesium ion does not exchange in acid solution with α-ZrP as shown in curve a, Fig. 2. This can be rationalized on a size basis, the ion being too large to diffuse into the α-ZrP cavities. The hydrated sodium ion is also too large to enter the cavities. Thus, unhydrated or partially hydrated ions must partake in the exchange process [28]. Once the ions are in the cavity, water molecules can follow (diffuse in) to rehydrate the cation and move the α-ZrP layers apart in the process. On this basis one can explain the fact that Na^+, K^+, and Li^+ readily exchange in acid solutions of the proper pH but Rb^+ and Cs^+ ions do not. These larger ions, however, do exchange in alkaline solution [34] but in large measure, hydrolysis and loss of crystallinity occur [9].

By control of the refluxing procedure it is possible to obtain zirconium phosphates with different degrees of crystallinity. Titration curves for a number of samples with different crystallinities are shown in Fig.5 [32]. The samples are designated by two numbers such as 0.8:48. The first number gives the molarity of acid used for refluxing an amorphous gel, and the second number gives the reflux time in hours. It is seen that there is a gradation of behavior from the two step process with crystals to a single smooth curve of increasing uptake with increased pH for the least crystalline sample. For sample 0.5:48 (and those of lesser crystallinity) the exchange is reversible, and a single solid solution phase is obtained at all loadings [32,34]. These gel-like samples swell in water so that their compositions are approximately $Zr(HPO_4)_2 \cdot 5H_2O$. The interlayer distance is quite large and sieving effects are not observed unless very bulky ions are exchanged [13]. Thus, hydrated ions can exchange with the gels, and the selectivity series at low loads is $Cs^+ > Rb > K^+ > Na^+ > Li^+$ [12,15]. At higher loadings repulsion effects become important and selectivity reversals occur [32,34].

With exchanger samples of greater crystallinity, distinct phases are observed which have rather broad solubility limits of the two exchanging cations. These limits narrow with increasing crystallinity [32,34] until in the most crystalline samples pure compounds are obtained (at least to the sensitivity of x-ray diffraction powder patterns in these systems). In the case of Cs^+ a half-exchanged phase is not observed as there is only one end point close to 75% of exchange [34]. Potassium ion behaves like sodium ion except that the half-exchanged phase is a monohydrate [31,52]. Lithium ion with highly crystalline a-ZrP forms a half-exchanged phase, a phase of composition $ZrLi_{1.33-1.67}H_{.67-.33}(PO_4)_2 \cdot 4H_2O$ and a fully exchanged phase $Zr(LiPO_4)_2 \cdot 4H_2O$ [5,36]. With less crystalline samples the half-exchanged phase is not obtained but only the latter two phases [30] with broadened solubility limits for Li^+.

Divalent ions do not exchange readily with crystalline a-ZrP in acid solution. However, in the case of Ca^{++} and Sr^{++} about 75% of theoretical uptake can be realized by addition of their respective hydroxides [6,26]. Only a single end point near the limit of uptake is observed. Barium ion exchanges very slowly, and this seems to be a size effect. For those divalent ions, the hydroxides of which are relatively insoluble, little exchange takes place. In general, however, as the crystallinity of the exchanger decreases, the affinity for divalent ions increases [2,4,12,15]. However, even for an exchanger of low crystallinity only slight differences in affinity for first row transition elements were observed [2]. Nevertheless, by proper choice of conditions it is possible to achieve certain desired results. For example, for industrial or reactor water purification a high sorption in nearly neutral solutions and at elevated temperatures is desired. Ahrland and Carleson found that Ni(II) and Cu(II) were completely removed from dilute, nearly neutral solutions at elevated temperatures using a semi-crystalline exchanger [3]. Under these conditions some phosphate ion is solubilized by hydrolysis, but this is prevented from entering the solution by sorption on hydrous zirconia.

Clearfield and Tuhtar have measured distribution coefficients for first row transition elements in acetate solutions on zirconium phosphates of varying crystallinity [36]. Since the K_d curves for different ions were not parallel, it was possible to choose an exchanger for a pair of ions which gave a high separation factor and to separate mixtures by column chromatography.

Several new developments have resulted from the studies of Alberti and his coworkers. They found that ions which do not readily exchange with crystalline hydrous zirconia are easily sorbed by the half-exchanged sodium phase, $ZrNaH(PO_4)_2 \cdot 5H_2O$ [7,11]. This sodium phase has an interlayer spacing of 11.8 Å. Thus, large ions are not prevented from entering the crystals. It was further found that the ions Cs^+ and Mg^{++} could be exchanged into crystalline α-ZrP in the presence of a high ($\sim$0.1M) concentration of NaCl [8] upon addition of a base of the ion. In the case of Mg^{++} exchange, solid MgO was added, and this dissolved by reaction with protons released by the exchange reaction. This technique and the others described above may be directly applicable to concentration, removal, and analysis of basic species from seawater.

Other Phosphate Salts. A large number of metal phosphates which exhibit ion exchange behavior are known. Only a few remarks concerning them will be included here. The interested reader may consult the review articles already referred to for further details [14,33,60,68,70].

Titanium phosphate and zirconium arsenate exist as amorphous gels but can be crystallized by methods refluxing procedures. The crystalline compounds are isomorphous with a-ZrP, but the ways leading into the cavities are of different sizes. This produces altered sieving characteristics, but these effects have not been explored in any detail.

Cerium phosphates are apparently not similar in structure to the zirconium phosphates. A large number have been prepared [44] including an interesting series of phosphate-sulfates. These compounds merit further study.

Acknowledgment: The author is grateful to the National Science Foundation for support of much of his work on inorganic ion exchangers.

REFERENCES

/1/ Ahrland, S.; Albertsson, J.; Johansson, L.; Nihlgard, B.; and Nilsson, L. 1966. Inorganic Ion Exchangers II. Sorption Rate and Dehydration Studies on Zirconium Phosphate and Tungstate Gels. Acta Chem. Scand. 18: 1357-1367.

/2/ Ahrland, S.; Albertsson, J.; Oskarsson, Å.; and Niklasson, A. 1970. Inorganic Ion Exchangers - VII. The Sorption of First-Row Transition Metal Ions on a Zirconium Phosphate Gel of Low Crystallinity, and a Study of the Reproducibility of the Gel. J. Inorg. Nucl. Chem. 32: 2069-2078.

/3/ Ahrland, S., and Carleson, G. 1971. Inorganic Ion Exchangers - VIII. The Purification of Water at Elevated Temperatures by a Combination of Zirconium Phosphate and Zirconium Hydroxide Gels. J. Inorg. Nucl. Chem. 33: 2229-2246.

/4/ Ahrland, S.; Bjork, N.; Blessing, R.H.; and Herman, R.G. 1974. Inorganic Ion Exchangers IX. The Sorption of Di-valent Transition Metal Ions on Semi-Crystalline Zirconium Phosphate. J. Inorg. Nucl. Chem. 36: 2377-2383.

/5/ Alberti, G.; Constantino, U.; Alluli, S.; Massucci, M.A.; and Pelliccioni, M. 1973. Crystalline Insoluble Salts of Tetravalent Metals XV. Influence of Preparation Methods on the Ion Exchange Behavior of Crystalline Zirconium Phosphate. J. Inorg. Nucl. Chem. $\underline{35}$: 1347-1357.

/6/ Alberti, G.; Costantino, U.; and Pelliccioni, M. 1973. Crystalline Insoluble Acid Salts of Tetravalent Metals. XIII. Ion Exchange of Zirconium Phosphate with Alkaline Earth Metal Ions. J. Inorg. Nucl. Chem. $\underline{35}$: 1327-1338.

/7/ Alberti, G.; Costantino, U.; and Gupta, J.P. 1974. Crystalline Insoluble Acid Salts of Tetravalent Metals - XVIII. Ion Exchange Properties of Crystalline $ZrNaH(PO_4)_2 \cdot 5H_2O$ Towards Alkali Metal Ions. J. Inorg. Nucl. Chem. $\underline{36}$: 2103-2107.

/8/ Alberti, G.; Costantino, U.; and Gupta, J.P. 1974. Crystalline Insoluble Acid Salts of Tetravalent Metals XIX. Na^+ - catalysed H^+-Mg^{++} and H^+-Cs^+ Ion Exchanges on α-zirconium phosphate. J. Inorg. Nucl. Chem. $\underline{36}$: 2109-2114.

/9/ Albertsson, J. 1966. Inorganic Ion Exchangers IV. The Sorption on Crystalline Zirconium Phosphate and its Dependence upon Crystallinity. Acta Chem. Scand. $\underline{20}$: 1689-1702.

/10/ Allen, L.H., and Matijevic, E. 1970. Stability of Colloidal Silica. II. Ion Exchange. J. Colloid Interface Sci. $\underline{33}$: 421-430.

/11/ Allulli, S.; LaGinestra, A.; Massucci, M.A.; Pelliccioni, M.; and Tomassini, N. 1974. Uptake of Transition Metal Ions by Crystalline Zirconium Phosphate. Inorg. Nucl. Chem. Letters $\underline{10.4}$: 337-341.

/12/ Amphlett, C.B.; McDonald, L.A.; and Redman, J.J. 1958. Synthetic Inorganic Ion Exchange Materials - I. Zirconium Phosphate. J. Inorg. Nucl. Chem. $\underline{6}$: 220-235.

/13/ Amphlett, C.B., and McDonald, L.A. 1962. Ion Sieve Properties of Zirconium Phosphate. Proc. Chem. Soc., 276.

/14/ Amphlett, C.B. 1964. Inorganic Ion Exchangers, Amsterdam: Elsevier.

/15/ Baetsle, L. 1963. Ion Exchange Properties of Zirconyl Phosphates - III. Influence of Temperature on Tracer Ion Equilibria. J. Inorg. Nucl. Chem. $\underline{25}$: 271-282.

/16/ Britz, D., and Nancollas, G.H. 1969. Thermodynamics of Cation Exchange of Hydrous Zirconia. J. Inorg. Nucl. Chem. $\underline{31}$: 3861-3868.

/17/ Caletka, R., and Zaitseva, T.D. 1969. Separation of Zir-
     conium and Hafnium from Other Elements by Adsorption
     from Mixed Solutions onto Silica Gel.
     Radiokhimiya 11: 510-515.

/18/ Caletka, R. 1970. Adsorption of Easily Hydrolysed Elements
     on Silica Gel. I. Adsorption of Zirconium and Hafnium from
     Solutions of Inorganic Acids. Radiokhimiya 12: 448-455.

/19/ Caletka, R. 1972. Sorption of the Polyvalent Elements on
     Silica Gel. I. Sorption of Protactinium from Solutions
     of HCl and H_2SO_4. Collec. Czech. Chem. Commun. 37: 1267-1276.

/20/ Chuiko, V.T., and Gavrilyuk, A.I. 1967. Adsorption (co-
     precipitation) of Nickel Microimpurities on Ferric
     Hydroxide from Electrolyte Solutions.
     Visn. L'viv Derzh. Univ., Ser. Khim. 9: 57-66.

/21/ Churms, S.C. 1965. Inorganic Ion Exchangers. I, II, III, IV.
     S. African Ind. Chemist 19: 26-92.

/22/ Clearfield, A., and Vaughan, P.A. 1956. The Crystal Struc-
     ture of Zirconyl Chloride Octahydrate and Zirconyl Bromide
     Octahydrate. Acta Cryst. 9: 555-558.

/23/ Clearfield, A. 1964. Crystalline Hydrous Zirconia.
     Inorg. Chem. 3: 146-148.

/24/ Clearfield, A. 1964. Structural Chemistry of Zirconium.
     Rev. Pure Appl. Chem. 14: 98-102.

/25/ Clearfield, A., and Stynes, J.A. 1964. The Preparation of
     Crystalline Zirconium Phosphate and Some Observations on
     its Ion Exchange Behavior. J. Inorg. Nucl. Chem. 26: 117-129.

/26/ Clearfield, A., and Smith, G.D. 1968. The Ion Exchange
     Behavior of Crystalline Zirconium Phosphate Towards Al-
     kaline Earth Cations. J. Inorg. Nucl. Chem. 30: 327-329.

/27/ Clearfield, A., and Duax, W.L. 1969. Crystal Structure of
     the Ion-Exchanger Zirconium Bis(Monohydrogen Orthoarsenate)
     Monohydrate. Acta Cryst. B25: 2658-2662.

/28/ Clearfield, A.; Duax, W.L.; Medina, A.S.; Smith, G.D.; and
     Thomas, J.R. 1969. On the Mechanism of Ion Exchange in
     Crystalline Zirconium Phosphate, I. Sodium Ion Exchange on
     α-zirconium Phosphate. J. Phys. Chem. 73: 3424-3430.

/29/ Clearfield, A., and Smith, G.D. 1969. The crystallography
     and Structure of α-zirconium Bis (Monohydrogen Ortho-
     phosphate) Monohydrate. Inorg. Chem. 8: 341-347.

/30/ Clearfield, A., and Troup, J.M. 1970. Mechanism of Ion
     Exchange in Crystalline Zirconium Phosphate. II. Lithium
     Ion Exchange of α-zirconium Phosphate.
     J. Phys. Chem. <u>74</u>: 314-317.

/31/ Clearfield, A.; Duax, W.L.; Garces, J.M.; and Medina, A.S.
     1972. Mechanism of Ion Exchange in Crystalline Zirconium
     Phosphates. IV. Potassium Ion Exchange of α-zirconium
     Phosphate. J. Inorg. Nucl. Chem. <u>34</u>: 329-337.

/32/ Clearfield, A.; Oskarsson, Å.; and Oskarsson, C. 1972.
     On the Mechanism of Ion Exchange in Crystalline Zirconium
     Phosphates. VI. The Effect of Crystallinity of the Ex-
     changer on $Na^+ - H^+$ Exchange. Ion Exch. Membranes <u>1</u>: 91-107.

/33/ Clearfield, A.; Nancollas, G.H.; and Blessing, R.H. 1973.
     New Inorganic Ion Exchangers. In Ion Exchange and Solvent
     Extraction 5, eds. J.A. Marinsky and Y. Marcus, pp. 1-120.
     New York: Marcel Dekker, Inc.

/34/ Clearfield, A., and Oskarsson, Å. 1974. On the Mechanism
     of Ion Exchange in Crystalline Zirconium Phosphates.
     IX. The Effect of Crystallinity on Cs^+-H^+ Exchange of
     α-ZrP. Ion Exch. Membranes <u>1</u>: 205-213.

/35/ Clearfield, A. Unpublished results.

/36/ Clearfield, A., and Tuhtar, D. to be published.

/37/ Dalton, R.W.; McClanahan, J.L.; and Maatman, R.W. 1962.
     The Partial Exclusion of Electrolytes from the Pores of
     Silica Gel. J. Colloid Sci. <u>17</u>: 207-219.

/38/ Donaldson, J.D., and Fuller, M.J. 1968. Ion Exchange
     Properties of Tin(IV) Materials. I. Hydrous Tin(IV) Oxide
     and its Cation Exchange Properties.
     J. Inorg. Nucl. Chem. <u>30</u>: 1083-1092.

/39/ Donaldson, J.D.; Fuller, M.J.; and Price, J.W. 1968. Ion
     Exchange Properties of Tin(IV) Materials. II. Cation Ex-
     change Column Chromatography on Hydrous Tin(IV) Oxide.
     J. Inorg. Nucl. Chem. <u>30</u>: 2841-2850.

/40/ Fryer, J.R.; Hutchison, J.L.; and Paterson, R. 1970. An
     Electron Microscopic Study of the Hydrolysis Products of
     Zirconyl Chloride. J. Colloid Interface Sci. <u>34</u>: 238-248.

/41/ Girardi, F.; Pietra, R.; and Sabbioni, E. 1970. Radio-
     chemical Separations by Retention on Ionic Precipitates -
     Adsorption Tests on 11 Materials.
     J. Radioanal. Chem. <u>5</u>: 141-171.

/42/ Heitner-Wirguin, D., and Albu-Yaron, A. 1965. Hydrous
     Oxides and Their Cation Exchange Properties.
     J. Appl. Chem (London) <u>15</u>: 445-448.

/43/ Heitner-Wirguin, D., and Albu-Yaron, A. 1966. Hydrous
     Oxides and Their Cation Exchange Properties - II. Struc-
     ture and Equilibrium Experiments.
     J. Inorg. Nucl. Chem. $\underline{28}$: 2379-2384.

/44/ Herman, R.G., and Clearfield, A. 1975. Crystalline
     Cerium(IV) Phosphates. I. Preparation and Characterization
     of Crystalline Compounds. J. Inorg. Nucl. Chem., in press.
     This article contains references to earlier work on this
     subject including phosphate-sulfates.

/45/ Keen, N.J. 1968. Extraction of Uranium from Seawater.
     J. Brit. Nucl. Energy Soc. $\underline{7}$: 178-183.

/46/ Kraus, K.A.; Phillips, H.O.; Carlson, T.A.; and
     Johnson, J.S. 1958. Ion Exchange Properties of Hydrous
     Oxides. In Proceedings of the Second International Con-
     ference on Peaceful Uses of Atomic Energy, 28,
     Paper No.15/P/1832, pp. 3-16. United Nations

/47/ Levi, H.W., and Schiewer, E. 1966. Adsorption Exchange of
     Cations on TiO_2. Radiochim. Acta $\underline{5}$: 126-133.

/48/ Linsen, B.G. 1970. Physical and Chemical Aspects of Adsor-
     bents and Catalysts. London: Academic Press.

/49/ see ref. 11, pp. 203-208, 248-262.

/50/ Maatman, R.W. 1965. The Behavior of Alkali Metal Cations
     in the Pores of Silica Gel. J. Phys. Chem. $\underline{69}$: 3196-3203.

/51/ Momma, T., and Iwashima, K. 1967. Manganese Dioxide and
     Metal Hydroxides as Scavengers for Radionuclides in
     Seawater. Radioisotopes (Tokyo) $\underline{16}$: 68-72.

/52/ Mounier, F., and Winand, L. 1968. Structure of Zirconium
     Phosphate. Bull. Soc. Chim. (Fr.), 1829-1832.

/53/ Muha, J.M., and Vaughan, P.A. 1960. Structure of the Com-
     plex Ion in Aqueous Solutions of Zirconyl and Hafnyl Oxy-
     halides. J. Chem. Phys. $\underline{33}$: 194-199.

/54/ Novikov, A.I., and Starovoit, I.A. 1969. Separation, Con-
     centration and Determination of Valence Forms of
     Pu(III,IV,VI) by Coprecipitation with Hydrated Oxides of
     Zirconium and Iron. Radiokhimiya $\underline{11}$: 339-347.

/55/ Okkerse, C. 1970. Porous Silica. In Physical and Chemical
     Aspects of Adsorbents and Catalysts, ed. B.G. Linsen,
     pp. 214-264. London: Academic Press.

/56/ Papavasileou, O.C. 1964. System $Th-NH_4OH-SiO_2$.
     Chim. Shronika (Greece) $\underline{29}$: 267-272.

/57/ Parks, G.A. 1965. The Isoelectric Points of Solid Oxides, Solid Hydroxides and Aqueous Hydroxo- Complex Systems. Chem. Rev. 65: 185-198.

/58/ Plachinda, A.S.; Chertov, V.M.; and Neimark, I.E. 1965. Interaction of Silica Gels of Various Pore Structures with a Solution of $Ca(OH)_2$. Ukr. Khim. Zh. 31: 567-573.

/59/ Plotnikov, V.I., and Kochetkov, V.L. 1967. Coprecipitation of Tungsten with Metal Hydroxides. Zh. Neorg. Khim. 13: 203-206.

/60/ Qureshi, M.; Qureshi, S.Z.; Gupta, J.P.; and Rathore, H.S. 1972. Recent Progress in Ion-Exchange Studies on Insoluble Salts of Polybasic Metals. Separation Sci. 7: 615-629.

/61/ Rijnten, H.T. 1970. Formation, Preparation and Properties of Hydrous Zirconia. In Physical and Chemical Aspects of Adsorbants and Catalysts, ed. B.G. Linsen, pp. 316-372. London: Academic Press.

/62/ Rijnten, H.T. 1971. Zirconia, Doctoral Thesis, Technische Hogeschool, Delft. pp. 92-108. Drukkerij. Gebr., N.V. Nijmegen.

/63/ Riskin, I.V., and Velikoslavinskaya, T. 1969. Sorption Capactiy of Titanium Oxide Hydrates. Zh. Prikl. Khim. 42: 1400-1402.

/64/ Rubanik, S.K., Baran, A.A., Strazhesko, D.N., and Strelko, V.V. 1969. Selective Adsorption of Groups I, II and III Cations on Ion Exchange Forms of Silica Gel. Teor. Eksp. Khim. 5: 361-367.

/65/ Sakellaridis, P.U., and Nobelis, F.Z. 1974. Sorption of Some Ions from Acid Solutions by Hydrous Zirconia. J. Inorg. Nucl. Chem. 36: 2599-2603.

/66/ Schiewer, E., and Levi, H.W. 1966. Exchange of Metal and Hydrogen Ions on Hydrous Titanium Dioxide. Radiochim. Conf. Abst. pap., Bratislava, 20-21.

/67/ Tien, H. Ti. 1965. Interaction of Alkali Metal Cations with Silica Gel. J. Phys. Chem. 69: 350-352.

/68/ Torracca, E.; Alberti, G.; Platania, R.; Scala, P.; and Galli, P. 1970. Preparation and Properties of Inorganic Ion Exchangers of the Zirconium Phosphate Type. Soc. Chem. Ind. (London), 156-157.

/69/ Unger, K., and Vydra, F. 1968. Sorption of $Zn(NH_3)_4^{++}$ and $Zn(en)_3^{++}$ on Silica Gels of Various Specific Surfaces. J. Inorg. Nucl. Chem. 30: 1075-1082.

/70/ Vesely, V., and Pekarek, V. 1972. Synthetic Inorganic Ion
     Exchangers I. Hydrous Oxides and Acidic Salts of Polyvalent
     Metals. Talanta 19: 219-262.

/71/ Vesely, V., and Pekarek, V. 1972. Synthetic Inorganic Ion
     Exchangers II. Salts of Heteropolyacids, Insoluble Ferro-
     cyanides, Synthetic Aluminosilicates and Miscellaneous
     Exchangers. Talanta 19: 1245-1283.

/72/ Vissers, D.R. 1968. Sorption of Orthophosphate on Crystal-
     line Metal Oxides. J. Phys. Chem. 72: 3236-3244.

/73/ Vissers, D.R. 1969. Kinetic Study of Orthophosphate Sorp-
     tion on Metal Oxides. J. Phys. Chem. 73: 1963-1965.

/74/ Vydra, F. 1967. Application of the Ion Exchange Properties
     of Silica Gel to the Separation of Metals.
     Anal. Chim. Acta 38: 201-205.

/75/ Vydra, F., and Galba, J. 1967. Sorption of Metal Complexes
     on Silica Gel. III. Sorption of Hydrolysis Products of
     Th^{4+}, Fe^{3+}, Al^{3+} and Cr^{3+}.
     Collec. Czech. Chem. Commun. 34: 3530-3536.

/76/ Vydra, F., and Galba, J. 1968. Sorption of Hydrolytic
     Products of Iron(III), Aluminum(III) and Chromium(III)
     on the Silica Column and its Analytical Use.
     Fresenius Z. Anal. Chem. 235: 166-172.

/77/ Vydra, G., and Galba, J. 1969. Sorption of Metal Complexes
     on Silica Gel. V. Sorption of Hydrolytic Products of Co^{++},
     Mn^{++}, Cu^{++}, Ni^{++} and Zn^{++} on Silica Gel.
     Collec. Czech. Chem. Commun. 34: 3471-3478.

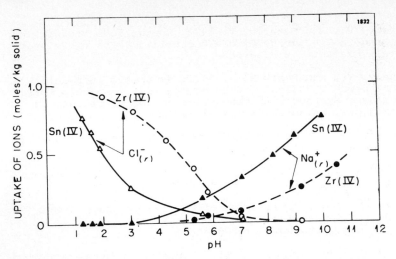

FIG. 1 - Anion- and cation-exchange properties of hydrous
Zr(IV) and Sn(IV) oxides

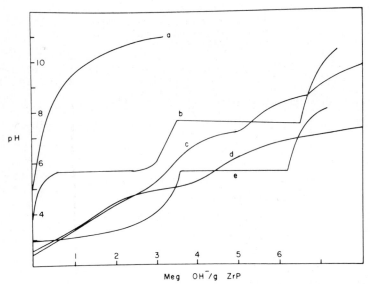

FIG. 2 - Potentiometric titration curves for zirconium phosphates
of different crystallinities. Curve a, crystalline ZrP titrated
with 0.1M CsOH. Curve b, crystalline ZrP titrated with 0.1M NaOH.
Curve c, gelatinous ZrP titrated with 0.1M NaCL + 0.1M NaOH.
Curve d, semi-crystalline ZrP titrated with 0.1M NaOH. Curve e,
crystalline ZrP titrated with 0.1M NaCL + 0.1M NaOH. (Curves
a,b,c, and e reproduced by permission from J. Inorg. Nucl. Chem.
26, 117 1964)).

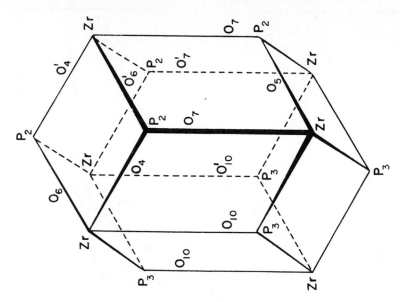

FIG. 4 – Idealized picture of a cavity formed by two adjacent layers in α–ZrP. To preserve clarity not all the oxygens have been shown. (reprinted by permiss. of Inorg.Chem.)

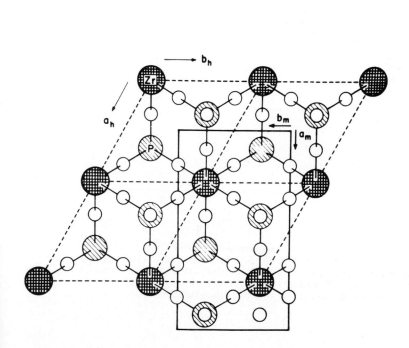

FIG. 3 – Idealized layer in the α–ZrP structure showing relationship of pseudo-hexagonal cell (broken lines) to the true monoclinic cell (solid lines). (reprinting by permission of Inorg. Chem.)

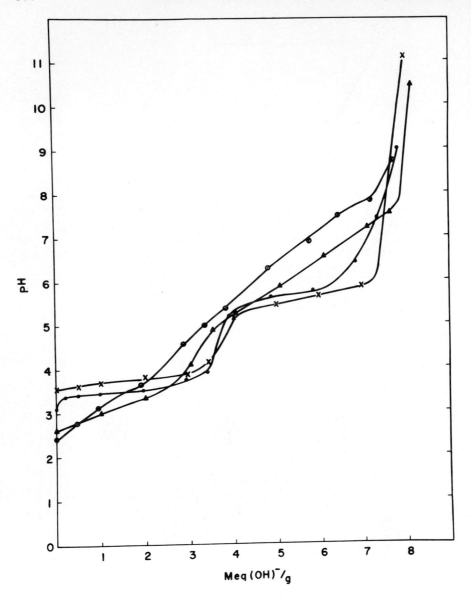

FIG. 5 - Potentiometric titration curves (forward direction
only) for zirconium phosphate samples: 0.8:48-⊘, 2.5:48-▲,
4.5:48-●, 12:48-×. Titrant: 0.1N NaOH + 0.1N NaCl.
(reprinted by permission of Ion Exch. Membranes)

Interfacial Electrochemistry of Hydrophobic Colloids

J. Lyklema
Laboratory for Physical and Colloid Chemistry of the
Agricultural University, De Dreijen 6, Wageningen,
The Netherlands.

Abstract: A review is given of some fundamental properties of charged interfaces with special reference to the distribution of charge and potential under conditions prevailing in sea water.

Introduction:

When a surface scientist is asked what he has to contribute to oceanography, he will start by realizing that in oceans two types of interfaces occur:

(a) the liquid-gas (LG) boundary between water and air and

(b) the solid-liquid (SL) interface between the water and the sea bottom and between the water and dispersed particulate material.

At all these interfaces *adsorption* occurs. Adsorption is important since it plays a role in many chemical and biological cycles. Moreover, the state of aggregation of dispersed, insoluble particulate matter depends to a large extent on what substances are adsorbed on the particle surfaces and how much. This latter problem belongs typically to the domain of the *stability of hydrophobic colloids*. Whether or not dispersed particles aggregate and set-

tle is also of substantial direct interest to oceanography, for
example in connection with the accumulation of trace elements and
biogenic molecules in marine sediments.

It is the purpose of this paper to outline adsorption as far as
charges are involved and the colloid chemical consequences of
this.   Adsorption of ions belongs automatically to this topic,
but we shall take the scope wider by also considering the sorption
of organic molecules, charged or not, on charged interfaces. All
these processes together will be collectively designated as *"elec-
trosorption"*.

Charged Interfaces and Electroneutrality

It is customary to speak of charged interfaces if one of the
adjoining phases bears a charge and the other one an equal but
opposite charge. Before discussing the mechanisms by which such
charges can be acquired it is good to realize that the determination of the surface charge (σ_o, usually in $\mu C/cm^2$) is to some
extent a question of definition, or for that matter, a question
of taste.   Interfaces *as a whole*, i.e. the entire transition
layer between the one homogeneous bulk phase and the other, are
always *electroneutral.*   Thermodynamically, it must always be possible to formulate adsorption as due to accumulation and/or ex-
pulsion of electroneutral combinations only, even if ions are involved.   The value assigned to σ_o then depends on where we situ-
ate the formal dividing plane between the two phases.
FIG. 1 illustrates this for the sea water-air interface. Going
from left to right a more or less gradual density increase is observed.   The thickness of the transition region (also a matter of
definition) is of the order of a few nm at room temperature.
Cl^- ions are bigger than H_2O molecules, but Na^+ ions are smaller.
The latter remain more strongly hydrated than the former, hence
the exterior liquid layer bears a slight excess of Cl^- ions,
followed by a layer with an excess of Na^+. Far enough from the
interface, the concentrations of Cl^- and Na^+ are of course equal
again.

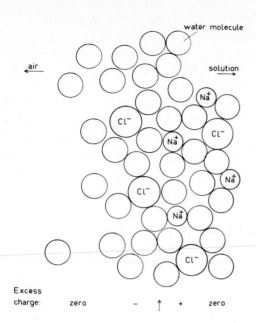

FIG. 1.   The sea water-air interface, schematic. (The concentra-
          tions of Na$^+$ and Cl$^-$ are exaggerated and other ions are
          omitted)

The picture shows that an unequal distribution of ions can give
rise to charged interfaces. In the case under consideration the
solution has a positive potential with respect to air. (Actually,
the ion distribution gives only part of the total potential difference because the preferential orientation of H_2O-dipoles in
the transition layer contributes also). However, the location
of "the" boundary between the two phases will determine how high
σ_o is: it is maximal if located at the arrow in FIG. 1 and zero
if located in one of the bulk phases.

Thermodynamically, the surface excess Γ_i of a substance i can be
related to the same of water Γ_w. For a NaCl-solution, according
to Gibbs

$$d\gamma = - \Gamma_w d\mu_w - \Gamma_{NaCl} d\mu_{NaCl} \tag{1}$$

By virtue of the Gibbs-Duhem relation ($x_w d\mu_w + x_{NaCl} d\mu_{NaCl} = 0$) it is possible to eliminate $d\mu_w$

$$d\gamma = - (\Gamma_{NaCl} - \frac{x_{NaCl}}{x_w} \Gamma_w) d\mu_{NaCl} \equiv - \Gamma_{NaCl}^{(w)} d\mu_{NaCl} \qquad (2)$$

where $\Gamma_i^{(w)}$ stands for the surface excess of i relative to that of water. Experimentally, γ of a NaCl-solution exceeds γ of pure water, hence $\Gamma_{NaCl}^{(w)} < 0$. In words: *NaCl is negatively adsorbed* at the air-water interface, relative to water. Thermodynamics does not inform us on the actual distribution of Cl^- and Na^+ ions. Obtaining this would require model considerations.

Mechanisms of charging interfaces

The most common mechanisms by which interfaces can acquire a charge are the following:

    a) dissociation of surface groups

    b) preferential adsorption of ions

    c) isomorphic substitution

Examples of group (a) are the dissociation of silanol groups on the surface of silica, schematically represented by

$$\equiv SiOH \; \rightleftharpoons \; \equiv SiO^- + H^+ \qquad (3)$$

Silanol groups can also adsorb excess protons:

$$H^+ + \equiv SiOH \; \rightleftharpoons \; \equiv SiOH_2^+ \qquad (4)$$

Reaction (3) renders the surface negative; reaction (4), positive. In this case, the choice of the surface charge is not difficult. In the case of reaction (3) it is the charge corresponding to the number of $\equiv SiO^-$ groups per unit area. The H^+ (or Na^+ in more alkaline solutions) is counted as belonging to the solution, regardless of whether these ions remain close by the surface (*counterions*).

Silica is a very acidic substance. Reaction (4) occurs only at
very low pH, so that in all cases of significance to oceanography silica is negatively charged. This is not necessarily so
with other oxides. Hematite (α-Fe_2O_3) is much more alkaline.   It
has a *point of zero charge* (p.z.c.) of 8.5, which means that below
pH 8.5 the surface is positively charged, whereas above pH 8.5 it
is negative.   At ambient sea water pH, it is possibly positively
charged, leading to attraction of dispersed hematite by silica or
clay particles (see below). Moreover, hematite is an effective
adsorbent for anions. In the soil, hematite plays an important
role in the phosphate fixation.

The determination and interpretation of p.z.c. involve some
problems.   One of them is that the actual value of the p.z.c.
usually depends on the crystal habit of the substance, on its
history and its age.   Very important is also the presence of ad-
sorbable ions.   If cations are strongly *specifically* adsorbed
(i.e. adsorbed through other than coulombic forces) they promote
reactions of type (3) suppressing those of type (4). In other
words, they tend to make the surface more negative.   Hence
in order to reattain the situation where the surface bears no
net charge,a lower pH is required than in the absence of such
cations.   This is tantamount to stating that *specific adsorption
of cations lowers the p.z.c.* By the same token, *specific adsorption of anions increases the p.z.c.* For sea water with its many
ions in high concentrations this can be an important point.
Generally,simple monovalent cations are only slightly specifically adsorbed.   Anions tend to adsorb more strongly than
cations of the same valency and polyvalent ions adsorb more
strongly than monovalent ones. The author does not know to what
extent this has been sorted out for oxides in the natural environment of the ocean.   Experience with model systems indicates
the importance of specific effects.   For example, Breeuwsma and
Lyklema (1973) have found that 10^{-3} N solutions of SO_4^{2-} increase
the p.z.c. of hematite by about one unit, whereas 10^{-3} N solutions of Mg^{2+} or Ca^{2+} decrease it by two pH units.   Considering the fact that in sea water Mg^{2+}, Ca^{2+} and SO_4^{2-} all occur

in concentrations $> 10^{-3}$ N it would be interesting to study their
competitive effect on hematite in oceans and estuaries.   Similar
features are bound to occur with other oxides.

What has been said for oxides applies mutatis mutandis to particles (and big molecules) of organic and biological origin.   These
systems can acquire a negative charge upon dissociation of carboxyl groups or become positive due to the uptake of a proton by
amino groups.   Other groups (imidazole, histidine ...) can also
contribute to the charge, though as a rule to a lesser extent.
For most proteinaceous substances the p.z.c. is below 5, implying
that as a rule,such materials in oceans are negatively charged.

In passing we note that p.z.c. and *isoelectric point* (i.e.p.)
are different notions. The isoelectric point is the pH where the
particle is electrokinetically uncharged.   Electrokinetics will
be treated extensively by Ottewill (this volume).In short, in
electrokinetics the division between moving and stationary phase
(the so-called *slipping plane*) does not coincide with what we
have taken as the physical boundary between particle and solution.
It is located more towards the solution side.   The electrokinetic
charge σ_e is the charge on the slipping plane.   It differs from
σ_o.   It depends on the way in which the charge is distributed
around the particles whether σ_e is higher or lower than σ_o.   The
two charges can even have different signs.

P.z.c. and i.e.p. are identical when there is no specific adsorption,   but with specific adsorption they move in different
directions.   For example, the i.e.p. of hematite in the presence
of Ca^{2+} is *higher* than 8.5 because electrokinetics measures σ_o
plus the envelope of adsorbed Ca^{2+}, and as this is more positive
than the same   without envelope it would require a higher pH to
render surface and envelope *together* again uncharged.   See also
below, FIG. 2.   In literature authors have often confused p.z.c.
and i.e.p.

The conclusion is that points of zero charge are important quantities, but that what is available in literature should be looked
upon critically.   A useful review, mainly of i.e.p.'s for oxides,
has been given by Parks (1965).

Mechanism (b), the preferential adsorption of ions, occurs to a large extent only if the adsorbing species has a particularly high affinity to the adsorbent, because the sorption must counteract the developing opposing potential difference generated by this process. As a rule of thumb a specific adsorption energy of RT is required per equivalent for every 25 mV of potential difference. The specific adsorption energy of simple monovalent cations is usually not enough to produce substantial potential differences. A few tens of mV can be obtained with simple monovalent anions or simple bivalent ions. Considerable potential differences can be obtained in two cases:

(i) if the adsorbing ion is *surface active* (soaps, fatty acids, polyelectrolytes), and

(ii) if the adsorbing ion is *potential determining* (p.d.), meaning that it is one of the constituent ions of the sorbent. The classical examples are Ag^+ and I^- for silver iodide. For potential-determining ion adsorption, Nernst's electrode potential law is valid, e.g. for AgI the surface potential ψ_o with respect to the p.z.c. follows from

$$F\psi_o = 2.3 \, RT(pI - pI^o) = - 2.3 \, RT \, (pAg - pAg^o) \qquad (5)$$

where $pI = - \log a_{I^-}$ and pI^o is the same at the p.z.c. Possibly HS^- ions are potential determining for sulphidic marine sediments.

In the case of the adsorption of KI of $AgNO_3$ on AgI the distinction between p.d. ions and counterions is obvious; so is the definition of σ_o. In the case of specific adsorption of other ions, whether surface active or not, it is to some extent a matter of convenience whether the charge they attribute is counted as "the" surface charge. We prefer the use of σ_o for surface charge in the strict sense of the charge on the surface proper, including the charge contributed by chemisorbed species, thereby acknowledging that the distinction between chemisorption and physical adsorption is not always unambiguous. The charge contributed by organic surface active ions, including polyelectro-

lytes,definitely belongs to the countercharge. For these substances the considerable specific adsorption energy is usually
derived from the many hydrocarbon segments they contain, each of
them contributing about RT upon adsorption.

Charging mechanisms (a) and (b) often concur. We noted already
that σ_o depends on the amount of specifically adsorbed countercharge.

Mechanism (c), isomorphic substitution,is typical for clay minerals. Isomorphic replacement of Si^{4+} by Al^{3+} or of Al^{3+} by Mg^{2+}
renders the crystals negative. It is a bulk charge rather than
a volume charge. Nevertheless,the adsorption and colloidal properties of clay particles resemble those of,say,SiO_2 and AgI.
The bulk charge is,of course,compensated by an equal but opposite
countercharge. Characteristically σ_o is a constant, independent
of pH and solution composition. Clays have no p.z.c.

Measuring surface charges

If the origin of the surface charge is known it is,in principle,
possible to determine its value.

For mechanisms (a) and (b) the standard technique is *potentiometric titration* (Lyklema and Overbeek, 1961 ; Tadros and Lyklema,
1968). The classical example is AgI, which can be titrated
with KI or $AgNO_3$. From such a titration it is possible to derive

$$\sigma_o = F(\Gamma_{AgNO_3} - \Gamma_{KI}) \tag{6}$$

as a function of pI or pAg, or,for that matter, as a function of
ψ_o. For silica, hematite,and other oxides by the same method

$$\sigma_o = F(\Gamma_{H^+} - \Gamma_{OH^-}) \tag{7}$$

is obtainable as a function of pH (but not without a lot of theory as a function of ψ_o).

Plots of σ_o(pI) or σ_o(pH) can be made only if the specific surface area and the p.z.c. are known. With respect to the latter,
the p.z.c. can be obtained from titration at various electrolyte
concentrations. In the absence of specific adsorption, σ_o is independent of ionic strength at the p.z.c. and once the p.z.c. in
the absence has been established it is not difficult to find
how much it shifts upon addition of specifically adsorbing substances. We note that surface charge plots can be made at various
concentrations of electrolytes and also in the presence of adsorbing organic substances.

Specifically adsorbed amounts of low- or high-molecular weight
ions can in principle be determined analytically. The practical
feasibility is usually restricted by the availability of large
enough adsorbing areas.

The conventional way in which σ_o of clay systems is expressed is
as the cation exchange capacity (CEC).

On double layer structure

It is clear from the above that the existence of charged interfaces implies the presence of an electrical double layer at that
interface. How such double layers are composed is a.o. important
for colloidal stability, sedimentation and electrokinetics.

The fundamental double layer parameters are *charge* and *potential*.
They are related quantities. At any location in a double layer
it is always possible to relate the charge per unit area to the
potential gradient, using Gauss' law of electrostatics in the
form

$$\iiint \rho dV = \varepsilon_o \iint (\vec{D}_n . \vec{dO}) \qquad (8)$$

where ρ is the space charge density, ε_o the permittivity of free
space and $\vec{D}_n$ the normal component of the dielectric displacement.
The integration in the LHS is carried out over a closed volume
and the integration in the RHS over the surface of that volume.
Applying (8) to a big particle (double layer thickness << parti-

cle radius) the LHS equals the total charge on the particle and the scalar product $(\vec{D}_n.\vec{dO}) \sim \varepsilon(d\psi/dx)_{x=0}dO$ if x is the distance from the surface and ε the relative dielectric constant at that place. Hence,

$$\sigma_o = \varepsilon\varepsilon_o(\frac{d\psi}{dx})_{x=0} \tag{9}$$

Alternatively, if Gauss' theorem would have been applied to the slipping plane, the corresponding relation between σ_e and the potential gradient at the slipping plane would have been obtained.

For a more detailed description of double layer composition in terms of charge and potential model considerations are required.

Generally, double layers consist of three parts.

a) The surface charge σ_o, whether restricted to the surface proper or not.

b) The Stern layer charge σ_m of specifically adsorbed ions in the immediate surroundings of the surface (Stern, 1924)

c) The diffuse layer charge σ_d of ions not specifically adsorbed. This charge can be spread over considerable depth due to thermal motion. It is essentially through this very part of the double layer that charged hydrophobic colloids "feel" each other's repulsion, with the ensuing possibility of electrostatic stabilization against aggregation. Also on behalf of this layer there is still some charge and potential left at the slipping plane, a feature that is responsible for electrokinetic effects. The diffuse part of the double layer is also known as Gouy-layer or Gouy-Chapman layer (Gouy, 1910, 1917; Chapman, 1913).

Because of electroneutrality

$$\sigma_o + \sigma_m + \sigma_d = 0 \tag{10}$$

Often, but not necessarily, σ_m and σ_o have opposite signs. If specific adsorption is very strong it is even possible that σ_m and σ_o have the same sign but more often specific adsorption is

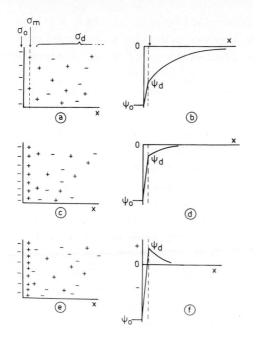

FIG. 2.   Some examples of charge- and potential distributions
           in double layers

superequivalent, i.e. σ_m and σ_o have opposite signs whereas
$|\sigma_m| > |\sigma_o|$. In that case σ_d has the same sign as σ_o.

FIG. 2 gives some illustrations. FIG. 2a visualizes to the left
a negative surface. It could be silica, a clay mineral or an
organic adsorbate at the water-air interface. The countercharge
is positive and there is some specific adsorption ($|\sigma_m|/|\sigma_o| = 0.4$).
Anions are negatively adsorbed. FIG. 2b gives the corresponding
potential distribution. The slipping plane is probably located
around the arrow. Usually ψ_d and the electrokinetic potential ζ
are taken as identical, hence $\zeta < \psi_o$. FIG. 2c gives the distribution at the same ψ_o if there is strong specific adsorption of
cations ($|\sigma_m|/|\sigma_o| = 0.875$). The surface charge is now more
negative than in case (a), but ψ_d is less negative (FIG. 2d).

Sols would be less stable and the electrophoretic mobility less
than in the first case. FIG. 2e gives the distribution in the
case of superequivalent cation adsorption and FIG. 2f the concom-
itant potential distribution. ψ_d and ψ_o have now different signs.
Somewhere between situations c and e, the electrokinetic potential is zero.

For the interpretation of colloidal phenomena, insight in the
charge-and potential distribution is important. Histori-
cally, the emphasis has been on diffuse double layers. The DLVO-
theory of colloidal stability (after Deryagin and Landau, 1941;
and Verwey and Overbeek, 1948) is to a large extent based on the
overlap of diffuse double layers. Actually, the role of the
Stern-layer in real systems is often considerable, because it is
the extent of specific adsorption that determines how much of σ_o
is left for the diffuse double layer part. In 0.1 M solutions of
monovalent cations,σ_m can easily amount to 30-50% of σ_o and in
10^{-3} M solutions of bivalent ions σ_m can become as high as 95% of
σ_o. Clearly, in sea water the role of the Stern-layer is domi-
nant. The Stern-layer is also responsible for the so-called
lyotropic sequence in the critical coagulation concentrations c_c
(that is the electrolyte concentration required to rapidly coagu-
late a hydrophobic sol). Even for a system with little specific
adsorption such as AgI, c_c for $RbNO_3$ is about a third lower than
the same for $LiNO_3$ (Lyklema, 1970).

The author is not aware of a systematic quantitative formulation
of σ_o and subsequent assessment of the ionic components of charge
of double layers in salt solutions with sea water composition.
However, a clever guess of the orders of magnitude is easily made,
using simplified double layer equations.

The thickness of a diffuse double layer is usually measured by
the distance over which the surface potential ψ_o, or rather the
potential ψ_d of the diffuse part of the double layer (see FIG. 2),
has dropped to ψ_d/e. This distance is approximately given by the
Debye length κ^{-1} (the measure is exact only for flat double layers and low potential) where

$$\kappa^2 = \frac{e^2 N_{Av} \sum_i c_i z_i}{1000 \; \epsilon\epsilon_o kT} \sim 10^{15} \sum_i c_i z_i^2 \quad cm^{-2} \tag{11}$$

for aqueous solutions at room temperature, if c_i in M. For a solution being about 0.5 M in (1-1) electrolyte and 0.05 M in
(2-2) electrolyte, roughly representative for sea water, one thus
computes $\kappa = 2.8 \times 10^7$ cm or $\kappa^{-1} = 0.36$ nm. As this is of the
order of magnitude of the radii of hydrated ions, the conclusion
is that *in sea water double layers are essentially non-diffuse*.
The diffuse part plays a significant role only in deltas, estuaries etc., where the salinity is low. In passing we recall that
the aggregation of suspended particulate matter in rivers upon
entering the sea is nothing other than the coagulation of sols by
electrolytes.

The conclusion that double layers in sea water are virtually non-
diffuse explains why ion adsorption, either on dispersed particles
or on the layers adsorbed at the very surface of the ocean, can be
so highly specific. At the same time it is not feasible to present
a general treatment. Specificity depends strongly on the nature
of the adsorbing surface and on the properties of the adsorbing
ion. Experiments are needed to sort these processes.

Experiments with model substances

The majority of double layer measurements have been done with
model substances like mercury droplets, silver iodide and latices.
By their very nature, these substances are so remote from particulate matter in oceans and from marine sediments that it is questionable whether the information, obtained with these model substances is relevant for oceanographic purposes. Relatively more
suitable is the double layer work on oxides, though systematic
investigations in mixed electrolytes appear to be unavailable.
For sake of illustration FIGS. 3 and 4 give some relevant examples. They are selected from work by Tadros and Lyklema (1968,
1969) and by Breeuwsma and Lyklema (1971, 1973).

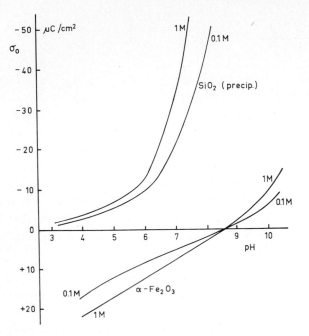

FIG. 3. Surface charge as a function of pH for precipitated
         silica and hematite (α-Fe$_2$O$_3$) in molar and decimolar
         solutions of KCl. Temperature 20°C.

FIG. 3 gives titration curves in KCl. The SiO$_2$-sample was a commercial precipitated product, ex BDH, the hematite has been synthesized. Products of other origin may show a somewhat different
behaviour, although the general features are probably retained.
The following is observed. Addition of electrolyte increases the
absolute value of σ_o. This is due to improved screening by counterions. In the absence of specific adsorption (as is the case
for KCl on these oxides) the intersection point of the curves at
different salt concentration is the p.z.c. which can thus be
determined. The 10^{-2} and 10^{-3} M KCl curves (not shown in the
figure) pass also through this point. As judged by the p.z.c.
values, hematite is more alkaline than silica. At solution pH-
values somewhat below 7 the particles are oppositely charged and
consequently attract each other. In practice this does not necessarily cause dramatic aggregation since in 10^{-1} and 1 M solutions the diffuse double layers are virtually compressed.

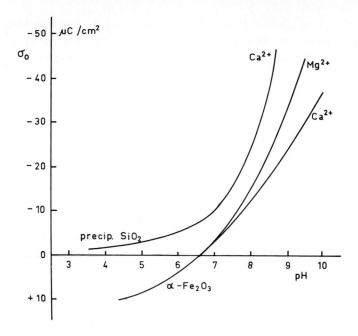

FIG. 4. Surface charge as a function of pH for precipitated
silica and hematite (α-Fe_2O_3) in 10^{-2} N solutions of
$MgCl_2$ and $CaCl_2$. Temperature $20^{\circ}C$.

FIG. 4 shows similar curves in more dilute $CaCl_2$ or $MgCl_2$ solutions. Because of the lower concentrations the absolute value
of σ_o would be less than in FIG. 3, but this lowering is counter-
acted if the bivalent cation would adsorb specifically. The latter is clearly the case with hematite at high pH where σ_o is much
more negative than in KCl. The stronger adsorption of Mg^{2+} as
compared to Ca^{2+} is possibly attributable to isomorphic substitution of lattice Fe^{3+} by Mg^{2+}, these two ions having approximately the same ionic crystal radius. The other feature indicating specific adsorption of earth alkaline ions on hematite is
the shift of the p.z.c. to lower values, a phenomenon
already discussed above. In the presence of bivalent ions the
charge contrast between SiO_2 and Fe_2O_3 at pH values below 7 is
much less than with monovalent ions.

As stated before, the negative surface charge can be attributed
to dissociated surface-OH groups. With about 4-5 of such groups per
nm^2 the surface could maximally carry a charge of approximately
65-80 $\mu C/cm^2$. Experimentally, this limit is easily exceeded with
SiO_2 at high pH and any type of counterion. The suggestion has
been put forward that in this case the charge is not confined
to the surface proper but has some depth into the solid (Lyklema,
1968). On hematite this is also likely with Mg^{2+} as the counterion, but not with Ca^{2+}.

Double layer studies like the ones described have also been done
with other types of silica and with other oxides, for example with
pyrogenic silica (Abendroth, 1970), quartz (Li and De Bruyn, 1966),
MnO_2 (Morgan and Stumm, 1964), Al_2O_3 (Herszyńska, 1964; Sadek
et al, 1970) and goethite (FeOOH) (Atkinson et al, 1967).

Further studies

Double layer investigations along the lines described can be pursued in various directions, especially

  (i) extension to mixed salt solutions as in sea water
  (ii) extension to incorporate the effect of adsorbed organic
  substances
  (iii) theoretical interpretation

Item (i) has not yet been done to the author's knowledge. Studies
of this type seem particularly appropriate in analyzing ion specificity, including adsorption antagonism or synergism. Item (ii)
has been systematically studied with AgI (Bijsterbosch and
Lyklema, 1965; Vincent et al., 1971) but not yet with oxides.
The AgI-work has given insight in the mode of attachment of the
organic substance and in its competition with water dipoles and
counterions. The method works also with adsorbed polymeric or
long chain surface active molecules (Koopal and Lyklema, 1975;
De Keizer and Lyklema, 1975). This can be of interest in the
assessment of the conformation of these molecules in the adsorbed
state. Knowledge of this conformation is, in turn, important in

connection with the possible role of long chain molecules in the
stabilization of particles against aggregation (*steric* stabilization, substituting the electrostatic repulsion which, as shown,
is largely suppressed in ocean water). Theoretical interpretation can go along several lines. Adsorption of counterions at
given σ_o can be described by isotherm equations, for example by
a modified Langmuir isotherm, the modification being the inclu-
sion of an electric contribution to the adsorption energy. Another approach is to describe the dissociation of $\equiv SiOH$ groups
in terms of acidity constants (pK's). If this is attempted it
should be realized that the standard Gibbs free energy of dissociation contains an electrical contribution which varies with
the potential. In practice this implies that the extent of dissociation is not solely determined by the intrinsic pK of the
group under consideration but also by how many neighbouring
groups are already dissociated. Still another theoretical analysis would consider interpretation of ion adsorption on a molecular scale.

Conclusion

In this survey, some general features of double layers and a number of results of experiments with model substances have been
discussed. Although these studies had no particular reference
to oceanographic problems it is nevertheless hoped that they do
contribute to a seminal insight in the important processes occurring at charged interfaces and that they may lead to suggestions for further investigations.

References

(1) Abendroth, R.P. 1970. Behavior of a Pyrogenic Silica in
       Simple Electrolytes. J. Colloid Interfac. Sci. 34: 591-596.
(2) Atkinson, R.J.;Posner, A.M.; and Quirk, J.P. 1967. Adsorp-
       tion of Potential Determining Ions at the Ferric Oxide-
       Aqueous Electrolyte Solution. J. Phys. Chem. 71: 550-558.

596   J. Lyklema

(3)   Bijsterbosch, B.H.; and Lyklema, J.   1965.   Electrochemistry
      of Silver Iodide.   Double Layer Properties in the Presence
      of Adsorbed Organic Molecules.   J. Colloid Sci. $\underline{20}$: 665-678.

(4)   Breeuwsma, A.; and Lyklema, J.   1971.   Interfacial Electro-
      chemistry of Haematite (α-Fe_2O_3).   Discussions Faraday Soc.
      $\underline{52}$: 324-333.

(5)   Breeuwsma, A.; and Lyklema, J.   1973.   Physical and Chemical
      Adsorption of Ions in the Electrical Double Layer on
      Hematite (α-Fe_2O_3).   J. Colloid Interfac. Sci. $\underline{43}$: 437-448.

(6)   Chapman, D.L.   1913.   A Contribution to the Theory of Elec-
      trocapillarity.   Phil. Mag (6) $\underline{25}$: 475-481.

(7)   Deryagin, B.; and Landau, L.   1941.   Theory of the Stability
      of Strongly Charged Lyophobic Sols and of the Adhesion of
      Strongly Charged Particles in Solutions of Electrolytes.
      Acta Physicochim URSS $\underline{14}$: 633-662 (Chem. Abstr. $\underline{39}$: 453^2).

(8)   Gouy, G.   1910.   Sur la Constitution de la Charge Electrique
      à la Surface d'un Electrolyte.   J. Phys. (4) $\underline{9}$: 457-468.

(9)   Gouy, G.   1917.   Sur la Fonction Electrocapillaire.   Ann.
      Phys. (9) $\underline{7}$: 129-184.

(10) Herczyńska, E.   1964.   Adsorption Isotherms of Potential
      Determining Ions.   J. Inorg. Nucl. Chem. $\underline{26}$: 2127-2133.

(11) De Keizer, A.; and Lyklema, J.   1975.   The Electrical Double
      Layer on Silver Iodide in the Presence of Adsorbed Dimethyl-
      dodecylamine Oxide.   An. Quím. Real. Soc. Españ. Fis. y Quím,
      to be published.

(12) Koopal, L.K.; and Lyklema, J.   1975.   Characterization of
      Polymers in the Adsorbed State by Double Layer Measurements.
      Faraday Discussions Chem. Soc. $\underline{59}$: to be published.

(13) Li, H.C.; and De Bruyn, P.L.   1966.   Electrokinetic and
      Adsorption Studies on Quartz.   Surface Sci. $\underline{5}$: 203-220.

(14) Lyklema, J.; and Overbeek, J.Th.G.   1961.   Electrochemistry
      of Silver Iodide.   The Capacity of the Double Layer at the
      Silver Iodide-Water Interface.   J. Colloid Sci. $\underline{16}$: 595-608.

(15) Lyklema, J.   1968.   The Structure of the Electrical Double
      Layer on Porous Surfaces.   J. Electroanal. Chem. $\underline{18}$: 341-348.

(16) Lyklema, J.   1970.   The Lyotropic Sequence in the Stability
      of Hydrophobic Colloids.   Croat. Chem. Acta $\underline{42}$: 151-160.

(17) Morgan, J.J.; and Stumm, W. 1964. Colloid Chemical Properties of Manganese Dioxide. J. Colloid Sci. 19: 347-359.

(18) Parks, G.A. 1965. The Isoelectric Points of Solid Oxides,
Solid Hydroxides and Aqueous Hydroxo Complex Systems. Chem.
Revs. 65: 177-198.

(19) Sadek, H,; Helmy, A.K.; Sabet, V.M.; and Tadros, Th.F. 1970.
Adsorption of Potential-Determining Ions at the Aluminium
Oxide-Aqueous Interface and the Point of Zero Charge.
J. Electroanal.Chem. 27: 257-266.

(20) Stern, O. 1924. Zur Theorie der Elektrolytischen Doppel-
schicht. Z. Elektrochem. 30: 508-516.

(21) Tadros, Th.F.; and Lyklema, J. 1968. Adsorption of Poten-
tial Determining Ions at the Silica-Aqueous Electrolyte
Interface and the Role of some Cations. J. Electroanal.
Chem. 17: 267-275.

(22) Tadros, Th.F.; and Lyklema, J. 1969. The Electrical Double
Layer on Silica in the Presence of Bivalent Counterions.
J. Electroanal. Chem. 22: 1-8.

(23) Verwey, E.J.W.; and Overbeek, J.Th.G. 1948. Theory of the
Stability of Lyophobic Colloids. Elsevier Publ. Cy., Amsterdam, New York,

(24) Vincent, B; Bijsterbosch, B.H.; and Lyklema, J. 1971. Com-
petitive Adsorption of Ions and Neutral Molecules in the
Stern Layer on Silver Iodide and its Effect on Colloidal
Stability. J. Colloid Interfac. Sci., 37: 171-178.

Electrokinetic Properties of Particles

R. H. Ottewill and L. R. Holloway
School of Chemistry, University of Bristol, Cantock's Close,
Bristol BS8 1TS, England.

Abstract: The application of electrokinetic methods to the examination of particulate matter is reviewed. Particular attention is given to the properties of oxides and clays. The use of electrokinetic methods to detect the adsorption of organic ions and hydrolysed ions on particles and to detect chemical reactions at surfaces is discussed.

Introduction

The movement of a particle, in an electrolyte solution, relative to the solution or the movement of a solution in laminar flow relative to a surface, causes part of the double layer to be moved away with the solution. The other part of the double layer remains, supposedly intact, near the surface. It is normally assumed that the two parts separate cleanly at an infinitely thin plane which is termed the plane of shear. The potential at this plane is known as the electrokinetic potential or the zeta-potential[6,26,31]. Physically there may well be a small region over which the shear process occurs and the ultimate reason for part of the double layer remaining near the surface may well be the increase in viscosity near the surface caused by

the very high field strength in the inner region of the double
layer[19]. A schematic diagram is given in Figure 1 showing the
position of the zeta-potential plane relative to that of the
surface potential, ψ_o, and the Stern (or outer Helmholtz)
potential, ψ_δ. In nature and in magnitude the zeta-potential
is probably close to the Stern potential and many authors
assume that they can be taken as identical; certainly as
$\psi_\delta \to 0$ so will $\zeta \to 0$. However, at the present time there is
no definitive treatment which explicitly relates the zeta-
potential to the other potentials in the electrostatic treatments of the undisturbed electrical double layer.

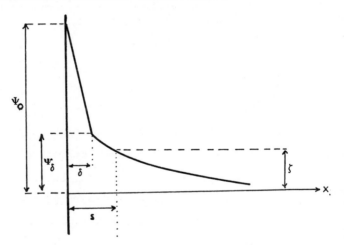

Figure 1:   Schematic diagram showing position of shear plane
             at distance, s, from wall

A number of electrokinetic effects are recognised and
these include :

   a)   Electrophoresis
             The movement of a particle in an electrolyte
   solution under the influence of an applied field.

b) Sedimentation potential

The generation of a difference of potential in a column of electrolyte solution by the movement of a particle, or particles, through it under the influence of a gravitational or centrifugal field. For a single particle of radius, a, sedimenting with a velocity, V, in an electrolyte solution of specific conductance, the potential generated is,

$$E = \frac{\varepsilon a \zeta}{\lambda} V$$

where ζ = zeta-potential and ε the relative permittivity of the solution.

c) Streaming potential

The potential, E, developed across a pair of electrodes at the end of a capillary or plug of powder when an electrolyte solution flows through it, in laminar flow, under an applied pressure P is given by,

$$E = \frac{\varepsilon \zeta}{4\pi\eta [\lambda + 2\lambda_s/r]} P$$

where r = capillary radius, λ_s = surface conductance and η = viscosity. It should be noted that λ_s becomes negligible when $\lambda \gg 2\lambda_s/r$.

d) Electro-osmosis

The movement of liquid in a capillary or plug of powder caused by the application of an electric field. The velocity of liquid flow per unit field strength is given by,

$$u = \frac{\varepsilon \zeta}{4\pi\eta}$$

The effects listed as a) to d) constitute the main electrokinetic phenomena but in addition, the electroviscous effect[26] and ultrasonic vibration potentials[30] are the consequence of electrokinetic effects.

The major part of the literature of electrokinetics reports measurements using the streaming potential method or measurements of mobility using the microelectrophoresis technique. The former method is extremely useful for coarse materials, such as minerals, which can be ground and sieved to obtain a powder with a particle size of the order of 100 μm or larger. The microelectrophoresis method is suitable for low particle number concentrations of materials which exist in the micron or sub-micron size range. The particles can be illuminated either directly or indirectly and viewed with a microscope; particles as small as 20 nm can be observed with an ultramicroscope, provided the refractive index of the particle is high. If precautions are taken to observe particles migrating in an electric field at the stationary level, i.e. the region where the velocity of the solution is zero, quite precise mobility results can be obtained[32]. Two pieces of equipment are, in fact, sold commercially for the measurement of electrophoretic mobilities[28,39].

The mobility, u, is related to the zeta-potential, by

$$u = \frac{\varepsilon \zeta}{6\pi\eta} \quad f(\kappa a, \zeta)$$

provided $\kappa a > 100$, then

$$u = \varepsilon\zeta/4\pi\eta$$

the so-called Smoluchowski equation which is identical with the equation for electro-osmotic flow.

If $\kappa a \ll 1$ then,

$$u = \varepsilon\zeta/6\pi\eta$$

giving the Hückel equation. The factor $f(\kappa a, \zeta)$ depends on the retardation and relaxation effects caused by the disturbance of the electrical double layer in the motion of the particle. The correction factors have been worked out and can be found in the papers of Wiersema, Loeb and Overbeek[36] and Ottewill and Shaw[25]. Since the correction factors are quite complicated, the basic data, i.e. the mobility, should be reported in preference to the derived data, i.e. the zeta-potential. The magnitudes of zeta-potentials are usually in the region 0-100 mV and seldom exceed 150 mV.

Despite the difficulties of converting mobilities into zeta-potentials and the uncertainty about the exact location of the plane of shear, and thus the uncertainty to some degree about the nature of the zeta-potential, electrokinetic measurements do provide an extremely important means of characterizing particulate material and of obtaining information about the behaviour of particles in various environments. Information which can readily be obtained from mobility measurements (or other electrokinetic measurements) include,

a) the isoelectric point. This is defined as the negative logarithm (base 10) of the concentration of potential determining ions at which the electrokinetic potential becomes zero; thus for electrophoresis, this corresponds to the point of zero mobility. In the present article, since H^+ and OH^- are the principle potential determining ions, the isoelectric point will be given in pH units.

b)   the behaviour of particles in solutions of "simple"
      electrolytes. The term simple is used to denote electro-
      lytes whose ions do not hydrolyse and whose ions do not
      interact with the surface.

c)   evidence for the specific adsorption of ions,

d)   evidence for the hydrolysis of ions and their subsequent
      adsorption on to particle surfaces,

e)   evidence for the adsorption of organic ions, as small
      ions, polyelectrolytes and neutral macromolecules,

f)   evidence for the occurrence of a chemical reaction at a
      surface with consequent change in the nature of the surface.

Since the salt concentration of sea water is very high,
only very small electrokinetic potentials would be expected.
However, in a recent paper, Pravdic[27] has examined a number of
sea sediments by a streaming current method. In 36% salinity he
finds that the electrokinetic potentials are usually positive
and can reach values as high as 138 mV.

The main role of electrokinetic phenomena would therefore
seem to be in obtaining information on particulate matter after
isolation from the sea-water environment. With this in mind this
article will be devoted to discussing the information which can
be obtained from the inorganic particulate matter most likely to
be found in sea-water, e.g. oxides and clays.

Behaviour of Oxides and Clays as a Function of
pH and Electrolyte Concentration

Most oxides in contact with water undergo surface hydrolysis
to form hydroxyl groups. The latter can then react with further
water molecules to form either negatively or positively charged
surfaces. This can be represented schematically as,

$$>\!\!M = O \quad \rightarrow \quad >\!\!M\!\!<^{OH}_{OH} \quad \xrightarrow[]{H_2O} \quad >\!\!M\!\!<^{OH_2^+}_{OH} \quad + \quad OH^-$$

$$\xrightarrow[H_2O]{} \quad >\!\!M\!\!<^{OH}_{O^-} \quad + \quad H_3^+O$$

Thus, eventually all the hydroxyl groups can become charged and since the equilibrium depends on the concentration of H_3O^+ and OH^- the latter are called the potential determining ions.

Alumina

An example of the behaviour of an oxide is shown in Figure 2 in which the mobility of α-alumina is plotted as a function of pH at four different concentrations of sodium chloride. In the three lower concentrations of sodium chloride the particles reach zero mobility at a pH value of 9.15 and hence at these salt concentrations, the isoelectric point of alumina is 9.15. At a sodium chloride concentration of 10^{-1} mol dm^{-3}, the isoelectric point moves to a somewhat lower pH (8.8), an effect which appears to be attributable to the specific adsorption of chloride ions to the alumina surface.

An examination of the mobility of the alumina particles at constant pH (4.0) as a function of the electrolyte concentration from the data given in Figure 2, shows that the mobility increases with ionic strength, reaches a maximum value at ca. 5×10^{-3} mol dm^{-3}, and then decreases again. On a straightforward application of double-layer theory the maximum is unexpected and it would be

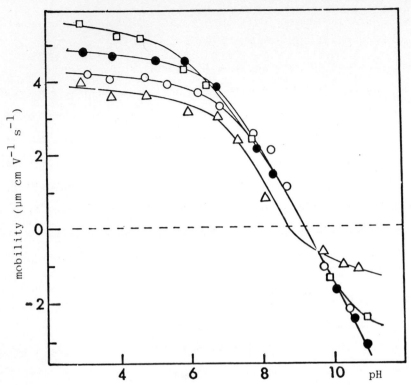

Figure 2:   Mobility against pH for alumina particles in various
            concentrations (mol dm^{-3}) of sodium chloride: —O— ,
            10^{-4}; —●— , 10^{-3}; —□— , 10^{-2}; —△— , 10^{-1}.

anticipated that the potential would decrease continuously with

increasing electrolyte concentration.   However, at low concentra-

tions of electrolyte, most of the current is concentrated in the

neighbourhood of the particle, i.e. there is a surface conduct-

ance term λ_s (see earlier).   In order to prevent an accumulation

of electricity in the region between the highly conducting

surface layer and the weakly conducting bulk liquid, a counter

e.m.f. is generated and thus the mobility is decreased.   This

effect usually becomes negligible in 1:1 electrolytes at concentrations of the order of 5 x 10^{-4} mol dm^{-3}. At higher
electrolyte concentrations, the increasing ionic strength
compresses the electric double layer and correspondingly decreases
the magnitude of the zeta-potential. The exact location of the
maximum in the mobility curve is not a simple matter and depends
on a number of factors, including whether the surface potential
or surface charge remain constant with increasing electrolyte,[14]
or whether the surface dissociation increases with increasing
electrolyte. Relaxation and discreteness of charge effects
could also play a role in determining the position of the
maximum.

Silica

The mobility against pH curves for silica particles at
different electrolyte concentrations are shown in Figure 3. For
this material the mobility does not reach zero within the range
of pH values examined. Extrapolation of the data indicates that
the isoelectric point lies below pH 2.0; with some silica
samples well defined isoelectric points have been observed. The
results indicate that the surface of silica is negatively charged
at all pH values above pH 2 owing to the loss of protons from the
surface.

Isoelectric Points of Oxides

From the data presented in Figures 2 and 3, it can be seen
that α-alumina has a basic surface, whereas silica has an
acidic surface. The isoelectric point of an oxide is a character-

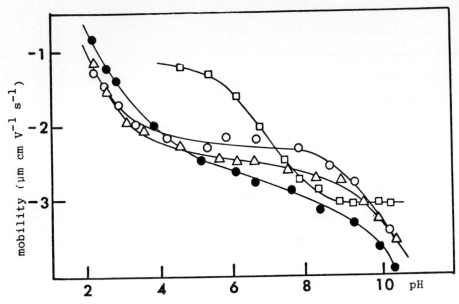

Figure 3: Mobility against pH for silica particles in various concentrations (mol dm^{-3}) of sodium chloride: —○— , 10^{-4}; —△—, 10^{-3}; —●—, 10^{-2}; —□—. 10^{-1}.

istic   of that material and the natural oxides fall into a spectrum of values. Some typical values are listed in Table 1. It must be remembered, however, that all oxides are soluble in water to an extent which depends on the pH. Thus the residence of several oxides in an aqueous environment may well result in them all becoming coated with solution products. For example, many materials stored as particulate dispersions in glass bottles will gradually become coated with silica.

Clay Materials

The principal elements from which a clay particle is constructed on an atomic level are 2-dimensional arrays of

Table 1

Isoelectric Points of Various Oxides

Material	Chemical Formula	Isoelectric Point	Reference
Natural α-alumina	Al_2O_3	8.4 ± 0.1	17
Linde "A" alumina	Al_2O_3	9.1 ± 0.1	38
Corundum	Al_2O_3	8.2 ± 0.1	4
Beryl	$3\ BeO, Al_2O_3, 6\ SiO_2$	3.3	8
Andalusite	$Al_2O_3\ SiO_2$	7.2	33
Mullite	$3\ Al_2O_3\ SiO_2$	8.0	33
Geothite	α-FeOOH	6.7	16
Hematite (Natural)	α-Fe_2O_3	6.7	15
Magnorite	MgO	12.5 ± 0.5	29
Mn(II) manganite	MnO_2	~ 2.0	12
α-manganese dioxide	MnO_2	4.6	12
β-manganese dioxide	MnO_2	7.3	12
γ- manganese dioxide	MnO_2	5.6	12
Silica powder	SiO_2	2.0 ± 0.1	37
Quartz (Brazilian)	SiO_2	3.7	9
Rutile (natural)	TiO_2	3.5	10
Zinc oxide	ZnO	10.3 ± 0.1	23
Zircon	ZrO_2	5.7	3

silicon - oxygen tetrahedra and two-dimensional arrays of
aluminium or magnesium hydroxyl octahedra[24] . The sheets of
tetrahedra and octahedra are superimposed in various ways in
the different types of clays, and it is possible to produce 2-
layer minerals (silica-alumina) or 3-layer minerals (silica-
alumina-silica). In many cases isomorphous substitution occurs
within the lattice, e.g. of Mg^{2+} for Al^{3+}, thus leaving the
crystal with a constant negative charge on the faces.

A typical example of a 3-layer clay is sodium montmorillonite,
a very commonly occurring expanding clay, which once dispersed can
exist in very thin sheets (ca. 1nm) with an extensive face area
(ca. 800 m^2 g^{-1}). In a typical case of a Wyoming bentonite this
was found to have a cation exchange capacity of 83.7 m equivalents
per 100 g of dry clay[2] . This corresponds to a surface charge
density of ca. 11.5 μC cm^{-2} and in 10^{-4} mol dm^{-3} salt solution to
a Stern potential of ca. 200 mV. Mobility against pH curves for
sodium montmorillonite[2] are shown in Figure 4. This material
shows an interesting behaviour in that the highest zeta-potential
is reached in 10^{-1} mol dm^{-3} salt solution. The Smoluchowski
equation gives a value of -50 mV for the zeta-potential. There
must be some uncertainty, however, about the calculation of zeta-
potential for measurements on such thin plates, since, as the
plates rotate, the lines of viscous flow and of the electric field
do not necessarily remain parallel to the particle surface.

With two-layer clays, e.g. kaolinite, which exist as much
thicker materials, the parallel arrays of silica tetrahedra and
alumina octahedra are often disrupted by fracture across the
planes in creating the edges. Thus the particle edges bear a
close resemblance to the oxide surfaces of silica and alumina and

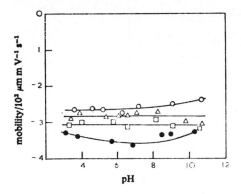

Figure 4:   Mobility against pH for alumina particles in various
concentrations (mol dm^{-3}) of sodium chloride: —□— ,
10^{-4}; —△—, 10^{-3}; —○—, 10^{-2}; —●—, 10^{-1}.

the charge determining mechanism of the clay edges is essentially

that of an oxide surface.   Hence for a material such as kaolinite

the face charge can remain essentially constant as a function of

pH whilst the net charge on the edges can change from positive to

negative as a function of pH,   i.e. the edge can have its own

point of zero charge.   The consequences of this on the electro-

phoretic mobility of kaolinite[7] are shown in Figure 5.   The

mobility of the particles, unlike montmorillonite, shows a varia-

tion with pH and even becomes positive at pH 4.   A region of

constant mobility is found over the pH range 5.5-8.0.   It is over

this range that the edges adsorb both anions and cations and it

has been suggested that the edges of a kaolinite crystal exhibit

a point of zero charge at about pH 7.0;   this value is close to

that found for some aluminosilicates by Smolik, Harman and

Fuerstenau[33] and by Johansen and Buchanan[17].

An important point when studying clays is to minimize the

exposure of the material to acid and alkali since attack on the

latter starts to occur fairly rapidly below pH 3 and above pH 10

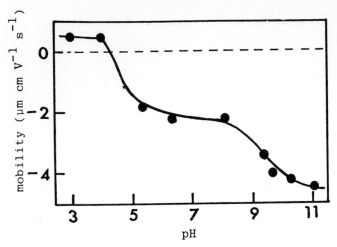

Figure 5:   Mobility against pH for sodium kaolinite
             particles in 10^{-4} mol dm^{-3} of sodium chloride

Inorganic Ion Interactions at Oxide Surfaces

The mobility of silica particles in various concentrations
of calcium chloride[13] is given in Figure 6.   In 10^{-4} mol dm^{-3}
calcium chloride solution, the results resemble those obtained
in sodium chloride solutions.   However, as the concentration of
calcium chloride is increased, the curves show a different
pattern of behaviour.   At 10^{-2} mol dm^{-3} a minimum is observed
in the curve and the mobility values above pH 7 decrease with
increasing pH.   This effect becomes more pronounced as the
calcium concentration is increased further.   The silica dispersions in 5×10^{-2} mol dm^{-3} were found to form large woolly flocs
on standing when the pH was higher than 10.7.   Increasing the
concentration of calcium chloride to 10^{-1} mol dm^{-3} lowered the
pH at which this occurred.   Stumm, Huang and Jenkins[34] found a
stoichiometric relationship between the critical coagulation

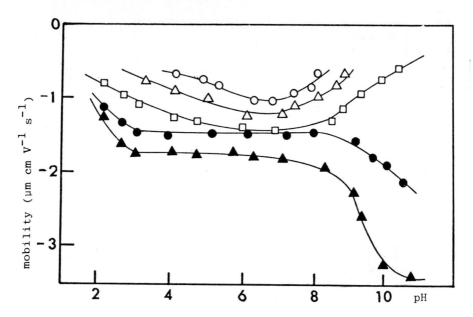

Figure 6: Mobility against pH for silica particles in
various concentrations (mol dm^{-3}) of calcium
chloride: ▲ , 10^{-4}; ● , 10^{-3}; □ , 10^{-2}; △ ,
5×10^{-2}; ○ , 10^{-1}.

concentration and the concentration of the dispersed phase and
considered that this was evidence for the reaction of the calcium
ion at the surface by a reaction such as,

$$\equiv SiOH \quad + \quad Ca^{2+} \rightleftharpoons \quad \equiv SiO\,Ca^{+} \quad + \quad H^{+}$$

$$= Si \begin{array}{c} OH \\ \\ OH \end{array} \quad + \quad Ca^{2+} \rightleftharpoons \quad = Si \begin{array}{c} O \\ \\ O \end{array} Ca^{2+} \quad + \quad 2H^{+}$$

A similar conclusion was reached by Greenberg[11] .

An alternative possibility is that Ca(OH)$^{+}$ is formed at[5,35]
pH values above 7.0 and that this reacts with the surface by
exchange,

$$\equiv Si\ OH\ +\ Ca(OH)^+\ \rightleftharpoons\ \equiv Si\ O\ Ca(OH)\ +\ H^+$$

by condensation,

$$\equiv Si\ OH\ +\ Ca(OH)^+\ \rightleftharpoons\ \equiv Si\ O\ Ca^+\ +\ H_2O$$

or by interaction with a charged site, via ion-exchange in the double layer,

$$\equiv Si\ O^-\ +\ Ca(OH)^+ \rightleftharpoons\ \equiv Si\ O\ Ca(OH)$$

The fact that the net charge on the particles is reduced favours the mechanisms other than the direct replacement of the hydrogen on the silanol group. Hence, although the electrokinetic technique does not of itself elucidate the reaction, it does provide direct evidence that a reaction has occurred.

In a similar manner the reaction of α-alumina with tetra-sodium pyrophosphate can be followed. In this case, reactions at the surface of the type,

$$> Al\ OH_2^+\ +\ H_2P_2O_7^{2-}\ \rightleftharpoons\ > Al\ H_2P_2O_7^-\ +\ H_2O$$

readily lead to reversal of charge.

Hydrolysed Ion Interactions at Oxide Surfaces

It is well known that many ions undergo hydrolysis reactions once a particular pH value has been reached. The hydrolysis products are frequently polymeric and as the pH is increased, in the case of a cation, result eventually in the formation of the hydrous oxide. The chemistry of the hydrolysis process is complex and there is not always universal agreement amongst authors as to the formulae and structure of the species formed. However, to demonstrate the effects of hydrolysis, we can follow the work of Matijević[20] who suggests that in the case of the aluminium ion the hydrolysis reaction can be represented as :

$$8 \ Al^{3+} \ + \ 20 \ H_2O \ \rightleftharpoons \ Al_8(OH)_{20}^{4+} \ + \ 20 \ H^+.$$

Whereas the Al^{3+} ion does not cause reversal of charge[21], once a hydrolysed species is formed, strong adsorption to the surface occurs and the sign of the original charge on the particle is reversed[21]. The concentration of salt required, at a specified pH, to bring the mobility or zeta potential to zero is termed the reversal of charge concentration.

Some data taken from the work of Matijević, Mangravite and Cassell[22] demonstrate the effect of aluminium ion hydrolysis on silica particles (Figure 7). The two curves marked with filled points show respectively the mobility against pH curves for silica and alumina. With 10^{-4} mol dm^{-3} aluminium nitrate, the mobility of the silica was slightly reduced. On the addition of 5.25×10^{-4} mol dm^{-3} aluminium nitrate at a pH value of ca. 4.5 the mobility was reduced to zero. Further additions caused reversal of charge. The mobility values at pH 4.5 as a function of aluminium nitrate concentration show this clearly. At pH values above 6.0 the aluminium ion is precipitated and under these conditions the silica mobility remains unchanged. According to these authors at 5.25×10^{-4} mol dm^{-3} two aluminium atoms are available for each aluminosilicate site and in order for charge neutralization to occur, the adsorbing counterion would require one positive charge for every two aluminium atoms. This was consistent with $Al_8(OH)_{20}^{4+}$ being the adsorbed species.

Effect of Surface Active Agents

Inorganic particles provide excellent surfaces for the

adsorption of surface active materials, particularly those with a charged head group where the sign of the latter is opposite to that of the particle. The adsorption of this type of material is again readily detected by electrokinetic measurements. Figure 8 shows the mobility of quartz particles plotted against the concentration of three different cationic surface active agents[18], hexadecyltrimethyl ammonium bromide (HTAB), dodecyl ammonium chloride (DAC) and N-dodecyl, propylene 1,3-diamine hydrochloride (DM 12). With HTAB reversal of charge occurred at 2.95×10^{-5} mol dm^{-3} and after this, the mobility became increasingly positive with increasing concentration of HTAB. At 10^{-2} mol dm^{-3} the mobility reaches the high value of 7.0 μm cm V^{-1} s^{-1}. With this type of system, interaction occurs between the cationic head group and the negative surface so that the hydrophobic alkyl chains are orientated towards the solution phase; as established by other techniques this leaves the surface hydrophobic and oleophilic. With increasing concentration, a second layer of surface active agent is adsorbed by chain-chain association, thus providing a high concentration of cationic head groups exposed to the solution phase; this surface is thus hydrophilic and has a high positive surface charge density.

Conclusion

Electrokinetic measurements provide a useful means of characterizing particulate material and of detecting the adsorption of surface active materials. Chemical reactions at the surface can also be detected by such measurements.

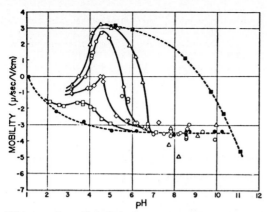

Figure 7: Mobilities of silica sols in the presence of various
concentrations of aluminium nitrate as a function of pH (solid
lines). $Al(NO_3)_3$ concentrations: 1.00×10^{-4} M($\square$), 5.25×10^{-4} M
($\diamondsuit$), 1.05×10^{-3} M (O), 2.10×10^{-3} M ($\triangle$); silica sol: 0.2g SiO_2/
100 cc. Dashed lines are for the silica sol in the absence of
$Al(NO_3)_3$ (blackened circles) and for aluminium hydroxide produced
from 1.05×10^{-2} M $Al(NO_3)_3$ in the presence of silica (full squares).
(From Matijević, Mangravite and Cassell[22]).

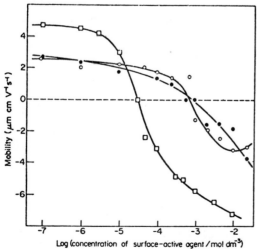

Figure 8: Electrophoretic mobility of quartz particles against
the logarithm of the molar concentration of surface-active agent
for three different cationic surface-active agents.
$\square$, HTAB in 10^{-3} mol dm^{-3} potassium bromide solution;
● , DM12 at pH 3; O , DAC at pH 3.

References

1. Buchanan, A.S. and Oppenheim, R.C. 1968. The surface
    chemistry of kaolinite. I. Surface leaching.
    Aust.J.Chem., 21: 2367.

2. Callaghan, I.C. and Ottewill, R.H. 1974. Interparticle
    forces in montmorillonite gels. Faraday Disc.Chem.Soc.,
    57: 110.

3. Cases, J.M. 1967. La détermination du point de charge nulle
    des nésosilicates en milieu aqueux. J.Chimie Physique,
    64: 1101.

4. Chernoberezhskii, Y.M., Zubkova, S.N., Usanova, S.D. and
    Afanas'eva, L.V. 1965. Investigation of the suspension
    effect. Colloid J. U.S.S.R.(Transl.) 27: 665.

5. Davies, C.W. and Hoyle, B.E. 1951. The dissociation constant
    of calcium hydroxide. J.Chem.Soc., 233.

6. Dukhin, S.S. and Derjaguin, B.V. 1974. Electrokinetic
    Phenomena. In Surface and Colloid Science, 7, ed.
    E. Matijević, pp 1-356. New York. John Wiley and Sons.

7. Flegmann, A.W. 1967. Studies on the colloid chemistry of
    kaolinite dispersions. Ph.D. thesis, University of Cambridge,
    England.

8. Fuerstenau, M.C., Somasundaran, P. and Fuerstenau, D.W.,
    Metal ion hydrolysis and surface charge in beryl flotation.
    Bull.Inst.Min.Met., 74: 381.

9. Gaudin, A.M. and Fuerstenau, D.W. 1955. Streaming potential
    studies - quartz flotation with anionic collectors.
    Trans. AIME., 202: 66.

10. Graham, K. and Madeley, J.D. 1962. Relation between the
    zeta-potential of rutile and its flotation with sodium
    dodecylsulphate. J.Applied Chem., 12: 485.

11. Greenberg, S.A. 1956. The chemisorption of calcium hydroxide
    by silica. J.Phys.Chem., 60: 325.

12. Healy, T.W., Herring, A.P. and Fuerstenau, D.W. 1966. The
    effect of crystal structure on the surface properties of a
    series of manganese dioxides. J.Colloid and Interface Sci.,
    21: 435.

13. Holloway, L.R. 1974. Chemical interactions at the oxide-
     solution interphase. Ph.D. thesis, University of Bristol,
     1974.

14. Hunter, R.J. and Wright, H.J.L. 1973. Adsorption at solid-
     liquid interfaces. II. Models of the electrical double
     layer at the oxide-solution interface. Aust.J.Chem.,
     26: 1191.

15. Iwasaki, I., Cooke, S.R.B. and Choi, H.S. 1960. Flotation
     characteristics of hematite, goethite and activated quartz
     with 18-carbon aliphatic acids and related compounds.
     Trans. AIME., 217: 237.

16. Iwasaki, I., Cooke, S.R.B. and Colombo, A.F. 1960.
     U.S. Bureau Mines Rept.Invest., 5593.

17. Johansen, P.G. and Buchanan, A.S. 1957. An application of
     the microelectrophoresis method to the study of the surface
     properties of insoluble oxides. Aust.J.Chem., 10: 398.

18. Lane, A.R. and Ottewill, R.H. 1975. The preparation and
     properties of bitumen emulsions stabilized by cationic
     surface active agents. In Theory and Practice of Emulsion
     Technology. London, Academic Press, pp 129-149.

19. Lyklema, J. and Overbeek, J.Th.G. 1961. On the interpreta-
     tion of electrokinetic potentials. J.Colloid Sci., 10: 501.

20. Matijević, E. 1967. Charge Reversal of Lyophobic Colloids.
     In Proceedings of the Fourth Rudolfs Research Conference,
     Principles and Applications of Water Chemistry, ed. S.D. Faust
     and J.V. Hunter, pp 32-369. New York: John Wiley and Sons.

21. Matijević, E., Mathai, K.G., Ottewill, R.H. and Kerker, M.
     1961. Detection of metal ion hydrolysis by coagulation.
     III. Aluminium. J.Phys.Chem., 65: 826.

22. Matijević, E., Mangravite, F.J. and Cassell, E.A. 1971.
     Stability of colloidal silica. IV. The silica-alumina
     system. J.Colloid and Interface Sci., 35: 560.

23. Mattson, S. and Pugh, A.J. 1934. The laws of soil colloidal
     behaviour. XIV. The electrokinetics of hydrous oxides and
     their ionic exchange. Soil Sci., 38: 299.

24. Olphen, H. van. 1963. An Introduction to Clay Colloid
     Chemistry. New York: John Wiley and Sons.

25. Ottewill, R.H. and Shaw, J.N. 1972. Electrophoretic studies on polystyrene latices. J.Electroanal.Chem. and Interfacial Electrochem., <u>37</u>: 133.

26. Overbeek, J.Th.G. 1952. Electrokinetic Phenomena. <u>In</u> Colloid Science 1, ed. H.R. Kruyt. p.232. Amsterdam: Elsevier.

27. Pravdić, V. 1970. Surface charge characterization of sea sediments. Limnol.Oceanog. <u>15</u>: 230.

28. Rank Bros., Bottisham, Cambridge, Cambs., England.

29. Robinson, M., Pask, J.A. and Fuerstenau, D.W. 1964. Surface charge of alumina and magnesia in aqueous media. J.Amer.Ceramic Soc., <u>47</u>: 516.

30. Rutgers, A.J. and Rigole, W. 1958. Ultrasonic vibration potentials in colloid solutions, in solutions of electrolytes and pure liquids. Trans.Faraday Soc., <u>54</u>: 139.

31. Shaw, D.J. 1969. Electrophoresis. London: Academic Press.

32. Smith, A.L. 1973. Electrical Phenomena Associated with the Solid-liquid Interface. <u>In</u> Dispersions of Powders in Liquids 2nd Edition, ed. G.D. Parfitt, pp 86-131. London: Applied Science.

33. Smolik, T.J., Harman and Fuerstenau, D.W. 1966. Surface characteristics and flotation behaviour of aluminosilicates. Trans.S.M.E., <u>235</u>: 367.

34. Stumm, W., Huang, C.P. and Jenkins, S.R. 1970. Specific chemical interaction affecting the stability of dispersed systems. Croat.Chem.Acta, <u>42</u>: 223.

35. Stumm, W. and O'Melia, C.R. 1968. Stoichiometry of coagulation. J.Amer.Water Works Assoc., <u>60</u>: 514.

36. Wiersema, P.H., Loeb, A. and Overbeek, J.Th.G. 1966. Calculation of the electrophoretic mobility of a spherical colloid particle. J.Colloid Interface Sci., <u>22</u>: 78.

37. Tadros, T.F. and Lyklema, J. 1968. Adsorption of potential-determining ions at the silica-aqueous electrolyte interface and the role of some cations. J.Electroanal.Chem. and Interfacial Electrochem., <u>17</u>: 267.

38. Yopps, J.A. and Fuerstenau, D.W. 1964. The zero point of charge of alpha-alumina. J.Colloid Sci., <u>19</u>: 61.
39. Zeta-Meter Inc., 1720, First Ave., New York 28, N.Y., U.S.A.

Origin and Fate of Organic Chemicals in the Sea – Group Report

D. J. Faulkner, Rapporteur
J. L. Bada   L. P. Hager
E. Bayer   A. Jernelöv
M. Blumer   J. P. Riley
M. Ehrhardt   K. L. Rinehart, Jr.
D. T. Gibson   A. V. Xavier

INTRODUCTION

During the course of the conference, the participants in the "Biosynthesis and Biodegradation" study group found themselves discussing a far wider range of subjects than the title of the session would suggest. In keeping with the aims of the conference, it was decided to change the title of the group report to the above. The overview contains a discussion of the problems facing marine chemists studying the organic chemistry of the sea, followed by some thoughts on biosynthesis and degradation and their contributions to the organic chemistry of the sea.

ORGANIC CHEMISTRY OF THE SEA

Organic compounds in the sea span a wide range in size, from methane to polymers, and in functionality, from hydrocarbons to complex multifunctional compounds.

The number of compounds is vast, and the discovery of new materials may uncover greater areas of study that are yet unknown. Thus, we now recognize hundreds of organic halogen compounds, in contrast to the few that were known five years ago, and this number is still multiplying. Similarly, we are just now

starting to recognize the complexity of the marine polymers and
of the materials returning to the sea from the sediments.

Organic compounds carry energy and information,and their participation is important in marine processes. Knowledge of their
structures also reveals information about the processes in which
they have been involved. This applies not just to the processes
of life; therefore, we should study not only the products of biosynthesis and biodegradation but also chemicals from other
sources.

The importance of the complex organic chemistry of the sea in
the operation of marine systems and the limited resources of man-
power necessitate the discovery of both rapid and economical
methods to enhance our understanding of marine organic chemistry.

We believe that this can be accomplished, or at least accelerated
in the following ways:

Transfer of Basic Knowledge to Marine Research

We need to understand the sources of organic compounds in the
sea, their interaction with the environment, the mode of their
participation in marine processes, and their fate. Also, we require efficient methods of analysis.

In Table 1 an attempt is made to assess the status of our knowledge in these marine areas and in the related basic fields,
especially in chemistry. It is apparent that there are three
principal fields in which marine chemists lack information, but
where basic facts are available, i.e., (a) the sources of organic
compounds, aside from plants and animals; (b) their interaction,
especially at low levels, with the biota and with particulate
and dissolved materials; and (c) their participation in chemical
processes, especially degradation and synthesis. New methods
for the concentration and analysis of organics have been developed and adapted to marine studies, but the marine chemist must
continue to assimilate this new technology.

TABLE 1 - Transfer of basic knowledge to marine organic chemistry.
An attempt is made to assess the state of knowledge in areas of marine organic chemistry and in those basic sciences relating to them. Those areas contained in "boxes" appear to offer the greatest potential for information transfer.

	knowledge	
	marine science	basic science
sources		
biochem. princ.	+++	+++
plants	+++	+++
animals	+++	+++
bacteria	+	+++
man	+	+++
sediment	+	++
air	−	++
internal reactions	−	−−
interaction		
- with life:		
toxicity	+(+)	+++
low level effects	−	++
pheromones	−	+++
- with dead material:		
modification of dissolved material	−	+
modification of particulates	−	+
processes:		
biodegradation	+(+)	+
chemical synthesis	−	++
chemical degradation	−	++
transport:		
food web	++	+
water	+	−
particulate	−	−
fate:		
small molecule	+	++
polymer, biological	+	++
polymer, chemical	−	++
methods:		
concentration	++	+++
separation, size	++	+++
separation, function	+++	+++
analysis (structure)	++	+++

Research Priorities

A functional asset of organic compounds is the information they
carry about the processes in which they have participated.
Clearly, unaltered biochemicals tell us most about their mode of
origin, while severely scrambled molecules reflect principally
the processes involved in the deep rearrangement of molecular
structures.

Table 2 suggests that slightly altered biochemicals may reflect
a particularly wide range of marine events. They are less well
known than either their biochemical precursors or the more deeply
altered products of diagenesis. To understand the formation and
composition of such compounds appears central to the unravelling
of the organic cycle in the sea, and the concentration of research efforts in this neglected area presents a new challenge
to marine organic chemistry.

TABLE 2 - Research priorities.
Organic chemicals in the sea carry information about those processes of formation and transformation in which they have been
involved. The type of retrievable information varies with the
degree of alteration of the original biochemical structure.
Slightly altered compounds may reflect a greater range of processes than their biochemical precursors or severely scrambled
transformation products.

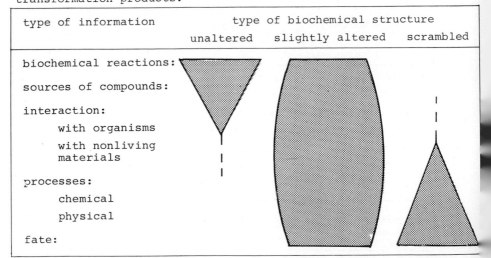

type of information	type of biochemical structure		
	unaltered	slightly altered	scrambled
biochemical reactions:			
sources of compounds:			
interaction:			
with organisms			
with nonliving materials			
processes:			
chemical			
physical			
fate:			

Information Exchange within Marine Organic Chemistry

Marine organic chemistry challenges specialists in diverse areas. We believe that a better mutual understanding of the overall goals of marine research and of the contribution which each group can provide is necessary. Thus, the study of sedimentary diagenesis contributes not only to our knowledge of fossil compounds but to the knowledge of organic cycles in the sea. Not only is the natural products chemist involved in the unravelling of metabolic pathways and the analytical definition of chemical structures, but his knowledge is also important to the ecologist and the chemist working on the transformation and fate of marine compounds.

It is hoped that this and possible future conferences further not only the understanding between scientists in the marine and basic fields but also the understanding among marine specialists in diverse areas.

BIOSYNTHESIS AND BIODEGRADATION

The principal quantitative source of organic carbon in the marine environment is the photosynthetic process in which phytoplankton fix and convert dissolved carbon dioxide to the organic compounds which they require for their metabolic processes. The annual primary production in the sea probably amounts to about 20×10^9 tons, a figure somewhat larger than that of the land. Over 90% of the plant material produced in this way will be rapidly consumed by the herbivorous zooplankton and may enter the food chain. Ingested organic compounds may be incorporated in the tissues of animals either unchanged or after partial breakdown and reassembly. Subsequently, the excretion products and dead organisms of both plants and animals will undergo biodegradation via a complex and largely unknown chain of reactions mediated by microorganisms, finally leading back to carbon dioxide. A small fraction of the intermediate degradation products will resist oxidation and will

be eventually incorporated into the sediments. Here further degradation will occur, and some of the degradation products may
diffuse back into the bottom waters.

In addition to organic compounds introduced into the sea by natural processes, an ever-increasing amount of material is entering through man's activities. Many of the compounds concerned
are known to be toxic or deleterious in other ways. However,
with the possible exception of petroleum products and DDT, practically nothing is known of the processes by which they are degraded, or indeed whether some of them are degraded at all.

Studies of the marine food chain have provided information concerning the gross transfer of organic material between the phytoplankton and the zooplankton in the surface waters. One of the
major differences between the marine and terrestrial environments
is that the photosynthetic organisms in the oceans are rapidly
consumed by invertebrates. In the process of obtaining energy,
invertebrates may degrade the molecular constituents of their
diet to smaller molecules which can either be excreted or used
for the biosynthesis of new molecules. Alternatively, a molecule from the dietary constituents can be employed without degradation as the starting material for the biosynthesis of a new
molecule. The simultaneous occurrence of biosynthesis, biodegradation, and bioconversion complicates the study of biosynthesis
in zooplankton. The problems of dealing simultaneously with both
biosynthesis and bioconversion must be overcome, since the invertebrates provide the greatest species diversity in the marine environment and also provide so many examples of chemical communication. The study of the biosynthesis of individual compounds
and their passage through the marine food chain will provide important specialized knowledge of the interdependence of marine
organisms.

Most of the techniques required for a study of the biosynthesis
of marine natural products are already available. In fact, most
biosynthetic pathways involving primary metabolism were first
elucidated using unicellular organisms. Adapting existing

procedures to study biosynthesis in marine algae and bacteria
should be a relatively simple task. The success of biosynthetic
studies using marine algae will depend on the development of
methods for their culture, as it is not feasible to study biosynthesis in situ. The study of biosynthesis in invertebrates
is complicated by the existence of both de novo biosynthesis and
the modification of dietary constituents. Undoubtedly, the most
difficult problems in biosynthesis will be encountered in chemical studies of symbiosis, which may be regarded as a problem of
biosynthetic interdependence.

The traditional approach to biosynthesis begins with the structural elucidation of related major and minor metabolites of an
organism. Hypothetical pathways linking the metabolites may
then be suggested on the basis of generalized biosynthetic theories (see, for example, Hager and White, Fig. 4, this volume).
After this stage, it is useful to have the organism in laboratory
culture, since the incorporation of labelled precursors must be
observed. In the initial incorporation studies, radioactively
labelled precursors are usually employed, but use of stable isotopes is sometimes advantageous for more detailed studies of individual steps when complex molecules must be specifically labelled. More sophisticated studies of the mechanisms of single
steps often involve the use of the enzyme systems controlling
them.

The generalized biosynthetic pathways of primary metabolites are
likely to be identical for all organisms. For this reason, the
marine natural products chemist should study the biosynthesis
of secondary metabolites, especially those which are uniquely
marine. Examples of these secondary metabolites are sterols
such as gorgosterol; neurotoxins such as saxitoxin, tetrodotox-
in and nereistoxin; marine pigments such as fucoxanthin and
peridinin; the algal polysaccharides of commercial importance
such as alginic acid; and the halogenated marine products such
as those described by Hager and White and Rinehart, et al.(this
volume). Examples of biosynthetic mechanisms which deserve

investigation are the halogenation of organic molecules, the
methylation of mercury and other metals, and the incorporation
of vanadium by tunicates.

Although few systems have been studied to date, the biosynthesis
of chemical messengers and their subsequent release into the
oceans promises to be an exciting research area. In particular,
those chemicals which trigger complex biosynthetic events, such
as the metamorphosis of crustaceans, are worthy of study. We need
to know the mechanisms of biosynthesis and the storage and release of chemical messengers, but most importantly, the chemistry
must be elucidated in order to predict the potential effects of
synthetic materials introduced into the ocean by man. A study
of the biosynthesis of chemical messengers may also lead to an
understanding of the evolution of hormones and pheromones.

Little information is available that describes the chemical reactions that occur during the biodegradation of organic compounds
in the marine environment. In terms of numbers of microorganisms
and turnover rates, surface waters and sediments are the principal sites of biodegradation (bioconversion?). Knowledge of the
biodegradative reactions that may occur in deep water is almost
nonexistent. To obtain an understanding of the contribution of
biodegradation to the nature of seawater, information is required
in the following areas:

(1) Identification of naturally occurring organic compounds in
    the surface zone and the deeper waters, in addition to the
    increasing amount of information that is available for
    sediments.
(2) Identification of synthetic chemicals in all three areas
    (e.g., PCB's).
(3) Identification of the microorganisms in the three regions
    that degrade the compounds implicated in (1) and (2).
(4) Elucidation of biodegradative reactions that occur in the
    three regions.

Such studies will increase our understanding of:

(1) The contribution of biodegradation to the productivity of
    the surface waters and the chemical composition in all three
    areas.
(2) The role of biodegradation in the possible transformation
    of synthetic pollutants.

Investigations are complicated by the complex nature of seawater and its interfaces. However, serious attempts should be made to correlate results obtained in the laboratory with observations made in the marine environment. For example, a considerable amount of information is available on the reaction sequences used by microorganisms to degrade many organic compounds. These intermediate degradation products may accumulate in certain regions of the marine environment where conditions are not favorable for further biodegradation. For example, current studies have shown that recent marine sediments contain a complex polycyclic aromatic hydrocarbon assemblage. Laboratory experiments have shown that microorganisms will oxidize alkyl-substituted aromatic hydrocarbons at the sidechain and also at the aromatic nucleus. In the light of these observations, it would seem possible that phenols and phenolic acids formed from polycyclic hydrocarbons could be formed and accumulate in the marine environment.

Although the correlation of results obtained by in situ measurements and laboratory experiments is a problematic discipline, the marine scientist should be challenged to utilize the background of basic information that is already available.

Many of the organic chemicals found in the oceans can be regarded as products of both biosynthesis and biodegradation. Less than 10% of this organic material has been characterized. Because of their possible significance to other disciplines, many of the components of the remaining 90% should be characterized as fully as possible using current instrumentation. Likely lines of approach include the use of macroreticular resins and high pressure membrane filtration for preconcentration, gas and high performance liquid chromatography for separation, and mass spectrometry and Fourier transform spectroscopy for identification. Enzymatic methods of analysis and radioimmunoassay techniques can be adapted to provide a quantitative analysis of individual compounds in seawater. In any investigation of organic compounds, avoidance of contamination both during collection of the sample and in subsequent analyses is most important. The analysis should be performed as rapidly as possible after collection, since the concentrations of many components could be rapidly altered by adsorption and biodegradation. Since it is possible to use many of the more elaborate instrumental techniques in a ship's laboratory, analysis of samples immediately after collection should be undertaken whenever possible. Failing this, the pre-concentration step should be accomplished at sea.

Oceanographic measurements of organic carbon must be interpreted with great care, since they represent a bulk measurement and take no account of individual compounds. Variations in the concentration of various classes of compounds with depth and location will provide more useful information. However, because of the enormous numbers of compounds present, a complete analysis is a formidable and unlikely task. Useful information can often be obtained by the determination of various classes of compounds, but in special instances it may be desirable to estimate the concentrations of individual compounds.

Studies of the organic composition of sediments present a similar problem which is further complicated by effects of bioconversion and early diagenesis. Nonetheless, the water-sediment interface promises to be an exciting area of investigation for the organic chemist.

REFERENCES

Hager, L.P., and White, R.H. 1975. A biosynthetic sequence of halogenated sesquiterpenes from Laurencia intricata. In Dahlem Workshop on the Nature of Seawater, ed. E.D. Goldberg. Berlin: Dahlem Konferenzen.

Rinehart, K.L.Jr.; Johnson, R.D.; Siuda, J.F.; Krejcarek, G.E.; Shaw, P.D.; McMillan, J.A.; and Paul, I.C. 1975. Structures of halogenated and antimicrobial organic compounds from marine sources. In: Dahlem Workshop on the Nature of Seawater, ed. E.D. Goldberg. Berlin: Dahlem Konferenzen.

A Biogenetic Sequence of Halogenated Sesquiterpenes from
Laurencia Intricata

R. H. White and L. P. Hager
Department of Biochemistry
University of Illinois
Urbana, Illinois 61801

Abstract: An analysis of the halogenated sesquiterpenes isolated from Laurencia intricata has been performed. Four new halogenated compounds, preintricatol, intricatene, acetoxyintricatol and cyclodebromointricatol are described. The isolation of these compounds supports a proposed biogenetic pathway which includes all of the compounds as biosynthetic intermediates or end products of this pathway. Bromine atoms appear to be introduced via oxidation of bromide ion to an electrophilic species.

Introduction:

Natural product research during the past five years has identified an abundance of new halogenated compounds unique to marine organisms (1,2). Very recently, a survey of approximately 1000 different species of marine plants and animals indicates that 25% of randomly collected species contain significant levels of organic halogens (3,4). This survey, which was carried out on board the research ship, the Alpha Helix, included preliminary gas chromatography and mass spectrometry analysis of those extracts which were rich in halogen-containing compounds. The latter chemical analyses indicated that not only were halogenated compounds abundant and widespread in marine species but also that there is a great diversity of halogenated compounds with many new structures still awaiting

identification. Thus, it seems appropriate to become concerned
with the function and biosynthesis of the halogenated compounds
found in marine organisms. With respect to the function and
biosynthesis, several questions come immediately to mind. For
example, do these compounds appear as the result of enzymatic
reactions which lead to unique structures or do they result from
purely chemical reactions between halogen anions with reactive
chemical species generated through intermediary metabolism. Certainly if the organisms which generate the halogenated compounds
synthesize them for specific purposes and uses, then one should
be able to discover the biosynthetic sequences which yield the
precursors and intermediates on the path toward the isolable
halogenated product. It is the purpose of this paper to examine
a biogenetic sequence of halogenated sesquiterpenes of Laurencia
intricata. It will be seen that each of these compounds fits
into a logical biosynthetic scheme which suggests that Laurencia
intricata has developed a purposeful pathway for synthesizing
a desired final product.

Members of the family Rhodomelaceae, genus Laurencia (red algae),
have supplied a wide range of halogenated natural products. These
products appear to be biogenetically derived from two independent
biosynthetic pathways, one pathway is based on a straight chain
C_{15} hydrocarbon and the other pathway is based on a sesquiterpene
hydrocarbon. In the straight chain C_{15} group are the compounds
laurencin (5), laurefucin (6), laueatin (7), and chondriol (8).
These compounds are further characterized by having a terminal
enyne function. In the sesquiterpene group are compounds such as
pacifenol (9), johnstonol (10), prepacifenol (11), caespitol (12)

and nidificene (13). These compounds have a bicyclic cyclohexane ring system. The separation and analysis of four new sesquiter-penes from Laurencia intricata is described in the following sections. As indicated above, each of these compounds fit logically into a consistent biosynthetic pathway which accounts for all of the compounds characterized.

Experimental:

Algae samples were collected at Key Largo, Florida on July 5-6, 1973 at long 80° 37.9', lat 24° 50.0' in shallow water 3-5 feet in depth. Each isolated clump of algae ($\sim$ 600g) was assayed separately for high organic lipid halogen (3) and only those containing the highest values (> 3% halogen in lipid) were subsequently extracted. Extraction was performed by grinding 100g portions of the wet algae with 200 ml portions of benzene-methanol (1:1) in a VirTis 45 tissue homogenizer (model 16-900). The lipid was isolated from the benzene layer after filtering and the addition of water to form a two phase system. It was then separated into 21 fractions on a 6 x 35 cm column of Brinkmann silica gel and then further separated by preparative thin layer chromatography (tlc) on Brinkmann preparative tlc plates (2.5mm) or analytical (0.25mm) plates. Fractions from the tlc plates were selected by screening with UV light, by sulfuric acid spraying followed by charing and by measuring the content of organic halogen after isolation and analysis.

Gas chromatography (GC) analysis was routinely performed on a 6' x 1/8" glass column containing 3% OV-17 on Gas Chromosorb Q programmed from 100° to 300° at 10° C/min. A Varian series 1700

gas chromatograph was used. The injector and detector were maintained at 300°C and helium was used as the carrier gas.

Low resolution gas chromatography-mass spectrometry was performed
with the CH-7 mass spectrometer interfaced with a Varian series
1700 gas chromatograph. For compounds of sufficient purity, i.e.,
single GC peak, mass spectra were obtained by direct insertion
on the CH-5 mass spectrometer. High resolution mass data by peak
matching and complete high resolution listings were determined on
the 731 mass spectrometer for each compound giving one tlc spot
in three different solvents and one GC peak. All spectra were
70 ev and the presence of halogen was confirmed by isotopic ratios
and high resolution mass measurement.

Proton magnetic resonance (PMR) data were collected on a Varian
HA-100 MHz NMR. The solvent in all cases was deuteriochloroform
containing 1% tetramethylsilane as reference. All data are reported as ppm from tetramethylsilane.

Results:

From 2 kg of wet algae were extracted 9 g of dark green oil that
contained 2.0% chlorine and 3.05% bromine. Four grams of this
material fractionated on silica gel gave the fractions shown in
Figure 1. The relative halogen content for each fraction is
proportional to the total organic halogen in each fraction. Sesquiterpenes were found in fractions 2, 4, and 11 which will be
described below. Because of the various methods used to purify
the halogenated compounds, the amount of pure material reported
as isolated does not reflect the total amount of the compound in
the original fraction.

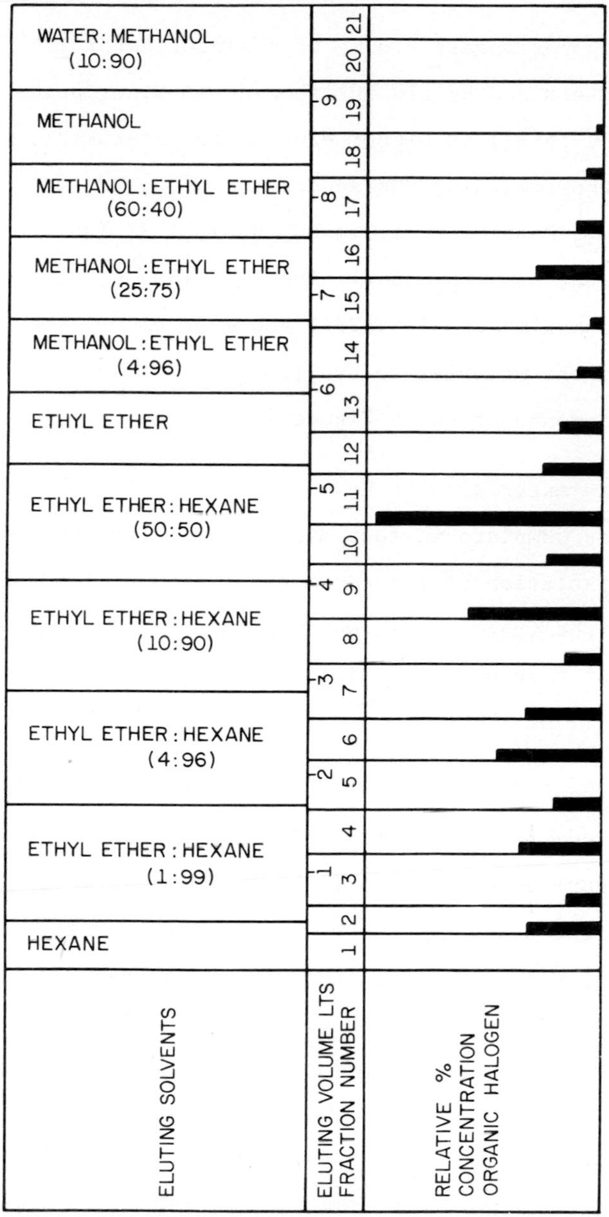

Figure 1. Elution and analysis of the lipid from Laurencia intricata. Four grams of algae lipid (2.10% chlorine and 3.05% bromine) was fractionated on a silica gel column 6 x 35 cm to give the fractions diagrammed. The material from each fraction was assayed to give the relative organic halogen (chlorine + bromine).

Fraction 2 yielded approximately 2.6 mg of preintericatol **2** which was pure as determined by tlc but showed two minor peaks (less than 10% of the total) at higher elution temperatures. This compound gave the following PMR spectrum: 5.15 (1H, m, $\underline{H}$-C=C), 4.40 (1H, m, $\underline{H}$-C-Br), 3.0-1.8 (10H, $\underline{H}_2$C), 1.72 (3H, s, C$\underline{H}_3$-C-Cl), 1.65 (6H, bs, (C$\underline{H}_3$)$_2$C=C), and 1.57 (3H, s, C$\underline{H}_3$-C=C). IR showed maxima at 3075, 2945 and 1458 cm^{-1}. The mass spectrum showed the material to be $C_{15}H_{24}ClBr$; M^+318, 320, 322 and gave the fragments shown in Figure 2.

Hydrogenation of this material with hydrogen over Pt in ethanol at one atmosphere was complete in four minutes as determined by tlc and led to the isolation of a new compound, $C_{15}H_{28}ClBr$; M^+322, 324, 326 which gave the fragments shown in Figure 2. Additional hydrogenation did not take place at higher temperatures (80°) or longer time periods (1 hr).

Intricatene **3**, $M^+C_{15}H_{23}ClBr_2$ 395.9838 (calcd for $C_{15}H_{23}{}^{35}Cl^{79}Br_2$ 395.9845) was isolated from fraction 4. Intricatene gave the mass spectral fragments shown in Figure 3. An IR maximum at 3090 cm^{-1} indicated the presence of a double bond as did the PMR spectrum which displayed signals at 5.22 (1H, s, $\underline{H}$-C=C), 4.82 (1H, s, $\underline{H}$-C=C), 1.67 (3H, s, C$\underline{H}_3$C-Cl), 1.23 and 1.12 (2 x 3H gem dimethyl). Treatment of the material with hydrogen over Pt in ethanol for 30 minutes at room temperature did not change the 3090 cm^{-1} IR absorption or the mass spectrum.

Two compounds, designated acetoxyintricatol **5** and cyclodebromo-acetoxyintricatol **6**, were isolated from fraction 11. Acetoxy-intricatol (76 mg isolated) was analyzed for $C_{17}H_{27}O_3ClBr_2$;

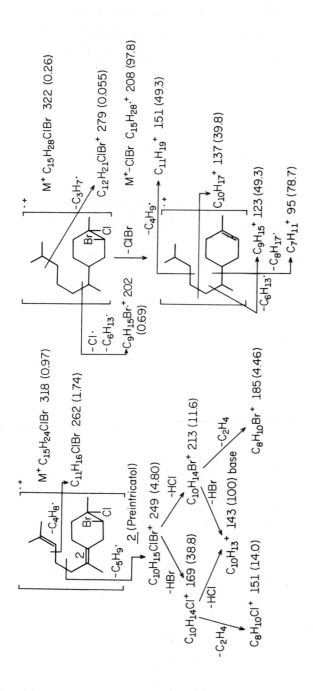

Figure 2. Fragmentation patterns for preintricatol and its hydrogenated product. Numbers in parentheses refer to the ion intensities as percent of the base peak. All ions containing halogens had the correct isotopic abundances for the compositions written.

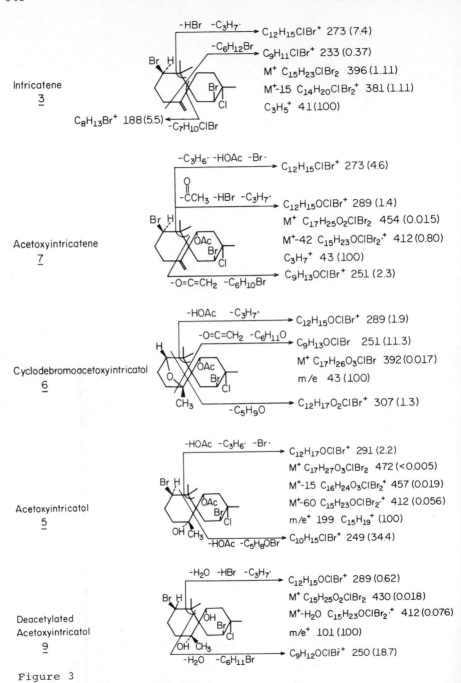

Figure 3

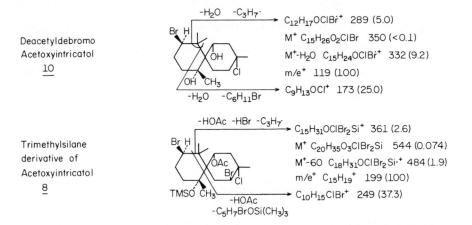

Deacetyldebromo
Acetoxyintricatol
<u>10</u>

$C_{12}H_{17}OClBr^{.+}$ 289 (5.0)

M^+ $C_{15}H_{26}O_2ClBr$ 350 (<0.1)

M^+-H_2O $C_{15}H_{24}OClBr^{.+}$ 332 (9.2)

m/e^+ 119 (100)

$C_9H_{13}OCl^+$ 173 (25.0)

Trimethylsilane
derivative of
Acetoxyintricatol
<u>8</u>

$C_{15}H_{31}OClBr_2Si^+$ 361 (2.6)

M^+ $C_{20}H_{35}O_3ClBr_2Si$ 544 (0.074)

M^+-60 $C_{18}H_{31}OClBr_2Si^{.+}$ 484 (1.9)

m/e^+ $C_{15}H_{19}^+$ 199 (100)

$C_{10}H_{15}ClBr^+$ 249 (37.3)

Figure 3. Comparison of the observed mass spectral fragments
for the compounds isolated from Laurencia intricata and their
derivatives. Numbers in parentheses refer to the ion intensities
as percent of the base peak. Ion compositions are based on
nominal masses, high resolution mass measurements and isotopic
abundances.

M^+472, 474, 476, 478; high resolution M-CH$_3$.-HOAc, 398.9568
(calcd for $C_{14}H_{20}O^{35}Cl^{79}Br^{81}Br$ 398.9550) and M^+-Br·-HOAc, 333.0617
(calcd for $C_{15}H_{23}O^{37}Cl^{79}Br$ 333.0621). Additional fragments observed are shown in Figure 3. The IR spectra ($\tilde{\nu}$ = 3500, 1720,
and 1250 cm^{-1}) showed the presence of a hydroxyl group and an
acetate ester. The PMR spectrum displayed signals at 5.31
(1H, dd, J=5.9 and 12.1 Hz, CH<u>O</u>C-CH$_3$), 5.06 (1H, dd, J=4.0 and
12.8 Hz, Cl-C-C(Br)-<u>H</u>), 4.23 (1H, dd, J=5.6 and 10.6 Hz, C<u>H</u>-Br),
3.20 (1H, bt, J=11.9 Hz, CH$_3$C-O-C-C<u>H</u>), 2.48 (1H, dd, J=4.0 and
12.8 Hz, <u>H</u>-C-C-Br), 2.44 (1H, dd, J-5.9 and 12.0 Hz, <u>H</u>-C-C^{CH_3}Cl),
and 2.6-1.8 (5H, m, <u>H</u>$_2$C). In addition, four singlet methyl signals (3H) were observed at 1.78 (<u>Me</u>-C-Cl), 1.52 (<u>Me</u>-C-OH), 1.15
and 1.16 (gem dimethyl) and an acetate methyl appeared at 2.12.

One D_2O exchangeable proton occurred at 1.6. The trimethylsilane derivative of acetoxyintricatol was formed by reaction with excess pyridine:hexamethyldisilazane:trimethylchlorosilane (5:5:1) for 10 minutes at 60°C. This material gave the fragments shown in Figure 3. Attempts to form the acetate by reaction of acetoxyintricatol with acetic anhydride-pyridine mixtures showed no change in the material by tlc. However, addition of acetic anhydride containing a small amount of sulfuric acid quickly produced a new product by dehydration.

Therefore, 15 mg of acetoxyintricatol in 1 ml acetic anhydride and 5 µl of sulfuric acid were heated at 60°C for 15 minutes in an airtight tube. Extraction and purification of the reaction mixture gave 8.4 mg of acetoxyintricatene $\underline{7}$. Mass spectral analysis showed the material to be $C_{17}H_{25}O_2ClBr_2$; M^+454, 456, 458, 460; high resolution M^+-42, 411.9850 (calcd for $C_{15}H_{23}O^{35}Cl^{79}Br_2$ 411.9850), IR ($\tilde{\nu}_{max}^{CCl_4}$ 3100, 1720, 1250 cm^{-1}), PMR 5.31 (1H, d, J=0.7 Hz, C=C$\overset{H}{\underset{H}{\diagdown}}$), 5.13 (1H, dd, J=4.8 and 11.8 Hz, C$\underline{H}$-OCCH$_3$), 4.90 (1H, d, J=0.2 Hz, C=C$\overset{H}{\underset{H}{\diagup}}$), 4.70 (1H, dd, J=5.0 and 8.8 Hz), and 4.55 (1H, dd, J=4.2 and 8.6 Hz). Three single methyl resonances were at 1.79, 1.12 and 1.00 with an acetate at 2.00.

Lithium aluminum hydride was used in an attempt to remove one or more halogens to further characterize the original molecule. The reaction between acetoxyintricatol and excess lithium aluminum hydride in ether followed by tlc, showed two products within 1 minute of mixing. The relative abundance of each product was constant for periods of up to one hour at room temperature. Thus 14 mg of acetoxyintricatol was added to 50 mg of lithium aluminum

hydride in 1 ml of ether, after 30 minutes water was added and
the ether soluble material purified by tlc. Two products were
isolated, the deacetyl compound $\underline{9}$, 3.8 mg, M^+-H_2O, 412, 414, 416,
418 $C_{15}H_{23}OClBr_2$; IR film 3450 cm^{-1}; PMR 4.42 (1H, dd, J=10.0 and

5.0 Hz, Cl-C-C$\overset{Br}{\underset{\underline{H}}{<}}$), 3.89 (1H, bd, J=5.0 Hz, $\underline{H}$-C-Br), 3.81

(1H, dd, J=10.0 and 9.0 Hz, $\underline{H}$-COH), 2.63 (1H, d, J=10.0 Hz,
HO-C-C-$\underline{H}$), 2.62 (1H, d, J=9 Hz, HO-C-C-$\underline{H}$), 1.80 (3H, s, $\underline{Me}$-C-Cl),
1.69 (3H, s, $\underline{Me}$-COH), 1.28 and 0.90 (2 x 3H, gem dimethyl); and
the deacetyldebromo compound $\underline{10}$, 1.3 mg, M^+-H_2O, 332, 334, 336
$C_{15}H_{24}OClBr$; IR 3450 cm^{-1}. Some of the principal fragments observed for these two compounds are summarized in Figure 3.

The second component of fraction 11 was cyclodebromoacetoxyintricatol 6 which was analyzed for $C_{17}H_{26}O_3ClBr$; M^+ 392, 394, 396,
high resolution M^+-59, $C_{15}H_{23}OClBr$ 335.0589 (calcd for
$C_{15}H_{23}{}^{37}Cl^{79}Br$ 335.0591 and for $C_{15}H_{23}{}^{35}Cl^{81}Br$ 335.0601). Additional fragments observed are shown in Figure 3. The IR spec-
trum, $\overset{\sim}{\nu}$ film   1720, 1250, 760 cm^{-1}, supported by the mass
        max
spectrum, indicated that an acetate was present but that no hydroxyl was present. The PMR spectrum displayed signals at 4.76
(1H, dd, J=3.2 and 9.5 Hz, $\underline{H}$-C-OAc), 4.32 (1H, dd, J=3.7 and
13.9 Hz, $\underline{H}$-C-Br), 3.71 (1H, dd, J=1.9 and 4.3 Hz, $\underline{H}$-C-O), 2.54
(2H, bd, J=8.2 and 9.5 Hz, H-C(OAc)-C$\underline{H}_2$), 2.17 (1H, dd, J=3.7

and 15.5 Hz, $\underline{H}$-$\overset{H'}{\underset{}{C}}$-C-Br), 2.05 (3H, s, C-O$\overset{O}{\underset{}{C}}$Me), 1.98 (1H, dd, 13.9

and 15.5 Hz, H-$\overset{\underline{H'}}{\underset{}{C}}$-C-Br), 1.80 (3H, s, $\underline{Me}$-C$\overset{Cl}{\underset{}{}}$), 1.75 (1H, s, O-C-$\underline{Me}$),
1.98-1.20 (4H, m, C-$\underline{H}$), 1.12 and 0.90 (2 x 3H, s, gem dimethyl).

Discussion:

Chemical Considerations - The structure proposed for preintricatol

2 is based on the following observations: 1) The compound contains
four singlet methyl resonances characteristic of a sesquiterpene.
Three of these had chemical shifts characteristic of vinyl methyl
resonances, the fourth had chemical shift characteristics of a
methyl group bonded to a carbon containing one chlorine and no protons; 2) Hydrogenation confirmed that the molecule contained two
double bonds and a ring, since only one vinyl proton was observed,
one of these double bonds had to be tetra substituted. With this
information the two double bonds and ring were placed in the sesquiterpene as shown in Figure 2. Further support for the assigned
structure comes from the observed fragments for preintricatol and
hydrogenated preintricatol reported in Figure 2. The ion
$C_{10}H_{15}ClBr^+$ 249, 251, 253 which appears for preintricatol is also
observed in both the mass spectra of acetoxyintricatol and the TMS
derivative of acetoxyintricatol shown in Figure 3.

From the PMR data, intricatene 3 is also a sesquiterpene but
lacks one methyl group. This is analogous to the chemically
derived acetoxyintricatene 7, in which this methyl group is transformed to an exocyclic vinyl group by dehydration of a tertiary
hydroxyl. The vinyl resonances for both of these compounds occur
at approximately the same values (5.31 and 4.90 for acetoxyintricatene and 5.22 and 4.82 for intricatene). Further support for
the structure comes from the mass spectrum fragments reported in
Figure 3. All compounds with the exception of acetoxyintricatol
showed the characteristic loss of a C_6 fragment containing one
bromine from the single bromine ring system. Apparently this same

compound has recently been isolated from Laurencia nidifica and
assigned the name nidificene (13). It was concluded that reduction
of the exocyclic double bond did not occur because of steric
reasons.

The most noted feature of the PMR of acetoxyintricatol is the
presence of five singlet methyl resonances. One of these resonances would have to be an acetate methyl due to the loss of
acetate as a mass spectral fragment and due to its chemical shift
(2.12). The remaining four methyls were assigned to the methyls
on the sesquiterpene backbone. In addition, three down field protons (5.31, 5.06 and 4.23) were each coupled to a unique set of
methylene protons. Dehydration to produce 7 showed that the
hydroxyl group was on a tertiary carbon containing a methyl group.
Comparison of these above observations to the previously identified compounds pacifenol (9), johnstonol (10), prepacifenol (11),
and caespitol (12) from other Laurencia species led to the proposed structure for acetoxyintricatol 5.

This structure was confirmed by total X-ray structure determination
(14). The characteristic fragments for this compound and its derivatives serve as models for the other compounds in Figure 3.

The mass spectrum of cyclodebromoacetoxyintricatol 6 showed it
to be (H + Br) less than acetoxyintricatol 5. The PMR showed
three down field single proton resonances coupled to a unique set
of methylene protons as in acetoxyintricatol and an acetate and
four methyl groups. Thus, the molecule could be formed from the
elimination of HBr from acetoxyintricatol by an intramolecular
cyclization. Model building showed that the entire conformation

of the molecule would be required to change, thus explaining the observed changes in chemical shifts for some of the protons. The stereochemistry of the molecule in Figure 3 is based on that determined for acetoxyintricatol. The changes in the coupling constants resulting in the conformation change observed in models agree with those expected for protons on vicinal carbons (15).

Consideration of these structures led to the biosynthetic pathway proposed in Figure 4. Either cis, cis or cis, trans farnesyl pyrophosphate could be the first step in the biosynthesis of compound 1. This compound was not isolated in the present study; however, several $C_{15}H_{24}$ hydrocarbons were observed in the GC-MS runs of different fractions during purification of the halogen-containing compounds. Trans addition of "ClBr" to the double bond in the cyclohexane ring would lead to preintricatol 2. Oxidation of the terminal double bond by a bromonium ion and cyclization of the acyclic portion of preintricatol 2 would result in the desired molecular framework. The resulting carbonium ion could then either add water and lose a proton to form intricatol or lose a proton to form intricatene 3 (Figure 4). Analogous reactions for the cyclization of acyclic terpenes by bromonium ion have been studied by Van Tamelem (16). The molecule intricatol was not identified in the extract. However, this does not eliminate the possibility of its presence in the extract since a large number of additional halogenated compounds were found to be present whose structures were not established. Thus whether intricatene was a biosynthetic intermediate or a side product from intricatol remains unknown. Oxidative hydroxylation of intricatol followed by acetate formation would then lead to acetoxyintricatol 5. Intramolecular nucleophilic attack of the free hydroxyl oxygen at the bromine

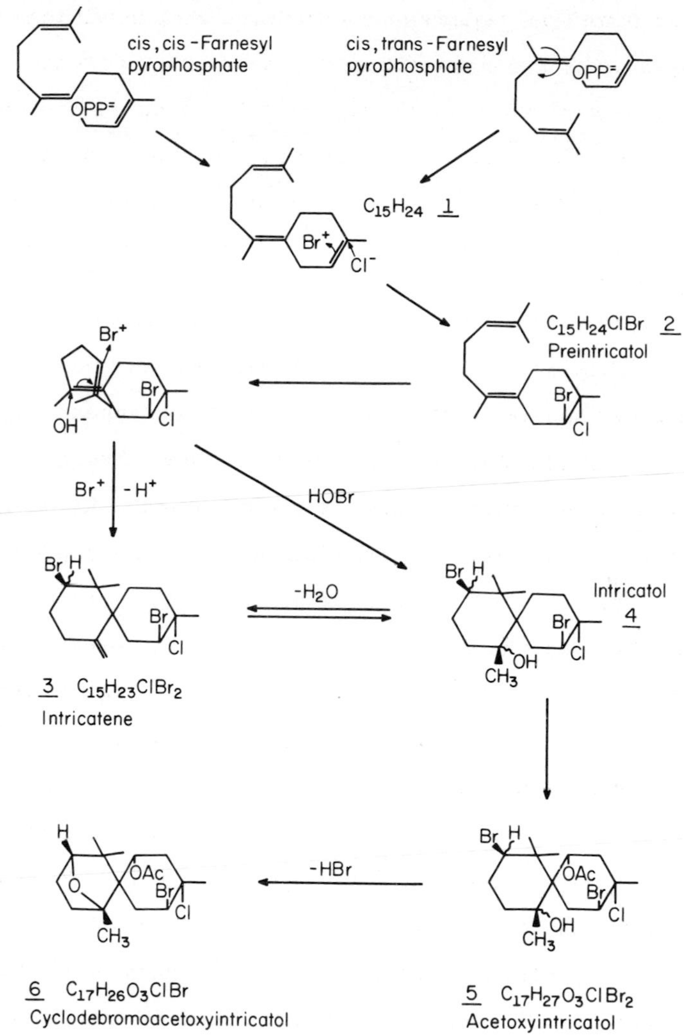

Figure 4. Proposed biogenetic pathway for the biosyntheses of the sesquiterpenes isolated from Laurencia intricata.

substituted carbon opposite it and subsequent loss of HBr would result in cyclodebromoacetoxyintricatol 6. No evidence was obtained for the occurrence of this reaction in vivo. Further support for the described biosynthetic pathway will have to await feeding studies on the isolated algae.

Biochemical Considerations - Several important biochemical consequences follow from the proposed biogenetic sequence for acetoxyintricatol. Most importantly, from the point of view of introducing halogens into marine natural products, the pathway indicates that Laurencia intricata must contain an enzyme or enzyme system capable of oxidizing bromide to form an electro- philic halogenating species. Chloride ion does not appear to be oxidized, but rather incorporated as chloride ion. There are appropriate analogies in the peroxidase field for this kind of specificity. Two peroxidases, chloroperoxidase and myleoperoxide are capable of utilizing hydrogen peroxide to oxidize chloride, bromide and iodide. On the other hand, horseradish peroxidase and other similar peroxidases can oxidize iodide but not bromide or chloride. Lactoperoxidase is intermediate between chloro- peroxidase and horseradish peroxidase in terms of halogen anion specificity. Lactoperoxidase can oxidize iodide and bromide but fails to oxidize chloride ion. In terms of the halogenation reactions in Laurencia intricata, a peroxidatic enzyme having the specificity of lactoperoxidase would explain the pattern of halo- gen incorporation. An electrophilic enzyme-bound bromine inter- mediate appears to be used as the cyclizing agent to close one of the cyclohexane rings in the conversion of preintricatol to in- tricatol. The other biochemical reactions proposed in the bio- genetic scheme are adapted from well established biochemical reactions.

Acknowledgement:

The experimental work described in this manuscript was supported by a grant (BMS 71-01280-A03) from the National Science Foundation.

References:

1. Siuda, J. F., and DeBernardis, J. F. 1973. Naturally occurring halogenated organic compounds. Lloydia 36: 107-143.

2. Fenical, W. 1975. Halogenation in the Rhodophyta. J. Phycology (in press).

3. Hager, L. P., White, R. H., Doubek, D. L., Hollenberg, P. F., Shaw, P. D., Rinehart, K. L., Jr., Johnson, R. D., Brusca, R. C., Krejcarek, G. E., Siuda, J. F., Guerrero, R., McClure, W. O., VanBlaricom, G. R., Sims, J. J., Fenical, W. O., and Rude, J. 1975. Halogenated natural products and anti-microbial activity in marine organisms. Proc. Nat. Acad. Sci. (U.S.A.) Submitted.

4. Hager, L. P., White, R. H., Hollenberg, P. F., Doubek, D. L., Brusca, R. C., and Guerrero, R. 1974. A survey of organic halogens in marine organisms. 4th Int. Food-Drugs From The Sea Conference, Mayaguez, Puerto Rico.

5. Irie, T., Suzuki, M., and Masamune, T. 1965. Laurencin, a constituent from Laurencia species. Tet. Lett.: 1091-1099.

6. Fukuzawa, A., Kurosawa, E., and Irie, T. 1972. Laurefucin and acetyllaurefucin, new bromo compounds from Laurencia nipponica Yamada. Tet. Lett.: 3-6.

7. Irie, T., Izawa, M., and Kurosawa, E. 1968. Laureatin, a constituent from Laurencia nipponica Yamada. Tet. Lett.: 2091-2096.

8. Fenical, W., Sims, J. J., and Radlick, P. 1973. Chondriol, a halogenated acetylene from the marine alga Chondria oppositiclada. Tet. Lett.: 313-316.

9. Sims, J. J., Fenical, W., Wing, R. M., and Radlick, P. 1971. Marine natural products. I. Pacifenol, a rare sesquiterpene containing bromine and chlorine from the red alga Laurencia pacifica. J. Amer. Chem. Soc. 93: 3774-3775.

10. Sims, J. J., Fenical, W., Wing, R. M., and Radlick, P. 1972.
     Marine natural products. III. Johnstonol, an unusual halo-
     genated epoxide from the red alga Laurencia johnstonii. Tet.
     Lett.: 195-198.

11. Sims, J. J., Fenical, W., Wing, R. M., and Radlick, P. 1973.
     Marine natural products. IV. Prepacifenol, a halogenated
     epoxy sesquiterpene from the red alga Laurencia filiformis.
     J. Amer. Chem. Soc. 95: 972-974.

12. Gonzalez, A. G., Darias, J., and Martin, J. D. 1973.
     Caespitol, a new halogenated sesquiterpene from Laurencia
     caespitosa. Tet. Lett.: 2381-2384.

13. Waraszkiewicz, S. M., and Erickson, K. L. 1974. Halogenated
     sesquiterpenoids from the Hawaiian marine alga Laurencia
     nidifica, Nidificene and Nidafidiene. Tet. Lett.: 2003-2006.

14. McMillan, J. A., Paul, I. C., White, R. H., and Hager, L. P.
     1974. Molecular structure of acetoxyintricatol, a new bromo
     compound from Laurencia intricata. Tet. Lett.: 2039-2042.

15. Karplus, M. 1963. Vicinal proton coupling in nuclear mag-
     netic resonance. J. Amer. Chem. Soc. 85: 2870-2871.

16. Van Tamelen, E. E. and Curphey, T. J. 1962. The selective
     in vitro oxidation of the terminal double bonds in squalene.
     Tet. Lett.: 121-124.

Structures of Halogenated and Antimicrobial Organic Compounds from Marine Sources

K. L. Rinehart, Jr., R. D. Johnson, J. F. Siuda,
G. E. Krejcarek, P. D. Shaw, J. A. McMillan, and I. C. Paul
School of Chemical Sciences, University of Illinois, Urbana,
Ill. 61801, U.S.A.

Abstract: During the eight-weeks' Alpha Helix Baja Expedition
of 1974, a total of 859 marine species were analyzed for organic
halogen content and antimicrobial activity. Species giving high
values in one or the other of the two analyses were then examined by gas chromatography-mass spectrometry on shipboard.
Using these techniques over 100 previously unreported halogenated organic compounds were found. Structures have been assigned
thus far to compounds in three classes: brominated terpenes of
the laurinterol family, metabolites of dibromo- and bromotyro-
sine, and brominated and iodinated aliphatic ketones.

Introduction:

Interest in the structures of natural products derived from
marine sources has increased in recent years as additional compounds of novel structures or bioactivity have been reported.
The field of marine natural products has been most extensively
reviewed by Scheuer [16], but also by others [3,14]. The compounds identified thus far have largely resulted from studies
which were less than systematic or comprehensive, being principally those compounds which crystallized from extracts or were
at least the major components in the extracts. Moreover, the
list of organisms examined is still relatively short. Even the
extensive studies directed toward establishing the structures of
marine toxins have been non-comprehensive in the sense that the
species extracted were those reported to be highly toxic on the
basis of occasional human fatalities, injuries or sickness, as

summarized in the extensive survey of Halstead [7].

Some systematic investigations have been carried out. Along
chemical lines, one can cite, for example, the extensive study
of terpenes from gorgonians carried out by Ciereszko, Weinheimer,
and Schmitz [23]. Along biological lines, the Burkholder and
Lederle groups have directed their efforts toward the discovery
of compounds having antimicrobial activity and have identified
a number of active compounds from sponges [2,17]. Following the
discovery of prostaglandins in the gorgonian Plexaura homomalla
[24], a systematic search for other gorgonians or corals which
might contain prostaglandins yielded mainly negative results
but the interesting observation that different specimens of P.
homomalla contain C-15 epimers of prostaglandin A_2 [15].

Perhaps the most comprehensive study is that presently being
supported by the National Cancer Institute in the U.S. [13].
This study, organized along the lines of their screen for anti-
tumor substances in plants, has not been in operation long enough
to produce dramatic results, but there are preliminary indications that 5-8% of the organisms extracted display anti-tumor
activity.

The Alpha Helix Baja Expedition 1974

The foregoing comments attest to the need for systematic studies
of the chemical constituents of marine species. In this vein
the Alpha Helix Baja Expedition 1974 was undertaken to investigate systematically two properties of the compounds present in
marine organisms: 1) the distribution of halogenated organic
compounds, and 2) the incidence of antimicrobial activity. In
addition, a number of species were analyzed for the occurrence
of prostaglandins and many of the larger samples collected were
extracted for subsequent investigation of their anti-tumor properties. The prostaglandin assay, involving a primary differential ultraviolet technique and a confirmatory gas chromatography-
mass spectrometry assay, identified no prostaglandins in

approximately 200 species assayed.   Results from the anti-tumor
assays are not yet available.

Halogen-containing Organic Compounds

During the eight-weeks' cruise of the R/V Alpha Helix in the
waters off Baja California and the West Coast of Mexico 859 different marine organisms were assayed--670 animal species and 189
plant species [6].   A representative sample of each organism
was homogenized in methanol-toluene and centrifuged.   The super-
natant was divided into two parts, for organic halogen assay and
for antimicrobial assay.   The first part was shaken with aqueous
sodium nitrate to remove inorganic halide and the toluene layer
was analyzed for organic halogen.   All of the 859 organisms
extracted aboard the Alpha Helix were examined for total halogen
content and most for organic bromine content.   Both analyses
involved combustion to halide ion.   Total halogen was then
determined by displacement from mercuric thiocyanate of thiocyanate ion, which in turn was assayed colorimetrically by reaction with ferric nitrate [5].   Bromide ion was determined by

$$2X^- + Hg(SCN)_2 \rightarrow HgX_2 + 2SCN^-$$
$$SCN^- + Fe^{+++} \rightarrow \underset{red}{FeSCN^{++}}$$

oxidation with chloramine T to bromine, which was then assayed
colorimetrically at pH 4.6 (as bromphenol blue) after reaction
with phenol red [1].   Iodide would presumably be determined in
the latter reaction as well, but preliminary studies carried out
on marine samples at Woods Hole [25] indicated iodine to be rare
in marine organisms.

Many of those extracts which showed high organic halogen content
were examined on shipboard by gas chromatography-mass spectrometry (gc-ms), employing methodology used earlier in our laboratory for examining mixtures of alkaloids [12]. For the identification of volatile halogen-containing compounds, gc-ms is an
ideal tool. Compounds are usually well separated by gc, while
ms can indicate immediately and conclusively the presence of
bromine or chlorine. Naturally occurring bromine is a mixture
of nearly equal amounts of two isotopes, ^{79}Br and ^{81}Br; thus,
all mass spectrometric ions containing one bromine atom appear
as doublets separated by 2 amu (atomic mass units), all ions
containing two bromine atoms appear as symmetrical triplets
(relative intensities, 1:2:1), all ions containing three bromine
atoms as quartets, etc., as shown in Figure 1. Similarly,
natural chlorine is a mixture of two isotopes, ^{35}Cl and ^{37}Cl, of
relative abundance 3:1 and all ms ions containing one chlorine
atom appear as doublets of relative intensity 3:1, separated by
2 amu. Mass spectral ions containing more than one chlorine
atom or combinations of chlorine and bromine give the patterns
shown in Figure 1, with all peaks separated by 2 amu. Natural
fluorine and iodine contain only one isotope (^{19}F, ^{127}I) and
cannot be detected by their isotopic abundance pattern, but compounds containing these halogens can usually be detected by the
loss of 19 or 127 amu from ions in their mass spectra or by the
presence of a peak at m/e 127. In any event, they occur far

less frequently than bromine or chlorine. The principal deficiency in the gc-ms method of determining halogenated compounds
is that only volatile, thermally stable compounds will be
observed. This problem can be alleviated in two ways. First,
one can trimsylate the sample prior to gc injection, rendering
it less polar and more volatile. Second, the sample can be
introduced into the ion source of the mass spectrometer via a
direct probe, thus lowering considerably the requirements for
volatility and thermal stability. Using all of these techniques,
over 100 previously unreported halogenated compounds were identified on board the R/V Alpha Helix.

Three species studied on board the Alpha Helix can be used to
illustrate the mass spectral method. The first is Laurencia
pacifica, a species previously reported by Sims [18] to contain
pacifenol and laurinterol. Our initial gc-ms analyses of the
L. pacifica extract (Figure 2) showed it to contain two major
mono-bromo components (Peaks C and D), each of molecular weight
294, and two major non-halogenated components (Peaks A and B) of
molecular weight 216. Previously reported compounds from
Laurencia species with these molecular weights would be laurinterol, isolaurinterol, aplysin, and laurenisol, all of molecular
weight 294, and debromolaurinterol and debromoaplysin, of
molecular weight 216 [8,9,10].

LAURINTEROL
(Irie, from *L.intermedia*
also debromo laurinterol)

ISOLAURINTEROL
(Irie, from *L.intermedia*)

LAURENISOL
(Irie, from *L.nipponica*)

APLYSIN
(Irie, from *L.okamurai*
also debromo aplysin)

In distinguishing among these possibilities laurenisol was first
eliminated, since it has been reported to be unstable at room
temperature [8], whereas our gas chromatograph was operated to
260°C. Of the remaining three brominated compounds, aplysin does
not have a hydroxyl group and can be eliminated, since trimsylation of the L. pacifica extract, followed by gc-ms, indicated
that both major mono-bromo compounds in L. pacifica were converted to monotrimsyl derivatives (mol. wt. 366). To distinguish
between the remaining two, laurinterol and isolaurinterol, a
major fragmentation of one of the two isomers (Peak D) was noted,
involving loss of 68 amu (C_5H_8). This can be rationalized well
for laurinterol by the mechanism shown in Figure 3, but not for
isolaurinterol, and peak C was assigned as isolaurinterol, peak D
as laurinterol. Parallel arguments were used to identify peak B
as debromolaurinterol and peak A as the previously unreported
debromoisolaurinterol. It is of some interest that we did not
detect pacifenol [18] by gc-ms; it may well have been thermally
unstable under our gc conditions.

Similar gc-ms studies identified the laurinterol family of
brominated terpenes as being far more widespread than the
Laurencia genus [8,9,10,18]. For example, laurinterol was
identified on shipboard in L. johnstonii, Rhodymenia californica,
and Corallina chilensis; isolaurinterol in L. johnstonii, L.
decidua, Centrocerus clavulatum, C. chilensis, and Asparagopsis
taxiformis; aplysin in L. johnstonii, L. decidua, C. clavulatum,
and A. taxiformis, debromolaurinterol in L. johnstonii and
Plocamium pacificum, debromoisolaurinterol and debromoaplysin in
L. johnstonii. All of these species are red algae.

More interestingly, extracts of a number of animal species were
observed to contain the same compounds. Both Ophioderma variega-
tum (a brittle star) and an unidentified bryozoan (phylum Ectoprocta) contained laurinterol, isolaurinterol, and aplysin, while
a Laxosuberites species (phylum Porifera) contained debromolaurinterol. These terpenes presumably reflect the diets of the
animals.

A second example of the use of gc-ms to assign structures to halogenated compounds is provided by the study of Verongia aurea, a red sponge [11]. The crude extract of V. aurea demonstrated high total halogen and bromine content, while gc-ms indicated a very complex mixture of bromine-containing compounds (Figure 4). The most abundant component had an apparent molecular weight of 306 and contained two bromine atoms. The compound displaying these characteristics was obtained in pure form when it crystallized from a concentrated ether solution of the extract. In characterizing the compound it was noted, however, that trimsylation followed by gc-ms gave a molecular ion at $\underline{m/e}$ 539 (323 + 3 x 72) for a tristrimsyl derivative instead of the expected $\underline{m/e}$ 522 (306 + 3 x 72). A direct probe mass spectrum obtained on shipboard indicated that the molecular weight of the crystalline compound was indeed 323; thus, the gc-mass spectrum reflected loss of 17 amu from the true molecular ion. Loss of 17 amu could have involved either OH or NH_3, but more likely the latter in view of the odd molecular weight. Subsequent losses of three carbon monoxide molecules would accord with a carbonyl group and two phenolic hydroxyl groups and, in view of the presumed relationship to other dibromotyrosine metabolites [3,20], the structure of a 2,6-dibromophenol-3(or 4)-hydroxy-4(or 3)-acetamide was proposed. This was placed on firmer ground when the crystals were subsequently shown by X-ray analysis [11] to be 3,5-dibromo-hydroquinone-2-acetamide.

Most of the other peaks in the gc trace also contained bromine and were regarded as being related to the dibromohydroquinone and the numerous other metabolites of dibromotyrosine [3,20] identified earlier by others. However, it was not clear what the true molecular ions were for the compounds in the original extract. Consequently, direct probe electron impact and field desorption mass spectra of the crude extract were obtained at the University of Illinois; these indicated a number of molecular ions different from those shown by gc-ms (Figure 5). To decide which compounds in the gc trace corresponded to which

molecular ions in the crude extract, column chromatographic
separation has been undertaken and individual components are now
being identified.   One of these is a mono-bromo analog of 3,5-
dibromohydroquinone-2-acetamide [11]; other structures will be
reported subsequently.

$$CH_3CH_2CH_2CH_2CX_1X_2\overset{\overset{+}{O^{\cdot}}}{\overset{\|}{C}}CHX_3X_4$$

$$M^{+\cdot}$$

1:   $X_1 = X_3 = H$; $X_2 = X_4 = Br$

2:   $X_1 = H$; $X_2 = X_3 = X_4 = Br$

3:   $X_1 = X_2 = X_3 = Br$; $X_4 = H$

4:   $X_1 = X_2 = X_3 = X_4 = Br$

5:   $X_1 = X_2 = Br$; $X_3 = H$; $X_4 = I$

A third example is provided by the red alga   Bonnemaisonia hamifera, which not only showed high total halogen and bromine content but also possessed a characteristically pungent, sweet odor.
The crude extract of B. hamifera was subjected to gc-ms analysis,
but the major peaks did not contain bromine or chlorine.   Consequently, the extract was chromatographed over a silicic acid
column and the individual fractions were examined by sniffing for
the characteristic odor and by gc-ms for halogenated compounds.
One fraction contained the nearly pure odoriferous compound (4).
This compound and the four related compounds shown were identified by their electron impact and field ionization gas chromatographic mass spectral fragmentation patterns [21] and, in part,
by synthesis as well.   Significantly, one of the compounds (5)
is the first organic compound shown to contain iodine, other
than iodotyrosine and related compounds [20].

Antimicrobial Compounds

Aliquots of the part of the toluene-methanol extract reserved for
antimicrobial assay (see preceding section) were transferred to

filter paper disks and the disks were applied to four agar
plates seeded with different organisms, a gram-positive bacterium (Bacillus subtilis), a gram-negative bacterium (Escherichia
coli), a yeast (Saccharomyces cerevisiae), and a fungus (Penicil-
lium atrovenetum). After incubation, zones of inhibition were
measured. A surprisingly high proportion of animal (13%) and
plant (17%) extracts indicated activity against B.subtilis, with
lower proportions active against the other organisms.

Rather strong correlations exist between the incidence of antimicrobial activity and the genus of the organism. There is an
especially high incidence of B. subtilis activity (32% of all
species) in the animal phylum Porifera (the sponges), as might
have been inferred from the several reports of antimicrobial
substances in sponges from the Lederle and Burkholder groups
[2,17]. However, other families also show high incidences of
antimicrobial activity. The animal phylum Ectoprocta and the
plant phylum Phaetophyta have high incidences of activity (23%,
28%) against B. subtilis, while the animal phylum Echinodermata
has activity (27%) against fungi. The generalizations established by this survey suggest families of organisms for further
investigation in other regions of the world.

Of course, a chemist is not satisfied with the identification of
a family or even a species possessing antimicrobial activity. He
seeks, rather, to identify the compound or compounds causing the
antimicrobial activity. Preliminary studies in this direction
were carried out during the Alpha Helix Baja Expedition, but time
limitations did not permit many detailed analyses. The principal
structural tool used on board the Alpha Helix was gc-ms and this
was highly successful in identifying halogenated compounds, as
detailed above, provided the compounds were sufficiently volatile
and stable to pass through the gc. However, while gc-ms is a
superb method for identifying compounds, it cannot indicate
whether they are antimicrobial. Thus, this tool could not be
used in assigning structures to the antimicrobial agents in crude
extracts. One could, however, infer from the predominance of
certain compounds in the extracts that they were responsible for

antimicrobial activity. This was the case, for example, with
extracts of Laurencia pacifica, which contained a large amount of
laurinterol, and of Verongia aurea, whose main constituent was
3,5-dibromohydroquinone-2-acetamide. The antimicrobial properties of laurinterol have been independently observed by others
[19,22].

Some of the extracts were chromatographed either on columns or
thick layer plates and the fractions separated were analyzed by
the usual procedure on seeded agar plates. Pure 3,5-dibromohydro-
quinone-2-acetamide was isolated from V. aurea and shown to be
active against B. subtilis and E. coli. Other chromatographic
fractions from V. aurea were also active. As noted above, chromatography of Bonnemaisonia hamifera yielded pure 1,1,3,3-
tetrabromo-2-heptanone (4), with weak antibacterial and anti-
fungal properties. Analogous brominated ketones have been
identified in the related red alga Asparagopsis taxiformis,
by us, by Fenical [4] , and by Moore, et al. [2a].

Studies are continuing on a number of other extracts. To date,
the studies based on the Alpha Helix Baja Expedition 1) have
assigned antimicrobial properties to members of the laurinterol
family, 2) have identified additional antimicrobial metabolites
of dibromotyrosine, and 3) have identified the aliphatic halo
ketones as a new class of antimicrobial compounds of marine
origin.

Conclusions

Gas chromatography-mass spectrometry has proved to be a uniquely
appropriate tool for the investigation of crude extracts of
marine organisms, allowing the identification of relatively
volatile halogenated organic compounds. It can be supplemented
by direct probe mass spectrometry for identifying less volatile
materials. The technique is sufficiently reliable to be used
routinely on shipboard. Employing this tool on the R/V Alpha
Helix and, later, at the University of Illinois, three classes
of halogenated compounds have thus far been studied in detail--

brominated terpenes, brominated tyrosine metabolites, and brominated and iodinated aliphatic ketones; over 100 previously unidentified halogenated compounds have been observed.

References

(1)   Archimbaud, M., and Bertrand, M. R.   1970.   Dosage de
bromure dans les eaux.   Chim. Anal. $\underline{52}$:   531-533.

(2)   Borders, D. B., Morton, G. O., and Wetzel, R. R. 1974.
Structure of a novel bromine compound isolated from a sponge.
Tetrahedron Lett. 2709-2712.

(2a) Burreson, B. J., Moore, R. E., and Roller, P. 1975.
Haloforms in the essential oil of the alga Asparagopsis taxiformis
(Rhodophyta). Tetrahedron Lett. 473-476.

(3)   Faulkner, D. J., and Andersen, R. J.   1974.   Natural
Products Chemistry of the Marine Environment.   In The Sea, Vol.
5, ed. E. D. Goldberg, pp. 679-714.   New York: Wiley-Interscience.

(4)   Fenical, W.   1974.   Polyhaloketones from the red sea-
weed Asparagopsis taxiformis. Tetrahedron Lett. 4463-4466.

(5)   Florence, T. M., and Farrar, Y. J.   1971.   Spectrophotometric determination of chloride at the parts-per-billion level
by the mercury (II) thiocyanate method.   Anal. Chim. Acta $\underline{54}$:
373-377.

(6)   Hager, L. P., White, R. H., Doubek, D. L., Hollenberg,
P. F., Shaw, P. D., Rinehart, K. L., Jr., Johnson, R. D., Brusca,
R. C., Krejcarek, G. E., Siuda, J. F., Guerrero, R., McClure,
W. O., VanBlaricom, G. R., Sims, J. J., Fenical, W. O., and
Rude, J.   1975.   Halogenated natural products and antimicrobial
activity in marine organisms.   Proc. Natl. Acad. Sci. U.S.,
submitted.

(7)   Halstead, B. W.   1965-1970.   Poisonous and Venomous
Marine Animals of the World.   Vols. 1-3.   Washington: U.S.
Government Printing Office.

(8)   Irie, T., Fukuzawa, A., Izawa, M., and Kurosawa, E.
1969.   Laurenisol, a new sesquiterpenoid containing bromine from
Laurencia nipponica Yamada.   Tetrahedron Lett. 1343-1346.

(9)   Irie, T., Suzuki, M., and Hayakawa, Y.   1969.   Isolation of aplysin, debromoaplysin, and aplysinol from Laurencia
okamurai Yamada.   Bull. Chem. Soc. Jap. $\underline{42}$:   843-844.

(10)   Irie, T., Suzuki, M., Kurosawa, E., and Masamune, T.
1970.   Laurinterol, debromolaurinterol and isolaurinterol,
constituents of Laurencia intermedia Yamada.   Tetrahedron $\underline{26}$:
3271-3277.

(11)   Krejcarek, G. E., White, R. H., Hager, L. P., McClure, W. O., Johnson, R. D., Rinehart, K. L., Jr., McMillan, J. A., Paul, I. C., Shaw, P. D., and Brusca, R. C. 1975. A rearranged dibromotyrosine metabolite from Verongia aurea. Tetrahedron Lett. 507-510.

(12)   Millington, D. S., Steinman, D. H., and Rinehart, K.L., Jr., 1974. Isolation, gas chromatography-mass spectrometry, and structures of new alkaloids from Erythrina folkersii Krukoff and Moldenke and Erythrina salviiflora Krukoff and Barneby. J. Amer. Chem. Soc., 96: 1909-1917.

(13)   Pettit, G. R., Day, J. F., Hartwell, J. L., and Wood, H. B. 1970. Antineoplastic components of marine animals. Nature 227: 962-963.

(14)   Premuzic, E. 1971. Chemistry of natural products derived from marine sources. Fortschr. Chem. Org. Naturstoffe 29: 417-488.

(15)   Schneider, W. P., Hamilton, R. D., and Rhuland, L. E. 1972. Occurrence of esters of (15S)-prostaglandin A_2 and E_2 in coral. J. Amer. Chem. Soc. 94: 2122-2123.

(16)   Scheuer, P. J. 1973. Chemistry of Marine Natural Products. New York: Academic Press.

(17)   Sharma, G. M., and Burkholder, P. R. 1967. Studies on the antimicrobial substances of sponges. II. Structure and synthesis of a bromine-containing antibacterial compound from a marine sponge. Tetrahedron Lett. 4147-4150.

(18)   Sims, J. J., Fenical, W., Wing, R. M., and Radlick, P. 1974. Marine natural products. I. Pacifenol, a rare sesquiterpene containing bromine and chlorine from the red alga, Laurencia pacifica. J. Amer. Chem. Soc. 93: 3774-3775.

(19)   Sims, J. J., Donnell, M. S., Leary, J. V., and Lacy, G. H. 1975. Antimicrobial agents from marine algae. Antimicrobial Agents and Chemotherapy 7: 320-321.

(20)   Siuda, J. F., and De Bernardis, J. F. 1973. Naturally occurring halogenated organic compounds. Lloydia 36: 107-143.

(21)   Siuda, J. F., VanBlaricom, G. R., Shaw, P. D., Johnson, R. D., White, R. H., Hager, L. P., and Rinehart, K. L., Jr. 1975. 1-Iodo-3,3-dibromo-2-heptanone, 1,1,3,3,-tetrabromo-2-heptanone, and related compounds from the red alga Bonnemaisonia hamifera. J. Amer. Chem. Soc. 97: 937-938.

(22)   Waraszkiewicz, S. M., and Erickson, K. L. 1974. Halogenated sesquiterpenoids from the Hawaiian marine alga Laurencia nidifica: nidificene and nidifidiene. Tetrahedron Lett. 2003-2006.

(23) Weinheimer, A. J., Schmitz, F. J., and Ciereszko, L. S. 1968. Chemistry of Coelenterates. VII. The Occurrence of Terpenoid Compounds in Gorgonians. In Transactions of the Drugs from the Sea Symposium 1967, ed. H. D. Freudenthal, pp. 135-140. Washington: Marine Technology Society.

(24) Weinheimer, A. J., and Sproggins, R. L. 1969. The occurrence of two new prostaglandin derivatives (15-epi-PGA$_2$ and its acetate, methyl ester) in the gorgonian Plexaura homomalla. Tetrahedron Lett. 5185-5188.

(25) White, R. H. 1974. Analysis of Organic Halogen Compounds in Marine Organisms. Ph.D. Thesis. Urbana: University of Illinois.

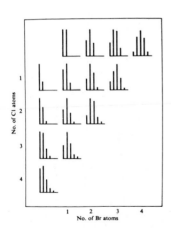

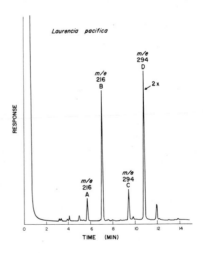

FIG. 1 -- Isotopic patterns for ions containing bromine and chlorine atoms. Adjacent lines are separated by 2 amu. [Taken from Shrader, S. R. 1971. Introductory Mass Spectrometry. Boston: Allyn and Bacon].

FIG. 2 -- Gas chromatographic trace of a Laurencia pacifica extract. Peaks: A, debromo-isolaurinterol; B, debromo-laurinterol; C, isolaurin-terol; D, laurinterol.

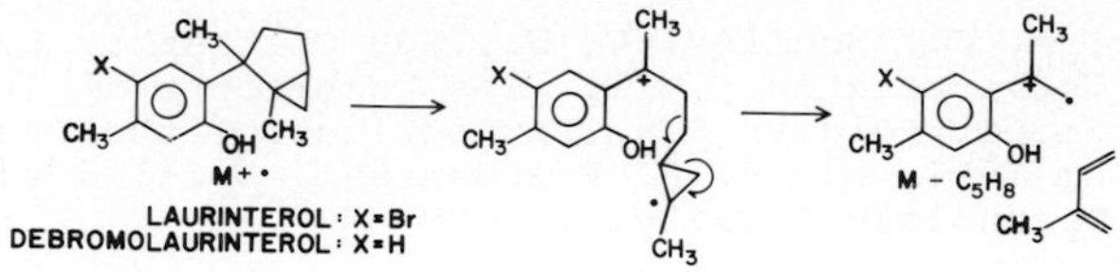

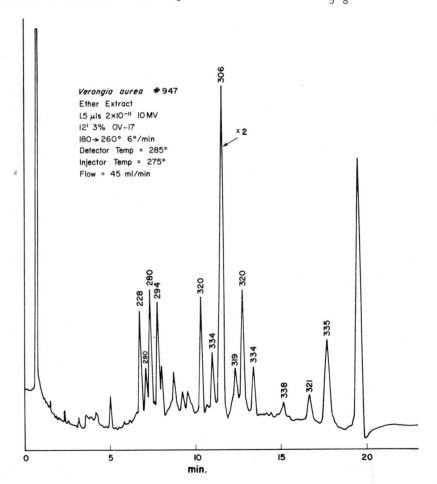

FIG. 3 -- Mass spectral fragmentation pathway of laurinterol and debromolaurinterol leading to loss of 68 amu (C_5H_8).

FIG. 4 -- Gas chromatographic trace of a Verongia aurea extract. The numbers for individual peaks refer to the ions of highest mass (apparent molecular ions, containing [79]Br or [79]Br$_2$) in the mass spectra of the components.

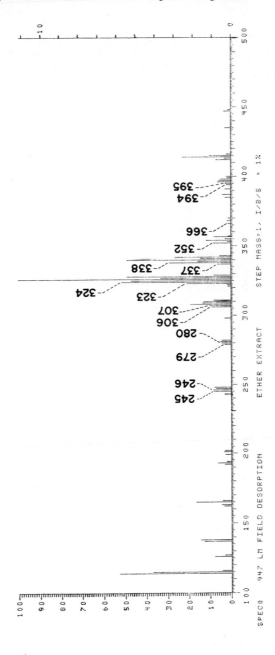

FIG. 5 -- Field desorption mass spectrum of a Verongia aurea extract. The numbers refer to the ions of lowest mass for ion clusters containing bromine (^{79}Br or $^{79}Br_2$).

Microbial Degradation of Hydrocarbons.

David T. Gibson
Department of Microbiology, The University of Texas
at Austin
Austin, Texas 78712 USA

Abstract: Many different hydrocarbons are synthesized by living organisms. Laboratory studies with single and mixed hydrocarbon substrates reveal that these compounds and structurally related molecules are subject to microbial degradation. Considerable information is available that relates to the mechanisms utilized by microorganisms for the degradation of n-alkanes, branched alkanes, and simple aromatic hydrocarbons. Thus, bacteria incorporate both atoms of molecular oxygen into aromatic hydrocarbons to form cis-dihydrodiols. The latter compounds are oxidized to catechols prior to fission of the benzene ring. Available evidence obtained from both laboratory and environmental studies, indicates that microorganisms can also metabolize the above compounds when they are present in crude oil. However, crude oil contains many classes of compounds that bear little structural resemblance to naturally occurring molecules. The microbial degradation of these compounds, particularly large polycyclic hydrocarbons and their sulfur-containing analogues, remains to be established.

INTRODUCTION

Hydrocarbons are organic molecules that contain only the elements of

carbon and hydrogen. They range in size from methane, the smallest

known organic compound, to large polycyclic compounds of unknown mo-

lecular weight that are found in crude petroleum. The biodegradation

of hydrocarbons has been the subject of intensive research since 1906

when Söhngen demonstrated the bacterial oxidation of methane (42).

Most studies have been directed towards the elucidation of the meta-

bolic pathways used by microorganisms to oxidize hydrocarbons to car-

bon dioxide and water. Usually these investigations have been limited
to the interactions between a single microorganism and a single hydrocarbon substrate. In addition, a considerable amount of effort has
been expended in a search for microorganisms that catalyze incomplete
oxidations of hydrocarbons to oxygenated derivatives. As a result of
these endeavours some general features of hydrocarbon degradation have
been obtained. They are as follows: (1) microorganisms from many
different genera are capable of metabolizing a variety of hydrocarbons; (2) degradation is initiated by the enzymatic incorporation of
molecular oxygen into the hydrocarbon molecule; (3) the degradation
of hydrocarbons does not occur under anaerobic conditions; (4) the
metabolic pathways used by microorganisms to degrade hydrocarbons
share many features in common with the pathways used to degrade a
variety of oxygenated substrates.

At this time a voluminous literature exists that pertains to the microbial degradation of hydrocarbons. It is beyond the scope of this article to describe the many hydrocarbon substrates that are subject
to microbial metabolism. Fortunately several excellent review articles
that cover this area are available (1,14,18,33,39,44,45). From this
information we can conclude that representative members of every known
class of hydrocarbons are subject to microbial degradation. Some examples are given in Table I and while the list is by no means complete
it is pertinent to note that most of these compounds are representative of the types of simple hydrocarbon structures that are present
in crude petroleum. The only exceptions are the olefinic compounds
which have never been detected as petroleum constituents. Nevertheless, the isolation of microorganisms capable of growth on hexade-
cene-1 has been used as an indicator of oil pollution (37) and a review entitled "Biodegradation of Hydrocarbons in the Sea" (13) ad-

TABLE 1

EXAMPLES OF HYDROCARBON STRUCTURES SUBJECT TO MICROBIAL DEGRADATION[1]

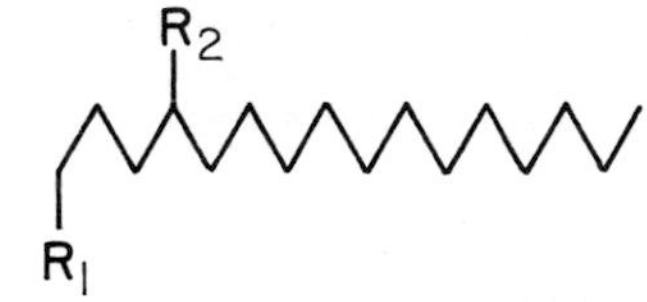

R_1, R_2 = H, Hexadecane
R_1 = phenyl, R_2 = H, 1-phenyldecane
R_1 = phenyl, R_2 = CH_3, 1-phenyl-4-methyldecane

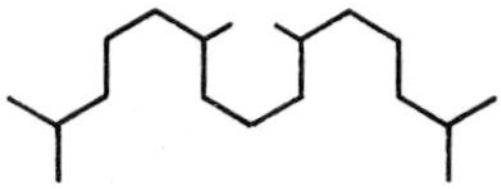

pristane

R = H, cyclohexane
R = CH_3, methylcyclohexane
R = $(CH_2)_3 CH_3$, n-butylcyclohexane

hexadecene

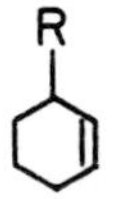

R = H, cyclohexene
R = CH_3, 3-methylcyclohexene

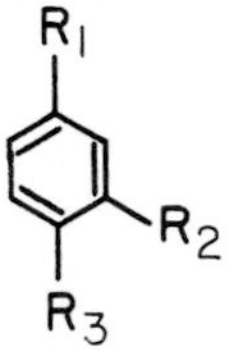

R_1, R_2, R_3 = H, Benzene
R_2, R_3 = H, R_1 = CH_3, Toluene
R_1, R_2 = CH_3, R_3 = H, m-xylene
R_1, R_2, R_3 = CH_3, 1,2,4-Trimethylbenzene

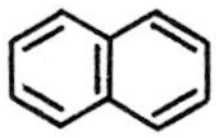

Naphthalene

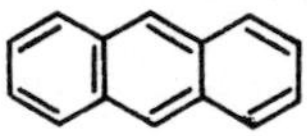

Anthracene

[1]Either to CO_2 and H_2O or to oxygenated derivatives.

dressed itself primarily to the ecological aspects of oil pollution
and alkane oxidation. The metabolic versatility of microorganisms
with respect to simple hydrocarbon substrates has resulted in the
misconception that the microbial degradation of crude oil is a well
established phenomenon. This is not the case. Paraffinic hydrocarbons normally account for less than twenty percent of most crude oils.
Even if they are removed from crude oil by microbial oxidation the
question still remains; what happens to the remaining oil components?
Apart from studies on alkane oxidation, there is little experimental
evidence available to support the statement "that many bacteria found
in the sea are capable of oxidizing a considerable part, if not all,
of the oil or oil products which are spilled into the marine environment" (13).

The problems associated with studies on the biodegradation of oil are
many orders of magnitude more complex than those encountered during
investigations of the metabolism of a single hydrocarbon by a single
microorganism. It is the purpose of this presentation to discuss the
types of information that can be obtained in these related, but by no
means identical, fields of scientific endeavour.

SOURCE OF HYDROCARBONS IN THE ENVIRONMENT

Over millions of years microorganisms, in their quest for sources of
energy, have evolved enzyme systems that are capable of metabolizing
almost every organic molecule that is synthesized by living matter.
These enzymes are synthesized in response to the presence of inducers
or derepressors. Consequently, the rate at which a molecule undergoes
biodegradation will depend on its structural relationship to naturally
occurring compounds. The wide distribution of microorganisms that are
capable of oxidizing certain hydrocarbons suggests that these hydro-

carbons, or structurally similar molecules, are natural components of
the environment. Thus, Clark and Blumer (9) have shown that the n-
paraffins in cultured plankton have a distribution pattern similar to
the n-paraffins found in some crude oils. n-Paraffins are the most
abundant alkanes that are produced by living organisms and chain
lengths up to C_{62} have been reported (30). However, it appears that
C_7-C_{36} alkanes and methane are the most common biological alkanes (35).
Pristane (2,3,10,14-tetramethylpentadecane) is an isoprenoid alkane
that is found in a variety of unicellular and multicellular organisms
(4). It seems probable that this hydrocarbon is produced by the biological transformation of phytol which is a constituent of chlorophyll.
Branched chain paraffins with methyl groups at C_2 and C_3 are found in
the waxes obtained from tobacco leaves, wool and sugar cane (27). Recently Ledet and Laseter (32) detected methyl branched alkanes ranging
in chain lengths from C_{15} to C_{35} and also alkyl-substituted cycloal-
kanes in the surface waters of the Gulf of Mexico. The authors suggested that these compounds could be produced by natural biological
sources. A list of the compounds identified in their investigation
is given in Table II.

Since n-alkanes and their branched chain derivatives are natural components of the environment it is not surprising to find that they will
serve as substrates for the growth of many different microorganisms.
The same is true for the terpenes which are the most abundant of all
biological hydrocarbons.

An alternative, and more serious, source of hydrocarbons in the environment is due to man's activities in the area of petroleum production,
transport and utilization. Blumer (6) has estimated that the marine
environment receives at least a million tons of crude oil per year due

TABLE II

HYDROCARBONS DETECTED AT THE AIR-SEA INTERFACE[1]

n-Hexadecane	Dimethyleicosane
n-Octadecane	2,6-Dimethylnonadecane
3-Methylpentadecane	Dimethyldocosane
3-Methylhexadecane	Nonadecylcyclohexane
3-Methylheptadecane	Decylcyclohexane
3-Methyloctadecane	Undecylcyclohexane
3-Methylnonadecane	Dodecylcyclohexane
3-Methyleicosane	Tridecylcyclohexane
3-Methylheneicosane	Tetradecylcyclohexane
2,6-Dimethylpentadecane	Pentadecylcyclohexane
Dimethyloctadecane	Pristane
3-Methyloctadecane	Phytane
2,6-Dimethylheptadecane	

[1]Reference (32).

to losses incurred during the transport of oil. While there is little doubt that oil is derived from biological sources, the majority of its constituents cannot be considered as natural components of the environment. It is probable that thousands of different compounds that bear little, if any, structural relationship to naturally occurring molecules are being continually added to the marine environment. At this time there is no sound reason to assume the existence of microorganisms that are capable of degrading these compounds. Molecules of nonbiological origin usually prove to be quite resistant to microbial degradation. Some typical examples are chlorinated hydrocarbons

such as DDT and polychlorinated biphenyls which are regarded as ubiq-
uitous environmental pollutants. It is conceivable that the recalci-
trance of certain molecules to biodegradation is due to insufficient
time for microorganisms to evolve the necessary enzyme systems. This
concept has been eloquently discussed by Hegeman (22).

In order to gain some appreciation of the types of compounds that may
be accumulating in the marine environment we must have some understanding of the constituents found in oil. Crude oil is a term used
to describe the fraction of petroleum that is a liquid which will flow
without great difficulty. It has little meaning in terms of composition. In addition, crude oils vary in composition according to their
source. Table III gives the general composition of some oils that are
produced in North America. The open chain paraffins are relatively
well characterized because they are the easiest to analyze. Although
the range of paraffins can vary from near zero to almost one hundred
percent, this class of compounds generally accounts for less than twenty
percent of most crude oils. Cycloparaffins constitute up to fifty per-

TABLE III

COMPOSITION OF CRUDE OIL FRACTION

| Crude Oil | Boiling Range °C | WEIGHT PERCENT | | | | |
		Paraffins & Cyclo-Paraffins	Aromatics	Neutral Nitrogen	Acids	Bases
Wilmington	370–485	37.8	42.7	9.4	5.3	5.0
Recluse	335–530	75.6	21.4	1.6	1.2	0.9
Gato Ridge	370–535	29.1	59.8	3.8	3.6	2.7
Prudhoe Bay	370–535	47.3	44.4	1.0	3.0	2.2
Ponca City	305–405	70.2	25.3	1.6	0.6	0.7

cent of many crude oils with cyclohexane and cyclopentane rings being
the basic structures. The possible combinations of cyclohexane and
cyclopentane rings together with the many positions available for substitution of alkyl sidechains account for the fact that this group of
hydrocarbons has resisted detailed analysis.

The aromatic hydrocarbons present in crude oil probably pose the greatest threat to the quality of the environment. Most known aromatic hydrocarbons are toxic to plants and animals. In addition, the carcino-
genicity of several polycyclic aromatic hydrocarbons is well documented (11). The aromatic fraction usually constitutes less than
twenty percent of total composition of most crude oils. The types of
aromatic compounds found in a narrow-boiling distillation fraction of
one crude oil are shown in Table IV. It is important to realize that
these are classes of compounds and that each class contains many different aromatic compounds. Also, for almost every class there are
analogous sulfur-containing compounds.

The larger molecules in crude oil are combinations of aromatic, cyclohexane and cyclopentane rings. Usually the ring structures contain
relatively short alkyl substituents. Obviously these molecules defy
description in terms of conventional hydrocarbon nomenclature. A
typical example is a group of compounds called the asphaltenes which
are found in petroleum fractions that boil over 500° C. Asphaltenes
can account for up to twenty percent of many crude oils. They are a
compound class that has defied structural analysis. Reported molecular weights vary from 500 to 500,000 and the asphaltenes have been
described as sheets of condensed aromatic rings that are stacked on
top of each other. Whether or not the sheets are linked with paraffin
bridges remains to be determined. Asphaltenes also contain large
amounts of sulfur, nitrogen and oxygen as well as the metals nickel

TABLE IV

HYDROCARBON TYPES IN THE 370° TO 535° C
DISTILLATE OF WILMINGTON, CALIFORNIA CRUDE OIL[1]

Monoaromatic Compounds

Alkylbenzenes
Indanes/Tetralins
Dinaphthenobenzenes
Trinaphthenobenzenes
Tetranaphthenobenzenes
Pentanaphthenobenzenes
Hexanaphthenobenzenes
Heptanaphthenobenzenes

Octanaphthenobenzenes
Naphthalenes
Naphtnenonaphthalenes or
   Diphenylalkanes
Dinaphthenonaphthalenes or
   Naphthenodiphenylalkanes
Trinaphthenonaphthalenes or
   Dinaphthenodiphenylalkanes
Tetranaphthenonaphthalenes or
   Trinaphthenodiphenylalkanes

Diaromatic Compounds

Alkylnaphthalenes
Naphthenonaphthalenes or
   Diphenylalkanes
Dinaphthenonaphthalenes or
   Naphthenodiphenylalkanes
Trinaphthenonaphthalenes or
   Dinaphthenodiphenylalkanes

Tetranaphthenonaphthalenes or
   Trinaphthenodiphenylalkanes
Pentanaphthenonaphthalenes or
   Tetranaphthenodiphenylalkanes
Hexanaphthenonaphthalenes or
   Pentanaphthenodiphenylalkanes
Heptanaphthenonaphthalenes or
   Hexanaphthenodiphenylalkanes

Polyaromatic Compounds

Naphthenophenanthrenes/Anthracenes
Dinaphthenophenanthrenes/
   Anthracenes
Trinaphthenophenanthrenes/
   Anthracenes
Tetranaphthenophenanthrenes/
   Anthracenes and/or
   Thienodibenzothiophenes
Pentanaphthenophenanthrenes/
   Anthracenes and/or
   Naphthenothienodibenzothiophenes
Alkyl Pyrenes
Alkyl Phenanthrenes/Anthracenes

Alkyl Benzopyrenes
Alkyl Acenaphthalenes
Naphthenoacenaphthalenes
Dinaphthenoacenaphthalenes
Trinaphthenoacenaphthalenes
Tetranaphthenoacenaphthalenes
Pentanaphthenoacenaphthalenes
Hexanaphthenoacenaphthalenes
Heptanaphthenoacenaphthalenes
Octanaphthenoacenaphthalenes
Naphthenopyrenes and/or
   Chrysenes
Naphthenobenzopyrenes

[1]Dooley, J.E., Hirsch, D.E. and Thompson, C.J. 1974. Analyzing Heavy
Ends of Crude. Hydrocarbon Processing. 53:140-146.

and vanadium. It seems probable that the composition of the asphaltene fraction varies with the age and location of the oil from which
it is derived.

At this time there is little evidence to indicate that many of the
above aromatic compounds and their sulfur-containing analogues are
subject to biodegradation by microorganisms. The environmental distribution of most of these types of molecule is largely unknown.
However, it is of interest to note that certain polycyclic aromatic
hydrocarbons, including benzo[a]pyrene and benzo[a]anthracene have
been found in marine and nonmarine sediments (28,36), soils (5),
plankton and marine animals (38). Suspected sources of these compounds include oil pollution, aerial transport of combustion products (8),
pyrolysis of wood and plant organic matter and biosynthesis by bacteria or higher plants (51). Since these compounds appear to be
natural components of the environment it is not surprising to find
that they are subject to microbial degradation (41).

BIODEGRADATION OF SINGLE HYDROCARBON SUBSTRATES

Techniques used to investigate the microbial degradation of aromatic
hydrocarbons will be presented. This approach, with minor variations,
may be considered typical of most investigations that relate to the
biodegradation of single hydrocarbon substrates.

A. Isolation and Growth of Microorganisms

The elucidation of the biochemical reactions that occur during the
microbial degradation of aromatic hydrocarbons was facilitated by
the isolation of pure strains of bacteria that could use these compounds as sole sources of carbon and energy for growth. A standard

enrichment culture procedure led to the isolation of pure strains of
microorganisms that degraded several aromatic hydrocarbons to carbon
dioxide and water. These organisms are listed in Table V.

TABLE V

BACTERIA CAPABLE OF GROWTH ON AROMATIC HYDROCARBONS

Organism	Growth Substrates
Pseudomonas putida, strain AB	Benzene, Toluene, Ethylbenzene
Pseudomonas putida, strain NP	Naphthalene
Beijerinckia species	Biphenyl, Phenanthrene
Nocardia species	ortho-xylene

Pseudomonas putida, strain AB and the Nocardia species would not grow
on the volatile hydrocarbons when these compounds were added directly
to the culture medium. It appears that saturating levels of benzene,
toluene, ethylbenzene and ortho-xylene are toxic to these two strains
of bacteria. However, when the hydrocarbons were introduced in the
vapor phase rapid growth was observed. The procedures used for growth
of these two strains of bacteria are shown in Figure 1. The solid hydrocarbons, naphthalene, phenanthrene, and biphenyl did not appear to
be toxic to microorganisms and were added directly to the culture medium. Available evidence suggests that microorganisms can only use
hydrocarbons that are in solution (48,49). If this is the case, it
may explain why there are no reports of microorganisms being able to
grow with aromatic hydrocarbons that contain more than three aromatic
rings. The solubilities of some aromatic hydrocarbons are shown in
Table VI. It is clear that compounds larger than anthracene will

TABLE VI

SOLUBILITY OF AROMATIC HYDROCARBONS IN WATER[1]

Hydrocarbon	Solubility, μgrams per liter
Benzene	1,860,000
Toluene	500,000
Ethylbenzene	175,000
n–Propylbenzene	120,000
n–Butylbenzene	50,000
Naphthalene	12,500
Phenanthrene	1,600
Anthracene	75
1,2–Benzanthracene	10
Chrysene	6
1,2,5,6–Dibenzanthracene	0.6*

[1]Data from Klevins, H.B. 1950. Solubilization of Polycyclic Hydrocarbons. J. Phys. Chem. $\underline{54}$:283-298.

*Approximate value.

never attain concentrations that are high enough to support signifi-

cant bacterial growth. This does not mean that these molecules will

not undergo microbial transformation. Nevertheless, the insolubility

of organic molecules probably plays a significant role in resistance

to biodegradation.

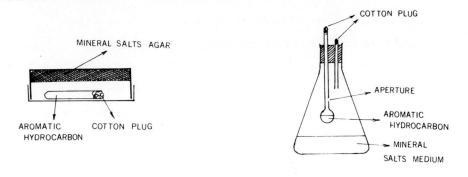

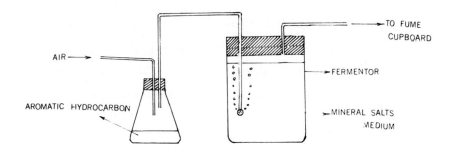

FIG. 1 - Methods used for growth of bacteria on volatile aromatic hydrocarbons.

B. Studies with Whole Cells

Growth of a microorganism on a single hydrocarbon substrate yields cells that contain all of the enzymes necessary to convert the hydrocarbons to carbon dioxide and water. Most of the enzymes that are involved in the initial states of degradation are inducible. That is, they are synthesized in response to the presence of the hydrocarbon substrate or its degradation products. This feature makes it possible to use the technique of simultaneous adaptation (43) to provide information as to the metabolic intermediates that

are formed during degradation. Thus, if a substrate (A) is metabolized according to the following sequence:

$$A \to B \to C \to D \to E \to etc.$$

cells grown on A will contain the enzymes that catalyze the degradation of A, B, C, D, and E. Also, the rates of oxidation of each
compound should be similar. Theoretically, cells grown on C should
contain the enzymes necessary for the oxidation of C, D and E but
not the enzymes for the metabolism of A and B. This theory has important practical applications since it provides a simple means of
predicting the intermediates that are involved in the degradation
of a growth substrate. For example, Pseudomonas putida strain AB
could theoretically oxidize toluene either at the methyl group or
at the aromatic nucleus. The ability of toluene-grown cells to oxidize suspected intermediates in the metabolism of toluene is shown
in Table VII.

TABLE VII

OXIDATION OF AROMATIC COMPOUNDS BY P. putida

Substrate	Rate of Oxygen Consumption μl O_2 per min.
Toluene	9.3
3-Methylcatechol	6.1
4-Methylcatechol	4.3
o-Cresol	2.1
m-Cresol	1.7
p-Cresol	0.9
Benzoic acid	0.0

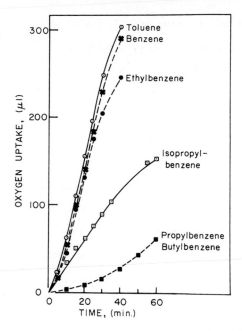

FIG. 2 - Oxidation of aromatic hydrocarbons by toluene-grown cells
of P. putida (13).

From this information it appears that the organism oxidizes toluene
through 3-Methylcatechol and that this reaction does not involve the
formation of o- or m-cresol. However, care must be taken in the interpretation of the data obtained from simultaneous adaptation experiments. The enzymes synthesized during growth on aromatic hydrocarbons
generally show broad specificity with regard to the substrates they
will attack. Thus, toluene-grown cells also catalyze the rapid oxidation of benzene, ethylbenzene and isopropylbenzene (FIG. 2). The
failure of intact cells to oxidize a suspected intermediate may be
due to a permeability barrier rather than an enzyme defficiency.
The most satisfactory way to establish a metabolic pathway is to iso-
late and identify each intermediate. In the case of aromatic hydrocarbon degradation this is not a simple task. Metabolic products

rarely accumulate in the culture medium. However, when P. putida was
grown on toluene, an analysis of the culture filtrate by thin layer
chromatography revealed the transitory accumulation of a phenolic
product. This compound was isolated and identified as 3-methylcate-
chol (15).

One of the most productive techniques for obtaining information relating to hydrocarbon degradation is the use of mutant organisms that
accumulate metabolic intermediates. Treatment of P. putida strain AB
with nitrosoguanidine led to the isolation of a mutant organism (P.
putida 39/D) that would no longer utilize toluene as a growth substrate. When P. putida 39/D was grown with glucose in the presence
of toluene a neutral compound was excreted into the culture medium.
An analysis of the infrared, ultraviolet and proton magnetic resonance spectra of this compound established its structure as 3-methyl-
3,5-cyclohexadiene-1,2-diol. The stereochemistry of the hydroxyl
groups was originally determined by condensing the diacetate of the
diol with maleic anhydride to yield a Diels-Alder adduct. The proton magnetic resonance spectrum of this compound (FIG. 3) revealed
that the coupling constants between H(A) and H(B) were 8.5 Hz, which
suggested that the compound formed from toluene by P. putida 39/D was
a cis-dihydrodiol (16). Subsequently, the absolute stereochemistry
of the microbial product was determined by chemical and spectroscopic
procedures (50) and also by analysis of X-ray diffraction data (29).
The results unequivocally established that P. putida oxidizes toluene
to 3-methyl-3,5-cyclohexadiene-1(S),2(R)-diol. An enzyme was detected
in the parent strain of P. putida that oxidized the dihydrodiol to
3-methylcatechol. The initial reactions in the oxidation of toluene
by this organism are given in Figure 4.

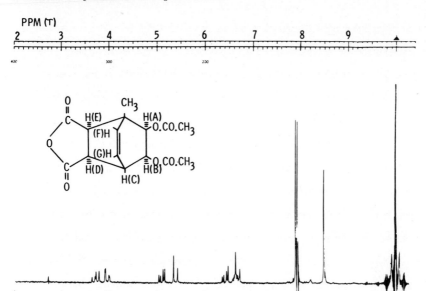

FIG. 3 - Proton magnetic resonance spectrum of the Diels-Alder adduct formed from the diacetate of 3-methyl-3,5-cyclohexadiene-1,2-diol (16).

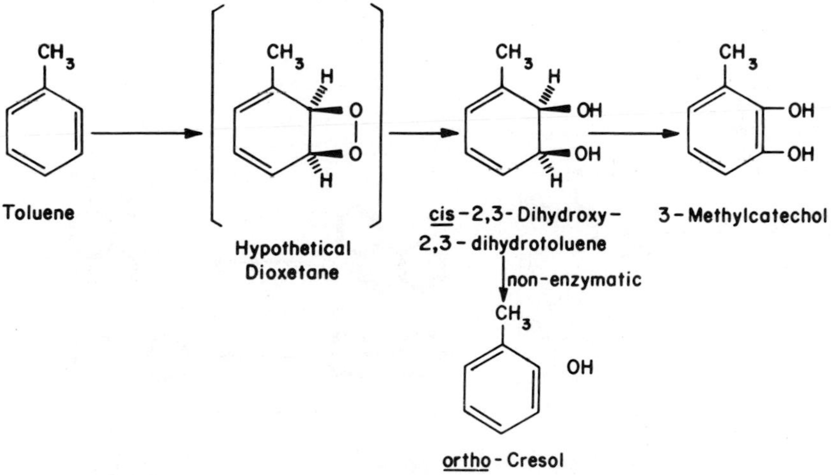

FIG. 4 - Initial reactions in the oxidation of toluene by P. putida. The further metabolism of 3-methylcatechol and related compounds is presented in Gibson, D.T., 1968. Microbial degradation of aromatic compounds. Science 161:1093-1097.

The discovery of a cis-dihydrodiol as an intermediate in the microbial degradation of an aromatic hydrocarbon was unexpected. However, the use of mutant organisms has allowed the isolation and identification of cis-dihydrodiols as intermediates in the bacterial degradation of benzene (17,23), ethylbenzene (19), naphthalene (26,25),
phenanthrene, anthracene (40), biphenyl (20), and para-xylene (21).
Some of these products are shown in Figure 5. In addition, $^{18}O_2$ incorporation studies have revealed that both atoms of a single molecule
of oxygen are incorporated into the aromatic nucleus. These results
are in direct contrast to those reported for the mammalian oxidation
of aromatic hydrocarbons (11). Mammals incorporate one atom of molecular oxygen into the aromatic nucleus to yield arene oxides. Subsequent enzymatic hydration leads to the formation of trans-dihydrodiols
which in turn are oxidized to catechols. The differences in mechanisms
utilized by bacteria and mammals to oxidize aromatic hydrocarbons are
illustrated in Figure 6. It should be noted that the dioxetane intermediate is hypothetical.

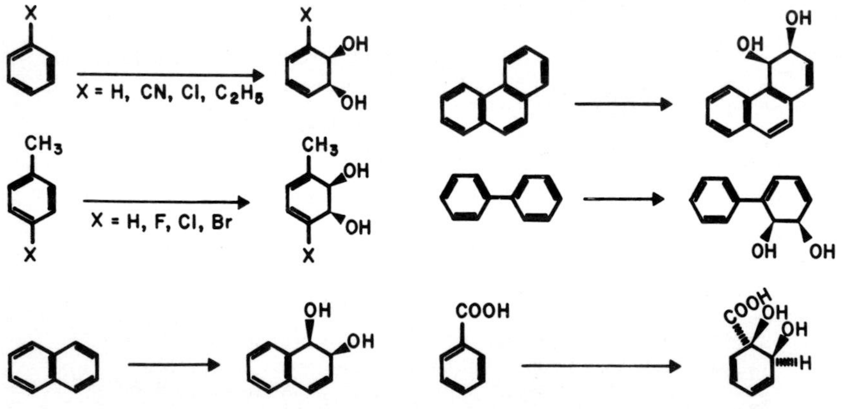

FIG. 5 - cis-Dihydrodiols produced by bacteria.

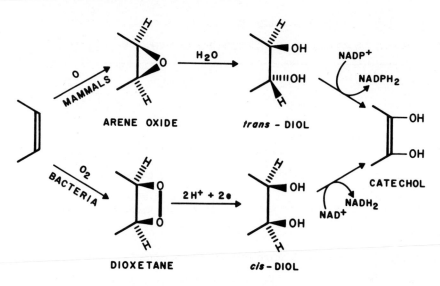

FIG. 6 - Initial reactions used by mammals and bacteria to oxidize aromatic hydrocarbons.

BIODEGRADATION OF MIXED HYDROCARBON SUBSTRATES (CO-OXIDATION)

Many microorganisms have the ability to oxidize a variety of hydrocarbons even though they cannot use these compounds as substrates for growth. The co-oxidation technique of Leadbetter and Foster (31) utilizes this observation. Thus, co-oxidation refers to the oxidation of nongrowth hydrocarbons when they are present as cosubstrates in a medium in which one or more different hydrocarbons are furnished for growth. This technique has widened considerably the spectrum of hydrocarbons that can be metabolized by microorganisms. The review of Raymond and Jamison (39) should be consulted for details. Table VIII lists some examples of co-oxidation:

TABLE VIII

CO-OXIDATION OF HYDROCARBON SUBSTRATES

Growth Substrate	Cosubstrate	Products	Reference
Methane	Ethane	Ethanol. Acetaldehyde. Acetic acid.	(14)
n-Hexadecane	Ethylbenzene	Phenylacetic acid	(12)
n-Hexadecane	p-Xylene	3,6-Dimethylcatechol. α,α-Dimethyl-cis-cis-muconic acid.	(24)

Two features of the co-oxidation phenomenon are apparent. The enzymes
induced by the growth substrate can have broad specificity which will
allow them to catalyze in incomplete oxidation of nongrowth substrates.
Thus, the enzyme system of a Nocardia species that oxidizes the methyl
group of hexadecane, also oxidizes the methyl group of ethylbenzene.
The resulting phenylacetic acid is resistant to further degradation
by this organism. In contrast, the nongrowth substrate may induce the
formation of enzymes that catalyze partial degradation of the inducing
substrate. In this case the growth substrate serves only to provide
for the synthesis of cellular constituents and need not necessarily
be a hydrocarbon. The oxidation of p-xylene to α,α-cis,cis-muconic
acid by a strain of Nocardia corallina is an example of this type of
metabolism.

Recently we have shown that cells of a mutant strain of Beijerinckia
oxidize biphenyl to cis-2,3-dihydroxy-2,3-dihydrobiphenyl (20). Cells
of this organism, after growth on glucose in the presence of biphenyl,
oxidize benzo[a]pyrene to the product shown below. The biphenyl ring

cis-9,10-Dihydroxy-9,10-dihydrobenzo[a]pyrene

structure can clearly be recognized in the benzo[a]pyrene molecule. This is the first report of the isolation and identification of a microbial degradation product from a polycyclic hydrocarbon that contains more than three aromatic rings. It is quite probable that similar co-oxidation reactions play a significant role in the biodegradation of hydrocarbons in the environment.

BIODEGRADATION OF CRUDE OIL

As stated previously, studies on the biodegradation of crude oil are complicated by the complex nature of the oil. The microbial degradation of certain oil components is well documented (2). However, the type of information obtained is limited by the analytical techniques that are available. The linear alkanes are easily analyzed by gas chromatography and mass spectrometry and there is little doubt that these compounds are rapidly removed during bacterial growth on crude oil. It is of interest to note that certain bacteria will rapidly degrade pristane under laboratory conditions (34,10). However, pristane and the related isoprenoid phytane are degraded slowly when they are present as constituents of crude oil. These compounds appear to be metabolized only after the removal of the n-paraffins (3). Also, temperature and the chemical composition of the oil play an important role in pristane biodegradation (46).

For many years it has been tacitly assumed that oil deposits are immune to microbial degradation. Variations in crude oil composition may be due to maturation processes within the reservoir, oxidation from the introduction of oxygen and reactions of the oil with sedimentary constituents such as elemental sulfur (47). The studies of Winters and Williams (47) on the composition of crude oil from different sites of a single oil deposit provide firm evidence for the microbiological alteration of oil within the reservoir. Table IX shows the extent of paraffin loss, the nitrogen content, and the

TABLE IX

CHANGES IN PROPERTIES OF CRUDE OIL SAMPLES
FROM DIFFERENT AREAS OF A SINGLE OIL DEPOSIT[1]

Sample	Extent of n-Paraffin Loss	% Nitrogen	Specific Rotation
1	All	0.14	1.05
2	Below C_{18}	0.14	0.80
3	Partial loss, entire range	0.09	0.46
4	None	0.05	0.48

[1]Adapted from the data of Winters and Williams (47).

specific rotation of different oil samples from the same field. Some increase in nitrogen content would be expected because the nitrogenous constituents of the oil would be concentrated by the removal of the paraffins. However, even if all the paraffin components were removed this would not result in a threefold increase in nitrogen content. The authors conclude that a large percentage of the nitrogen

TABLE X

LIGHT END ANALYSIS OF OIL SAMPLES
FROM DIFFERENT AREAS OF A SINGLE OIL DEPOSIT[1]

Sample	Extent of n-Paraffin Loss	n-C_7/MCH	3MH/MCH	CH/MCP[2]
1	All	0.15	0.50	0.61
2	Below C_{18} only	0.02	0.63	0.54
3	None	0.83	0.55	0.84

[1] From the data of Winters and Williams (47).

[2] n-C_7, normal heptane; MCH, methylcyclohexane; 3MH, 3-methylcyclohexane; CH, cyclohexane; MCP, methylcyclopentane.

present in the altered oil must be derived from microbial protein and related nitrogenous compounds. A twofold increase in optical activity of the altered oil is more than would be expected from just the loss of the n-paraffins, and could be explained by the microbial production of optically active compounds which were incorporated into the original oil. Table X shows the results of light end analysis of three different oil samples. The altered oils show changes in the methylcyclohexane/n-heptane ratio which is indicative of loss of the low molecular weight paraffins. Hydrocarbons other than the n-paraffins, but with similar volatilities do not show any significant changes.

Mass spectral analysis provides information that relates to the types of compounds in crude oil that are susceptible to microbial degradation. Table XI shows some of the compounds present in an unaltered and a partially degraded oil that were obtained from the same oil field. Clearly the paraffins are readily degradable. The large loss in paraffins distorts the data with respect to the other components.

TABLE XI

MASS SPECTRAL ANALYSIS OF CRUDE OILS
EFFECT OF BACTERIAL ATTACK[1]

Hydrocarbon Type	Volume Percent Total Crude Oil		Volume Percent Paraffin-free Basis	
	Unaltered	Degraded	Unaltered	Degraded
Paraffins	52.0	11.6	0	0
Non Cond Cycloparaffins	26.8	29.5	55.8	33.4
Cond Cyclopar 2-Ring	7.8	16.7	16.2	18.9
Cond Cyclopar 3-Ring+	5.0	12.7	10.4	14.4
Benzenes	5.6	7.6	11.7	8.6
Naphthenebenzenes	0.6	6.0	1.2	6.8
Dinaphthenebenzenes	1.0	4.9	2.1	5.5
Naphthalenes	0.7	4.4	1.5	5.0
Acenaphthenes, Dibzfurans	0.0	1.5	0.0	1.7
Fluorenes	0.1	1.0	0.2	1.1
Phenanthrenes	0.2	1.5	0.4	1.7
Naphthenephenanthrenes	0.0	0.6	0.0	0.7
Pyrenes	0.1	0.7	0.2	0.8
Chrysenes	0.0	0.3	0.0	0.3
Perylenes	0.0	0.2	0.0	0.2
Steranes				
4-Ring	0.1	0.7	0.2	0.8
5-Ring	0.1	0.6	0.2	0.7
6-Ring	0.0	0.2	0.0	0.2

[1]Data from J.C. Winters. The Chemistry of Petroleum. Presented in a symposium, Microbial Interactions with Hydrocarbons and Petroleum. Annual meeting of the American Society for Microbiology, Chicago, 1974.

Recalculation of the data on a paraffin-free basis allows a more valid comparison, and additional recalculations could be done to reach conclusions about the relative degradability of the different compound types. The results show that apart from the noncondensed cycloparaffins and simple benzenes very little degradation of the other components has occurred.

It is important to realize that the results presented above represent an example of the microbial degradation of oil in one particular

TABLE XII

CHANGES IN CHEMICAL COMPOSITION OF DIFFERENT
CRUDE OILS AFTER MICROBIAL DEGRADATION[1]

Crude Oil Fraction	% Change in Composition			
	Norman Wells	Prudhoe Bay	Lost Horse Hill	Atkinson Point
Asphaltenes	+0.46	+2.69	+5.36	+1.00
Saturates	−9.04	−6.65	−19.41	−0.93
Aromatics	+3.57	+1.30	−0.97	−1.99
NSO's[2]	+5.01	+1.37	+9.74	+1.90

[1]From data of Westlake et al. (46). Analyses were performed after
ten days growth of a mixed culture of microorganisms on the different crude oils.

[2]Nitrogen, sulfur and oxygen compounds.

environment. Also the changes observed are due to the interactions of
microorganisms with the crude oil over millions of years. Nevertheless, the results are typical of the type of information that can be
obtained in the laboratory (46). Table XII shows the changes in composition of different crude oils after they had been exposed to a
mixed culture of bacteria for ten days. Again the data appears distorted due to significant losses in the saturate fraction. Recalculation on a saturate-free basis reveals that the aromatic fraction
decreases slightly while the NSO fraction shows an increase. From
the results obtained with studies on the metabolism of single and
mixed hydrocarbon substrates we can tentatively assume that the small
decrease in the aromatic fraction is due to the biodegradation of
simple benzene derivatives. Also, the increase in the NSO fraction
suggests that some of the compounds in the saturate and aromatic
fractions only undergo partial metabolism. This could represent

an example of the co-oxidation phenomenon discussed earlier. The apparent increase in the asphaltene fraction is difficult to explain. It has been suggested that the bacterial degradation of crude oil leads to a significant increase in asphaltene content (3). This is unlikely since all available evidence suggests that asphaltenes are thermally-induced polymers formed from small aromatic hydrocarbons.

Space does not permit a detailed discussion of all aspects of oil biodegradation. The studies of Blumer et al., should be consulted for further information (7). However, it is apparent that knowledge in this area is meager. The paraffins and probably some simple cyclic compounds are removed from crude oil by microbial degradation. However, it is possible that many polycyclic compounds, particularly those that contain sulfur, are poor substrates for microbial degradation.

ACKNOWLEDGMENTS

The author is indebted to Dr. J. C. Winters for his valuable advice relating to the chemical composition of crude oil and also for his permission to use the data in Table XI. Dr. R. E. Kallio provided stimulating discussion. Some of the research presented was supported in part by Public Health Service grant ES-00537 from the National Institute of Environmental Health Sciences, grant F-440 from the Robert A. Welch Foundation and contract no. N00014-67-A-0126-0020, NR 306-054, from the Office of Naval Research, Naval Biology Program. The author is a recipient of Public Health Service Career Development Award 1-KO4, ES70088 from the National Institute of Environmental Health Sciences.

REFERENCES

(1) Abbott, B.J.; and Gledhill, W.E. 1971. The extracellular accumulation
     of metabolic products by hydrocarbon-degrading microorganisms. Adv.
     Appl. Microbiol. 14: 249-388.

(2) Ahearn, D.G.; and Meyers, S.P., eds. 1973. The Microbial Degradation
     of Oil Pollutants, and articles therein. Louisiana State University.
     Publ. No. LSU-SG-73-01. Baton Rouge, La. 70803. USA.

(3) Bailey, N.J.L.; Jobson, A.M.; and Rogers, M.A. 1973. Bacterial degra-
     dation of crude oil: comparison of field and experimental data. Chem.
     Geol. 11: 203-221.

(4) Blumer, M.; Mullin, M.M.; and Thomas, D.W. 1964. Pristane in the ma-
     rine environment. Helgolaender Wiss. Meeresuntersuch. 10: 187-201.

(5) Blumer, M. 1961. Benzpyrenes in soil. Science 134: 474-475.

(6) Blumer, M. 1969. Oil pollution of the ocean. Oceanus 15: (2) 2-7.

(7) Blumer, M.; Ehrhardt, M.; and Jones, J.H. 1973. The environmental
     fate of stranded crude oil. Deep Sea Research 20: 239-259.

(8) Blumer, M.; and Youngblood, W.W. 1975. Polycyclic aromatic hydrocar-
     bons in soils and recent sediments. Science 188: 53-55.

(9) Clark, R.C., Jr.; and Blumer, M. 1967. Distribution of paraffins in
     marine organisms and sediment. Limnol. Oceanog. 12: 79-87.

(10) Cox, R.E.; Maxwell, J.R.; Ackman, R.G.; and Hooper, S.N. 1974. Stereo-
     chemical studies of acyclic isoprenoid compounds. IV. Microbial oxi-
     dation of 2,6,10,14-tetramethylpentadecane (pristane). Biochim. Bio-
     phys. Acta. 360: 166-173.

(11) Daly, J.W.; Jerina, D.M.; and Witkop, B. 1972. Arene oxides and the
     NIH shift: The metabolism toxicity and carcinogenicity of aromatic com-
     pounds. Experientia. 28: 1129-1149.

(12) Davis, J.B.; and Raymond, R.L. 1961. Oxidation of alkyl-substituted
     cyclic hydrocarbons by a Nocardia during growth on n-alkanes. Appl.
     Microbiol. 9: 383-388.

(13) Floodgate, G.D. 1972. Biodegradation of Hydrocarbons in the sea. In
     Water Pollution Microbiology, ed. R. Mitchel, pp 153-171. New York:
     John Wiley and Sons, Inc.

(14) Foster, J.W. 1962. Bacterial Oxidation of Hydrocarbons. In Oxygenases,
     ed. O. Hayaishi, pp 241-269. New York: Academic Press.

(15) Gibson, D.T.; Koch, J.R.; and Kallio, R.E. 1968. Oxidative degradation
     of aromatic hydrocarbons by microorganisms. I. Enzymatic formation of
     catechol from benzene. Biochemistry 7: 2653-2662.

(16) Gibson, D.T.; Hensley, M.; Yoshioka, H.; and Mabry, T.J. 1970. Forma-
      tion of (+)-cis-2,3-dihydroxy-1-methyl-cyclohexa-4,6-diene from toluene
      by Pseudomonas putida. Biochemistry 9: 1626-1630.

(17) Gibson, D.T.; Cardini, G.E.; Maseles, F.C.; and Kallio, R.E. 1970.
      Incorporation of oxygen-18 into benzene by Pseudomonas putida. Bio-
      chemistry 9: 1631-1635.

(18) Gibson, D,T, 1971. The microbial oxidation of aromatic hydrocarbons.
      Crit. Rev. Microbiol. 1: 199-223.

(19) Gibson, D,T,; Gschwendt, B.; Yeh, W.K.; and Kobal, V.M. 1973. Initial
      reactions in the oxidation of ethylbenzene by Pseudomonas putida. Bio-
      chemistry 12: 1520-1528.

(20) Gibson, D.T.; Roberts, R.L.; Wells, M.C.; and Kobal, V.M. 1973. Oxi-
      dation of biphenyl by a Beijerinckia species. Biochem. Biophys.·Res.
      Commun. 50: 211-219.

(21) Gibson, D.T.; Mahadevan, V.; and Davey, J.F. 1974. Bacterial metabo-
      lism of para- and meta-xylene: oxidation of the aromatic ring. J.
      Bacteriol. 119: 930-936.

(22) Hegeman, G.D. 1972. The evolution of metabolic pathways in bacteria.
      In degradation of synthetic organic molecules in the biosphere, pp 56-
      71. Available from: Printing and Publishing Office, National Academy
      of Science, 2101 Constitution Avenue, N.W., Washington, D.C. 20418.

(23) Högn, T.; and Jaenicke, L. 1972. Benzene metabolism of Moraxella
      species. Eur. J. Biochem. 30: 369-375.

(24) Jamison, V.W.; Raymond, R.L.; and Hudson, J.O. 1969. Microbial hydro-
      carbon co-oxidation. III. Isolation and characterization of an α,α[1]-
      dimethyl-cis,cis-muconic acid-producing strain of Nocardia corallina.
      Appl. Microbiol. 17: 853-856.

(25) Jeffrey, A.M.; Yeh, H.J.C.; Jerina, D.M.; Patel, T.R.; Davey, J.F.; and
      Gibson, D.T. 1975. Initial reactions in the oxidation of naphthalene
      by Pseudomonas putida. Biochemistry 14: 575-584.

(26) Jerina, D.M.; Daly, J.W.; Jeffrey, A.M.; and Gibson, D.T. 1971. cis-
      1,2-Dihydroxy-1,2-dihydronaphthalene: A bacterial metabolite from
      naphthalene. Arch. Biochem. Biophys. 142: 394-396.

(27) Johns, R.B.; Belsky, T.; McCarthy, E.D.; Burlingame, A.L.; Haug, P.;
      Schnoes, H.D.; Richter, W.; and Calvin, M. 1966. The organic geo-
      chemistry of ancient sediments, 1-55. Part II, Technical Report on
      NsG 101-61, Series No. 7, Issue No. 8. Berkeley: University of Calif-
      ornia Press.

(28) Kern, W. 1947. Über das vorkommen von chrysen in erde. Helv. Chim.
      Acta. 30: 1595-1599.

(29) Kobal, V.M.; Gibson, D.T.; Davis, R.E.; and Garza, A. 1973. X-ray determination of the absolute stereochemistry of the initial oxidation product formed from toluene by Pseudomonas putida 39/D. J. Amer. Chem. Soc. 95: 4420-4421.

(30) Koons, C.B.; Jamieson, G.W.; and Ciereszko, L.S. 1965. Normal alkane distribution in marine organisms; possible significance to petroleum origin. Bull. Am. Assoc. Petrol. Geologists. 49: 301-204.

(31) Leadbetter, E.R.; and Foster, J.W. 1960. Bacterial oxidation of gaseous alkanes. Arch. Mikrobiol. 35: 92-194.

(32) Ledet, E.J.; and Laseter, J.L. 1974. Alkanes at the air-sea interface from offshore Louisiana and Florida. Science 186: 261-263.

(33) McKenna, E.J.; and Kallio, R.E. 1965. The Biology of Hydrocarbons. Ann. Rev.Microbiol. 19: 183-208.

(34) McKenna, E.J.; and Kallio, R.E. 1971. Microbial metabolism of the isoprenoid alkane pristane. Proc. Nat. Acad. Sci. U.S.A. 68: 1552-1554.

(35) Meinschein, W.G. 1959. Origin of petroleum. Bull. Am. Assoc. Petrol. Geologists. 43: 925-943.

(36) Meinschein, W.G. 1969. Hydrocarbons-Saturated, Unsaturated and Aromatic. In Organic Geochemistry, ed. G. Eglington and M.T.J. Murphy, pp 330-356. New York: Springer Verlag.

(37) Mulkins-Phillips, G.J.; and Stewart, J.E. 1974. Distribution of hydrocarbon utilizing bacteria in northwestern atlantic waters and coastal sediments. Can. J. Microbiol. 20: 955-962.

(38) Piccinetti, C. 1967. Diffusione dell'idrocarburo cancerogeno benzo 3,4 pirene nell'alto e medio adriatico. Arch. Oceanog. Limnol. Suppl., 15: 169-183.

(39) Raymond, R.L.; and Jamison, V.W. 1971. Biochemical activities of Nocardia. Adv. Appl. Microbiol. 14: 93-122.

(40) Selander, H.; Yagi, H.; Jerina, D.M.; Wells, M.C.; Davey, J.F.; Mahadevan, V.; and Gibson, D.T. 1975. J. Am. Chem. Soc., submitted for publication.

(41) Sisler, F.D.; and Zobel, C.E. 1947. Microbial utilization of carcinogenic hydrocarbons. Science 106: 521-522.

(42) Söhngen, N.L. 1906. Über Bacterien, welche Methan als Kohlenstoffnahrung und Energiequelle gebrauchen. Zentralbl. Bacteriol. Parasitenk. Infektionskr. Abt. 2. 15: 513-517.

(43) Stanier, R.Y. 1947. Simultaneous adaptation: a new technique for the study of metabolic pathways. J. Bacteriol. 54: 339-348.

(44) Treccani, V. 1974. Microbial degradation of aromatic compounds: in-
      fluence of methyl and alkyl substituents. In Industrial Aspects of
      Biochemistry, ed. B. Spencer. Federation of European Biochemical
      Societies.

(45) Van Der Linden, A.C.; and Thijsse, G.J.E. 1965. The mechanisms of
      microbial oxidations of petroleum hydrocarbons. Advan. Enzymol. 27:
      469-546.

(46) Westlake, D.W.S.; Jobson, A.; Phillippe, R.; and Cook, F.D. 1974. Bio-
      degradability and crude oil composition. Can. J. Microbiol. 20: 915-928.

(47) Winters, J.C.; and Williams, J.A. 1969. Microbial alteration of crude
      oil in the reservoir. Symp. on Petroleum Transformation in Geologic
      Environments. Div. Pet. Chem., Am. Chem. Soc., New York, N.Y., Sept
      7-12, Pap. PETR 86: E22-E31.

(48) Wodzinski, R.S.; and Bertolini, D. 1972. Physical state in which naph-
      thalene and bibenzyl are utilized by bacteria. Appl. Microbiol. 23:
      1077-1081.

(49) Wodzinski, R.S.; and Coyle, J.E. 1974. Physical state of phenanthrene
      for utilization by bacteria. Appl. Microbiol. 27: 1081-1084.

(50) Ziffer, H.; Jerina, D.M.; Gibson, D.T.; and Kobal, V.M. 1973. Abso-
      lute stereochemistry of the (+)-cis-1,2-dihydroxy-3-methylcyclohexa-
      3,5-diene produced from toluene by Pseudomonas putida. J. Amer. Chem.
      Soc. 95: 4048-4049.

(51) Zobell, C.E. 1971. Sources and biodegradation of carcinogenic hydro-
      carbons. API/EPA/USCG Conference, "Prevention and Control of Oil
      Spills", Washington, D.C., pp 441-451.

Curricula Vitae

Ahrland, Sten, Ph.D.

Born in Mariestad, Sweden, on August 4th, 1921.
Education in Chemistry at the University of
Lund, Lund, Sweden.

Present position:

Since 1971 Professor of Inorganic Solution
Chemistry at the Swedish Natural Science
Research Council. Working at the Chemical
Center of the University of Lund.

Fields of interest:

Equilibria in aqueous and non-aqueous solutions,
selective affinities of acceptors and donors,
inorganic ion exchangers.

Bates, Roger G., Ph.D.

Born in Cummington, Massachusetts, USA, on
May 20th, 1912. Education at the University of
Massachusetts, Amherst, Massachusetts and Duke
University, Durham, North Carolina.

Present position:

Since 1969 Professor of Chemistry at the University of Florida, Gainesville, Florida.

Fields of interest:

Acid-base properties in aqueous and non-aqueous
systems, single ion activities.

Bernhard, Michael, Dr.

Born in Berlin, Germany, on October 14th, 1925.
Education in Biology at the Humboldt University
of Berlin, the Philips University of Marburg and
the University of Naples, Naples, Italy.

Present position:

Since 1974 Senior Expert, Division of Environmental Research, Comitato Nazionale per l'Ener-
gia Nucleare.

Fields of Interest:

Chemical and biological oceanography, ecology,
marine pollution.

Biedermann, Georg, Ph.D.

<u>Born</u> in Budapest, Hungary, on November 9th, 1925.
Education in Chemistry, Physics and Mathematics
at the Universities of Budapest and Stockholm.

<u>Present position</u>:

Since 1964 docent at the Royal Institute of
Technology, Stockholm.

<u>Field of interests</u>:

Inorganic and analytical chemistry.

Campbell, Ian, Ph.D.

<u>Born</u> in Perth, Scotland, on April 24th, 1941.
Education in Physics at St. Andrews University.

<u>Present position</u>:

Since 1971 Research Officer in the Biochemical
Department of the University at Oxford.

<u>Fields of interest</u>:

The application of spectroscopy to biological
problems.

Clearfield, Abraham, Ph.D.

<u>Born</u> in Philadelphia, Pennsylvania, USA, on Novem-
ber 9th, 1927. Education in Chemistry and
Crystallography at Temple University, Philadel-
phia and Rutgers University, New Brunswick, New
Jersey.

<u>Present position</u>:

Since 1968 Professor of Physical and Inorganic
Chemistry, Ohio University, Athens, Ohio.

<u>Fields of interest</u>:

Crystal structure determinations, inorganic ion
exchangers, especially hydrous oxides and phosphates.

Edmond, John M., B.Sc., Ph.D.

Born in Glasgow, Scotland, on April 27th, 1943. Education in Chemistry at the University of Glasgow and in Marine Geochemistry at Scripps Institution of Oceanography, University of California.

Present position:

Associate Professor of Marine Geochemistry at Massachusetts Institute of Technology.

Fields of interest:

Geochemistry of marine and continental waters, chemistry of marine plankton, controls on the distribution of marine sediments, paleo-oceanography and paleo-climatology.

Eichhorn, Gunther L., Ph.D.

Born in Frankfurt am Main, Germany, on February 8th, 1927. Education at the University of Louisville, Kentucky, and Department of Chemistry, University of Illinois, Urbana, Illinois.

Present position:

Since 1958 Chief, Section on Molecular Biology, National Institutes of Health, Gerontology Research Center, Baltimore City Hospitals, Baltimore, Maryland.

Fields of interest:

Inorganic biochemistry, coordination chemistry, gerontology, catalysis, molecular biology.

Faulkner, D. John, Ph.D.

Born in Bournemouth, England, on June 10th, 1942. Education in Organic Chemistry at Imperial College, London, Harvard University and Stanford University.

Present position:

Associate Professor of Marine Chemistry at Scripps Institution of Oceanography.

Fields of interest:

Marine natural products, synthetic organic chemistry, chemical ecology.

Gibson, David T., Ph.D.

<u>Born</u> in Walefield, Yorkshire, England, on February 16th, 1938. Education in Microbial Biochemistry at the University of Leeds, England.

<u>Present position</u>:

Since 1975 Professor of Microbiology, Department of Microbiology, the University of Texas at Austin, Austin, Texas.

<u>Fields of interest</u>:

Bacterial metabolism, regulation and enzymology.

Goldberg, Edward D., Ph.D.

<u>Born</u> in Sacramento, California, USA, on August 2nd, 1921. Education in Chemistry at the University of California at Berkeley and at the University of Chicago.

<u>Present position</u>:

Since 1949 at the Scripps Institution of Oceanography, La Jolla, California, where he now occupies the position of Professor of Chemistry.

<u>Fields of interest</u>:

Marine geochemistry, geochronology.

Hager, Lowell P., Ph.D.

<u>Born</u> in Girard, Kansas, USA, on August 30th, 1915. Education at Valparaiso University and at the Universities of Kansas and Illinois.

<u>Present position</u>:

Since 1969 Head of Department of Biochemistry, University of Illinois at Urbana-Champaign.

<u>Fields of interest</u>:

Biochemistry, Biophysics.

Hansson, E. Ingemar

Born in Göteborg, Sweden, on June 23rd, 1937.
Education in Mathematics, Physics and Chemistry
at the Universities of Uppsala and Göteborg.

Present position:

Since 1973 Assistant Headmaster of Nils Ericson-
skolan, Science and Technical Gymnasium School,
Trollhättan, Sweden.

Fields of interest:

Chemical equilibria of seawater.

Harris, Gordon M., Ph.D.

Born in Chungking, China, on July 23rd, 1913.
Education in Chemistry at the University of
Saskatchewan, Canada, and at Harvard University.

Present position:

Since 1961 Larkin Professor of Chemistry at State
University of New York at Buffalo.

Fields of interest:

Chemical kinetics, mechanisms of reactions of
inorganic complex compounds, applications of isotopes to chemical problems.

Högfeldt, Erik H., Ph.D.

Born in Dalarö, Stockholms län, Sweden, on July
2nd, 1924. Education in Chemistry and Physics at
the University of Stockholm, Stockholm, Sweden.

Present position:

Since 1966 Associate Professor of Inorganic Chemistry at the Royal Institute of Technology, Stockholm, Sweden.

Fields of interest:

Ion exchange, extraction, solition chemistry and
thermodynamics, hydration in concentrated electrolytes.

Kester, Dana R., Ph.D.

Born in Los Angeles, California, USA, on January 26th, 1943. Education in Oceanography and Chemistry at the University of Washington, Seattle, Washington and Oregon State University, Corvallis, Oregon.

Present position:

Since 1972 Associate Professor of Oceanography at the University of Rhode Island, Kingston, Rhode Island.

Fields of interest:

Physical chemistry, marine chemistry, and chemical oceanography.

Liss, Peter Simon, B.Sc., Ph.D.

Born in Watford, England, on October 27th, 1942. Educated at University College, Durham University and the Marine Science Laboratories, University of of Wales.

Present position:

Since 1969 Lecturer in the School of Environmental Sciences at the University of East Anglia.

Fields of Interest:

Marine chemistry.

Lyklema, J., Ph.D.

Born in Apeldoorn, Netherlands, on November 23rd, 1930. Education at the Rijks Universiteit of Utrecht, Netherlands and at the University of Southern California, Los Angeles, USA.

Present position:

Professor of Physical and Colloid Chemistry at the Agricultural University, Wageningen, Netherlands.

Fields of interest:

Interfacial and colloid science.

Marcus, Rudolph A., Ph.D.

Born in Montreal, Canada, on July 21st, 1923.
Education in Physical Chemistry at McGill University, Montreal, Canada.

Present position:

Since 1964 Professor of Chemistry at the University of Illinois, Urbana, Illinois.

Fields of interest:

Theories of rates of chemical reactions, collision dynamics, and electrode processes.

Nürnberg, Hans Wolfgang, Dr. rer.nat.

Born in Cologne, Germany, on March 18th, 1930.
Education in Chemistry at the Universities of Bonn and Cologne, Germany.

Present position:

Since 1971 Professor of Physical Chemistry, University of Bonn; and since 1975 Head of the Institute for Applied Physical Chemistry at the Kernforschungsanlage, Jülich, Germany.

Fields of interest:

Electrochemistry, particularly polarography, applications for physical and analytical chemistry in environmental and electrical research and bioelectrochemistry.

Ottewill, R.H., B.Sc., M.A., Ph.D.

Born in London, England, on February 8th, 1927.
Education in Chemistry at Queen Mary College, London and Fitzwilliam College, Cambridge.

Present position:

Since 1973 Head of the Department of Physical Chemistry; and since 1971 Professor of Colloid Science, University of Bristol, England.

Field of interest:

Physical chemistry of disperse systems.

Parsons, Roger, D.Sc., F.R.I.C., Ph.D., A.R.C.S.

Born in London, England, on October 31st, 1926.
Education in Chemistry at Imperial College of
Science and Technology, London.

Present position:

Since 1963 Reader in Electrochemistry in the
School of Chemistry, University of Bristol. Also
since 1963 Editor of the Journal of Electroanalytical Chemistry and Interfacial Electrochemistry.

Fields of interest:

Structure of electrified interfaces, kinetics of
electrode reactions, physical chemistry of
electrolyte solutions.

Rinehart, Kenneth L., Jr., Ph.D.

Born in Chillicothe, Missouri, USA, on March 17th,
1929. Education in Chemistry at Yale University,
New Haven, Connecticut, and at University of California, Berkeley.

Present position:

Since 1964 Professor of Chemistry at the University of Illinois, Urbana, Illinois.

Fields of interest:

Antibiotics, marine natural products, mass spectrometry.

Schneider, Walter, Ph.D.

Born in Adliswil, Kt. Zürich, Switzerland, on
January 28th, 1928. Education in Chemistry at the
University of Zürich.

Present position:

Since 1964 Professor of Inorganic Chemistry, Eidg.
Technische Hochschule, Zürich.

Fields of interest:

Coordination chemistry.

Sherry, Howard S., Ph.D.

Born in New York, New York, USA, on November 18th, 1930. Education in Chemical Engineering at New York University, New York, New York and in Inorganic Physical Chemistry at the State University of New York at Buffalo, Buffalo, New York.

Present position:

Research Associate and Group Leader in Catalyst Research and Development, Mobil Research and Development Corporation, Paulsboro, New Jersey.

Fields of Interest:

Zeolites, catalysis and ion exchange.

Wagener, Klaus, Ph.D.

Born in Halle, Germany, on July 27th, 1930. Education in Physics and Physical Chemistry at the Universities of Göttingen and Zürich.

Present position:

Since 1968 Director, Institute of Physical Chemistry (now: Biophysical Chemistry), Nuclear Research Center Jülich, and Professor of Biophysics, Technical University, Aachen, Germany.

Fields of interest:

Environmental biophysics, chemical and atmospheric evolution, stable isotopes.

Warner, Theodore Baker, Ph.D.

Born in Chicago, Illinois, USA, on March 6th, 1931. Education in Chemistry at Williams College, Williamstown, Massachusetts and in Physical Chemistry at Indiana University, Bloomington, Indiana

Present position:

Since 1968 Head of the Electrochemistry Section, Ocean Sciences Division of the Naval Research Laboratory, Washington, D.C.

Fields of interest:

Physical chemistry, oceanography, geochemistry.

Whitfield, Michael, Ph.D.

Born in Cheshire, England, on June 15th, 1940.
Education in Chemistry at the University of Leeds,
England.

Present position:

Since 1970 Principal Scientific Officer at the
Marine Biological Association of the United Kingdom, Plymouth, England.

Fields of interest:

Marine chemistry, electrochemistry.

Wilkins, Ralph G., B.Sc., Ph.D., D.Sc.

Born in Southampton, England, on January 7th, 1927.
Educated at the University College, Southampton,
England.

Present position:

Since 1973 Head of Department of Chemistry, New
Mexico State University, Las Cruces, New Mexico.

Fields of interest:

Inorganic and bioinorganic chemistry.

Xavier, António V., Ph.D.

Born in Porto, Portugal, in August, 1943.   Educa-
tion in Chemistry and Molecular Biology at the
Universities of Porto and Lisboa, Portugal and
Oxford University, England.

Present position:

Since 1974 Associate Professor of the University
of Lisboa.

Fields of interest:

Molecular biology and inorganic biochemistry.

Participants

AHRLAND, S.
Inorganic Chemistry 1
Chemical Center
University of Lund
P.O. Box 740
220 07 Lund 7, Sweden

ANDERSEN, N.R.
Chemical Oceanography Program
Dept. of the Navy
Office of Naval Research
Code 482
Arlington, VA 22217, USA

BADA, J.L
Scripps Institution
of Oceanography
University of California
San Diego
La Jolla, CA 92037, USA

BATES, R.G.
Dept. of Chemistry
University of Florida
Gainesville, FL 32611, USA

BAYER, E.
Lehrstuhl f. Organische Chemie
der Universität Tübingen
Auf der Morgenstelle 18
74 Tübingen 1, F.R. Germany

BEASLEY, T.M.
International Laboratory
of Marine Radioactivity
Musée Océanographique
Principality of Monaco

BERNER, R.A.
Dept. of Geology and Geophysics
Yale University
Box 2161, Yale Station
New Haven, CT 06520, USA

BERNHARD, M.
C.N.E.N.
Laboratorio per lo Studio
della Contaminazione Radioattiva
del Mare
19030 Fiascherino (La Spezia), Italy

BERTINE, K.
Scripps Institution
of Oceanography
La Jolla, CA 92037, USA

BIEDERMANN, G.
Dept. of Inorganic Chemistry
Royal Institute of Technology
100 44 Stockholm 70, Sweden

BLUMER, M.
Chemistry Dept.
Woods Hole Oceanographic Institution
Woods Hole, MA 02543, USA

BRANICA, M.
Institute Rudjer Boskovic
Center for Marine Research
P.O. Box 1016
41001 Zagreb, Yugoslavia

CAMPBELL, I.D.
Dept. of Biochemistry
University of Oxford
South Parks Road
Oxford OX1 3QU, Great Britain

CLEARFIELD, A.
Dept. of Chemistry
Clippinger Research Labs
Ohio University
Athens, OH 47501, USA

DYRSSEN, D.
Dept. of Analytical Chemistry
University of Gothenburg
Fack CTH/GU
402 20 Göteborg 5, Sweden

EDMOND, J.M.
Dept. of Earth and
Planetary Sciences
54-1324
Massachusetts Institute
of Technology
Cambridge, MA 02139, USA

EHRHARDT, M.
Abt. Meereschemie
Institut f. Meereskunde
an der Universität Kiel
Düsternbrooker Weg 20
23 Kiel, F.R. Germany

EICHHORN, G.L.
Section on Molecular Biology
National Institutes of Health
Gerontology Research Center
Baltimore City Hospitals
Baltimore, MD 21224, USA

FAULKNER, D.J.
Scripps Institution
of Oceanography
University of California
San Diego
La Jolla, CA 92037, USA

GIBSON, D.T.
Dept. of Microbiology
University of Texas at Austin
Austin, TX 78712, USA

GOLDBERG, E.D.
Scripps Institution
of Oceanography
P.O. Box 1529
La Jolla, CA 92037, USA

HAGER, L.P.
Dept. of Biochemistry
University of Illinois
413 Roger Adams Laboratory
Urbana, Il 61801, USA

HANSSON, I.
Rotekullagatan 3
461 00 Trollhättan, Sweden

HARRIS, G.M.
Dept. of Chemistry
State University of
New York at Buffalo
250 Acheson Hall
Buffalo, NY 14214, USA

HÖGFELDT, E.
Dept. of Inorganic Chemistry
Royal Institute of Technology
100 44 Stockholm 70, Sweden

JERNELOV, A.
Swedish Air and Water Quality
Research Laboratory (IVL)
P.O. Box 5607
114 86 Stockholm, Sweden

KESTER, D.R.
Graduate School of Oceanography
University of Rhode Island
Kingston, RI 02881, USA

KRATOHVIL, J.
Dept. of Chemistry
Clarkson College of Technology
Potsdam, NY 13676, USA

KRAUS, K.A.
Nuclear Division
Oak Ridge National Laboratory
P.O. Box X
Oak Ridge, TN 37830, USA

KREMLING, K.
Abt. Meereschemie
Institut f. Meereskunde
an der Universität Kiel
Düsternbrooker Weg 20
23 Kiel, F.R. Germany

LISS, P.S.
School of Environmental Sciences
University of East Anglia
Norwich NOR 88C, Great Britain

LYKLEMA, J.
Laboratory for Physical
and Colloid Chemistry
Landbouwhogeschool
De Dreijen 6
Wageningen, The Netherlands

MacINTYRE, F.
School of Physics
Melbourne University
Parkvil', Vic. 3052, Australia

MARCUS, R.A.
Dept. of Chemistry
174 Noyes Laboratory
University of Illinois
Urbana, IL 61801, USA

MARTELL, A.E.
Dept. of Chemistry
Texas A&M University
College Station, TX 77843, USA

MARTIN, J.-M.
Groupe de Géologie Nucléaire
Laboratoire de Géologie Dynamique
Université de Paris 6
75230 Paris Cedex 05, France

MEYL, A.
Deutsche Forschungsgemeinschaft
Kennedyallee 40
53 Bonn-Bad Godesberg, F.R. Germany

MILLERO, F.J.
RSMAS
University of Miami
Miami, FL 33149, USA

MORGAN, J.J.
Environmental Engineering Science
California Institute of Technology
Pasadena, CA 91109, USA

MORRISON, G.H.
Dept. of Chemistry
Cornell University
Ithaca, NY 14850, USA

NANCOLLAS, G.H.
Dept. of Chemistry
State University of New York
at Buffalo
Acheson Hall
Buffalo, NY 14214, USA

NÜRNBERG, H.W.
Institut f. Angewandte
Physikalische Chemie
KFA Jülich
Postfach 365
517 Jülich, F.R. Germany

OTTEWILL, R.H.
Dept. of Physical Chemistry
University of Bristol
Cantock's Close
Bristol BS8 1TS, Great Britain

PARSONS, R.
School of Chemistry
University of Bristol
Cantocks Close
Woodland Road
Bristol BS8 1TS, Great Britain

PIRO, A.
C.N.E.N.
Laboratorio per lo Studio
della Contaminazione Radioattiva
del Mare
19030 Fiascherino (La Spezia), Italy

PRAVDIC, V.
Laboratory of Electrochemistry
and Surface Phenomena
Institute Rudjer Boskovic
P.O. Box 1016
Bijenicka 54
41001 Zagreb, Yugoslavia

PYTKOWICZ, R.M.
School of Oceanography
Oregon State University
Corvallis, OR 97331

RILEY, J.P.
Dept. of Oceanography
University of Liverpool
P.O. Box 147
Liverpool L69 3BX, Great Britain

RINEHART, K.L. Jr.
School of Chemical Sciences
454 Roger Adams Laboratory
University of Illinois
Urbana, IL 61801, USA

SCHINDLER, P.W.
Institut f. Anorganische Chemie
Freiestrasse 3
3000 Bern, Switzerland

SCHNEIDER, W.
Labor f. Anorganische Chemie
ETH Zürich
Universitätsstrasse 6
8006 Zürich, Switzerland

SHERRY, H.S.
Mobil Research and
Development Corporation
Billingsport Road
Paulsboro, NJ 08066, USA

STEFFAN, I.
Analytical Institute
University of Vienna
Währingerstrasse 38
1090 Wien, Austria

STUMM, W.
Institute for Aquatic Sciences
and Water Pollution Control
Swiss Federal Institute of
Technology EAWAG
8600 Dübendorf, Switzerland

WAGENER, K.
Institut f. Physikalische Chemie
der KFA Jülich
Postfach 365
517 Jülich, F.R. Germany

WARNER, T.B.
Ocean Sciences Division
Code 8334
Naval Research Laboratory
Washington, D.C. 20375, USA

WHITFIELD, M.
Marine Biological Association
The Laboratory
Citadel Hill
Plymouth PL1 2PB, Great Britain

WILKINS, R.G.
Dept. of Chemistry
New Mexico State University
Box 3C
Las Cruces, NM 88003, USA

WOOD, J.M.
Freshwater Biological
Research Institute
University of Minnesota
County Roads 15 & 19
P.O. Box 100
Navarre, MN 55392, USA

XAVIER, A.V.
Laboratorio de Quîmica Estrutural
Complexo Interdisciplinar
Instituto Superior Técnico
Lisboa 1, Portugal

Subject Index

Name Index